Fundamentals of Wireless Networking

Fundamentals of Wireless Networking

Ron Price
Spokane Community College

McGraw-Hill
Irwin

Boston   Burr Ridge, IL   Dubuque, IA   Madison, WI   New York   San Francisco   St. Louis
Bangkok   Bogotá   Caracas   Kuala Lumpur   Lisbon   London   Madrid   Mexico City
Milan   Montreal   New Delhi   Santiago   Seoul   Singapore   Sydney   Taipei   Toronto

McGraw-Hill
Irwin

FUNDAMENTALS OF WIRELESS NETWORKING

Published by McGraw-Hill/Irwin, a business unit of The McGraw-Hill Companies, Inc., 1221 Avenue of the Americas, New York, NY, 10020. Copyright © 2007 by The McGraw-Hill Companies, Inc. All rights reserved. No part of this publication may be reproduced or distributed in any form or by any means, or stored in a database or retrieval system, without the prior written consent of The McGraw-Hill Companies, Inc., including, but not limited to, in any network or other electronic storage or transmission, or broadcast for distance learning.

Some ancillaries, including electronic and print components, may not be available to customers outside the United States.

This book is printed on acid-free paper.

1234567890 DOC/DOC 09876

ISBN-13:   978-0-07-225668-0
ISBN-10:   0-07-225668-0

Editorial director   *Brent Gordon*
Executive editor   *Paul Ducham*
Managing developmental editor   *Jonathan Plant*
Editorial coordinator   *Lindsay Roth*
Marketing manager   *Rhonda Seelinger*
Senior media producer   *Victor Chiu*
Project manager   *Kristin Bradley*
Production supervisor   *Gina Hangos*
Designer   *Cara David/Jillian Lindner*
Lead media project manager   *Brian Nacik*
Cover design   *Jillian Lindner*
Typeface   *10/13 Times New Roman*
Compositor   *International Typesetting & Composition*
Printer   *R. R. Donnelley*

Library of Congress Cataloging-in-Publication Data

Price, Ron, 1947-
    Fundamentals of wireless networking / Ron Price. —1st ed.
      p. cm.
    Includes index.
    ISBN-13: 978-0-07-225668-0 (alk. paper)
    ISBN-10: 0-07-225668-0 (alk. paper)
    1. Wireless LANs. 2. Wireless communication systems. I. Title.
TK5105.78.P75 2007
004.6'8—dc22

                                                     2006040882

This book is dedicated to my awe-inspiring wife Connie and our truly gifted children: Jeana, Robert, Carly, Markus, Kirstin, and Jessica

About the Author

Ron Price is the School Chair for the schools of information technology and business at the *ITT Technical Institute* campus in Spokane, Washington. His experience in teaching and curriculum development in the computing, networking, and information technology areas extends over 26 years, with experience at the high school, community college, and university levels. In addition to his teaching, he has also served as a corporate executive and consultant in the telecommunications, multimedia, and online education fields.

Ron has written and published over twenty-five books on the topics of computer hardware, software, repair, networking, and career certifications, most under the pen name of Ron Gilster. Ron holds a number of vendor-neutral and vendor-specific IT certifications, including A+, Network+, CCNA, CWNA, AAGG, and others.

When not teaching and administrating, Ron spends his time writing, consulting, and developing curriculum for elementary and grade school students based on age-appropriate novels and biographies.

Contents at a Glance

Contents

Preface

"Ultimately, everything's going to be wireless."

—Jeff Hawkins, Founder of Palm Computing, Inc.

"Wireless is not an extension of the wired network. . . . It's [a network] *no longer defined by the length of your wires. It's where your people are."*

—William Nuti, CEO of Symbol Technologies, Inc.

For some time now, I have held the belief that networking, regardless of the medium in use, is just networking. A local area network (LAN) that includes both wired and wireless media is still just a network. A network isn't defined by its media. Rather a network is defined by the services and access to resources it provides its users. It is this philosophy that is my baseline premise in writing this book.

In my perfect world, networking should be approached with less focus on the medium and more emphasis on the mechanisms and services its can provide through its configuration and arrangement.

Another guiding force for this book is the subject matter outline and objectives of Plant3's *Certified Wireless Network Administrator* examination. Although not fully intended to be an exam preparation text, the topics and concepts listed in this exam's objectives have been included in the book.

Concept and Purpose

The concept and content of this book make two assumptions: the reader (student) has a basic knowledge of networking (most likely from a wired network perspective); and the reader wishes to learn the basic concepts of wireless communications and how they are applied in a wireless local area network (WLAN). If these assumptions are correct, then we are both in the right place to begin learning.

The purpose of this book is to expand the reader's knowledge and understanding of networking concepts and principles into the world of wireless communications and networking. Building from a foundation of radio frequency (RF) communications technology, the world of wireless local and personal area networks are explored at an intermediate level toward providing the reader with a thorough understanding of the use, application, and deployment of a wireless network.

Who Should Use This Book

This book is written for students in a first or second course in a program on computer networks. This book is also ideal for readers who are independently seeking better knowledge of wireless communications and networks. In a first networking course, the information contained in the appendices may prove helpful for building a foundation of networking concepts.

Elements of Pedagogy

This text employs a variety of pedagogical techniques intended to create a rich, realistic environment in which the student can actively pursue an understanding of wireless networking. The combination of the various approaches to learning used in this program of study is also intended to accommodate the widest possible range of cognitive styles for both the instructor and the students.

Chapter Learning Objectives

A statement of learning objectives for each chapter is presented in both performance and behavioral terms. The objectives state what the student should be capable of *understanding* and *doing* as a result of reading the chapter.

Figures and Tables

Clear and carefully designed figures and tables have been included to aid the student's understanding of the material. Wherever possible, the diagrams contained in each chapter are not only referenced in the body of the text, but are positioned such that they can serve as a repeated visual reference for the detailed explanations of the concepts.

Line Checks

After each major section and, in many chapters, after a topic of major importance, two or more review questions are inserted to give the student an opportunity to reflect on the material just covered. These questions are intended to help the student better understand and internalize the material.

What Do You Think?

Along with the Line Check review feature, a single question intended to make the student consider the application, reasoning, need, or future development of the major concept, feature, or application discussed in the preceding section is presented. There are no answers provided for these questions, as they are intended to encourage discussion among the students.

Key Terminology

Immediately following each chapter summary is an alphabetical glossary of the key terms presented in the chapter. This section can aid the student in reviewing the material contained in the chapter in preparation for either class discussion or examination. In addition, each of the key terms in the book has been used to create matching questions in the supplemental test bank.

Fill-in-the-Blank Questions

Each chapter contains 10 or more fill-in-the-blank questions intended to help students better understand the key terms and phrases used and their understanding of the material contained in the chapter. Each question is completed with one of the key terms listed in the chapter. The correct term for each question is provided in the Instructor's Manual supplement to this text.

Key Term Multiple-Choice Questions

Each chapter contains 10 or more multiple-choice questions intended to help students better understand the key terms and phrases used, and also their understanding of the material contained in the chapter. The correct answer to each question involves one or more of the key terms listed in the chapter. The correct response for each question is provided in the Instructor's Manual supplement to this text.

Lab Projects

Following the review questions, two or more projects are included to help the students better understand and master the subject matter of each chapter through a hands-on project. These projects are intentionally activity-rich, as opposed to equipment-rich, to enable their use in any classroom situation.

Advanced Lab Problems

In addition to the Lab Projects, the Advanced Lab Problems present the opportunity for the student to work on a more challenging application of wireless technology, either alone or as a part of a team. The Advanced Lab Problems are more equipment and application centered than the lab projects, but they also provide the student with a more in-depth experience. Each of the Advanced Lab Problems asks the students to assume a "real world" role, which requires them to perform one or more tasks as they would in an on-the-job situation.

Chapter Descriptions

Chapter 1—Introduction to Wireless Networks

This chapter introduces you to the characteristics, markets and applications, and issues of wireless networks. It also looks at the situations in which a wireless network may be appropriate, the variety of wireless networking technology available now and in the near future, and the advantages and disadvantages of wireless networking.

Chapter 2—Wireless Modes Technologies

This chapter provides an overview of the building blocks for local and wide area networking, and all networking in between, including the Open Systems Interconnection Reference Model (OSI) model, networking topologies, and media access methods.

Chapter 3—Wireless Network Devices

This chapter looks at the devices used to create a WLAN on two levels. The first is basic radio frequency (RF) components in wireless devices. Second is the WLAN connectivity and networking devices, as well as their role on a wireless network.

Chapter 4—Radio Frequency (RF) Communications

This chapter provides an overview of the basic operations, standards, and technologies that provide the foundation on which wireless data networking is built.

Chapter 5—Wireless LAN Standards

Included in the IEEE 802 standards are several that address the operation, characteristics, and construction of wireless LANs, personal area networks (PANs), and metropolitan or municipal area networks (MANs) that transmit data using radio frequency (RF) signals. This chapter focuses on the IEEE 802 wireless networking standards, their capabilities, and characteristics.

Chapter 6—Infrared and Other Networking Media

IR devices are now emerging for use in the wireless personal area network (WPAN) market, which is able to capitalize on the relatively short range of IR devices. In this chapter, you'll learn about the standards and operations of IR networking and other emerging standards that compete with IR for the WPAN market.

Chapter 7—Bluetooth and Wireless Personal Area Networks

In this chapter, we explore the Bluetooth wireless technology and how it can be applied to create a PAN or a HAN, the Bluetooth devices that are available or emerging to facilitate the creation of these networks, and a brief look at a few "real world" applications of this technology.

Chapter 8—Wireless LAN Planning and Design

The focus of this chapter is to review the recommended planning and design process used for wireless networking situations, especially the importance of performing a site survey and modeling a proposed network design.

Chapter 9—WLAN Configuration and Installation

To ensure that a new WLAN operates properly, giving its users the bandwidth and connectivity they need, a prescribed set of planning and testing steps should be followed. This chapter focuses on the steps to use, the information you should know, and the activities you should perform to plan, configure, and install a WLAN successfully.

Chapter 10—WLAN Antennas

In this chapter, you learn about the different types of antennas, how they operate, and where and why each has its most appropriate application. You also learn some of the safety issues associated with antenna installation and usage.

Chapter 11—WLAN Security

In this chapter, you learn about the various layers of security that can be applied to an 802.11 WLAN, ranging from "not much" to "almost excellent." You also look at the security protocols and services defined in the 802.11 standards, as well as the threats that exist from the outside world and how each protocol or service combats them.

Chapter 12—HAN, SOHO, and the Enterprise

Although its title may sound like a *Star Wars* sequel, this chapter focuses on the devices and processes used to install a wireless home area network (HAN) or small office/home office (SOHO), or an enterprise (corporate) wireless local area network (WLAN). Home and SOHO devices, and their installation procedures, are virtually the same, but the devices used and the installation practices applied in a corporate setting are different, even at the WLAN level.

Chapter 13—Troubleshooting WLANs and Wireless Devices

When wireless networks stop communicating, which they always do at some point, the true cause of the problem, whether it's obvious or not, must be identified before the problem can be resolved. This chapter focuses on the process of troubleshooting in general and the troubleshooting of wireless networks and their devices in particular.

Chapter 14—Wireless WANs

The focus of this chapter is to dispel some of the vagueness and confusion by explaining, in the context of wireless networks, just what WANs, metropolitan area networks (MANs), and a couple other area networks are, the technology used in each, and how they work.

Appendix A—Network Standards and Technologies

This appendix provides an overview of the building blocks on which local and wide area networking, and all networking in between, is built, including the OSI model, networking topologies, and media access methods.

Appendix B—WLAN Protocols and TCP/IP Utilities

This appendix reviews the protocols of the TCP/IP suite commonly associated with a WLAN. In addition, it covers the common TCP/IP utilities you need to know.

Appendix C—Network Addressing Basics

Appendix C provides a review of the network addressing schemes that allow a destination site to be specifically identified to anyone or anything wanting to send information to it across a network.

Appendix D—Network Media

This appendix provides an overview of the common network media. Every network uses at least one form of network medium, whether it is copper wire, fiber-optic cable, infrared beams of light, or radio frequency (RF) signals.

Acknowledgments

I sincerely wish to acknowledge those people who have been invaluable in the creation and production of this book, My thanks:

To Christopher Johnson and Jonathan Plant, the Osborne and McGraw-Hill acquisitions editors who believed in the project and kept it going through change after change.

To Jill Batistick, my project editor. Through her careful and skillful editing, she transformed what passes for my English into coherent sentences and paragraphs.

To Marcia, my copy editor. She was able to overcome my grammar-challenged writing to make it readable and, better still, understandable.

To the others at McGraw-Hill who contributed their efforts to making this book the very best it could be: Kristin Bradley, Thomas Casson, Ron Gilster, Sarah Hill, Lori Koetters, Jody McKensie, Lindsay Roth, Laura Stone, Jason Warzecha, and the Production and Art departments.

I am also indebted to a number of people who reviewed the manuscript, offering their praise and suggestions for improvement.

I would also like to thank the individuals, companies, universities, and trade and standards organizations for their kind permission to use their photographs and artwork. These people, companies, and organizations represent the pioneers and leading-edge developers who will take wireless networking and communications into the future.

—Ron Price

Fundamentals of Wireless Networking

Chapter 1

Introduction to Wireless Networks

LEARNING OBJECTIVES:

In this chapter, you learn how to:

Examine wireless technology and its applications.

Assess wireless networking technologies.

Identify wireless network applications.

Discuss the issues and constraints of a wireless network.

While some networking professionals see wireless networking as just networking with a radio frequency (RF) medium, wireless networking does have its own unique technologies, devices, and applications. True, if you have a general understanding of computer and data networks, you are more likely to understand the underlying principles, concepts, and applications of wireless networking quicker than someone who is totally new to networking—especially wireless networking. However, the differences between wired networks and wireless networks could fill a book and, in fact, they have—this book.

This chapter introduces you to the characteristics, markets and applications, and issues of wireless networks. In this chapter, we look at the situations in which a wireless network may be appropriate, the variety of wireless networking technology available now and in the near future, and the advantages and disadvantages of wireless networking.

Why Choose a Wireless LAN?

A wireless local area network (WLAN) can be considered in several situations:

- When installing a new LAN
- When extending an existing LAN
- When replacing an existing wired (or wireless) LAN

When you are installing a new LAN, you have a choice between a wired network or a wireless network. In many instances, a wired LAN is still a better choice over a wireless LAN. For example, a wired LAN can be much less expensive, more reliable, easier to manage, and especially in situations where the LAN is not likely to be moved or reconfigured, easier to troubleshoot. However, in those situations where installing cable is impractical, the network is temporary, or the LAN's physical configuration is likely to be dynamic, a wireless LAN can be a better choice.

You may want to extend a wired network for two reasons: to add additional workstations to the network or to provide users with the capability to access the network when they are away from their workstation. A wired network can be extended through additional wired networking or by installing a wireless solution. Essentially, the choice for the first situation boils down to whether you can or want to install additional cabling (a network cable has certain limits as to how long it can be). A wireless extension to a wired network can eliminate the need for new cabling to be installed. A wired network can also provide the capability for users to access the network when they are away from their primary workstation, but only when they are in places where they are able to connect to the network media. Adding a wireless capability to a wired network can enable users to access the network from virtually anywhere within the range of the wireless network's hardware.

CROSS-REFERENCE
See Appendix D for more information on network cabling and media.

Wireless networking is not the better solution in every situation. *RF communications*, which is the medium used by wireless networking, does have limitations and constraints that keep it from being totally effective in some instances. The materials used to construct the building, interference from other RF devices, or something as basic as the shape of the area in which the wireless network is to operate—among other factors—can reduce the effectiveness and efficiency of a wireless solution. On the other hand, these factors aren't generally an issue to a wired network.

Deciding between a WLAN and a wired LAN involves other considerations beyond the network medium, such as cost, ease of installation, scalability, and flexibility. The overall goal of any network is to support and fulfill the resource and data needs of the organization and the network's users. Let's consider these issues, and a few more, one at a time.

Cost Issues
Wireless networking is, first and foremost, a wire replacement technology, which means this: when you start adding up the costs of a wireless network in comparison to those of a wired network, the most obvious cost saving is the wire or cable.

A home or a small office/home office (**SOHO**) network is typically built around a device that provides a connection for the network to the Internet, even if the connecting device is as simple as a telephone modem, as illustrated in Figure 1-1. In the home network depicted in

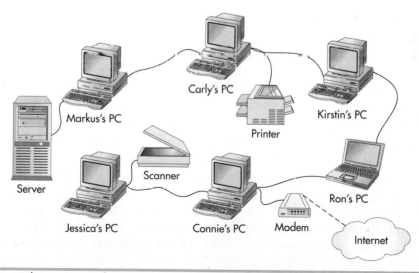

Figure 1-1   A home network using a shared Internet connection

Figure 1-1, the computers located around a home all connect to the Internet using a shared connection managed by Connie's PC. Another common home or SOHO network configuration connects each of the user computers directly to a cable modem or a digital subscriber line (DSL) bridge, as illustrated in Figure 1-2.

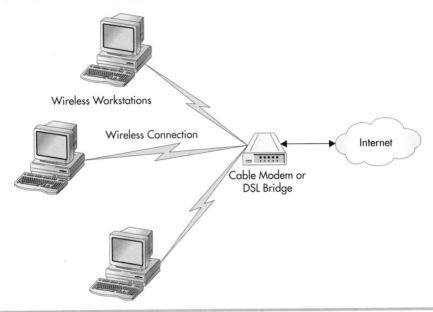

Figure 1-2 A wireless LAN using a cable modem or DSL bridge to connect to the Internet

The cost of the connecting device, which can be a switch, bridge, modem, or router, is typically about the same, regardless of the type of network installed. The real cost difference boils down to the cost of connecting the network's computers and peripheral devices to the connecting device.

NOTE

Chapter 3 discusses the functions and roles of wireless networking devices.

To state the obvious, a wireless network is, well, wireless, meaning it has no cabling requirements between the user workstations and the network access points. Figure 1-2 also illustrates how user workstations connect to the Internet connection device, which is most commonly referred to as the Internet gateway. No network is completely wireless; however, even a WLAN may require some cabling to connect the gateway to the service provider's network.

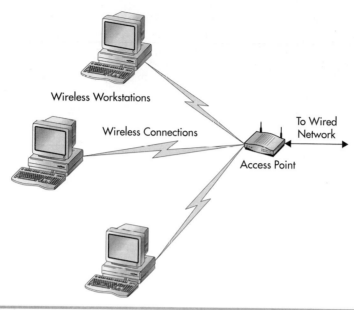

Figure 1-3   Wireless access points are often used to provide a connection to a wired network.

Figure 1-3 illustrates how a wireless network is connected to a wired network through its access point.

Another cost element related to the use of cable is the labor involved. Installing a wireless network not only saves the cost of the cable itself, but it also saves the cost of having the cable installed, either in real dollars paid to an installer or in the time involved for you to install the cable yourself. The real cost of installing network cabling in an existing facility or home must also include the finish and patch work required to repair the walls, floors, or ceiling after the cable is installed in, under, or above these surfaces. Of course, this assumes you wouldn't just string the cable across an open floor.

To summarize the cost issues between a wireless and a wired network:

- A wireless network eliminates the cost of cable runs between the network's workstations and peripheral devices to the Internet gateway.

- A wireless network eliminates the cost of installing the cable.

- A wireless network provides immediate connection anywhere in the wireless range of its access points, which is equivalent to running a direct connection to every user in a building. Obviously, a wireless network avoids the expensive cost of this type of wired network.

Scalability

The **scalability** of a network refers to the network's capability to change as needed to meet the expanding needs of an organization or home. As the number of computers or the complexity of the network changes, a network is scalable if it can easily be adapted to meet the changes without losing functionality.

A wireless network is generally more scalable than a wired network. When new workstations must be added to a WLAN—except for installing the radio network adapter in the workstation and configuring it to interface with the nearest access point—the workstation is almost automatically added to the network and in only a matter of minutes. While wireless networks do have some distance limitations, they are much less restrictive than those of wired networks, especially those using twisted-pair copper wiring (see Appendix D for more information on network media and cabling types). For example, the maximum segment length (the total length of the cabling connecting two network nodes) is around 100 meters (or roughly 330 feet). So, if a new workstation needs to be installed at a location more than 100 meters from the nearest gateway, additional equipment (such as a repeater—see Chapter 3) is required. In addition, the new workstation needs to be close to a network outlet jack, which is typically located on a wall, so it can connect to the network. Because of the safety hazards and potential performance issues involved, network cabling should not be left exposed for people to walk on or set furniture on.

 What Do You Think?

What are some of the safety issues involved with installing cable in an office or home environment?

To increase the scalability of a wired network, the number of workstations must be preplanned and the supporting infrastructure (cable, jacks, and power) must be preinstalled. On the other hand, a wireless workstation only needs to be within the range of the access point and, within that range, it can be anywhere at all.

Interoperability and Portability

In the early days of computer networks, manufacturers competed to establish their brand of equipment as a standard. The problem was this: not every manufacturer's equipment was completely compatible with the equipment produced by other manufacturers. When the International Organization for Standardization (ISO) developed the Open Systems Interconnection Reference Model (OSI), the computer networking world then had a design standard that assured all manufacturers who produced equipment adhering to the standard would be **interoperable**, which means they would have the capability to communicate effectively with each other.

CROSS-REFERENCE

Appendix A has additional information on the OSI model and other networking reference models.

Given the general framework provided by the OSI model, the Institute for Electrical and Electronics Engineers (**IEEE**—pronounced as "eye-triple-ee") began development of its networking standards for the data link and physical media layers of the networking model (see Appendix A). Data link standards define how a network node gains and maintains a link to the network media, and the physical media standards specify the characteristics of the media.

In the various networking standards, a physical layer standard (PHY) may define the electrical voltage, the current of a signal, and the pin assignment on a network connector, as well as the minimum and maximum distances and the speed requirements of the physical medium. The Layer 2 (data-link layer) standards, which are collectively referred to as a standard's Media Access Control (MAC), typically define how devices access and share the medium. Included in the MAC standards are the guidelines for device polling, medium contention, and token passing. The PHY and MAC specifications of the various wireless LAN standards are covered in Chapter 5.

The standards for both wired and wireless networks specify their PHY and MAC characteristics and methods. As long as the network devices in use on a network conform to the appropriate standards, the devices should have interoperability. Attempting to mix and match networking standards on a network may prove infeasible because the standards are incompatible and not interoperable. For example, an IEEE 802.11b wireless network interface can definitely not communicate with an IEEE 802.3 wired router.

For example, Carly purchased a notebook computer that includes an internal 802.11b wireless network adapter. She would like to install a wireless LAN in her home to share her printer with others and provide access to the Internet. Carly can assume that purchasing any 802.11b wireless router for her home network is safe because all 802.11b equipment should be compatible with all others. Similarly, Markus can be assured that all the 802.3 devices he wants to install in a wired network at his office are interoperable. However, a variety of devices are available to bridge between incompatible networking standards, such as network bridges, wireless access points, and others.

Standards-based systems provide the assurance that all equipment manufactured to the same standard will be interoperable. However, some vendors add additional features or slightly alter the standards to produce proprietary devices that are interoperable only with their devices. For example, devices manufactured under a vendor's proprietary 802.11b+ standard may not be fully interoperable with standard 802.11b devices.

The development of the network models and specific network standards provides network designers, installers, and users with the capability to assume a certain level of interoperability. As a standard matures, meaning as any shortcomings, errors, and omissions are corrected, the availability of products supporting the standard improves. This can increase the chances for the network to maintain both its scalability and its interoperability in new or add-on situations.

Another issue related to interoperability is portability. In the software world, *portability* refers to the capability of a software program to run on different operating systems (OSs) or hardware models. However, in the hardware world, and specifically in the networking hardware nation, portability refers to a device's capability to move from one standards-based networking environment to another. This could mean physically moving a computer (and its network adapter) from one WLAN to another or logically configuring a computer to interface with a different access point within a WLAN.

Integration with Existing Networks

Standards also provide the capability for one type of network to be integrated into another type of network. In fact, a common practice is for a WLAN to be added to an existing wired network to provide its benefits to one or two specific areas. In a home environment, perhaps the owners want to have the capability to connect to their wired home area network (HAN) using a wireless connection from their patio in the backyard. By installing a device designed to bridge between the wireless standard in use and the wired standard in use, this can be easily accomplished.

For an existing networked environment, "going wireless" doesn't necessarily require the removal of the existing network. Wireless networking can be used to extend an existing network to areas that have either not been cabled, or are too difficult or costly to cable. For example, a small insurance company remodels its office space to add two new offices in an area that was once an open warehouse area; the new offices can be connected into the existing SOHO network using a wireless access point that has the capability to connect to the wired network (see Figure 1-4).

? Line Check 1.1

1. What is the cost advantage of a wireless network in comparison to a wired network?

2. How does a wireless network meet the criteria for scalability?

3. Why are wireless networks largely interoperable?

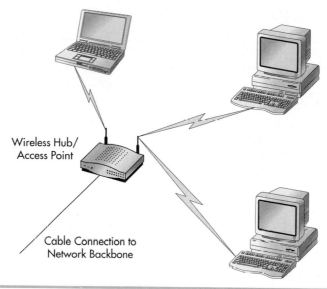

Wireless Hub/
Access Point

Cable Connection to
Network Backbone

Figure 1-4 A wireless access point can be used to integrate wireless devices into an existing wired network.

What Do You Think?

Identify a situation in which a wireless network is a better choice than a wired network. Are there situations where a wired network may be a better choice?

The Wireless Networking Market

In the wireless networking world, the availability of a wireless device typically precedes its application. Although most wireless devices have a fairly limited and narrowly defined application, several have been adapted to meet the demands of the ever-expanding market demand.

The marketplace for wireless devices is segmented into a variety of submarkets that are essentially defined by the function and purpose of the wireless devices themselves. The major markets for wireless devices are:

- Mobile personal devices
- Wireless networking devices

- Wireless Voice over IP (VoIP)
- RFID devices
- Health and medical care devices
- Commercial applications

Mobile Personal Devices

Wireless personal devices, which are also commonly referred to as mobile personal devices, first emerged as an electronic replacement for an appointment calendar, phone list, and address book in the form of the personal digital assistant (PDA). At the risk of describing something that is already obsolete by the time you read this, today's PDAs, like the one shown in Figure 1-5, include enough processing power and storage to replace the laptop and notebook computers of not so long ago.

Figure 1-5   A handheld mobile PDA device (Photo courtesy of Casio Computer Company, LTD.)

Figure 1-6   A mobile device that includes wireless communications capabilities. (Photo courtesy of Fujitsu Siemens Computers.)

In addition to the standard functions of PDAs, some mobile (meaning wireless) devices, like the one shown in Figure 1-6, include capabilities to enable their users to retrieve and send e-mail; browse the Web; participate in instant messaging sessions; capture, store, and send video images; play games; listen to music; or navigate using a Global Positioning System (GPS). Some mobile devices also include built-in cellular telephone capabilities. In fact, understanding where some mobile personal devices end and cellular phones begin has become difficult because the functions of several types of mobile devices have overlapped so much.

With the emergence of pocket PC mobile devices (see Figure 1-7), a user can carry in his hand more processing power (at typically less than $200) than most desktop computers had less than ten years ago.

The mobile device market will continue to grow as newer wireless communications standards mature and become available in more and more products. No longer must a person carry around separate PDA, cellular phone, and digital camera devices. These functions are now available as a single integrated device.

Figure 1-7   A pocket PC mobile device is capable of many computing functions. (Photo courtesy of Hewlett-Packard.)

Wireless Networking Devices

We won't go into this wireless device category too deeply at this point, because much of this book discusses these devices and their use when installing and configuring a WLAN. However, as a quick overview, here are the general classes of WLAN devices:

- **Network adapters**   These devices are either installed inside or attached to a PC to provide a radio link to a wireless network access point or another wireless device. Except for a few cases (such as in a Wireless Personal Area Network [WPAN]—see Chapter 2), a PC must have either a network interface card (NIC) or a network adapter to be a part of a wireless network. Desktop computers typically use NICs, like the one shown in Figure 1-8, and portable and mobile devices use PC Card network adapters (see Figure 1-9).

- **Access points**   Wireless access points (see Figure 1-10) provide two primary services to a WLAN. An **access point** serves as an interface point and bridge between wireless workstations and a wired network, so the wireless workstations can access the resources of the wired network. The second function of the access point is to provide wireless linkage between wireless workstations that may be out of range of each other.

Figure 1-8   A NIC for a wireless network connection (Photo courtesy of Cisco Systems, Inc.)

Figure 1-9   A PC Card wireless network adapter (Photo courtesy of Cisco Systems, Inc.)

Figure 1-10 A wireless access point (Photo courtesy of Cisco Systems, Inc.)

NOTE

For the remainder of the book, we refer to wireless access points as APs and not WAPs to avoid confusion with the Wireless Application Protocol (WAP), which is discussed in Chapter 5.

- **WLAN switches** A WLAN switch performs a variety of Layer 2 functions just like a LAN switch on a wired network. But the primary function of a WLAN switch is to reduce the amount of broadcast traffic passed from wireless network segments to a wired network. A wireless access point acts much like a wired hub in that all wireless traffic it receives is passed through to each of its interface ports, including an interface port to a wired network, if present. A switch forwards messages only to the interface port on which a particular destination address can be reached. This helps to maximize the total bandwidth and throughput of the network. A switch can also be used to create and manage one or more virtual LAN (VLAN) configurations (see Chapter 8 for more information about VLANs).

- **Print server** This specialized wireless networking device allows a printer to be connected independently to a wireless network. Two basic types of wireless print servers are available: standalone wireless devices (see Figure 1-11) and insertion modules that fit into the printer itself (see Figure 1-12). A *wireless print server* includes sufficient memory space to buffer incoming print files, so the sending workstation can free up the wireless medium and permit other stations to access the medium.

Figure 1-11   A standalone wireless print server (Photo courtesy of Cisco Systems, Inc.)

● **Wireless router**   A *wireless router*, while it performs the same basic function as a wired router, fits into the network structure in a slightly different way than its wired counterpart. A wireless router (such as the one shown in Figure 1-13) fits into the network between the connection to a service provider—DSL, cable, ISDN, fixed wireless, and so on—and either wireless workstations or wired workstations, or both. A wireless router includes and supports the functions of an access point, a wireless switch, and a router.

Figure 1-12   A printer insertion module that enables a wireless network connection (Photo courtesy of Hewlett-Packard)

Figure 1-13 A wireless router can support several wireless workstations, as well as wired workstations. (Photo courtesy of Cisco Systems, Inc.)

● **Wireless bridge** A *wireless bridge* (see Figure 1-14), which is also called a wireless Ethernet bridge, is used to connect two or more LANs (wired or wireless), typically between buildings in a campus setting or across a roadway. Wireless bridges, when used for a WLAN connection, are point-to-point (P2P) devices.

Figure 1-14 A wireless bridge is used to connect LANs in two separate buildings. (Photo courtesy of Cisco Systems, Inc.)

● **Wireless repeaters**   A *wireless repeater* can be used to extend the range of a WLAN as an alternative to adding additional access points or bridging the WLAN through the wired network. A *repeater* does exactly what its name suggests: it rebroadcasts the signals it receives after conditioning them for increased strength and clarity. Some wireless access points have built-in repeater capabilities, but standalone wireless repeaters are also available (see Figure 1-15).

Figure 1-15   A wireless repeater is used to increase the transmission range of a WLAN. (Photo courtesy of Buffalo Technology (USA), Inc.)

● **Antenna**   Wireless networks transmit using RF signals, which require an antenna to receive and transmit signals through the air. In a WLAN installation, a *standalone antenna* can be used to increase the signal strength or to overcome the weakness in a transmitted signal being received. Figure 1-16 shows an indoor omnidirectional antenna, but several types of antennas could be used. Antennas are discussed in more detail in Chapter 3.

Wireless Voice over IP (VoIP)

A wireless LAN, although generally thought of and used for transporting data, can also be configured to carry telephone signals around the LAN and provide support for mobile (roaming) users as well.

Figure 1-16 An auxiliary antenna can help overcome signal strength issues in a WLAN. (Photo courtesy of D-Link Systems, Inc.)

Voice over IP (VoIP) technology has been in existence for some time and is gradually being implemented on wired networks. *VoIP* layers voice signals onto a data network to achieve what is called voice and data convergence.

Because a wireless LAN is essentially an IP network that uses RF transmissions in place of wire media, the transmission of voice IP signals over the WLAN doesn't open too much new technology, as much as it finds a new application for the existing standards. Supporting both voice and data across a single network can prove less expensive and, in many cases, more reliable than maintaining two separate systems—one for voice and one for data. For example, in a large warehouse or factory, where two-way radios are used for communications, wireless VoIP can eliminate the cost of the "walkie-talkies" and their maintenance. In an office environment, new wireless VoIP telephones can be added quickly and without the need to install new cabling and connections.

Implementing wireless VoIP requires the use of telephones that include an RF transmitter and antenna. These telephones, which can be expensive, must also be compatible with the wireless networking standard in use on the WLAN. Another approach to wireless VoIP is the use of hand-held devices, such as palmtop computers, PDAs, and integrated devices, such as a Blackberry hand-held device (see Figure 1-17).

Figure 1-17   A woman is using a Blackberry as a wireless telephone. (Photo courtesy of Research in Motion, Ltd.)

Radio Frequency Identification (RFID)

Although few, if any, WLAN or PAN applications have been defined for it, radio frequency identification (**RFID**) is fast becoming a part of our daily lives. *RFID* is an RF-based system that has the capability to retrieve and store information in devices called *RFID tags*. Whether you realize it or not, RFID tags are already part of our daily lives.

An RFID system is made up of a transponder (embedded in a tag, button, or label) and a read/write unit. Both the transponder and the read/write unit have built-in internal intelligence and an antenna able to send, receive, and store data. Figure 1-18 shows examples of one type of RFID tag, which you may have seen attached to CDs, DVDs, and other merchandise.

The read/write unit constantly scans on its 13.56 MHz frequency for any transponders within its range (about 1 meter), sending out a signal that causes the transponder to respond with its encoded information. The read/write unit then decodes the signal and forwards the data to a designated control unit, such as a computer, security system controller, or even a point-of-sale system.

Figure 1-18 RFID transparent labels show their internal circuitry. (Photo courtesy of Texas Instruments, Inc.)

RFID tags are either active or passive. A *passive RFID tag* doesn't have a power source and uses power from the incoming signal to transmit its information. As a result, passive RFID tags are small and thin, with some as small as 4 millimeters square and thinner than an average sheet of bond paper. In fact, passive tags are small and thin enough to be inserted underneath an animal's skin. An *active RFID tag* has an internal power source, which allows it to transmit more information than is possible for a passive tag.

RFID tags are currently in use for animal identification, beer-keg tracking, car key and lock systems, and merchandise antitheft systems.

Wireless Applications in Medical and Healthcare

The potential for the application of wireless technologies in the medical and healthcare fields is virtually wide open. The capability to track and monitor patients outside of a hospital or medical facility is seen as one way to reduce hospital stays and reduce the cost of medical care.

One example is the Wireless Medical Telemetry System (WMTS). The *WMTS system* (see Figure 1-19) uses three frequency bands—608 to 614 MHz, 1.395 to 1.4 GHz, and 1.429 to 1.432 GHz—to receive or transmit information regarding the health or status of certain patients. Authorized physicians, hospitals, and other medical professionals can equip their patients with a radio transmitter that is connected to probes and sensors attached to a patient's body. Periodically, the patient's unit transmits its readings to the central system (on a closely coordinated frequency), which then analyzes the data and determines if any specific medical action is required. Figure 1-19 illustrates the concept of the WMTS system.

Another growing medical application for the use of wireless communications technology is what is referred to by a variety of names, including human area network, body area network, and Personal Area Network (PAN, with the emphasis on *personal*). For example, wireless sensors can be embedded into biomechanical devices, such as prosthesis arms and legs, and

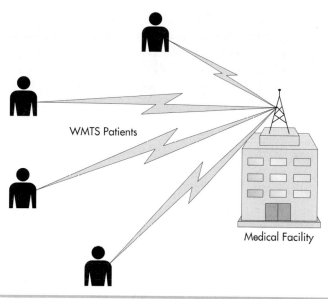

Figure 1-19   The WMTS system uses wireless technology to monitor patients.

communicate with body-mounted or embedded controller devices to control and monitor the movement of the artificial limb. Another example is the use of a micro-video camera mounted on a pair of eyeglasses that transmits images to a wireless receiver embedded inside the eyeball (see Figure 1-20) to provide sight to a vision-impaired person.

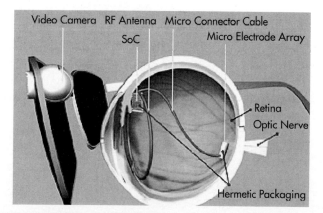

Figure 1-20   A wireless receiver embedded inside the eyeball receives images transmitted by a micro-video camera to provide sight to a vision-impaired person. (Image courtesy of the University of Southern California)

The basic concepts of this type of PAN include intrabody or interbody communications within a range of less than 1 meter to not more than 10 meters. An intrabody PAN includes wearable or embedded sensor and computing devices that communicate using wireless communications technology within the space of one person's body. For example, a device carried in a shirt pocket, such as a digital music player, can communicate with a wireless headset by either passing the signals through the wearer's body or using wireless communications. Interbody PANs are wireless systems that communicate from one person to another, but only if a linkage is established by the people touching skin-to-skin, such as with a handshake.

Industrial and Commercial Wireless Applications

As in the medical and healthcare industry, the potential for applications of wireless communications technology in manufacturing, retail, and services industries is virtually unlimited. The retail industry is already using RFID to identify and secure many of its goods, and at various levels of manufacturing, wireless sensors monitor production lines and processes and transmit alert notifications and readings when required or requested.

One example of this use of wireless communications technology is the inclusion of a wireless sensor, like the one shown in Figure 1-21, in spinning machinery where electrical or communications wiring would be virtually impossible to install, such as in a jet turbine engine, to supply strain and temperature, and to identity information in digital form.

Figure 1-21   A wireless microsensor can be embedded in many industrial applications. (Photo courtesy of MicroStrain, Inc.)

Line Check 1.2

1. What device provides the linkage between a PC and a wireless network?
2. What WLAN device works similarly to a wired network hub?
3. What embedded wireless device is used to identify and secure retail merchandise?

 What Do You Think?

What other uses can you foresee for embedded RF devices in industry, medicine, and other applications?

Wireless Networking Issues and Constraints

Several studies have projected that by the year 2008, more than 30 million users will be connected to a WLAN in the United States. This is the result of wireless networking becoming increasingly popular in corporations throughout the world, as literally thousands of companies deploy WLANs for entire buildings or campuses. In addition, it is also projected that more than 100,000 WLAN hot spots will be deployed in cities across the U.S. by 2008.

NOTE

See Chapter 2 for a discussion of hot spots.

As the deployment of WLANs continues to grow, the regulations, licensing requirements, and application standards that control and restrict the use of RF technology in the various types of wireless networks will undoubtedly continue to evolve.

The issues and constraints that impact the growth can be viewed as both constraints and facilitating factors to the growth of WLAN deployment. In the next few sections, you learn about each of the various issues that affect the use of WLANs. In addition, the public has expressed some health and safety concerns over the widespread deployment of RF technology, so you also learn about these concerns.

RF Bandwidth Allocation

Within the U.S. and in most developed countries of the world, the RF spectrum has been divided into a series of bands, which are then allocated, through licensing and registration, to specific usage or purposes. In the U.S., the Federal Communications Commission (**FCC**) is responsible for the allocation, licensing, registration, and management of the RF bands not used for government and military purposes. Table 1-1 lists some of the common RF bands managed by the FCC.

Band	Frequencies
AM radio	535 kilohertz (kHz) to 1.7 megahertz (MHz)
Short-wave radio	5.9 MHz to 26.1 MHz
Citizens' band (CB) radio	26.96 to 27.41 MHz
Alarm systems and garage door openers	40 MHz
Television channels 2–6	54 to 88 MHz
Radio-controlled (RC) aircraft	72 MHz
RC cars	75 MHz
FM radio	88 to 108 MHz
Television channels 7–13	174 to 220 MHz
Ultra high frequency (UHF) television	300 MHz to 3.0 GHz
Cellular telephones	824 to 849 MHz
Cordless telephone	900 MHz
IEEE 802.11b, 802.11g WLAN, and Bluetooth	2.4 to 2.4835 GHz
IEEE 802.11a WLAN	4.9 to 5.825 GHz

Table 1-1 Common FCC RF Spectrum Allocations

NOTE

To see the entire RF allocation for the U.S., visit **www.ntia.doc.gov/osmhome/allochrt.html**.

The allocated band for each type of RF application defines the frequency on which each type of signal is transmitted. As explained in more detail in Chapter 4, assigning each application to a different frequency allows multiple usage of the RF spectrum. Figure 1-22 illustrates how the RF spectrum is allocated.

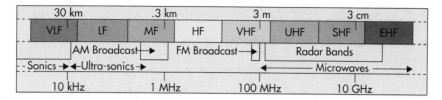

Figure 1-22   The RF spectrum is allocated in a series of frequency bands.

RF Band Licensing

Because many of the RF bands allocated by the FCC and other national communications authorities are fairly narrow, these bands are licensed to specific operators, either regionally or locally. In many cases, such as cellular telephone and point-to-multipoint fixed wireless, the operator is granted a license after the FCC conducts a public auction; the winning bidder is granted the license.

In the context of wireless networks in the U.S., use is largely unrestricted in two unlicensed bands. The Industrial, Scientific, and Medical (**ISM**) band is allocated in the 2.4 GHz to 2.4835 GHz band and is commonly used for a variety of purposes, including many wireless communications devices, such as some cordless telephones, baby monitors, emergency services radio, as well as wireless networking. This band was originally set aside, as its name describes, for use by manufacturers, scientific research, and the medical industry.

Unlicensed National Information Infrastructure (**UNII**—pronounced "you-nee") is the second unlicensed band primarily used for wireless networking. However, because UNII is unlicensed, it can be used for other purposes, such as broadband multimedia broadcasting. UNII is allocated to the 4.9 GHz to 5.825 GHz band, but is most commonly referred to as 5 GHz.

What Do You Think?

The next time you visit an electronics store, look over the wireless products available, and not just wireless networking products. Which of the bands previously discussed (Table 1-1) are required for the operation of these devices?

NOTE

See Chapter 4 for information about a technology called *spread spectrum* that allows many wireless devices to work within a single frequency band. Spread spectrum has made the wide-scale use of wireless networks possible.

RF Interference

Radio frequency interference (**RFI**) can be caused by a variety of environmental and electromagnetic sources, but the sources for RFI can be grouped into two general categories: broadcast and electrical.

Broadcast RFI sources include amplitude modulation (AM) and frequency modulation (FM) from radio stations, amateur radio (HAM), and citizens' band (CB) broadcast transmitters, as well as RF remote controls, wireless phones, cellular phones, microwave ovens, and so on. Each of these devices has either a transmitter or an emitter that sends out RF signals in a specific frequency. If the transmitter operates in a frequency close to another allocated frequency and begins to lose its precision, its signals can be picked up inadvertently by other devices.

Electrical RFI, which is also seen as electromagnetic interference (EMI), is caused by the normal operations of devices that produce electrical sparks or interrupt an electrical flow. Early RF transmitters used spark generation to spread RF signals over a wide frequency spectrum. Although the spark is contained within the transmitter, any wires connected to the transmitter become antennae for the electrical energy of the spark and emit signals over the same frequency spectrum. More commonly, RFI is created by devices like lighting dimmers, fluorescent lighting fixtures, television sets, computer displays, and some common light switches. In a not-so-extreme case, the source of RFI on a WLAN may be the very devices communicating over the network. If you have ever had an audio system that picked up static or played with a loud humming sound, such as an AM radio in your car, you have experienced the effect of RFI.

In the U.S., as well as most countries, formal regulations exist that require electronic and electrical devices to demonstrate they can still operate normally with certain levels of RFI and that they themselves don't generate RFI to interfere with other devices.

Most WLAN devices have some built-in tolerance for RFI and are able to withstand a certain amount of RFI in the medium. However, the best practice when designing and installing a WLAN is to avoid RFI sources and their disruptive impact on wireless communications.

Security

Security, or the lack thereof, is often cited as the reason why many companies and users are reluctant to install a wireless network. In a *wired network*, in which data flows through a cable from one distinct point to another, security is a physical access matter. However, a *wireless network* transmits its data through the air, which provides a less-restrictive opportunity for intercepting signals. In fact, while we look for broader and wider transmission ranges on WLAN devices, the range can often exceed the size of our buildings and homes. And, because RF signals can pass through walls and windows, physical access to the building or home isn't needed to intercept transmitted data.

As we discuss in Chapter 11, security continues to be a major issue in the use and deployment of WLANs.

Health and Safety Issues

Since the early 1990s, when a Florida court case raised the issue of the health effects of RF devices on human health, the public has felt some wariness about the safety of the long-term use of RF transmitters either as personal devices, such as a cell phone, or in an office or home setting. The allegation in that court case was that RF transmitters, if used frequently near a person's body, can cause cancer and other ailments. Because of a lack of related scientific evidence to support or refute the allegation, the case was dismissed. However, this uncertainty continues to cause some concern about the use of cell phones, cordless phones, and wireless networking devices.

The controversial defense made by the mobile phone and wireless networking industry is this: the energy in the RF bands used by these devices is nonionizing, which means its energy is not high enough to displace electrons from the atoms in living tissue and cause cancer. However, the claims that biological hazards exist suggest the heat radiating from these devices does the damage.

The bottom line, at least at this time, is until more information is available, the exposure standards published by nearly all developed nations are designed to protect humans from all identified RF energy hazards. Most of these standards deal with radiation and heat emissions, and are focused primarily on cell phones and computer display devices.

NOTE

A link between human ailments and the RF transmissions of WLAN devices has not yet been established or refuted.

? Line Check 1.3

1. What are the two RF frequency bands used in WLAN standards?
2. Are the two RF frequency bands used in WLAN standards licensed or unlicensed?
3. Why is RFI an issue for WLANs?

 **What Do You Think?**

Do you have concerns about the safety and health issues of RF communications? Why or why not?

Chapter 1 Review

Chapter Summary

Why Choose a Wireless LAN?

- The issues to be considered when making a decision between a wireless and a wired network are cost, ease of installation, scalability, and flexibility.

- Wireless networking is a wire replacement technology.

- No network is completely wireless; even a WLAN may require some cabling to connect the gateway to the service provider's network.

- A wireless network eliminates the cost of cable runs between the network's workstations and peripheral devices to the Internet gateway.

- A wireless network eliminates the cost of installing the cable.

- The scalability of a network refers to the network's capability to change as needed to meet expanding needs of an organization or home.

- Network models and standards provide network designers, installers, and users with a certain level of interoperability.

- Portability refers to a device's capability to move from one standards-based networking environment to another.

The Wireless Networking Market

- Most wireless devices have a fairly limited and narrowly defined application, but many can be adapted to meet other applications.

- The markets for wireless devices are: mobile personal devices, wireless networking devices, RFID devices, health and medical care devices, and commercial applications.

- Today's wireless personal devices include enough processing power and storage to replace the laptop and notebook computers of not so long ago.

- The general classes of WLAN devices are: NICs and network adapters, access points, WLAN switches, print servers, wireless routers, wireless bridges, wireless repeaters, and antennae.

- RFID systems have the capability to retrieve and store information in devices called RFID tags using wireless communications.

- The capability to track and monitor patients, as well as several embedded applications, using wireless communications technology are viewed as ways in which hospital stays and the cost of medical care can be reduced.

- The potential for applications of wireless communications technology in manufacturing, retail, and the services industries is virtually unlimited.

Wireless Networking Issues and Constraints

- Within the U.S., the RF spectrum is divided by the FCC into a series of bands, which are allocated to specific usages or purposes.

- The two unlicensed bands specified in the WLAN standards are ISM and UNII. ISM is allocated to the 2.4 GHz to 2.4835 GHz band and UNII is allocated to the 4.9 GHz to 5.825 GHz band.

- RFI is caused by a variety of environmental and electromagnetic sources. The sources for RFI can be grouped into two general categories: broadcast and electrical.

- Security is often the reason companies and users are reluctant to install a wireless network.

- A link between human ailments and the RF transmissions of WLAN devices has not yet been claimed or refuted.

Key Terms

Access point *(12)*
FCC *(24)*
IEEE *(7)*
Interoperable *(7)*
ISM *(25)*
Network adapter *(12)*
RFI *(26)*
RFID *(19)*

Scalability *(6)*
SOHO *(3)*
UNII *(25)*

Key Terms Quiz

Use the terms from the Key Terms list to complete the following sentences. Don't use the same term more than once. Not all terms will be used.

1. The device that provides the interface between a PC and the network medium is a(n) _____.

2. A(n) _____ is the WLAN device that provides communications support to wireless workstations and, in some cases, an interface to a wired network.

3. The acronym _____ represents the name given to a small office or home office that connects to a network.

4. The RF WLAN band that operates at approximately 2.4 GHz is _____.

5. The _____ is the agency of the U.S. government that regulates, licenses, and allocates RF frequency bands.

6. The RF WLAN band commonly known as the 5 GHz band is _____.

7. Networking devices from different manufacturers that are able to communicate are said to be _____.

8. _____ means a network technology can be resized to meet the needs of an organization.

9. The organization that develops and publishes the standards for WLANs is the _____.

10. _____ can disrupt communications and could cause the loss of data.

Multiple Choice Quiz

1. What is the wireless communications technology used in retail operations to identify and secure merchandise?

   A. ISM

   B. Micro sensors

   C. RFID

   D. UNII

2. What WLAN device provides communications management services to wireless workstations?

    A. Access point

    B. Antenna

    C. Network adapter

    D. Repeater

3. What WLAN device is installed in or attached to a PC to provide an interface to a wireless network?

    A. Access point

    B. Antenna

    C. Network adapter

    D. Repeater

4. What industry association develops, publishes, and maintains the standards for wireless networks?

    A. FCC

    B. IEEE

    C. ISM

    D. UNII

5. What is the term used to describe the capability for networking devices from different manufacturers to communicate effectively?

    A. Accessible

    B. Interoperable

    C. Portable

    D. Scalable

6. Which of the FCC's RF bands operates in the frequency range of 2.4 GHz to 2.4835 GHz?

    A. ISM

    B. RFID

    C. SOHO

    D. UNII

7. What is the term used to identify the broadcast or generated electrical signals that can disrupt wireless communications?

   A. ISM

   B. FCC

   C. RFI

   D. RFID

8. What is the acronym used to identify a single remote network that typically connects to another network to conduct its work?

   A. Enterprise network

   B. HOSO

   C. ISM

   D. SOHO

9. What is the term used to describe the capability of a network technology to be easily resized to meet the growing or changing requirements of an organization?

   A. Accessibility

   B. Interoperability

   C. Portability

   D. Scalability

10. Which of the FCC's RF bands operates in the frequency range of 4.9 GHz to 5.825 GHz?

    A. ISM

    B. RFID

    C. SOHO

    D. UNII

Lab Projects

1. Visit the web site for the FCC's RF band allocations at **www.ntia.doc.gov/osmhome/allochrt.html**. Identify at least three RF frequency band allocations that can be used in wireless networks. What are their frequency bandwidths?

2. Search the Internet and identify as many applications for the use of RF technology and wireless communications as you can in each of the following categories:

A. Retail sales

B. Medicine

C. Manufacturing

D. Home and building security

Case Problem

1. Working in a group of two to three classmates, design a wireless networking "dream home." Describe all the wireless communications technologies you would include in your home, whether or not they exist today. When you finish your design, do you think the majority of the features you've included are for entertainment, lifestyle, or household functionality?

Advanced Lab Project

The objective of this lab is to calculate the difference between scaling an existing wired network versus implementing wireless as part of the existing network.

Information for Laboratory: This lab requires the student to evaluate an existing company network. Using the worksheet provided, calculate the cost of scaling the wired network versus implementing wireless as an alternative to wired.

Estimated Completion Time: 20 minutes

Exercise I: The Acme Corporation recently expanded its Chicago operations. The office has been in Chicago for five years. During that time, the office IT manager has overseen the installation of a wired network.

The existing network currently consists of an Ethernet Switch and six wired workstations. The network is used to:

- Share files
- Access the Internet
- Access company e-mail
- Access a corporate database across the Web

The office has recently expanded and now occupies the entire first floor. The company now has 22 computers and 5 printers that need to be shared. The new sales department manager also purchased laptop computers for all six of his sales people and one for herself.

The sales offices are also used by corporate salesmen when traveling to Chicago. They typically need access to the Internet and a way to access e-mail. You have been asked to compare the cost of scaling the existing wired network versus installing wireless.

Facts: Cost per wired network connection will average $125.00 per cable segment

Use the following to record your findings:

Part One—Wired Network Calculation

Step 1 - Count the number of existing computer connections. Hint: They are colored blue.	$B =$ ___
Step 2 - Record the number of new computer connections needed. Hint: They are colored yellow in the diagram.	$Y =$ ___
Step 3 - Record the number of new printer connections needed. Hint: They are colored green.	$G =$ ___
Step 4 - Now account for the number of new cable runs for the Acme Chicago office. Hint: Count the new computers that need to be connected Y, all the printers that need to be shared G, and the seven new laptops purchased by the sales department. $Y + G + 7 =$ Total T.	$T =$ ___
Step 5 - Calculate the total cost of the new cable runs. Multiply T by $125.00. Record this value as C.	$C = \$$ ___

Part Two—Wireless Network Calculation

Step 1 - Record the total number of new computer connections needed. Hint: They are colored yellow and blue. The blue computers are currently on the wired network. *Note*: The blue computers *do not* have to be changed, but we will change them for this example.	$YB =$ ___
Step 2 - You must now account for the new laptops purchased by the sales department (7). (Hint: Add 7 to value YB.) *Note*: Most new laptops come with built-in wireless adapters. However, for this exercise we assume they did not.	$TC =$ ___
Step 3 - You decided Acme corporation will use USB wireless adapters to connect to the wireless network. The connectors are Belkin Wireless USB Network Adapters. You found them for $39.00 dollars each. How much will the wireless adapters cost Acme? (Hint: Multiply TC by $39.00.)	$A = \$$ ___
Step 4 - Calculate the cost of connecting the printers to the wireless network. You decided Acme corporation will use wireless print servers to connect the printers to the wireless network. Because all Acme printers have USB ports, you decided to use Linksys Wireless Print Server for USB. You found the wireless print server for $129.00 each. Multiply the number of printers (G) by $129.00. Record this value as PS.	$PS = \$$ ___

Part Two—Wireless Network Calculation (Continued)

Step 5 - Calculate the cost of the wireless access point needed to connect your workstations. *Note:* This process can be complicated. However, for this exercise, you determined Acme will need three wireless access points. You decided to use 3Com OfficeConnect Wireless Access Points. The access points are $79.00 each. How much will the wireless access points cost Acme Corporation? Hint: Multiply $79.00 by 3.	$AP = \$ \_\_\_$
Step 6 - Calculate the cost of running cable to each of the access points. All three access points will need a connection to the wired network. Hint: Multiply 3 by $125.00.	$W = \$ \_\_\_$
Step 7 - Calculate the total cost of using wireless to scale the Acme Chicago office. Hint: Add the cost of the wireless adapters A, plus the access points AP, plus the cost of the print servers PS, plus the cost of the cable runs to the new access points W. ($A + AP + PS + W = Z$)	$Z = \$ \_\_\_$

1. What is the difference in cost between the wired network and wireless network installations?

$$C - Z = \$ \_\_\_$$

2. What was more expensive—scaling your current network with wired runs or using wireless?

    ☐ Wired Network

    ☐ Wireless Network

3. How much would you save by leaving the existing computers on the wired network?

$$6 \times \$39 = \$ \_\_\_$$

4. What is the advantage of upgrading the existing computers to a wireless network?

Summary Discussion

As a wireless network professional, you may be required to demonstrate a cost analysis between expanding a wired network and installing a new wireless network. This exercise points out only the minimal costs you need to account for. In an actual cost analysis, you may need to expand the costs considered to include technician and user training, business interruption, and other intangibles associated with or created by the conversion.

Chapter 2

Wireless Modes Technologies

Perhaps the primary reason the Internet has grown as it has is because, in its infancy, networking models, practices, protocols, and standards were developed on which it could grow. Without these elements, networking as we know it today would be so segregated along proprietary lines, it would essentially be nonfunctioning.

This chapter provides an overview of the building blocks on which local and wide area networking, and all networking in between, is built, including the Open Systems Interconnection Reference Model (OSI) model, networking topologies, and media access methods.

CROSS-REFERENCE

The appendixes at the end of the book provide information on basic networking concepts, models, media, and components. Appendix A contains information on the OSI and TCP/IP networking models.

WLAN Modes and Topologies

Much like the topologies (see Appendix A), wireless networks can be configured into two operating modes: ad-hoc mode or infrastructure mode. In some instances, a wireless network can also support both modes, but in most cases, a wireless local area network (**WLAN**), meaning a local area network (LAN) operating on a radio frequency (RF) medium, is configured to only one mode.

Ad-hoc Wireless Networks

Ad-hoc mode, which is also called roaming mode, is applied to create a wireless network that allows devices to communicate directly with each other. Devices can move about within the network and connect with whatever wireless devices are within its range. Figure 2-1 illustrates a basic example of an ad-hoc wireless network. The three computers in this figure are able to link and communicate directly with one another, without the need or support of a wireless access point.

As shown in Figure 2-1, ad-hoc wireless networks create a peer-to-peer arrangement among the devices within range. However, as this figure shows, a wireless device in an ad-hoc network is able to associate and link with only those other devices within its range. Wireless ad-hoc networks can be like the one shown in Figure 2-1, a PC connecting to a cell phone or PDA within a personal workspace, a city or campus "hot spot," or a citywide mobile ad-hoc network (MANET).

The ad-hoc wireless network mode is best used in situations when a need exists to create an all-wireless network without installing wireless access points or in situations where a wired solution is impractical, such as across a wide area. An ad-hoc configuration can also serve as a backup to an infrastructure mode wireless network if a key access point stops working. Typically, an ad-hoc wireless network cannot connect to a wired LAN unless a wireless gateway designed for the purpose of bridging ad-hoc networks to a wired network is installed.

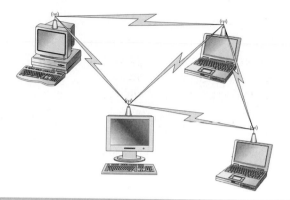

Figure 2-1   A basic ad-hoc wireless network

The nodes in an ad-hoc network communicate over virtual communications paths. Because an ad-hoc network may or may not include an access point, each of the nodes must have the capability to relay network signals from one node to another, creating a peer-to-peer network as needed. The virtual paths used to connect the peer pairs are created on the fly. This allows one node to communicate with another node through an intermediate node. For example, in Figure 2-2, node A is able to communicate with node F using the ad-hoc links between A and H, H and D, D and E, and E and F.

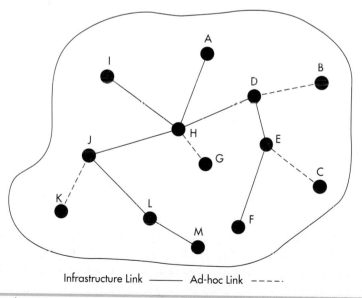

Figure 2-2   The dynamic topology of an ad-hoc network

Ad-hoc Attacks

Wireless networks are particularly vulnerable to an inside ad-hoc client or peer-to-peer attack. An ad-hoc client attack typically involves an inside client communicating directly with another inside client, bypassing any access point or wireless router on the ad-hoc network. By bypassing the access point or router, the attacker can typically also bypass and avoid any authentication systems on the WLAN. Inside ad-hoc attacks can be used to capture user names, passwords, IP addresses, or MAC addresses. The attacker may also be able to intercept other information about another inside wireless client, and then use it to defeat authentication and authorization safeguards. In most cases, an inside ad-hoc attack is intended to get the information needed to gain full access to an infrastructure network that may be accessed through the ad-hoc WLAN.

Figure 2-2 also illustrates the two types of connections that ad-hoc nodes can use. While both types of links, ad-hoc peer-to-peer (*A* to *H*) and ad-hoc on-demand (*B* to *D*), are virtual links, the peer-to-peer links remain in place because the device remains relatively fixed in location. The on-demand links remain in place only while the two devices are within range. In the example of node *A* communicating with node *F*, if *H* and *D*, or *D* and *E*, aren't actively communicating, the routing functions embedded in their network adapters are able to create the ad-hoc links that allow *A* and *F* to communicate.

Mobile Ad-hoc Networks (MANETs)

Wireless networks in support mobile devices are not a new concept. In fact, the Defense Advanced Research Projects Agency (DARPA), the technology research arm of the U.S. Department of Defense, has supported them since the early 1970s, when they were referred to as packet radio networks. In fact, packet radio networks have been around even before the Internet. When the first Internet protocols were developed, it was the mobile networks that provided much of the impetus for the development of these protocols.

A **MANET** is self-created when roaming wireless devices, typically mobile wireless routers, are connected over a wireless link. Within the dynamic topology of a MANET, which can change unpredictably, the roaming devices are able to move about freely and connect and disconnect to the network randomly. The first implementations of the MANET concepts were used for governmental and military use, such as the Joint Tactical Radio System (JTSR) and the Near-Term Digital Radio (NTDR) systems. However, the Internet Engineering Task Force (IETF) (see **www.ietf.org**) is developing MANET standards for use in Internet access. Figure 2-3 illustrates the creation of a MANET among wireless roaming devices, which could be located within buildings, cars, trucks, and in the pocket, purse, or briefcase of a person walking along a street.

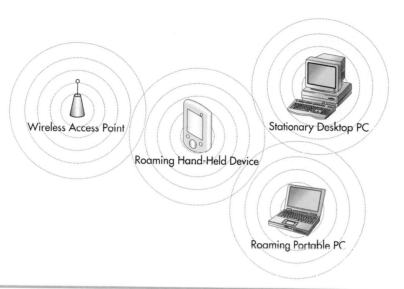

Figure 2-3   A MANET or ad-hoc wireless network is created dynamically by devices moving into range of other wireless devices.

The applications for which a MANET can be used range from small, fixed-position wireless networks to large-scale dynamic wireless metropolitan area networks (WMAN). Because of the breadth of this range, the protocols used to support a MANET must be efficient and designed to operate in a dynamic environment.

Wireless Ad-hoc Protocols

An ad-hoc protocol controls the manner in which roaming wireless devices associate and communicate. Ad hoc devices that are located in a single location or a MANET aren't arranged in a fixed topology. As a result, they must be able to create the network and its topology on-the-fly by discovering each other. This happens by each wireless node announcing its presence and listening for similar announcements from other wireless devices, called *new-near-nodes*, within its range.

Because a wireless ad-hoc network is, by definition, decentralized and its topology is dynamic, each of the wireless nodes must perform its own message forwarding. This means the network adapter in each ad-hoc node must have the capability to perform basic routing and switching functions. In a MANET, in which the wireless network adapters also have routing capability, the routing protocols in use must keep the size of the routing table small, while they keep the information in the routing table as current as possible for its dynamic network environment. WLAN standards and protocols are designed to work only within a fixed range "cloud" of wireless devices, supporting either ad-hoc or infrastructure networks without any routing capability. However, many of the high-level mobile wireless protocols are able to configure groups of WLAN devices into MANETs.

The primary protocols used in mobile wireless ad-hoc networking are:

- Ad-hoc On-demand Distance Vector (AODV)   *AODV* supports dynamic routing between mobile devices that provides for quick discovery of new-near-nodes and eliminates the need to maintain routes to nodes no longer active in the ad-hoc network.

- Destination Sequenced Distance Vector (DSDV)   *DSDV* maintains the ad-hoc network topology by periodically broadcasting routing updates. DSDV performs routing based on the "next-hop" destination for each wireless node active in the network.

- Dynamic MANET On-demand (DYMO)   *DYMO* is a MANET reactive routing protocol that efficiently performs route discovery and management functions.

- Dynamic Source Routing (DSR)   *DSR* includes the capabilities to perform both route discovery and maintenance. DSR is designed specifically for wireless ad-hoc networks comprised of mobile devices.

- Optimized Link State Routing Protocol (OLSR)   *OLSR* causes each node in an ad-hoc network to select one or more of its neighboring nodes to serve as a multipoint relay (MPR), which are the only nodes required to maintain routing information and forwarding control traffic.

Infrastructure Wireless Networks

An **infrastructure** *WLAN* (see Figure 2-4) is one in which the wireless stations usually remain in a relatively fixed location or area. These wireless devices associate (connect) through a designated access point and are bridged (linked) to a wired Ethernet network. An infrastructure WLAN also can provide connectivity for roaming wireless devices within its range. The advantages an infrastructure WLAN has over an ad-hoc wireless network are centralized security, scalability, and, often, better operating range. The disadvantage of an infrastructure WLAN over an ad-hoc network is primarily the cost of the access point(s) or other wireless network devices.

In an infrastructure WLAN, an access point serves as a communications hub and provides connectivity to wireless nodes, as illustrated in Figure 2-4. As in an ad-hoc network, the nodes on an infrastructure WLAN create their connections as required, but the connections are not peer-to-peer. The topology of an infrastructure WLAN is essentially a star, in which the wireless nodes all communicate with a central, clustering device (the access point) for access to network resources.

2

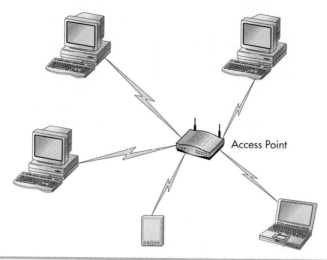

Figure 2-4   An infrastructure WLAN is created around an access point.

NOTE

Virtually all wireless network connectivity devices, such as routers, bridges, and so forth, have a wireless access point built-in.

The central device in an infrastructure WLAN is a wireless access point. To associate with the access point, the wireless nodes must be configured with the same service set identifier (SSID) and operate within the same WLAN standard(s) as the access point. In the majority of applications, an infrastructure WLAN is used to extend a wired network, which is accessed by the wireless nodes through the access point. In business, home, and small office/home office (SOHO) wireless networking environments, infrastructure WLANs are, by far, the most commonly used networking mode.

CROSS-REFERENCE

Chapter 3 provides more information about wireless access points and the other devices used in an infrastructure WLAN.

Basic Service Sets

Infrastructure WLANs are configured around an access point that is configured as either a Basic Service Set (**BSS**) or an Independent Basic Service Set (IBSS). A *BSS* access point provides point-to-point, fixed-point wireless bridging to a wired Ethernet network, as illustrated in Figure 2-5.

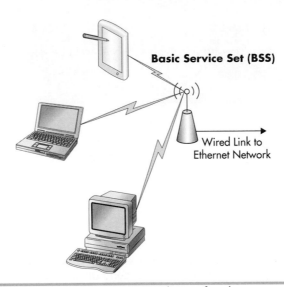

Figure 2-5   A wireless node operating in BSS mode is a fixed-point station.

IBSS mode wireless nodes are typically members of ad-hoc and peer-to-peer networks, in which the wireless devices connect to one another, generally without the use of an access point. IBSS mode devices are able to connect to each other whenever they are within each other's range, provided they agree to a few basic link parameters. Figure 2-6 illustrates the IBSS arrangement.

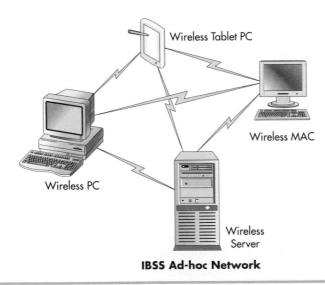

Figure 2-6   An ad-hoc network uses IBSS mode devices.

NOTE

An 802.11x wireless device cannot be configured to both BSS and IBSS at the same time.

NOTE

Another form of BSS that can be configured into a WLAN is an Extended Service Set (ESS), which is an access point that provides a wired link to an Ethernet network in a WLAN that includes more than one access point.

Peer-to-Peer WLAN

As previously discussed, an ad-hoc WLAN can be configured and operated with or without a wireless access point. When no access point is in the network, the wireless devices should be configured to operate in IBSS mode. A **peer-to-peer WLAN** can be established on older computers running open-license software, such as Linux, without the need for a wireless access point. Of course, a wireless NIC or network adapter is required for each computer.

Consider this example of peer-to-peer networking in action: working at her office desk, a salesperson updates the customer files on the company server from her tablet PC. She then joins the customer in the conference room and is able to recall her latest notes, as well as the customer's database information for use in her presentation to the customer.

WLAN Roaming

WLAN roaming has two general types: seamless and nomadic. *Seamless roaming* is more commonly associated with cellular telephones and *nomadic roaming* is used with WLAN devices.

Cellular telephones use seamless roaming. As the cell phone moves between cells (antennae), it disconnects from the cell it is leaving and establishes a connection to the next cell in an overlapping manner, which prevents a loss of service connectivity.

WLAN devices use nomadic roaming to move between links. As ad-hoc WLAN devices move through the range of two or more access points, routers, antennae, and other wireless radio devices, the device associates itself with that part of the network on an available channel. Figure 2-7 shows a simplistic view of how nomadic roaming works in a WLAN.

As an example of roaming, a salesperson can move about his office with his tablet PC, moving from one room to another, and remain reconnected to the network. In most cases, a roaming station is not actively executing an application while moving from one location to the next. However, what if the salesperson needs to be actively executing an application program while moving from his office to the conference room?

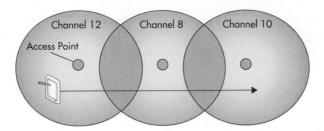

Figure 2-7   WLAN devices can roam among wireless base stations.

A number of factors can have an impact on how well a moving connection can remain linked to a WLAN, but the primary factors are

- 802.11 roaming
- The roaming configuration of the WLAN
- The duration of the movement

802.11 Roaming

Roaming on an 802.11 network uses a "break before make" sequence that breaks a roaming device's existing access point link before establishing a link with a new access point. The downside to this method is the possible loss of incoming data in the short period of downtime that can occur between the break and the make. For those applications that transmit using the Transmission Control Protocol (TCP), data loss is less of a problem because TCP includes mechanisms to prevent data loss; TCP requests a retransmission of any packet lost during the switchover from one access point to the next. For those applications that use the connectionless User Datagram Protocol (UDP), such as Voice over IP (VoIP) and streaming media, retransmission is not an option and any packets lost during roaming are simply dropped.

WLAN Roaming Configuration

Recall that an ESS is a grouping of two or more BSSs, which typically communicate over a distribution network (wireline network). In many respects, an ESS, which is a roaming domain, is much like a wired network's broadcast domain or a network subnet on which all nodes receive broadcast messages. Mobile wireless nodes are able to roam within an ESS without the need for changing their IP configuration because WLAN roaming occurs at Layer 2 levels. If a WLAN device roams across roaming domains, its IP configuration must be updated to configure the device as a member of the new roaming domain (subnet), which means any upper-layer activity, such as application-driven sessions, must be dropped.

Roaming Duration

When a wireless device moves about within a WLAN, it is roaming. To the network, *roaming* is the amount of time the wireless devices needs to disassociate (disconnect) from BSS

2

and establish an association with another BSS. The *roaming duration* is the time required for these two events to take place. Once the device is associated with an access point and communicating, the device is no longer roaming because it is now associated with the access point and a part of the BSS's infrastructure.

Line Check 2.1

1. Differentiate between ad-hoc and infrastructure wireless network modes.

2. In what type of network structures are the BSS and IBSS used?

3. What connection/reconnection sequence is used in 802.11 roaming?

What Do You Think?

Cellular telephones use a "make before break" connection/reconnection method when roaming. Why is this method inappropriate for 802.11 WLAN roaming and why is the "break before make" method better for WLANs?

Personal Area Networks (PANs)

A personal area network (**PAN**) is built around a personal operating space (**POS**), which is commonly defined as extending from 1 meter (about 3 feet) up to 10 meters (about 33 feet) in all directions around a person. In a wireless *PAN*, the operator is totally enveloped in a kind of networking bubble. When operating wireless communication devices, a person's *POS* remains present, regardless of whether the person is in motion or standing still.

One of the underlying concepts of a PAN is this: as a person moves through her daily activities, the opportunities to exchange data with others occur quite frequently as her POS comes into contact with another person's POS. A PAN is a network that exists around a single user.

Whenever the POSs of two or more individuals overlap, an opportunity occurs for the personal wireless devices of one person to exchange information with those of the other person(s). Examples of the devices commonly POSs and PANs are wireless PCs, cell phones, personal digital assistants (PDAs), and even watches. Inside the overlapping POSs, these devices discover each other and automatically establish an ad-hoc communications link. They are then able to transfer information to other devices. The same concepts hold true for home or office personal devices inside a POS, such as desktop computers or perhaps even a refrigerator, range, or microwave.

PANs are largely implemented as convenience networks built on one or more forms of cable replacement technology. For the most part, security is provided by the point-to-point nature of most PAN technologies, but this isn't the primary reason a PAN is implemented. Because of the nature of some PAN technologies, however, security will become an important issue in the not-too-distant future.

The advantage of a PAN is its capability to automatically detect and link to any device that falls within the POS in a seamless and transparent way. Some of the technologies you learn about in the chapter require some effort on your part to link with other devices and some require none. Not every technology is better for every possible PAN application, though. As the standards for the various PAN technologies become better defined, more devices will become available, which is likely when we finally begin to realize the original conceptualizations of just what a PAN can be.

The range of a PAN is generally only a few meters, which has proved effective because the needs of an individual rarely extend beyond that distance. A PAN is commonly used to interconnect a computer, its peripheral devices, and the devices used to connect to another network, such as an Internet gateway, as illustrated in Figure 2-8.

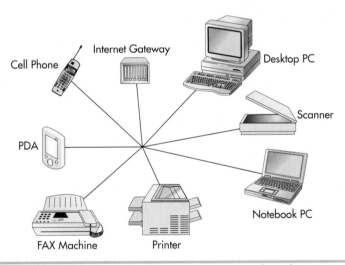

Figure 2-8   A personal area network (PAN) interconnects wireless devices into a network.

While our focus is on wireless PANs, a PAN can be created using wireline bus structures, such as the Universal Serial Bus (USB) or the IEEE 1394 (commonly known as FireWire) interfaces. Wireless PANs typically use cable replacement technologies, such as Bluetooth, the Infrared Data Association (IrDA) standard, ZigBee, or perhaps even radio frequency identification (RFID).

CROSS-REFERENCE

The wireless technologies listed in the preceding paragraph are discussed in Chapters 1 (RFID), 6 (IrDA), and 7 (Bluetooth).

Hot Spots

A *hot spot* is the general name given to a specific geographical location that provides wireless broadband services through an access point to which roaming wireless devices can connect using ad-hoc mode. Figure 2-9 shows one example of how hot spots are being implemented in public areas, campuses, and private businesses. Many cities, shopping centers, and universities have installed wireless hot spots, typically with a limited range, for their citizens, customers, and students.

Figure 2-9   A hot spot in a coffee bar is one example of how the number of hot spots continues to grow. (Photo courtesy of Northfield.org)

Line Check 2.2

1. Define and give an example of a WPAN.
2. What is required to implement a hot spot in a business, such as a coffee bar or restaurant?

What Do You Think?

Where do you see WPAN technology going in the next five to ten years? Think outside the box on this one, and remember, signals transmitted through the human body would constitute a WPAN as well.

Wireless Network Media

Network media are the physical communications links used to connect nodes on a network. Every network uses at least one form of network medium, whether it is copper wire, fiber-optic cable, or RF signals.

Although the "physical" medium of a wireless network is the air, eventually, all network transmissions end up on a cable of some kind, even wireless networks.

Radio Frequency (RF)

The primary medium used on WLANs is RF transmissions, but within the standards of wireless networking (802.11x) and the limitations of the public communications regulatory agencies (the Federal Communications Commission [FCC] in the U.S.). This means the medium used in wireless devices is actually the atmosphere. RF refers to that portion of the electromagnetic spectrum in which electromagnetic waves can be generated by an alternating current that is fed to an antenna (see Figure 2-10).

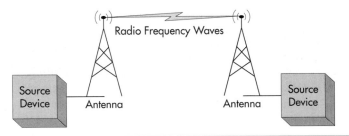

Figure 2-10   RF waves are transmitted through the air by an antenna.

CROSS-REFERENCE

Chapter 4 covers RF communications in detail.

RF communication is divided into the following major frequency groups:

- Very low frequency (VLF): 3–30 kHz
- Low frequency (LF): 30–300 kHz
- Medium frequency (MF): 300–3000 kHz
- High frequency (HF): 3–30 MHz
- Very high frequency (VHF): 30–300 MHz
- Ultra high frequency (UHF): 300–3000 MHz
- Super high frequency (SHF): 3–30 GHz
- Extremely high frequency (EHF): 30–300 GHz

When attached to a high-frequency AC power source, an antenna acts as a transmitting device, converting AC voltage and current into electromagnetic wave energy (as illustrated in Figure 2-10). Antennae also have the capability to intercept electromagnetic waves and convert their energy into AC voltage and current. The AC power source and the antenna form a basic RF circuit.

Chapter 2 Review

Chapter Summary

Define the Most Common Wireless Network Structures

- Wireless networks operate in one of two modes: ad-hoc and infrastructure. Ad-hoc mode is a roaming mode and is used on WLANs where some or all stations can move about within the range of the WLAN's access points. A WLAN infrastructure mode communicates through a base station or a wireless AP.
- Two types of wireless APs can be used in a WLAN: hardware AP and software AP.
- The RF transceiver of a wireless network adapter must be configured to communicate in either a BSS or an IBSS mode.
- WLAN devices use nomadic roaming to move between APs.

- A PAN encompasses a POS, which extends up to 10 meters in all directions around a person. A PAN is a network that exists around a single user.

- A hot spot is a geographical location with public wireless broadband services available to roaming wireless devices.

Identify WLAN Media Types

- The primary medium used on WLANs is radio frequency (RF) transmissions, but within the standards of wireless networking (802.11x) and the limitations of the public communications regulatory agencies (the Federal Communications Commission [FCC] in the U.S.).

Key Terms

Ad-hoc mode *(38)*
BSS *(43)*
Hot Spot *(49)*
IBSS *(44)*
Infrastructure *(42)*
MANET *(40)*
PAN *(47)*
Peer-to-peer WLAN *(45)*
POS *(47)*
WLAN *(38)*

Key Terms Quiz

Use the terms from the Key Terms list to complete the following sentences. Don't use the same term more than once. Not all terms will be used.

1. A(n) _____ is a public area in which users are able to connect to a wireless access point.

2. _____ access points provide point-to-point, fixed-point wireless bridging to a wireline network.

3. A(n) _____ is an ad-hoc node that allows other wireless nodes to connect together without the use of an access point.

4. A(n) _____ is a wireless network for mobile devices.

5. The _____ is the common name for a wireless Ethernet network.

6. In _____, wireless links are created between roaming wireless devices without an intermediary access point.

7. On a(n) _____ WLAN, the wireless stations remain in a relatively fixed location and establish links to an access point.

8. A _____ is built around a person, totally enveloping the person into a kind of networking bubble.

9. An ad-hoc infrastructure creates a _____, which generally does not include an access point.

10. The area around a user that is defined by the range of the wireless technology in use is called a(n) _____.

Multiple Choice Quiz

1. What wireless mode is being used by a student who uses a wireless connection to link to her lab partner's notebook PC in a study hall?

   A. Ad-hoc

   B. Infrastructure

   C. Fixed-base

   D. Roaming

2. What type of network is used to dynamically interconnect mobile wireless devices, which must include routing capabilities?

   A. Ad-hoc

   B. MANET

   C. MONET

   D. WLAN

3. What wireless network mode is being used when an office worker connects to a WLAN BSS from his desktop?

   A. Ad-hoc

   B. Infrastructure

   C. Fixed-base

   D. Roaming

4. What is the acronym used to indicate a network that provides support for a single user in a 10-meter range?

   A. CAN

   B. LAN

   C. MAN

   D. PAN

5. What is the working space, the size of which is defined by the wireless technology in use, surrounding a wireless user?

   A. POT

   B. PAT

   C. POS

   D. PAN

6. What type of base station is associated with ad-hoc and peer-to-peer wireless networking?

   A. BSS

   B. ESS

   C. IBSS

   D. DHSS

7. Which of the following is used to describe a public, campus, or building area where users are able to establish wireless connections to a network?

   A. CAN

   B. Hot spot

   C. Open source

   D. PAN

8. When an access point is used to link a wireless network to a wired Ethernet network, the access is considered to be a(n)

   A. BSS

   B. ESS

   C. IBSS

   D. SSS

9. What is the acronym given to a wireless network defined into a specific area?

    A. LAN

    B. CAN

    C. WAN

    D. WLAN

Lab Projects

1. Determine what wireless modes are in use in your school or business. Working with a team of two or three members, create a network diagram that illustrates the general layout and mode in use and how, if at all, they are interconnected.

2. Changes to the protocols, addressing schemes, and other fundamental issues of the Internet are implemented through the Request for Comments (RFC) process administered by the Internet Engineering Task Force (IETF). Access the Internet and find information about which RFCs have affected changes to TCP/IP.

Case Problems

1. If you were given the task to redesign the network in a standalone student computer laboratory, what wireless mode would you use and why? Would your choice be different if money wasn't an object? Draw a diagram of the lab representing the layout of your network.

2. What technological, social, or business developments over the past 15–20 years have been the major developments that have led to the rapid development of local area networks?

Advanced Lab Project

Use the Internet to locate three wireless hot spots near your city or in your town. Here is a popular web site that can locate hot spots: **http://www.jiwire.com/index.htm**. After locating each of the sites, explain why you think these businesses or organizations benefit by providing a free hot spot to their customers?

    a. Site One: _____

    b. Site Two: _____

    c. Site Three: _____

Chapter 3

Wireless Network Devices

LEARNING OBJECTIVES:

In this chapter, you learn how to:

List and describe wireless device components.

Define the usage of WLAN devices.

A wireless local area network (WLAN), like its wired LAN counterpart, is made up of several types of networking and connectivity devices. And, like wired devices, wireless devices play specific roles in creating and maintaining connectivity to a local network and, in some cases, to networks beyond the local network.

This chapter looks at the devices used to create a WLAN on two levels: the basic radio frequency (RF) components in wireless devices, and the WLAN connectivity and networking devices, and their role on a wireless network.

WLAN Radio Components

The wireless devices used to make up a WLAN are themselves comprised of a particular set of components. These components work together to allow each WLAN node to transmit, receive, and process the RF signals that form the network medium of the WLAN. The primary components in WLAN devices are its radio transmitter/receiver (transceiver) and its antenna.

As you would probably guess, a radio device is at the heart of any wireless device. Every WLAN device includes a radio transmitter/receiver (transceiver), which is also called a radio modulator/demodulator (modem).

The radio in an IEEE 802.11 device performs a number of essential functions to support communications across the WLAN:

- **Modulation** An 802.11 radio generates a carrier wave (either in the 2.4 or 5 GHz bands) and modulates the wave with a variety of keying and spread spectrum methods (see Table 3-1).

Standard	Data Rate	Modulation Method	Number of Phase Shifts	Spreading Method
802.11	1 Mbps	Binary Phase Shift Keying (BPSK)	1 (180 degrees)	Barker code
802.11	2 Mbps	Quadrature Phase Shift Keying (QPSK)	4 (0, 90, 180, and 270 degrees)	Barker code
802.11b	5.5 Mbps	QPSK	4	Complementary Code Keying (CCK)
802.11b	11 Mbps	QPSK	4	CCK
802.11a/g	54 Mbps	Orthogonal Frequency Division Multiplexing (OFDM)	–	–

Table 3-1 IEEE 802.11 Modulation Methods

● **Spread-spectrum encoding**   The radio modulates digital data streams by combining them into a bit sequence with a higher data rate to form what is called a chipping code. The chipping code divides the original data stream into the pattern used on a particular spread-spectrum transmission mode.

NOTE

A *chipping code* creates a redundant bit pattern for every bit transmitted to increase the capability of the transmitted signal to withstand interference and the capability to recover a bit damaged during transmission. IEEE 802.11 devices use the *Barker code,* which is ideal for modulated radio signals because of its 11-bit sequence.

3

Interference

Interference is perhaps the biggest single issue in maintaining consistent, quality wireless communications. *Interference* can cause intermittent reception and connectivity problems or completely trash a wireless signal to the point of making it undecipherable. You have probably witnessed interference when listening to an AM radio station or watching analog television. Interference can affect your wireless networking signal reception in many of the same ways.

Interference directly impacts the signal strength received by a wireless station. You can determine the affect of interference on a wireless signal using the wireless connection monitor included in Windows operating systems (OSs) or the client software that came with your network adapter. These tools enable you to monitor the signal strength, which should be relatively high when there is little or no interference or low when more interference is present.

There are two basic types of interference: in-channel and out-of-channel. *In-channel interference* (also called co-channel interference) on a wireless LAN can be caused by other devices that emit signals in the same frequency as the WLAN, such as a cordless phone, microwave oven, and the like. Another source of in-channel interference can be the access point in the wireless network. An *access point* can emit both transmitted (intermodulation) and spurious (harmonics) signals that can cause interference on the network.

Out-of-channel interference is the interference emitted by a device and received by other nearby devices. To avoid out-of-channel emissions, the sideband radiations are limited under the regulations of both the FCC and the 802.11x standards. However, reducing or limiting out-of-channel interference can become a delicate balance between range and coverage and the amount of interference a wireless network device produces.

- **Physical (PHY) layer splitting** A wireless radio divides its signal into two sublayers:

  - **Physical Layer Convergence Protocol (PLCP) sublayer** The PLCP sublayer provides the carrier features used by the Media Access Control (MAC) layer to sense the carrier and determine if the medium is in use.

  - **Physical Medium Dependent (PMD) sublayer** The PMD carries the modulated signal.

- **MAC controller** This is typically a microcontroller on the wireless network interface card (NIC) that runs (often in conjunction with the radio NIC device drivers running on a PC) the MAC layer protocols that buffer incoming and outgoing packets, and provide channel access and network management functions.

? Line Check 3.1

1. What modulation technique is used for 802.11 standards up to 11 Mbps?

2. What is the function of a chipping code?

3. What are the two sublayers of the 802.11 PHY?

WLAN Devices

Arguably, the most important components of any network are those that provide and support the communications links between a network's nodes. A network's communications and connectivity devices provide the links that attach a node to the network, allow it to share its resources, and facilitate its capability to communicate with other nodes across the network.

The primary connectivity components of a WLAN are

- Network adapters
- Access points
- Repeaters
- Bridges
- Switches
- Routers and gateways
- Antennas

Not all of these device categories are found in every WLAN. However, a typical WLAN includes at least one access point and one or more **network adapter**—all having either built-in or standalone antennas.

Each of these devices is discussed in the following sections.

Wireless Network Adapters

The most common wireless device you have to install and support is a wireless network adapter. For a computer—regardless of whether it is a desktop, notebook, tablet, or handheld computer—to communicate on a wireless network, it must be equipped with a wireless network adapter. The proper selection and configuration of a wireless network adapter can help to ensure the best operation of a WLAN.

When selecting a wireless card, several characteristics must be considered:

- Interface type (internal, USB, PCI, and so forth)

- Wireless standard (802.11a, 802.11b, 802.11g, Bluetooth, and so forth)

- Antenna type (detachable, nondetachable)

- Power output (40mW, 50mW, 200mW)

- Power modes (PSP, CAM)

A *wireless network adapter* can be connected to a computer as an internal built-in device, such as Intel's Centrino products and other RF-embedded devices, or as a peripheral device that attaches either externally or internally. External network adapters connect most commonly through a USB or another form or high-speed serial interface. An internally installed network adapter is typically in the form of an expansion card that is inserted into an expansion bus slot inside the computer's system unit.

The method used to attach a wireless network adapter defines its form factor. Although there are a variety of sizes, shapes, and interface types of wireless network adapters, they can be grouped into four general form factors:

- Internal expansion card network interface cards (NICs)

- Internal integrated network adapters

- External PC Card network adapters

- External USB network adapters

In addition, each type of network adapter form factor is available to interface with at least one of the three currently released IEEE 802.11x standards (802.11a, 802.11b, and 802.11g) and some interface with two or all three of these standards. Table 3-2 lists the common

Network Adapter Type	Advantages	Disadvantages
PC Card (PCMCIA)	No open-box installation required PC Card (16-bit) and CardBus (32-bit) models available Easily removed	Not compatible with most desktop PCs Relatively high-power requirements Size and power of antenna commonly lower than other types Poor antenna orientation
PCI and miniPCI expansion cards	Permanent installation	Requires open-box installation Antenna orientation can be weak
USB	No open-box installation required USB 2.0 features 480 Mbps peak transfer rate 802.11b operates at approximately the same speed as USB 1.1 USB devices can be easily removed Usable on either desktop or portable PCs	USB 1.0 features 12 Mbps peak transfer rate 802.11a/802.11g requires USB 2.0 Higher CPU usage More easily stolen

Table 3-2   Advantages and Disadvantages of Common Wireless NIC Types

advantages and disadvantages of each type of **NIC** in comparison to the other types. Wireless network adapters are also available to interface with the Bluetooth and HomeRF wireless standards.

Expansion Card Wireless NICs

An expansion card wireless *NIC* has been, at least until recently, the most common type of wireless network adapter in use. Even today, expansion card NICs continue to be the market choice when converting desktop computers for wireless networking.

An expansion card wireless NIC is installed inside a desktop computer's system unit (also known as "the case," "the box," or "the tower"), which encloses the computer's motherboard, internal hard disk drives, CD-ROM and DVD drives, and other internally mounted peripherals.

Although the most common expansion bus interface used for expansion card NICs (whether wired or wireless) is the Peripheral Components Interconnect (**PCI**), most modern motherboards also include expansion bus mounting slots for at least one or two other bus interfaces. We mention this only to help differentiate the PCI from the other bus interfaces, so you can readily identify a PCI slot from the other slots on a motherboard.

PCI expansion card slots are included on virtually all new computer motherboards, as well as nearly all motherboards manufactured in the past five years. Some motherboards may also include slots for the Industry Standard Architecture (ISA) or the Enhanced ISA (EISA) bus interfaces, but ISA/EISA wireless NIC cards are fairly uncommon (although they do exist and can be found, if you really want to install one). The other type of expansion slot found on motherboards is the Accelerated Graphics Port (AGP), which is used primarily by video cards. Figure 3-1 shows a motherboard with slots for all three of these interfaces. Table 3-3 shows a comparison of ISA, EISA, and PCI interface buses.

ISA/EISA   PCI   AGP

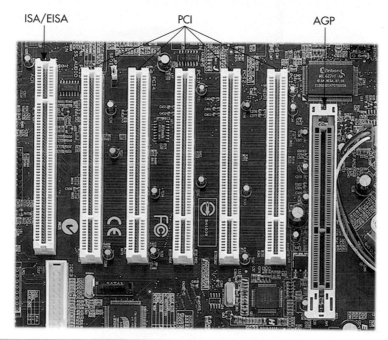

Figure 3-1   The expansion slots on a desktop computer motherboard (Original image courtesy of AOpen, Inc.)

Bus	Transfer Bits	Speed
ISA	8 or 16	8–10 MHz
EISA	32	8–10 MHz
PCI	32 or 64	33 or 66 MHz

Table 3-3   A Comparison of Motherboard Expansion Buses

NOTE

ISA/EISA slots are typically black in color, but like those shown in Figure 3-1, they can vary with the manufacturer.

Figure 3-2 An IEEE 802.11b wireless NIC expansion card (Photo courtesy of D-Link Systems, Inc.)

By far, the most commonly available expansion card NIC is the PCI 802.11b card, like the one shown in Figure 3-2, and all better wireless NICs are clearly marked with the 802.11x standard they support, typically with a label on the face of the card (see Figure 3-3). When installing a wireless NIC in a computer, you should recheck and verify that the IEEE 802.11x

Figure 3-3 Verify the 802.11x standard of a wireless NIC before installing it. (Original photo courtesy of Cisco Systems, Inc.)

standard of the card matches that of the other computers and wireless devices to be used on the network. This simple check can save troubleshooting and head scratching later.

Network Adapter Wireless Standard

Selecting the right wireless network adapter requires you to completely understand the differences and compatibilities of the 802.11x WLAN standards. You should also understand the situations in which each standard is likely the best solution. What can complicate the selection of the network adapter that is the best fit for a given WLAN installation is there are also several proprietary versions of the WLAN standards, such as the 802.11b-Plus standard, supported by several manufacturers. Although 802.11b-Plus devices are capable of transmitting at faster speeds than standard 802.11b devices, they may not be compatible to all other 802.11b devices. So, an important part of the decision process for WLAN network adapters is this: they should all support the same standard as the rest of the WLAN's devices.

NOTE

The IEEE 802.11b and 802.11g standards are mostly compatible, but 802.11a is incompatible with either 802.11b or 802.11g. And Bluetooth is incompatible with any of the 802.11 standards.

Antenna Type

Another consideration when selecting a wireless NIC is the antenna type. Wireless NICs come with either a nondetachable (the most common) or a detachable antenna.

A *detachable antenna* facilitates the use of an external antenna connected into the NIC. This is an important feature if you plan to perform site surveys with the PC. A nondetachable antenna cannot be removed from the NIC. However, several models of *nondetachable antenna* NICs also provide a connection jack for an external antenna, if the PC is located where its reception is limited or blocked. And some NIC models (see Figure 3-4) are configured only with a connection for an external antenna.

Power Output

One of the most important characteristics of a wireless NIC is its output power rating. Because battery power is limited in portable computers, power consumption can be an issue. Several different power management modes are available on NICs to help conserve power. The more common power modes available are

- **Constantly awake mode (CAM)**   *CAM* is designed for use on workstations and wireless devices that are always connected to an AC power source. However, this setting is the default for many NICs and, when used on portable devices, it can drain a battery fairly quickly.

Figure 3-4 An expansion card wireless NIC with a connection jack for an external WLAN antenna (Photo courtesy of D-Link Systems, Inc.)

- **Power savings polling (PSP)** This basic power-saving mode allows the NIC to be put to sleep to conserve power on the host computer and awakened by the network when messages have been queued for the station.

- **Fast PSP** This power-saving mode, also known as PSPCAM, combines the features of CAM and PSP. Fast PSP is good power-mode choice on PCs that switch between AC and DC (battery) power frequently.

- **Maximum power saving (MaxPSP)** *MaxPSP* is most commonly used when conserving power is more important than station or NIC performance. In *MaxPSP mode*, the wireless NIC is put into sleep mode after a preset period of inactivity and periodically awakened to retrieve any network traffic queued from it on the access point.

NIC cards are available with lower and higher output power. A higher output power capability can provide a greater RF range and possibly yield better throughput speeds. On most wireless NICs and network adapters, the output power rating ranges from 30 milliWatts (mW) to 200mW.

NOTE

You should use caution when choosing NICs with higher output power. Not only do they cost more, but they also can interfere with other nearby networks, by introducing in-channel interference.

Installing an Expansion Card NIC

Let's say you just purchased a PCI expansion card wireless NIC and can't wait to install it in your home PC. You want to connect to the WLAN your dad has installed in his home. Inside the packaging, you find the NIC, a user's guide, and an installation CD-ROM (Compact Disc—Read Only Memory). After reading the user's guide, you understand the installation process involves two major steps: (1) physically installing the NIC in the PC and (2) configuring the NIC using the PC's OS, which, in this case, is Windows XP, and the installation CD-ROM.

When installing an expansion card NIC, you should follow some handling and insertion guidelines to ensure the proper fit, contact, and operation of the card:

3

1. To ensure you are completely protected from electrical shock, shut down the computer using the normal shutdown procedure of the OS, turn the computer off with its power on/off switch if one exists, and then unplug the computer from the AC power source. Many newer computers have power to the motherboard even when the system is shut down. If a green or red light-emitting diode (LED) is lit on the back or front of the system case, power is flowing to the motherboard to facilitate its wakeup-on-LAN feature.

2. Remove the case cover following the information in the manufacturer's user's guide.

Electrostatic Discharge (ESD)

As a general rule, you should always wear an anti-ESD device such as a wrist or ankle strap, use an anti-ESD mat under the computer, or both—or more. Beyond what you can personally wear or set the computer on, a room can be treated or furnished to avoid ESD as much as possible.

ESD is created in nature in many ways, but the ESD you should be most concerned with is the static electricity your body generates walking across a carpet, working in an environment with low humidity, or even petting your dog or cat. If you've ever reached for a doorknob and gotten shocked, then you've experienced around 3,000 volts of ESD.

The electronic components in a computer run on 3 to 5 volts of electricity and, for the most part, as little as 30 volts of ESD can damage or destroy them. Consider that you can't feel ESD of less than 2,500 volts and that the blue spark of ESD is only visible when a discharge of 20,000 volts or more is involved.

Besides wearing an ESD strap, you can do a few other things to protect the inner components of a computer and yourself: apply antistatic carpet treatment to carpeted areas where you commonly work on your computer; store electronic components and expansion cards in ESD bags, even if only for a short time while you are working on a computer; place the computer on an ESD grounding pad while working on it; and last, but certainly not least, raise the relative humidity in the work area to above 45 percent.

If you are unable or unwilling to take these preventive steps, then at least while you're working inside a computer, keep a hand or forearm in contact with the computer's inner chassis at all times when touching any of the computer's electronic components.

3. Before starting to work on the computer, either put on an electrostatic discharge (ESD) protecting wrist (see Figure 3-5) or ankle strap and connect the clip end of its cable to the computer's inner chassis. This is a preventive measure to safeguard the electronic components, and especially the wireless NIC, against static electricity discharge that could damage or destroy electronic circuits.

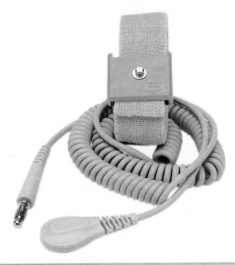

Figure 3-5 An ESD wrist strap can help to protect a computer's electronic circuits from static electricity discharge. (Photo courtesy of Desco Industries, Inc.)

4. Locate the expansion slot on the motherboard that is appropriate for the NIC card (typically a PCI). Expansion cards and their mating slots have a specific design, so make sure you don't put the card into the wrong slot—you could damage the card, the slot, or, perhaps, even the motherboard.

5. In most cases, you'll need to remove the slot cover (as illustrated in Figure 3-6) before the expansion card can be inserted and mounted properly. The slot cover is a placeholder for the front edge mounting of the NIC. Remove the screw holding the slot cover in place and keep the screw handy to use to secure the NIC later.

NOTE

Before removing the slot cover for an expansion slot, study the arrangement and placement of the cards already installed in the motherboard. Most wireless NICs are a bit thicker (side to side) than other cards, so you may need to rearrange the existing cards to create a space into which the NIC will fit without making contact with other boards. If the cards are touching, it can cause electrical shorts and damage one or both cards.

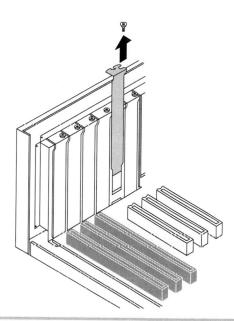

Figure 3-6   Before inserting an expansion card, you should remove the slot cover associated with the expansion slot in which the NIC is to be installed.

6. To insert the card, work from the inside of the case and move the antenna through the case slot inline with the expansion slot to be used. Align the card's edge contacts with the expansion slot and press the card down firmly and evenly into the slot. Don't press too hard; if the card bends or bows, you're pushing too hard.

7. Secure the card with the mounting screw, check again that there is clearance between the NIC and its neighboring cards, and then replace and secure the case cover.

Configuring a Wireless NIC

OSs are more ready for network adapters and NICs today than they have been in the past, and as a result, configuring a computer to interface with a network is far simpler than it once was. However, the key to a successful installation and configuration is to ensure that you have the most current and appropriate device drivers for the network adapter or NIC.

Network adapters and NICs have an almost infinite shelf life. You typically don't know how long the product has been on a vendor's shelf and how many updates have been made to the card or your computer's OS since the network adapter or NIC was manufactured. Changes to either card or its compatibility with a particular OS are typically incorporated into the network adapter's device driver, which is why you want to have the latest version of the device driver for your particular OS.

What this means is that the device drivers included on the installation disk or CD-ROM packed with the card may be slightly out-of-date. To avoid any potential version or compatibility problems with the NIC or its device drivers, after installing the NIC software from the disk or CD-ROM, you should go to the manufacturer's web site and download the latest drivers and updates, if any.

NOTE

Remember, in most cases, there is no Internet connection prior to installing the card anyway.

Configuring a Network Connection on a Windows XP Computer   The process used to configure a wireless network connection on a Windows XP system is essentially a Plug-and-Play affair. Windows XP is wireless-ready, which means it is able to recognize the wireless network adapter or NIC and, if the configuration is in place, connect to the network seamlessly.

In many cases, the installation disk that came with the network adapter or NIC will complete the more important configuration steps, but even in these cases, you should still review the configuration to ensure its correctness, as well as provide some important data the system will need to operate. The configuration areas you should review on Windows XP are the Network and Internet Connections control panel and the Wireless Connection properties window.

After installing the wireless NIC and closing the case, power up the computer. The OS should detect the NIC and automatically create an entry in the Network Connections folder.

To verify Windows XP has detected the NIC, perform the following steps:

1. Open the Control Panel from the Start menu.

2. Double-click the Network Connections icon.

   One of the network connections should be a wireless connection.

3. Right-click the wireless connection icon and choose Status from the pop-up menu to open the Wireless Network Connection Status window (see Figure 3-7).

   On this window, you can see the status of the wireless device (this should be Connected), how long the connection has been active (Duration), the data speed of the connection, and, perhaps, the most important part, the signal strength. Figure 3-7 shows the status of an 802.11g NIC. Notice that only two bars are showing for the signal strength. The best signal you can have will display five bars (increasing in height, left to right), but the connection should perform adequately with two bars or more. If only one bar shows, the orientation of the NIC's antenna or the position of the computer should be changed until sufficient signal strength is gained.

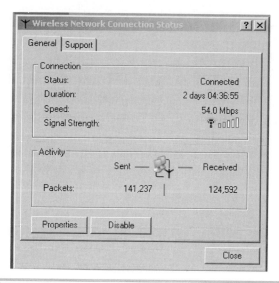

Figure 3-7   The Windows XP Wireless Network Connection Status window

4. On the Wireless Network Connection Status window, you should also find a Properties button. Click this button to display the Wireless Network Connection Properties window. If the NIC or adapter was installed using a proprietary installation disk or CD-ROM, the required protocols and services should already be installed and listed on the General tab of this window. If not, follow the manufacturer's installation instructions to configure the proper protocols and services. Figure 3-8 shows the configuration for the wireless NIC in a Windows XP system.

5. Choose the Wireless Networks tab on the Wireless Network Connection Properties window to display information regarding the connection of the wireless NIC. Figure 3-9 shows what this window should look like. The information on this tab, which concerns the configuration of the wireless LAN, should already be configured to the access point to which a connection has been made, if only one access point is detected by the NIC.

Your NIC may possibly detect more than one access point. How is this possible, you ask? Using hacking techniques called war-driving and phishing, an attacker can connect to a private WLAN by inserting an access point with stronger signal strength and the same service set identifier (SSID) close to the network's wireless stations to imitate the network's base station. This can cause the clients to associate with the "evil twin" access point and log in to the hacker's "honeypot" network, which can expose sensitive information like the user's passwords and access keys.

Two areas are on this window: *Available Networks*, which lists all the access points detected, and *Preferred Networks*, which lists the access points with which you want to connect. To update the configuration, add any of the available networks to the preferred list, using its SSID, and whether or not the Wired Equivalent Privacy (WEP) protocol is in use.

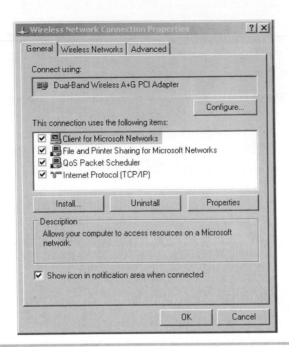

Figure 3-8   The Windows XP Wireless Network Connection Properties windows

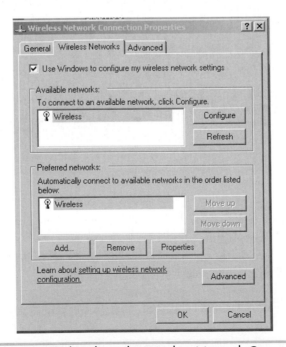

Figure 3-9   The Wireless Networks tab on the Wireless Network Connection Properties window on a Windows XP system

NOTE

See Chapter 11 for more information on WEP and other wireless network security issues.

6. Close each of the windows by clicking OK on each window. If the system requests you to restart the system, do so. You should be good to go on the wireless network after the system restarts.

Proprietary Wireless Network Monitors   Several wireless NIC manufacturers also provide proprietary connection management and monitoring software that can be used in addition to that of the OS. Figure 3-10 shows the display of one such product. These products perform many of the same functions as the OS functions described in the preceding section and may be redundant on those OSs that have wireless support built in, such as Windows XP. However, on early versions of Windows, this software is used to supplement the networking functions of the OS.

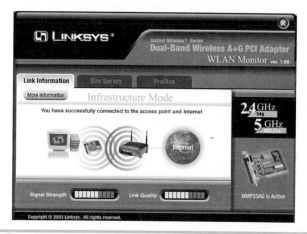

Figure 3-10   The Linksys PCI Network Monitor is a proprietary wireless network management and monitoring tool.

Wireless NICs and Linux   Luckily, most of the newer Linux commercial versions, such as Lindows 4, Mandrake 9, Red Hat 9, and SuSE 8.1, all include the capability to automatically discover and install the drivers for most wireless NICs, as long as they are 802.11b NICs, that is. Only the 802.11b (Wi-Fi) standard has widespread support in the Linux world.

NOTE

Remember, 802.11g access points are compatible with 802.11b NICs.

If your Linux system is not one of these releases, however, you may have a few more steps to perform. Check with the manufacturer of the wireless NIC to see if a Linux device driver is available for it—that is, if the NIC is Linux-compatible in the first place.

The chipsets on some wireless NICs do not include the code required for them to work on a Linux system. In fact, just because an earlier review for a NIC indicated it was compatible with Linux, the NIC may be incompatible in a later release. Manufacturers can change the chipsets and cause later releases of what was once a compatible NIC to be incompatible. So, when choosing a wireless NIC for use in a Linux system, ensure that the NIC's chipset is Linux-compatible. To verify whether a wireless NIC will work correctly on a Linux system, install the NIC on the computer, and then run the Linux utility LSCPI –v, which reports all the devices installed on the PCI bus. If the wireless NIC is included in the display from LSCPI, then the NIC is compatible and you can proceed with its configuration.

NOTE

Not that there isn't enough to check when installing a wireless NIC on a Linux system: make sure you are running version 2.1.11 or later of the LSCPI utility, which is a part of the pciutils library.

If the wireless NIC doesn't have a working device driver for your Linux system, a package of wireless utilities is available on the Internet—called wireless-tools.26 and created by Jean Tourrilhes—which contains utilities to manipulate wireless parameters, listing addresses, and signal strength, and to configure wireless device drivers.

PC Card/PCMCIA NICs

The standard used for PC card NICs, like the one shown in Figure 3-11, is the Personal Computer Memory Card International Association (**PCMCIA**), which defines three PC Card

Figure 3-11   A PCMCIA PC Card wireless NIC (Photo courtesy of 3Com Corporation)

types, based on their thickness and function. The *PCMCIA*'s *PC Card* standard defines a 68-pin connection mounted inside a PC's system unit to receive a removable media card. Table 3-4 lists the three card types and their characteristics. Virtually all wireless NIC PC Cards are PCMCIA Type II cards.

PC Card Type	Thickness (millimeters)	Applications
I	3.3	Memory
II	5.0	Modem, NIC, SCSI, audio
III	10.5	Hard disk, firewall

Table 3-4   PCMCIA PC Card Types

3

Before attempting to insert a PC Card NIC into a notebook computer, you should verify the PC Card types supported by the card slot. Although nearly all notebook computers have a PC Card slot, they are not all completely compatible with all PC Card types. Type I and II cards will fit and work in a Type III slot; Type I cards will work in a Type II slot, but Type II cards won't fit or work in a Type I slot.

For years, PC Cards have been advertised as being hot-swappable, which means the card can be inserted or removed without first powering down the computer. Many Type I cards, which are primarily memory cards, can be inserted and removed while the computer is running, but this isn't the best practice for PC Card NICs and other Type II or III cards. For the best performance and safety when working with a PC Card NIC, use the following guidelines:

- Use the OS to stop or disable the PC Card before removing it from the system when the computer is running and never remove the card while it is actively in use.

- Ensure the orientation of the card (correct side up) before inserting it into the PC Card socket. Putting the card in upside-down may damage the pins of the connector socket.

- When removing a PC Card, use the push buttons or ejectors built into the slot mounting. Don't use pliers or other gripping tools, as they can crush the circuitry inside the card.

After verifying that the computer's PC Card slot is compatible with the card type of the PC Card NIC, locate the PC Card slot on the computer, which is commonly one of two slots located on either the right or left side of the computer. To insert the card, follow these steps:

1. Insert the PC Card into either the top or bottom slot. Never attempt to install the card between the two slots.

2. Slide the card into the slot, pressing it firmly until it won't move any further. You should be able to feel the card snap onto the pins of the slot connector as you slide the card forward. Don't hit or force the card into place.

3. Start the computer and proceed to configuring the card for the OS and the wireless network.

USB Network Adapters

Two styles of Universal Serial Bus (USB) wireless network adapters are available: direct-connect and cable-connect. *Direct-connect* USB network adapters (see Figure 3-12) plug directly into an available USB jack on the computer (connecting a wireless network adapter into a USB hub can be done, but this is not recommended). *Cable-connect* USB network adapters (see Figure 3-13) are freestanding devices that connect to the computer through a USB cable.

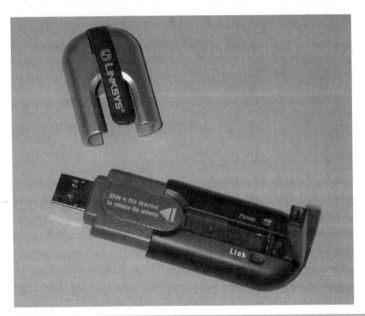

Figure 3-12 A USB network adapter that connects directly to a computer (Photo courtesy of Cisco Systems, Inc.)

The benefit of using a USB wireless network adapter is its ease of installation. All that is involved is to simply connect the network adapter to any available USB jack on the computer. However, like other network adapters or NICs, some configuration must still be performed on the computer itself.

If you have ever installed and configured a wireline NIC on a pre-XP Windows system, you will truly have an appreciation for how Plug-and-Play simplifies the configuration of a PC Card or USB network adapter.

3

Figure 3-13   A USB network adapter connected to a computer with a USB cable (Photo courtesy of Belkin Corporation)

PC Card, or PCMCIA, and USB wireless NICs are typically detected and configured by the later versions of the Windows OSs. However, if you are running a Windows version earlier than Windows 2000, you need to use the installation disk or CD-ROM that should be packed with the card. For the most part, the software on the disk will install and configure the card correctly for the OS version you are running. Once configured, the NIC monitoring and management functions listed earlier for Windows XP can be used to designate the access points to which the computer will connect (see the previous section "Configuring a Network Connection on a Windows XP Computer").

❓Line Check 3.2

1. List and describe three form factors commonly used with wireless network adapters and NICs.

2. Describe the process used to physically install a wireless NIC in a desktop computer.

3. What are the limitations involved with installing a wireless NIC in a Linux system?

What Do You Think?

Of the three most commonly used form factors for wireless network adapters and NICS, which do you think might be the best solution in each of the following situations? Why?

A. A desktop computer located in a small office environment

B. A portable computer used most frequently in outdoor locations

C. A Linux computer in a home wireless network

D. A notebook computer used in a virtual classroom setting

Wireless Network Access Points

A wireless **access point** is, in its most basic function, a distribution point, hub, and bridge for any and all wireless network adapters and NICs within its transmission range. An access point includes a radio transceiver used to communicate with wireless NICs using RF signals, a wireline 802.3 interface, and either bridging circuitry or bridging software. An access point aggregates the signals of the wireless NICs within its range and interfaces them to a wired network. The purpose of a wireless access point (see Figure 3-14) is to provide a communications link between a wireless node and other wireless and wired network services and resources.

Figure 3-14   A wireless access point (Photo courtesy of Cisco Systems, Inc.)

Access Point Considerations

Like other 802.11x wireless network components, wireless access points have a range of 29 meters (95 feet) for 802.11b in an enclosed area to the nominal range of 50 meters (163 feet) indoors to a maximum of around 400 meters (or about ¼ mile) outdoors. However, an access point's range can vary depending on the data rate, capacity, RF interference, the construction materials used in a building, power, connectivity, and the device itself.

Because an access point can be one of the most expensive components of a wireless LAN, assuming a high-quality device is used, the ratio of wireless NICs to access points tends to be high, in an attempt to maximize the cost of the access point. How many wireless access points are installed in a network depends on a number of considerations:

- **Coverage**   The design goal of a wireless LAN should be to provide linkage to every wireless LAN station first and an overlapping pattern of coverage cells to all WLAN NICs to allow for location flexibility to network stations.

- **Placement**   Typically, it is better to install wireless access points higher rather than lower inside a room or to build to minimize the opportunity for interference from walls, partitions, and any electrical or RF devices in use.

- **Network mode**   Access points can be configured for ad-hoc or infrastructure mode. If the access point is to support the roaming of the wireless devices in its vicinity, it should be configured to ad-hoc mode. However, if the access point is installed to support a fairly stationary wireless network, it should be configured to infrastructure mode, which is the most common use and configuration of an access point. Even in infrastructure mode, there is still some flexibility for relocating the stations within the range of the access point. When a station moves into the range of another access point, the software used to manage the NIC's connection to the network (the device management utility [DMU]) may need to be configured with the SSID of the new LAN.

- **Thin or fat**   The standard access point can be referred to as a *fat* device, which refers to a standalone, self-contained device that is able to provide all the functions required for WLAN functionality, including authentication, wireless encryption, and WLAN management. An emerging technology for access points is the *thin* access point, in which the access point is little more than an RF-to-RF linkage device and a radio-to-wire converter. An intelligent central controller that connects to the access point through either a wireless or a wired connection handles all other intelligent or fat functions and has the capability to individually configure and control each separate access point to the needs of the network. Figure 3-15 illustrates a WLAN employing thin access points.

Multiradio Access Points

With the continual evolution of wireless standards, many manufacturers now offer upgradeable, multiple-radio access points capable of supporting two or more different WLAN standards

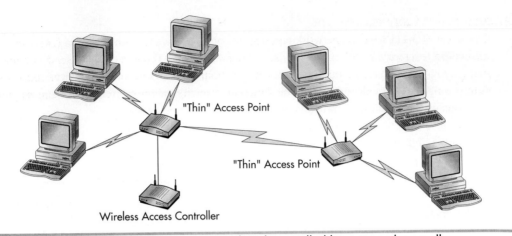

Figure 3-15 A thin access point is managed and controlled by a central controller.

simultaneously. Commonly, multiradio access points are used to service an existing WLAN on one standard, while also supporting new wireless devices on a different standard. For example, the Cisco 1200 AP and the Intermec MobileLAN WA22 (see Figure 3-16) both incorporate an 802.11b or 802.11g radio, as well as an 802.11a radio, in addition to providing standard wireless access point features, such as a connection to a wired network.

Figure 3-16 An access point with multiple built-in WLAN radios (Photo courtesy of Intermec Technologies Corp.)

Bridging Access Points

The *bridging function* in a wireless access point is used to connect two or more LANs together, allowing them to communicate and exchange messages. A wireless access point, if it includes bridging, will have either a point-to-point or a point-to-multipoint configuration. *Point-to-point bridging*, illustrated in Figure 3-17, provides a midpoint connection between the access points of two wireless LANs.

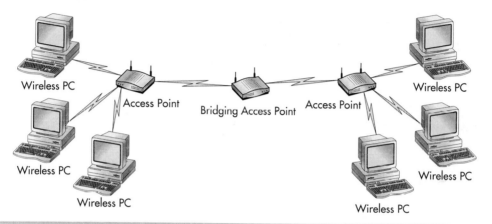

Figure 3-17   Point-to-point bridging

Multipoint bridging, illustrated in Figure 3-18, connects multiple wireless LANs together by providing a link point for the access point in each network. A point-to-multipoint bridging access point is commonly used as a base service set (BSS), which provides the connection point for the wireless LANs to the wired network.

Not all wireless access points provide bridging and, for the most part, wireless bridges (see the section "Bridges") are more commonly used in larger, corporate, campus, or commercial wireless networks. Although Figures 3-17 and 3-18 illustrate the use of wireless bridging in WLAN environments, more commonly, a wireless bridge is installed on the top of a building in a college, school, or commercial campus setting to link the wireless LANs in each building into a single, larger wireless network.

Stealth Access Points

Stealth access points don't broadcast their service set identifiers (SSIDs), which prevents the discovery of a wireless network and connection to the network by intruders. A *stealth access point* is purported as a security feature for wireless LANs, because to connect to a stealth access point, the SSID must be known and specified. By keeping the SSID secret, only those knowing it are able to connect to a wireless network.

Stealth mode access points are not defined in the 802.11*x* standards and are identified by vendors with a variety of names, including closed mode, private network, SSID broadcasting, and others.

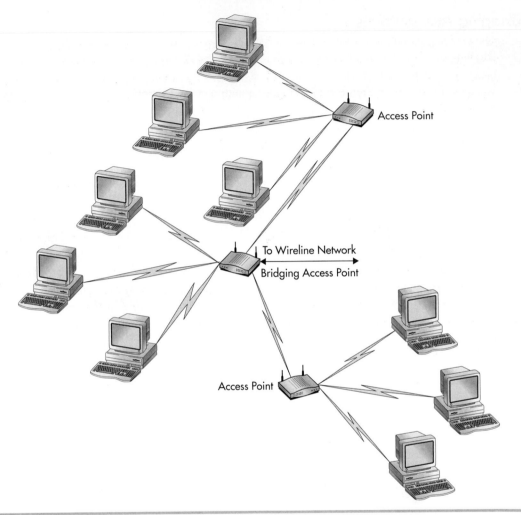

Figure 3-18   Point-to-multipoint bridging

🔍 Line Check 3.3

1. Describe the two primary modes that an access point can support in a wireless network.

2. What are the two connection modes supported by a bridging access point?

3. Describe the concept of a thin access point.

Wireless Repeaters

Every network medium, whether wired or wireless, has an effective range or distance at which the quality of its transmitted signal begins to degrade. Physical media, such as copper cables, have a distance limit at which point a phenomenon called attenuation begins to occur. Attenuation degrades the transmitted signal because the strength of the electrical impulses can no longer overcome the resistance of the cable, which is the friction in the cable caused by the electrical impulse passing through the molecules of the wire.

Like copper wire media, wireless media also suffers from attenuation. Wireless network signals are RF transmissions that are generally limited to the broadcast range of their transmitter and the power of its antenna, and their range can be impacted by electrical or thermal noise and the terrain over which it is transmitted.

In situations where the distance of a wireless transmitter must be extended beyond its normal operating distance, a repeater or signal extender is used to filter and re-energize the signal to extend its quality, strength, and effective range.

A repeater, like the one shown in Figure 3-19, isn't a complicated device. All a **repeater** does is receive a transmitted signal and retransmit the signal with its original strength restored and, in most cases, with much of the noise removed. However, the downside to repeaters and extenders is that they can add a small amount of delay (latency) to the signal. Too many repeaters or extenders on a wireless system may cause timing issues on high-speed networks.

Figure 3-19   A wireless repeater can increase the broadcast range of a wireless network signal. (Photo courtesy of Ahatpe Technical Company, Ltd.)

Bridges

A *network bridge* does about what its name implies—it creates a crossover point between two LANs or LAN segments operating on the same networking protocol. A simple **bridge** connects to two or more separate LANs or LAN segments and retransmits every message to both networks regardless of which network the message may be addressed to.

Most LAN bridges are what are called learning bridges. A *learning bridge* acts like a traffic cop for the networks it's serving. Messages transmitted between nodes on the same network are ignored, but a learning bridge forwards messages from one network that are addressed to a node on another network.

A learning bridge maintains a bridging table in which it keeps track of the physical address of a node that transmits a message addressed to another network. This allows the bridge to construct in its bridging table a cross-reference to which nodes are on which networks. Using the bridging table information, the bridge knows not to retransmit a message addressed to a node on the same network as the source device. The table also allows the bridge to decide which messages need to be forwarded to a different port than the one the message was received from. If a message is addressed to a node not included in the bridging table, the bridge records the source node's information, and then broadcasts the message to every one of its ports, except the port on which the message arrived.

For example, as illustrated in Figure 3-20, if node 1-A on network 1 transmits a message addressed to node 2-B on network 2, the bridge records the physical address and network of node 1-A in its bridging table. With this information in its bridging table, the bridge ignores any messages addressed to node 1-A sent by another node on network 1, assuming that node 1-A sensed the message on the medium at the same time as the bridge.

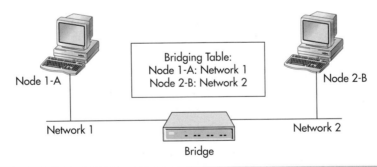

Figure 3-20   A bridge uses the entries in its bridging table to route messages arriving from different networks or network segments.

However, if a message addressed to node 1-A is transmitted by node 2-B on network 2, the bridge, after recording node 2-B's information in the bridging table, determines the message should be forwarded to network 1 to reach node 1-A using the information already in the bridging table.

The capability to reduce the amount of network traffic on a particular segment allows a bridge to improve the performance of the overall network and maximize the available bandwidth.

A wireless bridge is commonly used to provide a connection point between the WLANs in two buildings of a campus area network (CAN) and to jump a street, a landscaped area, or another type of open area between the buildings. Figure 3-21 illustrates the use of wireless bridges in a CAN environment. Figure 3-22 shows a wireless bridge unit.

3

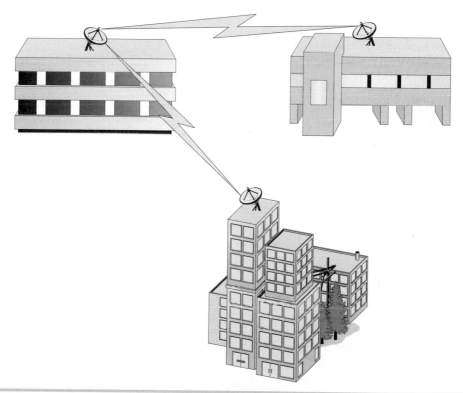

Figure 3-21   Wireless bridges are used to link buildings in a campus area network setting.

A wireless bridge commonly has a range of about two miles, which means a point-to-point wireless bridge can be used to link buildings that are some distance apart. The range of the bridge can vary, however, depending on a variety of (RF) factors, not the least of which is the capabilities of the bridge itself.

Figure 3-22   A wireless bridge (Photo courtesy of SMC Networks)

WLAN Switch

A **switch** can be likened to a multiport bridge, which was at one time essentially all a switch was. Today's switches do much more than simple bridging operations, though. A *LAN switch* is an intelligent device that is able to route messages according to a variety of factors, the least of which is the location of the destination node.

Switches create and maintain switching tables, which are similar to the bridging table maintained by a bridge. A switch keeps a bit more information than a bridge, however, which allows it to manage the network bandwidth and prevent problem messages or nodes from flooding the network or hogging up the bandwidth. A switch, like a hub, also shares its available bandwidth (transmission capacity) over the devices connected to it. However, some switches include the capability to buffer incoming and outgoing traffic to mitigate any fluctuations in the available bandwidth.

One of the mechanisms used by LAN switches to prevent undeliverable messages from clogging the network is the Spanning Tree Protocol (STP). The problem with an undeliverable message, such as a message with an unknown address, is it stays on the network, taking up the medium, which prevents other nodes from transmitting. A message in this situation is called a *network loop*. Although the exact electronics don't work this way, you can visualize the message continuing to circulate around and around the network looking for the node to which it is addressed, without ever succeeding. One of the primary functions of STP is to prevent loops on the network.

STP designates each port on a switch to be in either Forwarding or Blocking state. A *port* is a linking point on a switch through which the network medium is connected to the switch. When a port is in *Blocking state*, only messages that carry information about the status of other switches on the network are allowed to pass, with all other messages blocked. A port that's in *Forwarding state* allows all message types to be received and forwarded.

A port on a switch is changed to Blocking whenever a particular network path is experiencing delay or goes down (fails) and the switch is able to negotiate a new path through the network using other switches or bridges. When the problem is cleared up, the state of the port is changed back to Forwarding, which is the normal state for a port.

On a network, messages are forwarded through a switch using what is called *packet switching*, which is the switching method used on LANs and most WANs. Packets are switched (forwarded) between parts of the network according to their source and destination addresses (see Appendix C for more information on network addressing).

The most common methods used in packet switching to forward network messages by means of a LAN switch are

- **Cut-through switching** This type of switching method has lower latency (delay) than other switching methods because the switch begins to forward a message as soon as the source and destination addresses are received. This is typically at the beginning of the message block.

- **Fast-forward switching** This cut-through switching method can be prone to errors because it begins to forward a message as soon as its destination address is received. This means that good, as well as many bad, packets are forwarded without any filtering performed.

- **Store-and-forward switching** This type of switching adds the most latency to message processing because the entire message is read into a buffer (temporary storage area) before the switch begins taking action to forward the message. Some benefits counter the increased latency, however, including message filtering and traffic control. Plus, because the entire message is received, a store-and-forward switch is able to recognize and discard *runts* (incomplete messages) and *giants* (messages with extraneous data), which can increase undeliverable message traffic on the network.

- **Fragment-free switching** This switching method is a hybrid of the cut-through and the store-and-forward switching methods. *Fragment-free switching* buffers only the first 64 bytes of a message frame before forwarding it. The purpose of this switching method is to eliminate collision packets or the residue of a message that has suffered a collision on the medium. The assumption is this: a message that is at least 64 bytes long is okay.

NOTE

The normal forwarding mode for a network bridge is store-and-forward.

A feature unique to LAN switches is the capability to create a virtual LAN (VLAN, pronounced "vee-lan"). A VLAN is not required to be geographically or functionally fixed in place (such as within a single department of a company). A *VLAN* can be configured to logically create a network segment made up of nodes from a number of different physical segments. The primary benefit of a VLAN to a network administrator is that a specific network adapter (meaning a specific PC in most cases) can move to any location on the network and remain a member of the logical group created by the VLAN, thereby retaining the same level of access and security settings.

❓ Line Check 3.4

1. A wireless repeater is used to overcome what condition on the medium?
2. What is perhaps the most common usage for a bridge in a wireless network?
3. What type of switching is the fastest of the standard switching methods, although it can introduce higher transmission error rates?

Wireless Routers and Gateways

Regardless of the network media, wired or wireless, a **router** performs the same basic functions: determining the better route to be used to forward a message between source addresses and destination addresses on different networks and forwarding (routing) messages between networks.

If Markus in Washington State is sending an e-mail to his friend Martin in London, the message is routed over the Internet, moving from router to router until it reaches the network that includes the destination address (see Figure 3-23). When Markus clicks the OK button to send the e-mail message, the message's destination address is determined by the router to be located on a remote network and forwarded to the port connected to the Internet connection. To get from Markus's network to Martin's network, the message may pass through as many as 10 to 14 (or more) routers, with each making a similar determination about where the message should be forwarded.

To make this determination, each router on the path between Markus and Martin examines the destination address and looks it up in its routing table, which functions much like a directory in a large building. A router determines whether or not the destination address is located on the

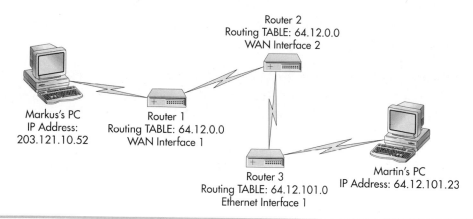

Router 2
Routing TABLE: 64.12.0.0
WAN Interface 2

Markus's PC
IP Address:
203.121.10.52

Router 1
Routing TABLE: 64.12.0.0
WAN Interface 1

Router 3
Routing TABLE: 64.12.101.0
Ethernet Interface 1

Martin's PC
IP Address: 64.12.101.23

Figure 3-23   A message is routed across the Internet until it arrives at the router servicing the destination node address.

network it services by looking for the address in its routing table. If the destination address is found in the routing table, the message is forwarded to the port through which that address can be reached. Eventually, the e-mail message arrives at the appropriate mail server and is stored in Martin's mailbox.

Routing tables can contain two types of routing entries: static or dynamic. A *static route* creates a fixed route for certain addresses to always use a specific port for forwarding. A *dynamic route* uses information gathering from other routers on the network to determine the route for a forwarded message. Instead of the network administrator specifically defining the route to take, as in static routes, routers talk to each other to learn about the network to dynamically decide which route to use.

Wireless Routers

In the purely technical sense, a wireless router or gateway isn't totally a wireless device. In most applications, a router integrated into a WLAN has the capability to communicate using RF transmissions with wireless access points and NICs. But unless the router is being used as a wireless switch or bridge within the WLAN, it is typically connected to either the wireline network or a network service provider's backbone.

Regardless of whether a router is wireless or wireline, it still performs the same basic function: routing network packets to the network path on which they can move closer to and, eventually, find their destination addresses. A wireless router combines the functions of a wireless access point with the standard functions of an IP multipoint router. Where a wireless access point provides connectivity between wireless stations within a single WLAN or network segment, a wireless router allows WLAN stations with connectivity to a wide area network (WAN) and to stations on other networks.

3

Power over Ethernet (PoE)

A new standard, IEEE 802.3af, is under development that defines a feature called Power over Ethernet (PoE) or Active Ethernet. PoE is not a new technology to the telecommunications industry; it has been used for many years on wireline networks. In fact, a similar technology is what allows your Telco-based telephone to operate during a power outage. However, *PoE* extends the earlier telecommunications technologies by adding the capability for wireless access points and other wireless network-capable devices to receive DC power over a network. In the new standard, devices that receive their power directly from a network are called powered devices (PDs).

PoE doesn't transmit electricity through the air—at least not yet—and any PoE device must be connected to a network cable to receive its power. DC power is transmitted over the network cable, which must be at least Cat 5e or better, by a device called a Power Sourcing Equipment (PSE) device or an injector, which is located at some central location on the network and before the need for DC power on the network cable.

PoE-compatible devices, such as wireless access points, accept the DC power from the cable through the RJ-45 jack used to connect the device to the network. Non-PoE devices can be converted to PoE power with the installation of a DC device called a picker or a tap, which is more formally called an Active Ethernet splitter. The DC power splitter receives the DC power on the Cat 5 cable and splits it off to a normal DC power jack.

What PoE brings to a WLAN is the capability to locate access points and other wireless devices where they can be connected to the Ethernet horizontal cabling without the need to also have an electrical power source available (such as high on a wall or in exterior locations).

Routers operate on Layer 3 (Network layer) of the OSI model. They use the information found in packet headers (the majority of which are Internet Protocol [IP] packets) and in their routing tables to determine which of the router's interface ports is connected to the better path for reaching the destination address in the packet header.

When a router receives an incoming packet, it examines the information in the IP packet header, primarily to extract the source and destination addresses, as well as any time or control information. The router then searches its access control and security information to determine if the source station is allowed access through the router. If not, the packet is allowed to time out and is discarded. If the source station is allowed access through the router, the destination address is matched to the entries in the routing table. This is used to determine which of the router's interface ports is linked to the better path for the packet to follow to its destination.

IP Packet Header   The information placed in an IP packet's typically 192-bit header (or five 32-bit segments) facilitates the actions of a router, as well as the IP processing at the destination network. Table 3-5 lists the fields of the IP packet header.

Field	Size (Bits)	Value/Usage
Version	4	Set to Binary 0100 (decimal 4) in all IPv4 packets.
IP header length (IHL)	4	The number of 32-bit segments included in the header; most commonly set to Binary 0101 (decimal 5).
Differentiated Services Code Point (DSCP)	8	Also called the Type of Service field. *DSCP* contains flags and values indicating precedence, delay, throughput, and reliability, which combine to indicate the quality of service (QoS) to be applied when processing the packet.
Total packet length	16	The total length of the entire packet, including the header and its data payload.
Identification	16	A numeric value that, together with the source address, provides a unique identifier for the packet. The identification value is also used to reassemble the packet at the destination network.
Flags	3	This field contains two single bit flags and one reserved bit. The Don't Fragment (DF) flag controls the fragmentation of a packet by routers. The More Fragments (MF) flag indicates a packet is the last of a sequence or more fragments remain.
Fragmentation offset	13	This binary number indicates the byte count at which the data in the packet payload should begin in the reassembled packet.
Time To Live (TTL)	8	*TTL* is used as both a hop count limit and a timing mechanism for a packet. The TTL value is set to a default value, which varies by the originating network OS, in the range of 30 to 255. As the packet moves through a router (hop), the TTL is decremented by 1 and if the TTL count reaches zero, the packet is discarded and not forwarded beyond that point.
Protocol	8	This field indicates the Transport layer protocol of the packet's data payload. Common entries are 1 for the Internet Control Message Protocol (ICMP), 6 for the Transport Control Protocol (TCP), and 17 for the User Datagram Protocol (UDP).
Checksum	16	*Checksum* is a calculated amount inserted each time the packet is sent and updated by each router that modifies the packet.
Source address	32	The IPv4 address of the network node that originated the packet.
Destination address	32	The IPv4 address of the network node to which the packet is intended.

Table 3-5 The Format of an IPv4 Packet Header *(Continued)*

3

Field	Size (Bits)	Value/Usage
Options	Variable	Options are not commonly used, but if they are, the IP header length must be increased to reflect more than five 32-bit segments. If options are included in a packet, they can indicate the type of routing handling and security to be applied to the packet.
Padding	Variable	The padding bits are used to fill out any unused portions of the 32-bit options segment, but only when an options field is included in the IP header.

Table 3-5   The Format of an IPv4 Packet Header

Checksum and the CRC

Quite a few computing and networking types use the terms "checksum" and "CRC" (which stands for cyclic redundancy check or cyclic redundancy code) interchangeably. Because they refer to essentially the same kind of data and processes, this is somewhat accurate. However, a checksum and a CRC are two different things.

Checksums can be 8-bits, 16-bits, 32-bits (the length used in IP packets), or longer. A checksum is computed by adding up (hashing) the bits in all the bytes (words) of a block of data (such as a network packet payload). When a checksum is included in a transmitted datagram by the sending side, the receiving side recomposes the checksum for comparison purposes when it receives the datagram. If the checksums are different, the assumption is that a transmission error occurred.

In contrast, a CRC is a bit more complex than a checksum in that it is calculated using division and either binary shifts or Boolean "exclusive or" (XOR) operations. A common algorithm used in composing a CRC is one that uses the input bits as polynomials coefficients to create a message polynomial and a generator polynomial. For example, the binary value 01100010 creates a message polynomial of $1 * X^6 + 1 * X^5 + 1 * X^1$. The generator polynomial uses constant coefficients and is divided into the product of the message polynomial, which yields a quotient and a remainder. The remainder is used to generate the CRC.

Perhaps the biggest downside to checksums and CRCs is they don't provide any information, which is why they are redundant. They are merely representations of the bits in a datagram. If only one bit is changed in a transmission, the receiving end CRC and checksum will result differently than the original. However, two or more bit changes can cancel each other out and mask a transmission problem.

While all the information in the IP packet header is important to the proper handling and forwarding of an IPv4 packet, the source and destination addresses and the TTL are, perhaps, the more important fields in the packet in the routing operation.

Routing Tables   Although the complexity and scope of the data included in a router's routing table depends on the routing protocol in use, the essential information stored in a routing table includes remote network addresses, perhaps a gateway router address for each remote network, and which of a router's interfaces is used to reach either the network or its gateway. Table 3-6 illustrates the simplified contents of a common routing table. In addition to the information shown in Table 3-6, a routing table, depending on the routing protocol in use, can include other information, called *metrics,* which indicate the speed, quality, and status of a particular route.

Destination	Gateway	Interface
64.111.0.0	64.111.10.1	s2
150.75.2.0		e1
172.168.1.0	172.168.1.10	e0
223.15.178.0		e3

Table 3-6   Sample Routing Table Entries

Router Protocols   First, two types of protocols are associated with a router: routing protocols and routed protocols. A router uses a routing protocol to talk to other routers to determine the better path available over which to forward a packet. A *routed protocol* is the protocol running on a network that creates and formats the packet and its data payload, so a router can forward it. The primary routed protocols in the TCP/IP suite are ICMP, IPv4, TCP, UDP, and Telnet. Other routable protocols include Novell's Internet Packet Exchange (IPX) and Apple Computer's AppleTalk.

Not all LAN protocols are routed protocols, however. For example, the Network Basic Input/Output System (NetBIOS), the NetBIOS Extended User Interface (NetBEUI), Systems Network Architecture (SNA), Local Area Transport (LAT), and Data Link Control (DLC) network protocols are not routable protocols. A nonroutable protocol typically employs a fixed point-to-point destination address that must be resident on the same network as the source device.

Routing protocols use some form of an algorithm to maintain the information in their routing tables and to determine the better path a packet should take to navigate through the Internet. The most commonly used routing protocols include Routing Information Protocol (RIP), the Border Gateway Protocol (BGP), the Interior Gateway Routing Protocol (IGRP), and the Open Shortest Path First (OSPF) protocol. Each protocol applies a different approach to determining the better of the available paths on which a packet can be forwarded.

WLAN Router Features WLAN routers provide a variety of LAN support features in addition to the basic functions of routing and serving as a wireless access point. Common features included on most WLAN routers are

- **Network Address Translation (NAT)** *NAT* allows network stations to share a single public IP address when communicating beyond the LAN and facilitates the use of private addresses within the LAN.

- **Port-based access control** **Transmission Control Protocol/User Datagram Protocol** (TCP/UDP) port numbers can be used to allow or deny access to the WLAN (incoming) or to the WAN (outgoing) based on the port number associated with the application initiating a network packet. For example, if you want to block Telnet requests from outside the WLAN, port 23 traffic can be blocked from the forwarding process.

- **Firewall** A *firewall* is a network mechanism that prefilters incoming packets before they reach the router or the network. Firewalls can be either standalone hardware or software, or integrated into a router, like the one shown in Figure 3-24.

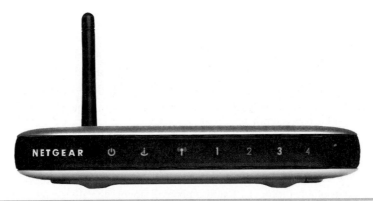

Figure 3-24 A wireless router often includes firewall functions. (Photo courtesy of Netgear, Inc.)

Firewalls

In networking, a firewall is a mechanism, either hardware or software, that is used to prevent certain inbound traffic from gaining access to a LAN or outbound traffic from gaining access to a WAN.

Although it is not commonly thought of as such, the most basic firewall service, and one of the most commonly implemented, is NAT. Even the most inexpensive routers include NAT, which eliminates an outside station from knowing any IP address other than that of the network gateway.

Another common router-based firewall function is Stateful Packet Inspection (SPI), which protects a LAN from network attacks. A router with SPI in its firewall functions looks at the packet header to determine if any special security handling is required. SPI routers have the capability to filter out advanced Denial of Service (DoS) attacks (see Chapter 11 for more information on DoS and other types of network attacks).

Two levels of firewalls can be implemented on a WLAN: personal software firewalls and dedicated hardware network firewalls.

A *personal firewall* is a software package most typically used in situations where a small network is connected to an open connection between the network and an Internet service provider (ISP). Because connection services like cable Internet and digital subscriber lines (DSL) are always on or available, the LAN is susceptible to hacker access. A personal firewall blocks incoming traffic not initiated from the network itself.

Some routers, like several models of WLAN routers, include firewall functions that go beyond the use of NAT for access control.

Dedicated network firewall appliances, like the Cisco Systems PIX Security Appliance from Cisco Systems, Inc., shown in the following illustration, can be extensibly configured to provide a wide variety of security filters for larger networks.

Wireless Gateways

The term "gateway" is a generic description used to describe a network device that joins two networks. In general networking, a *gateway* is the device or point at which a LAN connects to communication services beyond the LAN, such as a WAN or ISP connection. However, in wireless networking, gateway is used more to differentiate the multiple functions a wireless router can be used to support on a WLAN. While nearly every wireless router includes an access point function, it's the router's more advanced routing, switching, and security functions that fall under the description of a *wireless gateway.* Wireless gateways are also referred to as wireless routers and wireless base stations.

A popular use for wireless gateways (see Figure 3-25) is in support of hot spots, or areas of cities and buildings that are enabled for wireless station connections using a single base station. In these situations, most commonly, the gateway supports wireless fidelity (Wi-Fi) (802.11b) standards, but with the growing popularity and increased bandwidth and range of the 802.11a and 802.11g standards, many gateway devices include support for all three standards.

Figure 3-25 A wireless gateway is used as the base station in hot spot networks. (Photo courtesy of 3Com Corporation)

❓Line Check 3.5

1. What is the primary function of a network router?

2. Provide a brief overview of the actions taken by a router to determine how to forward a packet.

3. Describe the differences between a routing and a routed protocol.

What Do You Think?

Some say that without routers, there would be no Internet. Explain why you might agree or disagree with this statement.

WLAN Antennas

The dipole antenna built into most wireless NICs, access points, routers, and so on is generally adequate for the majority of small business and home wireless networks. However, in larger and enterprise WLANs, and especially those that must be bridged between buildings in a campus environment, an external antenna (such as the one shown in Figure 3-26) can be necessary to extend the range of the wireless devices. When choosing a WLAN antenna, you must consider the characteristics of wireless transmissions first, and then the specific characteristics of each type of antenna available.

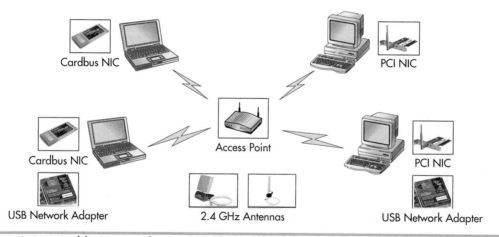

Figure 3-26   Building a Wireless LAN (Advanced Lab Project)

NOTE

See Chapter 10 for more detailed information on WLAN antennas.

When planning and designing a WLAN, you should consider several RF and antenna characteristics:

- An antenna's transmissions can be distorted by nearby metal and other objects, including walls and large furniture, as well as trees, buildings, and the like.

- Antennas both transmit and receive RF signals. Any nearby source of RF interference may be picked up and retransmitted by an antenna.

- Many RF antennas, such as cellular telephone antennas, may be polarized vertically, so an antenna with horizontal polarization may perform better in these situations.

- Any cable connections to an RF antenna should be free of splices, connectors, and other types of interconnections to minimize RF interference.

NOTE

WLAN antennas are not included in the WLAN standards, so the good news is you are free to choose an antenna. The bad news, though, is you are free to choose an antenna.

Line Check 3.6

1. What are three performance characteristics to consider when placing an antenna in a WLAN?

2. What type of antenna is most commonly built into WLAN devices?

Chapter 3 Review

Chapter Summary

List and Describe Wireless Device Components

- The primary components in a WLAN device are its radio transmitter/receiver (transceiver) and its antenna.

- Every WLAN device includes a radio transmitter/receiver (transceiver), which is also called a radio modulator/demodulator (modem).

- The radio in an IEEE 802.11 device performs a number of essential functions to support communications across the WLAN: modulation, spread-spectrum encoding, PHY layer splitting, and MAC control.

- Deploying one or more additional antennas can help to increase the range and the RF signal coverage of the WLAN and require fewer access points to provide connectivity to all wireless stations.

- The function of an antenna is to radiate and propagate signals generated by a transmitter, and to capture RF signals from the air and send them to a radio receiver. All antennas share four basic characteristics: frequency, gain, power, and radiation pattern.

- Polarization refers to the directionality or the orientation of the RF signals emanating from an antenna.

Define the Usage of WLAN Devices

- For a computer to communicate on a WLAN, it must be equipped with a wireless network adapter.

- WLAN adapters and NICs can be grouped into four general form factors: internal expansion cards, internal network adapters, external PC Cards, and external USB network adapters.

- The most common expansion bus interface for NICs is PCI, with some motherboards also supporting ISA and EISA.

- When installing an expansion card NIC, special handling and insertion should be used to ensure the proper fit, contact, and operation of the card. Precautions should always be taken to avoid ESD damage.

- The standard for PC Card NICs is PCMCIA, which defines three PC Card types that use a 68-pin connection.

- Two types of USB wireless network adapters can be used to connect to a network: direct-connect and cable-connect. Direct-connect USB network adapters plug directly into a USB jack on a PC and cable-connect USB network adapters connect to a PC through a USB cable.

- A wireless access point is a distribution point, hub, and bridge for wireless NICs.

- Wireless access points have a range of 29 meters to 50 meters indoor and 400 meters outdoors.

- The bridging function in a wireless access point is used to connect two or more LANs in a point-to-point or a point-to-multipoint configuration.

- A point-to-multipoint access point is commonly used as a BSS.

- A wireless bridge is commonly used to link buildings.

- Stealth access points prevent the discovery of a wireless network by intruders by not broadcasting its SSID. Stealth mode is also called closed mode and private network.

- A wireless router or gateway has the capability to communicate with wireless access points and NICs, as well as to a wireline network.

- Routers use the information in packet headers and their routing tables to determine which of the router's interface ports is connected to the better path for reaching the destination address in the packet header.

- Two protocol types are associated with a router: routing protocols and routed protocols. Routing protocols are used to forward packets to a network. A routed protocol is the protocol that creates and formats the packet and its data payload.

- Common WLAN router features are NAT, port-based access control, and firewall.

- Wireless gateways are commonly used to support hot spots for Wi-Fi.

- A wireless antenna can provide increased range and coverage in large facilities or between buildings.

- The characteristics to be considered when choosing a wireless antenna are distortion from nearby objects, RF interference, polarization, gain, and cable quality.

Key Terms

Access point *(78)*
Bridge *(84)*
Gateway *(88)*
Network adapter *(61)*
NIC *(62)*
PC Card *(62)*
PCI *(62)*
PCMCIA *(74)*
Repeater *(83)*
Router *(88)*
Switch *(86)*

Key Terms Quiz

Use the terms from the Key Terms list to complete the following sentences. Don't use the same term more than once. Not all terms will be used.

1. Most expansion card NICs are manufactured to interface with a(n) _____ slot inside a PC's system unit.

2. The type of radio network interface installed inside a computer's system unit in an expansion slot is a(n) _____.

3. The WLAN device used to provide a connection between two networks is a(n) _____.

4. The networking device that uses Layer 3 addresses to forward messages toward their destinations is a(n) _____.

5. Most notebook computers use a(n) _____ type of network adapter.

6. The WLAN device used to link two buildings to the network is a(n) _____.

7. The device that provides access to a wireless network for wireless nodes is the _____.

8. The wireless device used to overcome attenuation on the medium is a(n) _____.

9. The device that provides an interface for a computer to the network medium is the _____.

10. The Spanning Tree Protocol is implemented on a(n) _____ to prevent undeliverable messages from clogging up the network.

Multiple Choice Quiz

1. What type of WLAN device is used to interconnect two networks?
   A. Access point
   B. Bridge
   C. Gateway
   D. Router

2. What is the identity code called that is used between devices on a WLAN?
   A. BSS
   B. ESS
   C. SSID
   D. Stealth code

3. What type of WLAN device is used to forward packets from a local network to a WISP?
   A. Access point
   B. Bridge
   C. Gateway
   D. Router

4. What gateway security service allows all nodes on a network to share a single IP address on the Internet?

   A. Routed protocols

   B. Routing protocols

   C. NAT

   D. SSID

5. What high-speed, hot-swappable serial communication interface can be used to connect an external wireless network adapter to a PC?

   A. EISA

   B. ISA

   C. PCI

   D. USB

6. What device can be used to connect two buildings into a WLAN?

   A. Access point

   B. Bridge

   C. Gateway

   D. Router

7. What organization publishes standards for the design, form factor, and use of PC Cards?

   A. EIA

   B. IEEE

   C. PCMCIA

   D. TIA

8. Which of the following LAN devices implements the Spanning Tree Protocol (STP) to prevent undeliverable messages from clogging a network?

   A. Access point

   B. Bridge

   C. Repeater

   D. Switch

9. What is the device that provides connectivity and interface between a PC and the network medium?

    A. Access point

    B. Bridge

    C. Network adapter

    D. Router

10. A repeater can be used on a network to overcome the effects of what RF characteristic?

    A. Attenuation

    B. Crosstalk

    C. EMI

    D. RFI

Lab Projects

1. Install and configure a wireless NIC into a desktop PC. When the installation is completed, test the connection using the NIC's monitoring software. Record the detailed steps used to perform all phases of this task, including any problems you encountered and how they were resolved.

2. Install and configure a wireless PC Card NIC into a portable PC. When the installation is completed, test the connection using the NIC's monitoring software. Record the detailed steps used to perform all phases of this task, including any problems you encountered and how they were resolved.

Case Problems

1. A business wants to install a wireless network with only a single connection point to a wireless ISP (WISP). The business operates on two floors of an older brick-and-steel building with two-foot thick concrete and metal floors. Given only this information, respond to each of the following questions.

    A. Is it possible that the business operators can achieve their dream of a totally wireless LAN? If so, how. If not, why not?

    B. Is it possible that a portion of the network may need to be wireline? If so, which part of the network and why?

    C. What planning and design plan would you use in this situation?

2. If your school or college were to construct a new technology building, what options would be available to connect the new building into the existing campus wireline network? List at least three pros and cons for each identified networking option.

Advanced Lab Project

The objective of this lab is to be able to demonstrate the use of basic wireless LAN devices including antennas, NICs, and access points.

Information for Laboratory:

The selection, identification, and installation of WLAN devices are critical steps in the successful operation of a wireless network. The purpose of this lab is to enable students to install and configure wireless devices to form a WLAN (see Figure 3-26) and establish communications with a wireless access point. This lab should also demonstrate the use of standalone antennas in a WLAN.

This lab requires at least two desktop workstations on which a wireless NIC can be installed or attached, and two notebook or portable computers to which wireless network adapters can be connected.

The total list of equipment required by this lab is shown in Table 3-7.

Wireless Devices	Quantity Needed
802.11g Wireless Access Point	1
802.11g PCI NIC	2
802.11g Type II Cardbus NIC	2
802.11g USB Network Adapter	2
2.4 GHz Directional Indoor Antenna	1
2.4 GHz Omnidirectional Indoor Antenna	1

Table 3-7 Equipment List for Advanced Lab Project

NOTE

This lab can use all three types of NICs and network adapters, or it can be limited to one or two of the adapter types.

Estimated Completion Time: 45 minutes

1. Install either the expansion card NICs (see Figure 3-27) or the USB network adapters (see Figure 3-28) in the two desktop PC workstations. Install the device drivers using the media included with the device.

Figure 3-27 A PCI expansion card wireless NIC (Photo courtesy of D-Link Systems, Inc.)

Figure 3-28 A USB network adapter (open with its antenna raised) (Photo courtesy of D-Link Systems, Inc.)

2. Install either the PC Card (Cardbus) NICs (see Figure 3-29) or the USB network adapters in the two portable computers. Install the device drivers using the media included with the device.

Figure 3-29 A PC Card Type II NIC is designed primarily for use with portable PCs. (Photo courtesy of D-Link Systems, Inc.)

3. Use the configuration utility included with the adapter or NIC to configure the following settings on each device:

- SSID: FWL
- Channel: 6
- Mode: Infrastructure
- Transmit Rate (TxRate): Auto
- Preamble: Long Preamble
- Power Mode: continuous power mode (CPM) or constantly awake mode (CAM)

NOTE

Do not enable encryption!

4. Install and configure the access point (using the same settings included in the previous step). After the access point (like the one shown in Figure 3-30) is installed and configured, use the portable computers to test the RF range and signal strength of the WLAN by walking in an arc or circle around the access point, increasing the distance from the access point slowly. Measure and record the distance at which the PCs and the access point lose their association in each direction. Determine if distance is the only reason for signal loss or whether environmental objects may be causing interference.

Figure 3-30   A wireless access point with dipole antennas attached (Photo courtesy of D-Link Systems, Inc.)

5. Power down the access point and install the directional indoor antenna (see Figure 3-31). Perform the same activities described in Step 4 to track the distance and direction provided by this antenna. In most cases, the range (distance) of this antenna should be larger than that of the built-in dipole antennas of the access point, but narrower in its direction. Using the same walking patterns used in Step 4, determine if the range has increased and the beam width has narrowed.

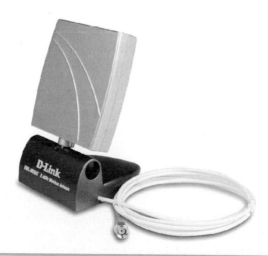

Figure 3-31   An indoor WLAN directional antenna (Photo courtesy of D-Link Systems, Inc.)

6. Replace the directional antenna with the omnidirectional antenna (see Figure 3-32) and retest the distances and direction of reception (using the same procedure used in Steps 4 and 5). Record your findings and discuss the impact that each of the different antennas could have on an actual installation design.

Figure 3-32 An omnidirectional antenna (Photo courtesy of Cisco Systems, Inc.)

7. (Optional) Using one or both of the portable PCs, attempt to retain the association with the access point from the exterior of the building. Perform an experiment similar to the one in Steps 4, 5, and 6 for each antenna type on the exterior of the building.

Chapter 4

Radio Frequency (RF) Communications

Whether used for voice, music, television, or data, RF wireless communications has been with us in one form or another for over 100 years. Despite the widespread use of radio and wireless communications around the world, people seem to treat RF wireless communications as if it's a fairly recent development. However, it isn't RF communications that's new; it's the fairly recent application to data networking that seems like a recent innovation.

This chapter provides an overview of the basic operations, standards, and technologies that provide the foundation on which wireless data networking is built.

RF Communications Basics

Almost every entity or body in the universe emits some form of radiation. *Electromagnetic radiation* is the type that alternates electrical and magnetic fields in a flow characterized by an oscillating waveform, or a wave pattern that alternates up and down within a frequency band. All types of electromagnetic radiation use waveforms, including **radio waves**, microwaves, infrared light, visible light, ultraviolet light, X-rays, and gamma rays.

RF devices communicate through the transmission and reception of electromagnetic waves. However, you should understand some differences in selection and application to know how wireless communications operate, especially on a data network.

Electromagnetic radiation is categorized by the length of each of its waves (a wavelength) or the number of wave cycles that occur in a fixed time period, such as a second, which is called its *frequency*. Figure 4-1 illustrates the alternating patterns of the electrical and magnetic waves that form electromagnetic radiation. The electrical and magnetic waves run at a 90-degree offset (polarization) to one another. One wavelength on either wave is one complete up and down (above and below centerline) cycle. The height of each wave (its amplitude) is created by the varying intensity in either field, electrical or magnetic. The direction of the flow of the radiation is its propagation.

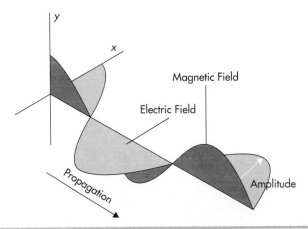

Figure 4-1 An electromagnetic wave consists of alternating electrical and magnetic waves.

Propagation of Radio Waves

In the context of RF waves, propagation represents how transmitted (or propagated) radio waves travel through the atmosphere. The general rule of *propagation* is the inverse-square law, which measures an electromagnetic wave's strength relative to the distance over which it is transmitted. The formula for the inverse-square law is $1/x^2$, in which x represents the distance from the wave's source (transmitter). For example, the strength of an electromagnetic wave using the inverse-square law after traveling three miles is the factor of 1/9 or 0.111. After five miles, the factor is reduced to 1/25 or 0.04.

However, radio waves transmitted from the ground rarely fit the inverse-square calculations. This is because radio waves propagate differently based on their frequencies. Table 4-1 lists some of the common radio wave frequencies and their propagation characteristics.

Frequency Range	Frequency Band	Propagation Characteristics
Low	300 kilohertz (kHz)	Propagate near the ground because of diffraction by the curvature of the Earth
High	1000 kHz	Don't propagate near the ground
Shortwave	3 MHz–30 MHz	Reflect back to Earth off the ionosphere; able to travel long distances
Very high	100 MHz	Line of sight, but will travel beyond the horizon
Extremely high	1 gigahertz (GHz)	Line of sight, but will travel beyond the horizon

Table 4-1   Radio Wave Propagation Characteristics

4

Radio Wave Properties

Electromagnetic energy, which includes RF energy, has two types of properties: wave properties and particle properties. Our focus is on the *wave properties*, which define the length, height, and speed of the radio wave. RF waves have seven such properties (see Table 4-2):

- **Amplitude:** Amplitude measures the scalar magnitude of a wave's oscillation from center. In effect, amplitude represents the height (or distance from center) of the wave at its peaks as it oscillates. In a sound wave, amplitude translates to loudness. In a radio wave, it translates to the strength or power of the signals. Figure 4-2 illustrates amplitude in a radio wave.

- **Frequency:** The **frequency** of a waveform represents the number of wave peaks that pass a given point in space in one second (see Figures 4-2 and 4-3). Frequencies are typically measured in the number of waves that occur in one second or in a fraction of a second,

Property	Measures
Amplitude	Height of wave at its crest
Frequency	The number of waves that occur in a set timeframe
Intensity	The energy propagated in a wave
Phase	The lag or lead a wave has to a reference wave
Polarization	The orientation of a wave's electrical field
Speed	How fast a wave travels through the atmosphere
Wavelength	The distance between two successive peaks on a sine wave

Table 4-2 Properties of a Radio Wave

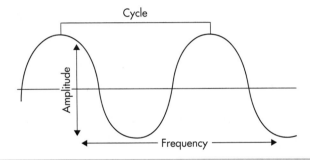

Figure 4-2 Amplitude and frequency are the vertical and horizontal measurements of a radio wave.

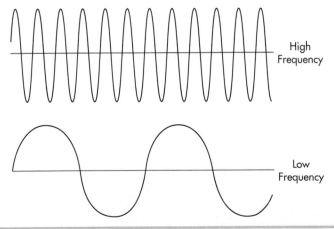

Figure 4-3 Frequency is the number of cycles (waves) that occur in specific timeframe. A high frequency has more waves (top) and a low frequency has fewer waves (bottom).

such the number of waveforms occurring in a millisecond (one-thousandth of a second). The common measurement used for expressing frequency is the **hertz** (Hz), which represents one waveform cycle per second. For example, an electromagnetic wave that has a frequency of 10,000 Hz has 10,000 waves pass a fixed point in one second. The hertz measurement is not used only for electromagnetic waves, but also for sound and other naturally occurring waveforms. Another common measure of a wave's frequency is its *period*, which represents the amount of time required for a wave to complete one cycle. The period of a wave is calculated by dividing one second by the number of cycles per second (frequency). For example: if the frequency of a wave is one megahertz (MHz) or one million cycles per second, its period is one-millionth of a second or one microsecond.

NOTE

The frequency of an electromagnetic or a sound wave is what causes its "vibration."

- **Intensity:** *Intensity* is the term used for how much energy is propagated along the wave. The wave intensity is normally expressed in voltage (volts) or power (watts).

- **Phase:** *Phase* measures how much ahead or behind a wave is to a reference frequency of the same wavelength. A wave that is exactly coincident to its reference wave is said to be *in-phase.* However, waves can be either a bit behind (*lag*) or a bit ahead (*lead*), in which case its phase is stated in the number of degrees (with 360 degrees representing a complete cycle) the wave is ahead or behind the reference wave. The point at which phase is determined is where amplitude is equal to zero (positive) or the bottom of the wave cycle. As the wave and the reference wave cross the zero amplitude point, the phase is measured ahead or behind, depending on which crosses first. For example, if a wave lags one-quarter of a wavelength behind its reference wave, the wave's phase is 90-degree lag, as illustrated in Figure 4-4.

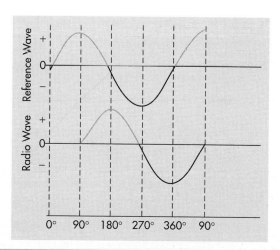

Figure 4-4   A radio wave that has a phase of 90-degree lag.

- **Polarization:** The *polarization* of a radio wave expresses the orientation of a wave's electrical field in relationship to its magnetic field. A wave's polarization can be vertical, horizontal, or circular. As depicted in Figure 4-1 earlier in the chapter, a wave's electrical and magnetic fields are perpendicular to one another. If the wave's electrical field is vertical, the wave has vertical polarization. When the electrical field is horizontal, the wave has horizontal polarization. If the electrical and magnetic fields are rotating or alternating, however, the wave has circular polarization and, depending on which way the wave is rotating, it can have left-hand polarization (counterclockwise rotation) or right-hand polarization (clockwise rotation).

- **Speed:** The nominal *speed* for an electromagnetic wave is the speed of light, but this is true only in a vacuum. As the atmospheric conditions through which a wave is traveling change, so does the speed of the wave. Another factor that impacts the speed of a wave is its frequency, which can have an even larger impact on the velocity of the wave. Because the changes in speed caused by the atmospheric conditions and the frequency of the wave are fairly small, the number $300 * 10^6$ meters per second is generally used for the speed of a wave.

- **Wavelength:** Radio waves typically vary cyclically in the direction of the wave's travel and, if the wave is continuous, as most radio waves are, the shape is described as *sinusoidal* (see Figure 4-5), which is why radio waves are often called *sine waves*. The speed of light is closely related to how rapidly the electric and magnetic fields in a radio

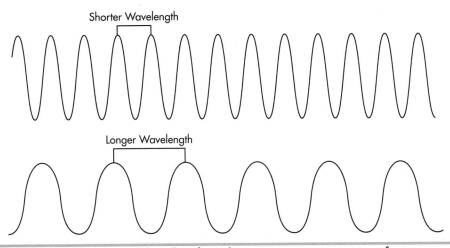

Shorter Wavelength

Longer Wavelength

Figure 4-5 This shows the wavelengths of an electromagnetic wave. More frequent waves have a shorter wavelength (top) and less frequent waves have a longer wavelength (bottom).

Speed of Light

Light, contrary to any logic, always travels at the same speed, regardless of the speed of the object emitting it. Measured in a vacuum, or in the absence of all other matter, light travels at a constant speed of 299,792,458 meters per second, or the equivalent of 186,000 miles per second and 700 million miles per hour.

At this constant speed, light emitted from the Earth would require 1.2 seconds to reach the moon (the same with RF waves, which is why a bit of a delay occurs when ground control speaks to the astronauts), 8.5 minutes for light from the Sun to reach Earth, and almost 6 hours for light from the Sun to reach the planet Pluto.

wave changes. How rapidly the fields change is also closely related to how far apart the strong parts of the electric fields are in the wave. For radio waves or light waves, the *speed of the wave* is essentially the speed of light. The wavelength of a radio wave is measured as the distance between two successive peaks on its sine wave. Figure 4-5 illustrates how a wavelength is measured.

Multipath Propagation

One of the problems that can occur, especially in wireless networking, is multipath propagation. *Multipath propagation* happens when an RF signal cannot take a clear and direct path between a transmitter and a receiver. In a home or office, walls, chairs, desks, and other furniture and objects can deflect an RF signal and cause it to bounce around an area in many directions. In these situations, a portion of the original signal may make it to the receiver unimpeded, while other parts of the signal may take an indirect route by way of the floor or ceiling. The delay caused by multipath propagation can be as much as 50 nanoseconds in a home or 300 nanoseconds in a large building or factory. Figure 4-6 illustrates how multipath propagation can be created in an outdoor setting. Because not all the channels carrying data arrive directly to the receiving station—a notebook PC in this case—because they deflect off buildings, trees, rocks, and so forth, some of the data signals arrive with some lag.

When multipath propagation happens, the delayed parts of the transmitted signal can overlap a signal also arriving at the receiver. When the data of one signal overlap those of another, a condition called intersymbol interference (ISI) occurs. The shape (amplitude, frequency, and phase) of the signal represents the data being transmitted and, if two signals are superimposed on

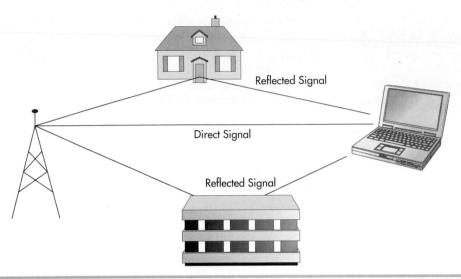

Figure 4-6   Multipath propagation is created by signals deflecting off obstacles, causing some channels to arrive later than others.

one another, the receiving device is unable to properly demodulate the signal back into its original data form.

The Relationship of Wavelength and Frequency

Electromagnetic waves travel at various propagation speeds, depending on the medium over which they are transmitted (see Table 4-3). For example, over fiber-optic cable, the constant speed of an RF wave is approximately 222,000 kilometers per second (kms) or two-thirds of the speed of light in a vacuum, regardless of their frequency or wavelength.

Medium	Propagation Speed
Air	300,000 kms
Cat 5e copper cable	200,000 kms
Fiber-optic cable	222,000 kms

Table 4-3   Propagation Speeds for RF Signals on Different Media

In fact, for any electromagnetic wave, its frequency times its wavelength should equal the speed of light. This means if you know either the wavelength or the frequency of an electromagnetic wave, you should be able to compute the other characteristic, as follows:

```
Speed of Light / Frequency = Wavelength
Speed of Light / Wavelength = Frequency
```

For example, on a wireless network, wavelength of the signal is calculated as approximately:

```
300 Mms (million meters per second) / 11 MHz (megahertz) =  27.3 meters
```

and its frequency is calculated as:

```
300 Mms / 27.3 meters = 11 MHz
```

Analog and Digital Waves

In the figures and discussion on radio waves to this point in the chapter, we have been showing and discussing analog radio waves. However, radio waves can also be used to transmit digital data. The waveform of the radio wave used to transmit digital data reflects the two-state electrical properties of binary data (representing ones and zeroes). Figure 4-7 shows an example of an electromagnetic wave carrying digital data. Notice how the state change is more abrupt when the electrical properties switch between the two values used for digital data.

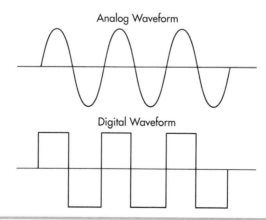

Figure 4-7 A comparison of an analog wave (top) to a digital signal (bottom)

⚡ Line Check 4.1

1. Radio waves are what type of energy?
2. What is a hertz? What is the meaning of MHz?
3. Describe the difference between an analog wave and a digital signal.

Radio Communications

Electromagnetic radiation is categorized into several radiation types. Table 4-4 lists the various categories (bands) of the electromagnetic spectrum (range) and their properties. Figure 4-8 illustrates the placement of each category (band) on the electromagnetic spectrum.

Category	Visible?	Wavelength (Centimeters)	Frequency (Hertz)
Radio waves	No	>10	$<3 * 10^9$
Microwave	No	10 to .01	$3 * 10^9$ to $3 * 10^{12}$
Infrared light	No	$0.01 - 7 \times 10^{-5}$	$3 \times 10^{12} - 4.3 \times 10^{14}$
Visible light	Yes	$7 \times 10^{-5} - 4 \times 10^{-5}$	$4.3 \times 10^{14} - 7.5 \times 10^{14}$
Ultraviolet light	No	$4 \times 10^{-5} - 10^{-7}$	$7.5 \times 10^{14} - 3 \times 10^{17}$
X-rays	No	$10^{-7} - 10^{-9}$	$3 \times 10^{17} - 3 \times 10^{19}$
Gamma rays	No	$<10^{-9}$	$>3 \times 10^{19}$

Table 4-4   Electromagnetic Radiation Categories

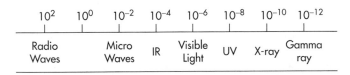

Figure 4-8   The electromagnetic radiation spectrum

Band	Frequencies
AM radio	535 kHz to 1.7 MHz
Short wave radio	5.9 MHz to 26.1 MHz
Citizens band (CB) radio	26.96 to 27.41 MHz
Television (Channels 2–6)	54 to 88 MHz
FM radio	88 to 108 MHz
TV stations (Channels 7–13)	174 to 220 MHz

Table 4-5   Common RF Spectrum Allocations

Radio waves are electromagnetic waves propagated (that is, transmitted or broadcasted) through the air and received by using an antenna. Radio waves are used to broadcast music, voices, images, and data using a variety of frequencies. Radio receivers are tuned to receive a particular range of frequencies or a specific frequency. In the United States, the Federal Communications Commission (FCC) assigns and licenses nongovernmental radio frequencies, determining who uses them and for what purpose each frequency is used. Table 4-5 lists some of the more common RF bands managed by the FCC.

4

Controlling the Air Waves

The various bands of the RF spectrum, which is within the electromagnetic radiation spectrum, are assigned both internationally and within each country's boundary. On the international level, the various classes of service of the RF spectrum are allocated and assigned by the International Telecommunication Union (ITU). In the United States and its possessions and territories, the RF spectrum assigned to the U.S. is divided into two primary bands: government and nongovernment.

In the U.S., the FCC allocates and assigns nongovernmental frequencies. The National Telecommunications and Information Administration (NTIA) allocates and assigns the radio frequencies used by agencies of the federal government with some assistance from the Interdepartmental Radio Advisory Committee (IRAC) that maintains the National Table of Frequency Allocations.

In many cases, the frequency band assigned to a particular RF application has as much to do with history as it does with science. For example, the primary reason the AM radio band (550 kHz to 1700 kHz) and the FM radio band (88 to 108 MHz) are assigned their respective spectrums is because the AM frequency range was assigned in the 1920s and FM's frequencies weren't assigned until the late 1950s.

Usage	Frequency
Alarm systems	40 MHz
Baby monitors	49 MHz
Cellular telephones	824–849 MHz
Cordless telephone	900 MHz
Garage door opener	40 MHz
Radio-controlled (RC) aircraft	72 MHz
RC cars	75 MHz
Wireless LAN	2.4–2.4835 GHz (802.11b/g) 4.9–5.825 GHz (802.11a)

Table 4-6 Allocations within the RF Spectrum

Within the nongovernmental RF spectrum allocations are more specific allocations for special purpose uses, as listed in Table 4-6.

NOTE

To see the entire RF allocation for the U.S., visit
www.ntia.doc.gov/osmhome/allochrt.html.

Transmitting RF Signals

A transmitted radio signal begins as an electrical current on a wire that represents voice, music, images, or data. The electrical current is created by the back and forth movement of electrons in the wire in an alternating and continuous pattern, which also creates an electromagnetic field around the wire.

As the electrical current moves through the wire, the electromagnetic field around the wire also moves along the wire and, eventually, moves into a radio transmitting antenna. The difference between the wire and the antenna is this: normally, the wire has an outer layer or jacket used to reduce the aura of the electromagnetic field, but the antenna does not. In fact, the antenna is designed to radiate the electromagnetic field created by the electrical current. Of course, the frequency and wavelength of the electromagnetic field have something to do with how far the radiated field travels through the air and how it's received or sensed by other antennas.

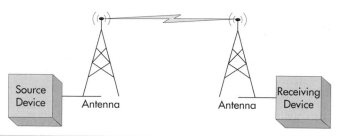

Figure 4-9   The electrical current on a wire is converted into an electromagnetic field by a transmitting antenna and travels through the air to be sensed by a receiving antenna.

A receiving antenna works just the opposite of a transmitting or radiating antenna. Where the transmitting antenna, in effect, converts the electrical current in a wire into a transmitted electromagnetic field, a receiving antenna converts the properties of a sensed electromagnetic field into an electrical current, as illustrated in Figure 4-9. Whether transmitting or receiving, the properties of the electrical current are maintained.

Transmitting Data with Radio Waves

To transmit any type of information using radio waves, the electrical current and its electromagnetic field must be converted (modulated) for transmission through the air. For the most part, two primary modulation methods are used: amplitude modulation (**AM**) or frequency modulation (FM). In its unmodulated state, a radio wave has a regular and even waveform, frequency, and wavelength. This unmodulated radio wave is called a *carrier wave*.

NOTE

Remember, *amplitude* represents the height of a radio wave and *frequency* represents the number of waves occurring in a given time.

Amplitude Modulation

One of the ways used to insert data into a radio wave is through AM, which varies the amplitude or the height of the wave. By varying the height of the transmitted radio wave to match the waveform of the transmitted data signal, the RF carrier signal is modulated into a data signal, as illustrated in Figure 4-10. In the top half of the figure, the signal carrying information is shown on top of the carrier wave of the medium, and in the bottom half of the figure, the amplitude of the carrier wave was modulated to reflect the waveform of the information signal.

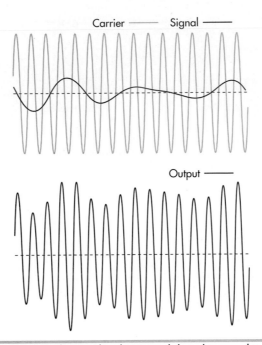

Carrier ――――   Signal ――――

Output ――――

Figure 4-10   The RF carrier signal's amplitude is modulated to combine with an information signal.

NOTE

Amplitude modulation (AM) is the same method used by AM radio stations to modulate their transmitted signal to a single channel (station) within the AM radio band.

Frequency Modulation

Another way to insert data into a radio wave is by using frequency modulation or **FM** radio transmissions. Where AM modulates the height (amplitude) of a transmitted radio wave, FM modulates the vibration rate or frequency of a signal. Like AM, simple or sine wave FM, in effect, merges the carrier wave with the information signal by varying the frequency of the carrier wave to match that of the information signal. Figure 4-11 illustrates how the resulting FM wave (bottom) combines an information signal and a carrier wave.

Transmitters and Receivers

A radio system typically either includes a transmitter or a receiver (or both), sometimes in the form of a transceiver, which combines both functions. A radio transmitter combines the data signal onto the carrier signal by modulating the signal's amplitude or frequency and energizes the modulated signal to the transmitter's antenna.

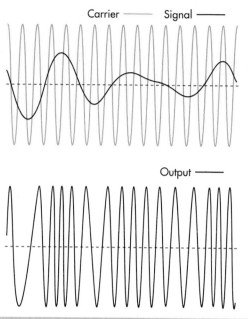

Carrier ——— Signal ———

Output ———

Figure 4-11   Frequency modulation combines the frequency pattern of a signal with the carrier wave.

In effect, a radio receiver is a decoder device because it essentially extracts the data signal from the carrier signal. It does this by demodulating the signal, and then passing the data signals to a processor, speaker, tuner, television, computer, or another device for processing.

Transceivers

In a wireless networking environment, the networking devices, such as access points and network adapters, incorporate transceivers that have the capability to both transmit and receive. Combining the transmitter and receiver into the same device saves space and promotes efficiencies of design and operations.

Because a transceiver performs both the transmitting and receiving operations for a wireless device, its transmissions are generally limited to *half-duplex communications mode*, which means it can both transmit and receive, but only one action at a time. When the transceiver is transmitting, that is all it's doing. As soon as the transceiver finishes transmitting, it switches over to receiving mode, until it needs to transmit again.

Line Check 4.2

1. What are the two types of modulation discussed in this section that are used to add data to a radio wave? What characteristic of a radio wave does each modify?

2. What is the RF frequency band allotted to wireless LANs?

3. Describe the functions of a transceiver.

What Do You Think?

RF signals are not just used for wireless communications. In fact, a home cable TV system transmits RF signals over its cable. What are some advantages to wireless communications and networking over a hard-wired communications approach?

RF Communications Standards

RF communications, commonly known as wireless communications, has become commonplace in today's society, even to the point of being taken for granted in many applications. However, the different wireless communications devices, such as garage-door openers, baby monitors, cordless and cellular telephones, and so forth use a variety of communications standards and protocols to communicate and transfer data.

As wireless communications has evolved from radio to analog radiotelephone to digital radio communications, several methods, services, and standards have emerged. Each new development in wireless communications develops a faster and more robust method of transmission.

Multiplexing Signals

Multiplexing is the method used to maximize the utilization of a limited transmission medium by interspersing message segments from multiple sessions onto the single medium. To understand multiplexing, let's first look at communications without it.

When two devices attempt to share a single communication medium, two options exist: (1) make one device wait until another device completes its communication session, or (2) make it possible for the two devices to share the line. The problem associated with either of these options is, of course, the delay involved for either or both of the devices, respectively. However, where the first option is fairly impractical, the second option provides the basis for a better solution—multiplexing. The basic forms of multiplexing used in communications are

- **Frequency-division multiplexing (FDM): FDM** applies a different frequency to each of the signal streams being combined onto a single transmission medium. Each signal is modulated onto a different and specific frequency (subchannel) within the carrier channel of the medium. All the uniquely modulated waves are then combined to create a composite signal for transmission (as illustrated in Figure 4-12). Special guard band frequencies are used to prevent the frequencies from "bleeding" over each other. FDM is the multiplexing technique used with telephone systems, as follows:

- **Code-division multiplexing (CDM):** *CDM* encodes a signal stream in such a way that it can be identified uniquely from other signals transmitted on the same link. The data is encoded using a pseudorandom numerical sequence, which is also called a *hamming code*.

- **Time-division multiplexing (TDM): TDM** is the multiplexing technique most commonly used for wire-line voice transmissions. TDM assigns each communications stream to a different time slot in a time sequence, and then transmits the time slots over a single transmission channel. For example, if three devices are transmitting over a single channel, device *A* may be assigned to slot 1, device *B* to slot 2, and device *C* to slot 3, and the transmitted block is constructed like that in Figure 4-13.

4

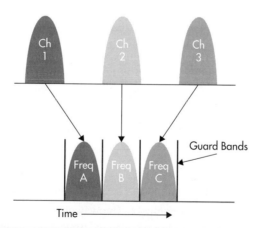

Figure 4-12   FDM combines multiple signal streams onto a single medium by modulating their frequencies.

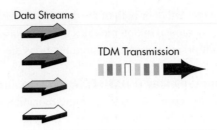

Figure 4-13   TDM sequences multiple streams into time slot divisions in a transmission.

- **Wave-division multiplexing (WDM):** *WDM* is used to combine transmitted data from different sources onto a fiber-optic cable link. Each data channel is assigned a unique wavelength, which results in minimizing the number of fiber-optic cable links required between two points, but it can also increase the effective bandwidth of the carrier link. Figure 4-14 illustrates how each signal is assigned a different wavelength on the cable.

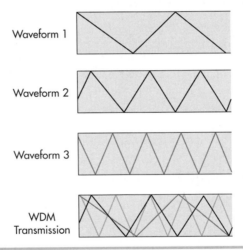

Figure 4-14   WDM combines multiple optical signals by assigning a different waveform to each signal.

Broadband systems use either FDM or TDM to share the media among multiple channels. TDM works much like a metered on-ramp to a freeway, with multiple lanes feeding the ramp. One vehicle from each lane is allowed to proceed at a time, but the lanes alternate access, so that within a given period of time, vehicles from each of the lanes are allowed to proceed. Let's continue this analogy: if four groups of cars (a group of red cars, a group of blue cars, a group of yellow cars, and a group of white cars) all need to reach a destination at about the same time traveling over a one-lane road, the only solution is to multiplex the cars onto the road.

FDM and Telephones

Multiplexing helps to maximize the utilization of communications lines, especially on busy circuits. One of the more common uses of multiplexing in communications is on the standard telephone network, which uses FDM to multiplex telephone calls on the carrier lines.

A telephone call signal requires about 3 kHz (kilohertz) of bandwidth on the line, but the telephone cables on which the signal will be transmitted are capable of much higher bandwidths. For example, if the line used to connect a local central office (CO) to a switching center is a 3 MHz (megahertz) line, which is the equivalent of 1,000 3 kHz signals, the line should be able to carry roughly 1,000 separate phone calls. However, because we need to think of bandwidth as width, and not length, the cable can only carry these calls if they are placed side-by-side (so to speak). To be able to tell one signal from another after they have been placed (multiplexed) onto the line, they must have a property that makes them unique. FDM alters the frequency of each signal to allow it to be separated (demultiplexed) from the others at the receiving end of the links.

4

Regardless of which group the first car is from (let's choose red), the cars can be allowed to proceed in the sequence of red, blue, yellow, white, red, blue, yellow, white, and so on. TDM is commonly implemented on wireless broadband networks.

FDM transmissions carry analog data, which are in continuously oscillating waves. Digital data has intermittent and alternating high- and low-frequency pulses, which represent the zeroes and ones of binary-encoded data, but don't connect into a wave (as illustrated in Figure 4-7 earlier in the chapter). To transmit digital data using FDM and broadband, the digital signal must be converted to an analog wave using a broadband modem, so it can be assigned to a single frequency on the medium. Cable TV is a common application of FDM transmissions.

Signal Switching

Signal switching involves the method used to create an end-to-end circuit path over which a transmitted stream travels between its source and its destination. The primary signal switching techniques used in RF communications are circuit switching and packet switching.

SDM

Another commonly referenced form of multiplexing—space-division multiplexing (SDM) —isn't really multiplexing at all. In *SDM*, separate data streams are applied to different conductors in a multiple conductor cable enclosed in a single jacket, such as Category 5 or 6 cable, or other multiple wire cables.

Circuit Switching

Circuit switching is the underlying switching and forwarding technology of first-generation wireless communication systems. Circuit switching uses mechanical and electronic switching to establish a circuit path between the source (the caller) and the destination (the receiver). *Circuit switching* creates a temporary dedicated, connection-oriented virtual circuit for each session, call, or transmission. After the call ends, the circuit is released and the session ends.

As illustrated in Figure 4-15, each time a telephone number is dialed, the switching equipment between the calling station and the called station creates a dedicated circuit through the intermediate switching facilities of the telephone system, which is formally known as the Public Switched Telephone Network (PSTN). At the end of the call (session), the circuit path is released, which terminates the session.

When a telephone call is dialed, the telephone number components are used, much like the network and host identity parts of an IPv4 address, to create the circuit over which signals will be routed. The area code, prefix, and last four (station) numbers are used to switch the circuits necessary to move the call from the caller to the station being called.

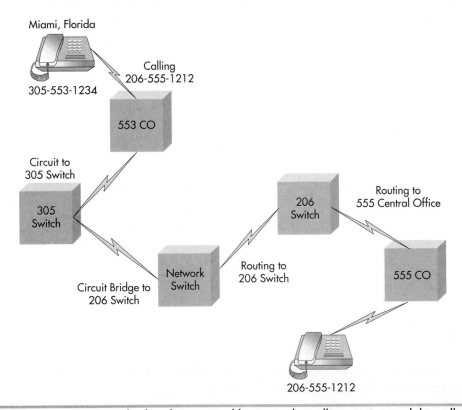

Figure 4-15   A circuit-switched path is created between the calling station and the called station

NOTE

Circuit switching is most commonly used in systems that require "real-time" communications, such as voice and live media transmissions.

Packet Switching

Where circuit switching creates a temporary dedicated path for a communication session, **packet switching** moves message segments across the network by forwarding or routing them between switching stations on the network. Packet switching creates no established communication path and the packets are routed between nodes using the better path available to each packet. When the packets of a single data stream are carried across a network connection, not all the packets will necessarily use the same physical path between their source and destination points. The packets that comprise a single message are reassembled at the destination network for delivery to the appropriate node.

Network packets, especially TCP/IP packets, include the addressing and administrative information needed to forward messages toward their destination network. The operation used to forward packets between network nodes until they reach their destination network is called *routing*. Routing involves determining the better of the available paths that could be used to forward a packet in the direction of its destination address. The primary network devices used to route packets are routers, for what should be obvious reasons.

4

NOTE

Packet-switching technology is the basis for nearly all wide area network (WAN) protocols, including TCP/IP, X.25, and frame relay. See Chapter 14 for more information about wireless WANs.

Circuit switching is best suited for communications systems that require fast and highly reliable transmissions that include little latency (delay). On the other hand, because the routing decisions being made by routers and switches add latency to the transmission, packet switching is better suited for data streams that are bursty and for which some delay is not a problem. Circuit switching is used for such data streams as audio, video, voice, and multimedia transmissions. Packet switching is used for such data streams as e-mail and downloading web pages.

NOTE

Newer packet-switching technologies are now being used to transmit audio, video, voice, and multimedia.

Bursty Data

Most of what is "normal" Internet traffic is bursty, which means the data streams are transmitted in delimited bursts, rather than a steady data stream. When a user requests a web page for download, the URL is entered and transmitted. The user waits for the download to complete, and then spends time reading or studying the web page before taking another action. In this sequence of events, long intervals (which are nearly infinite at times to the computer) occur during which nothing is being transmitted to or received from the network. While the network is not servicing one user, it is free to service another user. But even when it services all the users on a LAN, the data flows in and out are still rather bursty.

Two primary methods are used in packet switching:

- Virtual circuit packet switching
- Datagram switching

Virtual Circuit Packet Switching   In between full-scale packet switching and circuit switching is virtual circuit packet switching that constructs a virtual circuit (VC) between the end points of the communications session and all the intermediate points on the route between the end points. A *VC* is a logical circuit in which each of the intermediate nodes on the circuit is temporarily locked into a pathway that exists only during the session. A VC performs logically the same action as a circuit-switching system does physically. Once the VC is constructed, the packets of the data stream are transferred in sequence along the single path of the VC. Each VC is assigned a virtual circuit identifier (VCI) that is used to identify both the packets using the VC and the path itself to the network nodes.

The use of a VC eliminates much of the latency added by a standard packet-switching transmission. Like a standard circuit-switched network, however, if any intermediate leg of the virtual circuit fails, the whole circuit is unusable. Frame relay is the most commonly used virtual circuit WAN technology

Datagram Packet Switching   This type of switching is known by many different names. However, its most common name is routing. *Datagram packet switching* assumes that each packet contains all the information required to move it from its source to its destination. Along the way, each intermediate switching device looks at the information in the datagram's header and decides which node or device should receive the datagram next to reach its destination.

Generally, datagram packet switching uses two basic types of information to make its forwarding decisions: the shortest path and whether or not a switching device is along that

4

path to pass on the datagram. The length of a path is determined by the number of switching devices (such as routers) that must be passed through to reach a destination. Each device through which a datagram must pass is referred to as a *hop* (you read about the functions of routers in Chapter 3 and you can read more in Chapter 12). A lower number of hops mean a shorter path or route. Although a path may be the shortest in terms of hops, it may not have a device ready to receive a datagram, which means the path is unavailable and, perhaps, a slightly longer path must be used.

In case you haven't been overwhelmed with the feeling that this is all vaguely familiar, the primary implementation of datagram packet switching is the Internet and its use of the Internet Protocol (IP).

 ## Line Check 4.3

1. Define multiplexing.
2. What are the differences between the TDM and FDM multiplexing methods?
3. Describe the differences between packet switching and circuit switching.

What Do You Think?

In what situations is FDM more advantageous than TDM? And vice versa?

Wireless Evolution

The standards and protocols used to control the rate and quality of voice and data transfers on RF communications have evolved in a series of generations. Each generation has successively added additional and expanded capability, speed, and quality of service (QoS).

Narrowband Frequencies

Engineers pursued the goal of developing WLAN technology for almost two decades, trying to solve the issue of limited bandwidth availability. In the U.S., and around the world, regulatory agencies (the Federal Communications Commission [FCC] in the U.S.) are responsible for licensing and regulating the use of the public airways for broadcasting. Table 4-7 lists a few of the telecommunications regulatory agencies around the world.

Country	Agency
Australia	Australian Communications Authority (ACA)
Brazil	ANATEL
Canada	Canadian Radio Television and Telecommunications Commission
Denmark	Telestyrelsen National Telecom Agency
Egypt	Telecommunications Regulatory Authority (TRA)
France	ART (Autorité de Régulation des Télécommunications)
India	Telecom Regulatory Authority of India (TRAI)
Israel	Ministry of Communications
Japan	Ministry of Public Management, Home Affairs, Posts, and Telecommunications
Korea	Ministry of Communications and Informations
Mexico	Comisión Federal de Telecomunicaciones
Nigeria	Nigerian Communications Commission
Pakistan	Pakistan Telecommunications Authority
Singapore	Infocomm Development Authority of Singapore
Sweden	Post-och telestyrelsen (PTS)
UK	Office of Communications (Ofcom)
USA	Federal Communications Commission (FCC)
Taiwan	The Directorate General of Telecommunications

Table 4-7   Telecommunications Regulators around the World

The agencies listed in Table 4-7 typically oversee all the telecommunications in their country, including the licensing of narrowband frequency transmissions. *Narrowband frequency transmissions* are licensed exclusively to a single licensee for a particular geographical area. By limiting the amount of broadcast power that can be used, the FCC also protects the licensed areas from interference caused by adjacent broadcasters transmitting over the top of each other.

As the demand for wireless bandwidth began to grow, the industry faced a dilemma: How could additional bandwidth be made available for wireless LANs without interfering with one another? The answer lay in the licensing of existing bandwidth and the application of spread-spectrum transmission.

Wireless Generations

The standards and protocols used to control the rate and quality of voice and data transfers on RF networks, stationary or mobile, have evolved in a series of generations. Each generation has successively added additional and expanded capability, speed, and QoS.

The following table lists the generations and the protocols included in each.

Generation	Applications	Protocols
First-generation (1G)	Cellular phones transmitting analog voice	Advanced Mobile Phone System (AMPS)
		Narrowband Advanced Mobile Phone System (NAMPS)
		Extended Total Access Communications System (ETACS)
Second-generation (2G)	Circuit-based, digital, voice transmission systems	Code Division Multiple Access (CDMA)
		Global System for Mobile (GSM)
		Time Division Multiple Access (TDMA)
Second-and-one-half-generation (2.5G)	Packet-switching capabilities on high-speed circuits	General Packet Radio Service (GPRS)
		High-speed circuit switched data (HSCSD)
		Enhanced Data Rates for GSM Evolution (EDGE)
Third-generation (3G)	Megabit data rates for the transfer of data	Wideband Code Division Multiple Access (W-CDMA)
Fourth-generation (4G)	Broadband wireless access communication systems	WiMAX/Ultra Wide Band

4

Spread-spectrum transmission has long been a favorite technology of the military because it resists jamming and is hard to intercept. It is becoming popular for WLAN use as well because spread-spectrum signals, which are distributed over a wide range of frequencies (unlike narrowband transmission), and then recollected back onto their original frequency at the receiver, create what amounts to a transparent medium. Spread-spectrum transmissions are unlikely to interfere with other signals, even those transmitted on the same frequencies.

Spread-spectrum

One of the communication developments that advanced wireless communications between the first two generations of RF communication development was **spread-spectrum** communications. *Spread-spectrum communications* is a modulation technique characterized by its use of a wide frequency spectrum. Spread-spectrum modulates output signals to a much higher bandwidth than the bandwidth of the original signal's baseband information.

Spread-spectrum provides relatively secure digital communications for wireless LAN, digital cellular telephones, and other computer and radio modem devices. Spread-spectrum radio communications have been used in military applications because of its capability to resist jamming and its resistance to interception. Spread-spectrum signals are transmitted over a wide range of frequencies, and then modulated to a standard frequency by the receiver.

Spread-spectrum is a wide-band transmission technology using transmission power levels similar to narrowband (analog) transmitters. However, even though spread-spectrum signals occupy the same radio band, they transmit with little or no interference, which is the primary reason spread-spectrum began replacing narrowband technologies.

Another reason for the reliability of spread-spectrum signals is the use of noise-like signals. Through the use of what are called *spreading codes*, which are codes transmitted on higher frequencies than the information signals, spread-spectrum signals are hard to detect and intercept. The two types of spreading codes used are pseudorandom (PR) and pseudonoise (PN). In this context, "pseudo" means about the same as virtual, because these signals are not the same as interference or what is called Gaussian (measurable) noise. The use of noiselike signals makes spread-spectrum signals much harder to detect, intercept, jam, or demodulate than narrowband signals.

Spread-spectrum uses two primary signal structuring techniques (see Figure 4-16):

- **Direct-sequence spread-spectrum (DSSS): DSSS** uses amplitude modulation to combine the waveforms of the data and carrier signals, which is much like a normal AM signal, except the PN added to the signal causes it to be wider than a normal AM transmission. The IEEE 802.11B standard is based on DSSS. As illustrated in Figure 4-16, the amplitude of the resulting DSSS signal was modulated to reflect the rise and fall patterns of the original signal.

- **Frequency-hopping spread-spectrum (FHSS): FHSS** transmits signals by constantly switching the carrier signal between frequency channels, using a switching sequence that is known by both the transmitter and the receiver. PN is randomly applied to the carrier signal to create an evenly formed signal pattern. In Figure 4-16, the frequency of the resulting FHSS signal was modulated to incorporate the original signal.

NOTE

Some spread-spectrum systems also employ a hybrid of both direct sequence and frequency-hopping techniques, such as time-hopped systems.

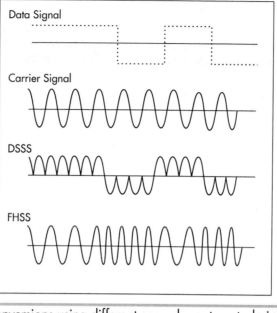

Figure 4-16   Signal conversions using different spread-spectrum techniques

Figure 4-16 illustrates the waveforms of a data signal and carrier signal (the top two waves, respectively) and the resulting signals after DSSS and FHSS modulation (the bottom two waves, respectively).

The primary benefit of using spread-spectrum signaling for wireless communications is that DSSS and FHSS signals can share a frequency with other types of transmissions without causing much interference. This allows the communications channel to be more efficiently used. However, not every country's regulatory body allocates the same number of channels or necessarily follows the same broadcast standards. Table 4-8 summarizes the channel allocations in several areas around the world.

Frequency-Hopping and the Actress

The basic concept that underlay frequency-hopping spread-spectrum communications was invented and patented in 1942 by actor and movie star Hedy Lamarr (using her legal name Hedy Keisler Markey) and musician George Antheil. Their design used paper rolls with punched holes (simiar to a player piano roll) to control the frequency shifts between transmitter and receiver.

Channel ID	Frequency Range (MHz)	Federal Communications Commission (FCC)—U.S.	European Telecommunications Standards Institute (ETSI)—Europe	France	Japan
1	2412	X	X		X
2	2417	X	X		X
3	2422	X	X		X
4	2427	X	X		X
5	2432	X	X		X
6	2437	X	X		X
7	2442	X	X		X
8	2447	X	X		X
9	2452	X	X		X
10	2457	X	X	X	X
11	2462	X	X	X	X
12	2467		X	X	X
13	2472		X	X	X
14	2484				X

Table 4-8 Channel Frequency Assignments around the World

Line Check 4.4

1. Describe the concept of spread-spectrum.
2. What are the basic differences between DSSS and FHSS?

What Do You Think?

What impact will the advancements in mobile phone technology have on data networks in the future?

Broadband, Baseband, Narrowband, and Wideband

Broadband data transmissions carry several channels simultaneously over a single transmission medium. As illustrated in Figure 4-17, *broadband* modulates multiple data streams into different frequencies for transmission of a single cable or wireless communications medium.

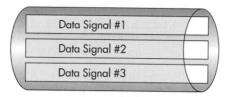

Figure 4-17   A broadband transmission carries multiple data steams, each with a different frequency.

4

Most networks transmit data using either baseband or broadband techniques. While most local area networks (LANs) are commonly baseband networks, a broadband network is used whenever multiple data services need to be carried over a single medium, such as closed circuit TV (CCTV), community antenna or cable TV (CATV), and multimedia transmissions.

In fact, cable television is a good example of how a broadband network transmits multiple streams. The cable network transmits multiple RF signal streams to a home, where either a cable-ready television or a set-top box demodulates the signal streams to different channels on a TV. In addition, most cable TV service providers now also provide Internet service connections over the same network that carries their audio and video streams.

Broadband Communications

Broadband networks, especially LANs, are typically laid out in a hierarchical tree-and-branch structure with the broadband backbone providing the root. At one end of the trunk cable is the gateway. The gateway provides the primary connection or access point to other broadband connections and other networks, such as the Internet, an enterprise network, or a company WAN. All transmissions from a LAN or to a LAN from outside the LAN pass through the network gateway, which modulates the incoming signals to the frequency used on the LAN or modulates the signals transmitted from within the LAN to the frequency used on the WAN.

In a wireless broadband network, the topologies implemented are the same as used in a microwave or satellite system: point-to-point, point-to-multipoint, and multipoint-to-multipoint. A broadband LAN is more commonly found in larger enterprises or in some smaller networking environments with the need for multiple data formats.

Broadband Loss and Gain

Because RF signals tend to lose their signal strength as they travel over a wire or through the air and because many devices on a broadband network can further weaken a transmitted signal, it may be necessary to reenergize the signal at certain points on the network.

In a broadband LAN environment, devices like splitters, couplers, and broadband equalizers can cause a signal to weaken—a condition called *signal loss.* The amount of signal loss incurred depends on the characteristics of the transmission media and those of the signal itself. Such factors as a cable diameter, the number of devices the signal passes through, the overall transmission distance, and the frequency of the signal can all contribute to signal loss on a broadband transmission.

To counteract the signal loss that occurs in a broadband transmission, signal amplifiers can be inserted into the network. In the broadband world, an *amplifier* is used to increase the amplification of a signal "as-is," meaning with its noise and all. Unlike a repeater in the baseband world, an amplifier doesn't reenergize or regenerate the signal. An amplifier is inserted into the media path at points where the signal needs to be reamplified to a desired level. The downside to an amplifier is that any interference, noise, or distortion the signal may have picked up along the way will also be amplified.

Amplification shouldn't be designed into a network without first considering the amount of amplification required. The design objective for adding amplification should be to create unity gain. *Unity gain* is the condition where the amount of gain added to a signal is equal to the amount of loss the signal suffers as it passes through the other components on the network or over a certain distance. The complicating factor in reaching unity gain on a network is that how much loss a signal suffers, along with how much gain is needed to offset it, depends on the frequency of the signal. So, the best location for an amplifier on a network should be carefully considered.

Broadband Services

Broadband services are available with capabilities that range from services that can be used for private homes through advanced technology transmission services that support global communications. Broadband transmission services are available in wireless and wired implementations.

Wireless Broadband Services   The transmission services used to transmit broadband signals are:

- **Microwave:** Microwave represents the portion of the RF spectrum between 1 GHz and 40 GHz, although recently the spectrum above 40 GHz has been approved for some uses.

- **39 GHz:** This is a microwave band used to extend fiber networks in last-mile applications. Using a wireless point-to-point, line-of-sight link to a fiber headend at a centrally located point, 39 GHz services are used to provide access to buildings without direct access to fiber-optic trunks. The 39 GHz spectrum is divided into two blocks: an *A* block and a *B* block.

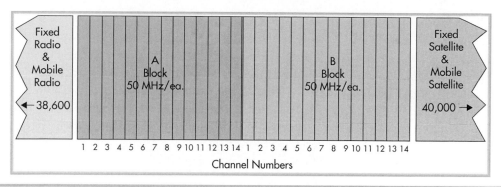

Figure 4-18   The channel allocations of the 39 GHz RF band

Each block is divided into 14 50 MHz channels, and then licensed to operators in matching channel pairs. For example, an operator may have a license to operate on Channel 12 with an *A* block channel and a *B* block channel. Figure 4-18 depicts the band allocation of the 39 GHz band.

- **Local Multipoint Distribution Service (LMDS):** *LMDS*, which uses three separate bands in the microwave spectrum (27.5 GHz to 28.35 GHz, 29.1 GHz to 29.25 GHz, and 31 GHz to 31.3 GHz), is used much like the 39 GHz service for point-to-multipoint access to Internet and telephone services. LMDS has a range of about three miles (line-of-sight) and uses TDM access to multiplex multiple customers into a single channel. Figure 4-19 illustrates the configuration used to provide a wireless LMDS link to a fiber-optic headend. The antenna/transceiver on the top of the building communicates on an LMDS channel to a fixed-point station connected into a fiber-optic network and the Internet. Inside the building, the rooftop unit is connected through a riser cable to the local network's gateway and through that to the network nodes.

- **Multichannel Multipoint Distribution Service (MMDS):** MMDS operates in the 2.5 GHz band of the microwave spectrum and was originally used to distribute cable television service via wireless transmission. New developments with MMDS are looking to make this service available to residential subscribers. Figure 4-20 illustrates an example of an MMDS system, in this case, a cable TV system that could also be used for cable-based Internet access.

- **Unlicensed National Information Infrastructure (UNII):** *UNII* uses two separate bands in the microwave spectrum: 5.15 GHz to 5.35 GHz and 5.725 GHz to 5.825 GHz. UNII is reserved for unlicensed, yet regulated, use. Commonly referred to as 5 GHz and 5.8 GHz wireless, UNII has several applications for small- to medium businesses and some residential customers as well. The UNII regulations restrict broadcast power and limit services to high-bandwidth, high-speed digital transmissions. UNII is used primarily for point-to-point Internet access. A wide variety of antenna styles are used for 5.8 GHz

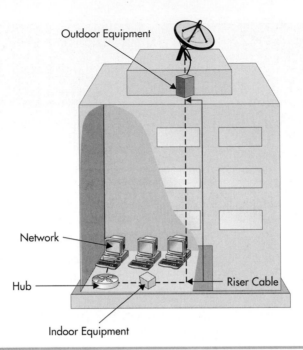

Figure 4-19   An example of an LMDS deployment providing Internet access to a building (Image courtesy of the Wireless Communications Association)

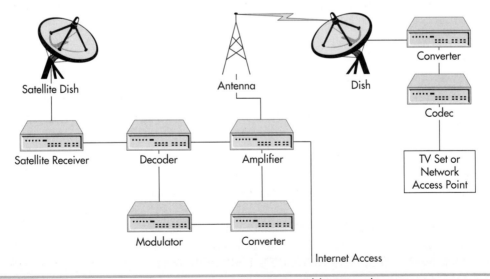

Figure 4-20   The devices and connections in an MMDS cable TV and Internet access system

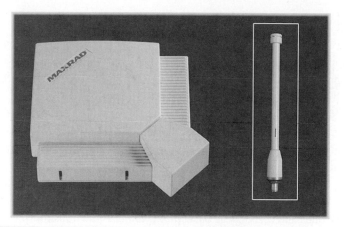

Figure 4-21   Two styles of 5.8 GHz antennas: a BWA directional panel and an omnidirectional pole antenna (Photo courtesy of MAXRAD, Inc.)

systems, including flat panels, poles, wire-grid parabola, dish, and even slim-line models that can attach directly to a computer monitor, wall, roof, or table. Figure 4-21 shows two of the more popular styles of UNII band antennas.

● **Industrial, Scientific, and Medical (ISM):** *ISM* is an unlicensed, unregulated RF band in the 915 MHz, 2.4 GHz, and 5.725 GHz bands. ISM provides between 2 and 11 Kbps of data transfer speed. At one time, ISM was set aside for the specific use of industry, science and technology, and medical communications, but it is no longer restricted to these uses. In fact, the 2.4 GHz frequency is the most commonly used band for wireless networking, including the IEEE 802.11 and Bluetooth technologies. However, the ISM bands are also used for cordless telephones, garage door openers, baby monitors, and other wireless products.

WiMAX

The networking standard for air interface networking is IEEE 802.16, which specifies fixed broadband wireless access (BWA) systems for point-to-multipoint communications. The original standard specified systems operating between 10 GHz and 16 GHz, but recently an amendment has been added to also include systems operating between 2 GHz and 11 GHz.

To ensure the interoperability between manufacturers and vendors, the Worldwide Interoperability for Microwave Access (WiMAX) technical group was formed to address the areas not addressed by the IEEE 802.16 standards. WiMAX is currently working on test and conformance specification for BWA systems, as well as interoperability issues.

Baseband Communications

Local area networks (LANs) communicate using baseband transmissions, which use the entire communications medium to transmit a single data stream. Using baseband simplifies the transmission process, but it does add the complexity of managing media access to prevent one transmission from colliding with another.

A baseband network transmits digital data streams, but because the origin data, such as data transmitted by a computer, is digital, the need for analog to digital modulation is eliminated. Some modulation may be needed, though, depending on the type of transmission media (such as infrared, to convert digital signals into pulsed light).

When data is transmitted over a baseband channel, a line driver within the transceiver of each node's network adapter generates voltage shifts on the channel to represent the changes between binary ones and zeroes. The *baseband channel* is the transport mechanism that carries voltage pulses to every node connected to or within range (in the case of wireless LANs) of the network medium.

Wireless Baseband LAN Communications

The 802.11 standard specifies baseband transmission over three types of physical (PHY) media:

- Infrared (IR)
- Radio frequency (RF)—Frequency hopping spread-spectrum (FHSS)
- Radio frequency (RF)—Direct sequence spread-spectrum (DSSS)

IR Baseband   The base 802.11 standard defines infrared (IR) pulse period modulation as one of its three PHY transmission media. *IR technology* uses high frequencies that are just below the visible light band to transmit digital data. Although IR is not typically used for wireless LAN implementations, it is an approved wireless networking medium.

Two types of IR technology are used to transmit data:

- **Directed (line-of-sight):** A directed or line-of-sight IR transmission must have a clear, unobstructed transmission path between the transmitter and receiver. IR transmissions have restrictive transmission criteria and are affected by variations in temperature across its range. IR cannot penetrate an opaque object, so anything placed in the path of a directed IR transmission breaks the beam. The drawback of direct IR technology is this: its effective range for computer peripherals and similar devices is about 1 meter or around 3 feet, which limits its use to personal area networks (PANs) and limited WLAN applications.

- **Diffused (reflective):** A diffused or reflective IR transmission is not limited to line-of-sight and its beam can be diffused and reflected around a closed room allowing IR receivers not in direct line of sight (LoS) to receive the transmitted data. The transmitter and receiver in a diffused IR system create what is called a cell, which is limited to a single room.

RF Baseband   Wireless RF communications are either FHSS or DSSS, which are the techniques used to spread data across the spectrum of an RF band for transmission purposes.

FHSS technology segments the 2.4 GHz RF band into 75 1 MHz channels. An FHSS transmission rapidly moves between channels using a channel sequence scheme known to both the transmitter and receiver. Figure 4-22 illustrates an example of how the signal of an FHSS transmission hops between frequencies. To avoid collisions with transmissions from other stations on the same band, each set of transmitters and receivers uses a unique frequency-hopping scheme.

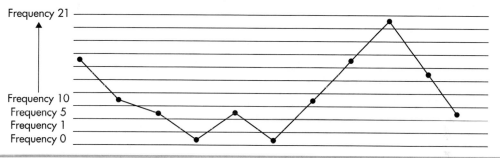

Figure 4-22   An example of the frequency hopping used in FHSS technology

DSSS technology divides the 2.4 GHz RF band into 14 22 MHz channels that slightly overlap each other. DSSS uses a process called chipping in place of frequency hopping. *Chipping* spreads the original digital bit using a *chipping code*, which is a higher data-rate bit sequence (as illustrated in Figure 4-23). DSSS modulates the original signal by applying Binary Phase Shift Keying (BPSK), Quadrature Phase Shift Keying (QPSK), or Complementary Code Keying (CCK). In effect, phase shift keying (PSK) rotates the phase of the electrical signal (see Figure 4-24) in such a way that it creates a digital wave sequence, which is horizontally as wide as the original data bit waveform is high. The differences among these three types of PSK are the number of bits used to convert the original data bit into a sequence of bits. Figures 4-25 and 4-26 illustrate how the application of BPSK and QPSK changes the transmitted signal, respectively.

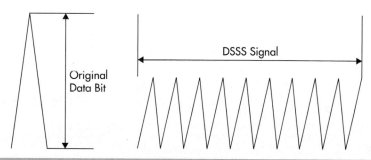

Figure 4-23   DSSS converts the original data bit (left) into a sequence of bits (right).

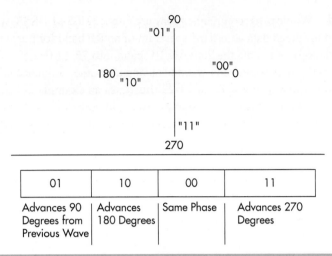

01	10	00	11
Advances 90 Degrees from Previous Wave	Advances 180 Degrees	Same Phase	Advances 270 Degrees

Figure 4-24 The phase shift positions used to shift the keying of a transmitted signal

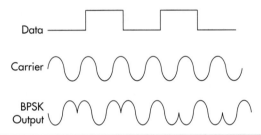

Figure 4-25 BPSK combines the data signal with the carrier to create a combined signal.

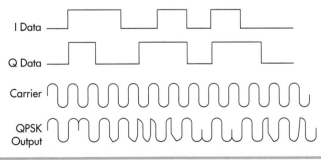

Figure 4-26 QPSK combines the in-phase bits (*I* data) with the Quadrature bits (*Q* data) with the signal carrier to create a combined signal.

Technology	Data Rates	Spreading Code Used	Modulation Used
2.4 GHz DSSS (802.11b)	1 Mbps	Barker Code	DBPSK
	2 Mbps	Barker Code	DQPSK
	5.5 Mbps	CKK	DQPSK
	11 Mbps	CKK	DQPSK
2.4 GHz DSSS (802.11g)	6 Mbps	BPSK	OFDM
	9 Mbps	BPSK	OFDM
	12 Mbps	QPSK	OFDM
	18 Mbps	QPSK	OFDM
	24 Mbps	16-QAM	OFDM
	36 Mbps	16-QAM	OFDM
	48 Mbps	16-QAM	OFDM
	54 Mbps	64-QAM	OFDM

Table 4-9   Modulation Technologies for 802.11b and g Networks

Table 4-9 lists the spreading code used with each data speed and type of modulation on 802.11b and 802.11g networks.

Wireless Baseband Media Access   The basic technique used in 802.11 Media Access Control (MAC) is Carrier Sense Multiple Access/Collision Avoidance (CSMA/CA), the same MAC method used in some wired networks. The difference between CSMA/CA and the Carrier Sense Multiple Access/Collision Detection (CSMA/CD) used by Ethernet networks is that CSMA attempts to avoid collisions before they happen, while CSMA/CD deals with collisions after the fact.

An 802.11 wireless LAN avoids collisions through a variety of actions. First, a wireless node waits for an allocation of time on the medium before transmitting its data. When the node is allotted a time slot, it then requests an acknowledgment from a nearby network access point (NAP). If the acknowledgment (ACK) is received, the node begins its transmission. If the acknowledgment is not received in a certain amount of time, however, the node assumes a collision has occurred and restarts its transmission process from the beginning.

Collisions can be caused on a wireless medium by what are called "hidden nodes." While each node can communicate with a nearby NAP, it may be unable to sense the transmissions of another node on the network. In other words, if one or more other nodes are hidden on the

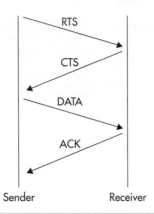

Figure 4-27 The RTS/CTS signal sequence

network from a node attempting to transmit, a collision can occur when one or more of these nodes also attempt to access the NAP. To overcome this problem, 802.11 nodes use a Request-to-Send/Clear-to-Send (RTS/CTS) procedure (illustrated in Figure 4-27) before attempting to transmit data.

Collision avoidance, including the ACK and RTS/CTS procedures, add additional processing to the actions required to transmit data on an 802.11 network. Because the wireless medium is less reliable (compared to cable media), more assurances must be gained before transmitting to make up for the lowered reliability.

Narrowband Communications

Narrowband typically is used to describe a single transmission channel that provides the capacity of a single voice-grade line, which ranges between 64 kilobits per second (Kbps) and 300 Kbps, but it can also be used to define any communications channel that has bandwidth up to 1.544 megabits per second (Mbps). Narrowband communications are commonly used for narrowband ISDN (NISDN), fax machines, and dialup networking.

Wideband Communications

Wideband refers to a communications system that uses multiple channels of a medium to provide high-speed transmission capabilities. Wideband operates in the space between narrowband and broadband, and it provides transmission speeds between 1.544 Mbps and 45 Mbps.

One version of wideband technology being developed for use in home automation and control and PAN applications is wireless ultra wideband (UWB) communications. *UWB* is a short-range system that uses multiple channels of a medium to transmit data. In addition, UWB applies Orthogonal Frequency Division Multiplexing (OFDM), which provides for more data throughput than a normal wideband link.

OFDM is an adaptation of FDM spread-spectrum technology that distributes data signals over multiple carriers transmitted on separate frequencies. Because the frequencies are spaced precisely apart, creating the orthogonal part of this modulation technique, each receiving device (or demodulator) sees only its specifically assigned frequency and no others.

Line Check 4.5

1. What are the differences between broadband and baseband communications?
2. Where is UWB technology being used?
3. How does OFDM ensure separation of frequency bands?

What Do You Think?

What is it about broadband communications that makes it compatible for the transmission of multimedia content across the Internet and local networks?

Chapter 4 Review

Chapter Summary

Define RF Communication Basics

- Electromagnetic radiation is alternate electrical and magnetic fields in a flow characterized by an oscillating waveform.
- All types of electromagnetic radiation have waveforms, including: radio waves, microwaves, infrared light, visible light, ultraviolet light, X-rays, and gamma rays.
- Wavelength is the distance between the peaks of two consecutive waveforms. The wavelength of a particular type of electromagnetic energy is used to identify and categorize that energy form.
- Frequency measures the number of wavelengths occurring in a specific time period, typically one second or a fraction of a second. Frequency is expressed in hertz (Hz).

- Radio waves are electromagnetic waves propagated through the air and received by an antenna. The range of a radio wave is determined by its frequency and amplitude.

- Radio waves are modulated using several methods. In this chapter, you learned about amplitude modulation (AM) and frequency modulation (FM). AM varies the amplitude or the height of the wave. FM modulates the vibration rate of the signal, represented by the number of wavelengths transmitted in the signal in one second.

- Transceivers can both transmit and receive.

Understand Radio Communications

- Multiplexing intersperses message segments from multiple sessions onto the single medium. The basic forms of multiplexing used in communications are frequency-division multiplexing (FDM), time-division multiplexing (TDM), and code-division multiplexing (CDM).

- Circuit switching uses mechanical and electronic switching to establish a circuit path between the source and destination for a single session.

- Packet switching doesn't create an established communication path and packets are routed between nodes using the better path available to each packet. Two packet-switching methods are most common: virtual circuit packet switching and datagram switching.

- A virtual circuit is a logical circuit in which each of the intermediate nodes on the circuit is temporarily locked into a pathway that exists for a single session.

Common RF Communications Standards

- The standards and protocols for voice and data transfers on RF communications have evolved in three generations. 1G protocols control the transmission of analog voice signals; 2G wireless technologies are circuit-based, digital, voice transmission systems; and 3G protocols provide megabit data rates that support the transfer of data other than voice communications.

- Spread-spectrum is a modulation technique characterized by its use of a wide frequency spectrum. Spread-spectrum uses two primary signal-structuring techniques: DSSS and FHSS.

Key Terms

AM *(121)*
Circuit switching *(128)*
DSSS *(134)*
FDM *(125)*
FHSS *(134)*

FM *(122)*
Frequency *(111)*
Hertz *(113)*
Multiplexing *(124)*
Packet switching *(129)*
Radio wave *(110, 119)*
Spread-spectrum *(134)*
TDM *(125)*

Key Term Quiz

Use the terms from the Key Terms list to complete the following sentences. Don't use the same term more than once. Not all terms will be used.

1. _____ uses mechanical and electronic switching to establish a circuit path between the source and destination for a single session.

2. _____ modulates the vibration rate of the signal, represented by the number of wavelengths transmitted in the signal in one second.

3. Frequency is measured in _____.

4. AM manipulates a transmitted radio wave by varying its _____.

5. _____ routes packets between nodes using the better path available to each packet.

6. A(n) _____ is an electromagnetic wave propagated through the air and received by an antenna.

7. _____ intersperses message segments from multiple sessions onto the single medium.

8. The number of wavelengths occurring in an oscillating radio wave in specific time is its _____.

9. _____ is a modulation technique characterized by its use of a wide frequency spectrum.

10. _____ uses amplitude modulation to combine the waveforms of the data and carrier signals.

Multiple Choice Quiz

1. What switching method uses mechanical and electronic switching to establish a circuit path between the source and destination for a single session?

   A. AM

   B. Circuit switching

   C. FM

   D. Packet switching

2. What are the two general types of spread-spectrum modulation?

 A. AMSS

 B. DSSS

 C. FHSS

 D. FMSS

3. What is the networking device used to forward packets on a packet-switching network?

 A. Hub

 B. LAN switch

 C. NAP

 D. Router

4. What type of electromagnetic wave is propagated through the air and received by an antenna to transmit data signals?

 A. Gamma rays

 B. Infrared light waves

 C. Radio waves

 D. Ultraviolet light waves

5. What signal transmission method intersperses message segments from multiple sessions onto the single medium?

 A. DSSS

 B. FHSS

 C. Modulation

 D. Multiplexing

6. What is the term used to describe the height of a radio wave?

 A. Amplitude

 B. Frequency

 C. Modulation

 D. Wavelength

7. AM manipulates a transmitted radio wave by varying its _____.

 A. Amplitude

 B. Frequency

   C. Modulation

   D. Signal strength

8. FM manipulates a transmitted radio wave by varying its _____.

   A. Amplitude

   B. Frequency

   C. Modulation

   D. Signal strength

9. Megahertz is used to state the _____ of a radio wave.

   A. Amplitude

   B. Frequency

   C. Modulation

   D. Wavelength

10. Which of the RF multiplexing methods uses times slices to carry multiple data streams on a single carrier?

   A. AM

   B. FDM

   C. FM

   D. TDM

Lab Projects

1. Search the Internet for information on amplitude modulation and frequency modulation. Then, describe how and why they are used to change the characteristics of a radio wave.

2. Determine whether broadband or baseband communications are used in each of the following applications at your school or business (if your school or business doesn't use one or more of the services listed, indicate which communications service should be used in each case):

   A. Downloading content from satellite broadcasts

   B. Intercampus television transmissions

   C. Building or lab networks

   D. Campus radio or television station

    E. Incoming cable television service

    F. Wireless campus networks

Case Problems

1. Do spread-spectrum technologies provide any benefit or enhancement for wireless networking security? Working in small groups, research this topic and report to the class or form teams for a debate on this topic.

2. Provide at least one application example for each of the following transmission modes:

    A. Narrowband

    B. Baseband

    C. Wideband

    D. Broadband

    E. Ultra wideband

3. What are the primary advantages or disadvantages broadband networks have over baseband networks? Should local area networks be converted to broadband? Why?

Advanced Lab Project

The objective of this lab is to introduce a product review process. The student will record the overall product features and technical specifications. The student will interpret several wireless devices including access points, routers, wireless adapters, and antennas to record important specifications.

    Information for Laboratory: This lab requires access to the Internet to download product manuals. The computer used to download these files needs the necessary software, including Adobe Acrobat to display the PDF files. The following equipment is also recommended to provide the opportunity to let students handle the actual equipment:

- 1–802.11g wireless router
- 1–802.11g wireless access point
- 1–802.11g PCI adapter
- 1–802.11g wireless Type II Cardbus NIC
- 1–802.11b/g wireless USB network adapter

Estimated Time: 20 minutes
Perform the following steps:

1. Go to the manufacturer's web site and locate the online product manuals for the devices you are using in this project.

2. Use the manuals to complete the following tables:

802.11g Wireless Router						
Wireless Standard						
Maximum Data Rate						
Wireless Frequency Range						
Wireless Transmit Power						
External Antenna Type						
Wireless Data Rates with Automatic Fallback:						
Indoor Operating Range						
Outdoor Operating Range						
Default Address of Router						
Admin Password						

802.11g Wireless Access Point						
Wireless Standard						
Maximum Data Rate						
Wireless Frequency Range						
Wireless Transmit Power						
External Antenna Type						
Wireless Data Rates with Automatic Fallback:						
Indoor Operating Range						
Outdoor Operating Range						
Default Address of Router						
Admin Password						

802.11g USB Wireless Network Adapter			
Wireless Standard			
Maximum Data Rate			
Interface Type			
External Antenna Type			
Wireless Data Rates			
Indoor Operating Range			
Available Channels:			

802.11g PCI NIC						
Wireless Standard						
Bus Type						
Maximum Data Rate						
Wireless Frequency Range						
Wireless Transmit Power						
Internal Antenna Type						
Wireless Data Rates with Automatic Fallback:						
Indoor Operating Range						
Outdoor Operating Range						
Power Consumption						
Modulation Technology:						

802.11g Cardbus Wireless Network Adapter					
Wireless Standard					
Bus Type					
Internal Antenna Type					
Frequency Range					
Wireless Data Rates					
Indoor Operating Range					
Outdoor Operating Range					
Modulation Technology					
Power Consumption					
Transmitter Output Power:					

4

REVIEW

Chapter 5

Wireless LAN Standards

The Institute of Electrical and Electronics Engineers (IEEE), which dates back to 1884 as the American Institute of Electrical Engineers (AIEE), is a professional organization with members in engineering, science, and education. The *IEEE* is best known for the standards it develops for the electronics, computer, and networking industries, including the IEEE 802 networking standard that has become the de facto industry standard for both wired and wireless local area networks (LANs).

Included in the IEEE 802 standards are several that address the operation, characteristics, and construction of wireless LANs, personal area networks (PANs), and metropolitan or municipal area networks (MANs) that transmit data using radio frequency (RF) signals. This chapter focuses on the IEEE 802 wireless networking standards, their capabilities, and characteristics.

The IEEE 802 Standards—An Overview

The 802 standards that specifically apply directly to wireless networks are listed in Table 5-1.

IEEE Standard	Defines
802.11	Wireless Networking
802.11a	54 Mbps Wireless Networking
802.11b	11 Mbps Wireless Networking
802.11g	54 Mbps Wireless Networking
802.11n	100 Mbps Wireless Networking
802.11r	Infrared Wireless Networking
802.15	Wireless Personal Area Network (WPAN)
802.16	Wireless MAN (WMAN)
802.20	Fixed Wireless Broadband

Table 5-1 The IEEE 802 Wireless Networking Standards

The IEEE 802.11*x* wireless local area network (WLAN) standards (802.11, 802.11a, 802.11b, 802.11g, 802.11n, and 802.11r) are discussed in this chapter. The remaining wireless networking standards listed in Table 5-1 are discussed in later chapters because each of these standards defines a particular type and application of wireless networking. IEEE 802.15, which defines wireless personal area networking, is discussed in Chapter 7, and the 802.16 and 802.20 standards, which define WMAN and fixed wireless broadband networking, respectively, are discussed in Chapter 14.

The IEEE 802 Committees

In February 1980, the IEEE formed a special committee to develop vendor-neutral standards for LANs. This committee was designated as the 802 committee using the year and month it was formed. After the 802 committee was organized, several subcommittees or task groups were formed to deal with specific networking issues.

Each of the subcommittees was assigned a sequential number to differentiate its work from that of the other subcommittees. For example, the 802.1 committee was assigned the task of developing standards to address network management issues, the 802.2 committee works on Layer 2 or data link layer standards, and the 802.3 committee works on media access control standards for bus networks (Ethernet). Notice that the committee's assigned number is also the primary number used for the standards, guidelines, or documents they publish. The full complement of 802 committees is:

- 802.1—Network management
- 802.2—Logical link control
- 802.3—Media access control for bus networks (Ethernet)
- 802.4—Media access control for token-passing bus networks
- 802.5—Media access control for token-passing ring networks
- 802.6—Metropolitan area networks (MANs)
- 802.7—Broadband Technical Advisory Group (TAG)
- 802.8—Fiber Optic TAG
- 802.9—Isochronous LAN
- 802.10—Security
- 802.11—Wireless LAN
- 802.12—Demand priority
- 802.13—Not used
- 802.14—Cable modems
- 802.15—Wireless PAN
- 802.16—Broadband wireless access
- 802.17—Resilient packet ring
- 802.18—Radio regulatory TAG
- 802.19—Coexistence TAG
- 802.20—Mobile wireless broadband

5

Line Check 5.1

1. Which of the IEEE 802 committees is tasked with the development of **WLAN** standards?

2. Which of the IEEE WLAN standards defines a physical layer that supports data speeds up to 11 Mbps?

The IEEE 802.11 WLAN Standards

A *WLAN* (also referred to as a local area wireless network or LAWN) is any local network that uses high-frequency radio waves to communicate between nodes. The default standards for WLANs throughout the world are defined in the IEEE 802.11 standards.

Like the standards that define WLAN, such as 802.3, 802.5, and so forth, the WLAN standards are focused on defining the physical media and the Media Access Control (MAC) functions for wireless networking. Wireless local area networking, as defined by the 802.11 standards, extends the standards that define wired networking to include three types of Physical layer wireless media: frequency-hopping spread spectrum (FHSS), direct-sequence spread spectrum (DSSS), and infrared (IR). The 802.11 MAC layer (the equivalent of the data link layer in a wired environment), as its name implies, is primarily focused on media access control. However, it also performs some tasks normally associated with higher layers in other networking standards, including frame fragmentation, retransmission, and acknowledgments.

As wireless networking technology has emerged, the standards have been upgraded and revised to keep pace, and in some cases, to even set the pace. As a result, several versions of the 802.11 standard have evolved and been adapted to specific wireless communications technologies, needs, and requirements. Table 5-2 lists the 802.11 WLAN standards and their operating characteristics.

Standard	RF Band	Speed
802.11	Infrared (IR) or 2.4 GHz	1 Mbps or 2 Mbps
802.11a	5 GHz	54 Mbps
802.11b	2.4 GHz	11 Mbps
802.11g	2.4 GHz	54 Mbps
802.11n	5 GHz	100 Mbps

Table 5-2 IEEE 802.11 Wireless LAN Standards

Within the IEEE 802.11 Working Group, a number of task groups were formed to focus on specific areas of wireless LAN specifications and standards, which are listed in Table 5-3.

Task Group	Area of Responsibility
802.11a	54 Mbps, 5 GHz standard
802.11b	Enhancements to 802.11 (legacy)
802.11c	MAC-level bridging
802.11d	Global compatibility
802.11e	Quality of service (QoS)
802.11f	Interaccess point roaming protocols
802.11g	54 Mbps, 2.4 GHz standard with compatibility with 802.11b
802.11h	5 GHz Dynamic Channel/Frequency Selection (DCS/DFS) and Transmit Power Control (TPC) for European compatibility
802.11i	Security enhancements
802.11IR	Infrared (IR) networking
802.11j	Standards extensions for Japan
802.11k	Radio resource measurement and reporting
802.11m	802.11 standards maintenance
802.11n	Higher throughput improvements
802.11r	Fast roaming wireless with Voice over IP (VoIP)
802.11s	Mesh networking to extend operating ranges

Table 5-3   The IEEE 802.11 Task Groups

The *802.11 standards* are a group of specifications that generally specify transmitting RF signals on a through-the-air medium between a wireless network node and a network base station or between two wireless network nodes.

The WLAN standards approved and adopted by the IEEE 802.11 group are:

- **802.11:** Now called the *802.11 legacy standard*, 802.11 defines 1 to 2 Mbps wireless networking using the 2.3 GHz RF band with FHSS and DSSS signaling and IR.

- **802.11a:** This extension to the 802.11 standard defines WLANs that provide up to 54 Mbps of data transfer in the 5 GHz RF band. **802.11a** also defines Orthogonal Frequency Division Multiplexing (OFDM) encoding that splits an RF signal into multiple substreams for simultaneous transmission on separate frequencies. *OFDM* is effective for transmitting large blocks of digital data with reduced crosstalk.

- **802.11b:** This extension to the 802.11 standard, which is also called 802.11 High Rate and Wi-Fi (wireless fidelity), defines WLANs that transmit 1 Mbps, 2 Mbps, 5.5 Mbps, and 11 Mbps in the 2.4 GHz RF band using DSSS signaling.

- **802.11g:** This extension of the 802.11 standard defines WLAN capable of transmitting up to 54 Mbps in the 2.4 GHz RF band, which makes it compatible with 802.11b systems.

- **802.11i:** Approved and adopted in June 2005, this standard improves WLAN security standards (see Chapter 11 for more information on this standard).

- **802.11IR:** Once included in the 802.11 legacy standard, IR WLAN specifications are now defined in a separate standard. 802.11IR defines a 2 Mbps WLAN that transmits on diffused optical technology.

Line Check 5.2

1. Which of the IEEE 802.11 task groups defines security standards for WLANs?
2. Which of the IEEE 802.11*x* standards is most associated with the name Wi-Fi?

Other Wireless Networking Standards

The European Telecommunications Standards Institute (ETSI) has developed and adopted the wireless networking standard used throughout Europe: HiperLAN. The ETSI wireless standards are:

- **HiperLAN/1** The European standard high performance radio local area network (HiperLAN/1) defines totally ad-hoc networking that provides up to 20 Mbps of bandwidth in the 5 GHz frequency band without the need for preset configuration or a central controller.

- **HiperLAN/2** The upgrade of the European HiperLAN standard, HiperLAN/2 provides up to 54 Mbps with strong security features. HiperLAN/2 is roughly the equivalent of IEEE 802.11a.

The IEEE 802.11 Legacy Standard

The original WLAN standard released by the IEEE as 802.11, which is now commonly referred to as the **802.11 Legacy** standard, was absorbed into the 802.11b standard that replaced it. When it was released in 1997, the 802.11 standard specified two data transfer speeds—1 or 2 Mbps—that could be transmitted using either IR signals or RF signals in the 2.4 GHz Industrial Scientific and Medical (ISM) band. IR signaling has been separated from the 802.11x RF standards in favor of the standards and protocols developed by the Infrared Data Association (IrDA) and the 802.11IR standard (see the section "The IEEE 802.11IR Standard").

The 802.11 MAC Layer

One lasting part of the 802.11 legacy standard was the common **MAC** layer used in all the 802.11x standards that followed. The primary functions of the common MAC layer are to manage and maintain communications between 802.11 transmitters and receivers (wireless network interface cards, network adapters, and access points) by coordinating and controlling access to the shared RF channels and applying the appropriate protocols.

Each of the 802.11x standards defines how the 802.11 physical layer (**PHY**) is used and the 802.11 MAC layer adapts to each standard to perform carrier sensing, data transmission, and the reception of message frames. As illustrated in Figure 5-1, the 802.11 MAC layer operates between the 802.11x PHY layer in the protocol and services stack of a wireless system. The MAC layer performs a variety of services and provides a form of translating buffer between the wireless medium and the protocols in use on the network, and the operating system (OS) and application software running on a host PC.

Because the RF medium used by 802.11x PHY layers is a shared medium, a wireless station must first gain access to the medium before it can transmit. Two methods are used to control and coordinate access to the shared RF medium:

- Distributed coordination function (DCF)
- Point coordination function (PCF)

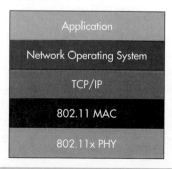

Figure 5-1   The 802.11 MAC layer operates on top of the 802.11x PHY layer

Distributed Coordination Function (DCF)

DCF is a mandatory part of the MAC functions in 802.11 and it operates much like the CSMA/CA protocol. On an 802.11 network, the stations share the medium, but unlike Ethernet and the Carrier Sense Multiple Access Collision Detection (CSMA/CD) protocol, wireless stations cannot merely test the medium to check whether it is in use. Wireless stations can be placed at some distant apart and, although they share a common access point, they may not be in range of each other. Without some mechanism to indicate when the transmission channel is available, wireless stations would create frequent collisions on the medium.

If you've ever called a technical support service and been told that the wait should be 3, 5, or even 30 minutes, you have experienced something like how access to a wireless medium is controlled. DCF uses a navigation allocation vector (NAV) to inform a station how long it must wait to access the medium and transmit its frames.

Before a station transmits a frame, it calculates the amount of time it needs to completely transmit the frame—based on the frame's length and the data transfer speed, which is the NAV—and places this value in the header of the frame. Each of the other stations receives the transmitted frame and extracts the NAV, and then uses it as the basis to calculate the NAV for its frame. Each station also uses the NAV as a countdown timer and, when the received NAV is zero, a station can attempt to transmit its frames.

The assumption here is that seldom should two or more stations need to transmit at exactly the same instant. However, if a station attempts to transmit on the medium and the channel is in use, DCF, like CSMA/CD, generates a random back-off timer, which is the amount of time the conflicting stations must wait before attempting to retransmit. Each station receives a different random period and this helps to ensure the stations don't attempt to retransmit again at the same time.

Because WLAN stations can't sense activity on the medium, in addition to the fact that a wireless NIC can't use its receiver while transmitting, message acknowledgments are also used. After completely receiving a frame, the receiving station transmits an ACK frame to the network, indicating no errors were detected and all is well. If the sending station doesn't receive an ACK in a certain time period, the assumption is that either a collision occurred or RF interference prevented the message from reaching its destination, and it retransmits the frame.

Point Coordination Function (PCF)

PCF is an optional media access control method for 802.11*x* wireless LANs that, unfortunately, is not currently implemented on many access points or NICs. PCF works something like the old adage, "Speak only when spoken to." An access point with PCF enabled polls the wireless stations using the sequence configured in a PCF polling list whenever the medium is idle and no DCF-based traffic is active to see if any of the stations are ready to transmit. A PCF station cannot transmit until the access point polls it. When DCF traffic requires the medium, PCF polling is disabled until the medium is once again idle. PCF, if implemented, allows the WLAN to transmit both synchronous data (such as streaming media) using DCF and asynchronous (like e-mail or web pages) using PCF.

IEEE 802.11 MAC Layer Operations

The 802.11*x* MAC layer has separate operational functions, depending on whether the network is an infrastructure network or an ad-hoc network. An *infrastructure network*, because its topology remains fairly constant, can use more structured MAC layer functions. An *ad-hoc network* requires the use of PHY discovery protocols before the MAC layer functions can be activated.

Three required and four optional functions are performed by the MAC layer on an 802.11*x* infrastructure network:

- Scanning for signals
- Device authentication
- Network association
- Data encryption
- RTS/CTS handshake
- Frame fragmentation
- Power conservation

Scanning for Signals

The 802.11 WLAN standard defines two methods a wireless NIC or network adapter can use to search the medium for an access point:

- **Passive scanning:** An access point periodically broadcasts a signal, called a *beacon*, which is used by any wireless NICs within range to identify the access point and determine the strength of its RF signal. A NIC may be able to receive signals from more than one access point, in which case the NIC compares the signal strength of the access points' beacons to determine which is the strongest. An access point's beacon contains information about the access point including its service set identifier (SSID), data rates, and more. Passive scanning is the default and mandatory standard for 802.11*x* networks.

- **Active scanning:** *Active scanning* is an optional scanning method that is essentially the reverse of passive scanning. When active scanning is in use, the wireless NICs broadcast a probe frame and any access points within range reply with a probe response frame. Active scanning allows a wireless NIC to connect to an access point (of its choosing) without needing to wait for a beacon from the access points within its range. The downside to active scanning is additional frames (probe and response) add traffic on the medium.

NOTE

A unique 32-character SSID, which is called a *network name*, is used to identify each WLAN and to differentiate one WLAN from another. All the access points, NICs, and wireless devices on a WLAN must use the same SSID. The SSID can also be used as a password when a mobile device attempts to join an infrastructure network.

Device Authentication

A critical process on any network, and especially on a WLAN, is mutual authentication, in which a network's nodes are identified to the network and the network edge devices (access points, routers, and so forth), and vice versa. On a wired network, client devices are connected to the same medium as network edge devices, so the client devices are assured they are connecting to the correct network. In a wireless environment, however, a client device must authenticate the network and the network must authenticate the device to ensure the device is connected to the correct network. This two-way authentication is called *mutual authentication*. The authentication process is used to establish access between the WLAN's stations, both as a security step and a way to avoid man-in-the-middle attacks.

IEEE 802.11*x* WLANs implement two levels of authentication: open systems authentication and shared-key authentication. *Open systems authentication* (see Figure 5-2) requires a wireless device to request authentication by sending an authentication request to an access point. The access point responds with an authentication approval. In effect, the access point authenticates any device with the correct SSID.

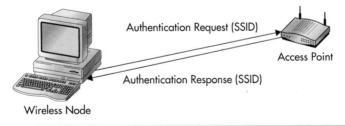

Figure 5-2 The exchange of frames in an open systems authentication process

The *shared-key authentication process* is an optional process in which public encryption keys are exchanged between wireless stations over a secure RF channel outside the 802.11*x* communications channel.

Because of the lack of a robust authentication process in the 802.11 standards, proprietary authentication methods have emerged, such as Cisco Systems' Lightweight Extensible Authentication Protocol (LEAP) and Wi-Fi's Protected Access (WPA).

Cisco's *LEAP* is a wireless centralized and user-based authentication process that eliminates security issues through the use of dynamic Wireless Equivalent Privacy (WEP) keys, mutual authentication, and user-based authentication, which adds another layer of authentication of just verifying the SSID of the devices.

Man-In-The-Middle (MTTM) Attacks: The Danger of Shared-Key Authentication

A man-in-the-middle (MTTM) attack occurs when an attacker is able to intercept, read, and, perhaps, modify frames transmitted between two stations, usually undetected.

As explained in Chapter 13, MTTM attacks most typically occur when a public encryption key is used to secure the authentication data between a station and an edge device. When a public key is in use, an MTTM attack would happen something like this:

If the user on station A wants to communicate directly with the user on Station B, user A requests the public encryption key from user B. However, if the evildoer on station X wants to alter or replace the messages from user B to user A, user X can intercept the public key message from user B and forward his own public key to user A.

User A uses the encryption key from user X to encrypt messages, believing the key is user B's and transmits the message. User X intercepts the message, decrypts it, either changes the message or replaces it, and sends the message on to user B.

The upshot of this attack is the attacker now receives all the traffic between users A and B, as illustrated in the following:

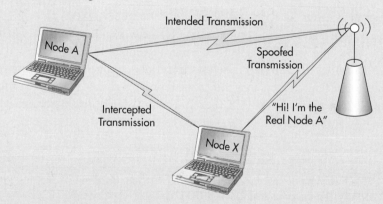

An MTTM attack can happen on any network that uses public encryption keys (or no keys at all), but a WLAN is all the more vulnerable. The defense against MTTM attacks is the use of signed keys, which are issued by a security certificate authority (see Chapter 13).

CROSS-REFERENCE

For more information on WEP and its role in authentication, see Chapter 13.

While WPA is similar to LEAP, it is vendor-neutral, where Cisco is proprietary to Cisco products and the Cisco security suite of products. Nearly all Wi-Fi devices apply WPA.

Network Association

After a wireless NIC has received authentication from an access point, the NIC must be associated with an access point before it can begin transmitting frames on the medium. The association process allows the NIC to synchronize with the access point and the bandwidth of the medium.

To initiate the association process, a wireless NIC transmits an association request frame to the access point that contains the network SSID and the data transfer rates the NIC supports. The access point replies with an association response frame that includes an association identity code, SSID, and the data rate on which the association is granted. When the association process is completed, the NIC can begin transmitting data frames, subject to the availability of the medium.

Data Encryption

An optional feature of the 802.11 MAC layer is the use of WEP. Using WEP, a wireless NIC encrypts the data (payload) of each data frame using a common 40-bit encryption key before transmitting the frame. The receiving station is able to decrypt the frame's data using the common key. Because the 802.11 standard doesn't define special handling for the common key, WEP is susceptible to interception and MTTM attacks. However, the 802.11i task group is currently defining security improvements for the 802.1x wireless standards.

Ready-To-Send/Clear-To-Send (RTS/CTS) Handshake

An optional feature that can be activated on 802.11x networks, Ready-To-Send/Clear-To-Send (RTS/CTS), allows the network to control the transmission of larger than normal data blocks. With RTS/CTS activated, each station defines a maximum frame length. Whenever a remote station wants to transmit a frame longer than the receiving station's maximum frame length, the sending NIC must activate RTS/CTS for the transmission of that frame.

NOTE

The length of the maximum frame varies with the 802.11x standard in use and the data rate of the medium, but the default length is 1,000 bytes.

RTS/CTS is a form of flow control in which the receiving station can signal the sending station that it wants to interrupt a transmission. Because its incoming data buffers are nearly full, it needs time to process the data in its incoming data buffer or it must tend to higher priorities.

To activate RTS/CTS, a NIC transmits an RTS frame to the access point or another wireless device. The access point then responds with a CTS frame that includes a duration value and indicates the NIC can begin transmitting its data frame. The duration value is placed in the header of the CTS frame and indicates to the other nodes on network the amount of time they must wait to allow the frame transmission to complete. The exchange of RTS and CTS frames is referred to as a handshake and the RTS/CTS handshake must be performed for each frame,

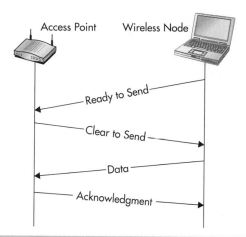

Figure 5-3   The RTS/CTS handshake

whenever the frame size exceeds the maximum frame length. Figure 5-3 illustrates the actions involved in the RTS/CTS handshake. Understand that Figure 5-3 shows only the first few of the frames exchanged when the session is established, and the data and acknowledgement exchange continues throughout the session while data is being transmitted.

RTS/CTS is especially helpful in the situation where two nodes are "hidden" from each other. A hidden nodes situation (see Figure 5-4) is created when two nodes are outside each other's operating range. For hidden nodes to communicate, they must associate with a third node that falls within the range of both of the hidden nodes. Using RTS/CTS in this situation helps to reduce the number of transmission collisions that would otherwise occur.

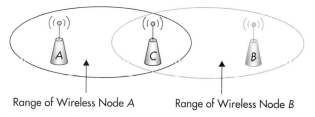

Figure 5-4   Nodes A and B are "hidden" from each other and must communicate through Node C

Frame Fragmentation

An optional function that can be applied on the 802.11 MAC layer is fragmentation. *Fragmentation* allows a transmitting node to divide a data frame into smaller frames (fragments) to avoid the possibility of having to retransmit larger frames, if enabled. The most typical reason for retransmitting a frame is when RF interference causes bit errors in the frame. Using fragmentation, it is more efficient to retransmit a shorter frame than a longer one.

With fragmentation in use, each node can define a maximum segment length, which is used to determine when an incoming frame must be fragmented by the transmitting station, with each fragment not longer than the maximum frame length.

Power Conservation

Another optional function of the 802.11 MAC layer is a power save mode that can be used in portable computers and devices to conserve battery power. If the NIC's power save mode is enabled, it allows the NIC to reduce its power requirements during idle periods and notify its access point that the NIC is switching to a sleep state. This is done by the NIC setting a bit in a notification frame header to ON. The access point then buffers messages for the sleeping station until it is notified that the station is changing back to active state. The NIC must change to active state periodically to receive buffered messages, after reestablishing authentication and association.

Phase-Shift Keying

The two primary types of signal modulation used with WLAN transmissions are frequency-shift keying (FSK) and phase-shift keying (PSK). The modulation method defined in the 802.11 standard for transmitting and receiving digital RF signals is *PSK*, which varies the phase of the transmitted signal. Several different phase modulation schemes can be used with PSK:

- **Biphase modulation:** Digital signals are divided into signal pulses and the state of each successive pulse (bit) is based on the state of the preceding bit, using signal phases of 0 and 180 degrees. When the bit value doesn't change (for example, when a one bit follows another one bit), the phase remains constant. When the value of the transmitted bit changes from one to zero or zero to one, the phase is shifted 180 degrees.

- **Four-phase modulation:** Adding additional signal phases allows binary data phase changes to occur quicker, which results in faster modulation than possible when two signal states are used. Four-phase modulation applies phase angles (the number of degrees at each phase shift step) of 0, 90, 180, and 270 degrees, which allows each phase shift to represent two signal elements.

- **Eight-phase modulation:** In eight-phase modulation, the phase angles available are 0, 45, 90, 135, 180, 225, 270, and 315 degrees and each phase shift can represent four signal elements.

Figure 5-5 illustrates the resulting signal waves from amplitude and phase shift methods.

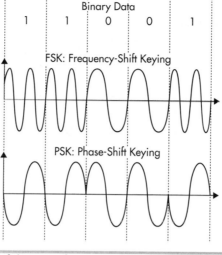

Figure 5-5   A comparison of the waveforms resulting from FSK and PSK modulation methods

5

CROSS-REFERENCE

FSK, PSK, and other WLAN modulation techniques are discussed in more detail in Chapter 4.

Signal Modulation

To attach data to an electronic (wired or wireless RF) or optical (such as an IR signal) carrier signal, the signal must be modulated. Any form of electrical signal, whether direct current (DC), alternating current (AC), or optical signal, can be modulated, but in RF communications, AC is modulated to carry data from the transmitter to the receiver using a range of radio frequencies.

Some of the more common examples of RF modulation are amplitude modulation (AM), frequency modulation (FM), and phase modulation (PM). *AM* radio is transmitted with the amplitude of the signal modulated, *FM* radio modulates the frequency of the signal, and *PM* modulates a data signal by slightly delaying the data portion of the signal from that of the carrier, which puts the two signal streams in separate phases.

The phase of an electronic signal is determined by a comparative position of its waveform at a particular point in time. A waveform completes a complete cycle in a 360-degree linear distance, as shown in Figure 5-6. When phase shifting modulation is applied to a signal, the data signal wave is inserted with a displacement that is relative to the carrier wave, with both waves having the same frequency, as illustrated in Figure 5-7.

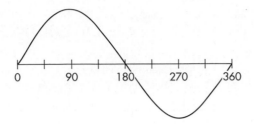

Figure 5-6   A waveform has a 360-degree cycle length.

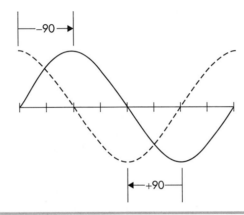

Figure 5-7   An analog signal after a phase modulation of 90 degrees

 # Line Check 5.3

1.   What are the three mandatory functions performed on the 802.11 MAC layer?

2.   Describe the actions of the optional RTS/CTS function of the 802.11 MAC layer.

3.   What is the purpose of the authentication function on a wireless network?

What Do You Think?

Do 802.11 MAC functions like RTS/CTS and fragmentation improve or degrade the performance of a WLAN when in use?

The IEEE 802.11b WLAN Standard

The *IEEE 802.11b WLAN standard*, which is also known as 802.11 High Rate or Wi-Fi (Wireless Fidelity), is an extension to the IEEE 802.11 standard improving throughput and increasing data transfer rates to 5.5 Mbps and 11 Mbps. Like 802.11, 802.11b operates on the 2.4 GHz RF band. Because of its higher data transfer speeds, 802.11b provides functionality similar to that of a wire-based Ethernet network.

Specifically, the 802.11b **PHY** layer defines wireless communications that operate in the 2.4 to 2.483 GHz unlicensed RF ISM band, in either infrastructure or ad-hoc mode, and requires a minimum of two pieces of wireless equipment:

- A wireless station, such as a desktop PC, notebook, or other portable computing device, with a wireless NIC

- A wireless access point or a bridge between wireless stations, and a distribution system or wired network.

In the following sections, you look at the primary operating characteristics and modes of the 802.11b standard:

- The 802.11b physical layer (PHY)

- The 802.11b PLCP and PMD sublayers

- The 802.11b infrastructure mode

- The 802.11b ad-hoc mode

802.11b Physical Layer

Like the other 802.11*x* PHY definitions, the 802.11b PHY defines the RF medium used to provide an interface between wireless devices and how data is transmitted over its communication channels. And, like the other 802.11*x* PHY, the 802.11b PHY is an extension of the 802.11 PHY. The 802.11b PHY defines two higher data transfer rates—5.5 Mbps and 11 Mbps—and the use of Complementary Code Keying (CCK) with Quadrature Phase Shift Keying (QPSK) modulation (discussed in Chapter 4) and the use of direct sequence spread-spectrum (DSSS) transmission.

CCK is the modulation scheme used for the 5.5 Mbps and 11 Mbps data transfer speeds defined in the 802.11b specification. CCK applies a set of mathematical formulas to DSSS codes, which allows the DSSS codes to represent more data per cycle and achieve higher data rates. CCK works only with DSSS. It does not work with any of the frequency-hopping or infrared technologies.

QAM combines two amplitude modulation (AM) signals onto a single channel, which effectively doubles the available bandwidth of the channel. QAM is used with pulse amplitude modulation (PAM) in wireless system transmissions. The term "quadrature" refers to the 90-degree (one-quarter of a cycle) phase shifts used to differentiate two carriers.

The 802.11b PHY also defines the use of dynamic rate shifting (DRS), which allows the transmission rate to be adjusted to a lower rate when interference is experienced. An 802.11b transmitter can adjust the transmission speed down from 11 Mbps to 5.5 Mbps, 2 Mbps, or 1 Mbps in an electrically noisy environment, which can occur as devices begin to move out of range. If the interference subsides, the transmitter can begin to increase the rate, settling at the highest rate on which the least amount of interference is present.

802.11b PLCP and PMD Sublayers

The IEEE 802.11b PHY is divided into two parts: the Physical Layer Convergence Protocol (PLCP) and the Physical Medium Dependent (PMD) sublayer.

Physical Layer Convergence Protocol (PLCP)

The 802.11b PLCP performs the carrier sense (CS) portion of CSMA/CA and also provides a common service access point (SAP) through which the MAC layer passes and receives data from the PHY layer.

The process used for carrier sensing is Clear Channel Assessment (CCA), which measures the voltage on the medium and compares it to a threshold, which varies with the type of transmission technologies in use. If the current measured on the medium exceeds the threshold, the medium is assumed to be in use. At or below the threshold, the medium is assumed to be idle.

Physical Medium Dependent (PMD)

The PMD sublayer of the 802.11b PHY defines the methods and characteristics of the transmit and receive functions including the type of modulation and spread-spectrum used.

802.11b Infrastructure Mode

In infrastructure mode, an 802.11b network includes at least one wireless station and one access point connected to a distribution system. The distribution system could be a wired network, a cable Internet system, a satellite Internet access, or another type of network access. In a WLAN with a single access point, the access point is connected directly to the network. In a wireless infrastructure network, two configurations can be used: Basic Service Set (BSS) and Extended Service Set (ESS).

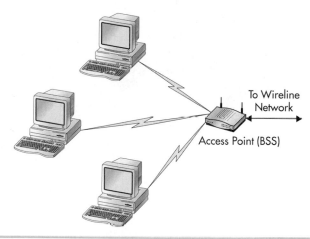

To Wireline
Network

Access Point (BSS)

Figure 5-8   An access point or BSS provides a link to a wired network for wireless stations.

Basic Service Set (BSS)

In infrastructure mode, all the wireless stations on the WLAN communicate directly and only with an access point to create a **BSS**. Commonly, the access point in a BSS serves as a bridge between the wireless nodes and a distribution system, such as a wired network, as illustrated in Figure 5-8.

Extended Service Set (ESS)

An **ESS** combines two or more BSS stations and their wireless nodes into an extended wireless networking arrangement. As illustrated in Figure 5-9, within an ESS, frames are forwarded from one BSS to another. This arrangement allows wireless nodes to change locations and move from one BSS to another within the ESS, without the node or the network being reconfigured. As shown in Figure 5-9, an ESS is made up of two or more BSS groupings.

802.11b Ad-hoc Mode

IEEE 802.11b ad-hoc networks are formed on an Independent Basic Service Set (IBSS) or the equivalent of a peer-to-peer wireless network. In this arrangement, no base station (access point) is involved and the wireless stations communicate directly to any other station within range.

Ad-hoc mode is essentially a peer-to-peer wireless network structure in which any wireless station within range of any of the ad-hoc stations is able to communicate. Ad-hoc networks are best used in small networks, such as home or small office networks, but they can also have some use in portions of a larger network, such as in visiting workers offices, conference rooms, or customer areas.

5

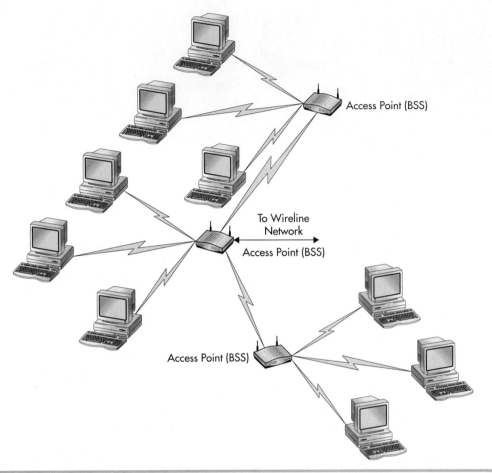

Figure 5-9 An ESS connects multiple wireless BSS together.

☞ Line Check 5.4

1. What are the two topology structures commonly used with 802.11b WLANs?

2. Describe the function of the 802.11b PLCP and PDM.

3. Describe the functions of CCK and QAM.

Wi-Fi

The *Wi-Fi Alliance* is a nonprofit trade organization that focuses on three primary areas of 802.11 WLAN development and implementation: encouraging the use of Wi-Fi systems worldwide by promoting the standardized 802.11 technologies in wireless networking products; promoting and marketing Wi-Fi products for use in home networks, small office networks, and enterprise networks; and testing and certification of Wi-Fi products and systems to ensure interoperability. Wireless devices that have been tested and approved by the Wi-Fi Alliance carry the following logo (which is the logo of the Wi-Fi Alliance):

5

Wi-Fi was originally formed to focus on 802.11 technologies, but it also promotes and tests 802.11a and 802.11g products. So, where the general term "Wi-Fi" referred only to 802.11b products and systems, the term now extends to include all 802.11 products.

Wi-Fi is also involved with developing applications for wireless networking systems, such as its Wireless Internet service provider (WISPr, pronounced "whisper") initiative. *WISPr* is involved with promoting ISPs to provide wireless Internet services to homes and businesses, as well as promoting the implementation of hot spots in businesses and city areas.

What Do You Think?

Why do you believe there has been such wide acceptance and use of the 802.11b standard?

The IEEE 802.11a WLAN Standard

Like all 802.*x* standards, IEEE 8021.11a defines the PHY and MAC layers for wireless networking. However, the 802.11a standard defines the operation of a WLAN using Orthogonal Frequency Division Multiplexing (OFDM) technology to achieve up to 54 Mbps of bandwidth on the 5 GHz

Unlicensed National Information Infrastructure (UNII) RF band using 12 20 MHz channels. The fact that 802.11a operates in the UNII band eliminates the interference problems common to the 2.4 GHz systems, such as 802.11b, Bluetooth, and many consumer electronics products. One disadvantage of operating in the 5 GHz band is this: if you want to retrofit an existing network, 802.11a is incompatible with 802.11b systems. However, several access points and NICs are on the market with support for both standards built in.

NOTE

In the math world, "orthogonal" refers to items placed at 90-degree angles. In the context of computing and especially WLANs, however, *orthogonal* is used to describe items that do not overlap, are mutually independent, and expand to span an entire space.

802.11a Modulation

IEEE 802.11a modulation converts digital data into analog waveforms using a variety of modulation methods, depending on the data transfer rate in use. For example, at 54 Mbps, the 802.11a PMD applies QAM that varies the signal using different amplitude levels, as well as phase shifting. At 6 Mbps, the PMD uses Binary Phase Shift Keying (BPSK), which shifts a single carrier to represent binary data.

Orthogonal Frequency Division Multiplexing (OFDM)

Unlike DHSS and FHSS, **OFDM** can be referred to as either a modulation method or a multiplexing technique. OFDM is not a form of spread-spectrum technology. OFDM divides a 20 MHz RF channel into 48 narrowband subchannels, and then splits a data signal into 48 separate carriers, one on each subchannel. This arrangement supports data transfer speeds of 6, 9, 12, 18, 24, 36, 48, and 54 Mbps, of which 6, 12, and 24 Mbps data rates are mandatory on all 802.11x devices. The subchannels are overlapped, which results in saving about 50 percent of the available bandwidth. This arrangement (see Figure 5-10), along with transmitting signal

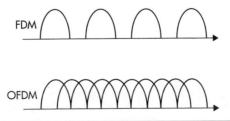

Figure 5-10 A comparison of how FDM and OFDM modulate a signal for transmission

bits as parallel data and using frequency-division multiplexing (FDM), enables OFDM to handle transmission problems common to other 802.11x standards: crosstalk and multipath propagation.

Multipath propagation occurs when an RF signal cannot take a clear and direct path between a transmitter and a receiver. In a home or office, walls, chairs, desks, and other furniture and objects can deflect an RF signal, causing it to bounce around an area in many directions. In these situations, a portion of the original signal may make it to the receiver unimpeded, while other parts of the signal may take an indirect route by way of the floor or ceiling. The delay caused by multipath propagation can be as much as 50 nanoseconds in a home or 300 nanoseconds in a large building or factory.

When multipath propagation happens, the delayed parts of the transmitted signal can overlap a signal also arriving at the receiver. When the information symbols of one 802.11x signal overlap those of another, a condition called intersymbol interference (ISI) occurs. The shape (amplitude, frequency, and phase) of the signal represents the data being transmitted and, if two signals are superimposed on one another, the receiving device is unable to properly demodulate the signal back into its original data form.

Not a new technology, OFDM has been used with Asymmetrical Digital Subscriber Line (ADSL) service. OFDM is used in both 802.11a, 802.11g (see the section "IEEE 802.11g"), and HiperLAN/2, the European high-speed WLAN standard (much like 802.11a) because of its support for high-speed data transmission rates.

? Line Check 5.5

1.   How does OFDM differ from spread-spectrum technologies?

2.   What problems can be caused by multipath propagation and ISI?

3.   What is the advantage of 802.11a using the 5 GHz band?

The IEEE 802.11IR Standard

An often overlooked standard in the 802.11x standards is 802.11IR, which defines a PHY that transmits data using optic diffusion to provide the 1 Mbps or 2 Mbps data rates specified in the 802.11 legacy standard. Because few suppliers of 802.11IR equipment exist, this standard is rarely implemented.

Optical diffusion is a transmission method that bounces IR light beams off of ceilings and walls to support connectivity within a single room or small office. Because IR signals operate in the terahertz (THz) range, or the trillion hertz range, the light transmissions are invisible to humans and beyond the defined control of the regulatory agencies around the world, including the Federal Communications Commission (FCC) in the United States. The high frequency of

IR light makes it highly reflective, which allows IR transducers on PCs and portable computers both to transmit and receive in an enclosed area.

Despite its lower speeds, 802.11IR does offer a few advantages, as well as a few disadvantages, when compared to the RF WLAN standards:

- *Security:* Unlike RF signals, IR light doesn't penetrate walls, ceilings, or floors, which makes it virtually impossible for anyone outside the immediate area to intercept transmitted signals. However, IR light goes through a window (because it's visible light) to be intercepted by someone outside its source room. So, while IR is generally secure, it can and does have its weaknesses as well.

- *Interference:* The THz frequencies of IR transmissions aren't susceptible to RF interference, like all RF-based standards.

- *Range:* IR light transmissions are limited to a single room, so an access point (BSS) is required in each area to provide connectivity throughout a building. This could be a cost issue in comparison to the range of RF access points and NICs.

- *Compatibility:* Few of the IR networking products on the market are fully compatible with the 802.11 standards and many operate on proprietary standards, which reduce their interoperability with other manufacturers' equipment.

❓Line Check 5.6

1. Explain the functions of optical diffusion.
2. List the advantages and disadvantages of 802.11IR compared to other 802.11x standards.

Cutting-Edge IEEE 802.11x Standards

The IEEE 802.11 task groups are continuing to improve the standards for WLANs and provide for standards that provide higher data rates as well as compatibility with the 802.11a and 802.11b standards.

IEEE 802.11g

The 802.11g PHY defines a wireless system that operates in the 2.4 GHz frequency band, which makes it compatible with 802.11b and the Wi-Fi standards, although with data rates up to 54 Mbps. And because the 802.11g standard also uses the same CCK mode used on 802.11b and OFDM, used in 802.11a (although in the 2.4 GHz band), it conceptually has compatibility with both of these standards.

Data Speeds versus Throughput

There is a difference between the rated data transfer speed of a medium and its throughput. The *data speed* is the maximum rate bits can be transmitted across a medium and *throughput* refers to the speed realized by the user. Rarely is a medium able to achieve its rated speed because of the bandwidth requirements of the protocols in use or the transmission overhead. For example, an 802.11b medium, which has a rated speed of 11 Mbps, yields only about 6 Mbps in actual throughput. IEEE 802.11a and 802.11g, with data speeds up to 54 Mbps, typically provide throughput between 18 and 22 Mbps.

Another impediment to maximizing throughput on a WLAN is the distance between the transmitting station and an access point. Unless the station and the access point are sitting right next to each other, the distance of the transmission lowers the throughput of the link. The dropoff in throughput is also impacted by the amount of wood, metal, concrete, wiring, and other construction materials located between the communicating devices.

And the last, but certainly not least, impact on the throughput speed of a WLAN is the number of stations sharing the medium's bandwidth. Access points are shared devices and, as such, divide its bandwidth to each of the stations connecting to it.

5

The 802.11g PHY transmits over three channels, as does 802.11b. Because of the advantage of the eight channels used by the 802.11a PHY, many believe that 802.11g may have a limited future. Products are now emerging that offer 802.11a+g support that can provide a fairly smooth transition to 802.11a networks.

IEEE 802.11n

The IEEE **802.11n** standard is in development to increase the throughput of the 802.11 standards to as much as 100 Mbps through standardized modifications made to the 802.11 PHY and MAC layers. Although not completely defined at this time, the operating frequency is likely to be in the 5 GHz range, which should make it compatible with 802.11a.

❓ Line Check 5.7

1. What is the rated transfer speed of 802.11g?

2. To which other 802.11x standard is 802.11g compatible?

3. What is the target throughput rate of the 802.11n standard development?

Chapter 5 Review

Chapter Summary

The IEEE 802 Standards—An Overview

- The IEEE 802 standards define local, personal, and wide area networking.
- The IEEE 802 standards that specifically apply to wireless networks are: 802.11, 802.15, 802.16, and 802.20.

The IEEE 802.11 WLAN Standards

- The de facto WLAN standards used throughout the world are the IEEE 802.11 standards.
- The IEEE 802.11x WLAN standards are: 802.11 legacy, 802.11a, 802.11b, and 802.11g.
- The IEEE 802.11 Legacy standard defines 1 and 2 Mbps WLAN networks on the 2.4 GHz band using RF and IR transmissions.
- The IEEE 802.11 standard defines the MAC layer functions for WLANs.
- Each 802.11x standard defines the PHY layer and how it interfaces to the 802.11 MAC.
- Two methods are used to control and coordinate access to the shared RF medium: DCF and PCF.
- Three required functions are performed by the MAC layer on an 802.11x infrastructure network: scanning, authentication, and association.
- Four optional functions are available in the 802.11 MAC: encryption, RTS/CTS handshake, frame fragmentation, and power conservation.
- IEEE 802.11 MAC defines the use of PSK, which varies the phase of the transmitted signal. Several different phase modulation schemes can be used with PSK: biphase modulation, four-phase modulation, and eight-phase modulation.

The IEEE 802.11b Standard

- The IEEE 802.11b WLAN standard is also known as 802.11 High Rate and Wi-Fi.
- IEEE 802.11b adds data transfer rates of 5.5 Mbps and 11 Mbps to the 802.11 Legacy Standard.
- IEEE 802.11b operates in both infrastructure and ad-hoc modes. In an infrastructure network, two configurations are used: BSS and ESS.

- An IEEE 802.11b ad-hoc network is formed on an IBSS, which is equivalent to a peer-to-peer wireless network.

- The 802.11b PHY defines the use of CCK with QPSK modulation and DSSS.

- CCK is the modulation scheme used for the 5.5 Mbps and 11 Mbps data transfer speeds in the 802.11b specification.

- QAM combines two AM signals onto a single channel to double the bandwidth of a channel.

- IEEE 802.11b PHY is divided into PLCP and the PMD sublayer.

- PLCP performs the carrier sense portion of CSMA/CA and provides a SAP for the MAC layer; carrier sensing is performed by CCA.

The IEEE 802.11a Standard

- IEEE 802.11a PHY defines a WLAN using OFDM to provide 54 Mbps on the 5 GHz RF band on 12 20 MHz channels.

- OFDM divides a 20 MHz RF channel into 48 narrowband subchannels.

- When the transmission of one 802.11x signal overlaps another, the result is ISI.

- An 802.11 safeguard against multipath propagation problems is the CRC.

The IEEE 802.11IR Standard

- Optical diffusion bounces IR light beams off ceilings and walls using the THz band.

Cutting-Edge IEEE 802.11x Standards

- The 802.11g PHY defines a WLAN in the 2.4 GHz band that is compatible with 802.11b, with data rates up to 54 Mbps.

- The IEEE 802.11n standard is in development to increase the throughput of the 802.11 standards to as much as 100 Mbps.

Key Terms

802.11a *(161)*
802.11b *(162)*
802.11g *(162)*
802.11 Legacy *(163)*
802.11n *(181)*
BSS *(175)*
ESS *(175)*

MAC *(163)*
Multipath propagation *(179)*
OFDM *(178)*
PHY *(163, 173)*
WLAN *(160)*

Key Term Quiz

Use the preceding vocabulary terms to complete the following sentences. Not all the terms will be used.

1. The IEEE 802.11x standards define the use of wireless media to create a(n) _____.

2. ISI is the condition caused by _____.

3. The original standard developed by the 802.11 Task Group is now called _____.

4. The IEEE 802.11a standard specifies _____ modulation.

5. The _____ and _____ standards produce rated speeds of 54 Mbps.

6. The 802.11x topology that connects access points to extend a network is _____.

7. The _____ standard is being designed to support 100 Mbps of throughput.

8. _____ is the 802.11x topology in which a wireless station communicates only with an access point.

9. The 802.11 _____ defines the physical media of a WLAN.

10. The use of CSMA/CA is defined on the 802.11 _____.

Multiple-Choice Quiz

1. Which of the following wireless transmission phenomena cause(s) ISI?

    A. Singlepath propagation

    B. Multipath propagation

    C. DSSS

    D. FHSS

2. What is the modulation method used with 802.11a PHY?

    A. DSSS

    B. FHSS

    C. QAM

    D. OFDM

3. On which 802.11*x* topology are frames forwarded between access points with the same network?

    A. BSS

    B. ESS

    C. DSSS

    D. Peer-to-peer

4. Which of the following IEEE 802.11 standards does not define a PHY layer?

    A. 802.11a

    B. 802.11b

    C. 802.11i

    D. 802.11g

5. Which of the following IEEE 802.11 standards is under development to produce 100 Mbps of throughput?

    A. 802.11c

    B. 802.11h

    C. 802.11i

    D. 8021.11n

6. What term is used to represent the physical layer of an 802.11*x* standard?

    A. PYC

    B. PHY

    C. WLAN

    D. BSS

7. What is the current designation for the original IEEE 802.11 standard?

    A. 802.11a

    B. 802.11b

    C. 802.11 Legacy

    D. 802.11*x*

8. What is the term used to represent the IEEE 802.11 layer that controls access to the medium?

   A. BSS

   B. MAC

   C. WLAN

   D. PHY

9. What is the 802.11b topology that arranges wireless stations in a peer-to-peer network?

   A. BSS

   B. ESS

   C. Infrastructure

   D. Ad-hoc

10. What networking structure do the 802.11 standards define?

   A. WLAN

   B. WPAN

   C. WMAN

   D. BSS

Lab Projects

1. Install an 802.11x NIC in a desktop computer and a compatible 802.11x access point in a computer lab or classroom, following the manufacturer's installation guidelines. Connect the access point to a network distribution service, such as an Ethernet hub. After the computer is able to connect to the network, install a second wireless device using the same 8702.11x standard. Compare the installation process of the first computer to that of the second computer.

2. In a building, install two 802.11x access points at the opposite ends of a long building, connecting only one to the building's wired network. Install one or more computers in range of each access point and establish a network connection on each computer. What 802.11x topologies are in use in this model?

Case Problems

1. You decided to install wireless networking into your home. Which of the IEEE 802.11*x* standards would you use? Why?

2. Wire Bound Industries has decided to install wireless networking in a new addition to their headquarters building and to connect the WLAN back to the wired network established in their existing facilities. Describe the topology they should use for the new WLAN and diagram the connection to the existing network.

Advanced Lab Project

Among the issues facing the designers of a wireless network is security. In addition to the security features of the WLAN standards and devices, such as Wired Equivalent Privacy (WEP) and Wi-Fi Protected Access (WPA), security can also be enhanced by implementing a standard that has the range to provide coverage to all the areas to be included in the WLAN, but not too much beyond the facility. The capability to limit a wireless signal to specific areas should be considered during the security phases of the WLAN design project.

Project Objective: The objective of the project is to determine if you are able to receive a wireless signal from the access point when the PC is placed outside the planned area, either inside or outside the building.

Information for Laboratory: This project exposes you to the considerations of physical security in a WLAN design project. In it, you will need a computer, preferably a portable PC, equipped with a wireless network adapter and a compatible wireless access point.

Project Tasks:

1. Prepare a design diagram for a WLAN to be installed in your school or a representative small business. The diagram should indicate where the wireless access points are to be located around the areas of the building to be included in the network's coverage. Consider the operating ranges of the various standards and how each fits with the overall physical design of the WLAN.

2. Ensure that the design includes at least one of the following types of locations for the access points: near an outside wall, near a hallway wall, and near the physical center of the building.

3. Choose one of the access point locations as a starting point and install the access point. Ensure its configuration is compatible with that of the wireless adapter of the PC (your instructor can help you with this, if needed).

5

REVIEW

4. Using the wireless PC, determine the following for each location:

   a. What is the physical distance (in feet) the PC can move away from the access point before losing its capability to connect?

   b. Can the PC associate with the access point from immediately outside the nearest exit from the building (door)?

   c. How far beyond the exterior of the building can the PC continue to associate with the access point?

5. If you are able, repeat this process with different WLAN standards and compare the results.

6. Write a brief statement explaining why you would or would not use a WLAN for a network in the part of the building tested. If a WLAN is recommended, include which WLAN standard you would recommend.

Chapter 6

Infrared and Other Networking Media

LEARNING OBJECTIVES:

In this chapter, you learn how to:

Understand IR operations.

Understand IR networking.

Describe IrDA standards and protocols.

Identify other limited range media.

Although infrared (IR) networking was included in the first version of the 802.11 wireless local area network (WLAN) standards, it has yet to gain the popularity of other wireless communications media. This is likely because of two situations: (1) few manufacturers have, in the past, developed IR networking devices; and (2) IR networking has been limited in its effective range, until recently. However, IR devices are now emerging for use in the wireless personal area network (WPAN) market, which is able to capitalize on the relatively short range of IR devices. In this chapter, you learn about the standards and operations of IR networking.

Also in this chapter, you learn about other media standards that are emerging to compete with IR for the WPAN market. These standards include ultra wideband technology, ZigBee, induction wireless technology, Home Phone Networking Alliance (HomePNA), HomeRF and Shared Wireless Access Protocol (SWAP), and powerline communications (PLC).

NOTE

Another competing technology to IR, and, perhaps, IR's major competition, is Bluetooth. Bluetooth technology is covered in Chapter 7.

IR Operations

The primary components in an **infrared (IR)** device are a light-emitting diode (LED) and an IR receiver. An **LED** is an electronic device that emits a light source or beam that can be used to encode data. An *IR receiver* is a light-sensing device that is able to "see" the light source and also decode the data carried in the light stream.

A key operational factor for nearly all IR devices is that the light source and the receiver must have a line-of-sight (**LoS**) orientation. *LoS orientation* means the source and receiving devices must be placed and aligned on the same plane, so they are directly opposite each other with a clear and unobstructed path between them. Its LoS requirement is, perhaps, the most limiting factor that has kept IR from becoming a widely used networking medium. However, newer IR technologies are emerging that are able to operate without a direct LoS, which makes IR a better solution for larger WPAN applications. Many new computer models, especially portable computers, have built-in IR ports, but several types of add-on or add-in peripheral devices, like the one shown in Figure 6-1, can be used to configure a PC with an IR port.

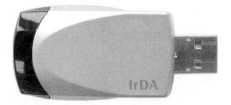

Figure 6-1 A USB IR port

Note that light-emitting diodes (LEDs) are used in several common devices, including digital clocks, remote controls, watches, ballpark display screens, traffic lights, car dashboards, and even some home appliances. Essentially, an LED is a small light bulb, but unlike ordinary household incandescent light bulbs, an LED doesn't have a filament to burn out and it doesn't produce much heat. An LED produces light by exchanging free electrons and photons.

In the following subsections, you learn about the electronic components used to create and receive the light beam on which IR operates.

Understanding Diodes

A *diode* is an electronic device that consists of two primary electrodes and a buffering space, which is used as a junction between the two electrodes. The two *electrodes* in a diode are made up of materials that have atoms, which are positively charged (P-type) and negatively charged (N-type). *N-type materials* have extra or free electrons that can be attracted away from an atom by a positively charged material. The atoms in *P-type materials* have space for additional electrons that can be added by attracting them from a negatively charged atom.

Inside a diode, the N-type material is placed adjacent to the P-type material and, without any external current being applied, a depletion zone is created at the junction of the two materials, as illustrated in Figure 6-2. In the *depletion zone*, the free electrons from the N-type materials fill the voids (holes) of the P-type materials, creating insulator through which a current or charge cannot flow.

6

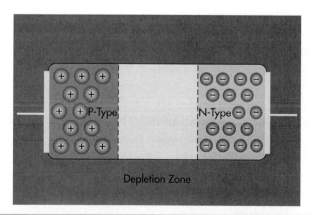

Depletion Zone

Figure 6-2   In a diode, without an external power source, a depletion zone is created between the P-type and N-type materials.

When a negative electrical charge is applied to the N-type side of the diode and a positive charge is connected to the P-type side, the free electrons of the N-type material move toward the positive side and the holes of the P-type atoms move toward the negative side, eliminating the depletion zone. If the charge is high enough, the free electrons continue to move toward the positive terminal, creating a current, as illustrated in Figure 6-3.

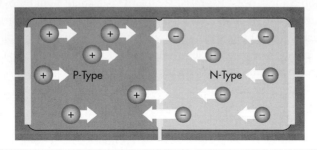

Figure 6-3 When a power source is applied to the negative side of the diode, the free electrons move toward the power source, creating a current.

Creating Light

The energy released by the interaction of the electrons and holes of the N-type and P-type materials releases particles called *photons*, which are light particles. Depending on the materials used in the diode, some diodes produce visible light (higher frequency) and some produce lower-frequency light that is invisible to the human eye. For example, a silicon diode creates low-frequency infrared light that is invisible to the human eye. The amount, frequency, energy, and color of the light produced by a diode depend on the materials used for the N-type and P-type areas of the diode.

The IR light used in most computer networking applications is produced by a diode laser. A *diode laser* (see Figure 6-4) uses a microscopic chip to generate a coherent, concentrated light beam. The light-producing element in a solid-state diode laser is similar to that of an

Figure 6-4 Diode lasers (Photo courtesy of Blue Sky Research)

LED, and the diode lasers used in most computing and home and personal entertainment products have a maximum output between 3 and 5 milliWatts (mW).

IR Networking

The IR technology used in cable replacement networking applications is near infrared (NIR), which has almost the same properties as visible light. The frequency of *NIR* is low enough in the optical frequency spectrum (see Figure 6-5) that it is invisible to the human eye. IR light behaves like visible light and reflects off solid objects, such as walls, ceilings, and floors. And, like visible light, IR won't pass through an opaque object.

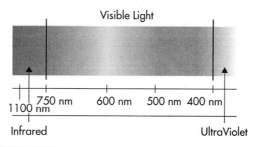

Figure 6-5   Infrared light falls below and outside the visible light spectrum.

6

Where other forms of wireless networking, such as radio frequency (RF) technologies, require at least two devices, IR networking is generally limited to connecting *only* two devices. While the most common use of IR is connecting two devices using LoS communications, diffused IR allows devices not in LoS to connect.

The two types of IR technology used to connect devices are as follows:

- **Directed IR (DIR):** Directed or LoS IR requires the transmitter and receiver to have a direct line of sight. Any opaque obstruction will block the IR beam, preventing the receiver from receiving the signal. All *DIR* technologies are limited to narrow, point-to-point transmissions that originate from a light-emitting source, such as a light-emitting diode (LED), a laser diode, or, perhaps, even a high-power laser. Another limitation of DIR is that the linked devices must remain motionless, which eliminates any use for connecting mobile or roaming devices. One of the benefits of DIR, and IR in general, is its inherent security. Because it is directed point-to-point, invisible, and resistant to interference, IR transmissions are both reliable and secure. However, you still have that LoS issue to deal with.

- **Diffused IR (DFIR):** Unlike directed IR, *DFIR* spreads its signal over a wider angle (up to 180 degrees), which allows it to reflect off surfaces in an enclosed space, such as a single room. DFIR is both non-LoS and nondirectional, meaning the transmitter and receiver don't have to be inline to receive the IR signal. The transmitted IR signal expands, like the light from a light bulb, to fill a space, and it uses the ceiling and walls of the space to bounce the signal between the transmitter and receiver. DFIR is not limited to the range of directed IR (less than 1 meter), but it is limited to operating in a single enclosed room. Most DFIR devices are both transmitters and receivers (transceivers) that emit diffused IR beams and detect IR beams transmitted by other devices, as illustrated in Figure 6-6.

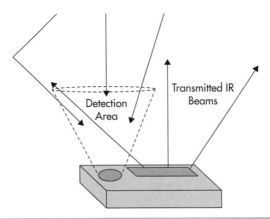

Figure 6-6　A diffused IR transceiver includes light-emitting circuits (transmitting), as well as light-sensing (detecting) circuits.

　　The infrared receiver or port on a desktop, notebook, or other portable computer serves as the network adapter for IR networking. It receives and decodes the light beam transmitted by an IR device. Each IR device has a device ID that allows the base station, typically a computer, to identify which device is transmitting. Beyond device identification and the LoS requirement, IR networking also requires a standard shared protocol.

　　IR transmitters or emitters, as they are most commonly called, use a pattern of light pulses to encode data for transmission. The receiving station or port, using a standard shared protocol, is able to decode the light pulses into a data stream. The basic IR encode/decode circuitry, called Serial IR (SIR), is patented by Hewlett-Packard.

The Infrared Data Association (IrDA) Standards

The **IrDA** is an independent trade organization that creates and publishes standards aimed at establishing an interoperable, low-cost data connection using IR technology.

The first IrDA standard, IrDA 1.0, defined the physical layer specification (**IrPHY**) of the IrDA data link. *IrDA 1.0* provided for a communications link that supported up to 115.2 Kbps of bandwidth. The IrPHY defines the guidelines for point-to-point (P2P) communications between IrDA-enabled devices, including modulation, viewing angle, optical power, data rate, and noise immunity. The standard also includes specifications for the use of IrDA devices where ambient light and IR interference sources may be present.

IrPHY is currently in version 1.3 and includes options for standard and low-operating power levels. Standard power *IrPHY* has an operating range up to 100 centimeters (cm) or about 3.25 feet. The standard power option is the option most commonly associated with computer networking. Low-power *IrPHY*, which is used with handheld devices, specifies the physical layer guidelines for communications up to 20 cm (about 0.6 feet). Table 6-1 summarizes the IrDA versions and their characteristics.

IrDA Version	Data Rate	Power Option(s)
1.0	115.2 Kbps	Standard
1.1	4 Mbps	Standard
1.2	115.2 Kbps	Low
1.3	115.2 Kbps to 4 Mbps	Low and Standard

Table 6-1   IrDA Versions and Their Characteristics

6

The IrDA link operates in *half-duplex mode*, which means an IrDA transceiver cannot send and receive at the same time because the transmitter and receiver aren't separate and isolated devices. Using half-duplex communications from a combined transceiver means IrDA also has built-in latency of about 10 milliseconds to allow for the switchover between transmit and receive.

Ambient light can be a source of interference to an IR transmission. Most IR computer-related systems use an LED laser and an ambient-light rejection process to ensure the data link works in a wide range of ambient light situations. IrDA specifications define the methods used to reject normally encountered levels of sunlight, fluorescent light, and incandescent light.

As illustrated in Figure 6-7, the IrDA protocol stack consists of four layers: IR hardware, serial communications, IrDA data link protocols, and IR application interface protocols. Within the IrDA data link protocols area, the IrDA defines two mandatory protocols: the IR Link Access protocol (IrLAP) and the IR Link Management protocol (IrLMP).

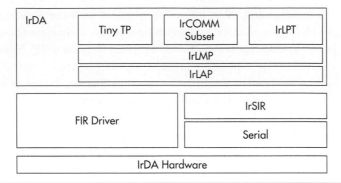

Figure 6-7 The IrDA protocol stack

IrDA Data-link Protocols

The two mandatory data-link protocols in the IrDA standards are as follows:

- **IrLAP:** *IrLAP* corresponds to the data-link layer of the OSI model and is based on the half-duplex High-level Data Link Control (HDLC) and Synchronous Data Link Control (SDLC) protocols. IrLAP specifies the guidelines for device-level software that seeks out other devices (called sniffing), finds other devices (discovering), connects, transfers data, and disconnects.

- **IrLMP:** *IrLMP* sits on top of the IrLAP layer in the IrDA protocol stack (see Figure 6-7) and provides services to the system's transport and application layer activities. IrLMP has two components:

  - **Link Management-Information Access Service (LM-IAS):** *LM-IAS* maintains a database of other IrDA devices that have been discovered within its range and an inventory of the services provided by each discovered device.

  - **Link Management Multiplexer (LM-MUX):** *LM-MUX* services the LM-IAS layer, the transport layer functions, and the applications of its local device. LM –MUX also provides for linking multiple IrDA devices on the IrLAP layer.

IrDA also defines the following three optional standards that can be used in specific applications:

- **Transport Protocols (Tiny TP):** *Tiny TP* provides what are considered to be standard transport layer activities, like those performed by the Transmission Control Protocol (TCP), including managing the virtual channel between devices, performing error detection and correction, and encapsulating data.

- **Infrared Communications Protocol (IrCOMM):** *IrCOMM* provides serial and parallel port emulation to enable existing devices, such as printers and modems, to use IR communications without change.

- **Infrared Link Printer Transport (IrLPT):** *IrLPT* replaces Tiny TP for communications directly with printers.

IR Interface Standards

In addition to the original IrDA Serial Infrared (SIR) standard based on the Motorola patent for IR communications, several newer and faster standards have been developed. Table 6-2 summarizes the primary IR standards now available, detailing the data transfer rate, the operating range, and whether the standard uses Directed IR (DIR) or Diffused IR (DFIR) communications.

IR Standard	Data Rate	Range	Directed or Diffused
Serial Infrared (SIR)	115.2 Kbps	1 meter	Directed
Fast Infrared (FIR)	4 Mbps	1 meter	Directed
Very Fast Infrared (VFIR)	16 Mbps	1 meter	Directed
IrDA Control (IrDA-C [formerly IrBus])	75 Kbps	8 meters	Directed
IrGate	10 Mbps	10 meters	Diffused
Advanced IR (AIR)	4 Mbps	8 meters	Diffused

Table 6-2 IR Interface Standards

6

If you want to create a WPAN using one of the IR standards listed in Table 6-2, you may have trouble finding devices for anything other than SIR and FIR. The other standards have either just been announced or are still in development (such as AIR). Diffused IR products have yet to make inroads into the WPAN world, and they are primarily in use in the home control and home entertainment areas.

? Line Check 6.1

1. What are the two characteristics that limit the IR medium to WPAN applications?
2. What is the operating range of an IrDA device?
3. Explain the operations of diffused IR?

What Do You Think?

Using the information in Table 6-2, could an IR network be integrated with a wired or a wireless network in a home or office? How?

Other Limited Range Technologies

In addition to IR communications, several other technologies are emerging for use in short-range communications and applications. The most popular of these technologies are:

- Ultra wideband (**UWB**)
- ZigBee
- Induction wireless
- Home Phoneline Networking Association (HomePNA)
- HomeRF and SWAP
- Powerline communications (PLC)

Ultra Wideband Technology

Ultra wideband (UWB) has been widely used by the military and other government agencies for some time, but it is just becoming approved for use in commercial and home networking applications. *UWB* transmits in the 3.1 to 10.6 GHz RF band and it has been primarily used for short-range, high-resolution, high-bandwidth radar and imaging systems. UWB's signals are able to pass through just about everything in its path, including walls, the ground, and even human bodies.

UWB provides 40 Mbps to 600 Mbps of bandwidth, which will make it ideal for WLANs and WPANs transmitting multimedia and other high-bandwidth applications. UWB is a low-power system that transmits billions of short-pulse radio signals that spread encoded data over a wide frequency range. The receiving station uses the pulse sequence to translate the signal pulses back into data.

The initial products now in development should be more suited to WPANs than WLANs with a range of about 10 meters and data rates near 100 Mbps. Other developers are hoping to increase both the range and the data speed to extend the technology to the WLAN market. Because it operates at low power with a wide spectrum, UWB is relatively interference-free compared to other RF technologies.

When UWB is released for use, the expectation is that the first application UWB will dominate is home multimedia networks and WPANs. UWB will facilitate the wireless connection of every multimedia device in a home over a high-bandwidth network allowing TVs, PCs, DVDs, and other audio-video devices to stream multimedia content throughout a home.

ZigBee

Originally created by Philips as RFLite, **ZigBee** is a low-power, low-cost, simpler RF communications standard, often compared to Bluetooth. However, ZigBee is aimed at creating WPANs by connecting up ZigBee-equipped sensors and controllers.

NOTE

Understand that like Bluetooth, ZigBee is available on a system chip that will be incorporated into consumer and commercial products to provide wireless communications capabilities

ZigBee transmits at 20 Kbps (extended range), 40 Kbps, and 250 Kbps in the 2.4 GHz RF band and uses frequency-hopping spread-spectrum (FHSS) over 25 channels of 4 MHz each. At 250 Kbps, ZigBee has a range of 30 meters and, in its extended range mode, ZigBee supports a range of 134 meters. ZigBee promises to connect up to 254 devices.

ZigBee's claim to fame will come from its energy savings. For example, if a home or office space were to have 50 802.11 always-on devices, the electrical power consumption would be around 1.67 mW. However, if these devices were ZigBee (802.15.4) equipped and, if instead of being always on, the devices were power cycled under the 802.15.4 standards, the power consumption would drop to a mere 75 watts.

The ZigBee standard defines two types of ZigBee devices:

- **ZigBee Network Coordinator:** The functions of this device are:
  - Establishes network
  - Maintains information about the network nodes
  - Manages network nodes
  - Operates in receiver state
  - Routes messages to network nodes
  - Transmits network beacons

6

- **ZigBee Network Node:** The functions of the network nodes are:

  - Conserves battery power or operates on low electrical power

  - Monitors for pending data

  - Requests data from network coordinator

  - Scans for available networks

  - Sleeps when not in use and can sleep for extended periods

  - Transfers application data to network coordinator

Induction Wireless Technology

Induction wireless, or what is called near-field magnetic communications, applies magnetic induction instead of radio frequency or other close-range communications technologies. An RF antenna transmits a signal that includes both electric and magnetic fields, but induction wireless transmits only the magnetic field. The induction wireless antenna, which is small, resembles the winding in a transformer more than it does an RF antenna.

Induction wireless as it exists today has a range of about 3 meters and transmits at data rates up to 204.8 Kbps on the 11.5 MHz frequency. It is an extremely low-power, and because it is a short-range technology, it is also an inherently secure technology. This technology was developed and has been patented by Aura Communications for use in the next generation of headsets, portable communication devices, portable entertainment playback devices, and other wearable PAN devices. Figure 6-8 shows an induction wireless cell phone headset.

Figure 6-8   An induction wireless cellular phone headset and its recharging dock (Photo courtesy of Aura Communications)

A consumer wearing an induction wireless MP3 player would, perhaps, have the playback unit in her purse or backpack and wear a wireless headset that receives digital music signals transmitted by the playback unit. In cellular phone applications; the induction wireless transceiver creates a 3-meter magnetic aura, unique to each user, which receives signals directed to the unit.

HomePNA

The Home Phoneline Networking Alliance (**HomePNA**) standard defines a networking protocol that transmits data and control signals over a home's existing POTS (Plain Old Telephone Service) twisted-pair telephone wiring. Using *HomePNA* network adapters, you can connect a PC into the telephone lines and transmit data to other HomePNA adapters on the system (as illustrated in Figure 6-9).

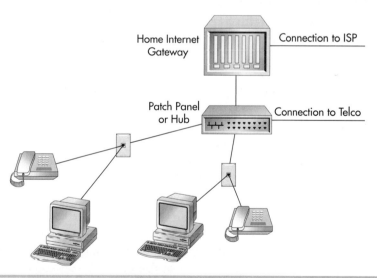

Figure 6-9   The construction of a HomePNA network

6

NOTE

Understand that HomePNA and PLC (covered in the section "Powerline Communications") are considered to be "wireless" only because they don't introduce any *new* wiring in a home or office. These technologies use existing wiring already in place for the telephone (HomePNA) or the electrical services (PLC).

SPIKE—Wireless Personal Area Gaming Network

The xiSPIKE (SPIKE) wireless gaming control platform, developed by Eleven Engineering, Inc. of Canada, is designed specifically to provide wireless control for video games and similar applications. SPIKE's wireless 900 MHz RF communications feature short-haul transmissions of low-latency, error-free, high-bandwidth, data packets, which are well-suited for applications where speed and reliability are required. The next version of SPIKE will include 2.4 GHz RF communications. Gaming systems equipped with the SPIKE technology feature the xiSPIKE logo, which indicates a system equipped with this wireless technology. The following illustration of the logo is shown with the permission of Eleven Engineering, Inc.

Beyond video games, Eleven Engineering sees the SPIKE technology as also being ideal for other applications, such as real-time data acquisition, infant monitors, medical monitoring equipment, computer peripherals, and wireless access points connected to high-speed wireline networks.

The benefit of a HomePNA system is it requires no additional wiring to be installed to network a home. In fact, the network doesn't require any hubs, routers, or additional connection points to implement a network within a home. However, if you want to connect to outside networks, such as the Internet, these devices must be interconnected into the system.

In its current definition, HomePNA 2.0, a phoneline network can support up to 50 nodes at a 10 Mbps data rate. The network nodes can be up to a maximum of 500 feet apart. Because the data signal uses a different frequency than that used for voice or fax machines, the data network is able to share the line without complication.

HomePNA adapters use standard RJ-11 telephone plugs to connect into standard telephone jacks, like the ones in nearly every room of a home. The HomePNA adapters scan the telephone wiring sensing for transmissions in its specific frequency and examining the transmission for Layer 2 addressing before processing it. Because HomePNA is supported in all versions of the Windows operating system since Windows 98 SE, implementing this type of a LAN is as simple as connecting a HomePNA adapter to a computer, connecting it into a phone jack, and configuring Windows accordingly.

HomeRF and SWAP

Another cable replacement wireless technology, although less well-known than Bluetooth, is the specification produced by the Home Radio Frequency Working Group (HomeRF) for the wireless transmission of Ethernet networking.

A second standard developed by the HomeRF Working Group is SWAP, which is an open specification that allows a broad range of consumer devices such as PCs, computer peripheral devices, cordless telephones, and enabled appliances to share and communicate voice and data inside, and in the close proximity of, a home. The objective of SWAP is to provide high-quality, multiple-user, and low-cost voice and data communications in the 2.4 GHz ISM RF band.

The following sections discuss these standards in detail.

HomeRF

Some mild confusion exists between HomeRF and SWAP but, basically, *HomeRF* is an emerging standard that, essentially, is a subset of the International Telecommunications Union (ITU) specifications for wireless Ethernet transmissions. HomeRF provides for a maximum broadcast range of 40 meters (a bit more than 131 feet) and provides for a bandwidth of 1.2 Mbps.

As illustrated in Figure 6-10, three major layers are in the HomeRF protocol stack. The lowest layers define the physical media and Media Access Control (MAC) methods, the middle layers consist of existing networking and telephony protocols, and the top layer is made up of other existing higher layer protocols and applications.

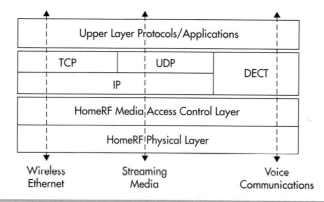

Figure 6-10   The HomeRF/SWAP protocol stack shows the paths taken through the stack by its primary network applications.

Wireless Ethernet transmissions are made much like those of the 802.11 standards, using the Transmission Control Protocol (TCP) and Internet Protocol (IP) protocols. Likewise, streaming media is transmitted using UDP and IP, much the same as other networking technologies. Of course, the difference between HomeRF/SWAP networking and other networking technologies exists in the physical (PHY) and MAC layers.

Voice communications over a SWAP network use the Digital European Cordless Telephone (DECT) standard, which defines wireless and data communication systems restricted to single buildings or campus-sized areas.

SWAP

SWAP is a telecommunications industry standard that permits PCs, peripherals, cordless telephones, and some appliances to communicate using wireless transmissions. The SWAP standard uses a MAC method similar to the Carrier Sense Multiple Access/Collision Avoidance (CSMA/CA) method used in 802.11 communications, but also includes an extension to provide for voice transmissions.

SWAP operates either as an ad-hoc service between SWAP-enabled devices or as an infrastructure networking service controlled by a central connection or access point. In ad-hoc network operations, SWAP devices are all peers, without master and slave designations, with the control functions distributed among the peers. SWAP ad-hoc networks support only data transmissions.

In infrastructure network operation, a connection point, such as the one shown in Figure 6-11, is used to control and coordinate the network and provide a gateway to the telephone company's Public Switched Telephone Network (PSTN). Security is provided by the assignment of a unique network ID to each device.

Figure 6-11   A HomeRF/SWAP connection point (Photo courtesy of Siemens Information and Communication Mobile [ICM] LLC)

The operating characteristics of a SWAP network are:

- Utilizes a broadcast range of up to 45.7 meters (150 feet)
- Broadcasts in the 2.4 GHz ISM band
- Transmits using FHSS

- Supports both Time Division Multiple Access (TDMA) for voice transmissions and CSMA/CA for high-speed data transmissions

- Connects up to 127 nodes

- Provides bandwidth of 1 Mbps or 2 Mbps, depending on the frequency-shift method employed

- Supports up to six full-duplex voice transmissions simultaneously

- Provides both encryption and data compression algorithms

Table 6-3 shows a comparison among Bluetooth, 802.11b, and the SWAP technologies.

Wireless Service	Bandwidth	Range	Data Transmission	Voice Transmission
Bluetooth	1 Mbps	10 meters	PPP	IP and cellular
IEEE 802.11b	11 Mbps	50 meters	TCP/IP	IP
SWAP	1.6 Mbps	50 meters	TCP/IP	IP and PSTN

Table 6-3   A Comparison of Wireless Networking Services

CROSS-REFERENCE

See Chapter 7 for more information on Bluetooth technology.

6

Powerline Communications (PLC)

PLC networking is most commonly associated with home automation systems or the central control (from a PC or specialized control unit) of a home's lighting, security, heating and cooling, and other systems.

NOTE

Although more commonly known as X-10, powerline communications (PLC) is a signaling technology that transmits control and data signals over a home's existing electrical alternating current (AC) service wiring. Note, don't confuse PLC with the research and service trials currently under way to transmit broadband signals over high-tension power lines, which is called Broadband over Power Line (BPL).

Like HomePNA, PLC systems require an interface adapter to modulate digital signals into specific frequency signals that are transmitted over the 110 or 220 volt wiring in a home.

A PLC system uses three types of interface devices: receivers, transmitters, and two-way receiver/transmitters:

- **PLC receivers:** The device to be controlled over the PLC network is connected, typically using its power cord and plug, into a receiver. The receiver accepts control signals addressed to its specific unit code and responds accordingly to turn on, turn off, or alter the electrical signal passing through to the device.

- **PLC transmitters:** Transmitters are commonly controlled by IR or RF remote control devices and encode the commands for transmission on the electrical lines to the appropriate receiver. A *PLC transmitter*, which is also called a control module, can send up to 256 coded signals using low-voltage frequency signaling.

- **PLC Two-way receiver/transmitters:** These specialized devices (see Figure 6-12) combine the functions of PLC receivers and transmitters to both transmit and receiver PLC control signals.

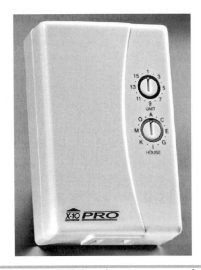

Figure 6-12 A two-way PLC control module (Photo courtesy of Smarthome, Inc.)

As shown on the PLC device in Figure 6-12, each PLC device is configured to a unique address setting using the dials on the face of the device. Two levels to the coding scheme are used to assign a unique code to each PLC device: a house code and a unit code. For each of the 16 house codes (*A* through *P*), 16 unit codes can be used (1 through 16). The combination of house codes and unit codes can be set to allow up to 256 separate PLC devices to be addressed on the AC wiring in a single home or office. The house code can be used to establish separate control zones in a home or to segregate the controls for different home systems.

Figure 6-13 illustrates an integrated PLC network in a home. When the intruder breaks into the home, a motion detector senses his movement and transmits an alarm event using an IR signal to a two-way control module. The control module then transmits a PLC command code over the home's AC wiring addressed to a home-security control system running on a PC. The PC then automatically dials an outgoing telephone call to the homeowner, who is out for the evening, displaying a text message on her cell phone that the intruder alarm has been activated in her home and also places a call to the local police department with the same information.

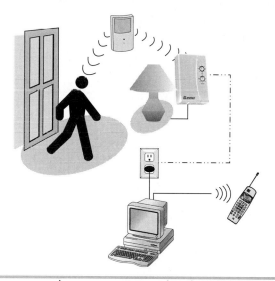

Figure 6-13 A PLC home control system activating the alarm to report an intruder

6

Line Check 6.2

1. What is the transmission medium for each of the following technologies?

   a. IrDA

   b. HomePNA

   c. PLC

2. What advantage would a HomePNA or PLC network have over a UTP Ethernet network?

3. What method is used to uniquely identify up to 256 PLC devices in a single home?

What Do You Think?

What do you foresee for home control and entertainment systems in the future, in terms of networking and integrating these systems together?

Chapter 6 Review

Chapter Summary

Understand IR operations and networking

- The primary components in an IR device are a light-emitting diode (LED) and an IR receiver.

- Nearly all IR devices must have a LoS orientation.

- An LED produces light by exchanging free electrons and photons.

- A diode is an electronic device that consists of two primary electrodes: P-type and N-type.

- The energy released by the interaction of N-type and P-type materials releases photons.

- IR technology is used in cable-replacement networking applications.

- Two types of IR technology are used to connect devices: DIR and DFIR.

Describe IrDA Standards and Protocols

- The Infrared Data Association (IrDA) is an independent trade organization that creates and publishes standards aimed at establishing an interoperable, low-cost data connection using IR technology.

- The IrDA standard defines the IrPHY specification. IrPHY version 1.3 includes options for both standard and low-power and operating range up to 100.

- IrDA links operate in half-duplex mode and have a built-in latency of 10 milliseconds.

- The IrDA protocol stack consists of four layers: IR hardware, serial communications, IrDA data link protocols, and IR application interface protocols. IrDA defines two mandatory protocols: IrLAP and IrLMP.

Identify Other Limited Range Media

- UWB is widely used by the military and other government agencies, but it has been approved for commercial and home-networking applications.

- UWB transmits in the 3.1 to 10.6 GHz RF band and its signals are able to pass through nearly everything in its path, including walls, the ground, and even human bodies. UWB provides 40 Mbps to 600 Mbps of bandwidth.

- ZigBee is a low-power RF communications standard often compared to Bluetooth.

- ZigBee transmits at 20 Kbps (extended range), 40 Kbps, and 250 Kbps in the 2.4 GHz RF band. It uses FHSS over 25 channels of 4 MHz each. At 250 Kbps, ZigBee has a range of 30 meters and, in its extended range mode, ZigBee supports a range of 134 meters.

- Induction wireless transmits only a magnetic field. It has a range of about 3 meters and transmits at data rates up to 204.8 Kbps on the 11.5 MHz frequency.

- HomePNA defines a networking protocol that transmits data and control signals over a home's existing POTS twisted-pair telephone wiring.

- Also known as X-10, PLC transmits over a home's existing electrical AC service wiring. PLC systems require an interface adapter to modulate digital signals into specific frequency signals transmitted over the 110- or 220-volt wiring in a home.

Key Terms

Diffused IR *(194)*
Directed IR *(193)*
HomePNA *(201)*
Infrared (IR) *(190)*
IrDA *(194)*
IrPHY *(195)*
LED *(190)*
Line-of-sight (LoS) *(190)*
PLC *(205)*
UWB *(198)*
ZigBee *(199)*

Key Term Quiz

Use the terms from the Key Terms list to complete the following sentences. Don't use the same term more than once. Not all terms will be used.

1. The communications and networking technology that transmits over a home or office's existing AC wiring is _____.

2. The band of light just below visible light is _____.

3. The communications and networking technology that transmits over a home or office's existing telephone wiring is _____.

4. IR devices must be aligned into _____ to communicate effectively.

5. _____ is a low-power, low-cost, simpler RF communications standard, often compared to Bluetooth.

6. _____ requires devices be LoS-oriented.

7. _____ transmits in the 3.1 to 10.6 GHz RF band and its signals are able to pass through walls, the ground, and even human bodies.

8. The IR technology that spreads its signal up to 180-degrees, allowing it to reflect off surfaces in an enclosed space, is _____.

9. _____ defines the physical layer interface and functions of the IrDA standards.

10. An electronic component that uses electricity to cause a reaction between P-type and N-type materials to release photons is a(n) _____.

Multiple-Choice Quiz

1. Which type of IR technology uses reflected light rays to communicate?

   A. DIR

   B. DFIR

   C. FIR

   D. SIR

2. The letters in the term LED stand for _____.

   A. Light-emulating diode

   B. Laser-emitting diode

   C. Light-emitting diode

   D. Limited-emissions diode

3. Which of the following IR technologies does *not* require LoS orientation?

   A. DFIR

   B. DIR

    C. FIR

    D. SIR

4. Which of the following is *not* a data-link control protocol within the IrDA standards?

    A. IrLMP

    B. IrLAP

    C. IrPHY

    D. Tiny TP

5. What is the technology that communicates over existing AC power lines in a home or office?

    A. IrDA

    B. HomePNA

    C. PLC

    D. ZigBee

6. What is the communications technology that communicates over existing telephone lines in a home or office?

    A. IrDA

    B. HomePNA

    C. PLC

    D. ZigBee

7. What orientation must standard IrDA devices have to communicate?

    A. Level-plane

    B. Parallel

    C. Line-of-sight

    D. Serial

8. What type of light band is just below the visible light band?

    A. Ambient

    B. Infrared

    C. Ultraviolet

    D. X-ray

6

REVIEW

Lab Projects

1. Using a portable PC (notebook, Pocket PC, or the like) or a desktop computer equipped with either an internal or external IrDA adapter and the appropriate device drivers or software, test the range of the operating range with a IR-enabled device. Begin your test by operating the device at a 3-foot distance. Increment the distance by 3 feet and test again. Continue incrementing the distance between the PC and the Bluetooth adapter until the device fails to communicate. Record the distance at which the devices no longer communicate effectively.

2. Using the same equipment used in Lab Project 1, experiment on the width of the angularity within which the IrDA devices will communicate. Start by operating the device directly in front of the adapter. Move to the left or the right, a few feet at a time, to determine the angularity of the devices' line-of-sight (LoS). Note the position, relative to your starting point, at which communication fails.

Case Problems

1. Using what you learned in this chapter, and from your research, would IR networking be an effective choice for a home, office, or school network? Why? In what specific applications would IR not be an effective choice?

2. Using the Internet, research IrDA security options. Should users be concerned about using IR for PAN applications? Which uses might they want to avoid, under the current specifications?

Advanced Lab Project

You have been assigned the task of recommending a PAN technology for use in a new set of automated study carrels, connected into the school's LAN, to be installed in your school's library. Each carrel is 4 feet wide and 3.5 feet deep, with 5 feet assigned to the seating area for each carrel. Each of the 12 carrels to be installed is separated from its neighbors by a 5-foot-tall fabric-covered metal divider on both sides, including the carrels at each end of the row.

Prepare a comparative analysis that studies the use of IR in this situation, listing the pros and cons.

Chapter 7

Bluetooth and Wireless Personal Area Networks

LEARNING OBJECTIVES:

In this chapter, you learn how to:

Understand the Bluetooth technology and its operations.

Work with WPAN concepts and the IEEE 802.15 standards.

Review WPAN technology.

Although the 802.11*x* standards provide sufficient capability to create ad-hoc networks in a home or small office environment, several other wireless technologies can be more adaptable for specific networking and communications situations. A wireless local area network (WLAN) can be overkill in a situation where the wireless network requires only a few meters of range. When all you want to do is use a wireless keyboard and mouse, or use a wireless headset with your cell phone or an audio device, the 802.11 technology is likely not the best solution. Two terms, personal area network (PAN) and home area network (**HAN**), have emerged to describe limited area networks to serve the specific connection needs of an individual, a home, or a small office. A *PAN* is a communications network that connects computing and other devices in the immediate vicinity of an individual to support the activities of that individual. A *HAN* is a communications network limited to the immediate vicinity—inside and outside—of a home that connects a wide range of devices, such as personal digital assistants (PDAs), computers, peripheral devices, telephones, video and DVD players, TVs, video games, security systems, appliances, and several other types of digital devices into a single centrally controlled network.

Chapter 6 introduced infrared wireless communications, as well as the technologies— powerline communications (PLC), Home PhoneLine Networking Alliance (HomePNA), HomeRF, and ZigBee—that can be used to create a PAN or a HAN. In this chapter, we explore the **Bluetooth** wireless technology and how it can be applied to create a PAN or a HAN, the Bluetooth devices that are available or emerging to facilitate the creation of these networks, and a brief look at a few "real world" applications of this technology. First, let's look at the Bluetooth technology, its protocols and operations, and how it compares to infrared (IF) technology, and then briefly review the WPAN technologies discussed here and in Chapter 6.

Understanding the Bluetooth Technology and Its Operations

Bluetooth, the RF networking technology with the odd-sounding name, incorporates a radio frequency transceiver and a full set of networking protocols on a single chip that is small enough to be included in cellular and cordless phones, PDAs, portable PCs, headsets, and several other devices in the near future.

Bluetooth is an RF-communications standard used to form ad-hoc PANs within a 10-meter (a bit under 33 feet) range. Bluetooth, which is primarily a cable-replacement technology, uses a frequency-hopping radio link to connect devices. Although commonly thought of as a particular type of connection, Bluetooth is merely an adaptation of many existing protocols and RF communications capabilities that defines the characteristics and operation of a particular type of short-range ad-hoc networks.

The Origin of the Name Bluetooth

The name Bluetooth was assigned to this technology by Telefonaktiebolaget LM Ericsson, the Swedish mobile telephone giant, when they first developed the basic ideas for the technology in the mid-1990s.

Bluctooth is actually the name of a Danish king, Harald Blatand. Harald was the son of King Gorm the Old, who ruled Jultland, the main peninsula of Denmark. When King Gorm died, Harald became king and took over Norway on the request of his sister, who was then the Queen of Norway, after her husband died.

The Bluetooth specifications are named after King Harald, or Bluetooth—as he was called because of an uncharacteristically dark beard and his fondness for blueberries, which stained his teeth blue. However, despite the fact that Harald may have had blue teeth, it is far more likely the name is derived from the name Blatand.

Ericsson chose the Bluetooth name for this new technology in the hope that, in the same way King Blatand united Denmark and Norway, Bluetooth would unite the mobile communications world.

To the right is the logo of the Bluetooth Special Interest Group (**SIG**), which combines the Nordic characters for *H* (Harald) and *B* (Blatant). The logo is shown courtesy of the Bluetooth SIG.

To understand the desire for technologies such as Bluetooth and even infrared (IR), you only have to image your cell phone or your cordless phone requiring a connecting cable or cord. Cable replacement technologies such as Bluetooth, IR, and even the wireless networking standards (IEEE 802.11) free us from the tether of a connecting cable. You can imagine what the world would be like if cell phones required a connecting cable. Suffice it to say, we would not likely have cell phones. The same basic idea behind eliminating cables has been extended to personal computing, in the form of a PAN or HAN.

The Bluetooth standard is developed, managed, and controlled by the Bluetooth SIG. The *SIG* is responsible for the development, promotion, testing, and conformance issues surrounding the Bluetooth technology. The Bluctooth SIG consists of literally thousands of electronics manufacturers and developers who are looking to integrate the Bluetooth technology into their products, which can range from computers and mobile phones to keyboards and headphones, and so on. The use and application of the Bluetooth specification is controlled by the SIG. Approved products are allowed to display the Bluetooth SIG's logo.

7

NOTE

For more information about the Bluetooth SIG and Bluetooth technology, in general, visit their web site at **www.bluetooth.com**.

The documentation that defines Bluetooth divides the standards into two parts: the *Bluetooth Specification*, which defines its technical operation and protocol architecture and the *Bluetooth Profiles*, which define its range of applications. You'll learn about the Bluetooth Profiles in the section "Bluetooth Profiles," but first you need to understand the technology by looking at the protocols, transmission operations, and networking capabilities of Bluetooth.

 Pathfinders

Telefonaktiebolaget LM Ericsson

In 1994, Ericsson, as this company is more commonly known around the world, decided to develop a low-power, low-cost radio interface that could be built into cellular telephones, mobile phones, portable computers, and their accessories to replace the need for connecting cables. During the ongoing engineering of this technology, however, it was discovered that the interface could also serve as a universal bridge, which could be used to form private ad-hoc groups of linked devices. Ericsson engineers Dr. Japp Haartsen and Dr. Sven Mattisson (shown in the following illustration) are credited with being the coinventors of the Bluetooth technology.

In 1998, Ericsson joined with other companies interested in pursuing this new technology, which had been designated as Bluetooth, to form the Bluetooth Special Interest Group (SIG). The original SIG companies are Ericsson, IBM, Intel, Nokia, and Toshiba. Today, the SIG also includes thousands of associate companies interested in promoting Bluetooth technology.

Bluetooth Protocols

Bluetooth is implemented in a device as an integrated microprocessor module, referred to as an *application module* (see Figure 7-1), which includes all the circuitry required to establish ad-hoc connections, and transmit and receive data to and from other Bluetooth-enabled devices. A developer who wants to create a Bluetooth-enabled product integrates an application module into their product and writes software that operates within the Bluetooth protocol stack to carry out its particular function.

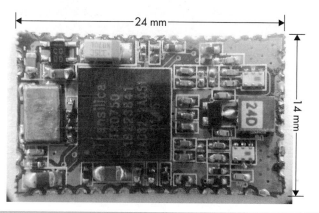

Figure 7-1   A Bluetooth application module (Photo courtesy of Cal-Comp Electronics [Thailand] Public Company Limited)

The Bluetooth specification defines seven operational layers (see Figure 7-2):

- **Radio frequency communications:** The *Radio layer* of the Bluetooth specification defines the operations of the Bluetooth transceiver (transmitter/receiver) operating in the 2.4 GHz Industrial, Scientific, and Medical (ISM) radio frequency band.

- **Baseband communications:** The Bluetooth Link Controller (LC) controls the functions of baseband protocols and media access and link control functions.

- **Link management:** The link managers on the devices, on either side of a connection, create, set up, and control the links established with other devices.

- **Host control:** The Bluetooth Host Controller Interface (HCI) provides a command interface to the LC and the LMP, as well as access to hardware status and control data.

- **Logical link control:** The Bluetooth Logical Link Control and Adaptation Protocol (L2CAP) provides for networking functions, such as high-level multiplexing, packet segmentation and reassembly, and the management of quality of service (QoS) data.

- **Serial port emulation:** The Bluetooth RFCOMM layer emulates the function of serial ports through the L2CAP protocol.

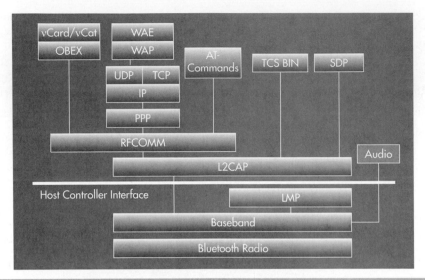

Figure 7-2 The Bluetooth protocol architecture. The protocols shown in gold are Bluetooth-specific protocols, and those shown in green, purple, and grey are standard telephony and networking protocols.

- **Service discovery:** The Service Discovery Protocol (SDP) provides the means for applications to discover the services provided by or available on another Bluetooth device and to determine the characteristics of available services. The discovery process, as well as the networking operations, of a Bluetooth connection is carried out by its protocol architecture.

The protocols included in the Bluetooth protocol stack, as depicted in Figure 7-2, include:

- **Bluetooth Radio layer:** This is the lowest defined layer of the Bluetooth specification. While it is not a protocol, it does define the requirements and operations of the Bluetooth transceiver device, transmitting and receiving radio frequency (RF) signals in the 2.4GHz ISM band.

- **Baseband:** This is the physical layer protocol of the Bluetooth specification and it lies on top of the Bluetooth Radio layer in the Bluetooth stack. The *Baseband layer* manages the physical channels and provides links to and from other communication services, including error correction, hop selection, and Bluetooth security. This protocol works with the LMP to carry out data-link level functions, such as link connection and power control. It also manages the asynchronous and synchronous communications links, packet handling, and performs the paging and inquiry processes as a part of the device discovery within the range of a Bluetooth device.

- **Link Manager Protocol (LMP):** The Bluetooth *LMP* performs the link setup, configuration, and authentication process within the Bluetooth stack. After the Link Manager (LM) of one Bluetooth device discovers the LM of another Bluetooth device, the LMP then communicates with the remote LM (through its LMP) to establish a link.

- **Host Controller Interface (HCI):** The Bluetooth **HCI** provides a command interface between the baseband controller and the LM.

- **L2CAP:** The **L2CAP** resides on Layer 2 (data-link layer of the OSI model) and provides, as its name implies, the link functions for the Baseband protocol. L2CAP provides both connection-oriented and connectionless services to upper-layer protocols through protocol multiplexing, frame segmentation, and reassembly services. L2CAP frames can be up to 64KB in length. L2CAP supports two link types from the Baseband layer: Synchronous Connection-Oriented (SCO) for voice traffic and Asynchronous Connectionless (ACL) for data traffic. *SCO* is used to support real-time voice traffic and *ACL* is used to transport data.

- **RFCOMM:** *RFCOMM* is the cable replacement protocol in the Bluetooth protocol stack. It creates a virtual serial port through which RF communications can be passed using standard Electronics Industries Association/Telecommunications Industry Association (EIA/TIA) 232 standards, which is the most commonly used serial port communications standard.

- **Object Exchange Protocol (OBEX):** Originally specified by the Infrared Data Association (IrDA), OBEX is used to transfer data, graphics, and voice objects between devices. OBEX is used in several devices, such as PDAs, mobile phones, and computer systems.

- **vCard/vCal:** A protocol used to store and transfer virtual business cards and personal calendars on mobile devices.

- **Point-to-Point Protocol (PPP):** A Transmission Control Protocol/Internet Protocol (TCP/IP) standard protocol that transports IP datagrams across a point-to-point link.

- **Internet Protocol (IP):** The foundation addressing and packet management protocol in the TCP/IP protocol suite.

- **Transmission Control Protocol (TCP)/User Datagram Protocol (UDP):** *TCP* provides for many packet-handling, error-detection, and transmission controls and services, while *UDP* omits these controls and services to provide transmission speed.

- **Wireless Application Protocol (WAP):** *WAP* is a secure protocol that provides the capability for users to display network information on handheld wireless devices, such as mobile phones, pagers, and PDAs.

- **Wireless Application Environment (WAE):** Creates a World Wide Web (WWW) environment on wireless mobile and handheld devices.

7

- **AT command set:** The *AT command set* includes the control commands used to control dial-up modem functions and actions. The AT command set was developed by the Hayes Corporation for use in its modems, but soon became the industry standard for controlling modem communications.

- **Telephone Control Specification—Binary (TCS BIN):** *TCS BIN* is a bit-oriented protocol used to establish voice and data links between Bluetooth devices.

- **Service Discovery Protocol (SDP):** Bluetooth requires an **SDP** to identify and manage the services available on portable devices moving into and out of range with each other. The Bluetooth SDP is specifically designed for Bluetooth devices.

Table 7-1 organizes the protocols of the Bluetooth architecture into their primary functionality.

Protocols	Protocol Type
Baseband, LMP, L2CAP, SDP	Bluetooth core protocols
RFCOMM	Cable replacement
TCS BIN, AT command set	Telephony control
IP, OBEX, PPP, TCP, UDP, vCard, vCal, WAE, WAP	Adapted protocols

Table 7-1   The Protocols of the Bluetooth Architecture

Line Check 7.1

1. What is the function of the HCI in the Bluetooth stack?
2. List the seven Bluetooth operational layers.
3. What protocol is used to transfer data, graphics, and voice objects between devices in the Bluetooth protocol stack?

What Do You Think?

Why is a standardized protocol stack necessary in any wireless specification?

TCP versus UDP

Transmission Control Protocol (TCP)is the more commonly used protocol for transmissions over the Internet. This is primarily because TCP provides a guaranteed delivery for transmitted data packets and it also provides for error detection. On the other hand, User Datagram Protocol (UDP) is used whenever speed is an issue, such as with streaming media. UDP is also used when a guarantee of delivery is not required because, unlike TCP, UDP doesn't provide any controls or packet handling services.

Bluetooth Transmitters

The Bluetooth radio specifications define RF communications using frequency-hopping spread-spectrum (FHSS) within the RF band of 2.402 gigahertz (GHz) and 2.480 GHz using 79 channels. However, in some countries, for instance, France, the range of the RF band is temporarily reduced to only 23 channels because of existing out-of-band regulations there and in other countries.

The Bluetooth specification defines three RF transmitter classes: Classes 1, 2, and 3. Class 1 transmitters have a range of up to 100 meters, as illustrated in Figure 7-3. Many Class 1 Bluetooth products, either because of size or the power available, are more likely to have a range of 40 to 75 meters. For example, the compact flash interface card shown in Figure 7-4 includes a Class 1 transmitter with an advertised range of 40 meters. In all cases, the range of any of the transmitter classes is defined as the maximum range possible across an open and unobstructed space.

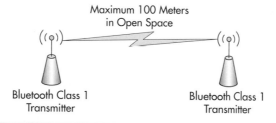

Figure 7-3   Bluetooth Class 1 transmitters have a nominal range of 100 meters.

Most Bluetooth devices include a Class 2 transmitter, with a maximum range of 10 meters or about 33 feet (see Figure 7-5). Class 2 transmitters are generally accepted as the default transmitter standard for most Bluetooth products. However, some plug-in network adapter dongles, like the one in Figure 7-6, include a Class 1 Bluetooth transmitter, which gives it a range comparable to the IEEE 802.11b wireless LAN standards at about 100 meters or about

7

Figure 7-4 A Bluetooth compact flash interface card (Photo courtesy of ANYCOM, Inc.)

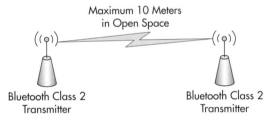

Figure 7-5 Bluetooth Class 2 transmitters have a nominal range of 10 meters.

Figure 7-6 A Bluetooth USB dongle (Photo courtesy of Belkin Corporation)

Class	Range	Maximum Transmission Power	Minimum Transmission Power
3	10 centimeters	1 milliWatt (mW)	No minimum
2	20 meters	2.5 mW	.25 mW
1	100 meters	100 mW	1 mW

Table 7-2   Bluetooth Transmitter Characteristics

330 feet. When two different transmitter classes are connected, though, the lesser transmitter standard establishes the characteristics of the link. Table 7-2 summarizes the Bluetooth transmitter classes arranged by order of transmission power.

Like all low-power RF transmitters, the actual range realized by any Bluetooth installation depends on two criteria: the power source and the operating environment. The power source may be unable to produce the amount of energy required to drive a transmitter at its maximum output power. The environment can also affect the operation of a Bluetooth transmitter, in any class. For example, a Bluetooth Class 2 transmitter may only achieve a range of 5 meters or less in a room filled with large furniture and metal studs in the walls. In addition, when two Bluetooth devices have different class transmitters, the communications between them operate at the lower of the two classes (see Figure 7-7).

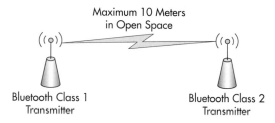

Figure 7-7   Two Bluetooth devices with different transmitters use the range of the lowest class.

Bluetooth Networking

Most Bluetooth networking devices incorporate either a Class 1 or Class 2 RF transmitter, but for the most part, the operating range for Bluetooth networks is generally considered 10 meters. Bluetooth networks are created in an ad-hoc fashion through the discovery processes of the link manager in each device. Like a WLAN ad-hoc network, Bluetooth devices create an ad-hoc connection and, correspondingly, a network link, just by entering each other's operating range.

An ad-hoc Bluetooth network is called a **piconet** (see Figure 7-8), which can include up to eight Bluetooth devices, regardless of the device type or its Bluetooth application. When more than eight devices are attempting to associate with a piconet, the piconet is divided into two or

7

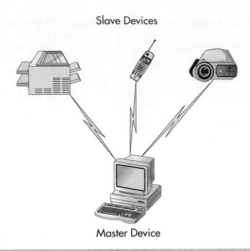

Slave Devices

Master Device

Figure 7-8 A Bluetooth piconet

more piconets, and then interconnected into what is called a **scatternet** (see Figure 7-9). The devices that are a part of different piconets within the scatternet can communicate, but they must do so through other devices to reach each other (something like how "hidden" nodes of a WLAN must communicate).

Bluetooth technology transmits data using a pseudorandom (PR) frequency-hopping spread-spectrum (FHSS) on 79 channels of 1 MHz each (or 23 channels in some countries). In each connection, one of the devices takes on the role of the master device and the other becomes the slave device. This arrangement allows the units to know in advance which of the available channels is in use. The *master device* communicates a channel-hopping sequence to the slave device, so the *slave device* can know the channel on which signals will arrive.

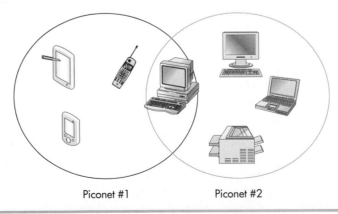

Piconet #1   Piconet #2

Figure 7-9 One or more piconets combine to form a scatternet.

Figure 7-10   A Bluetooth network access point (Photo courtesy of ANYCOM, Inc.)

Bluetooth technology can also provide a link into a wired network in much the same way that 802.11 access points do. Installing a Bluetooth access point, such as the one in Figure 7-10, that is connected to a wired network can provide access to the wired network for any Bluetooth device within range of the access point.

The Bluetooth specifications set some limitations on the number of devices and their formations in a Bluetooth wireless network. These formations, **piconets** and scatternets are explained in the following sections.

Piconets

As explained earlier in the chapter, when two Bluetooth devices are within range of and discover each other, the device initiating the link becomes the master and the discovered device becomes the slave. In addition to setting the frequency-hopping synchronization for their communications, the master/slave relationship is also the basis for the formation of the ad-hoc Bluetooth piconet. A piconet is formed around a unique master device, which sets the communications pattern for any other device (up to a total of eight devices) joining the network. Bluetooth devices each have a unique clock signal and device address, which are combined to provide a unique identity used to differentiate one Bluetooth device from every other Bluetooth device. The difference or offset between one device's clock signal and the clock signal of another device is the basis for the FHSS sequence used between the devices.

An example of a piconet is when a user's Bluetooth handheld PDA or pocket PC moves into the 10-meter range of a Bluetooth-enabled desktop computer. The computer's Bluetooth LM discovers the LM of the portable device and establishes an ad-hoc connection. Depending on the applications running on either device, the user may be able to access her Internet or e-mail, transfer a personal calendar, or remotely access software on the master, which, in this case, could be either device.

7

A Bluetooth device cannot act as a master for two piconets. If a piconet master device is also linked to another piconet in a scatternet, it must participate as a master device in one piconet and a slave device in a second piconet, as illustrated earlier in Figure 7-9. The device could also cease being a master device and become a slave device in two or more piconets. The slaves that share the same master device all belong to the same piconet by definition and, to remain as a member of a piconet, each slave must interact with the master on a time interval negotiated between the master and the slave.

However, if the master leaves the piconet, the other devices must elect a new master and the piconet is reformed. When a Bluetooth device is a member of two piconets, it can be used as a link between the piconets. In this situation, the device, in effect, serves to bridge the two piconets.

Bluetooth piconets are formed using a master/slave arrangement. Any Bluetooth device is capable of serving as either a master or a slave, depending on the networking situation it encounters on-the-fly.

A Bluetooth piconet can be formed using one of two methods:

- A master device actively scans for slave devices and, when it detects one in its range, it can invite the device to join a piconet as a slave.

- A master device can passively wait for a slave to contact it, and then invite the slave to join the piconet as a slave.

If one of the slave devices is turned off or moves out of range, this has no effect on the piconet or on the remaining devices on the piconet unless, of course, only two devices were in the piconet to start.

Scatternets

When two or up to ten piconets are connected through one or more common devices, they form a Bluetooth scatternet. A scatternet is a group of nonsynchronized piconets that connect through a common device that serves as a bridge between the piconets. However, to communicate effectively across a scatternet, a Bluetooth device must have point-to-multipoint communications capabilities. Otherwise, it is limited to point-to-point communications with the devices in its piconet.

Scatternets, while defined in the Bluetooth specifications, aren't the most efficient way to utilize Bluetooth technology. Scatternets are ad-hoc structures (like the WPAN shown in Figure 7-11) and because the piconets that make up a scatternet aren't synchronized to each other, communicating from one end of the network to the other can be awkward or virtually impossible at times. Also, remember, the piconets can be formed and dissolved frequently, and in a matter of only a few seconds.

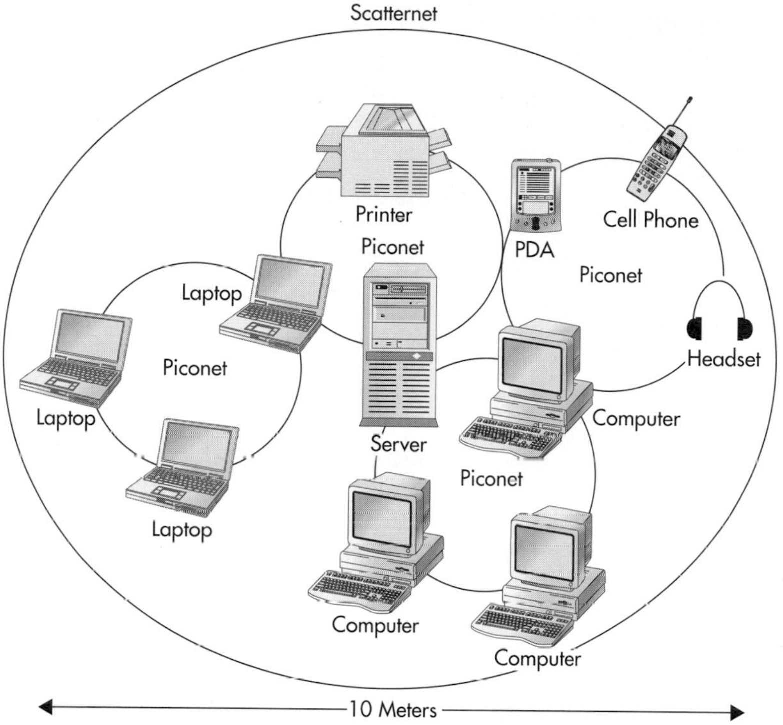

Scatternet

Printer
Piconet

Cell Phone

PDA

Piconet

Laptop

Headset

Piconet

Laptop

Computer

Laptop

Server

Piconet

Computer

Computer

Computer

← 10 Meters →

Figure 7-11 A scatternet can cluster several piconets into a **WPAN**.

Line Check 7.2

1. What is the nominal operating range of a Bluetooth Class 2 transmitter?

2. What would be the operating range between a Bluetooth Class 1 transmitter and a Bluetooth Class 2 transmitter?

3. How many devices can be included in a Bluetooth piconet?

What Do You Think?

Why do you think one of the devices in a piconet must be designated as a master?

Connecting Bluetooth Devices

While some Bluetooth devices continuously scan for other Bluetooth devices in an effort to "discover" them, many Bluetooth devices require the user to activate the discovery (masters) or search (slaves) mode, usually for a short period. Bluetooth devices must be turned on to perform discovery or be discovered.

Many Bluetooth devices do continuously search for other Bluetooth devices, such as Bluetooth headsets for cell phones, MP3 players, USB Bluetooth adapters (see Figure 7-12), and mouse devices, which have built-in Bluetooth capabilities. On some Bluetooth devices, one or more buttons are used to activate Bluetooth scanning. Other Bluetooth devices, including PCs, must be configured for a Bluetooth connection before its scan functions can be activated.

Figure 7-12   A USB Bluetooth adapter provides Bluetooth capability to a PC. (Photo courtesy of Novell, Inc.)

NOTE

The actual method used to activate or configure a device for Bluetooth functionality varies by manufacturer and device type.

Using PIN Codes

Bluetooth attempts to prevent just anybody from accessing or connecting to your Bluetooth device. The Bluetooth standards define security options that can be built into a Bluetooth device. A common security method used on several Bluetooth device types is to require that a personal identification number (PIN) code be entered on the master device when attempting to establish an association with a slave device (see Figure 7-13). For example, a Bluetooth modem may require that a PC provide a PIN number when the PC attempts to initialize a connection with it. The use of a PIN number is intended to prevent any unauthorized Bluetooth device to create an association with another. Several types of Bluetooth devices have a preset, built-in PIN code that is unique to a Bluetooth device.

Figure 7-13   Some Bluetooth devices require the master device to provide a preset PIN code to establish a connection.

Pairing Bluetooth Devices

Another method of establishing an association between two Bluetooth devices is a process called pairing. *Pairing* applies the use of a PIN code, but enables the user to specify the PIN. This user-defined PIN code, which must be configured into both Bluetooth devices, is then exchanged and verified by the devices when attempting to associate (see Figure 7-14). Because most Bluetooth-enabled cell phones don't have a built-in PIN code, the same PIN code configured on the connecting device must be entered into the cell phone when attempting to pair with another Bluetooth device.

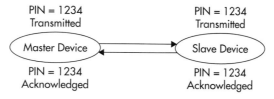

Figure 7-14   Pairing uses a user-defined PIN code to be exchanged between two Bluetooth devices.

7

Bluejacking and Toothing

Some seemingly harmless activities have become popular among Bluetooth users, especially those that gather in fairly crowded places: Bluejacking and Toothing.

Bluejacking involves sending messages from a Bluetooth device to any other nearby Bluetooth devices, surprising the recipient. This activity even has a web site dedicated to it: **www.bluejackq.com/**.

Toothing is a bit more goal-oriented than bluejacking. In *toothing*, as in bluejacking, the communications are to other Bluetooth users in an immediate (10 meters) area, but the objective is not surprise as much as it is to arrange for casual meetings and, perhaps, even a date.

NOTE

The Bluetooth security options, including the requirement of a PIN code, can be disabled on many Bluetooth devices, although this is not recommended.

 ## Line Check 7.3

1. Why is it important to use a PIN code when connecting two Bluetooth devices?

2. Describe the Bluetooth discovery process.

 ## What Do You Think?

Which method of connecting Bluetooth devices do you believe would be the most secure? Why?

Bluetooth Profiles

Unlike other wireless and cable replacement technologies, Bluetooth applications are required to follow a set of guidelines published by the Bluetooth SIG. These application guidelines are defined in the Bluetooth specifications as Bluetooth Profiles. The profiles describe how Bluetooth is to be implemented in user applications using descriptions of a variety of scenarios in which Bluetooth provides the wireless communications technology. The primary purpose behind the *Bluetooth Profiles* is to ensure interoperability between devices that provide the same or similar applications.

The Bluetooth Profiles specifically define how a particular type of application will implement a vertical path through the Bluetooth protocol stack, as well as the range of parameters an application needs to use with each of the protocols in use.

NOTE

New Bluetooth Profiles are in development at any time. If you want to keep current with the profiles, you should visit the Bluetooth News web pages (www.bluetooth.com/news/) regularly.

The Bluetooth Profiles don't define specific applications, such as a wireless cell phone headset. Rather, they define specific groupings of Bluetooth protocols and services that are

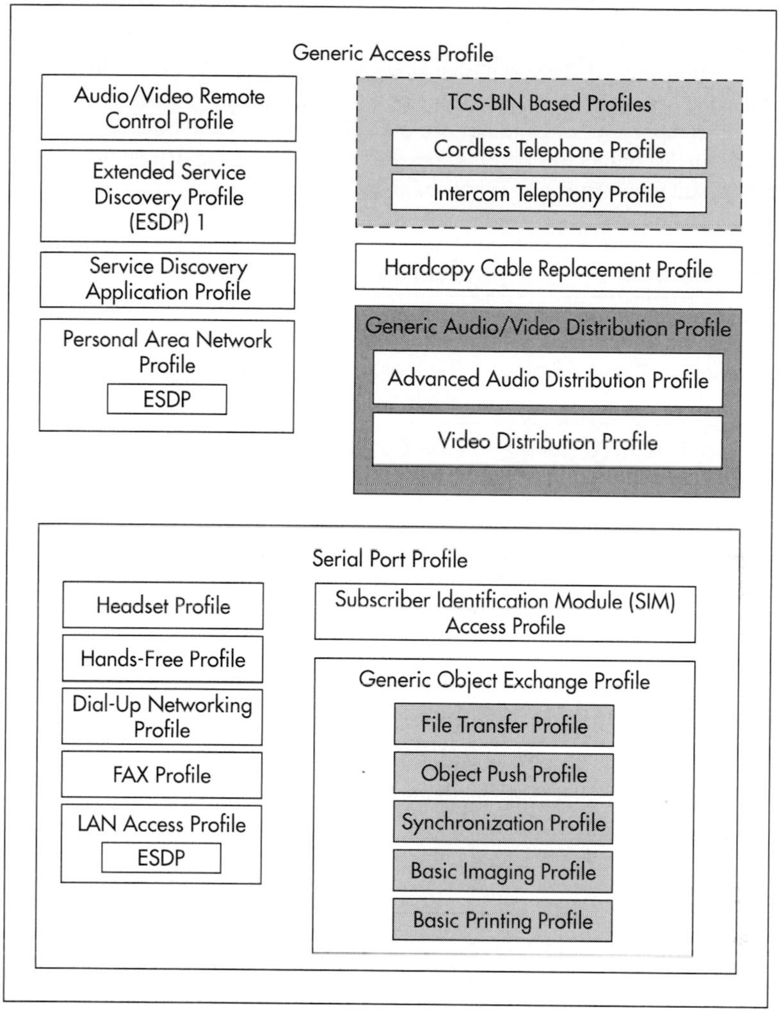

Figure 7-15   The Bluetooth Profiles showing profile dependencies

dependent on each other to accomplish a particular function. Figure 7-15 illustrates the profile dependencies for Bluetooth applications. Within this hierarchy of profiles, notice the Headset Profile is dependent on the Serial Port Profile and, in turn, the Generic Access Profile. Each profile is dependent on the profile in which it is a member. Table 7-3 lists the Bluetooth Profiles and a brief description of what each defines. For more information on the Bluetooth Profiles, see the Bluetooth tutorials provided by PaloWireless at **www.palowireless.com**.

NOTE

Figure 7-15 and Table 7-3 contain only enough examples of the Bluetooth Profiles to illustrate the hierarchy and relationships among the various profiles. Many more profiles, either approved or pending, are available for Bluetooth devices. To see a more complete list of Bluetooth Profiles, as well as a good summary on the Bluetooth technology, visit **www.trust.com/service/help/bluetooth/**.

Profile	Defines
Generic Access Profile	The use of the Link Controller and the Link Manager Protocol
Audio/Video Remote Control Profile	The features and procedures that ensure interoperability between Bluetooth devices with audio/video control functions
Extended Service Discovery Profile	How Bluetooth devices use the Service Discovery Protocol (SDP) to discover other devices with Universal Plug and Play (UPnP) services
Service Discovery Application Profile	The features and procedures for a Bluetooth application to discover services in other Bluetooth devices
Personal Area Network Profile	How two or more Bluetooth devices form an ad-hoc network and access a remote network through a network access point
Serial Port Profile	How the RFCOMM serial port emulator is used in Bluetooth devices
Headset Profile	The duplex link to a Bluetooth headset that is controlled by an audio gateway, such as a mobile phone
Hands-Free Profile	The means for the remote control and voice connections of hands-free devices, such as a cell phone connected to a Bluetooth in-car kit
Dial-Up Network Profile	The Bluetooth link to a dial-up modem
FAX Profile	How to transfer a fax over a Bluetooth link
LAN Access Profile	How Bluetooth devices access a LAN through the Point-to-Point Protocol (PPP) and how PPP is used to create a network between two Bluetooth devices
SIM Access Profile	The protocols and procedures used to access a SIM card over a Bluetooth link
Generic Object Exchange Profile	How a Bluetooth device uses OBEX for file transfer, object push, and data synchronization
File Transfer Profile	How data files are transferred between Bluetooth devices

Table 7-3 Bluetooth Profiles and What They Define

Profile	Defines
Object Push Profile	The processes used to push files from a Bluetooth server to a Bluetooth client
Synchronization Profile	The processes used to synchronize files and data between two Bluetooth devices
Basic Imaging Profile	The Bluetooth services and device features required to exchange JPEG images
Basic Printing Profile	The device requirements for Bluetooth-enabled printers
Generic Audio/Video Distribution Profile	A generic definition for distributing audio/video content between Bluetooth devices over an ACL channel
Advanced Audio Distribution Profile	The protocols and procedures used to distribute high-quality audio content
Video Distribution Profile	The device requirements to transfer video content between two Bluetooth devices
Hard Copy Cable Replacement Profile	The device requirement to print or scan documents on a Bluetooth-enabled device
Cordless Telephone Profile	How telephone calls are forwarded to a Bluetooth cordless telephone
Intercom Profile	Voice communications over short ranges between Bluetooth devices

Table 7-3   Bluetooth Profiles and What They Define (*continued*)

NOTE

A profile for TCS-BIN doesn't specifically exist, but the cordless telephone and the intercom profiles are based on the services of the TCS-BIN protocol.

Subscriber Identification Module (SIM) Cards

A Subscriber Identification Module (SIM) card is inserted into any mobile phone or other communications device employing Global System for Mobile Communications (GSM). The *SIM card* is a small plug-in circuit board that identifies the device, the service subscriber, and security data, and it provides memory for storing personal data, such as telephone numbers and other personal directory information.

Line Check 7.4

1. What is defined by the Personal Area Network Profile?
2. What is defined by the Serial Port Profile?

What Do You Think?

Why has the Bluetooth SIG created the application profiles?

Bluetooth versus Infrared (IR)

Depending on your WPAN needs, in some instances, Bluetooth or IR may provide the best solution. Of course, connecting your network with cabling is still an option, but assuming you are only interested in a wireless network, we should compare these two technologies—even before we look at a few others—to understand the applications in which each may be the better choice.

- **Bandwidth:** Bluetooth has a raw data transfer rate of 1 Mbps. IrDA FIR or VFIR provide up to 4 Mbps and 16 Mbps, respectively.

- **Range:** If the distance from your base station (most likely your computer) to any of the devices on your WPAN is more than 1 meter, then it's likely that, unless you install the IR devices very carefully, Bluetooth, with its 10 to 100 meter range would be your choice (depending on your environment, of course).

- **Environment:** The space in which your WPAN is to be installed can also impact your decision. If LoS is an issue, then IR may not be the better choice. Bluetooth's RF can move through or around some objects in its path, although they tend to diminish its range to a certain extent.

- **Convenience:** This could also affect your decision. To transmit data between IR devices involves aligning the LoS of the devices and pressing a button. Because the users place the devices into position for communications, there is no mystery about where the transmitted data is going and who may be intercepting it. However, Bluetooth's ad-hoc connections aren't as trouble-free as they may sound. A Bluetooth device discovers all the other Bluetooth devices within its range, which not only means your laptop computer may be connecting to your PDA or cell phone, but also those of everyone else in your immediate vicinity.

Bluetooth cannot distinguish one device from another, so the user must indicate which of the devices on the piconet should be included in an exchange.

- **Interference:** IR devices are essentially interference-free, unless they are pointed directly at the sun or another bright light source. On the other hand, Bluetooth operates in the ISM 2.4 GHz band, along with a host of other devices, such as 802.11b WLAN access points and NICs, cordless telephones, microwave ovens, and even garage door openers and some baby monitors. And, while you are discouraged from using your RF devices on board a commercial airplane, you may use your IR devices (except during takeoff and landing).

- **Number of devices:** DIR is a point-to-point technology and, unless you install a DFIR system, you are limited to one device linking to one other device. Bluetooth is both a point-to-point and a point-to-multipoint technology, so if you have multiple devices to which you want to connect, you should use Bluetooth or look into DFIR.

- **Cost:** IR ports and adapters are inexpensive to add to a PC or any other processor-based device, but adding Bluetooth to each of your devices is still a relatively expensive undertaking.

- **Control:** When you are using IR for the communications technology in a **WPAN**, you must physically perform a series of actions to complete a transmission. Bluetooth is constantly scanning the area to discover any Bluetooth devices that move within its range, whether or not you know about it.

If you are determined to choose between Bluetooth and IR, it is also possible that you could do both. Interface modules are in development to provide both Bluetooth and IR connectivity in a single module.

CROSS-REFERENCE

7

See Chapter 6 for more information on LoS devices.

Understanding WPAN Concepts and the IEEE 802.15 Standards

A wireless personal area network (WPAN) involves several computing and peripheral devices that are able to communicate to form a single ad-hoc system, whether in a home, office, car, or a public place. *WPAN* technologies are wire replacement services that are grouped together under the general category of wireless connectivity (WiCon) systems.

An example of a WPAN is a computer able to connect to a wireless (RF or IR) keyboard, mouse, and printer or a PDA device that is able to use wireless communications to synchronize e-mail or a personal calendar with a desktop computer.

IEEE 802.15 Standards

In 1997, the Institute for Electrical and Electronics Engineers (IEEE) formed an ad-hoc group within its Portable Applications Standards Committee (PASC) to study the need for standards in the personal networking area. In 1999, this group was formalized as the 802.15 Working Group for wireless personal area networks (WPAN).

Since 1999, the **IEEE 802.15** working group has expanded to include several task groups and subgroups (see Table 7-4), each of which is focused on a specific communications technology or PAN variation.

Task Group	Focus
802.15.1	Wireless PAN
802.15.2	Coexistence of PANs
802.15.3	High-data rate PAN (2.4 GHz to 55 Mbps)
802.15.4	ZigBee low-data rate PAN

Table 7-4   IEEE 802.15 Task Groups

Within the responsibility for each of the task groups listed in Table 7-4, more specific groups are focused on one or more particular technology. For example, the use of the Bluetooth technology for a WPAN is assigned to the 802.15.1a subgroup within the 802.15 task group. The standards listed in Table 7-4 are discussed in the following sections.

IEEE 802.15.1

The *802.15.1 standard* for wireless PAN, which is officially named the IEEE Standard 802.15.1–2002, is based on the Bluetooth foundation specifications. This standard defines the lower layer transport functions of Bluetooth:

- **Baseband: Baseband** is the physical (PHY) layer of Bluetooth and manages the physical channels and links. The *Baseband layer* serves as the link controller and operates on top of the Bluetooth Radio layer in the Bluetooth protocol stack. As the LC, Baseband works with the LM to provide link connection and power-control management.

- **Link Manager Protocol (LMP):** The *Bluetooth LMP* performs link setup, authentication, link configuration, and the discovery of other Bluetooth devices.

- **Logical Link Control and Adaptation Protocol (L2CAP): L2CAP** is a Layer 2 (data-link layer of the OSI model) protocol that provides both connection-oriented and connectionless data services, including multiplexing, segmentation, and reassembly, which allow upper layers to transmit and receive packets of up to 64KB in length. The Bluetooth specification for L2CAP defines two link types: Synchronous Connection-Oriented (SCO) links and Asynchronous Connectionless (ACL) links. *SCO* links support real-time voice traffic over fixed bandwidth and *ACL* links support best-effort traffic, such as IP data packets. However, in the 802.15.1 standards, only ACL links are specified.

● **Radio:** The Bluetooth *Radio layer* defines the requirements of the Bluetooth transceiver and its operations in the 2.4 GHz Industrial, Scientific, and Medical (ISM) RF band.

IEEE 802.15.2

The *802.15.2 Coexistence Task Group* for WPANs has developed a recommended practices standard that facilitates the coexistence of WPANs (802.15) and wireless LANs (802.11). This standard, which has the self-explanatory name of the "IEEE 802.15.2–2003 Recommended Practice for Telecommunications and Information Exchange Between Systems—Local and Metropolitan Area Networks; Specific Requirements—Part 15.2: Coexistence of Wireless Personal Area Networks with Other Wireless Devices Operating in Unlicensed Frequency Band," defines a coexistence model and a set of coexistence mechanisms to ensure the coexistence of WPAN and WLAN devices operating in the same general area.

IEEE 802.15.3

This task group, which is officially named the High Rate (HR) Task Group for WPANs, has developed and published a new standard for high-data rate (meaning 20 Mbps or higher) WPANs. In addition to providing for high-data transfer rates, the standard also provides low-power and low-cost solutions for portable digital imaging and multimedia applications.

The *802.15.3 standard* specifies WPAN capabilities that include data rates of from 11 Mbps to 55 Mbps on ad-hoc peer-to-peer WPANs. The use of Ultra wideband (UWB) technology for WPANs is specified under the 802.15.3 standards.

7

IEEE 802.15.4

The *802.15.4 task group* has developed a standard for low-data rate, low-complexity WPAN alternatives powered by multimonth to multiyear batteries operating in unlicensed RF bands. This standard also specifies WPANs that operate on a mesh networking topology, either in full mesh or partial mesh. A *full-mesh topology* connects every node directly to each of the other nodes. In a *partial-mesh topology*, a node is connected only to those other nodes with which it exchanges data most frequently.

The projected applications for this technology are sensors, interactive toys, smart identity badges, remote control units, and a variety of home automation applications. The primary RF technologies identified with this standard is ZigBee and a low-power, low-rate version of UWB.

Reviewing WPAN Technology

Table 7-5 summarizes the primary characteristics of the WPAN technologies discussed in this chapter, as well as Chapter 6. Which of the technologies discussed is the better choice? The answer is best summed up by Gilster's Law: You never can tell; and it all depends. The application drives the selection of the WPAN technology that best suits the needs of any WPAN implementation.

WPAN Technology	Data Rate	Range
Bluetooth (Class 1)	1 Mbps	100 meters
Bluetooth (Class 3)	1 Mbps	10 meters
DFIR	10 Mbps	Single room
IEEE 802.11b	11 Mbps	100 meters
Magnetic induction	204.8 Kbps	3 meters
IrDA	9.6 Kbps to 4 Mbps	1 meter
ZigBee	Up to 250 Kbps	30 meters

Table 7-5   A Comparison of the Primary WPAN Technologies

NOTE

Another WPAN and home area network (HAN) technology, HomeRF and its Shared Wireless Access Protocol (SWAP), is now an open standard available to schools and companies wanting to use it as a teaching tool or to develop other technologies. The sponsoring organization, the HomeRF Working Group, was disbanded in 2002 and no new development effort is being made.

Line Check 7.5

1. What wireless communications technology is the basis for the 802.15.1 standard?
2. Ultra wideband communications technology is included in which of the 802.15 standards?
3. The 802.15 standards are focused on what particular application of networking?

What Do You Think?

Consider your personal needs and requirements for setting up a WPAN at home or in your office space. Explain why one particular WPAN technology may best satisfy your needs.

Chapter 7 Review

Chapter Summary

Understand the Bluetooth Technology and Its Operations

- The Bluetooth Radio layer operates in the 2.4 GHz ISM band.

- Bluetooth incorporates an RF transceiver and a full set of networking protocols on a single chip.

- The Bluetooth SIG is responsible for the development, promotion, testing, and conformance issues surrounding the Bluetooth technology.

- Bluetooth is defined on two levels: PHY and MAC.

- A Bluetooth piconet connects up to eight devices in active mode and up to 255 devices in parked mode. Bluetooth piconets are combined into a scatternet.

- The Bluetooth specification defines three transmitter classes: Classes 1, 2, and 3, each of which defines a different operating range.

- The nominal broadcast range of a Bluetooth Class 2 transmitter, the most commonly used transmitter, is 10 meters (about 33 feet).

- The use of the Bluetooth technology in applications is defined in a series of application profiles.

WPAN Concepts and the IEEE 802.15 Standards

- A PAN is built around an area called personal operating space (POS). A **POS** is commonly defined as extending up to 10 meters (about 33 feet) in all directions around a person.

- The 802.15.1 standard is based on the Bluetooth foundation specifications and defines the lower-layer transport functions of Bluetooth: Baseband, LMP, L2CAP, and Radio.

7

REVIEW

- The 802.15.2 Coexistence Task Group for WPANs has developed a recommended practices standard that facilitates the coexistence of WPANs (802.15) and wireless LANs (802.11).

- The 802.15.3 task group has developed a new standard for 20 Mbps or higher WPANs that also specifies the use of UWB technology for WPANs.

- The 802.15.4 task group has developed a standard for low-data rate, low-complexity WPAN alternatives powered by multimonth to multiyear batteries. The primary RF technology identified in this standard is ZigBee and a low-power, low-rate version of UWB.

Review WPAN Technology

- The requirements of a particular application are what drive the selection of a specific WPAN technology.

Key Terms

Baseband *(218, 236)*
Bluetooth *(214)*
HAN *(214)*
HCI *(219)*
IEEE 802.15 *(236)*
L2CAP *(219, 236)*
LMP *(236)*
Piconet *(223, 225)*
POS *(239)*
Scatternet *(224)*
SDP *(220)*
SIG *(215)*
WPAN *(227, 235)*

Key Term Quiz

Use the terms from the Key Terms list to complete the following sentences. Don't use the same term more than once. Not all terms will be used.

1. The IEEE standard that defines personal area networks is _____.

2. The acronym WPAN refers to _____.

3. The WPAN technology that forms ad-hoc devices into a piconet is _____.

4. A network that provides a communications connection between devices inside a home is a _____.

5. The physical layer of the 802.15 standard is provided by Bluetooth's _____ layer.

6. The Bluetooth _____ performs link setup, authentication, link configuration, and the discovery of other Bluetooth devices.

7. _____ is a Layer 2 Bluetooth protocol that provides connection-oriented and connectionless data services.

8. The Bluetooth standard is developed, managed, and controlled by the _____.

9. A Bluetooth _____ connects up to 8 devices in active mode and up to 255 devices in parked mode.

10. Multiple Bluetooth piconets are connected into a _____.

Multiple Choice Quiz

1. What is the acronym used for a network that provides a communication connection between devices in a home?

   A. AIR

   B. HAN

   C. PAN

   D. POS

2. What is the RF communications standard that can organize up to eight devices into a piconet?

   A. Bluetooth

   B. IrDA

   C. UWB

   D. ZigBee

3. Which of the IEEE 802 standards defines the technologies used to form and manage personal area networks?

   A. 802.3

   B. 802.11

   C. 802.15

   D. 802.16

4. Which of the following acronyms is used in reference to a PAN that employs wireless communications technology?

   A. CPAN

   B. PPAN

   C. TPAN

   D. WPAN

5. Which of the following is Bluetooth's Physical layer?

   A. Baseband

   B. Broadband

   C. Wideband

   D. Ultra wideband

6. Which Bluetooth protocol performs link setup, authentication, link configuration, and the discovery of other Bluetooth devices?

   A. L2CAP

   B. LMP

   C. Radio

   D. SIG

7. Which Layer 2 Bluetooth protocol provides connection-oriented and connectionless data services?

   A. L2CAP

   B. LMP

   C. MAC

   D. PHY

8. What ad-hoc logical structure does Bluetooth form with less than eight Bluetooth devices?

   A. Micronet

   B. Piconet

   C. Scatternet

   D. Supernet

9. What ad-hoc logical structure does Bluetooth form when more than eight Bluetooth devices are present within the range of a master device?

    A. Multiple piconets

    B. Multiple scatternets

    C. Multiple piconets organized into a scatternet

    D. Multiple scatternets organized into a piconet

10. What is the space normally associated with a wireless personal area network (WPAN)?

    A. Enclosed room

    B. Single building or home

    C. Personal operating space

    D. Desktop

Lab Projects

1. Using a portable PC (notebook, Pocket PC, or the like) or a desktop computer equipped with either an internal or external Bluetooth adapter and the appropriate device drivers or software, test the range of the operating range with a Bluetooth-enabled device. Begin your test by operating the device at a 3-foot distance. Increment the distance by 3 feet and test again. Continue incrementing the distance between the PC and the Bluetooth adapter until the device fails to communicate. Record the distance at which the devices no longer communicate effectively.

2. Using the same equipment used in Lab Project 1, experiment on the width of the angularity within which the Bluetooth devices will communicate. Start by operating the device directly in front of the adapter. Move to either the left or the right, a few feet at a time, and circle the Bluetooth adapter at about the same distance, and then increase the distance by 3 to 5 feet, until you reach a point at which the devices will no longer communicate effectively. Note the position, relative to your starting point, and the distance at which the communications failed.

Case Problems

1. Using what you learned in this chapter, Chapter 6, and from your research, would Bluetooth networking be an effective choice for a home, office, or school network? Why? In what specific applications would Bluetooth not be an effective choice?

2. Using the Internet, research Bluetooth security options. Should users be concerned about using Bluetooth devices for PAN applications? Which uses might they want to avoid, under the current specifications?

Advanced Lab Project

You have been assigned the task of recommending a PAN technology for use in a new set of automated study carrels, connected into the school's LAN, to be installed in your school's library. Each carrel is 4 feet wide and 3.5 feet deep, with 5 feet assigned to the seating area for each carrel. Each of the 12 carrels to be installed is separated from its neighbors by a 5-foot-tall fabric-covered metal divider on both sides, including the carrels at each end of the row. Prepare a comparative analysis that recommends a PAN technology and the better choice for connecting to the LAN, choosing from Bluetooth, IrDA, DFIR, PLC, and HomePNA. List the pros and cons for using each these technologies in this application and discuss the reasons behind your recommended choice.

Chapter 8

Wireless LAN Planning and Design

In small wireless networking situations, such as a home network or a one or two-person office, you don't need to perform much in the way of planning or design. In these situations, only three primary tasks are required. First, you need to place a wireless access point or router near the Internet service terminal device, such as a cable, DSL modem, or bridge. Then, connect the access point to the service terminal device with a cable. And, finally, you need to locate a power source for both devices. In larger networking situations, however—the entire floor of a corporate network, the extension of a wired LAN segment, or the setup of an exterior hot spot—a bit more consideration, planning, and design must be performed to help ensure the effective and efficient operation of the wireless network.

The focus of this chapter is to review the recommended planning and design process that should be used for wireless networking situations, especially the importance of performing a site survey and modeling a proposed network design.

WLAN Design Considerations

Wireless networking, including IEEE 802.11x wireless local area networks (WLANs), has a number of limitations and performance issues that must be considered during the planning and design phases of a WLAN installation project. These limitations and issues, some obvious and some rather subtle, if not addressed during the WLAN design process, can cause the network to have intermittent problems or to fail altogether.

The issues that must be addressed during planning and design are, categorically:

- RF design issues
- WLAN site qualification
- Capacity and coverage
- Existing network issues

RF Design Issues

Perhaps the most important design issue with any WLAN design is that it communicates using radio frequency (RF) radio waves. Obviously, a wireless network transmits RF waves, but if RF transmissions are affected by their environment and surroundings, a WLAN could develop operational problems. You should never assume that any setting is able to support RF communication because it doesn't necessarily work the same in every situation.

IEEE 802.11 WLANs primarily operate on the 2.4 GHz Industrial, Scientific, and Medical (ISM) frequency band. While ISM has, in general, proven fairly reliable, some characteristics of the ISM band can affect a WLAN's performance:

- **Competing devices**   Because the ISM RF frequency band is unlicensed, many different types of wireless devices also use this band, such as Bluetooth devices, cordless telephones, emergency services (police and fire protection) radio communications, and even some baby monitors. For example, if a company incorporated Bluetooth headsets into its call center operations, that company shouldn't be surprised that its 802.11b 2.4 GHz WLAN began to have problems in the call center area.

- **Distance**   At some distance, all RF signals will lose at least some signal strength. This translates to a loss of bandwidth and signal integrity for a wireless network as the distance approaches the outside edges of a wireless device's effective range. Depending on an antenna's power (gain), the distance of its operating range may be longer or shorter, even in comparison to the same or similar devices in the same network. In a WLAN situation, an 802.11b device can only provide its full 11 Mbps bandwidth within the first 30 meters (100 feet) around of its antenna or transmitter. Over each successive 30 meters in distance, around 50 percent of its bandwidth (as illustrated in Figure 8-1) is lost. The bandwidth loss is reduced for each additional 30 meters of distance from a transmitter to the point where, at around 100 meters, its bandwidth is decreased to only 1 Mbps. Likewise, the 802.11a standard, which transmits on the 5 GHz frequency band, loses around one-third of its bandwidth every 25 meters. This reduction in bandwidth is caused by the access point automatically reducing its data transfer speed when the signal begins to weaken. Lower frequency signals are better able to penetrate any interference in the path of the signal, which grows as the distance increases. Having only one WLAN node communicating at 1 Mbps can slow the entire WLAN because of the time required for the access point to communicate with the slow node.

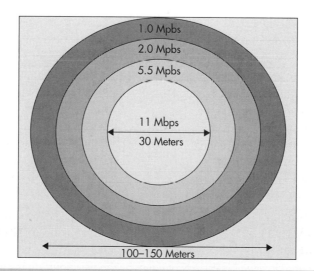

8

Figure 8-1   The bandwidth of an 802.11b signal fades as its distance increases.

- **Metal boxes**   In RF terminology, a **metal box** is any metallic or magnetic object that blocks or absorbs a transmitted RF signal. A metal box can be a building, an air conditioning unit, a vault or large safe, a large machine, metal partitions, and the like.

- **Stationary objects**   Not only can metal boxes block or interfere with an RF transmission, but also the walls of a building, rock walls and fireplaces, trees and large bushes, and other large stationary objects can deflect or block RF signals. Different stationary objects create different levels of attenuation in the RF signal. Table 8-1 lists many common objects and their effect on an RF signal.

- **Shared bandwidth**   The bandwidth of WLAN devices is *shared bandwidth*, which means all active wireless devices are competing for the available bandwidth. The number of wireless nodes on a WLAN that must compete for the bandwidth can reduce the overall performance of the network.

Because of these issues and many specific to a particular location, any proposed WLAN area may have spots in which wireless reception can change from outstanding to poor in only a few meters. Before a WLAN can be planned into an area, large or small, the area should be physically and carefully modeled using a site survey (see the section "Site Surveys").

WLAN Site Qualification

Qualifying a particular site for the installation of a WLAN is a relatively simple process. The qualification process addresses the scope and size of the network to be installed, as well as the capability for the site to support the bandwidth requirements and the number of nodes to be deployed. Verifying or qualifying a site's capability to support a WLAN is similar to performing a feasibility study to determine whether or not you should proceed with a site survey.

The bandwidth of an 802.11 WLAN is shared bandwidth and, if the preliminary design calls for a large number of devices or users to compete for bandwidth, the performance of the network may be impacted. The general rule used to plan a WLAN layout is 20 concurrent (active) users per wireless access point. This restriction addresses the number of channels available more than it does any bandwidth issues that may be caused by a large number of users. Using one 802.11 standard over another can increase the available bandwidth, but not the number of available channels. For example, 802.11a has potentially five times more bandwidth than 802.11b, but only a few more channels. Higher bandwidth may not always be the solution to supporting more nodes on a wireless network.

Another concern for a WLAN design is the type of traffic it will be carrying. WLANs work well with large numbers of small, bursty packets, such as those used to retrieve e-mail and web pages from the Internet. *Bursty* means the data is transmitted in bursts, rather than in a continuous stream. However, a WLAN may not be the best solution in situations where most of its traffic would be transferring large data files.

Obstruction	Degree of Attenuation	Example
Open space	None	Cafeteria, courtyard
Wood	Low	Inner wall, office partition, door, floor
Plaster	Low	Inner wall (old plaster lower than new plaster)
Synthetic materials	Low	Office partition
Cinder block	Low	Inner wall, outer wall
Asbestos	Low	Ceiling
Glass	Low	Nontinted window
Wire mesh in glass	Medium	Door, partition
Metal tinted glass	Low	Tinted window
Human body	Medium	Large group of people
Water	Medium	Damp wood, aquarium, organic inventory
Bricks	Medium	Inner wall, outer wall, floor
Marble	Medium	Inner wall, outer wall, floor
Ceramic (metal content or backing)	High	Ceramic tile, ceiling, floor
Paper	High	Roll or stack of paper stock
Concrete	High	Floor, outer wall, support pillar
Bulletproof glass	High	Security booth
Silvering	Very High	Mirror
Metal	Very High	Desk, office partition, reinforced concrete, elevator shaft, filing cabinet, sprinkler system, ventilator

Table 8-1 Degree of Attenuation by Common Materials. (Used with permission from Intel Corporation.)

Consider this: even the general rule of supporting 20 or more wireless nodes with a single access point requires nearly perfect conditions. The nodes and the access point must have clear, unobstructed lines of sight between them. However, in nearly every situation, an area or room will have a few architectural features, furniture, metal boxes, and, perhaps, other obstructions that may impede the signal, with the results being similar to those caused by distance. Unless you are absolutely sure a wireless solution is required, the best solution for many networking challenges may still be a wired network.

Bursty Data

Internet providers and most LAN administrators depend on the bursty nature of network use to help avoid some bandwidth issues. Users spend most of their time using a network waiting, reading, studying, and otherwise sitting idle (in terms of on-air or on-wire activity). In a vast majority of instances, a user transmits a relatively small amount of data to the network, such as a web page download request or the body of an e-mail message. The amount of actual clock time required by the NIC to transmit the data to the network (wired or wireless) is small (typically milliseconds at most), so in terms of the amount of potential circuit time available, the NIC is largely idle most of the time.

Data is transmitted to and received from the network by an NIC in small groups of bursts with relatively long periods of circuit idleness in between. This bursty nature of network operations allows the network's bandwidth to be oversubscribed to a larger group of users than might otherwise be possible if the bandwidth were divided equally and dedicated to the network nodes.

Line Check 8.1

1. List and explain two RF design issues that must be addressed when planning a WLAN.

2. Describe the relationship of distance and bandwidth on an 802.11b signal.

3. Explain the concept of shared bandwidth and how it may impact a WLAN.

What Do You Think?

What might be the repercussions of not performing a WLAN design when planning a wireless network in a large corporate or school setting?

Capacity and Coverage

A WLAN designer often concentrates on ensuring sufficient **coverage**, which means he attempts to provide the same level of signal strength to all the network's nodes. However, the designer should work to strike a balance between **capacity**, meaning the number of nodes and amount of shared bandwidth available to each node, and coverage. If the design focuses only on coverage, enough bandwidth may not be available across the network to support every node. When the design emphasizes capacity, in most cases, the resulting WLAN should typically also provide adequate coverage.

It seems intuitive that you should plan for coverage to ensure that all the nodes on the network are able to associate with a network access point. Planning for capacity may go against the designer's goal of providing adequate RF signal coverage to all nodes. Equally, if not more, important is for the WLAN design to ensure adequate bandwidth is available to support the applications and traffic to be transmitted across the network. Ensuring capacity to every node almost always ensures coverage to every node.

Remember, users with wireless nodes expect the same performance as their co-workers with wired nodes. Planning a network only to provide coverage may not adequately address the need to consider the bandwidth available and how applications will perform on the network.

WLAN Coverage

As previously (see Figure 8-1), distance inversely affects the bandwidth of an RF signal because, as the distance increases, the bandwidth—and, perhaps, even more important, throughput—decreases. A typical 802.11b WLAN access point has an RF range of about 100 meters (about 330 feet). To maximize the coverage of the access point, the access point should be placed in the center of or, at a minimum, in a location that provides the most coverage to the area it is to support.

In larger areas, meaning areas that exceed the 100-meter coverage of a single access point, multiple access points should be planned, so they overlap and provide for seamless roaming within the WLAN's coverage area. Remember, each of the overlapping access points should be set to operate on a different channel to prevent crosstalk. Also remember that WLAN RF technologies use a "break before make" handoff method, which means that an existing connection will be dropped before a new connection is established, so it is best to not overlap the signal coverage of the access points too much.

Another benefit to including additional access points in the design (and placing the access points closer together) is this design can provide a level of redundancy, which can continue to provide the service to users if an access point fails. A further benefit of redundant access points is it provides for the capability to balance the capacity and coverage loads as the WLAN grows.

8

WLAN Capacity

One of the considerations when planning the capacity of a WLAN is the number of non-overlapping channels available on the various 802.11 standards. IEEE 802.11b and 802.11g provide three nonoverlapping channels, which should be enough capacity for typical bursty Internet and e-mail activities. The 802.11a standard provides for eight nonoverlapping channels, although only four are available in most Pacific Rim countries. Increasing the number of nonoverlapping channels available to the network also increases the capacity and potential throughput of the WLAN. Choosing the 802.11a standard over the 802.11b/g standards provides the maximum number of channels, bandwidth, and capacity to the WLAN. However, because this additional capability does come at a higher price, the need for the additional capacity must justify its cost.

The capacity of a WLAN is dependent on the capability of its access points to support the amount of data traffic at any given time. Because bandwidth is shared by the nodes connecting to an access point, the number of simultaneous users possible depends on just what those users are transmitting across the network. The capacity of an access point can change based on its load, as well as the types and amounts of data its users are transmitting. For example, an 802.11b access point, which has up to 11 Mbps of bandwidth (within 10 meters), can support

The Incompatibilities of 802.11a and 802.11b

The 802.11a and 802.11b (and generally the 802.11g) standards are not interoperable because of a variety of incompatibilities, which include:

- **Modulation technology** 802.11a uses the Orthogonal Frequency Division Multiplexing (OFDM) modulation scheme and 802.11b uses the direct-sequence spread-spectrum (DSSS) modulation method. Because DSSS is more power-efficient than OFDM, 802.11a wireless devices use more power than 802.11b devices.

- **RF Frequency** 802.11b operates on the 2.4 GHz RF band (as does the 802.11g standard) and 802.11a operates on the 5 GHz band. While the 2.4 GHz band is much more crowded with many types of wireless devices, it does have a lower absorption rate and is able to penetrate walls and objects better than the 5 GHz band. The trade-off is the 5GHz is far less crowded by other devices.

- **Operating range** Because the RF spectrum of the 802.11a standard (5 GHz) has a higher absorption rate, it generally has a shorter range (around 50 meters) than the 802.11b standard (about 100 meters).

- **Data transfer rate** The 802.11a standard provides data rates up to 54 Mbps, which is about five times faster than the 11 Mbps of the 802.11b standard.

- **Coverage** An 802.11a access point is able to support more wireless nodes than an 802.11b access point because of its higher bandwidth and additional RF channels.

- **Cost** 802.11a devices are generally more costly than 802.11b devices. Because an 802.11a WLAN requires more access points, an 802.11a network is much more expensive to implement.

50 nodes that are mostly idle, as many as 25 nodes accessing e-mail and mid-sized data files, or 10 to 15 nodes that are active on the network and transmitting or receiving mid- to large-sized data files. The general rule of 20 nodes is based on the nodes transmitting a mix of traffic.

The easiest way to increase the capacity of a WLAN is to include more access points, but another way is to use different WLAN standards where additional and localized capacity is needed. Of course, you can also do both. For example, if the employee lunch room or the company's lobby is to be a hot spot, it's likely that 802.11b provides adequate capacity and compatibility for most users. However, for the engineering area, conference rooms, and areas where large file transfers demand more bandwidth and throughput, the 802.11a or 802.11g standard may better satisfy the WLAN's requirements for higher bandwidth.

Because the 802.11b and 802.11g standards are generally compatible and will interoperate to a certain extent, these two standards have been used together in a number of situations where using two standards is appropriate. Many newer user devices, such as personal digital assistants (PDAs), wireless network adapters, and even access points, include support for multiple WLAN standards. Although a few WLAN devices have support for 802.11a, 802.11b, and 802.11g, they are rare. The devices available for supporting more than one 802.11 standard generally combine either 802.11b and 802.11g or 802.11a and 802.11g, such as the USB wireless network adapter shown in Figure 8-2.

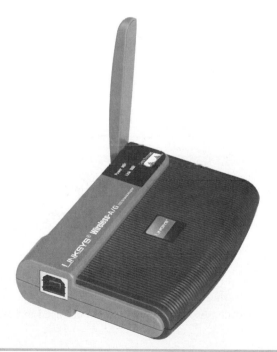

8

Figure 8-2   A dual-band wireless network adapter (Photo courtesy of Cisco Systems, Inc.)

WLAN Mode and Topology

As discussed in Chapter 2, a WLAN can be configured into two basic modes of operation and three standard topologies. WLANs operate in either ad-hoc or infrastructure modes, and they can be configured into an Independent Basic Service Set (**IBSS**), a Basic Service Set (BSS), or an Extended Service Set (ESS). The ad-hoc operational mode establishes an IBSS topology. Infrastructure mode requires either BSS or ESS for the WLAN's topology.

Ad-hoc Mode   Ad-hoc operations on a WLAN provide nodes with the capability to directly connect to each other, in a way similar to peer-to-peer operations on a wired network. Just as a wired peer-to-peer network doesn't require a central server, an *ad-hoc WLAN* doesn't require a central access point. In most corporate or large business settings, however, an ad-hoc WLAN may prove to be chaotic and most likely less secure than management wants to have in use.

Each of the wireless nodes in an ad-hoc WLAN is an IBSS. An *IBSS* can provide access to peripherals, a wired network, a modem connection, and other services, depending on the permissions granted by the IBSS's user (see Figure 8-3).

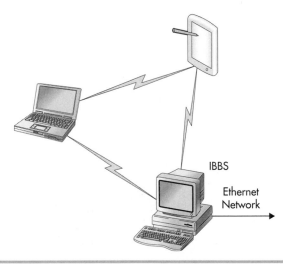

IBBS

Ethernet Network

Figure 8-3   An ad-hoc WLAN is created from two or more IBSS devices.

In some instances, an ad-hoc WLAN can be effective for a small area of the overall network, such as in a conference room, an employee break area, or a company-sponsored public hot spot. But, in most cases, ad-hoc WLANs are not used in business settings.

Infrastructure Mode   The most common mode used for larger WLANs is *infrastructure*, which requires the use of at least one access point, also called a base station, connected to a wired network infrastructure or a WAN gateway. A WLAN implemented with 20 or less wireless nodes and a single access point creates a **BSS** topology (see Figure 8-4).

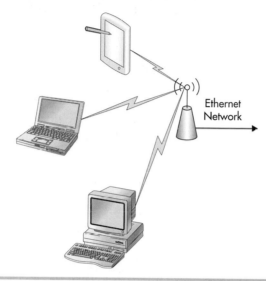

Ethernet
Network

Figure 8-4   A BSS requires the inclusion of an access point (base station).

When multiple access points must interact to access a single wired network connection, as pictured in Figure 8-5, an ESS topology is created. On larger networks that must provide coverage to an area larger than the range of the wireless devices, an **ESS** topology should be used.

Line Check 8.2

1. Define the difference between the considerations of coverage and capacity.
2. What issues must be considered when designing for coverage?
3. What issues must be considered when designing for capacity?

8

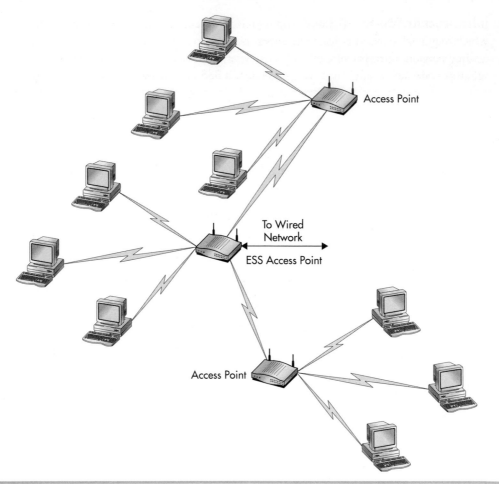

Figure 8-5   Multiple access points in a single WLAN create an ESS topology.

What Do You Think?

What performance issues might arise from mixing two or more WLAN standards within a building or area?

Existing Network Issues

Although an 802.11 WLAN may be installed as a first network in many small office or home network situations, its most common application, certainly in a business setting, is to extend an existing Ethernet or Token Ring wired network. A WLAN can quickly and inexpensively extend an existing wired network, eliminating the need to physically install cabling and terminations. In addition, a new WLAN installation can also be used to extend an existing wireless network. Both of these WLAN applications have their advantages, disadvantages, and issues, as you learn in the following sections.

NOTE

For definitions, explanations, and more information on Ethernet, Token Ring, or other networking technologies, see Appendix A.

Extending an Existing Wired Network with a WLAN

A thorough knowledge of an existing wired network to which a WLAN is to be attached is an absolute requirement for the design of the WLAN for several reasons, including:

- **Dynamic Host Configuration Protocol (DHCP) usage:** If a WLAN is being installed as an extension to or an overlay of an existing wired network, the recommendation is that the wired network's DHCP server be used for the wireless nodes as well. This provides the capability for the wireless node to take advantage of the Network Address Translation (NAT) services of the gateway router and to retain its DHCP configuration while roaming. The DHCP services on any wireless devices should be disabled. However, because many WLAN routers include DHCP capability and can act as a DHCP server for its wireless nodes, you do have the option, in a completely wireless network, of using this service for the WLAN.

- **Roaming:** For users to roam from one access point to another within a WLAN, the access points must all be located on the same IP subnet and serviced by the same router, which is typically part of the wired network.

- **Throughput:** Use the peak and nonpeak throughput and capacity statistics of the existing network to determine if the WLAN may cause a capacity issue for the existing wired nodes on the same bandwidth domain. The wired network may require some modifications to accommodate the WLAN interface.

8

Extending an Existing Wireless Network

The issues to consider when extending an existing WLAN with additional WLAN devices are essentially the same issues to consider when you design a new WLAN. When planning a wireless extension to a WLAN, consider these issues:

- **Coverage** Adding a single node to a WLAN typically does not impact the coverage of the existing network. However, adding multiple devices and an additional access point can impact the coverage scheme of the entire network. In this case, the coverage of the network must be reevaluated.

● **Capacity** Because WLAN bandwidth is shared bandwidth, adding additional nodes can impact the nodes on the existing network. It may be necessary to implement additional access points to maintain the capacity expectations of the overall network.

● **Compatibility** As previously discussed, not all 802.11 standards are compatible within the same WLAN. If a different WLAN standard is to be used for the extension, ensure that you have no interference issues for existing nodes.

● **Topology** Adding additional nodes to an existing WLAN may require adding one or more access points to the network, which could force the network's topology to move from a BSS to an ESS.

● **Expandability** Never assume the current expansion of a WLAN is the last expansion that will be made to it. Future expandability of the WLAN depends on the choices made for the WLAN standard and wireless devices, as well as the mode and topology of the network.

If additional access points must be installed, the design issues of overlap, redundancy, and roaming must also be considered. You must carefully consider the topology of the WLAN and whether the addition of one or more access points requires the insertion of an ESS topology to provide bridging between two or more access points or a change in the WLAN standard used on all or part of the network.

Another method that can be used to extend an existing network, especially one that has the available capacity to support additional wireless nodes, is the use of a wireless repeater. A wireless repeater works just like a repeater on a wired network to regenerate the signal to extend its range. As a part of a WLAN, a *wireless repeater* receives the transmitted signals on the network and retransmits them, as they are—interference and all—so nodes located beyond the effective range of the access point are able to communicate on the network.

 Line Check 8.3

1. Differentiate between the capacity and the coverage of a WLAN.

2. Explain the importance of investigating all existing wired and wireless networks when you plan the installation of a new WLAN.

What Do You Think?

Why are the issues listed in the section "Extending an Existing Wireless Network" vitally important to the effectiveness of a WLAN in the future?

Performing a Site Survey

A site survey can be one of the most important steps in the preparation, planning, and installation of a new WLAN, especially in larger networks and facilities. The primary purpose of a **site survey** is to ensure that all nodes and users are able to connect to the WLAN, and that they have sufficient signal strength and bandwidth for their network applications, regardless of whether they are stationary or mobile.

The importance and need to perform a site survey depends on the complexity of the WLAN to be installed. The complexity of the WLAN also helps to determine how extensive the site survey should be. If a WLAN is to be installed in a single room, a small two- or three-room office, or a typical home, it is likely that a single access point would provide all the coverage and capacity needed. So, conducting a site survey in these situations may be more than is needed and would be an intuitive exercise. However, in a multiple-floor, multiple-department WLAN for a corporate office or a similarly complex WLAN situation, a site survey is an absolute requirement to ensure the resulting WLAN meets the user's and the company's requirements.

In essence, a WLAN site survey is a preliminary test of a proposed WLAN site. The site survey tests an area to determine how RF signals will perform in its environment and the amount of RF interference (**RFI**) or electromagnetic interference (**EMI**) present. The reasoning behind why you would conduct a site survey is that, regardless of the type of antennas in use, radio waves don't always travel the same distance in every direction. Walls, doors, people, and several other types of obstacles (see the previous Table 8-1) can cause the radiation pattern of radio waves to become irregular and even unpredictable, a condition called *multipathing*. So, to fully understand how radio waves will behave in a certain area, a site survey should be performed, certainly before the actual installation of a WLAN proceeds.

Conducting the Site Tests

By assessing the signal strength of an access point in a particular area, you are better able to determine the number and placement of the access points required to meet the design objectives of the WLAN. Using a variety of antenna types and sizes, and different combinations of access point configurations, you should be able to identify the right mix of components and configurations required to provide the proper coverage and capacity needs for a proposed WLAN.

In general, WLAN industry experts agree that the following steps should be included in a WLAN site survey:

- Gather as much documentation as possible, including facility diagrams, drawings, blueprints, wiring plans, and information that identifies the locations of computer systems, existing network infrastructure, power outlets, and where any potential sources of interference, such as metal firebreaks, walls, and doors, are located.

8

- Perform a walk-through and visual inspection of the area in which the WLAN will be installed. Note any building features that may cause performance problems on the network.

- Use a device specifically designed for site surveys or special software in a portable PC, which can be used to determine the radio coverage and interference patterns in all areas to be included in the WLAN (see the section "Site Survey Tools" for more information).

- Based on the results of the preceding step, you should be able to identify the best locations for and the positioning of the WLAN's access points and antennas.

- Identify the areas of the WLAN where additional antennas, access points, or repeaters may be needed to overcome interference, signal loss, or range problems.

- Locate the available power sources (outlets) and determine if any existing (or planned) electrical systems are likely to generate interference. You also need to determine if backup power, such as an uninterruptible power supply (UPS), may be required to safeguard against power loss or degradation (highly recommended).

- After determining the potential locations for the access points, install an access point in each location and retest the area using the site survey device or software previously used in the process. Test from the location of each of the user stations to be included in the network, noting the data transfer rate, bandwidth, and signal strength of each location. If a location is not supported adequately, adjustments may be needed in the placement of the access point or by adding an antenna or repeater.

- Absolutely document every test, finding, and even your suspicions or assumptions during the site survey. If problems arise after the network is installed, you can refer to your notes to see if any warning signs or other red flags occurred that may have forewarned of a potential problem and, knowing the source of the issue, you can easily correct it.

Site Survey Tools

The equipment required to carry out a site survey can be as simple as a single access point and a portable PC with a wireless network adapter or as complex as a full-scale site survey kit costing thousands of dollars. But, for the most part, the equipment needed to perform an indoor site survey in most facilities includes:

- **Access point:** To survey an area for a single BSS, a single access point is needed. However, if the area is larger or the WLAN topology requires an ESS, more than one access point will be needed.

- **Antenna:** One or more types of indoor antennas may be required if the distance requirements exceed the range of the bandwidth required by the network. A variety of antenna cables, connectors, and mounts may also be needed. Double-faced tape can work well in situations where an antenna may need to be placed where no mountable surface exists.

- **Network adapter:** Either an internal-mount PC Card-type wireless NIC or an external network adapter is needed for the portable PC to be used to test and model the wireless configuration of the WLAN.

- **Paper:** Every reading, measurement, finding, and decision made during the site survey should be documented on copies of a floor plan, blueprints, or on plain paper for use during the final design and planning phases of the installation project.

- **Portable (notebook, handheld, or laptop) PC:** The portable PC has two particular uses in a site survey: (1) to test connectivity between itself and the wireless access point and (2) to execute the site survey utility software, if used. This can provide detailed planning information, such as signal, channel, and bandwidth coverage and capacity, as well as signal strength to different parts of the WLAN's coverage area.

In addition to the previous, other specialized devices or tools that can be used as a part of a site survey are:

- **Battery pack and AC/DC converter:** In situations where power outlets may be unavailable in every possible access point location, a battery pack and power converter can be used to provide AC power to the access point for testing and modeling purposes.

- **Network or protocol analyzer (sniffer):** This device can be used to receive and analyze packets being transmitted by a nearby network, which is transmitting its signal into the area being considered for another WLAN. A *protocol analyzer* is able to determine the channels being used and the distance from the transmitter, the bandwidth, and the signal strength. This information can help you to determine if the overlap is likely to provide interference.

- **Site survey software:** Several software packages are available to perform both the RF environmental testing and the data analysis required in a site survey. The previous Figure 8-2 shows one version of site survey software that can be loaded on to a handheld device or a portable PC equipped with a radio network adapter. Figure 8-6 shows an example of the display from one of the many site survey software packages available, this one from AirMagnet, Inc. Many wireless system manufacturers, such as Cisco Systems (**www.cisco.com**), Symbol Technologies, Inc. (**www.symbol.com**), and others provide site survey software at no charge when you purchase their equipment. (See the section "Site Survey Software" for more information.)

- **Site survey devices:** Several types of special-purpose site survey devices are also available, such as the one shown in Figure 8-7. These handheld and tabletop devices can provide better portability when you are surveying a large area.

8

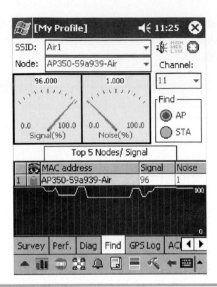

Figure 8-6 A screenshot of the AirMagnet Surveyor site survey software (Image courtesy of AirMagnet, Inc.)

Figure 8-7 A handheld special-purpose site survey device (Photo courtesy of Berkeley Varitronics Systems, Inc.)

● **Spectrum analyzer:** Although more commonly used for troubleshooting interference issues, a *spectrum analyzer* can be either a dedicated piece of hardware or a specialized software program running on a computer. An *RF spectrum analyzer* is a specially designed RF receiver that is able to receive a wide range of signals, but usually within a user-defined range. An RF spectrum analyzer also displays a line pattern in a logarithmic scale on a built-in oscilloscope or, in the case of spectrum-analysis software running on a PC, on the PC's monitor. A spectrum analyzer, like the one shown in Figure 8-8, is used to identify and isolate sources of low-power narrowband interference.

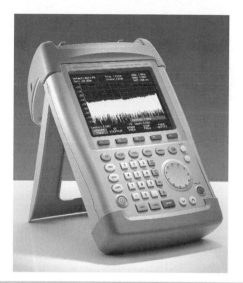

Figure 8-8   A handheld WLAN spectrum analyzer (Photo courtesy of Rohde & Schwarz GmbH & Co. KG)

Line Check 8.4

1. Explain the primary purpose for conducting a site survey.
2. List the major activities that should be included in a site survey.
3. What equipment should be used for conducting a site survey?

What Do You Think?

What is the risk a WLAN designer runs by not performing a site survey?

8

WLAN Modeling and Testing

During a site survey, the planned location for each WLAN access point, antennas, and other devices, as appropriate, should be modeled to determine how well each location supports its objective and if some building features or interference sources may be present that weren't apparent during the planning of the WLAN.

NOTE

What if an NIC and an access point will not communicate, or the site survey software continues to indicate that the NIC cannot associate with a wireless access point, or a network signal cannot be found? Before panicking, check to ensure that both devices are using the same 802.11x standard.

Before the actual installation begins, each of the identified WLAN locations should be tested using an access point and a wireless-enabled computer (a portable PC is best for this activity). Ultimately, the objective of the design and the installation is to create a wireless environment that provides overlapping coverage for every wireless device on the network. Figure 8-9 illustrates this objective.

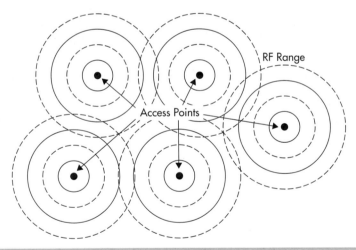

Figure 8-9 Overlapping the RF ranges of wireless access points in a WLAN ensures coverage throughout an area.

Modeling a wireless network as a part of a site survey provides a number of benefits, such as coverage, range, and, perhaps, even more important, cost savings by minimizing the number of access points required.

Range and Coverage Modeling

Using a floor plan layout diagram, the PC should be placed at each location at which a wireless station (computer, printer, and so forth) is either currently or will be located in the area. Nearly all wireless NICs include software to monitor the signal strength (as well as the configuration of the link) received by the PC. Figure 8-10 shows an example of the display screen produced by the software included with Linksys NICs. Because this software displays the strength of the signal being received by the network adapter or NIC, it can be used to gauge the quality of the planned location of the access point.

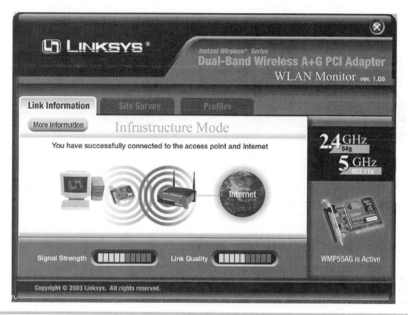

Figure 8-10   Most wireless NICs are shipped with monitoring and configuration software.

NOTE

Also important is to test how far an access point's signal extends outside a building. Knowing whether or not someone with a network traffic sniffer outside the building, for instance, in the parking lot, can receive the WLAN's signals is a good idea.

Being able to determine the efficiency and effectiveness of each access point location prior to making any final installations is far better than the alternative, just in case reality doesn't perform at the level hoped for in the design. This is especially true if the access points are to be placed on custom shelving, above a false ceiling, or mounted to a wall.

Also important is that the area in which the WLAN is to be installed has all its major features already installed. The WLAN may work great in an empty room, but after all the 5-foot tall paneling, metal desks, copy machines, cordless phones, and other office accoutrements are in place, the signal strength may not be the same as before the space was obstructed.

Bandwidth Modeling

The bandwidth of a WLAN is shared bandwidth and the number of stations attempting to share the bandwidth can affect the performance, especially in terms of throughput. In areas where a relatively large number of stations will exist, more than one access point may be needed to support the bandwidth demand.

Just how many access points are needed to support a certain number or range of wireless stations is dependent on the 802.11x standard in use, whether the network is indoor or outdoor, and how bursty the network access is by users. Depending on the demand from the stations, the number of stations an access point can support can vary greatly. Splitting the stations and access points to different channels is one way to control which stations are sharing bandwidth, but often, this can be a trial-and-error proposition.

To run a bandwidth test on a new wireless network requires an increasing number of stations be linked to one or more access points in a particular area until the signal strength of the shared signal begins to fall below acceptable levels.

Pilot Network Modeling

A *pilot network*, a small subset of an entire planned network, in one or more portions of the area to be networked, can be an effective way to demonstrate the working elements of the wireless network architecture and environment to achieve user acceptance. As the site survey testing explained previously in this section, a pilot network allows the organization, including management and other network users and decision-makers, to observe the network's functionality in a "live" environment.

Site Survey Software

Several manufacturers offer site survey software that establishes a two-way data network using stationary and mobile devices at various points within the proposed radio coverage area. This software then provides statistics and advisory information regarding coverage and capacity of the WLAN.

Site survey software can provide measurements of several critical WLAN criteria either in display or printed report form. The more common parameters covered by site survey software are:

- **Access point criteria:** If more than one access point is included in the site survey (which is recommended for large areas likely to require more than one access point), site survey software displays information to indicate which access points provide coverage to different locations in the area, which access point provides the strongest signal, and if signal overlap exists.

- **Receive signal strength indicator (RSSI):** This measurement indicates which access point is providing the strongest signal on each channel at each location.

- **Signal strength:** This measurement indicates the strength of the signals from each access point, which access point has the strongest signal, and, in some cases, it provides a ranking of the signal strengths for all the access points available to a particular location. On many site-survey programs, a map of the area is created to indicate the overall signal strength detected. As shown in Figure 8-11, different colors are used to indicate the relative signal strength.

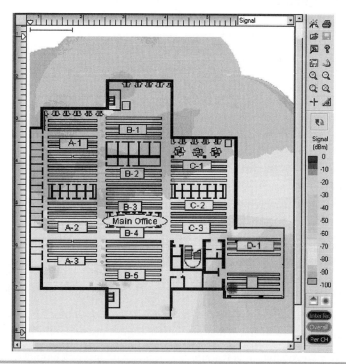

Figure 8-11 The signal strength display of the AirMagnet Surveyor site survey software (Image courtesy of AirMagnet, Inc.)

- **Signal-to-noise ratio (SNR):** This measurement indicates the amount of interference to a particular location. If multiple access points are active, the access point with the strongest signal is assumed as the associated BSS and all others as interference.

𝓠 Line Check 8.5

1. Why is it important to verify a WLAN design by modeling the network layout?

2. Explain the difference between a bandwidth model and a pilot network model.

Chapter 8 Review

Chapter Summary

WLAN Design Considerations

- IEEE 802.11 WLANs have a number of limitations and performance issues that must be considered during the planning and design phases of a WLAN installation project, including RF issues, site qualification, and capacity and coverage.

- The 2.4 GHz RF band can be affected by competing devices, distance, metal boxes, and stationary objects.

- Site qualification is a relatively simple process that addresses the scope and size of the network to be installed. Site qualification also addresses the capability for the site to support the bandwidth requirements and the number of nodes to be deployed.

- The general rule used to plan a WLAN layout is 20 concurrent (active) users per wireless access point.

- The design of a WLAN can be a trade-off between capacity and coverage.

- A typical 802.11b WLAN access point has an RF range of about 100 meters.

- To maximize the coverage of the access point, it should be placed in the center of an area or, at a minimum, in a location that provides the most coverage for the area it services.

- One planning consideration is the number of nonoverlapping channels available on 802.11 standards. IEEE 802.11b and 802.11g provide three nonoverlapping channels and 802.11a standard provides for eight nonoverlapping channels.

- An 802.11b access point can support 50 nodes that are mostly idle, as many as 25 nodes accessing e-mail and mid-sized data files, or 10 to 15 active nodes transmitting or receiving mid- to large-sized data files.

- An 802.11 WLAN is commonly installed as a first network in many small office or home network situations, but its most common application is to extend an existing Ethernet or Token Ring wired network.

- A thorough knowledge of an existing network is an absolute requirement for the design of the WLAN for several reasons, including DHCP usage, roaming, and throughput.

Perform a Site Survey

- Before installation begins, each WLAN location should be tested in an area that contains, as close as possible, all the equipment, furniture, and other items it will have while operating.

- A pilot network can be an effective way to verify the working elements of a wireless network architecture and its operating environment for user acceptance.

- A WLAN has shared bandwidth that can affect overall performance. Where a relatively large number of stations are to be located, more access points may be needed to provide sufficient bandwidth.

- Balancing the number of nodes per access point is another way to maximize the available bandwidth to any one station.

- To test or model a WLAN supporting ad-hoc mode, move a wireless-capable PC in and out of the range of the access points.

Key Terms

Capacity *(250)*
Coverage *(250)*
BSS *(255)*
EMI *(259)*
ESS *(255)*
IBSS *(254)*
Metal box *(248)*
RFI *(259)*
RSSI *(269)*
Site survey *(259)*
SNR *(267)*

Key Term Quiz

Use the terms from the Key Terms list to complete the following sentences. Don't use the same term more than once. Not all terms will be used.

1. _____ is the type of interference picked up by an antenna from other nearby transmitters.

2. Any large metallic object in the vicinity of a RF transmitter is referred to as an _____.

3. The _____ of a WLAN refers to its capability to support a certain number of nodes.

4. The type of interference commonly emitted from electrical motors is _____.

5. When a WLAN is configured into ad-hoc mode, each node is referred to as a(n) _____.

6. The process used to verify the capability for a facility or space to support a WLAN is an _____.

7. The distance, bandwidth, and range of a wireless access point is considered as a part of its _____.

8. A WLAN that includes only a single access point is in the _____ topology.

9. _____ is used to measure which of the multiple access points is providing the strongest signal on each channel at each location.

10. _____ indicates the amount of interference present in a particular location.

Multiple Choice Quiz

1. Which of the following is a type of wireless network interference that can originate from a nearby radio wave transmitter?

   A. Crosstalk

   B. EMI

   C. SNR

   D. RFI

2. What is the primary purpose for conducting a site survey?

   A. To perform acceptance testing on a new WLAN installation.

   B. To ensure that a WLAN design provides sufficient signal strength and bandwidth to planned stationary or mobile nodes.

   C. To qualify a particular part of the interior or exterior of a facility as a possible site for a WLAN.

   D. To verify an existing WLAN meets the requirements for connecting to a WWAN.

3. Which of the following can cause interference in an RF transmission?

   A. Metal box

   B. Humans

   C. Walls, floors, ceilings

D. Mirrors

E. Competing RF devices

F. All of the above

4. When planning a WLAN, what characteristic addresses the number of nodes supported by each access point and the bandwidth of the WLAN?

A. Capacity

B. Coverage

C. Depth

D. Topology

5. When planning a WLAN, what characteristic addresses the range and signal strength of the transmitted signal of the WLAN?

A. Capacity

B. Coverage

C. Depth

D. Topology

6. What term is used to designate the nodes in an ad-hoc network?

A. Extended Service Set

B. Basic Service Set

C. Independent Basic Service Set

D. Extended Basic Service Set

7. What type of interference is emitted by nearby electrical motors, appliances, or faulty connections?

A. Crosstalk

B. EMI

C. SNR

D. RFI

8. What is the WLAN topology in use on a network with more than one access point?

A. Extended Service Set

B. Basic Service Set

C. Independent Basic Service Set

D. Extended Basic Service Set

9. What is the receive signal strength indicator used to measure?

A. The weakest signal on any channel within the range of an access point.

B. The strongest signal on a particular channel at a specific location.

C. The channel that has the least signal-to-noise ratio.

D. The SSID of the access point with the strongest signal.

10. What is the measurement used to indicate the amount of interference to a particular location?

A. Crosstalk

B. EMI

C. SNR

D. RFI

Lab Projects

1. Install and configure a wireless access point, connecting it to either an existing wireline or wireless network. Your instructor will provide you with the required configuration settings.

2. Configure a wireless network adapter in a portable PC. Move the PC around within and out of the range of a wireless access point or router. Were you able to maintain the connection while moving the PC? What may have caused you to lose the signal at times?

Case Problems

1. In early 2004, the city of Spokane, Washington, installed a network of 802.11b wireless switches and routers to provide wireless network service to its downtown area, covering an area of over 16 square blocks. This system allows anyone with a PC configured for 802.11b or 802.11g wireless networking to access the public network from anywhere in the downtown area. Create a diagram that shows the placement of the wireless devices required to create a similar system in the downtown area of your town or city, or a nearby city.

2. If you were to implement a wireless network design in your school or business, would you choose to implement an infrastructure or an ad-hoc wireless topology, or a combination of the two? In what areas would you implement each and why?

Advanced Lab Project

The ability to perform a complete site survey and understand its results and their impact on the overall design of a WLAN is an essential skill for a wireless networking professional. In this lab, you use site survey software to perform a site survey on your wireless lab, school, or a local business with or looking to install a wireless network.

If site survey software is unavailable, download a demonstration version of a site survey software package from one of the following sites:

- AiroPeek—WildPackets, Inc.: **http://www.wildpackets.com/support/downloads**

- Hive—Berkeley Varitronics Systems, Inc.: **www.bvsystems.com/Products/Software/Hive/hive.htm**

- VisiWave—AZO Technologies, Inc.: **www.visiwave.com**

Install the site survey software on a portable PC and, following the steps listed in this chapter, perform a site survey for the following situations:

- A new WLAN installation, where no other WLANs exist

- An existing WLAN installation

- A new WLAN installation, where an existing WLAN exists (the existing WLAN will not be connected to the new network)

8

REVIEW

Chapter 9

WLAN Configuration and Installation

In too many wireless local area network (WLAN) installations, there is a tendency to "throw and go," meaning the devices are placed in a way that allows the network to "work," yet fairly haphazardly. While this approach can and often does work, eventually, link and range problems can begin appearing, especially if the network begins to grow in size.

To ensure that a new WLAN operates properly, giving its users the bandwidth and connectivity they need, a prescribed set of planning and testing steps should be followed. This chapter focuses on the steps you should use, the information you should know, and the activities you should perform to plan, configure, and install a WLAN successfully.

WLAN Planning

A WLAN is created when at least two radio-equipped devices establish a communications link for the purpose of sharing data, information, or resources. A WLAN can be created completely from mobile devices, completely from stationary devices, or from some combination of the two types of devices. A WLAN can be standalone without Internet access, used only for Internet access, or to interface or extend an existing wired network, including Internet access.

Regardless of its structure, purpose, or application, a WLAN network has several operating characteristics common to every use and purpose, including its setup, modes, power consumption settings, and devices.

NOTE

Throughout this book, we refer to computers and PCs interchangeably. In today's networked environment, the vast majority of computers being connected to networks are personal computers (PCs). So, if you read "computers," this also means "PCs." And, if you read "PCs," this also means "computers." Also, remember, when a PC or computer is attached to a network, it becomes a node, a client, or, perhaps, even a server.

WLAN Configurations

The first issue for consideration is the operating configuration of the WLAN. Making the right choice is basic to the successful installation and operation of the WLAN. Each of the two configurations that can be implemented has advantages and disadvantages, but the needs of the organization and its users should be the overriding factor in making your choice.

The two operating configurations that can be used in a WLAN are

- Infrastructure
- Ad-hoc

Each of the WLAN connection modes, their structure, and differences are discussed in the sections that follow.

CROSS-REFERENCE

Chapter 2 includes additional information about the infrastructure and ad-hoc connection modes of WLANs.

Infrastructure WLANs

In an office setting, the most common configuration used for WLANs is infrastructure. In this configuration, the devices in the WLAN must associate with and connect through a wireless access point. However, depending on the number of access points included in the WLAN, the network can take one of two configurations:

- **Basic Service Set (BSS):** A WLAN that includes only one access point is configured as a BSS. The access point provides point-to-point wireless bridging between the wireless devices associated with it and also serves as a gateway to either a wired network or WAN (meaning Internet) services, or both. Figure 9-1 illustrates a WLAN configured as a BSS.

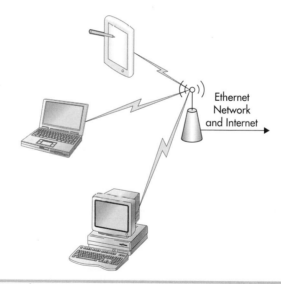

Figure 9-1   A WLAN configured as a BSS, which is built around a single access point

- **Extended Service Set (ESS):** If a WLAN is large enough to require two or more access points, with at least one of the access points serving as a gateway to a wired network, WAN services, or both, the WLAN is configured as an ESS. An *ESS* is a WLAN that operates with two or more access points, which means it combines two or more BSS WLANs, as illustrated in Figure 9-2.

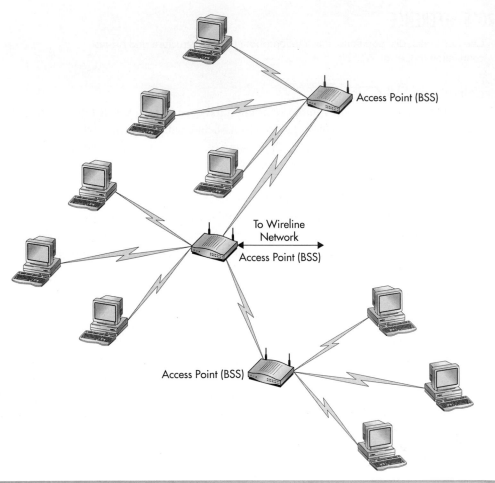

Figure 9-2 An ESS includes multiple access points and addressable nodes.

Ad-hoc WLANs

An **ad-hoc** wireless network, which is also commonly referred to as a peer-to-peer or just peer network, is created between wireless devices without the use of a centralizing device, such as an access point. An ad-hoc WLAN connects its wireless devices directly to and through one another. A common misconception is that ad-hoc networks are created only from roaming stations and, while this can be essentially true, not all "roaming" stations roam. A small office/home office (SOHO) WLAN, which is made up of only stationary desktop PCs, can

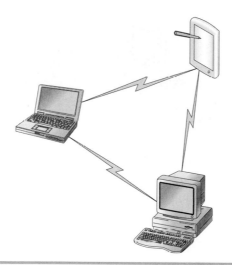

Figure 9-3   Wireless devices forming a WLAN using ad-hoc mode links

also be set up completely with an ad-hoc connection mode. Figure 9-3 illustrates how wireless nodes use an ad-hoc link to form a WLAN.

To connect to a WLAN, the radio frequency (RF) transceiver in a PC's wireless network interface card (NIC) or network adapter must be configured to communicate in ad-hoc mode. When an ad-hoc device establishes an association with another ad-hoc device, an Independent Basic Service Set (**IBSS**) is formed. What binds ad-hoc devices into an IBSS is the use of a Common Service Set Identifier (SSID).

The devices in an *IBSS* provide services to one another at varying levels. The amount of service one ad-hoc device can provide to another depends on the applications, services, and associations of the devices. Within an IBSS, one or more of the ad-hoc devices, commonly a stationary PC, may be associated with an access point that is configured to ad-hoc mode. In this situation, roaming devices beyond the range of the access point can gain access to the resources and services of an infrastructure WLAN or a wired network. Not all IBSS WLANs connect to an access point. In fact, the general lack of an access point is what defines the IBSS. Figure 9-4 illustrates an IBSS arrangement.

NOTE

Wireless devices cannot be configured to both BSS and IBSS modes at the same time.

9

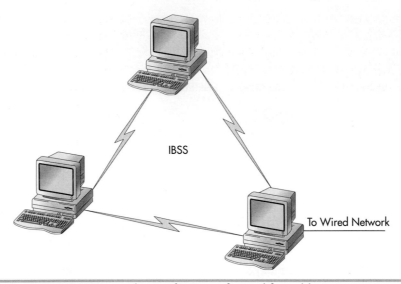

Figure 9-4   An IBSS WLAN is made up of PCs configured for ad-hoc connections.

Line Check 9.1

1. Describe the configuration and operation of an infrastructure WLAN.

2. Describe the configuration and operation of an ad-hoc WLAN.

3. How does an IBSS differ from a BSS?

What Do You Think?

Which of the WLAN configurations described in this section would provide the best performance and security? Why?

SSID, Beacons, and Association

Nearly all access points are assigned default Service Set Identifiers (**SSIDs**) by their manufacturers, which are used as low-level pass-codes by wireless devices wishing to associate with a particular access point. For example, Cisco Systems (including Linksys) assigns the default SSID "tsunami" to its systems and NetGear uses "wireless" as its default SSID. When configuring a WLAN, you can use the default SSID, but it helps to provide somewhat higher security to change the SSID to a private code word or letter/number combination. Although the role of the SSID in a security scheme can be highly overstated, a unique and secret code can help to prevent some, but not necessarily all, unauthorized access.

NOTE

The SSID is also referred to as the NetID and the ESSID by some manufacturers.

CROSS-REFERENCE

The role of the SSID in a WLAN security scheme is discussed in Chapter 11.

The SSID and Device Association

Before one wireless node can communicate with another, the two stations must first create an association, which is a discovery, recognition, request, and acceptance process between the stations.

An access point broadcasts what is called a beacon frame periodically to help wireless nodes within its range locate and identify it as a BSS. A *beacon frame* contains a variety of information a wireless node can either use immediately or at some point in the future to associate with the access point and transmit on the wireless medium. The beacon frame includes the fields shown in Figure 9-5 and described in Table 9-1.

Time Stamp	Beacon Interval	Cap. Data	SSID	Rates	FH Set	DS Set	CF Set	IBSS Set	TIM
64 bits	16 bits	16 bits	32 bits	64 bits	56 bits	24 bits	64 bits	32 bits	256 bits

Figure 9-5   The fields included in a BSS beacon frame

As indicated in Table 9-1, the SSID can be suppressed on many access point models. Suppressing the SSID in the beacon frame is typically done as a security measure, although the amount of security this provides is limited. The SSID is included in the probe and management frames that are exchanged as part of the sequence of frames used to establish an association between a BSS/ESS and a wireless node. When the SSID is not broadcast in the beacon frame, which is called *stealth mode*, the wireless nodes must be manually configured with the WLAN SSID.

9

Field	Contents
Timestamp	Value of access point's synchronization timer
Beacon interval	Number of 1024 microsecond units between beacon transmissions
Capability	Facilities and settings required of stations to gain association
SSID	BSS keyword used for association. Optional—can be suppressed on many access point models
Rates	The transmission speeds supported
PHY parameters	Frequency hopping (FH), direct sequence (DS), and contention free (CF) parameter sets
IBSS	Optional—used only by IBSS to provide information on the IBSS transmitting the beacon
TIM (Traffic Indication Map)	Sent when a node in power-saver mode has messages buffered on a BSS

Table 9-1 Beacon Frame Fields

To establish an association, a wireless node begins the process by broadcasting a probe request, looking for responses from any BSS within range. The probe request may contain a particular SSID or it can be structured to locate any WLAN within range. The probe request has essentially two fields: the SSID and a list of the node's supported rates. In a BSS/ESS WLAN, the BSS/ESS responds with a probe response, but in an IBSS WLAN, the last station to transmit a beacon frame responds with a probe response. The contents of a probe response frame are much like those of a beacon frame, except the probe response doesn't include the optional delivery traffic indication map (**DTIM**) data and the probe response is only broadcast to the medium in response to a probe request. A DTIM is a special type of traffic indication map (TIM) that is included in a beacon frame that is used to inform any wireless stations on a BSS that are in power-save mode just where on the BSS their messages are being buffered. However, the probe response frame, which includes its SSID, is transmitted in clear text, regardless of what encryption method is in use. Figure 9-6 illustrates the sequence of frames transmitted between a node and a BSS during the association process. The sequence goes like this:

1. The wireless node broadcasts a probe request frame.

2. The access point (BSS) broadcasts a probe response frame.

3. With the information from the probe response frame, the wireless node transmits an authentication request frame and waits for an acknowledgment.

4. The wireless node transmits an association request frame, seeking to be added to the WLAN.

5. The BSS responds with an association response frame.

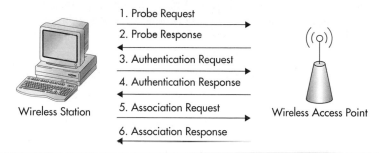

Figure 9-6 The sequence of frames transmitted between a node and an access point during the association process

WLAN Management Frames

WLANs use several types of management and control frame types. The following are the common WLAN frame types:

- **Management frames:**

  - **Association:** This series of frames is used to establish and manage a formal communications link between a wireless node and an access point.

    - **Association request frame:** The series begins when a wireless node transmits an association request frame asking the access point to synchronize with the node's NIC. The *request frame* contains information about the node's NIC or network adapter, which the access point analyzes for acceptance. If the NIC is accepted for association, the access point allocates its resources appropriately and creates an association identity for the node.

    - **Association response frame:** After an access point accepts and analyzes an association request frame, it sends an association response frame indicating whether the association request was accepted or rejected. If the BSS accepts the request, it responds with association information, including an association ID and the supported data rates.

    - **Disassociation frame:** When a wireless station wants to terminate an association with an access point, it sends a disassociation frame. This can be done when a user wants to suspend the communications session or the station is shut down using its operating system's shutdown procedure. The access point is able to release any resource allocations assigned to the station.

9

- **Reassociation request frame:** If a wireless station loses its connection with an access point, it immediately transmits a reassociation request frame. Depending on how long the station is disconnected or if its reassociation request is rejected, it may need to restart the association process.

- **Reassociation response frame:** A reassociation response frame containing either an acceptance or a rejection is sent to the node requesting reassociation. If accepted, the access point requests and forwards any data frames remaining on the node's previous access point intended for that node.

- **Authentication frames:** In the authentication process, an access point accepts or rejects the Layer 2 identity of a wireless node's NIC or network adapter.

  - **Authentication frame:** The authentication process begins with a wireless node sending an authentication request frame to an access point, which contains its identity. If open system authentication (OSA) is in use (*OSA* is generally the default method for most systems), the node transmits an authentication frame to which the access point responds with an authentication frame indicating its decision to accept or deny authentication. If optional shared-key authentication (OSKA) is in use, the node first sends an authentication frame and the access point responds with an authentication challenge frame. The node responds to the challenge frame with an encrypted version of the challenge data and the access point responds with either an acceptance or rejection.

  - **Deauthentication frame:** A *deauthentication frame* is sent by one wireless node to another when it wants to terminate a secure communications session.

- **Beacon frame:** A WLAN BSS broadcasts a *beacon frame* periodically to announce its presence and to share information about its communications link and medium.

- **Probe frames:**

  - **Probe request frame:** A wireless node sends a probe request frame when it wants to get the information it needs to establish an association with an access point or IBSS. Typically, a wireless node broadcasts a probe request frame during startup to see which, if any, access points are within its range.

  - **Probe response frame:** An access point or IBSS station responds to a probe request frame with a probe response frame that contains the information required to establish an association.

- **Control frames:**

  - **Request to Send (RTS) frame:** RTS/CTS (Clear to Send) communications is an optional transmission control method for WLANs used to reduce the number of frame collisions on the medium when one or more hidden nodes are associated with the same access point. A node wanting to transmit sends an RTS frame to its base station before sending a data frame.

- **Clear to Send (CTS) frame:** After receiving an RTS frame, a wireless node or base station responds with a CTS frame, which indicates it is ready to receive a data frame from the sending station.

- **Acknowledgement (ACK) frame:** During a CTS/RTS communications session, an ACK frame is transmitted to indicate that no errors were detected in the frame last received by the receiving station. If errors are found in a transmission, the frame timers are allowed to default, which causes the frame to be retransmitted.

Wireless Roaming

A WLAN device configured for ad-hoc mode is able to move around the network and connect to other ad-hoc devices. This allows the device to connect to the network from anywhere it is within range of another device. Two general types of roaming are used in wireless mobile networking: seamless and nomadic.

Seamless roaming is more commonly associated with cellular telephones and other mobile radio devices. In *seamless roaming*, a cell phone moves between cells (antennas) and disconnects from one cell to establish a connection to the next cell in an overlapping manner to prevent a loss of service connectivity.

WLAN devices use nomadic roaming. In *nomadic roaming*, as ad-hoc WLAN devices move through the range of two or more access points or other wireless radio devices, the roaming device seeks to associate itself with the access point with the strongest signal on an available channel. Figure 9-7 shows a simplistic view of how nomadic roaming works in a WLAN. As the wireless device moves through the range of each access point, it seeks out an available channel on which to initiate an association request with that access point.

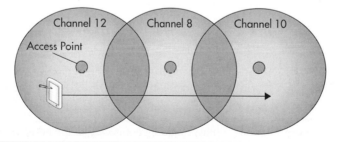

Figure 9-7   WLAN devices roam between wireless access points seeking an open channel on which to associate.

9

When multiple access points are placed in relatively close proximity to support roaming within an ESS WLAN, each access point should be configured to a separate channel. The channel on which an access point communicates is part of its configuration. Any wireless NICs or network adapters that come into its range automatically adjust their transceiver to the frequency and channel of the strongest signal (access point) it detects.

While roaming (see the next section), the wireless NIC scans for signals from access points and seeks to associate itself with the access point with the strongest signal. This is why when access points are within range of each other, their channels should be set to minimize the amount of frequency overlap as much as possible.

In the U.S. and Canada, Wi-Fi (802.11b) defines 12 available frequency channels that can be assigned to access point devices, but because of the nature of 802.11 transmissions, only three frequency channels (Channels 1, 6, and 11) are effectively usable because the frequencies used on these channels don't overlap. Each 802.11b channel represents a center frequency that has only 5 MHz of separation from the next frequency (see Figure 9-8). When you consider that the 802.11b signal requires 30 MHz of frequency bandwidth, each channel overlaps those above or below it, which results in only three channels being available for assignment.

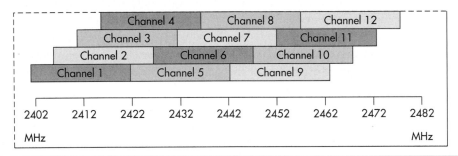

Figure 9-8 The 802.11b frequency channels defined for the U.S. and Canada

CROSS-REFERENCE

For more information on 802.11 channels and their characteristics, see Chapter 4.

The success in the layout of a WLAN that supports roaming is in the placement and channel assignments of the access points. However, other issues also impact the effectiveness of a roaming environment. For example, let's say a salesperson needs to move her tablet PC from her office into a conference room, while remaining connected to the network. If she doesn't need to be actively executing an application while roaming from one location to the next, the node will transmit a reassociation request to the new access point. But what if she needs to be actively executing an application while moving from her office to the conference room?

A number of factors can have an impact on how well a moving connection can remain linked to a WLAN, but the primary factors are as follows:

- WLAN roaming

- The roaming configuration of the WLAN

- The duration of the movement

The following sections discuss each of these issues in turn.

WLAN Roaming   Unlike cellular telephones, WLAN roaming operates in a "break before make" sequence. This means that before a roaming WLAN device establishes a link with a new access point, it breaks its link to its current access point. The downside to this method is the possible loss of incoming data in the short period of downtime between the break and the make. For those applications that transmit using Transmission Control Protocol (TCP), data loss is less of a problem because TCP includes mechanisms to prevent data loss. TCP requests a retransmission of any packet lost during the switchover from one access point to the next. For those applications that use the connectionless User Datagram Protocol (UDP), such as Voice over IP (VoIP) and streaming media, retransmission is not an option and any packets lost during roaming are simply dropped.

WLAN Roaming Configuration   Recall that an Extended Service Set (ESS) is a grouping of two or more BSSs, which are typically connected to a wired network. In many respects, an *ESS,* which is a roaming domain, is much like a wired network's broadcast domain or a network subnet on which all nodes receive local broadcast messages. Mobile wireless nodes are able to roam within an ESS without changing their IP configuration because WLAN roaming occurs at Layer 2 levels. If a WLAN device roams from one ESS (roaming domain) to another, its IP configuration must be updated to configure the device as a member of the new ESS. Any upper-layer activities, such as application-driven communications sessions, are canceled when the wireless node leaves an ESS.

An answer to the problem of interrupting running applications when roaming from one wireless network to another is the concept of Inter-Network Roaming (INR) that many companies are attempting to implement on local and wide-area levels. Essentially, *INR* would allow a LAN-to-WAN roaming that would allow many Internet-related applications to continue running when a mobile device moves from one connection point to another.

Roaming Duration   *Roaming* is essentially the time required for a wireless device to disassociate itself from one access point and to reassociate with another access point. The duration of a roaming action is the time needed for these two events to take place. Once the device is associated with an access point and communicating, the device is technically no longer roaming. It is now associated with the access point, just like any fixed base devices within the access point's range.

9

Line Check 9.2

1. Why is it important to verify a WLAN design by modeling the network layout?
2. What is the purpose of the beacon frame?
3. What connection-transfer method does a roaming wireless device use when moving from one access point to another?

What Do You Think?

What are some of the advantages and disadvantages of implementing a network in ad-hoc mode, instead of implementing the network in infrastructure mode?

Installing and Configuring WLAN Devices

Installing WLAN hardware devices (access points, routers, bridges, NICs, or network adapters) should follow the plan developed during the planning design phase (see Chapter 8) and any adjustments made during the design modeling. Generally, after the issues of providing capacity and coverage have been resolved, perhaps the next issue that must be resolved when deciding where to place an access point is the location of AC electrical power sources into which the DC power transformer is plugged. NICs and network adapters must be inserted into each computer or attached to each device to be connected to the WLAN.

Once the hardware devices are in place, the configuration or setup activities must be performed for each device, as applicable. The major steps involved in this process are:

- Configuring the access points
- Configuring wireless NICs and network adapters

Each of these steps and the processes involved are discussed in the following sections.

Configuring Access Points

Straight out of its box, a wireless access point is configured with default values. These default values allow the access point to work in most situations, but they may not be appropriate to the specific needs of your WLAN. Important to the effective operation of the access point is that you address each of the major features and settings during the configuration process. The process of configuring an access point can be divided into three general steps:

- Setting the wireless connection configuration
- Setting the administrative configuration
- Setting the networking configuration

Setting the Wireless Connection Configuration

Virtually all 802.11x access points can be configured from a PC using one of three connection types: wireless access, serial cable connection, or through a crossover Ethernet cable. While not all access points support all three of these links, most do. Read the manufacturer's documentation for the connection methods available for any particular access point.

NOTE

In most cases, a notebook or laptop PC should be used to configure an access point, if for no other reason than its portability.

Wireless Access   From a PC equipped with a wireless NIC or network adapter, you should be able to access an operating access point using a web browser and the default IP address of the access point. The documentation for the access point should specify its default IP address, which is typically something like 192.168.0.1 or another private network IP address.

CROSS-REFERENCE

Private and public IP addressing is discussed in Appendix C.

Enter the access point's IP address in the location or address bar of the browser, as follows:

```
http://192.168.0.1
```

Most access points include a small web server that should respond with the configuration data of the access point in web page format. Figure 9-9 shows a screen capture of the HTTP configuration interface for an access point.

NOTE

Some access points expect the PC to be configured with an IP address that falls within the same private network address scheme, such as 192.168.0.2 (where the 2 could be any address between 2 and 254, inclusive).

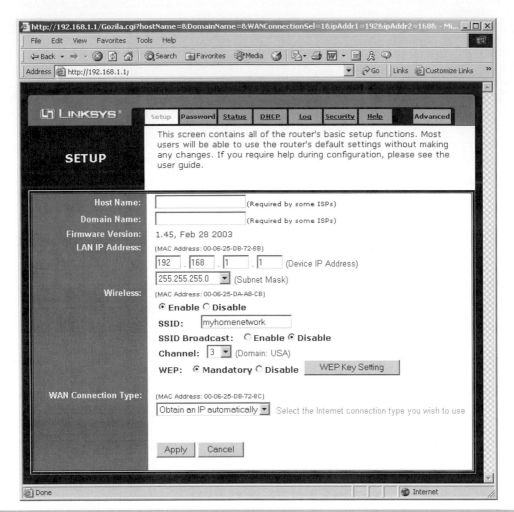

Figure 9-9 The configuration interface of a Linksys access point is accessible using a web browser.

Serial Access   A PC can be connected directly to a wireless access point using a serial cable. The serial cable must be terminated on at least one end with a DB-9 connector, as shown in Figure 9-10. Once the serial connection is made, terminal emulation software, such as Windows HyperTerminal, can be used to view the menus and control screens of the access point's configuration.

Unlike the web page interface displayed by a wireless access (described in the preceding section), the data displayed for a serial connection is typically character-based and not all that user-friendly. In addition to this downside, you must be within 15 feet of the access point to make the serial connection.

Figure 9-10 A PC can be connected to an access point for configuration purposes using a serial cable. (Photo courtesy of Datum Systems)

Ethernet Cable Access Another, yet less common, method you can use to connect to an access point is using a Cat 5 Ethernet crossover cable between a PC's Ethernet NIC and the access point. Using this connection method, the device name or default IP address can be used to access the web page configuration interface. Figure 9-11 illustrates a notebook PC directly connected to an access point using an Ethernet crossover cable.

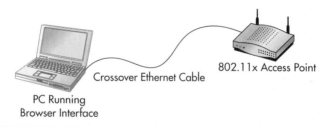

Crossover Ethernet Cable

802.11x Access Point

PC Running
Browser Interface

Figure 9-11 An access point can be configured directly from a PC using an Ethernet cable.

Setting the Administrative Configuration of an Access Point

The primary settings you should review for configuration on a wireless access point are as follows (listed in alphabetical order because their sequence varies from device to device):

- **Administrative control:** Even the most advanced encryption and authentication schemes can be easily defeated if the access point itself is not secured. An access point can be secured in two ways: disabling the serial (console) port and resetting the administrative user name and password. The default values are universal for a manufacturer's devices and easily obtained, which can enable an unauthorized person to reconfigure an access point to allow easy access to transmitted data.

9

- **Authentication:** If your access point offers Wi-Fi Protected Access (WPA), it should be enabled to provide a higher level of encryption and authentication over the standard 802.1 OSA or SKA, which is commonly supported. Although, if WPA is unavailable, OSA and SKA should be enabled to provide at least a minimum of security. Some access points also support 802.1x authentication methods that use an external authentication server.

- **Beacon interval:** This setting indicates the amount of time between the access point's beacon transmissions, which is typically preset to 10 milliseconds (ms) or 10 beacon transmissions every second. For the vast majority of cases, this setting should be sufficient for supporting both fixed and roaming devices. Increasing the beacon interval can speed a network slightly by reducing the transmission overhead. However, a longer beacon interval can also reduce the capability for roaming devices to associate with an access point. The recommendation is that this setting is ignored and allowed to operate at its default value.

- **Data transmission rate:** An 802.11b access point operates by default at 1, 2, 5.5, or 11 Mbps, which allows the access point to choose the appropriate data rate for the quality of the RF link. When data compression methods are applied to wireless data transmissions, 802.11b is able to transmit at 22 Mbps and 802.11g is able to support 100 Mbps. However, some access points enable you to lock in a specific data rate, as an all or nothing. Access points that support more than one 802.11 standard, such as 802.11a/g devices, let you choose which of the two standards, or both, you want to use.

- **Encryption:** Wired Equivalent Privacy (WEP) provides a minimum level of security to a WLAN. Most of the better access points allow WEP to be enabled on all communications. WEP, which is detailed in Chapter 11, encrypts only the data payload in a packet, leaving the headers unencrypted. If WEP is enabled, each access point, NIC, network adapter, and wireless device on the WLAN must be configured with the same encryption key. WEP can be enabled with either 40-bit or 128-bit keys. If 40-bit keys are used, a 10-character encryption key, expressed in hexadecimal characters (0-9, *a-f,* or *A-F*), must be supplied. If 128-bit keys are used, the encryption key consists of 26 hexadecimal characters. Of the two choices, 128-bit keys provide for better security. Higher-end access points also offer other forms of encryption, with dynamic WEP the most common. WEP only provides a minimum level of communications protection, and then only while wireless signals are being exchanged with an access point. It doesn't protect data stored on laptops, especially if drives are shared unrestricted.

- **Fragmentation:** When enabled, fragmentation helps to reduce the amount of data that may need to be retransmitted because of transmission collisions on the medium or as a result of RF interference. Typically, fragmentation is disabled or set to the highest fragment size (2,048 bytes), which is the same as disabling fragmentation. Fragmentation is only used in unicast (point-to-point) transmissions and can be applied to overcome link quality issues. The fragment size can be set as low as 256 bytes.

- **IP address:** Just like all other network devices, an access point must be configured with an IP address. In most cases, an access point is assigned a default IP address (such as 192.168.0.225 or similar) by the manufacturer, which should be changed to fit the IP addressing plan in use on the WLAN. An access point can be configured with a static (unchanging) IP address or it can be configured to obtain its IP address from a Dynamic Host Configuration Protocol (**DHCP**) server, either within a LAN or at an Internet service provider (ISP). (DHCP is discussed in detail in the following section.)

- **RF channel:** Setting access points that are within range of each other to operate on different radio frequency (RF) channels avoids the problem of interference between the access points. On 802.11b WLANs, the channels used should be as far apart as possible to provide sufficient frequency separation to avoid channel crosstalk. For example, if three 802.11b channels were needed, using Channels 1, 6, and 11 would ensure enough frequency separation. The channels of the 802.11a and 802.11g standards don't overlap, so the need for frequency separation is eliminated. On WLANs using 802.11a/g, configuring each access point to a different channel provides the separation needed. If the access point includes an automatic channel selection feature that sets the RF channel automatically after determining which channels within range are already in use, you may want to enable this feature.

- **Request to Send/Clear to Send (RTS/CTS):** RTS/CTS is typically enabled in situations when an access point is servicing wireless nodes that are "hidden" (meaning out of range) from each other. Because the nodes cannot sense each other on the medium, RTS/CTS is used to prevent possible collisions. In most common installations, RTS/CTS is disabled.

- **Transmit power:** Typically, the transmit power setting on an access point is at its highest value—100mW in the U.S.—to provide the maximum range for the access point and its network. However, if multiple access points are to be placed within each other's range, you can scale back the transmit power to reduce the chance of signal overlap and interference. A lower transmit power setting can also add to the security of a WLAN by reducing the amount of signal that can be received outside the physical area of the network.

NOTE

You should update the firmware of an access point before installing it in the WLAN and starting its configuration to ensure you have the latest updates and features. The best place to look for an update to the firmware of your access point is on the manufacturer's web site.

9

Setting the Networking Configuration of an Access Point

The primary setting for an access point, as far as its capability to support an Ethernet network over its wireless interface, is its Dynamic Host Configuration Protocol (DHCP) configuration.

DHCP can be used to configure the IP address and other network settings of an access point and the network nodes automatically when they connect to the network, typically at startup.

In many installations, the access point is directly connected to the Internet gateway device that connects to the network of an ISP. In these installations, the access point will likely be supplied with its Internet configuration, including its IP address, by the ISP. In turn, the access point can then provide DHCP configuration data to the wireless node associated with it. DHCP on a WLAN works in exactly the same way it does on a wired network. The access point acts as the DHCP server to the WLAN. Like a wired network DHCP server, the access point must be configured with a range of available IP addresses and the related information needed to configure a DHCP client (wireless node).

Here is a brief overview of how DHCP works: When a DHCP client boots up or requests to renew its DHCP configuration, it sends a request packet to the network that includes its MAC address. In effect, this packet says to the network, "Hello, I'm 00:22:33:AB:CD:EF and I need my IP data, so I can join the network." The DHCP server (in this case, the access point) receives this request and responds with the data needed to configure the client for IP communications. The information provided includes an IP address, the IP address of the default gateway, the subnet mask of the assigned IP address, and, possibly, the IP address of a default Domain Name System (DNS) server. Figure 9-12 shows the results of an ipconfig command on a Windows XP computer that lists the information provided to a DHCP client.

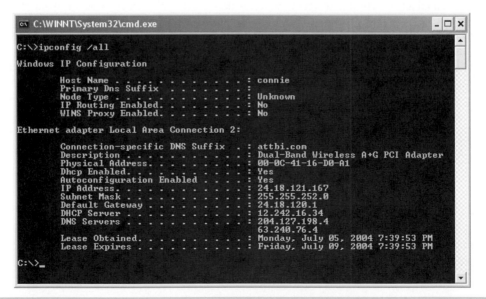

Figure 9-12   IPCONFIG lists the information supplied to a DHCP client.

At the bottom of the information displayed in Figure 9-12 are two lines that state when a lease was obtained and when it expires. What lease, you ask? DHCP doesn't permanently assign IP data to a network node. Instead, the IP configuration is assigned to the node temporarily. One of the features of DHCP is this: it can be used to manage a network on which there are more nodes than available IP addresses, although this is rarely an issue on a network using a private IP address block.

When the DHCP server assigns IP configuration data to a node, it sets a lease period duration, at about the middle of which, the node starts the process to renew its lease or release the IP address for others to use. The default period for a DHCP lease is 72 hours, but a network administrator can shorten or lengthen this time, depending on the needs and demands of the network. In situations where the network has ample IP addresses, the lease period rarely becomes an issue. However, in situations where a limited pool of IP addresses must be shared by a larger number of nodes, at the end of the lease period, or when the node disconnects from the network—whichever comes first—the IP address assigned to one node can be reassigned to a different node.

Multiple Radio Access Points

Some access point models are available with multiple radio transceivers. This feature allows an access point to provide simultaneous support for multiple wireless nodes and multiple wireless standards. In areas where the wireless standard being used by roaming devices could vary, a multiple radio access point can simultaneously support two or more wireless standards, such as 802.11b and 802.11a. The following illustration shows an Intermec access point with two internal radio transceivers, as evidenced by its two sets of antenna. This photo is courtesy of Intermec Technologies Corporation.

9

Pathfinders

Phil Karn—KA9Q

Phil Karn (shown in the photo) is credited with the first definition of the access methods now incorporated into the IEEE 802.11 standards. In late 1985, Karn developed an implementation of the RF packet-radio Internet protocols for low-end PCs, working on a Xerox 820 running CP/M and, later, an IBM PC running MS-DOS. Karn named this system KA9Q after his HAM radio call letters.

KA9Q was the first PC-based network operating system (NOS) that could support an Internet client, a server, and an IP packet router simultaneously, while handling multiple client and server sessions at the same time. The KA9Q NOS became the basis for many low-end routers and was influential in the development of many of the Internet protocols. In fact, KA9Q is also embedded in the software of Qualcomm's CDMA cellular telephones.

Karn holds a BSEE from Cornell University and an MSEE from Carnegie Mellon University. He is currently a Principal Engineer at Qualcomm in San Diego, California. (Mr. Karn's photo is courtesy of Qualcomm, Inc.)

DHCP is almost a necessity on wireless networks and, especially, on those that support roaming. The utility gained from being wireless would be defeated if you had to manually reconfigure the IP settings of a PC each time you moved from one roaming domain to another or happened to move a wireless station from one access point to another. DHCP allows a wireless node to obtain the information it needs to join a network automatically.

Line Check 9.3

1. What are the three most common methods used to connect to a wireless access point for configuration purposes?

2. Why is it important to change the administrative access settings on an access point?

3. Explain the purpose and functions of DHCP.

What Do You Think?

Why would the use of a wireless access point as a gateway device not be the best practice?

Configuring Wireless NICs and Network Adapters

Perhaps the most difficult part of configuring a wireless NIC or network adapter on a PC is physically installing the card. NICs must be installed inside the system unit of a desktop PC in an available expansion slot. A network adapter is installed in various ways, but the most common are to connect an external network adapter to a PC through a Universal Serial Bus (USB) port or to insert a PC Card network adapter into a PCMCIA slot.

NOTE

PC Cards are widely advertised as being "hot-swappable" and, for the most part, they are. When installing a PC Card network adapter, however, the recommendation is that you power off the PC, insert the card while the PC is powered off, and then restart the PC. However, if you are using a USB card, it can be inserted while the PC is running without any danger to the card.

Configuring a Wireless Network Interface on a Windows XP PC

Because nearly all wireless NICs and network adapters are Plug-and-Play (PnP) devices, the hardware side of configuring a WLAN interface involves setting software parameters on the Windows XP operating system (OS). To completely and properly configure a network interface on a Windows XP PC involves a series of steps that must all be completed to ensure the PC will be able to communicate on the WLAN. The following steps should be performed to complete the configuration of the wireless interface on a PC:

- Verify the hardware acceptance
- Configure the WLAN settings on Windows XP
- Configure the authentication and security settings
- Verify the WLAN configuration

Each of these configuration steps is detailed in the following sections.

Verifying Hardware Acceptance　After you install a wireless NIC or a PC Card network adapter, and then you restart the PC, Windows XP automatically detects and adds the

9

interface to its list of available network interfaces in its Network Connections folder. Even if this process seems to proceed as it should, you should verify that Windows XP has, in fact, recognized the card.

To verify that Windows XP has recognized and accepted the wireless card, perform the following steps:

1. Click Start and choose Control Panel from the Start menu.

2. Click the Network and Internet Connections icon on the Control Panel.

3. Click Network Connections.

On the Network Connections window, you should see an icon labeled Wireless Network Connection (or words to that effect).

4. Click the Wireless Network Connection icon to open the Wireless Network Connection Status dialog box, shown in Figure 9-13.

Figure 9-13 The Windows XP Wireless Network Connection Status dialog box

The status dialog box shown in Figure 9-13 is the same dialog box used for wired network adapters, with one addition—the graphic with the ascending signal strength bars. If the wireless adapter is functioning, the bars should show green to indicate the strength of the RF signal the network adapter is receiving.

Configuring WLAN Settings on Windows XP   The next step in the configuration process is to set the WLAN settings through the Properties button on the Network Connection

Status dialog box. To configure the WLAN settings for the wireless NIC or network adapter on a Windows XP system, perform the following steps:

1. Click the Properties button on the Wireless Network Connection Status dialog box to display the Wireless Network Connection Properties window, shown in Figure 9-14. If you've configured a wired network adapter on Windows XP in the past, you'll recognize this window. However, when you are configuring a wireless adapter, an additional tab, labeled Wireless Networks, is added.

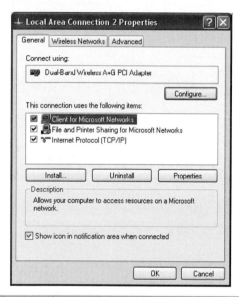

Figure 9-14   The Windows XP Wireless Network Connection Properties window

2. Click on the Wireless Networks tab to display the Wireless Networks dialog box (see Figure 9-15).

    This dialog box is used to configure the PC and its wireless network adapter for communications with any detected access points.

3. Ensure that the Use Windows To Configure My Wireless Network Settings check box is selected. This is the default setting.

    This dialog box has two sections: the top part is the Available Networks area and the bottom part is the Preferred Networks area.

4. If no access points are listed in the Preferred Networks area, you can manually add an access point connection by clicking the Add button. This displays the Wireless Network Properties connection configuration dialog box shown in Figure 9-16.

9

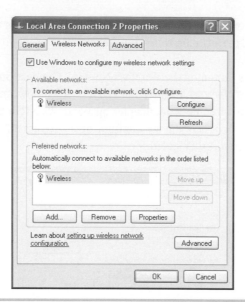

Figure 9-15 The Windows XP Wireless Network Connection Properties Wireless Networks dialog box

Figure 9-16 The Windows XP Wireless Network Connection Properties preferred networks add dialog box

5. Enter the SSID of the access point you want this PC to be associated with and check the boxes for Data Encryption and Network Authentication, as appropriate. Be sure these settings match those of the access point indicated by the SSID.

6. Click the OK button on this and the higher-level windows to save the configuration.

Another way to configure a wireless adapter to an access point is to use the Available Networks area of this window. If you use this method, the following steps replace Steps 4 through 6 of the preceding process.

4. On the Windows XP Wireless Network Connection Properties Wireless Networks dialog box, shown in Figure 9-15, click the Refresh button.

   The Refresh button causes Windows to scan for nearby access points and list any it detects in the Available Networks list.

   To configure the PC to a particular access point, click that access point from the Available Networks list, and then click the Configure button to display the Wireless Network Connection Properties dialog box, shown in Figure 9-16.

5. Enter the SSID of the access point you want this PC to be associated with and check the boxes for Data Encryption and Network Authentication, as appropriate. Be sure these settings match those of the access point indicated by the SSID.

6. Click the OK button on this and the higher-level windows to save the configuration.

   The Available Network you have configured will display in the Preferred Networks area on the Wireless Networks Properties window (see Figure 9-15).

NOTE

Steps 5 and 6 in this process are identical to the Steps 5 and 6 used to add a Preferred Network in the preceding process.

Configuring Authentication and Security   Windows XP includes support for 802.1x security and authentication (see Chapter 11). To configure this feature on a wireless connection, choose the Authentication tab on the Wireless Network Connection Properties window (see Figure 9-17).

If you choose to enable the 802.1x security feature, you need to select the Extensible Authentication Protocol (**EAP**) type being used. The primary choices are RADIUS (Remote Authentication Dial-In User Service), a smart card, or a certificate.

9

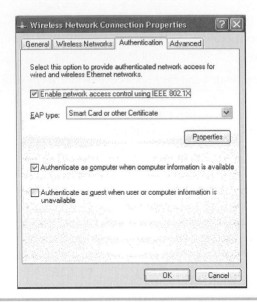

Figure 9-17 The Windows XP Wireless Network Connection Properties Authentication dialog box

NOTE

The IEEE 802.1x is not just a wireless networking feature. It can also be applied to wireline Ethernet networks.

Verifying a Windows XP Configuration   To verify the configuration of a wireless NIC on a Windows XP system, use the TCP/IP ipconfig command. To execute this command, shown earlier in Figure 9-12, use the following steps:

1. On the Start menu, choose Run to open the Run dialog box.

2. In the box labeled Open: (see Figure 9-18), enter the command **cmd** and click OK.

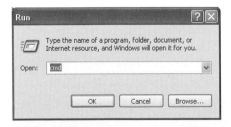

Figure 9-18 The Windows XP Run dialog box

This action opens a Command Prompt window, or as some people call it, a DOS command window. Another way to access the Command Prompt window is to use the mouse to navigate through the Start | All Programs | Accessories | Command Prompt selections.

3. At the command prompt, which should be something like that shown in Figure 9-19, enter the command **ipconfig/all** (to display all network adapters on the PC). The results should be similar to the information shown earlier in Figure 9-12.

Figure 9-19   The Windows XP command prompt window

Configuring Roaming PCs on Windows XP

When a Windows XP PC is roaming, the Available Networks function on the Wireless Networks Connection Properties window (Figure 9-15) can be used to detect and add networks to the Preferred Networks list. Once this has been configured and the network is added to the list, any time the PC roams into the range of the access point, it is automatically connected.

If an office setting has multiple overlapping access points, all or some of the access points can be added to the Preferred Networks list and prioritized.

Configuring WLAN Cards on Linux

Unfortunately, not every wireless NIC or network adapter is compatible with Linux and not every wireless NIC manufacturer develops device drivers for Linux. Wireless device manufacturers typically offer different chipsets on their different wireless cards, which results in some cards working with Linux and others being incompatible. However, the following sections explain the process used to configure a network interface on a Linux system, assuming the card and its device drivers are compatible.

9

NOTE

For an up-to-date list of the wireless cards that are compatible with Linux (plus other helpful Linux-related wireless information), check the web site of the Linux-WLAN group at **www.linux-wlan.org**.

Configuring a Wireless NIC on a Linux PC   Most new Linux distributions, such as Linspire, Mandriva, Red Hat, and SuSE, have the capability to automatically detect, recognize, and install the appropriate device drivers for any Linux-compatible wireless NICs and network adapters. In most cases, the card manufacturer should provide a Linux configuration script or program to configure the WLAN settings for the NIC. Follow the manufacturer's instructions for loading, expanding, and executing the configuration script on a Linux system.

The following instructions are an example of the steps performed to configure a Linksys NIC on a Linux system for a connection to a WLAN:

1. Log on as root.

2. Access the manufacturer's web site to download the latest version of the device driver for your particular Linux distribution.

3. Use the tar command to expand the tarball containing the device driver file, for example:

   ```
   # tar zxvf linux-wlan-ng*.tar.gz
   ```

4. Move to the directory in which the expanded version of the linux-wlan-ng files are located, for example:

   ```
   # cd linux-wlan-ng
   ```

5. Enter the command to execute the configuration script, such as:

   ```
   # ./Configure
   ```

6. The configuration script should display a series of prompts that use your responses to configure the NIC as needed for your WLAN. Figure 9-20 shows a sample of the configuration script used to configure a wireless NIC.

7. Next, the device drivers need to be compiled and installed. Enter the following commands (one at a time) at the command prompt:

   ```
   # make all
   # make install
   ```

8. Restart the system.

9. To enable the wireless NIC device to begin scanning the network, enter the command

   ```
   # ifconfig wlan0 up
   ```

10. If you want to enable DHCP for the wireless connection, enter the command

    ```
    # dhcpcd wlan0
    ```

Setting the SSID   All the wireless device configuration files should be located in a single directory, which is typically the /etc/wlan directory. In this directory, a file named /etc/wlan/wlan. conf should be edited to assign the SSID of the network to which the NIC should associate.

"Build Prism2.x PCMCIA Card Services (_cs) driver? (y/n) [y]:" type **y** for yes, and hit **Enter**

"Build Prism2 PLX9052 based PCI (_plx) adapter driver? (y/n) [n]:" type **n** for no, and hit **Enter**

"Build Prism2.5 native PCI (_pci) driver? (y/n) [n]:" type **n** for no, and hit **Enter**

"Build Prism2.5 USB (_usb) driver? (y/n) [n]:" type **n** for no, and hit **Enter**

"Linux source directory [/usr/src/Linux]:" by default this should be where your kernel is located, if it's located in a different place please input the path. Else hit **Enter**

"pcmcia-cs source dir [/usr/src/pcmcia-cs-3.1.XX]:" by default this should be where your card services are located, if it's located in a different place please input the path. Else hit **Enter**

"Build for Kernel PCMCIA? (y/n) [n]:" type **n** for no, and hit **Enter**

"PCMCIA script directory [/etc/pcmcia]:" by default this should be where your PCMCIA scripts are located, if it's located in a different place please input the path. Else hit **Enter**

"Alternate target install root directory on host []:" hit **Enter**

"Module install director [/lib/modules/2.*.**]:" this will depending on where your module directory is, and the *.** depends on what kernel you're running, if you've got another install directory please input it. Else hit **Enter**

"Target Architecture? (i386, ppc, arm, or alpha) [i386]:" this prompt is for the type of processor you use, **i386** is Intel/AMD based systems (IBM Clones). If you're running a IBM clone, just hit **Enter**, else input the type of Architecture you're using and hit **Enter**

"Prefix for build host compiler? (rarely needed) []:" just hit **Enter** here unless you're sure

"Compiling with a cross compiler? (y/n) [n]:" Type **n** and hit **Enter** unless you're compiling with a cross compiler.

"Build for debugging (see doc/config.debug) (y/n) [n]:" Type **n** and hit **Enter**

Figure 9-20 The prompts included in the configuration script for a wireless NIC on a Linux system

The contents of wlan.conf file should include at least the following entries and, commonly, much more:

```
# Specify all the wlan interfaces on the server
WLAN_DEVICES="wlan0"
# Specify whether the server should scan the network channels
# for valid SSIDs
WLAN_SCAN=y
# Specify expected SSIDs and the wlan0 interface
SSID_wlan0="linksys"
ENABLE_wlan0=y
# Select Station Mode
IS_ADHOC=n             # y|n, y - adhoc, n - infrastructure
# Infrastructure Station Start
AuthType="opensystem" # opensystem | sharedkey (requires WEP)
# Use DesiredSSID="" to associate with any AP in range
DesiredSSID="linksys"
```

9

The boldface lines in this example are the entries that should be added to enable scanning for valid SSIDs, assign the SSIDs, set the topology mode, and set the authentication type, if any, of the access point to which this PC should associate.

Verifying the Configuration   To verify the configuration, use the Linux command ifconfig to display the configuration of the wireless NIC and its device driver. Figure 9-21 shows a sample ifconfig display.

```
# ifconfig -a

wlan0 Link encap:Ethernet HWaddr 00:06:25:09:6A:B5
inet addr:192.168.1.100 Bcast:192.168.1.255 Mask:255.255.255.0
UP BROADCAST RUNNING MULTICAST MTU:1500 Metric:1
RX packets:47379 errors:0 dropped:0 overruns:0 frame:0
TX packets:107900 errors:0 dropped:0 overruns:0 carrier:0
collisions:0 txqueuelen:100
RX bytes:4676853 (4.4 Mb) TX bytes:43209032 (41.2 Mb)
Interrupt:11 Memory:c887a000-c887b000


wlan0:0 Link encap:Ethernet HWaddr 00:06:25:09:6A:B5
inet addr:192.168.1.99 Bcast:192.168.1.255 Mask:255.255.255.0
UP BROADCAST RUNNING MULTICAST MTU:1500 Metric:1
Interrupt:11 Memory:c887a000-c887b000

#
```

Figure 9-21   A portion of the results displayed by the Linux ifconfig command

? Line Check 9.4

1. What is the 802.11 security standard supported by Windows XP?
2. What TCP/IP utility can be used to verify a wireless NIC installation?
3. What step should be performed before you begin configuring Windows XP for a WLAN connection?

What Do You Think?

What are the advantages and disadvantages of choosing a Windows XP system? A Linux system?

Configuring Other WLAN Devices

Some larger WLAN installations may require additional WLAN devices beyond an access point. These devices may be needed to extend the broadcasted signal or to provide routing, security, and other services to the WLAN. In the following sections, we look at the major wireless devices likely to be included on a WLAN, which are:

- Wireless repeaters
- Wireless routers
- Wireless bridges
- Wireless switches

In the following sections, we briefly discuss these devices, their uses, and the processes used to configure them.

Wireless Repeaters

Every network medium, whether it is wired or wireless, has an effective range or distance at which the quality of its transmitted signal begins to degrade. Physical media, such as copper cables, have a distance limit at which point a phenomenon called attenuation begins to occur. *Attenuation* degrades the transmitted signal because the strength of the electrical impulses can no longer overcome the resistance of the cable (this is the friction in the cable caused by the electrical impulse passing through the molecules of the wire).

Like copper wire media, wireless media also suffer from attenuation. Wireless network signals are RF transmissions that are generally limited to the broadcast range of their transmitter and the power of their antenna. Their range can be impacted by electrical or thermal noise, and the terrain over which they are transmitted.

In situations where the distance of a wireless transmitter must be extended beyond its normal operating distance, a repeater or signal extender is used to filter and reenergize the signal to extend its quality, strength, and effective range (see Figure 9-22).

9

Figure 9-22 A wireless repeater can increase the broadcast range of a wireless network signal. (Photo courtesy of Ahatpe Technical Co., Ltd.)

Repeaters aren't complicated devices. All they do is receive a transmitted signal and retransmit it with its original signal strength restored and, in most cases, with much of the noise removed. However, the downside to repeaters and extenders is they can add a small amount of delay (latency) to the signal. Too many repeaters or extenders on a wireless system may cause timing issues on high-speed networks.

Wireless Routers

Regardless of the network media, wired or wireless, a router performs the same basic functions: determining the better route to be used to forward a message between source addresses and destination addresses on different networks and forwarding (routing) messages between networks.

If Markus in Washington State is sending e-mail to his friend Martin in London, the message is routed over the internetwork, moving from router to router until it reaches the network that includes the destination address (see Figure 9-23). When Markus clicks the OK button to send the e-mail message, the message's destination address is determined by the router to be located on a remote network and forwarded to the port connected to the Internet connection. To get from Markus's network to Martin's network, the message may pass through as many as 10 to 14 (or more) routers, with each making a similar determination about where the message should be forwarded.

To make this determination, each router on the path between Markus and Martin examines the destination address and looks it up in its routing table, which functions much like a directory

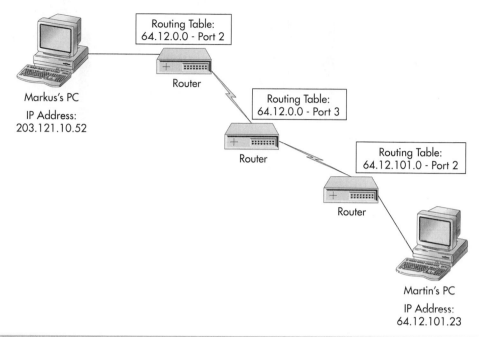

Figure 9-23   A message is routed across the internetwork until it arrives at the router servicing the destination node address.

in a large building. A router determines whether or not the destination address is located on the network it services by looking for the address in its routing table. If the destination address is found in the routing table, the message is forwarded to the port through which that address can be reached. Eventually, the e-mail message arrives at the appropriate mail server and is stored in Martin's mailbox.

Routing tables can contain two types of routing entries: static or dynamic. A *static route* creates a fixed route for certain addresses to always use a specific port for forwarding. The router uses a variety of routing metrics and algorithms to determine a *dynamic route*.

Routers versus Access Points

While a wireless router (see Figure 9-24) looks much like a wireless access point, a wireless router provides a WLAN with the capability to connect to several networks, while an access point serves as a bridge to a single network. In addition, a router works at a higher layer (Layer 3) than an access point (Layer 2), which means IP addresses are the basis used for making decisions about where a packet should be forwarded. An access point ignores the IP address and generally forwards all packets.

9

Figure 9-24 A wireless firewall router (Photo courtesy of 3Com Corp.)

Wireless routers also implement a number of security and functionality features not offered in the majority of access points. The primary features offered by a wireless router, but not commonly offered by access points, are:

● **DHCP support:** Most wireless routers provide internal DHCP support and include the functionality of a DHCP server for all nodes on a WLAN, typically from a pool of private IP addresses.

● **Firewall services:** Most wireless routers also include some form of firewall service that can be used to prevent unauthorized access to all traffic not originated on the local WLAN. Many wireless routers also include some level of exclusion between allowing all traffic to access the WLAN and no traffic being passed through the router.

● **Network Address Translation (NAT):** This service allows multiple WLAN devices to share a single public IP address, which is typically provided by an ISP or a wireless Internet service provider (WISP). Without NAT, each individual device would require its own unique IP address from the service provider.

● **Port-based control:** Transport layer segments, which are encapsulated into IP packets, contain a port number that identifies the protocol, service, or application that originated or should process the data payload. Many wireless routers allow for port-based filtering that can be used to block or allow packets containing certain port numbers through to the WLAN.

In addition, a wireless router helps to improve the overall performance of a WLAN by blocking broadcast packets and not allowing them to propagate throughout the entire network.

In addition, because the IP address is used to make forwarding decisions, only those nodes on the addressed subnet see forwarded messages, instead of all nodes seeing every message, as is the case with an access point.

Configuring a Wireless Router or Internet Gateway

One basic rule exists when it comes to incorporating a wireless router into a WLAN: one router serves one WLAN. A wireless router is typically wireless on only one side, with the other side directly connected to a DSL, cable, or wireless Internet service modem, bridge, or adapter with a cable. You would include a router in your WLAN for several reasons, but the primary reasons are that you are setting up a new WLAN in a home or office, you are rebuilding all or a portion of an existing network to be wireless, you want to operate a wireless network using only a single public IP address, or you want to extend an existing WLAN.

A wireless router should be installed in a fairly central location to the WLAN, especially if the WLAN doesn't include any access points. The location of a wireless router is less critical to the whole WLAN if access points are also in use. Remember, a wireless router also includes a built-in access point, so you generally need at least one less access point anyway.

The process used to configure a wireless router is much like that used to configure a wireless access point (see the previous section "Access Point Configuration"), because most of the configuration involves setting up the internal access point.

Most wireless routers, like most wireless access points, provide a web-based configuration function that can be accessed from a wireless-equipped PC using a web browser. The previous Figure 9-9 shows an example of a user interface for a wireless router configuration function.

The areas in which the configuration of a wireless router differs from that of a wireless access point are:

- **NAT:** In most wireless routers, enabling *NAT* involves selecting a check box on the router configuration screens (accessed in the same way as on an access point) and either indicating that you want to receive an IP address using DHCP from a service provider or entering a static IP address. In either case, the IP address assigned to the router is the public IP address used in all public network packets.

- **WPA security:** Not every wireless router supports WPA security, but many manufacturers offer a firmware upgrade to add this feature to some models. If you want to enable WPA, visit the manufacturer's web site to see if an upgrade is available. When configuring WPA on the router, you also need to indicate the EAP type you want to use. Remember, if WPA is enabled on the router, then it also needs to be enabled on all access points and wireless NICs and network adapters. Microsoft has a download update to add WPA support to Windows XP.

9

- **Protocol support:** If the wireless router is serving as an Internet gateway for a connection to a DSL link, the service provider may require that Point-to-Point Protocol on Ethernet (PPPoE) be enabled, which is commonly supported in most wireless routers. Another protocol group commonly supported by wireless routers that is enabled as required is virtual private network (VPN) pass-through, which includes support for IP Security (IPSec), Point-to-Point Tunneling Protocol (PPTP), and Layer Two Tunneling Protocol (L2TP).

- **Routing protocols:** Most routers use the Routing Information Protocol (RIP), which is commonly referred to as RIP-1, as the default routing protocol. Some also support RIP-2, which is an upgraded version of RIP-1 that corrects some inefficiency in RIP-1, especially on larger networks. Networks with a large number of ad-hoc nodes should install a wireless router that supports Ad-hoc On-demand Distance Vector (AODV) or Dynamic Source Routing (DSR) routing protocols.

Line Check 9.5

1. What functions does a wireless router perform that aren't performed by a wireless access point?

2. Explain the benefit of enabling NAT on a wireless router.

3. What is the most commonly implemented routing protocol on wireless routers?

Routing Protocols

Essentially, two types of routing protocols exist: distance vector and link-state.

A *distance-vector routing protocol*, such as RIP, Interior Gateway Routing Protocol (IGRP), and Enhanced IGRP (EIGRP), exchanges route information with other nearby routers. Route information is advertised (transferred) as a vector that combines direction and distance. *Direction* indicates the path leading to the next upstream router along a path, while *distance* is a value (metric) that indicates the number of hops (routers) encountered along the path to the destination network.

A link-state protocol, such as the Open Shortest Path First (OSPF) and the Intermediate System to Intermediate System (IS-IS) routing protocols, requires each router in an internetwork to maintain a map of all or a portion of the network. Changes in the state of the network (this primarily means the status of the routers on the network) are broadcast to the network using a link state advertisement (LSA) packet, which causes all other routers to reconfigure their routing tables to reflect this information.

What Do You Think?

Would internetworking as we know it today be possible without routers? Briefly describe the limitations that would exist if routers weren't available.

Wireless Bridges

A *network bridge* does just about what its name implies—it creates a crossover point between two LANs or LAN segments operating on the same networking protocol. A *simple bridge* connects to two or more separate LANs or LAN segments and retransmits every message to both networks, regardless of which network the message may be addressed to.

Most LAN bridges are what are called learning bridges. A *learning bridge* acts like a traffic cop for the networks it's serving. Messages transmitted between nodes on the same network are ignored, but a learning bridge forwards messages from one network that are addressed to a node on another network.

A learning bridge maintains a bridging table in which it keeps track of the physical address of a node that transmits a message addressed to another network. This allows the bridge to construct in its bridging table a cross-reference to which nodes are on which networks. Using the bridging table information, the bridge knows not to retransmit a message addressed to a node on the same network as the source device. The table also allows the bridge to decide which messages need to be forwarded to a different port than the one the message was received from. If a message is addressed to an address not included in the bridging table, the bridge records the source node's information, and then broadcasts the message to every one of its ports, except the port on which the message arrived.

For example, as illustrated in Figure 9-25, if node 1-A on network 1 transmits a message addressed to node 2-B on network 2, the bridge records the physical address and network of node 1-A in its bridging table. With this information in its bridging table, the bridge ignores

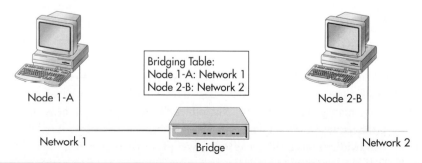

Bridging Table:
Node 1-A: Network 1
Node 2-B: Network 2

Node 1-A

Network 1

Bridge

Node 2-B

Network 2

9

Figure 9-25   A bridge uses the entries in its bridging table to route messages arriving from different networks or network segments.

any messages addressed to node 1-A sent by another node on network 1, assuming that node 1-A sensed the message on the medium at the same time as the bridge.

If a message addressed to node 1-A is transmitted by node 2-B on network 2, however, the bridge, after recording node 2-B's information in the bridging table, determines the message should be forwarded to network 1 to reach node 1-A using the information already in the bridging table. As you can see, the capability to reduce the amount of network traffic on a particular segment allows a bridge to improve the performance of the overall network and maximize the available bandwidth.

A wireless bridge is commonly used to provide a connection point between the WLANs in two buildings of a campus area network (CAN) and to jump a street, a landscaped area, or another type of open area between the buildings. Figure 9-26 shows a wireless bridge unit.

Figure 9-26   A wireless bridge (Photo courtesy of SMC Networks)

LAN Switch

A LAN switch can be likened to a multiport bridge, but LAN switches do much more than simple bridging operations. A *LAN switch* is an intelligent device that is able to forward messages according to a variety of factors, the least of which is the location of the destination node.

Switches create and maintain switching tables, which are similar to the bridging table maintained by a bridge. However, a switch keeps a bit more information than a bridge, which allows it to manage the network bandwidth and prevent problem messages or nodes from flooding the network or hogging up the bandwidth. A switch, like a hub, also shares its available bandwidth (transmission capacity) over the devices connected to it, but some switches include the capability to buffer incoming and outgoing traffic to mitigate any fluctuations in the available bandwidth.

Switching Methods

One of the mechanisms used by LAN switches to prevent undeliverable messages from clogging the network is the Spanning Tree Protocol (**STP**). The problem with an undeliverable message, such as a message with an unknown address, is that it stays on the network, taking up the medium, which prevents other nodes from transmitting. A message in this situation is what is called a *network loop*. Although the exact electronics don't work this way, you can visualize the message continuing to circulate around and around the network looking for the node to which it is addressed, without ever succeeding. One of the primary functions of *STP* is to prevent loops on the network.

STP designates each port on a switch to be in either Forwarding or Blocking state. A *port* is a linking point on a switch through which the network medium is connected to the switch. When a port is in *Blocking state*, only messages that carry information about the status of other switches on the network are allowed to pass, with all other messages blocked. A port that's in *Forwarding state* allows all message types to be received and forwarded.

A port on a switch is changed to Blocking whenever a particular network path is experiencing delay or goes down (fails), and the switch is able to negotiate a new path through the network using other switches or bridges. When the problem is cleared up, the state of the port is changed back to Forwarding, which is the normal state for a port.

On a network, messages are forwarded through a switch using what is called *packet switching*, which is the switching method used on LANs and most WANs. Packets are switched (forwarded) between parts of the network according to their source and destination addresses. Network addressing is detailed in Appendix C.

The most common methods used in packet switching to forward network messages by means of a LAN switch are:

- **Cut-through switching:** This type of switching method has lower latency (delay) than other switching methods because the switch begins to forward a message as soon as the source and destination addresses are received, which is typically at the beginning of the message block.

- **Fast-forward switching:** This cut-through switching method can be prone to errors because it begins to forward a message as soon as its destination address is received. This means collision packets, as well as good packets, are forwarded without any filtering performed.

- **Store-and-forward switching:** This type of switching adds the most latency to message processing because the entire message is read into a buffer (temporary storage area) before the switch begins taking action to forward the message. Some benefits counter the increased latency, however, including message filtering and traffic control. Plus, because the entire message is received, a store-and-forward switch is able to recognize and discard *runts* (incomplete messages) and *giants* (messages with extraneous data), which can increase undeliverable message traffic on the network.

9

- **Fragment-free switching:** This switching method is a hybrid of the cut-through and the store-and-forward switching methods. *Fragment-free switching* buffers only the first 64 bytes of a message frame before forwarding it. The purpose of this switching method is to eliminate collision packets or the residue of a message that has suffered a collision on the medium. The assumption is a message that is at least 64 bytes long is OK.

NOTE

The normal forwarding mode for a network bridge is store-and-forward.

Virtual LANs

A feature unique to LAN switches is the capability to create a virtual LAN (**VLAN**, pronounced "vee-lan"). A VLAN is not required to be geographically or functionally fixed in place (such as within a single department of a company). A *VLAN* can be configured to logically create a network segment made up of nodes from a number of different physical segments. Figure 9-27 illustrates the basic concepts of a VLAN with some, but not all, of a WLAN's nodes included in a VLAN.

The primary benefit of a VLAN to a network administrator is that a specific network adapter (meaning a specific PC in most cases) can move to any location on the network and remain a member of the logical group created by the VLAN, thereby retaining the same level of access and security settings.

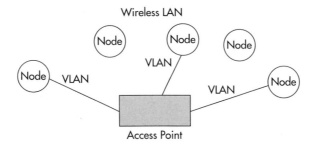

Figure 9-27 A diagram of a simple wireless VLAN shows how some nodes can be included in the VLAN and others can be excluded.

The benefits of a VLAN on a wired network are performance and security. Performance is improved because broadcast traffic is contained to only members of a VLAN and not sent to the entire network. Security is enhanced because nodes that are not members of a VLAN are isolated from access to those resources controlled by the VLAN, even though they may be a part of the same physical network.

NOTE

A VLAN only controls traffic that is outbound from the switch or access point.

Two types of VLANs are implemented on networks:

- **Port-based:** This type of VLAN is generally limited to networks with a single switching device (LAN switch or access point) and associates nodes by their MAC addresses to a particular interface port.

- **Tagged:** A *tagged VLAN* is able to incorporate multiple switches and access points (provided that all the switches or access points provide VLAN support). Each VLAN within the physical network is assigned a tag or identity, and the tag is then associated with an interface port on the switch or access point. When a message is forwarded from one switch to another for a node in a particular VLAN, the VLAN's tag is included with the message. This allows the remote switch to forward the message appropriately.

Wireless switches, routers, and access points typically implement a VLAN on either a node or a group basis. When a node-based VLAN is configured, the access point can allow certain nodes to access a wired network, but prevent wireless nodes from accessing each other's resources. A *group-based wireless VLAN* creates logical groups of nodes (associating their MAC addresses with the group ID [tag]). A node that is a member of a group VLAN can then access the resources of the other nodes in the same group.

Line Check 9.6

1. What is the purpose of a WLAN bridge?

2. Differentiate store-and-forward from cut-through switching.

3. Describe the purpose of a VLAN.

Chapter 9 Review

Chapter Summary

Plan for a WLAN Installation

- A WLAN is made up of at least two radio-equipped devices that establish a communications link for the purpose of sharing data, information, or resources.

- WLANs are created from mobile devices or stationary devices, or both.

9

REVIEW

- Two operating configurations can be used in a WLAN: infrastructure and ad-hoc.

- An infrastructure WLAN includes at least one access point.

- An infrastructure WLAN can be configured as either a BSS or an ESS.

- An ad-hoc network directly connects wireless nodes without the use of an access point.

- An ad-hoc WLAN creates an IBSS, which is bound by the use of a common SSID.

- WLANs use several types of management and control frame types, including management frames, authentication frames, beacon frames, probe frames, and control frames.

- A roaming wireless device uses either seamless or nomadic roaming.

- IEEE 802.11b defines 12 available channels, of which only three (Channels 1, 6, and 11) are generally used.

Install and Configure WLAN Devices

- You should follow the plan developed during the planning design phase when installing a WLAN.

- The major steps involved in installing and configuring a WLAN are configuring the access points, and configuring wireless NICs and network adapters.

- The process of configuring an access point can be divided into three general steps: setting the wireless connection configuration, setting the administrative configuration, and setting the networking configuration.

- A wireless access point can be configured through a web browser interface or through a direct connection with a serial cable or an Ethernet crossover cable.

- The primary settings on a wireless access point are: administrative control, authentication, and its operating features, including DHCP, encryption, and IP address.

- Each device to be included on the WLAN must have a network interface (either a NIC or a network adapter) installed.

- Other WLAN devices may need to be installed in the network, including wireless routers, repeaters, switches, and bridges.

Key Terms

Ad-hoc mode *(278)*
BSS *(277)*
DHCP *(293)*

DTIM *(282)*
EAP *(301)*
ESS *(277)*
IBSS *(279)*
NAT *(310)*
SSID *(280)*
STP *(315)*
VLAN *(316)*

Key Term Quiz

Use the terms from the Key Terms list to complete the following sentences. Don't use the same term more than once. Not all terms will be used.

1. The _____ is used as a keyword so that wireless network adapters are able to associate with wireless access points, routers, and other WLAN devices.

2. The protocol used to automatically assign IP configuration data to a node is _____.

3. A WLAN configured without an access point is in _____ mode.

4. _____ is a service implemented on an Internet gateway that allows a WLAN's nodes to share a common public IP address.

5. A(n) _____ provides point-to-point wireless bridging between wireless nodes and, commonly, to a wired network.

6. The field used to inform a wireless node that a queue of messages has been created while the node was in sleep mode is the _____.

7. Wireless nodes configured for _____ don't require an access point.

8. A(n) _____ WLAN operates with multiple access points.

9. When a wireless node is configured for 802.1x security, the type of _____ must also be indicated.

10. A network made up of workstations that may or may not be physically adjacent to which the same access and security rules apply is called a(n) _____.

Multiple Choice Quiz

1. Wireless nodes on a WLAN that directly connected to each other are configured in which WLAN mode?

    A. Ad-hoc mode

    B. Architecture mode

    C. Infrastructure mode

    D. Roaming mode

2. What is the Internet gateway service that allows a WLAN's nodes to share a common public IP address outside the WLAN?

    A. DHCP

    B. IP

    C. NAT

    D. TCP

3. What protocol is used to automatically assign IP configuration data to a WLAN node when it starts up?

    A. DHCP

    B. IP

    C. NAT

    D. TCP

4. What keyword must be used between wireless devices when one device attempts to associate with another device?

    A. BSS

    B. ESS

    C. IBSS

    D. SSID

5. You choose to enable 802.1x security on a WLAN. As a part of the configuration, you must indicate the EAP type in use. Which of the following is not a primary EAP type available on a Windows XP system?

    A. Certificate

    B. Default

    C. RADIUS

    D. Smart card

6. Which of the following service set modes is most associated with a WLAN and a single access point?

    A. BSS

    B. ESS

    C. IBSS

    D. EIBSS

7. Which of the following service set modes is associated with an ad-hoc WLAN?

    A. BSS

    B. ESS

    C. IBSS

    D. EIBSS

8. Which of the following service set modes is most associated with a WLAN containing multiple access points?

    A. BSS

    B. ESS

    C. IBSS

    D. EIBSS

9. What field in a beacon frame is used to inform a wireless node that it has traffic buffered on a BSS?

    A. Announcement traffic information message (ATIM)

    B. Inactivity threshold period (ITP)

    C. Link state advertisement (LSA)

    D. Delivery traffic indication map (TIM)

10. Which of the following is not associated with power management and power-saving procedures on a wireless radio NIC?

    A. CAM

    B. PSP

    C. ITP

    D. DHCP

9

REVIEW

Lab Projects

1. Install and configure a wireless access point connecting it to either an existing wireline or a wireless network. Your instructor will provide you with the required configuration settings.

2. Install and configure a wireless expansion card NIC into a PC running either Windows XP or Linux. Configure the NIC for infrastructure mode. Write down the steps performed and the outcome or results of each step. Use a wireless access point in your lab and its configuration data to finalize the configuration of the network adapter. Verify your configuration using the appropriate command.

3. Configure a wireless network adapter for ad-hoc mode and move its PC around within the range of a wireless access point or router. (You may need to make a configuration change to the access point or router to support ad-hoc devices.) Were you able to maintain the connection while moving the PC?

Case Problems

1. In 2005 the city of Spokane, Washington, upgraded its network of 802.11b wireless switches and routers to include 802.11g wireless network service to its downtown area, extending its area to over 30 square blocks. This system allows anyone with a PC configured for 802.11b or 802.11g wireless networking to access the public network from anywhere in the downtown area. Create a diagram that shows the placement of the wireless devices required to create a similar system in the downtown area of your town or city, or a nearby city.

2. If you were to implement a wireless network design in your school or business, would you choose to implement an infrastructure or an ad-hoc wireless topology, or a combination of the two? In what areas would you implement each and why?

Advanced Lab Project

One of the best ways to understand the processes used to configure a wireless access point and a PC with a wireless network interface is to install and configure one of each. This lab uses the information in this chapter, along with any information supplied by the manufacturer of the access point and network adapter, either in print or on its web site, to guide you through the installation and configuration of these devices.

Equipment Needed: You need a wireless access point, a PCI expansion card wireless network interface that operates on the same WLAN standard, and a PC running either Windows XP or a major commercial release of the Linux operating system.

Follow the instructions included in this chapter and those provided by the manufacturer to install and configure a wireless access point, install and configure a PCI wireless NIC, and configure the PC for the NIC. Establish communications with the access point across the wireless network to verify your installation.

Chapter 10

WLAN Antennas

LEARNING OBJECTIVES:

In this chapter, you learn how to:

Explain the operations and characteristics of WLAN antennas.

Describe the cables, connectors, and other devices used with WLAN antennas.

Radio frequency (RF) antennas were briefly introduced in Chapter 3, but to understand how, when, where, and why you would install an antenna in a WLAN installation, you also need to study antennas and their associated devices a bit more.

In this chapter, you learn about the different types of antennas, how they operate, and where and why each has its most appropriate application. You also learn about some of the safety issues associated with antenna installation and usage.

WLAN Antenna Basics

A transmitted radio signal begins as an electrical current representing voice, music, images, or data signals on a wire. The *electrical current* is created by the back and forth movement of electrons in the wire in an alternating and continuous pattern, which also radiates an electromagnetic field outside and around the wire.

As the electrical current moves through the wire, the electromagnetic field moves along with the current and, eventually, the current and the electromagnetic field both move into the radio's transmitting antenna. While the wire has an outer covering or jacket that is used to reduce the aura of the electromagnetic field outside and around the wire, an antenna has no such covering. In fact, *antennas* are designed to radiate the electromagnetic field created by an electrical current. In other words, where the design of a wire attempts to control or suppress the electromagnetic field, an antenna is designed to freely radiate it. Just how far an antenna is able to radiate its signals depends on the power of the antenna, as well as the frequency and wavelength of the electromagnetic field. The direction in which these signals radiate is controlled by the antenna's design or type.

 Pathfinders

Guglielmo Marconi—"The Father of Radio"

When Marconi began his experiments in the late 1890s, radio waves were known as "Hertzian waves" (after Heinrich Hertz's earlier discoveries). Marconi didn't actually discover radio waves, but he did develop the technology able to produce and detect radio waves over long distances. His discoveries and developments created a purpose and usefulness for what we now know as radio and radio frequency communications.

Since the early 1900s, when Guglielmo Marconi and Karl Braun were awarded the Nobel Prize for Physics for their work in the development of electromagnetic wave transmissions, radio frequency (RF) antennas have been independent components of an RF transmitter/receiver (transceiver). Prior to the work of Marconi, antennas had been a component of the radio transmitter's power circuitry, which had limited their range.

(continued)

The following is a portrait of Marconi, courtesy of The Guglielmo Marconi Foundation, U.S.A., Inc.

As you might guess, a receiving antenna works just the opposite of a transmitting antenna. Where the *transmitting antenna* converts an electrical current into a transmitted electromagnetic field, a *receiving antenna* transforms a sensed electromagnetic field into an electrical current and places it on a wire. Whether transmitting or receiving, the frequency, wavelength, and amplitude of the electrical current remain the same.

Wireless local area network (WLAN) antennas operate like any RF antenna, which, in fact, they are. In the next few sections, you learn about the basic characteristics, operating requirements, and the various types of WLAN antennas.

Wireless Antenna Basics

While it may appear that the *transmission medium* in a wireless network is the air, in fact, the medium is transmitted radio waves. Although wireless network is often described as using an air interface, this is not quite accurate. If air were the actual medium for wireless RF communications, if there were no air, no communications could exist. Radio waves can be transmitted in a vacuum, as they are in outer space. The early pioneers in wireless communications, including Marconi and Hertz (see the above "Pathfinders" sidebar) struggled with this concept, so they proposed "ether" (which is where we get the term "Ethernet") as the "substance" that allowed radio waves to propagate even when no air is present.

dBi and dBd

The amount of gain for an antenna is measured as either an isotropic source (dBi) or a dipole source (dBd). An antenna doesn't have a power source of its own; it merely uses the energy in an electrical or magnetic current and refocuses it over a broader or narrower area. The amount of power (or *gain*) in an antenna's signal is simply a reflection of the energy in the signal it receives.

An *isotropic source* is a reference standard that represents the gain emitted by a radiation pattern that disperses equally in all directions, forming an imaginary spherical shape, around a fixed transmission point. *Isotropic gain* is a relative measurement stated as dBi (decibels of gain referenced to an isotropic source). For example, if an antenna has 2.5 dBi of gain, it means the antenna has two and one-half times the amount of gain in one or more portions of its radiation pattern compared to the same points in the imaginary isotropic sphere. On the other hand, *dBd* measures antenna gain against a standard of 2.15 dBi of gain, which represents the standard gain of a reference dipole antenna.

To convert dBi to dBd, you use a simple set of formulas:

- dBd to dBi: dBi = dBd + 2.15

- dBi to dBd: dBd = dBi − 2.15

A wireless antenna, such as the antenna of a wireless NIC, access point, or standalone antenna, inserts and extracts RF energy to and from the air. But the RF energy, in the form of radio waves, is the medium and not the air. The function of an RF antenna is twofold:

- To radiate and propagate the signals sent to it by a radio transmitter

- To capture transmitted RF signals from the air and transfer them to a radio receiver

Virtually every wireless device has a built-in antenna, but standalone antennas can also be installed as a part of a WLAN to improve its range and reception (see the section "Choosing a WLAN Antenna").

All RF antennas share five basic characteristics:

- **Frequency:** WLANs use antennas tuned for either 2.4 GHz (802.11b/g) or 5 GHz (802.11a). An antenna only works efficiently when the frequency of the antenna and radio matches. An antenna tuned to one frequency will not operate with a transmitter tuned to another frequency. However, some WLAN devices, like the access point in Figure 10-1, can be designed and equipped to receive more than one frequency.

Figure 10-1   A WLAN access point with a set of antennas for 2.4 GHz and 5 GHz (Photo courtesy of Intermec Technologies Corp.)

- **Gain:** An antenna's **gain** indicates its capability to increase its signal power, which is measured in decibels (dB). As a rule-of-thumb, an additional 3 dB of gain means the power of the transmitted signal has been doubled. Antenna manufacturers typically specify gain as referenced in decibels to either an isotropic source (dBi) or a dipole source (dBd). In the U.S., the Federal Communications Commission (FCC) has established guidelines for the amount of gain or loss a WLAN transmission can have. These guidelines are published in the FCC Part 15.247 standard that also defines and, in many cases, restricts the effective isotropically radiated power (**EIRP**) produced by an antenna. The *EIRP* represents the transmit final output (**TFO**), or the total transmission power, of an RF radio transmitter, plus any gain from the antenna and minus any loss from the antenna's cable.

- **Power.** Antennas are designed to handle a specific amount of TFO from the transmitter. In the case of 802.11, the antenna is generally rated greater than 1 watt to handle the maximum peak TFO of the radio NIC or access point. For most applications, the antenna power specification won't be of too much concern to you because of the relatively low-power levels at which WLANs transmit.

- **Radiation Pattern.** The **radiation pattern** defines the shape and width of the radio wave propagation produced by an antenna. However, all real antennas are unable to generate a perfect omnidirectional radiation pattern. The most commonly used WLAN antenna is the dipole antenna (see Figure 10-2), which transmits in a region shaped something like a doughnut, with the antenna in the center "hole."

10

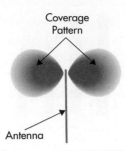

Coverage
Pattern

Antenna

Figure 10-2 A diagram showing an example of the radiation pattern from a dipole antenna

• **Polarization:** Within the context of antennas, **polarization** refers to the orientation of the electrical flux of an electromagnetic signal. Generally, polarization is either horizontal or vertical (see Figure 10-3), but it can also be made to alternate between wave cycles. In general, the physical orientation of an antenna to the Earth's surface determines the polarity of the signals it broadcasts. An antenna that is set perpendicular (vertical) to the ground produces electromagnetic waves that have vertical polarization. An antenna set parallel (horizontal) to the ground produces waves with horizontal polarization. In short-range communications, such as on a WLAN, it is best for all the wireless devices to have the same polarization. However, in long-range communications, the polarization matters much less because the Earth's atmosphere can change the polarization of a signal. Some wireless devices transmit using a circular polarization, which can rotate in either a clockwise or a counter-clockwise direction. When circular polarization is used, the communicating devices should all use the same rotation direction.

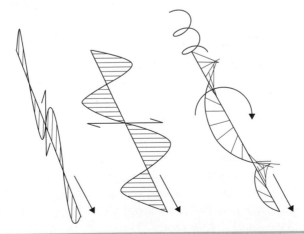

Figure 10-3 Left to right: vertical polarization, horizontal polarization, and circular polarization

NOTE

Except in rare cases, omnidirectional and sector antennas use vertical polarization, and parabolic and Yagi antennas (all of which are covered in the following section) can be configured for either horizontal or vertical, as required by the communications environment.

Decibels

Alexander Graham Bell developed the decibel (dB) as a measurement of the difference in amplitude between two signals, including changes made to a single signal as a before and after measurement. Technically, a *decibel* is one-tenth of a *Bel*, the unit Bell described. A decibel is the equivalent of 10 times the logarithm (log) of a signal's power and 20 times the log of a signal's voltage. A decibel states the difference measurement between a signal's present power or voltage to zero dB. Because a Bel can become too large a number to work with conveniently, the decibel, or 0.1 Bel, is far more commonly used.

The actual formula used to calculate the decibel measurement between two signals is:

$DB = 10 \log_{10} * (P_1 / P_2)$, in which P_1 and P_2 are the before and after signal strengths

In RF communications, the decibel measures the change in milliWatts (one-one thousandth of a watt), in which 0 **dBm** is equivalent to one milliWatt and 1 dBm is about 1.259 milliWatts. However, most communications technicians need to calculate decibels, except to possibly compute signal loss on a circuit. The following table lists the relative signal gain in terms of decibels and the resulting increase or loss in signal strength.

Decibels	Relative Change in Signal Strength
0	1
1	1.26
3	2
10	10
20	100
30	1,000
50	100,000
100	10,000,000

Line Check 10.1

1. What creates the current in an electrical stream?

2. What is an antenna's gain?

3. Explain polarization as it affects an RF antenna.

What Do You Think?

Radio frequency communications are all around us. List the different types of RF communications operating in your area. Can you identify the antennas used by each type of RF communications?

WLAN Antenna Requirements

The requirements, and the restrictions and regulations, for WLAN antennas are measured using a variety of measurement units, including watts, milliWatts, and decibels. However, the performance requirements for an antenna, which are typically stated as power and gain levels, are commonly stated in terms of one calculated value or another. The sections that follow define the common measurement units and the formulas used to state and measure the performance of an antenna.

Watts and Decibels

Before you learn about the actual measurements and formulas, let's discuss the measurement units themselves. Because the number of watts, kilowatts, and milliWatts involved in radio transmission can become large, many of the measurements are converted into smaller and easier to use decibel numbers using logarithmic calculations. Regardless of whether watts, kilowatts, or milliWatts are in use, the formula to convert it into decibel reference is:

dBx = 10 log (power in x)

So, if the measurements are in milliWatts, the power rating is stated in dBm. If the measurements are in watts, the power is stated in dbW. And, if kilowatts are used, the power is in dbK. However, in the context of WLAN power, dBm is most commonly used. Table 10-1 lists the power equivalents of dBm to milliWatts.

Power (dBm)	MilliWatts (mW)	Power (dBm	MilliWatts (mW)
−40	.00010	0	1.0
−37	.00019	3	1.9953
−35	.00032	5	3.1623
−33	.00050	7	5.0119
−30	.001	10	10.0
−27	.002	13	19.953
−25	.00316	15	31.623
−23	.00601	17	50.119
−20	.01	20	100.0
−17	.01995	23	199.53
−15	.03162	25	316.23
−13	.0501	27	501.19
−10	.10	30	1.00w
−7	.1995	33	1.99w
−5	.3162	35	3.16w
−3	.5012	37	5.01w
		40	10.00w

Table 10-1 Decibels and MilliWatt Equivalents

On a simpler scale than the numbers in Table 10-1 is the information in Table 10-2, which shows the power in *x* watts and its conversion to decibels (dBx – where *x* is *m*, *K*, or *W*). As shown in Table 10-2, when the power in watts doubles, the increase is 3 dB.

Antenna Power and Gain

Two methods are used to calculate the power and gain output from an RF antenna: EIRP, which is also referred to as the equivalent isotropically radiated power, and effective radiated power (ERP). **EIRP** is used to compare an antenna's gain to the equivalent gain of an isotropic antenna. *ERP* is used to measure the gain produced by a directional antenna in a particular direction.

10

xW	dBx
1	0
2	3
4	6
8	9
16	12
32	15
64	18
128	21

Table 10-2   Power (xW) to dBx Conversion

Isotropic Antennas

The performance and radiation patterns of virtually all real antennas are based, at least in part, on a theoretical antenna that is called an **isotropic** antenna. In theory, an *isotropic antenna* is able to transmit its radio waves equally (in pattern and strength) in all directions at once.

To visualize the conceptual model of an isotropic antenna, imagine an antenna shaped like a small solid ball, like a BB or a small ball bearing, which radiates a spherical transmission pattern. As the following illustration shows, the result would be something like the BB being suspended exactly in the middle of the inside sphere of a beach ball. Because no antenna can produce a radiation pattern that is perfectly spherical, and because a spherical pattern would be a bit unpractical anyway, an isotropic antenna doesn't exist.

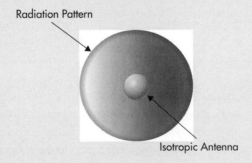

Radiation Pattern

Isotropic Antenna

Effective Isotropically Radiated Power (EIRP)   **EIRP** represents the amount of power an isotropic antenna would need to produce to match the maximum gain of a transmitting antenna. In other words, EIRP is a measurement that indicates the maximum power an antenna can produce in a particular direction. EIRP is calculated as the power of the WLAN interface card, plus the antenna's gain, minus any loss from cable and wire. When a transmitter places a signal on the circuit (line) that leads to the antenna, its power level is reduced by losses that occur on the cable and its connectors.

In the United States, the FCC has set a limit of +36 dBm (or 4 watts) EIRP on omnidirectional WLAN antennas, which can be achieved with 1 watt of power and 6 dB of antenna gain. If the gain of the antenna is 8 dB, then the power must be lowered by 2 dB to provide for a total of 36 dBm total EIRP. The total EIRP for an antenna cannot exceed 36 dBm.

For the most part, commercially available WLAN components and devices conform to this regulation, so you have little need to worry about it. However, if you are inclined to build your own access points or antennas, you should determine the EIRP for each of the transmitters.

Assuming the gain of an antenna (typically, a directional antenna) is specified in dBi, its EIRP is calculated as follows:

1. Determine the total output power of the WLAN network adapter from its specifications or the manufacturer's web site. It is commonly stated in dBm.

2. Determine the amount of loss between the transmitter and the antenna (cable loss) in decibels.

3. Determine the gain of the antenna from its documentation or the manufacturer's web site. It is typically stated in dBi.

4. Using the following formula, calculate the EIRP:

   Total output power of network adapter − Loss in cable + Antenna gain = EIRP

For example, if the output power by a wireless NIC is 15 dBm, the cable loss is 4.5 dB, and the antenna gain is 14 dBi, then the EIRP is 24.5 dBm (15 − 4.5 + 14).

The FCC's rule for directional antennas is this: for every dB of gain in excess of 6 dB, the power is required to be lowered only by one-third (.33) of a decibel. This means a directional antenna with 6 dB of gain doesn't need to lower its power at all. However, for an antenna with 9 dB of gain, the power must be lowered by 1 dB to produce an EIRP of 38 dBm (see Table 10-3).

The gain of the antennas in use in a WLAN is important for you to know, especially any standalone antennas incorporated into the design. But equally important is that you know the propagation and the radiation patterns of the WLAN's antennas. In most cases, all you need to know about the characteristics and performance criteria of an antenna is included on an antenna's specification sheets or its manufacturer's web site.

10

Directional Antenna Gain	Power	Total EIRP
6 dB	30 dBm	36 dBm
9 dB	29 dBm	38 dBm
12 dB	28 dBm	40 dBm
15 dB	27 dBm	42 dBm

Table 10-3   Directional Antenna EIRP

Effective Radiated Power (ERP)   The radiated power (RP) of an antenna is the actual amount of power delivered to the antenna by a transmitter. ERP is a calculation that determines how a directional antenna propagates its energy in one specific direction. The difference between RP and ERP measurements is similar to the difference between a standard light bulb and a spotlight. Even if the two light sources produce the same wattage (for instance, 100 watts) at a certain distance, the spotlight seems brighter because it focuses its light into a single narrow beam, where the light bulb spreads its light in all directions. RP would be the equivalent of the energy from the standard light bulb and ERP measures an antenna's output to be similar to that of the spotlight.

Most wireless systems use ERP to determine the amount of gain produced by antennas transmitting on unlicensed frequency bands (such as 2.4 GHz). In the U.S., the FCC's Code of Federal Regulations, Title 47, Part 15, permits spread spectrum systems to have up to 1 watt (1,000 mW) of maximum transmitter power and only 36 dBm (4 watts) of ERP.

ERP is calculated by adding an antenna's gain (in dBi) to the power of the signal the antenna receives (in dBm). For example, an antenna with 15 dBi of gain that receives a signal with 15 dBm of power has an ERP of 30 dBm (1 watt):

ERP = 15 dBi (gain) + 15 dBm (power) = 30 dBm

Calculating EIRP and ERP   EIRP and ERP are calculations used to determine different power and gain properties of RF antennas. EIRP is used to compare the output of an antenna relative to the radiation of an isotropic source. ERP is used to determine the power and gain produced by an antenna in a specific direction. The formulas used to calculate EIRP and ERP are:

EIRP: total output power – cable loss + antenna gain
ERP: gain + power

❓Line Check 10.2

1. How is EIRP calculated?

2. When an antenna's power in watts doubles, what is the increase in decibels?

3. What is the maximum EIRP allowed by the FCC for an omnidirectional antenna?

Antenna Types

A wide variety of antenna types are used in RF communications for an even wider array of applications. Some antennas are designed for outdoor use, some for indoor use, and some are built into wireless networking devices.

An RF antenna has two general functions: receiving and transmitting. In its receiving functions, an antenna converts electromagnetic energy detected from the air into an electrical current (voltage) for transmission over a circuit. In its transmitting role, an antenna converts an electrical current (voltage) into modulated waves of electromagnetic energy that are radiated into the air.

NOTE

Chapter 3 lists the physical characteristics of the most common WLAN antennas.

Antennas are generally grouped into two basic categories:

- **Directional:** A **directional** *antenna* transmits and receives signals to and from one general direction. There are two general types of directional antennas: highly directional and semidirectional. *Highly directional antennas*, such as many parabolic antennas, transmit signals in a narrow, concentrated beam in a focused direction. Highly directional antennas, commonly used in point-to-point and bridging situations, must be carefully aligned to ensure proper communications. A *semidirectional antenna*, such as a patch antenna and many applications of the Yagi antenna, can increase the gain of a signal by as much as 10 times over that of an omnidirectional antenna. Semidirectional antennas are commonly used to extend a WLAN or a wireless metropolitan area network (MAN) over a larger area. All directional antennas transmit and receive in the same directional pattern.

- **Omnidirectional:** An **omnidirectional** *antenna* transmits its signals in what is essentially a circular pattern around the antenna. Figure 10-4 shows the standard dipole type of omnidirectional antennas typically attached to a WLAN device.

10

Figure 10-4 An access point with dipole omnidirectional antennas (Photo courtesy of Cisco Systems, Inc.)

Figure 10-5 illustrates the shape of the radiation produced by an omnidirectional antenna, which is something like the shape of a doughnut. The signals radiate in all directions from and around the antenna, which would be located in the center hole. Figure 10-6 illustrates a top view of the radiation pattern of a directional antenna. Although the radiation pattern of the directional antenna does splay out a bit, it is generally focused into a single direction.

The next few sections describe the various types and styles of antennas included in these two general categories.

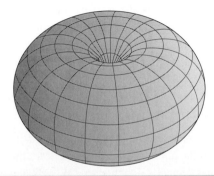

Figure 10-5 An omnidirectional antenna broadcasts to a circular area around the antenna.

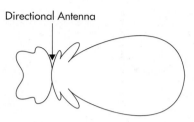

Figure 10-6   The broadcast pattern of a directional antenna.

Directional Antennas

Directional antennas are configured so their transmitted signals are broadcast in a relatively narrow beam width (as illustrated earlier in Figure 10-6). The primary types of directional antennas are:

- **Parabolic** Also called a dish antenna, a *parabolic antenna* is the most directional of the wireless antennas. Parabolic antennas are most commonly used for point-to-point RF transmission of up to 20 miles. WLAN parabolic antennas, which can be a round dish, a wire grid (see Figure 10-7), or a special WLAN type called a backfire, can be several inches to feet in diameter.

Figure 10-7   A wire grid parabolic antenna is commonly used for customer sites by wireless ISPs. (Photo courtesy of Pacific Wireless).

10

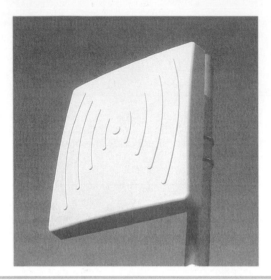

Figure 10-8   A patch antenna is a directional antenna that transmits and receives to and from a single direction. (Photo courtesy of Telex Communications, Inc.)

- **Patch:** The patch antennas used in WLAN applications are generally flat, rectangular, thin panels that are mounted on a wall or ceiling. *Patch antennas* are a type of directional antenna that transmits in an area directly related to its mounting surface, as shown in Figure 10-8. Patch antennas are used when a WLAN's physical topology is fairly flat.

- **Sector:** Perhaps without realizing it, you have probably seen many sector antennas around town, typically on the top of buildings, on towers, and occasionally on top of water towers, as part of a fixed wireless service. A *sector antenna* (see Figure 10-9) is a directional outdoor antenna that transmits only to one specific sector (slice) of the 360-degree transmission spectrum, as illustrated in Figure 10-10. Sector antennas can be configured to as little as a 10-degree sector and as much as a 180-degree sector, with 60 degrees as a common sector. Unless you are planning to start a wireless Internet service provider (WISP) business, it is unusual for a WLAN to incorporate a sector antenna.

- **Yagi-Uda array (Yagi):** This type of antenna, most commonly referred to as a Yagi antenna, was originally developed by two Japanese engineers: Hidetsugu Yagi and Shintaro Uda. *Yagi antennas* are purely directional antennas that are used primarily in citizens' band (CB) and amateur radio (HAM) systems. However, a Yagi antenna (see Figure 10-10) can also be used in a WLAN application for point-to-point transmissions, such as between two buildings on a CAN. Although not commonly referred as a Yagi antenna, the typical TV antenna used on homes is a form of a Yagi antenna. A Yagi antenna uses a directional sector of from 15 to 60 degrees, which makes them more single-direction than a sector antenna.

Figure 10-9   A sector antenna array is on a pole mounting. Each of the sector antennas broadcasts to a different sector. (Photo courtesy of PCTEL, Inc.)

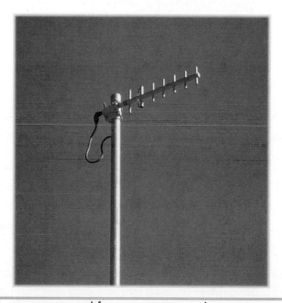

Figure 10-10   A Yagi antenna is used for transmitting and receiving in narrow sector bands. (Photo courtesy of PCTEL, Inc.)

Smart Antennas

A new breed of WLAN antenna is emerging that may help to solve many of the complex layout and coverage design issues that many WLAN designers encounter. To get a general understanding of how a smart antenna works, stand in the center of a darkened room with your eyes tightly closed and have someone walk about the room saying your name (sort of like a dark-room game of "Marco Polo"). As the other person moves about the space, you can generally locate them in the room by the sound of their voice. A *smart antenna* is able to track the location of a roaming wireless station as it moves about inside its range and adjust its radiation pattern to provide coverage to the station in each new location.

Smart antenna systems are also known as *adaptive antenna systems* because in essence that is exactly what they do: adapt the shape, size, and power of their signal to accommodate a roaming station. Smart antennas initially will likely be implemented in mobile telephone applications but, eventually, they should find their way into WLAN applications as well.

Smart antennas implement several new technologies, but the most prevalent is the Multiple-In/Multiple-Out (MIMO) antenna, which is projected to be the basic antenna technology in IEEE 802.11n systems.

Smart antennas come in three types: dual-antenna systems that can automatically choose which of its antennas will better receive an incoming signal, the maximal ratio combining antenna that combines the signals received by its two antennas, and MIMO, which can use two or more antennas to enhance its transmit and receive signal strength.

Omnidirectional (OD) Antenna Types

Omnidirectional (OD) antennas radiate RF signals equally in all directions on a general horizontal direction, much like how the ripples radiate from the point where a pebble is tossed into a pond. Typically, *OD* antennas are most commonly dipole antennas, but they can also be domes and other wall- or ceiling-mounted antennas designed to mount on a ceiling, wall, or desk, as shown in Figure 10-11. OD antennas are used to provide coverage over a large area when the location of the receivers is not fixed or known. The downside of an omnidirectional antenna is it can also pick up random signals and RF noise, which can be rebroadcast, weakening its signal.

Choosing a WLAN Antenna

The built-in antenna included in most wireless NICs, access points, routers, and so on is generally adequate for the majority of small business and home wireless networks. However, in larger and enterprise WLANs, and especially those that must be bridged between buildings in a campus environment, an external antenna may be necessary to extend the range of the wireless devices.

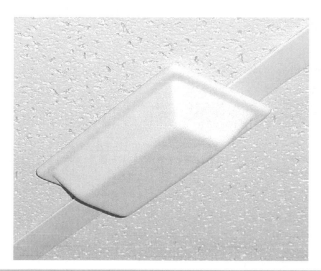

Figure 10-11   A ceiling-mount omnidirectional antenna (Photo courtesy of Telex
Communications, Inc.)

When choosing a WLAN antenna, you must consider the characteristics of wireless
transmissions first, and then the specific characteristics of each type of antenna available
(see the preceding section "WLAN Antenna Basics"). The wireless antenna characteristics you
should consider are:

- The range of the antenna and whether it meets the coverage and capacity requirements of
  the WLAN.

- The type of antenna should be such that it blends in or is functional to its surroundings.
  It doesn't make sense to put a parabolic antenna in the middle of an office space.

- The radiation emanating from an antenna can be distorted by nearby metal and other
  objects, including trees, buildings, and the like.

- Antennas are also used for receiving RF signals and any nearby source of RF interference
  can be picked up and retransmitted in an antenna's outgoing transmission.

- Many RF antennas, such as cellular telephone, may be polarized vertically, so a horizontal
  antenna generally performs better in these environments.

- Cabling connecting to an RF antenna should be free of splices, connectors, and other types
  of interconnections to minimize RF interference.

WLAN antennas are not included in the WLAN standards, so the good news is you are
free to choose an antenna. The bad news is you are free to choose an antenna.

10

Line Check 10.3

1. What are the two basic types of WLAN antennas?

2. Which type of antenna transmits in a circular pattern, both horizontally and vertically?

3. What type of antenna is the kind most commonly attached to WLAN access points and other devices?

What Do You Think?

In which of the following WLAN environments would you recommend the use of an external (not necessarily outside a building) antenna?

A. A WLAN contained completely inside a medium-sized, open-plan concrete building.

B. A WLAN that bridges at least three buildings on a campus setting.

C. A WLAN in which two buildings are located one mile apart.

D. A home WLAN.

Antenna Installation

Locating and installing antennas in a WLAN is an essential step in ensuring the proper operation and performance of the WLAN and its RF communications. Although rare in occurrence, locating an antenna in the wrong place can damage or even destroy WLAN devices and, perhaps, even cause personal harm to installers, technicians, and users.

The criteria that must be considered when deciding on the use of antennas in a WLAN design are:

- Alignment
- Cabling
- Mounting
- Placement
- Safety

Alignment

Alignment is typically not a problem for omnidirectional, semidirectional, or directional antennas that have wide vertical and horizontal beam width. In these situations, aiming two such devices toward each other is generally enough to associate the devices with reasonably good signal quality. This is a common situation when installing access points or wireless routers in a WLAN setting.

However, in situations where a highly directional antenna is being used to connect to a bridging device across a campus or between two buildings, the *alignment* of the devices can be critical to their capability to associate and maintain a quality link between the devices. Wireless bridges and many directional antennas come with software to assist you in establishing the best alignment possible between wireless devices.

Cabling

The cabling used to connect most standalone antennas to a wireless transceiver is most commonly **coaxial** cabling (shown in Figure 10-12). *Coaxial* cable, like the cable used to connect your television set to the cable TV source, has either a solid copper wire or a stranded copper wire core that is covered by a dielectric plastic sheath, which is then covered by a braided copper or aluminum wire sheath. All of these layers are then collectively enclosed with a relatively thick vinyl outer jacket. Both the inner core and the braided sheath carry electrical currents, which is why they are separated by a dielectric (nonconducting) layer.

Figure 10-12   A cut-away view of a coaxial cable

Antenna Cable Types

No single standard grade or size of coaxial cable exists, and some manufacturers have a preference for the type of coaxial cabling and connectors used to connect an antenna to a transceiver. Coaxial cable is available in either 50-ohm or 75-ohm impedance, which must be matched to the system to which it's being attached, and a variety of cable diameters and shielding characteristics. For the most part, 50-ohm cabling is used and is available in RG-8, RG-8X, and RG-58 standards, with RG-58 having the smaller diameter. Many current standards are now calling for RG-213 (single-shield) or RG-214 (double-shield) cable.

NOTE

RG, when used to designate cable, refers to an older U.S. military cable specification. One of the cable categories was "radio grade," which included coaxial cabling. Although no longer used by the military, RG is still used in the cabling industry.

One of the more important parts of installing the cabling on an antenna system is protecting the cable and its connections from moisture. Once moisture gets into the cable or a connector, it can cause erratic and intermittent signal problems in the link. Several types of coaxial cable-specific tape and sealers are available on the market to help waterproof a cable and its connectors. Once moisture gets into a cable, it is far easier and less expensive (in terms of time) simply to replace the cable altogether than to try to get the moisture out.

Connectors

Only a few types of connectors are commonly specified for use with coaxial cable, antennas, and transceivers. The most common connector types are:

● **N-type:** *N-type connecters* are threaded coaxial connectors that are slightly larger in size than the other common coaxial connectors. N-type connectors are commonly on circuits as high as 18 GHz. See Figure 10-13.

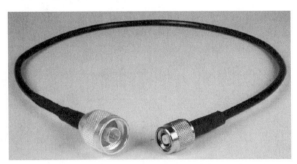

Figure 10-13   An adapter cable with an N-type connector (left) and an RP-TNC connector (right) (Photo courtesy of BusyBits.Com, Australia)

● **Subminiature version A (SMA):** The **SMA** is a subminiature coaxial connector with a screw-type coupling mechanism. This connector has 50-ohm impedance and supports frequencies up to 18 GHz. The SMA (see Figure 10-14) is one of the most commonly used RF connectors.

● **Threaded Neill-Concelman (TNC):** The **TNC** *connector* (see Figure 10-15) is a threaded version of the Bayonet Neill-Concelman (BNC) connector, commonly used on audio networks. TNC connections support frequencies up to 12 GHz, with special frequency TNC versions that support 11 GHz to 18 GHz. The TNC connector is commonly used in cellular telephone and RF antenna installations.

Figure 10-14 SMA connectors are commonly used to attach detachable antennas.

 **Pathfinders**

Neill and Concelman

In the early days of connecting coaxial cabling together for communications and networking purposes, two engineers, Paul Neill of Bell Laboratories and Carl Concelman, developed two connector types: the N-type connector and the C-type connector, respectively, which have merged over time into the NC connector family. The two most commonly used of the NC connectors are the Threaded Neill Concelman (TNC) and the Bayonet Neill Concelman (BNC) connectors.

Figure 10-15 A TNC connector is commonly used with coaxial cable in antenna connections.

Cabling Antennas

As the RF signal moves through the coaxial cable between the transceiver and the antenna, the cable introduces loss for both transmitter and receiver. The longer the cable runs between the transceiver and the antenna, the greater the amount of loss. To minimize the signal loss, the length of cable runs should be as short as possible and low-loss antenna cable should be used.

The amount of signal strength loss that occurs as a signal travels through a cable is impacted negatively by the cable's length and the signal's frequency, and somewhat positively by the cable's diameter. First, the positive side: as the diameter of a coaxial cable increases, the amount of signal loss incurred decreases (but typically at a higher material cost per foot). The length of the cable run increases the amount of loss the signal will incur and higher frequencies (carried over higher numbered channels) suffer more loss than lower signal frequencies.

The loss on a cable increases with both the frequency and the distance over which the signal is transmitted. One way to demonstrate the affect of loss on a cable is by comparing the difference between the wattage of an input power signal and the resulting power output (POut) from a circuit. Table 10-4 demonstrates the loss numbers for a standard (RG-58) coaxial cable at various distances with an input signal (PIn) of 50 watts.

PIn	MHz	dB Loss/100 feet	POut
50	50	2.5	28
50	100	3.8	21
50	200	5.6	14
50	400	8.4	7
50	700	11.7	3

Table 10-4 Signal Loss (in dB) for RG-58 Cable

A number of manufacturers are producing low-loss and ultra-low-loss coaxial cables that reduce the amount of signal loss suffered by longer cable runs. A low-loss cable can reduce the dB loss per 100 feet to around 4.4 dB as compared to the 11.7 dB loss per 100 feet for non-low-loss cabling.

Some installation tips that can help you to avoid introducing loss producing problems into the cable are:

- When installing the cable, don't pull so hard on the cable that you might stretch it. This could increase the amount of loss a cable suffers.

- Don't sharply bend or kink the cable. The coaxial cable used with antennas typically has a minimum bend radius of around 3 centimeters (or about 1.2 inches).

- Minimize the length of every cable run.

- Install lightning protection (see the section "Safety during Installation ")

- Seal all openings through which the coaxial cable passes with a good sealing material, such as *Coax-Seal*, which is a hand-moldable sealing material.

Mounting

Whether they are indoor or outdoor types, standalone antennas generally must be mounted to a surface. Yes, some antennas can sit on a table top or floor but, for the most part, antennas need to be attached to a wall, a ceiling, or some other surface. Depending on the size and type of the antenna, a variety of mounting options can be used, including:

- **Articulated mountings:** An *articulated mounting* is a mounting option that is jointed and, typically, allows an antenna's position to be adjusted slightly without the need to remove and physically reposition the entire mounting point. Virtually all antennas on wireless access points, NICs, and other WLAN devices have an articulated mounting. Figure 10-16 illustrates a wireless NIC with an articulated mounting in its antenna.

- **Ceiling mountings:** A *ceiling mounting* is attached to a ceiling crossbeam or the rigid crossbars of a suspended ceiling. The previous Figure 10-11 showed a ceiling-mount antenna.

Figure 10-16   A wireless network interface card (NIC) with an antenna that includes an articulated mounting (Photo courtesy of Cisco Systems, Inc.)

10

Figure 10-17 An antenna mounted to a mast (Image courtesy of Kenbotong Communications, Ltd.)

- **Ground plane mountings:** A *ground plane mounting* is typically attached to a pole, post, or mast. Figure 10-17 illustrates the installation of a ground plane antenna.

- **Mast, pillar, and post mountings:** These types of antenna mountings most commonly consist of mounting flanges that tighten around a metal or fiberglass pole, post, or pillar using u-bolts or screw-type clamping mechanisms (as shown in Figure 10-18). The mast, pillar, or post can be attached directly to the side of a building, to a tripod mounted either permanently or temporarily on a rooftop, or to a pole or post installed in the ground.

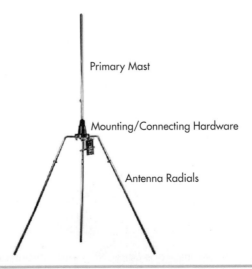

Figure 10-18 A ground plane antenna is typically mounted to the top of a mast or pole. (Original image courtesy of Decade Transmitters, Inc.)

Figure 10-19   A tabletop antenna mounting with dipole antennas (Photo courtesy of Cisco Systems, Inc.)

- **Table mounts:** A *tabletop antenna mount* works like a candlestick holder in that the antennas are inserted into receiver holes (as shown in Figure 10-19). Obviously, this type of mount is used indoors, in situations where the infrastructure of a WLAN needs to remain somewhat flexible.

- **Wall mountings:** *Wall-mount RF antennas*, like the one shown in Figure 10-20, are designed to fit flat against a wall and blend into the décor as much as possible. This type of antenna either mounts to a mounting plate (which is attached to the wall directly) or directly to the wall though screw holes provided by the manufacturer.

10

Figure 10-20   A wall-mounted antenna (Photo courtesy of Kenbotong Communications, Ltd.)

Placement of a WLAN Antenna

The primary rule-of-thumb for locating a WLAN antenna is to place the antenna as close to the users as possible. An antenna doesn't need to be all that close to an access point or another wireless device, but it should be placed in the immediate proximity of the users it services. Often this means the antenna is connected by cable to an access point or the like, so it can be placed where it provides the most service to network users.

When coaxial cabling is used to connect the antenna back to a wireless access point, switch, bridge, or router, the cable run should not be more than 30 meters (about 100 feet). This is regardless of the distance rating of the coaxial cable, which may be as high as 200 meters or more.

Indoor antennas should be placed as high as possible to provide for enhanced coverage, but also align the antenna, so users directly beneath or close to the antenna's location also have coverage. Omnidirectional antennas should be placed as close to the center of a coverage area as possible. Outdoor antennas should be mounted to avoid any large obstructions, such as trees, other buildings, rocks, and the like that may fall in their radiation patterns.

Safety during Installation

WLAN antennas, which are electrical devices, can be dangerous in certain situations to the installer and to the user. The safety guidelines for working with and using RF antennas are essentially the same as for any electrical device and are mostly based on common sense. However, the following are safety guidelines you should know and follow to ensure a safe installation for all concerned.

- **Avoid metal obstructions:** An antenna should not be installed where it is near heating and air conditioning ducts, metal ceiling trusses or building superstructures, or large bundles of cabling, whether structured cabling or electrical lines. Nearby metal objects can create multipath conditions, which can cause transmission problems by reflecting portions of a signal, so they arrive at a receiver at different times.

- **Avoid power lines:** An antenna should not be placed near overhead power lines. The rule-of-thumb is this: a power line should not be closer than twice the height of the antenna (including its mounting or tower) outdoors and no closer than 24 inches indoors. Placing an antenna too close to a power line can cause an electrical short between the two, which could be dangerous for anyone working on the system. Placing an antenna too close to a power line could destroy the antenna and any equipment connected to it.

- **Handling precautions:** When power is being applied to an antenna, especially high-gain antennas, you should never touch the antenna with any part of your body. And, you should not point the transmitting end of the antenna toward your body, which could be the equivalent of climbing into a microwave oven. An antenna in any of the unlicensed bands transmits high RF power over point-to-point links and putting any part of your body in the transmitting beam is dangerous.

- **Install grounding rods:** An outdoor RF antenna should be connected to a grounding rod as required by the National Electrical Code (NEC) and likely local electrical codes as well. A grounding rod with 2 ohms or less of resistance is another way to protect anyone working on the system in the event of a lightning strike or electrical arc from an external power source.

- **Install lightning arrestor:** Lightning is said to strike the highest object it can find and, in many locations, an outside, metal, RF antenna may just be that object. If lightning directly strikes or merely strikes in its immediate vicinity, an exterior WLAN antenna and its cabling can be severely damaged, not to mention the power surge that will travel down the cable to any attached devices, such as an access point. The installation of a **lightning arrestor** (see Figure 10-21) designed for the frequency in use (2.4 or 5 GHz) in-line between the antenna and the access point, or other wireless device, prevents the energy surge associated with a lightning strike from causing damage to any downstream equipment. Regardless of the energy in the lightning, a lightning arrestor limits the exiting energy to less than 50 volts per 100 nanoseconds, a level nearly all RF and electrical devices are able to handle.

Figure 10-21   A lightning arrestor is used to reduce the electrical energy of a lightning strike to protect RF and electrical devices. (Photo courtesy of PCTEL, Inc.)

Lightning

Lightning is a constant threat to RF communications and electrical devices. *Lightning* is composed of an average of four electrical strokes that occur in a series. The time duration and the electrical energy of each stroke varies quite a bit but, on average, a lightning stroke lasts around 30 microseconds and has about 10^{12} watts of energy. In addition, a lightning stroke heats the air around it to around 20,000 degrees Centigrade, which is about three times hotter than the surface of the sun (it is the heat expansion in the air that causes the sound of thunder).

Line Check 10.4

1. List three types of connectors commonly used with antenna and cabling.

2. What are the general guidelines when choosing the placement of a WLAN antenna?

3. What device can help to protect an antenna and other downstream devices from a lightning strike?

 ## What Do You Think?

What are the two greatest safety issues surrounding the installation and operation of an RF antenna? Do you believe the general public is aware of the dangers posed by RF antennas? Is this a situation that should be corrected? If so, how?

Chapter 10 Review

Chapter Summary

Explain the Operations of a WLAN Antenna

- Transmitted radio signals begin as an electrical current, which is caused by the alternating and continuous movement of electrons, on a wire. The current also radiates an electromagnetic field outside and around the wire.

- An antenna is designed to radiate the electromagnetic field of an electrical current.

- How far, and the direction in which, an antenna radiates a signal depends on the antenna's power, the frequency and wavelength of the electromagnetic field, and the design of the antenna.

- Whether an antenna is transmitting or receiving, the frequency, wavelength, and amplitude of the electrical current are maintained.

- All antennas share five basic characteristics: frequency, gain, power, radiation pattern, and polarization.

- Several basic measurement units and formulas are used to measure and state the power levels emitted by an antenna, including watts, milliWatts, and decibels.

- A transmitter places a signal on the TFO circuit that leads to an antenna. line losses occur on the line, and the antenna adds gain to the signal before it is radiated. The power of the signal radiated by the antenna is EIRP.

- Whenever an antenna's power in watts doubles, the increase is equivalent to a gain of 3 dB.

Explain Characteristics of WLAN Antennas

- Antennas are generally grouped into two basic categories: directional and omnidirectional.

- The performance and radiation patterns of virtually all antennas are based on a theoretical antenna—an isotropic antenna.

- Directional antennas are configured so their transmitted signals are broadcast in a relatively narrow beam width. The primary types of directional antennas are parabolic, patch, sector, and Yagi.

- Omnidirectional antennas radiate equally in all directions on a general horizontal plane. Omnidirectional antennas are commonly dipole antennas, but they can be domes and other wall or ceiling-mounted antennas.

Describe the Cables, Connectors, and Other Devices Used with WLAN Antennas

- The criteria that must be considered when deciding on the use and placement of an antenna in a WLAN are alignment, cabling, mounting, placement, and safety.

- The cabling used to connect most standalone antennas to a wireless transceiver is most commonly 50-ohm coaxial cabling in the RG-8, RG-58, RG-213, or RG-214 standards.

- The most common connector types for coaxial cable and antennas are N-type, SMA, and TNC.

- Depending on the size and type of the antenna, the mounting options that can be used are: articulated, ceiling, ground plane, mast, pillar, post, table top, and wall mountings.

● A WLAN antenna should be placed as close to WLAN users as possible. Indoor antennas should be placed as high as possible. Outdoor antennas should be mounted to avoid any large obstructions, such as trees, other buildings, rocks, and the like that may fall in their radiation patterns.

Key Terms

coaxial *(345)*
dBm *(331, 333)*
directional *(337)*
EIRP *(329, 333, 335)*
gain *(329)*
isotropic *(334)*
lightning arrestor *(353)*
omnidirectional *(337, 342)*
polarization *(330)*
radiation pattern *(329)*
SMA *(346)*
TFO *(329)*
TNC *(346)*

Key Term Quiz

Use the terms from the Key Terms list to complete the following sentences. Don't use the same term more than once. Not all terms will be used.

1. The radiation patterns and other properties of virtually all actual antennas are based on the properties of the _____ antenna.

2. The power added to the signal by an antenna is called _____.

3. A(n) _____ is used to help protect cabling and electrical devices connected to an antenna from damage by an electrical surge.

4. The area to which an antenna broadcasts its signal is defined by its _____.

5. A(n) _____ antenna is the type built into most standard WLAN devices.

6. A(n) _____ antenna broadcasts its signal in one general direction.

7. The total power of the signal generated by an antenna is its _____.

8. The most common type of cable used with antennas is _____ cable.

9. _____ and _____ are the common connector types used with the cabling for antenna systems.

10. To ensure the signal is received properly, both the transmitter and receiver should use the same _____.

Multiple Choice Quiz

1. What is the calculation used to measure the total power produced by an antenna?

   A. EIRP

   B. Power

   C. Radiation

   D. EIRP

2. What conceptual antenna is used as the base for all real antennas?

   A. Omnidirectional

   B. Directional

   C. Isotropic

   D. Microwave

3. What device can be added between an antenna and an access point to help reduce the potential damage from electrical storms?

   A. Grounding rod

   B. Lightning arrestor

   C. Lightning rod

   D. SMA

4. What measurement is used to state the total power produced by an antenna?

   A. EIRP

   B. TFO

   C. Radiation

   D. Pout

5. What type of cabling is most commonly used between an antenna and a WLAN access point?

    A. UTP

    B. STP

    C. Coaxial

    D. Fiber optic

6. Which of the following is not a commonly used connector standard for coaxial cable and antenna applications?

    A. N-Type

    B. RJ-45

    C. SMA

    D. TNC

7. Which of the following is not a type of antenna used in WLAN systems?

    A. Earth station

    B. Patch

    C. Ceiling-mount

    D. Parabolic

8. What type of antenna is used to aim a radiation pattern to a specific area?

    A. Directional

    B. Omnidirectional

    C. Isotropic

    D. Smart

9. What is the term used to describe the power added to a signal by the antenna?

    A. Attenuation

    B. Gain

    C. Loss

    D. Voltage

10. What characteristic of a transmitted signal must be configured on both a transmitter and a receiver to ensure signals are properly received?

   A. Power

   B. Gain

   C. EIRP

   D. Polarization

Lab Projects

1. In an existing WLAN served by an access point with built-in (but detachable) antennas, make a note of each station able to associate with the access point through its built-in antennas. Remove the detachable antennas and connect the access point to an external omnidirectional antenna. Move the antenna to different locations around the WLAN and check each of the WLAN's stations to verify each is still able to associate with the access point. What general location seems to provide the best coverage?

2. Repeat Project #1 using an external directional antenna. Do you have the same results? Why? Based on your findings, what is the general radiation pattern of the antenna?

Case Problem

Gotcha Covered Insurance Company has a small WLAN installed in its offices. Because of their recent growth, they have added three more agents and constructed additional office space to the rear of their building. Their current WLAN access point is unable to provide association to any of the new offices and they want to solve this problem in the least expensive, yet most effective, way possible. Moving the access point has not proven effective for all stations. What do you recommend?

Advanced Lab Project

The Commercial Ceilings Division of Armstrong World Industries has developed a ceiling tile ("i-ceilings") that contains an embedded WLAN antenna. This product was recently installed in an elementary school in Florida with much success. Read the article in the following sidebar for more information on application.

   A. If you were to apply this ceiling tile/antenna technology to your school or a local business, how many panels would be required to provide for adequate coverage and capacity?

   B. Does the use of these panels add any complexity to the overall WLAN design?

   C. Do you believe this product and similar products represent a lasting innovation? Why?

Florida School Rates an A+ for Its Wireless Capability

(www.armstrong.com/commceilingsna/article1012.html)

Ceiling panels have wireless antennas embedded in them to provide connectivity anywhere in the facility.

Considering that it's only four years old, the Terrace Community School, a rapidly growing charter school for fifth to eighth graders in Tampa, Florida, is quickly making quite a name for itself. Its fifth-grade students recently ranked first in the Hillsborough County School District in math in the state's aptitude tests, while its eighth graders ranked first on the reading test and writing test, and ranked second on the math test.

However, academics aren't the only factor contributing to the school's reputation. The school recently moved from its small, original facility to a much larger space located in the city's Museum of Science and Industry. And, when it made the move, it quickly became one of the leaders in the Tampa area in terms of technology, as well as academics. The reason: the entire school is now wireless capable.

One of the major elements contributing to that capability is a unique ceiling system that has wireless antennas embedded in the ceiling panels, thereby providing wireless connectivity for the students anywhere in the school.

Laptops Best Solution to Computer Needs

Armstrong's i-ceilings Wireless System provides the students and faculty of the Terrace Community School with wireless connectivity for their laptops anywhere in their facility, from the classroom to "The Commons." Even though "The Commons" is located nearly 75 feet from the classroom area, students do not lose connectivity. Only four i-ceilings Antenna Panels are required to provide the 17,000-square-foot school with coverage.

According to William McKelligott, Head of the School, the original facility was a traditional one. However, when the decision was made to move to the new building, it gave McKelligott and other school administrators the opportunity to think ahead.

"We knew that computers are tremendous tools for instruction, and that we wanted to provide our students with these tools," he states. "However, we also knew that we did not want a computer lab, nor did we want computers in only one or two classrooms. We wanted the students to be able to use computers anywhere in the school if they wanted to."

Greg van Stekelenburg, Head of the school's Technology Committee, concurs. "However," he says, "the problem was deciding how to handle all the wiring, especially in an existing facility. Would we drop cables from the ceiling, run wires from the walls, or install ports in the floor? After some investigation, we eventually decided that laptops in conjunction with wireless connectivity were, by far, the best solution."

The decision to go wireless is working out extremely well. The school has 80 laptops thus far as a result of two grants. It has also established its own Wireless Local Area Network (WLAN) for e-mail, shared data, and access to the Internet.

In order to obtain WLAN coverage within a building, antennas are usually mounted onto the ceilings or walls. However, the Terrace Community School decided instead to install an i-ceilings™ Wireless System to provide its students and faculty with wireless connectivity throughout the facility.

Ceiling System Provides Wireless Coverage

Manufactured by Armstrong, the unique new system features a special Antenna Panel that has a set of antennas embedded in the ceiling panel to enable in-building wireless connectivity. The panels can handle both voice and data connectivity. However, the school is only utilizing the data capability at the present time.

Antenna Panels provide very efficient and effective coverage because the ceiling plane is considered to be the best location for omnidirectional antennas. They are also quick and easy to install, since they simply lay into the grid like standard ceiling panels.

From an aesthetic point of view, Antenna Panels look just like ordinary ceiling panels so that they blend in with the overall ceiling. And, because the antennas are embedded in the ceiling, they are invisible from below. This makes the room more visually pleasing, and creates a more comfortable atmosphere for both students and teachers. It also helps eliminate the potential for damage, vandalism and theft that can occur with visible antennas.

Four Antenna Panels Cover 17,000 Square Feet

The school is not only pleased with the aesthetics but also the coverage. Terrace Community School occupies the second and third floors in one of the museum wings. Its administrative offices are located along one side of a long corridor on the second floor, and twelve classrooms along the other.

To provide wireless connectivity on this floor, i-ceilings Antenna Panels are located in the third, sixth, and ninth classrooms. Access points are also installed there, directly above the Antenna Panels. Two more rooms are located on the third floor, with an antenna panel and access point located midway between them.

Considering that only four Antenna Panels are providing coverage for all 17,000 square feet of the facility, van Stekelenburg reports that the quality and range of the signal are strong. As a case in point, he notes that students spend a lot of time in an area known as "The Commons." It is located on the third floor about 75 feet from the classroom area, and students must cross a breezeway to get there.

"Students go there after school and do their homework while waiting for their ride home," he states. "They'll take laptops with them, and even though there are two walls and quite a distance between them and the antenna panels, they don't lose connectivity."

Wireless System Offers Academic Benefits

McKelligott, too, is delighted with the system, but more from an instructional point of view. "The use of computers challenges students to think," he says, "in the sense that they have to select and organize information for academic success. This forces them to become much more analytical in their thinking, which is one of the keys to academic success. Computers are one of the best tools by which to accomplish this, and wireless technology facilitates the process."

The Armstrong i-ceilings Wireless System provides the students and faculty of the Terrace Community School with wireless connectivity for their laptops anywhere in their facility, from the classroom to "The Commons." Even though "The Commons" is located nearly 75 feet from the classroom area, students do not lose connectivity. Only four i-ceilings Antenna Panels are required to provide the 17,000-square-foot school with coverage.

Chapter 11

WLAN Security

Security is a hot topic these days and it couldn't be any hotter for wireless networks than it already is. Wireless networks, especially wireless local area networks (WLANs), are inherently insecure. Anyone with the ability to intercept a radio transmission is able to steal data, gain access, or perform an ever-widening array of evil deeds to a wireless network, and worse, to the users on that network.

Not all wireless networks are intended to be secure: it depends on the purpose and goals of the network. For example, in a community WLAN that is intended to create a hot spot, so anyone in the coverage area can gain access to the network, the focus is hardly on protecting the network from the end user or vice versa. On the other hand, wireless networks in many commercial companies, such as banks, must implement strict user control, authentication, and data privacy procedures. For the most part, home networks are somewhere in the middle, and which of these two extremes a particular home network is closer to depends on the knowledge and skill level of the family member who installs and manages it.

In this chapter, you learn about the various layers of security that can be applied to an 802.11 WLAN, ranging from "not much" to "almost excellent." You also look at the security protocols and services defined in the 802.11 standards, as well as the threats that exist from the outside world and how each protocol or service combats them.

Wireless LAN Security Basics

When wireless systems were first introduced, the manufacturers and vendors claimed that security and privacy were inherent characteristics of the transmission methods in use. An early claim regarding the security of a wireless network was that the necessary receivers that could be used to intercept WLAN signals didn't really exist. Spread-spectrum systems, including WLAN transmitters and receivers, modulate their signals into a wide transmission band. The belief was this: because the radio frequency (RF) receivers that could be used to intercept signals were predominantly narrowband receivers, those wideband transmissions were safe from interception. Unfortunately, it didn't take long before someone determined that WLAN receivers themselves were the devices that were said not to exist.

The need to secure a wireless network became even more of a priority after stories began to surface about people driving around with high-gain antennas on their cars and using special software to detect wireless networks, a practice called *wardriving* (see the sidebar "Wardriving and Warchalking" on page 391).

Securing wireless networks has become a priority for the industry and, in June 2004, the Institute for Electrical and Electronics Engineers (IEEE) announced the adoption of the 802.11i security standard, which is aimed at vastly improving the overall security and privacy of wireless network data and SSIDs and denying access to unauthorized intruders.

Several protocols and methods can be used to secure WLAN transmissions and prevent unauthorized access to the network. The most commonly used methods are:

- Wired Equivalent Privacy (WEP)
- MAC address filtering
- A variety of authentication protocols
- Data encryption

These security methods and the specific protocols used to implement them are discussed in the following sections.

WEP

The need for some security was apparent early in the development of the IEEE 802.11 standards, so a security protocol, Wired Equivalent Privacy (**WEP**), was included in the 802.11b standard. *WEP* is designed to provide a WLAN with security and privacy equivalent to that expected on a wireline network. WEP is an optional element of a wireless network but, if used, it provides more security than if it is not used at all.

WEP Goals and Shortcomings

One fairly major issue with this goal was that much of the security surrounding a wireline network is physical in nature and includes such security elements as controlled building access, locked office doors, cables in the walls and floors, and the like. A wireless network is much harder to secure because radio waves are transmitted through the air and can pass through walls.

WEP encrypts the data payload in each transmitted packet in an attempt to keep the data private between network adapters and the access points. When WEP encryption was added to the other commonly implemented security measures, such as passwords and authentication, the concept was that the network would be secure.

Unfortunately, a number of software programs, such as AirSnort and WebCrack, are readily available. They can decipher the WEP encryption and allow intruders to gain access to the network. These programs are purported to be WLAN "tools" that can be used to recover encryption keys by passively monitoring wireless transmissions and, after gathering enough encryption samples, compute the encryption key.

Although WEP was never intended to serve as the only security measure in use on a network, many home and small office networks depend on it to provide security on their networks. However, because WEP is applied only on the two lowest OSI layers (data link and physical layers), it doesn't provide end-to-end security for transmitted data.

WEP Encryption

Each packet is encrypted by WEP using an **RC4** (Rivest Cipher 4), an encryption cipher developed by Dr. Ronald Rivest of RSA Data Security, Inc., which accepts encryption keys of arbitrary lengths and generates a pseudorandom number. That number is then combined with the data stream using the Boolean algebra exclusive OR (XOR) function to output encrypted data.

The encryption key, used by WEP as the seed to the pseudorandom number generator in RC4, has two parts: a 24-bit initialization vector (IV) chosen by the network user or administrator and a WEP key, supplied by the wireless device. This is either 40 bits or 104 bits in length, yielding a total length for the WEP key of 64 bits or 128 bits. The 24-bit IV limits the encryption to 16,777,216 different RC4-encrypted streams for each IV, regardless of whether 40 or 104 bits are used for the remaining portion of the key. One of the weaknesses in WEP is that the IV is transmitted in plain unencrypted text in each packet. Because the IV is rarely changed, and it is reused over and over, a packet snooper could gather enough packets in a matter of minutes to crack the key.

Figure 11-1 illustrates the process involved to encrypt and transmit a single packet between a wireless node and an access point. The PC prepares the data for transfer and passes it to the network adapter. The network adapter applies the WEP and encryption process, and then transmits the encrypted data along with other information, including the IV, to the access point. The access point deciphers the encrypted data using the IV. If the packet is forwarded to another wireless node, the WEP process is performed by the access point before transmission. When you consider that multiple packets are transmitted across the network to send even an instant messaging (IM) note that just says, "Hi," you get a sense of how often this process is performed and the number of packets that are transmitted on the wireless media.

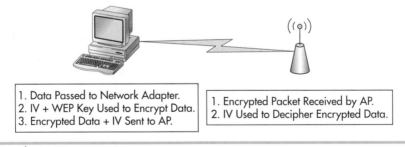

1. Data Passed to Network Adapter.
2. IV + WEP Key Used to Encrypt Data.
3. Encrypted Data + IV Sent to AP.

1. Encrypted Packet Received by AP.
2. IV Used to Decipher Encrypted Data.

Figure 11-1   The WEP encryption process

When a user transmits a message to a wireless network on which WEP is activated, the NIC or network adapter in or attached to the user's PC encrypts the body of the transmitted frame and its cyclic redundancy check (CRC) checksum using an RC4 cipher before transmitting the message to the network medium.

Random Number Generators and Seeds

A *random number seed* is a numerical value used to initialize a random number generator. A *random number generator* is an algorithm that generates a series of numbers that have no apparent relationship to each other and no apparent sequence. In other words, the generated series of numbers should represent the values that could be chosen completely at random from an infinite set.

 Pathfinders

Dr. Ronald L. Rivest

Dr. Ronald L. Rivest (shown in the photo below) is the Viterbi Professor of Computer Science at the Massachusetts Institute of Technology (MIT) and a cofounder of RSA Data Security, now known as RSA Security, Inc.

Dr. Rivest is best known in the computing world for his work in cryptography, algorithms, and computer and network security. Drawing on his extensive experience in cryptographic design and analysis, Dr. Rivest developed the Rivest-Shamir-Adleman (RSA) encryption method, working with his partners, Adi Shamir and Leonard Adleman, also of MIT.

Dr. Rivest holds a bachelor degree in Mathematics from Yale University and a PhD from Stanford University in computer science. In addition to his work in computer and network security, Dr. Rivest has also worked extensively in computer algorithms, machine learning, and very-large-scale integration (VLSI) design.

In the encryption process, WEP uses a key schedule or seed that consists of the shared key supplied by the sending node (as configured by its user) and a random number IV. Even if the shared key doesn't change, the IV is unique to each transmitted frame. The key schedule (the combination of the shared key and the IV) is then used to a generate a pseudorandom number that is the same length as the frame's data payload, plus a 32-bit integrity check value (ICV), which functions much like the CRC in the data payload.

When the encrypted message frame is received by an access point or another wireless NIC, it is deciphered (decrypted) for processing, and the ICV is recalculated and compared to the ICV transmitted in the frame. If the two ICVs match, then the message frame is accepted and processing continues. If the ICVs don't match, however, the receiving node either rejects the frame (drops it) or signals the sender to retransmit the frame. If the message is to be transmitted on to a wireline network, it remains decrypted. WEP only encrypts data frames transmitted between 802.11 WLAN nodes.

Although not specified in the 802.11 standards, the sending node uses a unique IV for each transmitted frame in most cases. This is intended to overcome the vulnerability created when transmitted messages contain the same data, such as in e-mails that begin with the words "From," "Reply," or "Forward." When these messages are encrypted, the encrypted stream is either the same or similar, which could provide an interceptor with a pattern that could be used to break the encryption. Using a unique IV overcomes this situation for the most part.

How Critics View WEP

WEP has been in use since 1999, which has been long enough for evildoers to fix on its methods and processes, not to mention its encryption results. Those who are critical of WEP's capability to provide truly secure communications on a WLAN cite the following issues:

- **Short IV:** The same 24-bit IV is commonly used repeatedly, regardless of the packet's contents and on a fairly busy network. The IV pattern can be recognized easily within a short time frame.

- **Static shared keys:** Because 802.11 doesn't include any provisions for the dynamic exchange of keys between nodes, the same keys are used over and over by a node, sometimes for weeks, months, and, perhaps, even years. This situation, if it goes on for any length of time, gives a hacker plenty of opportunity to decipher the encryption keys and gain access to a WEP-enabled network. One of the solutions to this problem is the use of the 802.1x security standard (see the section "IEEE 802.1x Security").

Activating WEP is still better than nothing. WEP does a good job of keeping most people out, at least those who are easily deterred. But true hackers are around who can exploit the weaknesses of WEP and access WEP-enabled networks.

MAC Address Filtering

Many of the early manufacturers of wireless access points and routers chose not to implement WEP and developed MAC address filtering as an alternative method for securing a WLAN.

Like all 802.x networks, 802.11 WLAN nodes are identified using a 48-bit device identifier, more commonly known as a MAC address. Defined on the MAC (Layer 2) sublayer, the MAC address identifies the manufacturer and a globally unique device ID. The concept behind MAC address filtering is this: because IT departments are responsible for issuing wireless NICs to network users and the installation of wireless connectivity (WiCon) devices, they should be able to manage a list of MAC addresses allowed to access the WLAN.

When a wireless access point or router is installed and configured, a list of the MAC addresses allowed to connect to the network is entered. The access point can then scan its list of allowable MAC addresses to determine if a node is on the approved list. However, an attacker using a listed MAC address is permitted to associate with the access point and participate on the network.

The downfall of this approach is that the MAC address is transmitted in several of the administrative and association frames exchanged between two wireless nodes. Even if MAC filtering is used with encryption, a dedicated hacker can eventually learn one or more of the MAC addresses on a WLAN.

MAC address filtering is not a part of the 802.11 standards and provides only marginal security to a wireless network.

Line Check 11.1

1. WEP was defined in which of the 802.11x standards?

2. In the WEP process, what elements are used to generate the encryption key?

3. What is often cited as the major fault in WEP security?

Authentication

Before wireless access points and wireless NICs or network adapters establish an association with each other, a series of management frames is exchanged. However, even before this can begin, these devices must first be aware that each other exists.

Wireless access points, depending on their configuration, may transmit beacon frames, which include their SSID. Wireless nodes receiving a beacon frame determine, based on its signal strength, if they want to associate with the access point transmitting the beacon. A wireless station transmits probe frames, which includes its station ID and the SSID to which it has been configured and the authentication method it wants to use. An access point receiving a transmitted probe frame responds based on how it has been configured for establishing an authentication method. Within the 802.11 standards and, as a part of WEP, two authentication methods are defined: open system authentication and shared key authentication.

Open System Authentication

The standard default authentication method is open system authentication (OSA), which provides for no authentication to be performed. Using OSA, any wireless node is allowed to associate to an access point using a randomly generated shared key.

Authentication implies the use of a shared key that is used to continually verify than an association exists between two devices. Under OSA, however, the node and the access point don't establish a single shared key that remains in use throughout the association session. Each station generates and transmits its own randomly generated key and requests that the receiver accept the key temporarily for the association. The key is then used only to establish the association. A new key is generated and used to maintain the association between the devices. In effect, *OSA* involves a two-step authentication process, in which a node transmits its identity and shared key, and the access point responds with acceptance and the data required to establish an association. All the frames involved in establishing an association using OSA are transmitted as open (not encrypted) text.

Shared Key Authentication

As shown in Figure 11-2, shared-key authentication (SKA) follows a sequence of actions to authenticate a node attempting to associate with an access point. After receiving an association request—in the form of an 802.11 registration request frame—the access point generates a random number challenge key and transmits it to the requesting node. The node then signs (applies) its preset shared key to the challenge key using a Boolean XOR operation and sends the signed key back to the access point for verification. The access point then performs the same signing operation and compares the results. If the signature of both keys matches, the node is authentication and the association is established.

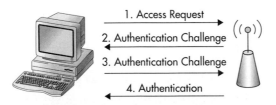

1. Access Request
2. Authentication Challenge
3. Authentication Challenge
4. Authentication

Figure 11-2   The shared key authentication (SKA) process

Because the challenge key and the signed challenge key are both transmitted in open text, a hacker can easily use an intercepted message to determine the IV used by the RC4 encryption algorithm and decipher a frame's data payload. This knowledge also gives the intruder the ability to respond to any challenge frames and provides the capability to freely join the network.

 Line Check 11.2

1. On a wireless network, what is the purpose of the authentication process?

2. What are the two standard authentication methods defined in the 802.11x standards?

3. What is the security risk associated with using OSA?

 What Do You Think?

Does authentication have more, less, or about the same importance on a wireless network than on a wireline network?

Extensible Authentication Methods

The most commonly used authentication methods consist of only a user name and a password, which are verified to grant or deny access. Because most network administrators and their organizations want to have more security than is available through user name/password authentication, the Extensible Authentication Protocol (**EAP**) was developed for point-to-point communications. *EAP* provides the means to override standard or proprietary authentication methods and to allow other authentication methods be applied, including passwords, challenge keys, and public key infrastructure certificates. Although originally developed to work with the dial-up Point-to-Point Protocol (PPP), EAP has been adapted for use on wireless networks.

In the dial-up world, standard EAP is interoperable and compatible with most authentication methods in use. When a user dials into a remote access server (RAS) that is using EAP to authenticate the PPP connection, the authentication processes normally performed by the RAS are pushed aside and authentication processing is passed to an authentication server, such as a Remote Authentication Dial-In User Service (RADIUS) server that supports EAP.

On an 802.11 wireless network, the authentication and security methods are divided into three primary areas:

- **Authentication framework:** The *authentication framework* is the actual mechanism that performs the authentication process, including login processing, service classes, protocol support, and functions used in performing user or device authentication. Each of the various authentication types constitutes an authentication framework.

- **Authentication algorithm:** The 802.11x standards define the use of two primary *authentication algorithms*: RC4, which is used in WEP and the Wi-Fi Protected Access (WPA) protocol, and Advanced Encryption Standard (AES), which is used in 802.1x and EAP.

- **Data frame encryption:** *Data frame encryption* applies the encryption key to the data payload in a frame for secured transmission (see the section "Data Encryption").

802.1x Security

The standard 802.11 authentication methods concentrate more on authorizing the association between wireless devices and less on verifying the user's or the node's identity. However, if the network administrator and the company's management want to extend the focus of the authentication system, the authentication method in use must be of sufficient scalability (extensibility) and able to handle all the WLAN's nodes.

On a small network, meaning a network with a single access point, the capability of the security method to scale to fit the number of users is not typically an issue. On a large enterprise wireless network, however, the authentication method must be able to scale to support hundreds, or even thousands, of wireless nodes and users. Of course, an enterprise network of this size also requires centralized administration of the authentication process.

In an effort to improve the overall security of WLANs, including the enhancement of the authentication methods defined in the 802.11 standards, the 802.11i task group is working to incorporate the **IEEE 802.1x** authentication framework, which was developed for all 802 networking. The *802.1x* standard allows for centralized authentication of wireless users or nodes and is able to work with multiple authentication algorithms simultaneously.

EAPoL

The 802.1x protocol, which is EAP encapsulation over LAN (EAPOL), has the capability to dynamically apply a multiple encryption key using EAP. EAP supports multiple authentication methods, including Kerberos, one-time passwords, digital security certificates, and public key authentication.

In general, 802.1x authentication starts with what the standard calls an *unauthenticated supplicant* (meaning a wireless node) attempting to associate with an authenticator (a wireless access point). The authenticator responds to the node's registration frame by enabling one of

Kerberos

Kerberos is a form of authentication protocol that provides strong authentication for client/server applications. Kerberos, which was developed by the Massachusetts Institute of Technology (MIT), uses a process called authentication by assertion. *Authentication by assertion* provides a low level of security because all that happens is this: when a network node (client) accesses a network service (server), the client declares (asserts) it is both acting on behalf of the user and using a secret key encryption for its transmissions. MIT freely distributes Kerberos.

its ports to pass EAP packets between the node and an authentication server, also known as an authentication, authorization, and accounting (AAA) server. An *AAA server* is typically located on the wireline network to which the access point is attached. Until the authentication server has authenticated the node, all other traffic transmitted by the node is blocked. Once the authentication server has authenticated the node to the network, the port is unblocked for all other traffic types.

Here are step-by-step details of the 802.1*x* authentication process:

1. When a network node is started or connects to the WLAN, it transmits an EAP-start frame on the wireless media.

   This frame is, in effect, a request to enter the network. This is similar to the node asking a door person at a night spot to be permitted to enter the club.

2. The access point that receives the EAP-start frame replies with an EAP-request identity frame.

   The access point is asking the node to identify itself. The club's door person asks, "Who're you?"

3. The node responds with an EAP-response frame that contains its identity (MAC address and other information) intended for the authentication server. The access point blocks all traffic from the node that is not EAP-related, as illustrated in Figure 11-3.

   This is similar to the node showing a club's door person its driver's license.

Figure 11-3   EAP authentication uses a port-control procedure.

4. The authentication server then applies an authentication algorithm to verify the node's identity information, using a digital certificate or another of the EAP authentication types.

In effect, the door person verifies the picture on the ID and that the "birth date" of the node is valid.

5. The authentication server then sends back either an accept or a reject frame to the access point, indicating it was either able or unable to verify the identity information provided by the node.

Either the driver's license is good or fake, altered or unaltered, or the node can't be identified from the information provided.

6. Depending on the response from the authentication server, the access point transmits an EAP-success or an EAP-rejection frame back to the node. If the authentication server has successfully authenticated the node, the access point stops blocking the node's normal traffic and allows it to pass to the network. If the node is rejected, however, its port remains in EAP-only status.

The node is either permitted to enter the club or is turned away.

The 802.1x standard is available in most wireless access points and routers, typically with a proprietary version using the 802.1x standard as a delivery method for any other security schemes implemented, such as 802.11 WEP and other dynamic key management methods. If a dynamic key method is in use, the 802.1x authentication server returns session keys to the access point with the EAP-accept frame, which the access point then uses to build, sign, and encrypt an EAP-key frame sent to the node immediately after the EAP-accept frame. The wireless node uses the information in the EAP-key frame to create its encryption keys, which can be changed by the node as needed.

EAP Types   Remember, the 802.1x authentication standard doesn't provide authentication itself. And it must rely on another protocol or service to perform authentication. The authentication process is supported by an authentication server or service running on the network. When 802.1x is in use, an EAP type must be designated for the network's authentication method. In most cases, the EAP types that can be chosen when configuring a wireless NIC or network adapter or an access point or router are:

● **Message-Digest Algorithm (MD5):** *MD5* provides only basic EAP support. MD5 is not recommended for WLAN implementation because it provides only one-way authentication, meaning it doesn't include a provision for mutual authentication between wireless nodes and the network. In addition, MD5 doesn't provide a means to generate dynamic WEP keys.

Server-side and Client-side Digital Certificates

Server-side digital certificates are used to verify that the data being requested, whether from a web site or a wireless network host, is, in fact, from the source intended and not an imposter. This is done by checking that the requested source is the responding source.

Client-side certificates are essentially the same as server-side certificates. They differ only in how they are used. *Client-side certificates* require that each node or user be issued a unique certificate, which can then be used to verify the user or node is exactly who they say they are and not an imposter.

- **Protected Extensible Authentication Protocol (PEAP):** *PEAP* has the capability to securely transport authentication data between wireless devices. PEAP supports a variety of authentication protocols, including legacy password-based protocols, by creating tunnel PEAP nodes and the authentication server. PEAP authenticates WLAN nodes with server-side only certificates, which simplifies the implementation and administration of a WLAN.

- **Transport Layer Security (EAP-TLS):** *EAP-TLS* provides for both certificate-based authentication and mutual authentication between wireless nodes and the WLAN, using client-side and server-side certificates to perform the authentication. EAP-TLS also has the capability to dynamically generate user-based and session-based WEP keys to secure WLAN communications. Because certificates must be managed on both the client and server side, EAP-TLS is often not implemented on large, enterprise networks. EAP-TLS authentication is often referred to Smart Card or Certificate authentication. In fact, when you are configuring a Windows XP node for this EAP type, the choice listed in the Wireless Properties dialog box is "Smart Card or other Certificate."

- **Tunneled Transport Layer Security (EAP-TTLS):** *EAP-TTLS* is an extension of EAP-TLS that provides for certificate-based, mutual authentication of a WLAN node and WLAN using an encrypted tunnel. EAP-TTLS requires only server-side certificates.

NOTE

Cisco Systems has developed its own proprietary version of the EAP standard, which it calls Lightweight Extensible Authentication Protocol (LEAP). *LEAP* authentication supports dynamic key encryption and mutual authentication, and is included on Cisco's Aironet wireless devices and on some Linksys (a subsidiary of Cisco) devices as well.

Tunneling

The concept of tunneling through a network can conjure up some fairly wild images. In reality, a *tunnel*, or channel, through a network is created by encapsulating the packets of one network protocol inside packets of another network protocol. Another way to explain tunneling is this: it encapsulates (places) unsecured ordinary packets (such as FTP, HTTP, and the like) inside encrypted, secured packets (like IP).

It's better to think of tunneling more in terms of encapsulation and less about the literal meaning of the word. In the context of networking, and especially virtual private networks (VPNs), *tunneling* merely refers to the transmission of secured, private data over an insecure transmission medium, such as wireless networks or the Internet.

Table 11-1 summarizes the features and characteristics of the EAP authentication methods.

EAP Type	Developer	Certificates Required	Dynamic WEP Keys	Authentication	Security Level
MD-5	Microsoft	Client/Server	No	One-way	Low
PEAP	Microsoft	Server	Yes	Mutual	High
TLS	Microsoft	Client/Server	Yes	Mutual	Very High
TTLS	Funk Software	None	Yes	Mutual	High

Table 11-1 IEEE 802.1x Authentication Method Characteristics

Remote Authentication Dial-In User Service (RADIUS)

Although not a totally secure authentication method, RADIUS is also supported by many wireless access points and routers. Typically referred to by EAP systems as a legacy password-based authentication method, RADIUS can provide a minimum level of access security to a WLAN.

Commonly used by dial-up Internet service providers (ISPs), RADIUS is used to verify a user name and password against a database of authorized users, which is maintained by the network administrators.

NOTE

Microsoft's implementation of RADIUS is its Internet Authentication Server (IAS).

Since 2003, some wireless access points, like the Intermec MobileLAN access point (see Figure 11-4), have included an embedded authentication server (EAS) to support not only RADIUS, but also EAP-TLS, EAP-TTLS, and MAC address filtering.

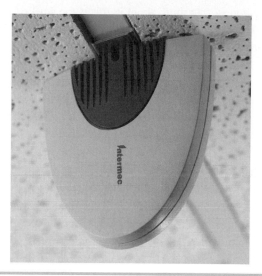

Figure 11-4   A wireless access point with an embedded authentication server mounted on an office ceiling (Photo courtesy of Intermec Technologies Corp.)

The Case for Authentication Services on a WLAN   In summary, a wireless network should (must) employ some form of secure access method to authenticate authorized nodes and users. Because imposters (hackers) can join a wireless network with relative ease, some method must be implemented on the access point to allow the access point to determine which requests are from authorized users and which are from imposters. An imposter can attempt to join the network by representing (spoofing) itself as one of the network nodes. Depending on the level of the threat and the nature of the resources available through the network, an authentication method should be chosen that is appropriate to the security level desired, ranging from none at all to a server-side digital certificate.

Line Check 11.3

1. What are the three major parts of an 802.11 authentication and security method?
2. What are the four primary EAP types?
3. What is the 802.1x authentication protocol?

Data Encryption

Literally dozens of encryption forms were used within the past century, most of which have been chronicled in spy novels, movies, and true-life stories about secret messages, spies, and espionage. And, when you stop to think about it, this is the stuff of WLAN security as well.

Since early in human history, people have wanted to conceal the meaning of their messages and they have developed a variety of schemes, algorithms, and mathematical formulas to accomplish just that. Some are simple, such as the decoders that came with chocolate milk powders and syrups that could be used to decode the secret messages from Captain Video and Captain Midnight in the 1950s. The decryption tools (decoders) used on today's wireless networks are much more complex than these early decryption methods. In fact, their complexity is such that it is often easier to trust that they work rather than trying to understand exactly how they do so.

Basic Encryption Methods

In the earliest forms of cryptography, letters and numbers were concealed through a substitution method that replaces each letter in a text stream with symbols, letters, numbers, or even pictures. Substituting one character for another in a consistent pattern transforms the original message and its meaning into a stream of what amounts to gibberish or gives it an entirely different meaning to the uninformed reader.

One form of a substitution encryption is the transposition method in which standard alphabet characters are replaced on a one-to-one basis using what is called a monoalphabetic method. In the *monoalphabetic method*, each alphabetic character is replaced with another alphabetic character a certain number of positions later or earlier in the alphabet. For example: in a plus-five substitution, A is replaced with F, B is replaced with G, C is replaced with H, and so on. The last five letters in the alphabet are replaced with the first five letters (V is replaced with A, for example). Using this very simple encryption form, the stream BOXKRKY TKZBUXQOTM translates to Wireless Networking.

Cryptography

Two basic types of cryptography are used to encrypt data on computer systems: symmetric and asymmetric. A *symmetric* encryption system uses the same key (secret key) to both encrypt and decrypt a transmitted message. An *asymmetric* encryption system uses a public key to encrypt data and a **private key**, which is unique to the public key, to decrypt data. A symmetric encryption system is called a *secret key system* and an asymmetric encryption system is called a *public key system*.

Public key or asymmetric systems are the most commonly used encryption method used to encrypt and decrypt transmitted data. This is primarily because the encryption key doesn't need to be transmitted with the data. Symmetric key systems have a major limitation—finding a way to transmit the secret key without it being intercepted.

Letter	Number	Letter	Number
Q	1	F	14
W	2	G	15
E	3	H	16
R	4	J	17
T	5	K	18
Y	6	L	19
U	7	Z	20
I	8	X	21
O	9	C	22
P	10	V	23
A	11	B	24
S	12	N	25
D	13	M	26

Table 11-2   The Translation Table for a Simple Transposition Encryption Scheme

Another form of transposition encryption uses a seed or key word to establish relative positions for letters in the alphabet. Table 11-2 lists a simple transposition scheme that can be used to decode the string 2 8 4 3 19 3 12 25 5 2 9 4 18 8 25 15.

Several other, and more complex, methods have been used over the 4,000 years in which cryptography has been used, including mechanical devices, such as the Jefferson cylinder in the 1700s; the Wheatstone disk in the 1800s; the Enigma rotor machine (see Figure 11-5) of

Figure 11-5   The rotors inside the German Enigma machine were used to encrypt text messages.

World War II; and mathematics-based algorithms, such as the Vigenère and Beauford ciphers. Today's data public key encryption methods use a Boolean algebra operation (exclusive OR [XOR]), such as the Rivest-Shamir-Adleman (RSA) or RC4 (Rivest Cipher 4) ciphers.

Wireless Encryption Methods

One of the limitations with WEP is that it uses a symmetric key encryption method, which means each end of a wireless transmission must use the same key to encrypt and decrypt the message. The problem is this: the same encryption key must be stored and used by the NICs and network adapters, as well as in the access points. This presents a network administration problem in that, when the encryption keys are changed, they must be distributed to the network's nodes. The result of this requirement is the same keys may be used for extended periods on a WLAN, giving attackers the opportunity to intercept and defeat the encryption method using a variety of software that is readily available for this specific purpose.

Symmetric Key Encryption   The most commonly used symmetric key encryption algorithm is the Data Encryption Standard (DES) or one of its later enhancements or variations. DES uses a 56-bit encryption key and a block cipher encryption method. The *block cipher method* used by DES breaks a data stream into 64-bit blocks to which the encryption key is then applied. Figure 11-6 illustrates a simplified view of a symmetric encryption process.

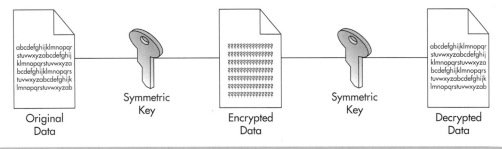

Figure 11-6   A symmetric encryption process uses the same private key to encrypt and decrypt a message.

DES, which is also referred to as single DES, repeats its primary algorithm 16 times for each 64-bit block of data. The encryption key used by DES is actually 64 bits in length, but because the right-most (least significant) bit in each of the 8 bytes is used as a parity bit, the key is effectively 56 bits long.

The process used to convert first the key, and then the data in DES involves a series of permuted choice (PC), subkey rotation (SR), and substitution (S) tables used to modify the encryption key before it is XORed with the data. DES uses four different encryption modes:

- **Electronic code book (ECB):** *ECB* is the regular DES algorithm that divides data into 64-bit blocks and each block is encrypted individually. Because ECB adds no additional encryption steps to the standard DES process, it is considered the weakest of the DES encryption methods.

- **Cipher-block Chaining (CBC):** In *CBC*, each ECB block of encrypted data is XORed with the next block, which makes each succeeding block dependent on the preceding block. Because the first block has no preceding block, a 64-bit IV is used instead. Because CBC adds one additional step to the encryption process, it is considered more secure than ECB.

- **Cipher Feedback (CFB):** *CFB* is used when the data stream to be encrypted is less than 64 bits in length. Dummy bytes are added to the end of the data before it is encrypted. CFB is similar to CBC for security, but because of its additional processing, it is much slower.

- **Output Feedback (OFB):** *OFB* passes the output of the DES process back through the encryption process. The result is only the original encrypted data block and the output of the DES process are needed to decipher a block. This means, because the key is not required to decipher a block, this mode is less secure than the CFB mode.

Triple DES (3DES) is a variation of the DES algorithm that first encrypts a data block using a 112-bit key (168 bits less parity bits), then it decrypts the data, and then encrypts it again. Other variations are DES-X and Generalized DES (G-DES).

Asymmetrical Encryption   An *asymmetrical encryption* uses two keys: a **public key** that is not secret and a private, secret key. The public key is essentially known to everyone, while the **private key** is known only to the recipient of the encrypted message. For example, if Markus wants to send an encrypted message to Carly, he uses Carly's public key to encrypt the message. Carly then uses her private, secret key to decrypt the message when it arrives, as illustrated in Figure 11-7.

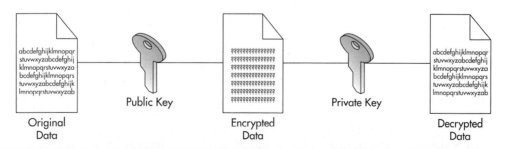

abcdefghijklmnopqr
stuvwxyzabcdefghij
klmnopqrstuvwxyza
bcdefghijklmnopqrs
tuvwxyzabcdefghijk
lmnopqrstuvwxyzab

Public Key

?????????????????
?????????????????
?????????????????
?????????????????
?????????????????
?????????????????

Private Key

abcdefghijklmnopqr
stuvwxyzabcdefghij
klmnopqrstuvwxyza
bcdefghijklmnopqrs
tuvwxyzabcdefghijk
lmnopqrstuvwxyzab

Original
Data

Encrypted
Data

Decrypted
Data

Figure 11-7   An asymmetrical encryption system uses a public key to encrypt data at the sending end and a private key to decrypt the data at the receiving end.

Pathfinders

Diffie, Hellman, and Merkle

Public key encryption, also known as the *Diffie-Hellman-Merkle encryption*, which is a patented security algorithm still used to secure network transmissions, was developed in 1976 by Whitfield Diffie, Martin Hellman, and Ralph Merkle. The following shows each of these pioneers, with Diffie on the left, Hellman in the center, and Merkle on the right.

NOTE

Diffie's photo is courtesy of Sun Microsystems, Hellman's photo is courtesy of Stanford University, and Merkle's photo is courtesy of Georgia Institute of Technology.

Dr. Whitfield Diffie, currently a vice president and chief security officer at Sun Microsystems, is responsible for developing Sun's security vision and strategies. During the 1990s, Dr. Diffie worked extensively on cryptography public policy and testified numerous times before congressional committee on security and cryptography. Dr. Diffie holds a bachelor degree in mathematics from MIT and a doctorate from the Swiss Federal Institute of Technology.

Dr. Martin Hellman, Professor Emeritus of Electrical Engineering at Stanford University, has been a long-time contributor to the computer privacy debate, starting with the issue of DES key size in 1975 and culminating with service on the National Research Council's Committee to Study National Cryptographic Policy. Many of Dr. Hellman's recommendations have since been implemented.

Dr. Ralph Merkle is currently the Director of the Georgia Institute of Technology's Information Security Center and has continued to work in computer security and cryptography. In addition to his contributions to public key cryptography, Dr. Merkle is also the developer of Merkle Trees, which is used in several authentication methods. Dr Merkle's current research focuses on computer security, as well as nanotechnology.

The public key and the private key of what is called the public key infrastructure (PKI) are related to the point that only the *public key* can be used to encrypt data and only the associated *private key* can then be used to decrypt it. While the two keys are related, it is virtually impossible to deduce the private key from the public key.

On a wireless network, a sending device, such as a NIC or an access point, uses a public key to encrypt data before transmitting it on the wireless media. The receiving device then uses its private key to decipher the data and vice versa.

Wireless NICs or network adapters can be configured manually with a public key or provided with one automatically by the network Base Service Set (BSS). Figure 11-8 shows the Windows XP Wireless Network Properties dialog box that contains the settings for public key encryption. In this case, the NIC supports only WEP security and is configured to automatically receive its key from the BSS.

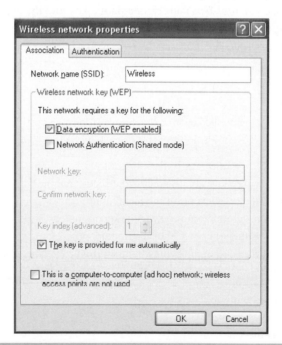

Figure 11-8   The Windows XP Wireless Network Properties dialog box's Association tab is used to configure a NIC for a public key.

On a wireless network, typically, it is better to allow the BSS to supply its public key to ensure no mistakes are made entering the key manually. If the key is off by one character, the encryption and decryption processes do not produce the same result. WEP keys are distributed periodically by encrypting the key with the public key of the receiving station and decrypted by the station using its private key.

Digital Signatures So, how does someone across a network know you are who you say you are? In the offline world, you could sign a document with your signature and have a notary public verify its validity. In the online world, a digital signature serves the same purpose as the notary public, verifying you as the source of a document or message.

A *digital signature* is an application of PKI used on networks to verify that the originator of a document, image, or message is a trusted source. In the context of network security, trust means the public and private keys used to encrypt and decrypt a message have been verified and expressly issued to a particular person by a **certificate authority** (CA).

A CA is similar to an online notary public and passport office that protects the security and trustfulness of the PKI system. When you want to obtain a digital certificate for your private key, you submit a private key (typically generated by the CA's application process). After verifying that you are who you say you are, the CA signs your public key with its own private key, which is also called a *root key*. Your signed public key and the digital signature of the CA together make up your digital signature, which can be used like an online passport that has been stamped with the official seal of the CA.

NOTE

For more information on the public key infrastructure (PKI) and a list of public key certificate authorities, visit **www.pki-page.org**.

When you want to transmit a digitally signed document, a hash total is made of the document and signed with your private key. At the receiving end, the validity of the document and its source are verified by decrypting the hash total of the document using your public key, and comparing it to a hash total computed by the receiving end. If the two hash totals match, the receiving station has the assurance that the document is secure. Although the receiver didn't see you transmit the document, your digital signature verifies its source, because only you have your private key.

❓ Line Check 11.4

1. What are the two types of encryption keys used in the PKI architecture?

2. What mechanism can be used to assure a receiving station of the source and security of a transmitted document?

3. Who verifies and issues digital signatures?

IEEE 802.11i

In June 2004, the IEEE approved the 802.11i security standard, entitled the "MAC Enhancements for Enhanced Security," which defines the security measures available to 802.11a and 802.11b networks. This enhancement of the 802.11 standards incorporates the Advanced Encryption Standard (AES)—newly developed cryptography algorithm—that incorporates the security standards of 802.1x, and defines the use of Temporal Key Integrity Protocol (TKIP) and Wireless Robust Authenticated Protocol (WRAP). The **802.11i** standard effectively defines a robust set of security measures to protect the entire process of association, authentication, and message transmission.

The 802.11i standard consists of three elements arranged into two layers. The lowest layer includes the encryption algorithms of Temporal Key Integrity Protocol (TKIP) and a counter mode that incorporates the Counter Mode with Cipher-Block Chaining Message Authentication Code Protocol (CCMP). The top layer is 802.1x for authentication processing.

TKIP and *CCMP* are encryption protocols that provide for enhanced security over the methods included in WEP. TKIP is an interim addition intended for legacy devices that can be upgraded through a firmware update. CCMP is intended for new and future WLAN devices.

The major features specified as a part of the 802.11i standard are:

- AES
- TKIP
- CCMP
- 802.1x authentication

AES

The Advance Encryption Standard (AES) provides a level of security that satisfies the high-level standards of the Federal Information Processing Standard (FIPS) required by many government agencies. To use AES requires a dedicated circuit, which may require many WLANs to upgrade or replace their existing hardware.

TKIP

The Temporal Key Integrity Protocol (**TKIP**)– (pronounced "tee-kip") is the next generation of WEP. *TKIP* provides dynamic per-packet encryption keys, a message integrity check, and a mechanism for assigning new keys to network nodes, all of which correct flaws with WEP.

Originally referred as WEP2, TKIP is still just an interim solution, focusing primarily on the issues that surround the security issues of periodically reusing keys to encrypt data in WEP. TKIP uses 128-bit temporal keys that are combined with the wireless node's MAC address and a 16-octet IV to produce the key used to encrypt the data payload of a frame using the RC4 algorithm. A *temporal key* is used for only a certain time period or number of packets. The TKIP temporal keys are used for only 10,000 packets before they are dynamically exchanged.

NOTE

Wi-Fi released an early version of TKIP in early 2003 under the name WPA, which is replaced with the release of 802.11i. Wi-Fi refers to the 802.11i standard as WPA2.

CCMP

CCMP is a block cipher mode protocol that performs both encryption and authentication. CCMP combines a counter-mode encryption process and CBC-MAC authentication, both of which have been around for many years. The encryption process uses any block cipher, such as AES, in combination with a secret key for that cipher. CBC-MAC is only as strong as the encryption algorithm, but 802.11i specifies it with the strength of AES.

802.1x Authentication

The 802.1*x* standard uses the EAP authentication method (see the previous section "EAP Types"), which can be supported on a network with both wired and wireless components.

Line Check 11.5

1. What cryptography algorithm was incorporated into the 802.11i standard for future WLAN devices?

2. What security protocol issues temporal keys?

Security Threats to WLANs

Primarily because they are wireless, 802.11 networks are uniquely vulnerable to outside attacks and interception. Unlike a wireline network, a wireless network's media cannot be physically secured and an attack can be launched from almost anywhere within the media's range, which could be the next cubicle, the next building, the parking lot, or even the street.

An attack on a wireless network can take a wide variety of forms and, unless you understand the different types of attacks that could be made, protecting against them is difficult. Not all attacks are particularly dangerous and devastating to a WLAN. Some are frivolous and harmless, but any attack, even those that are harmless, could lead to something far more dangerous.

In designing and implementing the security for a WLAN, the more you know about the threats that exist, the better your chances are of protecting the network.

The network shown in Figure 11-9 illustrates a fairly common network installation. The network has three primary segments, the Internet gateway, the wireline network supporting several workstations, servers, peripheral devices, and a wireless segment supporting several wireless nodes.

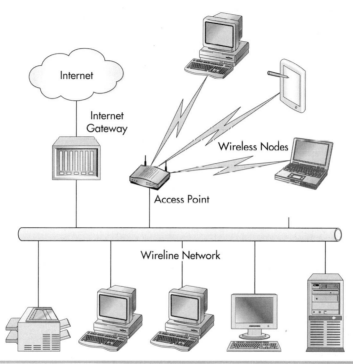

Figure 11-9   This common network implementation is vulnerable to a variety of security threats.

While several types of threats can be made against the wired segment of the network shown in Figure 11-9, let's focus on the security and the potential threats that can be made against the Internet gateway, the access point, and the wireless nodes, and, especially, the threats that would originate from outside the network.

The threats you should protect your network against the most are not much different than those that threaten a wireline network. Most network administrators are already familiar with them. The most common and frequent of the attacks made on networks are:

- Client-to-client
- Denial of service (DoS)
- Insertion
- Interception

Client-to-Client Attacks

Because two wireless nodes have the capability to communicate directly with one another and bypass their access point, a wireless node should be protected from other nodes on the WLAN. Any node that is configured—more than likely in the spirit of sharing resources—with TCP/IP services, such as a web server or the Windows Print and File Sharing, can be attacked by another node on the WLAN, taking advantage of any misconfiguration.

Another common client-to-client attack is a smaller version of the most common attack made on networks, the denial of service (DoS) attack (covered in the next section, "Denial of Service Attacks"). The purpose of a **DoS attack** is to flood a node with an overload of incoming messages to the point that all other functions of the computer are interrupted or cease altogether. An alternative form of the DoS attack is configuring another network node with the same MAC or IP address as another node, disrupting communications to the target node.

Denial-of-Service (DoS) Attacks

A DoS attack has only one objective: to prevent any access to a network's resources by internal or external nodes. The most common DoS attack involves flooding an Internet gateway, web server, or internal network server with packets or frames that must be processed, monopolizing the system's resources to the point that all other user functions are severely interrupted or prevented entirely.

Types of DoS Attacks

There isn't just one type of DoS attack. A DoS attack can attack a network almost on every layer of the OSI Reference model. Here is a brief description of the types of DoS attacks that can happen on each layer:

- **Application layer:** Attacks that target the application layer typically involve the transmission of seemingly legitimate requests to a network-ready application running on a server or node. For example, a flood of HTTP page requests are sent to a web server, which overloads the web server attempting to fulfill the requests and prevents other (legitimate) requests for accessing the server.

- **Transport layer:** Transport layer DoS attacks are most commonly made against a network's operating system (OS) environment, which typically manages the number of connections made to network hosts. When a remote device is attempting to establish a TCP connection, it transmits a synchronization (SYN) packet to request the opening of a TCP link. Because most network operating systems (NOS) have limits to the number of links they can process per second and the number of established links they can support, a *SYN flood*, as this attack is called, overloads the NOS on one or both of these limits, crowding out requests made by legitimate network nodes and services.

- **Network layer:** Attacks made on the network layer target the transmission capabilities of the network by flooding the transmission media with more packets than it can process effectively. For example, if an attacker were to continually transmit over 100 Mbps of data to a 10 Mbps network, the network infrastructure would be unable to retransmit all the incoming data to the network. The result is that some of the data in the network queue, including legitimate network traffic, for retransmission would be dropped. The upshot of this type of attack is this: network throughput is disrupted and the collision level and retransmissions also begin to rise, causing further disruption on the network. The most common type of network layer attack is a ping flood, in which excessive quantities of Internet Control Message Protocol (ICMP) echo request packets are transmitted to the targeted network overloading the network's gateway, which denies access to the Internet by network nodes.

- **Data-link layer:** Data-link layer attacks can target an entire wireless network or a single network node. The most typical data-link layer attack is a flood of empty and invalid frames that the network server then broadcasts across the network tying up the network media. This type of attack is only effective on networks or network segments that don't include a WLAN switch or router, which commonly does not forward broadcast messages beyond a single segment. However, if this type of attack is generated from within a network, the network segment of the source device is affected.

- **Physical layer:** The physical layer of a WLAN is attacked primarily by blocking, jamming, or removing the transmission means. On wired networks, such as wide area network (WAN) links over which Internet requests are transmitted, damage to the physical media can create a DoS situation, although in most cases, inadvertently. The most infamous of the physical layer DoS situations is called Backhoe Fade, which means the signal strength has faded to nothing because the main carrier line (typically, fiber-optic cable) has been cut. Another fairly common physical layer attack is posed by lightning storms. The best protection against these types of occurrences is redundancy.

WLAN DoS Attacks

The physical layer on a wireless network is especially vulnerable to attack. The good news about wireless networks is they transmit using RF signals; the bad news is wireless networks transmit using RF signals. This may seem like double-talk, but the area in which a wireless network is most vulnerable to an attack is on its physical layer.

Unlike a wired network, where the attacker must have access to the physical medium and where the evidence of the attack is typically visible, a wireless network's medium can be attacked from a distance with no evidence left behind, other than the results of the attack itself.

Because the 802.11 PHY standards are readily available and its specific radio frequencies are spelled out, an evildoer is able to flood these frequencies with interference and electromagnetic noise. If enough interference and noise is added to the transmission frequencies, the RF medium becomes unusable, which effectively knocks any wireless nodes within range off the network.

Insertion Attacks

Also called unauthorized or illicit use attacks, *insertion attacks* involve an attacker adding an unauthorized device to a wireless network primarily for access to the Internet gateway or the wired network behind the WLAN's access point. Insertion attacks are only possible if an attacker is able to bypass the security settings of a WLAN.

Insertion attacks can happen on two levels: the insertion of a wireless node, such as a notebook computer or a wireless PDA, or the insertion of an unauthorized access point or router. The simplest way to prevent the insertion of an unauthorized node is to require a user looking to add a node to an access point to enter a password. Without a password, any device, configured with minimal settings, can associate with an access point.

Most insertion attacks are inadvertent. If an employee adds an unauthorized access point to a network that is not properly configured at the same security levels as the rest of the network, this can create a hole in the security through which an outside attacker can enter. The threat is even more pronounced if the access point is connected to the wired network directly. Although less common, a crafty attacker could also physically insert an access point into the network and gain access to the network resources from inside or even outside the building.

NOTE

Another form of unauthorized use occurs when an attacker gains entry to a WLAN through an existing access point configured for OSA authentication.

Interception Attacks

Interception attacks are more common on wireline networks, especially on those with poor physical security for the media, but because of the general nature of RF transmissions, these attacks may become more common on WLANs, as well.

Four general types of interception attacks exist:

- **ARP spoofing:** The Address Resolution Protocol (ARP) is a Layer 2 protocol used on TCP/IP networks to resolve IP addresses to MAC addresses. When a node wants to communicate with another node on the same network, it may only have the other node's IP address,. So, the node broadcasts a frame on the network, asking the other node assigned to a particular IP address to respond with its MAC address, which is then used to transmit messages across the WLAN. Unfortunately, in *ARP spoofing*, this same process can be used by an attacker to fool the network into addressing packets to his computer by supplying its MAC address in response to ARP requests. Once the ARP information is set, packets are routed through the attacker's computer, captured, and then forwarded on to the legitimate recipient, with the interception undetected. ARP spoofing is also called ARP poisoning.

Wardriving and War Chalking

Back in the days when only dial-up modems could be used to access a remote network for good or evil, hackers would dial a sequence of phone numbers looking to find one that would reach a modem. This practice became known as *wardialing*, a term based on the actions of the young computer hacker in the movie *War Games*.

In the wireless network world, there is no need to dial sequential numbers to gain access. To find a wireless network, all one has to do is carry a wireless networking-equipped laptop or notebook computer as they walk around (warwalking), drive around (wardriving), or fly over (warflying) business areas or residential neighborhoods to discover any number of unsecured wireless access points.

War drivers, walkers, and flyers then mark the house or building with one of three symbols, which were adapted from the symbols used in the past by hobos to indicate which houses would give food, drink, or shelter. The following illustrates these symbols. Where a word or acronym is used in a symbol, the actual value detected would be inserted at that position.

Symbol	Meaning
SSID ⤬ Bandwidth	Open Node
SSID ◯	Closed Node
SSID (W) Access Contact Bandwidth	WEP Node

So, if you have a wireless network, you may want to check any suspicious chalk marks around or on your home. Not all the chalk marks on the street, sidewalk, or the side of your house may be from children. An evildoer may have detected your network and is sharing his good fortune with fellow warriors.

- **Monitoring:** If a WLAN connects a wireless access point into a hub on the wired network, any network traffic passing through the hub may also be transmitted across the wireless network. This situation allows an attacker who has gained access to the network or who is sniffing the network's traffic to view potentially sensitive data flowing across the wireline or wireless networks.

- **Sniffer:** Wireless sniffers are software programs installed on WLAN nodes or servers that capture transmitted RF traffic off the media for analysis and monitoring. For the most part, these products are intended for use by a network's administrators, but they can also be used for less-than-honorable purposes. A *wireless sniffer* captures a transmitted packet as raw data and has the capability to extract addressing information from the packet header. A wireless sniffer, such as CommView, Kismet, and Sniffer Pro, can be installed on a wireless node that has gained insertion into a WLAN and can be located outside a building, but within range, of course.

- **Session hijacking:** An attacker that can sniff a WLAN's traffic also may have the capability to insert packets into the network to use a legitimate node's identification information to carry out whatever access the legitimate user may have.

Protecting a WLAN

Configuring a WLAN for the proper security may not, as yet, totally protect it from outside attacks, but this can prevent most of the truly damaging attacks to the network and its resources. The following is a list of suggested actions and configurations you can apply to a WLAN to help secure it from outside evildoers.

- Develop a company, corporate, or personal WLAN security policy that defines exactly what is to be allowed and, more specifically, what is not to be allowed on the network. The policy should be detailed to the point of listing the configuration elements of the access points and routers to be installed in the network.

- Implement the 802.11 standard that provides only the range needed to support the network. Installing the latest and greatest technology may not be the best solution in terms of security. If 802.11b serves the needs of the organization, then 802.11g isn't necessary.

- If the WLAN is small enough that a network sniffer won't be used for analysis and monitoring purposes, disable broadcast pings on the access point. This eliminates the capability for 802.11b sniffers from seeing the access point.

- Configure the network with dynamic privacy keys and 802.1x. Avoid static privacy keys as they negate the role of 802.1x in the security scheme.

❓ Line Check 11.6

1. Which type of attack has the objective of monopolizing a network's resources, so they are no longer available to the network's users?

2. What type of device or software can be used to intercept network traffic on a WLAN?

3. What first step should be performed for the installation of a WLAN in an area that requires a high level of security?

 **What Do You Think?**

Which of the attack threats described in this chapter do you believe pose the largest threat to a WLAN? Why?

The TLAs of Security

This chapter, like most discussions on wireless networking, includes a large number of three-letter-abbreviations (TLAs) or acronyms, plus a considerable number of four-letter-abbreviations (FLAs). To help you remember all the concepts discussed, Table 11-3 includes a reminder of the meanings of each of these TLAs and FLAs.

TLA/FLA	Meaning/Description
802.11i	A security standard that features 128-bit AES for encryption
802.1x	A port-based network control standard that provides multiple authentication methods
AES	Advanced Encryption Standard
ARP	Address Resolution Protocol
CA	Certificate authority
CCMP	Counter Mode Cipher-Block Chaining Message Authentication Code Protocol
DES	Data Encryption Standard
DoS	Denial of service
EAP	Extensible Authentication Protocol
EAPOL	EAP over LAN
EAP-TLS	EAP-Transport Layer Security
EAP-TTLS	EAP-Tunneled Transport Layer Security
ECB	Electronic code book
ICV	Integrity check value
IV	Initialization vector

Table 11-3   The Meanings of Common 802.11 Security Terms *(continued)*

TLA/FLA	Meaning/Description
LEAP	Lightweight Extensible Authentication Protocol
MD-5	Message-digest algorithm 5
OSA	Open system authentication
PEAP	Protected Extensible Authentication Protocol
PKI	Public key infrastructure
RADIUS	Remote Authentication Dial-in User Server
RC4	Rivest Cipher 4
RSA	Rivest-Shamir-Adleman
TKIP	Temporal Key Integrity Protocol
WEP	Wired Equivalent Privacy
WRAP	Wireless Robust Authenticated Protocol

Table 11-3   The Meanings of Common 802.11 Security Terms

Chapter 11 Review

Chapter Summary

Understand WLAN (802.11) Security Basics

- In June 2004, the IEEE announced the adoption of the 802.11i security standard, aimed at improving the overall security and privacy of wireless network data and SSIDs, and denying access to unauthorized intruders.

- WEP, included in 802.11b, is designed to provide a WLAN with security and privacy equivalent to that expected on a wireline network. WEP is an optional on a wireless network.

- A wireless network is hard to secure physically because radio waves are transmitted through the air and can pass through walls.

- WEP encrypts the data payload in each transmitted packet.

- WEP is applied on the data link and physical layers, but it doesn't provide end-to-end security for transmitted data.

- WEP uses RC4 encryption, which accepts encryption keys of arbitrary lengths and generates a pseudorandom number that is combined with the data stream to produce encrypted data.

- The WEP encryption key has two parts: a 24-bit initialization vector (IV) and a WEP key that is either 40 bits or 104 bits in length, yielding a total length for the WEP key of 64 bits or 128 bits.

- Wireless access points transmit beacon frames, which include its SSID. Wireless nodes receiving a beacon frame determine if they want to associate with the access point transmitting the beacon. A wireless station transmits probe frames, which include its station ID and the SSID.

- WEP includes two authentication methods: OSA, which allows any wireless node to associate to an access point using a randomly generated shared key, and SKA, which follows a sequence of actions to authenticate a node attempting to associate with an access point.

- EAP provides the means to override standard or proprietary authentication methods and to allow other authentication methods to be used, including passwords, challenge keys, and public key infrastructure certificates.

- The 802.1x standard allows for centralized authentication of wireless users or nodes, and is able to work with multiple authentication algorithms simultaneously. The 802.1x authentication protocol is EAPOL.

- The EAP authentication types are: MD-5, PEAP, EAP-TLS, EAP-TTLS, and LEAP

- MAC filtering bases access to the WLAN on when a list of the MAC addresses allowed to connect to the network is entered.

Describe Security Enhancements in 802.11i

- The 802.11i security standard defines the security measures available to 802.11a and 802.11b networks. The major features of 802.11i are: 802.1x authentication, access point to node security, AES, and TKIP and CCMP.

Define Security Threats to 802.11 Networks

- Wireless networks are uniquely vulnerable to outside attacks and interception.

- The most common attacks made on networks are: client-to-client, DoS, insertion, and interception.

- The objective of a DoS attack is to prevent any access to a network's resources by internal or external nodes. The common forms of DoS attacks are: application request flood, SYN flood, bandwidth flood, invalid frames flood, and physical media disruption.

- Insertion attacks involve adding an unauthorized device to a WLAN to access network resources.

- The four general interception attacks are: ARP spoofing, monitoring, sniffer, and session hijacking.

Key Terms

Authentication *(369)*
Certificate authority *(384)*
DoS attack *(388)*
EAP *(371)*
IEEE 802.1x *(372)*
IEEE 802.11i *(385)*
Public key *(378, 381)*
Private key *(378, 381)*
RC4 *(366)*
TKIP *(385)*
WEP *(365)*

Key Term Quiz

Use the terms from the Key Terms list to complete the following sentences. Don't use the same term more than once. Not all terms will be used.

1. The network security standard for all IEEE networks is _____.

2. The legacy WLAN security protocol, specified in 802.11b, is _____.

3. _____ is used to provide access to a network to users and networking devices.

4. In June 2004, the IEEE approved the _____ WLAN security standard.

5. The interim protocol added to WEP to enhance its security capabilities is _____.

6. Digital signatures are issued by a(n) _____.

7. The encryption cipher used in WEP is _____.

8. In PKI, a message is encrypted using the receiver's _____.

9. A(n) _____ is one of the most common security threats to a network.

10. In PKI, a receiving station decrypts a message using its _____.

11. The 802.1x standard prescribes the use of EAP for authentication.

Multiple Choice Quiz

1. What is the authentication protocol that supports multiple methods?

   A. AAA

   B. EAP

   C. WEP

   D. WPA

2. Which of the following is used to decrypt a PKI-encrypted message at the receiving end?

   A. Dynamic key

   B. Private key

   C. Public key

   D. Static key

3. Which of the following security threats has the primary objective of overloading a network's resources, resulting in the resources becoming unavailable to the network's users?

   A. Denial of service

   B. Intrusion

   C. Interception

   D. ARP spoofing

4. Which of the following is used to encrypt a message using PKI at the sending end?

   A. Dynamic key

   B. Private key

   C. Public key

   D. Static key

5. What is the cipher method used in the WEP security protocol?

   A. 3DES

   B. DES

   C. PKI

   D. RC4

6. Who verifies and issues digital signatures?

   A. CA

   B. IEEE

   C. PKI

   D. RSA

7. Which of the following is *not* an enhancement to the security capabilities of WEP in the 802.11i standard?

   A. 802.1*x*

   B. EAP

   C. TKIP

   D. WPA

8. What is the 802.11i security protocol that issues temporal keys?

   A. AES

   B. EAP

   C. TKIP

   D. WPA2

9. What is the process used to confirm the identity of a person or to prove the integrity of specific information?

   A. Association

   B. Authentication

   C. Certification

   D. Encryption

10. What is the IEEE general security standard for networks?

    A. 802.1*x*

    B. 802.11i

    C. 802.3

    D. 802.15

Lab Projects

1. Understanding the nature of an attack, you should observe it first hand. Using a wireless sniffer, such as CommView for Wi-Fi (www.tamos.com), create an intrusion attack on your WLAN, list the network connections and IP statistics, and then attempt to decrypt individual packets to simulate this type of attack from an outside attacker.

2. Visit the web site of a certificate authority and list the steps required and the cost for obtaining a digital certificate for an individual and an entire WLAN.

Case Problems

1. A major university has made the decision to phase in a conversion of the wireline networks inside all teaching buildings to wireless networks. Its first task is to convene a panel of administrators, faculty, and students to determine what the security policy should include for the first phase of buildings, which includes the science building, the engineering building, the library, and the redesign of all student computer labs into hot spot facilities. Working in a team of four to six classmates, assume roles that represent the various constituencies that would be on the university's panel. What are your group's recommendations to the university regarding its wireless security policy?

2. Design a security policy for a home WLAN. What issues are the most important, what safeguards can be implemented, and what is the threat level to a home WLAN?

Advanced Lab Project

This project is intended to enable you to witness the difference between OSA and higher levels of authentication methods defined in the 802.1x standard.

To carry out this experiment, you need a WLAN with an access point that supports both OSA and one or more EAP authentication methods, at least two associated wireless nodes, and one node not associated with the network.

First, configure the access point and nodes for OSA authentication. Roam the independent node into the network's range. Is this node able to easily join the network?

Now, configure the access point and nodes with each of the EAP authentication methods supported. Is the roaming node able to join and participate on the network as easily as it was able to do under OSA?

Chapter 12

HAN, SOHO, and the Enterprise

LEARNING OBJECTIVES:

In this chapter, you learn how to:

Identify home and small office WLAN devices.

Install WLAN devices.

Although its title may sound like a *Star Wars* sequel, this chapter focuses on the devices and processes used to install a wireless home area network (HAN) or small office/ home office (SOHO), or an enterprise (corporate) wireless local area network (WLAN). Home and SOHO devices, and their installation procedures, are virtually the same, but the devices used and the installation practices applied in a corporate setting are different, even at the WLAN level.

Home and Small Office WLAN Devices

Before we get to the devices used in small home and office WLAN devices, we need to define each of the three networking environments that were organized into the two general networking groups covered in this section:

- **Home area network (HAN):** A **HAN** is a network (wired or wireless) that is installed to support the needs of the occupants of a single home. A HAN can be installed to provide Internet access, create a home intranet, or to monitor and control an integrated home automation system that may include audio/visual, heating/air conditioning, lighting, appliances, and more. A HAN can also integrate telephone services.

- **Small office/home office (SOHO):** A **SOHO** network is typically associated with telecommuting, which is the context from which this term was originally coined. A SOHO network (wired or wireless) is most commonly installed to support the needs of a single individual. A SOHO network is connected directly to an Internet source, which it accesses (or should access) using a virtual private network (VPN) client to interact with a company or enterprise network and its resources.

NOTE
Home and SOHO networks are generally grouped together because of their similarities.

- **Enterprise:** An **enterprise network** (wired, wireless, or both) is the internal network of a medium-to-large company or corporation. An enterprise network is typically a *nexus*—meaning a network of networks—in which many smaller LANs are combined into a single wide area network (WAN) that services a single enterprise and, perhaps, its customers and suppliers as well.

The following sections discuss these networking environments in detail.

HAN/SOHO Devices

Five general types of devices can be used to create a home or small office WLAN:

- Wireless network interface cards (NICs) and network adapters
- Wireless access points
- Wireless routers
- Wireless repeaters or signal boosters
- Antennas

You can refer to Chapter 3 for detailed information on each of these WLAN device types. In this chapter, you can find the information you need to complete the layout and installation of a WLAN in these environments.

Wireless Interface Devices: NICs, WNAs, and WICs

As WLAN technology begins to mature, the number and types of wireless interface devices continues to expand. A PC can be equipped with a wireless network adapter in a variety of ways but, in general, a wireless interface is installed inside a PC's system unit, connected to an external port on a PC or built into the system circuitry of the PC.

Network interface cards (NICs), wireless network adapters (WNAs), integrated mobile technology (IMT), and wireless interface cards (WICs) have evolved from a generic group of terms used interchangeably into each having its own fairly specific meaning (listed oldest to newest):

- **Network interface card (NIC)**   Unless you are completely new to computers and networking, chances are you are familiar with this term. A *NIC* is an expansion card form of network adapter that is installed inside the system unit of a PC in an available expansion slot, most commonly in a Peripheral Components Interconnect (PCI), shown in Figure 12-1.

- **Wireless network adapter (WNA)**   A *WNA* is designed primarily with portable systems in mind. There are three general types of WNAs:

  - **External WNA**   An *external WNA* is plugged into a PC to provide it with connectivity with a wireless network. The most common forms of external WNA devices connect through an available Universal Serial Bus (USB) connection. Figure 12-2 shows a USB WNA that can be connected into its own base.

  - **PC Card/PCMCIA WNA**   A *PC Card/PCMCIA WNA* is plugged into the PC Card connector on a PC as a hot-swappable device. Like nearly all WNAs, this WNA type (see Figure 12-3) is self-contained with a built-in antenna and radio-frequency (RF) transceiver capabilities.

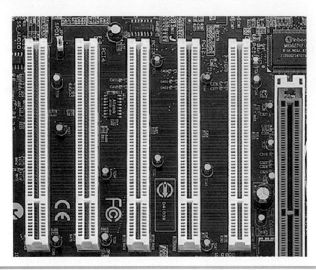

Figure 12-1 Nearly all NICs, wired or wireless, are installed in PCI slots. The slot to the extreme right is an Advanced Graphics Port (AGP) slot.

- **Compact Flash (CF) WNA**   Except for some detailed engineering stuff, the difference between a PC Card WNA and a CF WNA is essentially size and connector type. *CF WNAs* (such as the one shown in Figure 12-4) are primarily designed for use with hand-held devices, such as PocketPCs, PDAs, and the like.

- **Integrated mobile technology (IMT)**   Most new PCs (desktop or notebook) have a wireless network interface (adapter) built into their system circuitry. PCs built on the Centrino mobile technology from Intel or the Turian mobile technology from AMD, to name the most popular, have the capability to associate with a WLAN right out-of-the-box (after a bit of configuration, of course).

Figure 12-2 This USB wireless network adapter includes its own base jack for use with a USB hub. (Photo courtesy of Belkin Corporation)

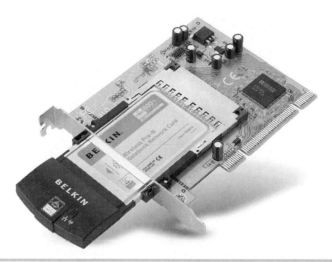

Figure 12-3   A PC Card WNA for use with notebook PCs (without the mounting hardware) or a desktop PC (using the mounting hardware) (Photo courtesy of Belkin Corporation)

Wireless Access Points

A **wireless access point** (see Figure 12-5) provides RF connectivity to the network adapters installed in user PCs and other radio-equipped devices within its range. To establish an association, the access point and the wireless devices must be configured with the same settings. In home and small office WLANs, a single access point can in essence be the central controller of the wireless network and supply any security services in use to protect the network's transmissions. In an enterprise setting, which may have several access points in

Figure 12-4   A Compact Flash (CF) WNA is designed for use with hand-held devices. (Photo courtesy of Cisco Systems, Inc.)

Figure 12-5   A wireless access point is the central device in a home or office WLAN. (Photo courtesy of U.S. Robotics Corp.)

a single location, an access point is used much like a hub in a wired network to connect fixed position and roaming devices for a single defined area.

Wireless Routers

Virtually all routers perform a standard set of networking functions, which include message forwarding, network address translation (NAT), and gateway services. In addition to these features and others, a wireless router also includes the functions of a wireless access point.

In home and small office settings, a **wireless router** is commonly used to bridge signals from the wired connection of an Internet service provider (ISP) or a wireless ISP (WISP) and the wireless workstations of the home or office WLAN. The line from a wireless receiver, a cable splitter, or a DSL splitter connects into the router, which commonly includes the function of an access point for wireless connections, as well as a small number of wired connection jacks, as shown in Figure 12-6. Having both wired and wireless capability provides flexibility in any network application.

Figure 12-6   The connections found on commonly configured wireless routers (Photo courtesy of Fiberline Europe)

Wireless Repeaters and Signal Boosters

Although they both work to increase the gain of a transmitted signal, repeaters and signal boosters go about it in different ways. A **wireless repeater** (such as the one shown in Figure 12-7) is a free-standing wireless device that receives a transmitted signal, increases its gain (power), and rebroadcasts it to extend its range and coverage. On the other hand, a **signal booster** (see Figure 12-8) is installed between an antenna and an access point or router. A signal booster filters out any noise or interference from both the inbound and outbound signals, and it boosts the power of the outbound signal to extend its range.

Figure 12-7   A wireless repeater (Photo courtesy of Buffalo Technology [USA], Inc.)

Antennas

In a home or small office setting, an external antenna is typically not needed because the omnidirectional dipole antennas built into access points and routers generally provide sufficient range and coverage for the wireless network. In some situations, though, an irregularly shaped home or building, such as one that is unusually long, tall, or narrow, may need to install an antenna to reach a location in an extreme corner of the building.

Antennas (such as the one shown in Figure 12-9) can be attached or connected to nearly any wireless device as long as it is equipped with a connector into which a plug on a cable from an antenna can be attached. Those wireless devices with one or more built-in (and detachable) antenna include a connector that can be accessed after the attached antenna has been removed (such as the one shown in Figure 12-10).

Figure 12-8 A wireless signal booster (Photo courtesy of Micronet Communications, Inc.)

Figure 12-9 A standalone omnidirectional dipole antenna (Photo courtesy of D-Link
Systems, Inc.)

12

Figure 12-10   A wireless NIC with a detachable antenna (Photo courtesy of D-Link Systems, Inc.)

NOTE
See Chapter 10 for more information on wireless network antennas and cabling.

Line Check 12.1

1. List three ways in which a PC can have a wireless network adapter installed on it.

2. What wireless device generally is used to provide basic RF connectivity to radio-equipped PCs?

3. What type of RF antenna is most commonly built into wireless devices?

 What Do You Think?

Future-proofing refers to installing systems that provide compatibility and interoperability with emerging technologies and systems not yet developed. Can you think of any possible future-proofing reasons to replace a wired HAN with a wireless HAN?

Enterprise Wireless Devices

Contrary to popular belief, the wireless devices used in a wireless SOHO network and those that should be included in an enterprise are not, nor should they necessarily be, of the same performance level, range, and standards. A fairly common perception is, especially among network technicians with little wireless network experience, that the requirements and quality of SOHO devices is adequate for use in an enterprise setting, with the enterprise WLAN only needing more of them.

The basic differences between the devices appropriate at each of these two levels of WLANs should be apparent when you, as the network planner, answer the following questions. These questions aren't in any particular order of importance:

- How many simultaneous users will be accessing the WLAN at any one time?
- What is the coverage and capacity required by the WLAN?
- What is the sensitivity of the data and information transmitted across the WLAN?
- What is the uptime requirement for the WLAN?
- What are the threat, risk, and exposure levels of the WLAN to intruder attacks?
- Is the WLAN an extension of a wired network?

This list is far from complete, but these questions should raise the issues for which SOHO and enterprise WLAN devices require different operating capabilities, features, and overall quality. A SOHO or HAN may have only one or two simultaneous users during its peak operating times, while an enterprise WLAN may have as much as 40 percent of its users "on the Net" at any one time. Home and SOHO devices are engineered around the lower end of the issues raised in the previous list. This is primarily so they can be priced appropriately to the HAN/SOHO application. Enterprise WLAN units are designed for higher traffic flow, more secure operations, and the network operations functions (routing and switching) required in a larger network.

In general, HAN/SOHO WLANS are standalone networks. On the other hand, an enterprise WLAN is typically an extension to and integrated with one or more wired networks. The enterprise WLAN might also need to support voice and video traffic, in addition to normal network data flows. An enterprise WLAN may also need to support a wider range of network protocols and services than is typically required of a SOHO WLAN, such as Simple Network Management Protocol (SNMP), Remote Access Dial-In User Service (RADIUS), Extensible Authentication Protocol (EAP), as well as other network access, authentication, and management tools.

WLAN devices designed for use at the enterprise-level typically have been engineered to provide some features not always required at the HAN/SOHO level. These features include the following:

- **Security:** Enterprise-level wireless devices usually offer standards-based, installation-specific, scalable security systems to complement the security levels provided by the wired portion of an **enterprise network**.

- **Upgradeability:** Wireless enterprise devices are *multimode* (supporting more than one 802.11 standard) and have the capability to be upgraded in place for both hardware and software enhancements.

- **Manageability:** Enterprise WLAN devices must be able to communicate with and report to the network management tools used to monitor and control all forms of networking in an enterprise. These forms include event logging, the application of upgrades, the management of configuration changes, and the troubleshooting of network issues.

The differences of HAN/SOHO and enterprise-level wireless devices are implemented in three basic wireless device types:

- Enterprise-level WLAN access points
- Wireless bridges
- Wireless routers

The following sections discuss what makes them appropriate to the enterprise WLAN and not so appropriate to the SOHO environment.

Enterprise WLAN Access Points

Many enterprise networks have been expanded to include wireless network segments. In most of these instances, standard, full-function (thick) access points are connected to the existing Ethernet network. This approach is intended to maximize all existing networking devices, while extending the system with a wireless segment.

Thick access points commonly provide a wide variety of enterprise-level features, which increases their prices over access points designed for HAN or SOHO applications. However, thick access points aren't designed to function as one of a group of access points on a network. As a result, they don't share information, which could help improve the performance of the network on the whole.

Better suited for use in larger WLANs, in which multiple access points are deployed, is the thin access point. As explained in Chapter 3, a *thin access point* interacts with an access point controller or wireless switch that consolidates several functions, which the controller performs for all the access points associated with it. The functions commonly off-loaded from the access points to the wireless switch or controller are association processing, authentication, encryption, security protocols, and address processing.

Wireless Bridge

Wireless bridges are used to connect two WLANs together, often at a distance, such as across a street, across a campus, or across a fairly short distance in a city. A wireless bridge that is used to connect the WLAN segments in two adjacent buildings is typically mounted outdoors and is designed for this use. Notice the rugged outdoor vase on the wireless bridge shown in Figure 12-11.

Figure 12-11 A wireless bridge with a case appropriate for outdoor installation (Photo courtesy of D-Link Systems, Inc.)

Wireless bridges can be implemented in two different modes:

- **Point-to-Point (P2P): P2P** mode connects two WLAN segments using a pair of wireless bridges, with one bridge configured as a master and one bridge configured as a slave (this why P2P is also referred to as master/slave mode).

- **Point-to-Multipoint (P2MP):** The **P2MP** mode creates a network among wireless bridges, either configured with one master and multiple slaves or with each bridge able to communicate with all other bridges in P2MP mode.

Some wireless bridges can also be configured to provide both bridging in a P2P or a P2MP mode, as well as provide access point services to wireless infrastructure workstations within its range. Others feature a more advanced operating mode in which enterprise-level access points include a wireless LAN access point (WLAP) mode that provides for simultaneous access-point-to-access-point bridging and access-point-to-wireless-workstation communications.

Wireless Routers

To be truly effective in an enterprise network setting, a wireless *router* must be able to interface with other routers located on the same internal network or the same WAN. This means the protocols, switching methods, and addressing of the wireless router must be compatible with the other routers, both wired and wireless, on the network.

Nearly all wireless routers are both 802.11- and 802.3-compatible, but some only support proprietary routing protocols and interface modes of the manufacturer. Because of this, typically, a good idea is, when mixing wired and wireless devices on a network, that they be from the same manufacturer or at least otherwise support the same standards-based functionality.

Wireless routers can be used for a range of enterprise network purposes, including:

- **Connecting WLANs and LANs:** If a wireless enterprise network includes any public areas, such as patio, cafeteria, or recreation areas for employees, a wireless router can be used to provide access back to the local network (wired or wireless) of each employee using a portable PC equipped with a wireless network adapter.

- **Improving overall network performance:** Routers, of any type, do not forward broadcast messages or any other message traffic that doesn't contain a valid and specific Internet Protocol (IP) address. Therefore, inserting a router into a network usually means an increase in the overall performance of an enterprise network. The performance improvement is primarily due to the elimination of broadcast messages across the whole network. In effect, local message traffic, including broadcast messages, stays local, which frees up bandwidth and improves throughput. This in turn, translates to better throughput for all network users.

- **Improving security:** Higher-end wireless routers generally include added layers of security not commonly offered on HAN/SOHO access points or bridges, including firewall and access control filtering protection (to its wired side), IP Security (IPSec), 802.1*x* security, and Wired Equivalent Privacy (WEP), or better, encryption.

Line Check 12.2

1. Describe the essential differences between an enterprise WLAN and a SOHO WLAN.

2. What are the two basic modes of transmission associated with wireless bridges?

3. How does a wireless router improve the throughput of an enterprise LAN?

What Do You Think?

What arguments can you make against using wireless networking technology for the entire networking solution of a large corporation?

Installing a WLAN

One consideration that affects a WLAN on any level is its logical (IP) addressing. Because IPv4 (see Appendix C) addresses are becoming increasingly scarce, more and more ISPs and WISPs are implementing the Dynamic Host Configuration Protocol (**DHCP**), which can be used to automatically configure a wireless workstation when it starts up or connects to the network, for all subscribers (not just their dial-up subscribers!). On the other hand, some are also restricting a subscriber to a single static IP address. In either case, the IP addresses for the multiple stations on a WLAN have evolved into more of a local issue.

IP addressing is also an important component of an overall security scheme in any setting. Whether in a SOHO setting where only a single station exists, in a wireless HAN where several PCs share a single Internet connection, or in an enterprise WLAN where a dozen stations access enterprise resources and the Internet, how IP addressing is handled can enhance or defeat the performance and security of the network.

Another feature found in nearly all wireless routers is Network Address Translation (NAT). *NAT* allows the workstations on the network behind the router to share a single public address on a WAN or the public network. This feature maintains tracking records to indicate which internal station was accessing which external address and publishes its single IP address to the world.

In lieu of assigning the same assigned IP address to every station on a network, private IP addressing (see Appendix C) can be used and assigned to the workstations automatically using DHCP (see Appendix B). When a workstation powers up, it requests an IP configuration set from the DHCP server, which then provides its next available address from the pool of addresses it has been configured with by the network administrators. By configuring and activating NAT and DHCP, any IPv4 addressing issues should be resolved for a WLAN of any size.

NOTE

Another approach to solving any addressing issues caused by IPv4 is to implement IPv6 (see Appendix C), provided all upstream networks support it.

Assuming you have already advanced beyond the choice of whether or not to install a wireless network (and have chosen to install a wireless network, of course), you now need to choose the mode (ad-hoc versus infrastructure), standard(s) (802.11a, b, or g), and design (layout and device placement) of the WLAN. With these choices made, you are ready to begin installing the wireless network.

A few differences exist among the installation of an HAN, a SOHO, and an enterprise network, as you might guess. Those differences are discussed in the following sections.

Installing a HAN WLAN

In most cases, physically installing a wireless network in a home requires little beyond installing a wireless NIC or network adapter on each PC to be included in the network and installing an access point. The detailed steps required to complete the installation involve setting the logical configuration of the access point and the network adapters.

NOTE

Chapter 9 includes additional information on installing and configuring WLAN devices.

Whether a wireless router or access point is being installed as the core of the network, it should be installed as close to the physical center of the network space as possible. Remember, the devices closer to the router or access point will have better throughput than those further away. So, you want to place the router or access point in a location that makes it, as much as possible, about the same distance from every workstation.

In a wireless HAN setting, you need to decide if you want the workstations on the wireless network to be able to communicate directly with each other (ad-hoc mode) or if they should communicate only through an access point (infrastructure mode). Unfortunately, on virtually all HAN-level access points or routers, you must choose one or the other. Ad-hoc mode may provide the better level of flexibility for a home network, but this depends on the needs of the users.

Security is the one area often overlooked in home WLANs and it shouldn't be. Commonly access points are installed fairly close to an outside wall, which means that because most built-in antennas are omnidirectional, at least half of the signal coverage is outside the home. One way to correct this situation is simple: replace the built-in omnidirectional antenna with an external directional antenna that limits the signal coverage pattern to the areas of the home where the signal is needed and not beyond.

Another way to limit the coverage area of the network is to choose a standard appropriate for the area being served. The three-mile range of 802.11g may be overkill if you truly don't need 54 Mbps of throughput in the vicinity immediately around the access point.

Installing a SOHO WLAN

Similar to a wireless HAN, a wireless network in a SOHO situation involves the physical installation of the wireless devices and their configuration. However, because a small office or home office involves working on private, proprietary, or confidential business-related projects, security can be more of a consideration.

Connecting to a corporate or enterprise network from a SOHO is best done through a VPN and, if privacy is important on the public network (Internet), a wireless router should be used as a gateway device. Wireless routers are available to connect to any Internet service medium, including cable, wireless receiver, or telephony-based service (DSL, frame relay, and so forth).

The configuration of a SOHO network should include address filtering, firewall protection, SSID stealth, WEP, IPSec, and, if available, 802.1*x* security. If a VPN client is in use, private key encryption is typically in use but, if not, you may want to implement it regardless.

Infrastructure mode provides another layer of security because it helps to prevent direct access from an external roaming device into the SOHO's primary workstation.

Line Check 12.3

1. What are the three general steps performed to install a WLAN?

2. What IP addressing options should be considered for any WLAN?

3. Why is security typically more of an issue for a SOHO than a HAN?

Installing an Enterprise WLAN

The primary installation issues for any enterprise WLAN are RF signal propagation and providing the best coverage patterns based on the locations of the access points. Every building has unique architectural features, even if they exist behind the walls, ceilings, and floors of seemingly "identical" spaces. When a wired network is installed, the characteristics of the network's medium are contained to the cable and its immediate environment. If properly installed, a wired network has few environmental concerns once it is activated. However, a wireless network can suffer unexpected interference from sources that may not have existed at the time the network was installed.

The installation of an enterprise WLAN must anticipate and address the following issues:

- **Bandwidth:** The capacity of the WLAN must provide sufficient bandwidth to satisfy the requirements of all associated stations.

- **Coverage:** The WLAN coverage must provide every station with continuous connectivity, including mobile or roaming stations moving across WLAN cells.

- **Security:** The security mechanism implemented on the WLAN must be able to withstand attacks and protect the resources of the individual stations, as well as those of the enterprise on the whole.

Enterprise WLAN Bandwidth

The bandwidth requirements of the WLAN are determined by the needs of the users located in a particular coverage area. Determining the bandwidth needs of the WLAN helps to determine which of the 802.11 standards should be implemented.

Remember, the bursty nature of network data and the bandwidth requirements at peak load are not necessarily the same as the bandwidth requirements of the network at all times. A trade-off of cost and higher bandwidth capacity definitely exists and there is a best fit between cost and capacity.

The amount of bandwidth required by a WLAN determines the number of access points the network will need and the transmission speed at which it must operate. To estimate the amount of bandwidth a WLAN must provide, you need to consider the following:

- What are the number of and the requirements of the most commonly accessed applications?
- What applications do users in certain coverage areas (cells) access regularly?
- What oversubscription factor do you want to apply (10:1 is common)?

Enterprise WLAN Coverage

Installing the right number of access points in just the right locations to provide the exact RF signal coverage required by a WLAN can be tricky because of RF attenuation and the distances of the network. Figure 12-12 illustrates that as the distance from an 802.11b access point increases, the available bandwidth (as well as the WLAN's throughput) decreases.

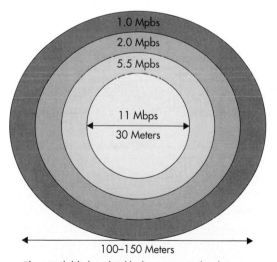

The available bandwidth decreases as the distance
between an access point and a node increases

Figure 12-12   The bandwidth available to a WLAN node decreases as the distance between itself and its base station (access point) increases.

To correctly configure a network with the proper number of access points, a coverage ring (similar to that illustrated in Figure 12-12) must be drawn for each planned infrastructure workstation on the network. The result should be a diagram that includes all infrastructure devices with which a node can associate with at least some bandwidth (see Figure 12-13). As the bandwidth decreases, fewer numbers of workstations can be supported—remember, WLAN bandwidth is a shared bandwidth. In coverage areas with reduced bandwidth, it may be necessary either to move one or more of the workstations or to add an additional access point.

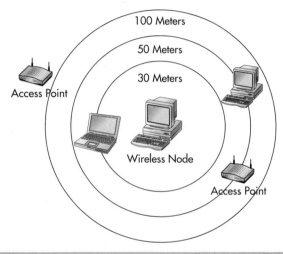

Figure 12-13   A coverage ring diagram for an infrastructure node on a planned WLAN

NOTE

Overlapping access point coverage areas create coverage redundancies and help to provide for the continuity of coverage.

Given the distances and the layout of the WLAN's layout plan, a common association rate should be chosen to determine the number of access points required to provide sufficient bandwidth to the WLAN. The number of access points is estimated by dividing the distance to the furthest point from the center of the network by the distance associated with the association bandwidth. For example, if the distance from the center of an 802.11b network to the workstation furthest from the center is 100 meters and a data rate (bandwidth) of 5.5 Mbps is chosen as the association data rate for the network, 100 meters is divided by 40 meters (the approximate distance of 5.5 Mbps bandwidth). This computation yields the information that 2.5 or 3 access points are required to provide 5.5 Mbps to the entire network.

Multiplying the calculated number of access points (3) by one-half of the association data rate yields the throughput capacity of the WLAN. Continuing the same example, multiplying

3 by 2.75 Mbps gives 8.25 Mbps of throughput capacity on the WLAN. Comparing this number back to the amount of bandwidth required by the applications completes the circle on determining if this is sufficient bandwidth to support the network. If not, additional access points may be required. The reason only one-half of the association data rate is used is this: the amount of overhead processing and traffic associated with 802.11 standards literally cuts the effective throughput in half.

NOTE

If the WLAN standard to be used is 802.11g, and 802.11b stations will also be supported, then the throughput rate will vary so much in practice, it is usually better to use 802.11b rates to estimate the number of access points required.

Routers in Enterprise WLANs

In nearly all enterprise wireless network situations, a wireless router is used as the gateway device for any WLAN segment. As previously mentioned, this helps to promote the overall performance of the enterprise network by capturing all broadcast and locally addressed traffic to the local segment. In addition, a router typically has the capability of bridging the wireless network to the wired network, regardless of its medium.

Security is arguably the most important consideration for an enterprise WLAN and all facets of the WLAN's coverage, range, and security protocols and services must be carefully analyzed. In addition, the security protocols and services in use must be able to interoperate with those in use on the wired network, as well as with all the wireless bridges, switches, routers, and access points installed on the WLAN or wireless wide area network (WWAN), if required.

NOTE

Chapter 11 discusses WLAN security protocols and features.

Enterprise WLAN Issues

To help minimize support, maintenance, and security issues of an enterprise WLAN, here are some design and installation tips:

- **Don't trust it:** You should approach and work with a WLAN much like you would a public network—completely untrustworthy. A firewall (hardware or software) should be installed between the wired network and the WLAN to prevent unauthorized wireless users from accessing or attacking the wired network, which is typically where the enterprise's resources are located.

- **Shape the network:** The radiation pattern coverage of the antennas in a WLAN can be controlled by using directional antennas in place of omnidirectional antennas, especially on access points and routers located close to the outside edges of the coverage area or buildings. The power levels of the radio transmitters can also be adjusted, so lower power is used where the signal doesn't have far to travel.

- **Set the infrastructure:** Disable ad-hoc mode on each workstation to prevent unauthorized roaming wireless devices from gaining access to the network through one of the WLAN's stations. Use the same make, model, and brand of NICs or network adapters to standardize their operations and features, register their Media Access Control (MAC) addresses, and enable address filtering.

- **Avoid defaults:** Change the default settings, especially for SSIDs and IP addresses, and disable SSID broadcasting on all wireless access points and routers. Physically secure the access points and routers in an out-of-sight location. If available, create VLANs to further separate traffic types across the WLAN.

- **Change the channels:** Each access point in an enterprise WLAN establishes a cell on the network, and each cell should be configured with an RF channel that does not overlap the channels of neighboring cells. If the cells are located close to one another or a large number of roaming or ad-hoc connections will occur, then using 802.11a or 802.11g is probably better, because of the increased number of channels available.

- **Tighten security:** If available, upgrade the WLAN's devices to implement 802.1*x*, 802.11i, or Wi-Fi Protected Access (WPA) to ensure the highest available levels of security are in use. In any case, be sure whatever encryption method is in use, that it encrypts at least the data payload, if not the entire packet.

- **Prevent failure:** One of the major issues for an enterprise network of any type (wired or wireless) is keeping the network up and available without failure. Because even the best electronic devices can fail, some means of ensuring the continuity of the network must be implemented as well. Several newer network architectures and devices, such as Aruba's Virtual Router Redundancy Protocol (VRRP), Bluesocket's Hot Failover, and Cisco's Structured Wireless Aware Network (SWAN), are addressing the issue of high-availability for wireless networks. These features help to ensure that the router and gateway for a WLAN remains active and functioning automatically in the event of a device failure.

- **Remain ever vigilant:** Install and use a form of WLAN traffic analyzer or monitor to monitor the network for unauthorized access attempts or successes. Several products are available, with more coming, to monitor and analyze WLAN packets.

NOTE

Chapter 13 discusses the use of packet sniffers, analyzers, and monitors.

Line Check 12.4

1. Describe the process used to determine the number of access points that should be installed on a WLAN to provide the level of bandwidth required.

2. Why should a wireless router be used as the gateway device for all WLAN segments on an enterprise network?

3. Why should the default settings on access points and routers be changed during installation?

What Do You Think?

Discuss what you think are the trade-offs between installing systems that absolutely never fail and systems that are reliable but, occasionally, suffer some downtime. Is a happy medium available?

Chapter 12 Review

Chapter Summary

Identify Home and Small Office WLAN Devices

-   A HAN is a network installed to support the needs of the occupants of a single home.

-   A SOHO network is installed to support a single individual through a connection to the Internet using a VPN to interact with an enterprise network and its resources.

-   An enterprise network is the internal network of a company or corporation.

-   Five general types of devices can be used to create a home or small office WLAN: wireless NICs and network adapters, wireless access points, wireless routers, wireless repeaters or signal boosters, and antennas.

-   A wireless access point provides RF connectivity to the network adapters installed in user PCs and other radio-equipped devices within its range.

- In an enterprise network setting, a wireless router must be able to interface with other routers located on the same internal network or the same wide area network. This means the protocols, switching methods, and addressing of the wireless router must be compatible with the other routers, both wired and wireless, on the network.

- A wireless repeater is a free-standing wireless device that receives a transmitted signal, increases its gain, and rebroadcasts it. A signal booster filters out any noise or interference from both the inbound and outbound signals, and it boosts the power of the outbound signal to extend its range.

- Enterprise networks must integrate with wired networks for data and voice traffic support, as well as enterprise network functions.

- WLAN devices designed for use on enterprise-level networks are engineered to provide additional features beyond those required at a HAN or SOHO level.

- Wireless bridges are used to connect two WLANs together, such as across a street, across a campus, or across a fairly short distance in a city. Wireless bridges are implemented in variations of two primary connection modes: P2P and P2MP.

- P2P bridging connects two WLAN segments using one bridge configured as a master and one bridge configured as a slave.

- P2MP mode is configured with one master and two or more slaves.

- An enterprise wireless router must be compatible with other routers on the same internal network or the same wide area network, including protocols, switching methods, and addressing.

- Wireless routers can be used for a range of enterprise network purposes, including: connecting WLANs and LANs, improving network performance, and improving security.

Install WLAN Devices

- Three steps are used to install a WLAN: design and approach, purchase the equipment, and install and test.

- A key consideration affecting all WLAN installations is IP addressing because IPv4 addresses are becoming increasingly scarce.

- NAT allows workstations to share a single public address on the public network.

- Private IP addressing can be used in conjunction with DHCP to dynamically assign IP configurations to network workstations.

- Wireless routers or access points should be installed as much in the center of a network as possible.

- Connecting to a corporate or enterprise network from a SOHO is best done through a VPN. A wireless router should be used as a gateway device.

- The primary installation issues for an enterprise WLAN are RF signal propagation and coverage.

- The installation of an enterprise WLAN must anticipate and address the following issues: bandwidth, coverage, and security.

- Determining the bandwidth needs of a WLAN helps to set the 802.11 standard, the number of access points, and the transmission speed of the network.

- In enterprise WLANs, a wireless router is the gateway device for any WLAN segment.

12
REVIEW

Key Terms

DHCP *(414)*
Enterprise network *(402, 411)*
HAN *(402)*
P2P *(412)*
P2MP *(412)*
Signal booster *(407)*
SOHO *(402)*
Wireless access point *(405)*
Wireless repeater *(407)*
Wireless router *(406)*

Key Term Quiz

Use the terms from the Key Terms list to complete the following sentences. Don't use the same term more than once.

1. A(n) _____ is recommended as the gateway device for any WLAN connected to an enterprise network.

2. A network that connects the resources for an entire company or corporation is a(n) _____.

3. _____ bridging connects two WLAN segments using one bridge configured as a master and one bridge configured as a slave.

4. A(n) _____ is a wireless device that increases the gain of a transmitted signal.

5. A(n) _____ is a network installed to support the needs of the occupants of a single home.

6. _____ can be used to automatically assign IP configurations to network workstations.

7. A(n) _____ filters out noise or interference from an inbound or outbound signal and boosts the power of an outbound signal to extend its range.

8. A(n) _____ provides RF connectivity to network adapters installed in user PCs and other radio-equipped devices within its range.

9. One type of _____ bridging is configured with a master and two or more slaves.

10. A(n) _____ network typically supports a single individual and provides a connection to an enterprise network and its resources.

Multiple Choice Quiz

1. What mode of network bridging transmits only between two fixed points?

    A. Dedicated

    B. P2P

    C. P2MP

    D. Switching

2. What type of network connects the internal data and system resources of an entire company or corporation?

    A. Enterprise network

    B. LAN

    C. WAN

    D. WLAN

3. What type of wireless device is used to increase the gain of a transmitted signal?

    A. Amplifier

    B. Lightning arrestor

    C. Wireless Repeater

    D. Signal booster

4. What wireless device should be installed as the gateway of any enterprise network WLAN segment?

    A. Wireless access point

    B. Wireless bridge

    C. Wireless repeater

    D. Wireless router

5. What acronym is used to describe a network installed to support the needs of the occupants of a single home?

    A. HAN

    B. CAN

    C. LAN

    D. SOHO

6. What type of wireless device provides RF connectivity to network adapters installed in user PCs and other radio-equipped devices within its range?

    A. Access point

    B. Bridge

    C. Repeater

    D. Router

7. What type of network supports a telecommuter with a connection to an enterprise intranet and its resources?

    A. HAN

    B. CAN

    C. LAN

    D. SOHO

8. Which of the following protocols is used to dynamically assign IP configurations to network workstations?

    A. DHCP

    B. IP

    C. TCP

    D. IPSec

9. What type of wireless networking device is used to filter out noise or interference from a signal, as well as to boost its power between an antenna and an access point?

    A. Amplifier

    B. Wireless bridge

    C. Wireless repeater

    D. Signal booster

10. What wireless bridging mode connects bridges in a one-to-many fashion?

    A. Dedicated

    B. P2P

    C. P2MP

    D. Switching

Lab Projects

1. Perform an access point coverage study (such as that described in "Coverage" in the section "Installing an Enterprise WLAN"). Determine first the bandwidth requirements for an existing or a proposed WLAN, and then, using coverage rings, determine the best association data rate, number of access points, and whether or not the antennas should be replaced to better serve the network.

2. Working in a small group of three or four, use the Internet and recent IT trade periodicals to locate research regarding the cost of failover and high-availability WLAN devices for enterprise networks. Prepare a cost-benefit analysis that compares the cost of implementing a zero-tolerance, high-availability network versus the cost of providing minimal failure recovery devices (perhaps an uninterruptible power supply [UPS]). Discuss the feasibility of both approaches and how we place a value on data and security with your group.

Case Problems

1. Drawing on what you have learned by this point in the book and your course, create a detailed checklist of the steps that should be performed when installing a wireless LAN as an extension of an existing wired enterprise network. Be as complete as possible. Identify from the steps you've listed what you consider as the most important step of the entire process.

2. Perform a site survey on your home and prepare an installation plan to install a SOHO WLAN, which you will use to telecommute to your new job as the sales manager of XYZ Widgets Manufacturing Company. XYZ is located three states and over 500 miles away. A part of your job is to prepare employee performance evaluations each month along with detailed and summary sales reports, which are to be submitted into the CEO's intranet mail box as documents. You are also required to participate in a live video-teleconference meeting on your PC to review new product proposals and R&D projects each week.

    What requirements do you believe this SOHO installation must address to satisfy the previous job requirements now and in the future?

Advanced Lab Project

Using the design for an enterprise WLAN developed in an earlier chapter or a new WLAN specified by your instructor, work with at least one of your classmates to develop coverage circles for each access point and each infrastructure wireless node. Annotate the distances between nodes on the coverage circles and complete a planning matrix similar to the following:

Node ID	Location	Distance in Feet to Nearest AP	Computed Bandwidth Available

After you complete your diagrams and the bandwidth matrix, develop a list of coverage recommendations that should be implemented to ensure that each 802.11b infrastructure node has at least 5.5 Mbps of bandwidth.

Chapter 13

Troubleshooting WLANs and Wireless Devices

LEARNING OBJECTIVES:

In this chapter, you learn how to:

Understand network troubleshooting procedures.

Troubleshoot wireless network problems.

Describe WLAN troubleshooting tools.

When wireless networks stop communicating, which they always do at some point, the true cause of the problem, whether it's obvious or not, must be identified before the problem can be resolved. This chapter focuses on the process of troubleshooting in general and the troubleshooting of wireless networks and their devices in particular.

Troubleshooting is the process used to identify the source of a hardware or software problem. Using a sequence of tests and trials, the object of troubleshooting is to isolate the cause of a problem through a process of elimination of potential causes for a particular problem. Technically, the process used to "troubleshoot" software is commonly called "debugging," but to avoid any confusion with what computer programmers do, let's stick with troubleshooting for both hardware and software. We look at the basic troubleshooting procedure and how it can be applied to troubleshooting and diagnosing wireless networking problems and issues to resolve association, throughput, coverage, and other performance issues. Whether you are troubleshooting your own small office/home office (SOHO) network or working as a network technician who is troubleshooting a larger network, the process and procedure is the same. In this chapter, the focus is on larger networks, but the steps described can be applied to smaller networks, as well. Because this book is about wireless networks, the discussion and examples are WLAN-related. However, for the most part, the same process also holds true for wired networks.

Network Troubleshooting Procedures

Over the long haul, the best way to consistently identify the root cause of networking problems and performance issues is to use a structured **troubleshooting** procedure. Several versions of a standard troubleshooting and diagnosis process exist, but for identifying and resolving networking problems—especially wireless networking problems—a six-step approach, as illustrated in Figure 13-1, is recommended.

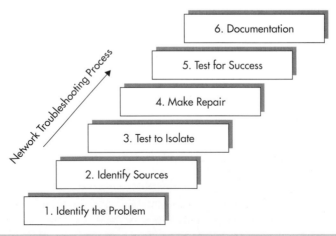

Figure 13-1   The six steps of a network troubleshooting procedure

The six steps of a comprehensive wireless network troubleshooting procedure are:

1. **Identifying the problem**   The first step to solving any problem is to identify the real cause of the problem and solve it. Otherwise, you run the danger of treating symptoms and not solving the actual problem, which will likely recur.

2. **Identifying potential causes of the problem**   On a computer, and most certainly on a network, performance problems can have a variety of causes. On a PC, a failing power supply can appear to be a hard-disk issue and, on a network, a connection issue could be configuration, hardware failure, interference, or simply range. During the diagnosis part of the troubleshooting process, consider any and all potential causes for a particular problem.

3. **Testing to isolate the problem**   After you determine what you think is the most likely cause of a problem on a network, attempt to reproduce the problem through testing until you are certain of its cause and any possible remedies. Hardware and configuration issues are more easily identified and resolved through a testing process than most protocol-related issues.

4. **Fixing the problem**   Obviously, you want to fix the problem by making the change or adjustment you've decided is the right solution. While you are applying your fix, you should document—in detail—everything you do, including any parts that had to be removed or any software changes made to apply the fix. This record not only can help you if a related problem occurs in the near future, but it could also help the next person to work on the system understand what happened in the past to this particular workstation, server, or network device.

5. **Testing the solution**   After the problem is identified, isolated, and resolved or repaired, you should test to verify that the change or adjustment you made is, in fact, solving the problem. You should also involve the user in the testing because until she tells you the problem is fixed, the issue is still active.

6. **Documenting the process**   As previously mentioned in Step 4, you should document the repair process. However, you may also want to write up a summary of the problem, whom it was reported by, how the solution was tested and verified, and what form of followup will be performed to ensure the fix continues to resolve the issue.

These steps are discussed fully in the following sections.

Identifying the Problem

In most cases, users notice and report network problems before network administrators can detect the cause and take corrective action. Users also tend to report the result of a problem or the result they see. For the most part, users can only tell you about what they saw, heard, or smelled.

Users can only report a problem they are experiencing, even though the real problem may be somewhere else on the network. For example, a user may report they are unable to log into a network, which, seemingly, is a single user problem. However, the root cause of this problem could be in a variety of areas. The underlying cause could be environmental, network configuration, hardware or software failure, one or more network protocols, or, perhaps, just plain old operator error.

For the most part, the majority of user-reported issues can be resolved by a trained and skilled network administrator fairly easily. Generally, because of his or her experience and knowledge, a technician who witnesses a network problem first-hand can readily diagnose, identify, and resolve a network problem.

This isn't always the case, however,. Users may not always be able to replicate the problem, so all you have to go on is what the user is telling you. This means, in this case, you are facing a problem typically reported by an unhappy user, who may or may not be able to accurately describe exactly what is happening (or what is not happening).

Typically, the best immediate source of information about a network problem is the user who reported the issue. The sooner you can interview the user after the report, the better the information you can gather. An old technician's joke is where one tech says to the other, "You go see what the problem is and I'll start fixing it." Because of the complexity of networks, it is difficult to begin fixing a problem before you know what the problem is or what it could be.

When interviewing users to learn exactly what they experienced, follow these simple steps:

- **Listen**   Hear what the user is saying. Don't try to show off your vast knowledge of technology and make suggestions as to what could be the problem. This will only confuse the user. Some users may attempt to impress you with their half-vast computing knowledge. In these cases, focus on exactly what happened or didn't happen, and exactly what the user was attempting to do when the problem occurred.

- **Understand**   If you don't understand what the user is trying to explain, ask him or her to repeat it, perhaps again and again, until you do understand. Don't jump to conclusions. Verify your understanding of the situation by paraphrasing what you understand back to the user. In most situations, rarely is an emergency so urgent that there isn't time to repeat this process as many times as necessary to gain understanding.

- **Repeat the problem**   An important part of truly understanding what users are experiencing is to have them repeat exactly what occurred. What may sound like a common problem that you've solved in the past could be an entirely different situation altogether. If the problem cannot be repeated, this doesn't necessarily mean it didn't happen or won't happen again, and it doesn't mean that you shouldn't investigate it. Perhaps all you can do is tell the user to call you if the problem recurs, leaving the evidence as is. You need to give the user the assurance that you are concerned about the problem and that you believe it exists.

● **Gather the facts**   Note all the details of the system environment, including what programs were running when the problem occurred, what exact operation or activity the user was attempting, whether any hardware or software changes had recently been installed or removed, and whether or not the problem has happened before and was not reported. If the user says the problem occurs all the time, you need to take him at his word and treat the situation as serious.

Some users tend to have more problems than others. A common cause for many user problems is a lack of training or ability. However, even "problem" users can have real system problems. Don't assume every problem reported by certain users is an operator error. Treat each issue as important as all other issues. The user is as much a part of the network as the PC, the operating system (OS), and the networking devices. Sometimes you need to fix that part of the system to resolve the issue.

13

NOTE

Although the documentation step is listed last in this six-step series, it should begin in this part of the troubleshooting process.

Identifying Potential Causes of the Problem

The size and complexity of a network can add to the difficulty of locating the root cause of a network problem. On smaller networks, the problem is likely easy to isolate and resolve, but on larger networks, what may seem like the apparent cause of a problem may not be the cause at all. Instead, it might just be a "red herring." Before assuming a certain device or piece of software is the sole cause of the issue, determine what could cause the component to fail or perform as it is in the particular situation at hand. If the source of the problem could be caused by connected or related components, you need to continue your investigation further by looking into those components. For example, consider a situation in which only a single workstation (out of multiple workstations) is unable to connect to a single access point (regardless of whether the network has more than one). In such a case, the problem is most likely in either the network adapter or the access point. If other workstations are able to connect and communicate with the access point in question, the problem is obviously with the workstation's network adapter. However, if more than one station is unable to connect to a particular access point, then the access point appears to be malfunctioning.

A network problem is typically caused by one of four general sources:

● The user (as in "user error")

● The network adapter in a network PC or its configuration

- Network devices, such as access points, routers, switches, bridges, and so forth

- The transmission medium, including radio frequency (RF) signals and the cabling of a wired network

User Errors

As previously mentioned, training, or the lack thereof, can often be the cause of a network problem reported by a user. If the user has not been properly trained with the knowledge required to operate a PC on a network, it is possible that an inadvertent errant key stroke or mouse click could cause the PC to disconnect from the network or cause any number of software problems that might appear to be a network problem to the user.

If properly configured and set up, the network connection for a network workstation should be all but transparent to a user. About the only evidence he may see that indicates he is connected to a WLAN infrastructure should be the wireless networking icon (see Figure 13-2) located in the lower-right part (on the taskbar tray) of the Windows screen.

Figure 13-2   The wireless networking icon on a Windows XP desktop

Network Adapter Issues

For the most part, communication-linkage problems on a wireless network are caused by one or more of a small set of common issues. Where you start the investigation into the cause of a WLAN problem depends on the scope of the problem. If many network users are unable

The Problem of User Training

User training is a common problem in many companies and organizations. Training users to be competent in the areas they should know to work on a network workstation is too often overlooked as an important part of a network installation. The dilemma of user training in most businesses (and most individuals as well) is this: when business is slow, often either no funds are available to pay for user training or the perceived need is low; when business is good, no time is available to spare for user training, although the need is more apparent. As a result, training for network users often falls on the network administrators, who should approach this task as a matter of survival—both for the user and themselves.

to connect to the network or are experiencing throughput issues (but other users are able to connect and work normally), the problem is one of many access points is creating the trouble. If every user is experiencing the same problem on a single access point network, however, you should probably start with the access point. But the problems on a wireless network may not always be the fault of the WLAN devices, especially on networks connected through an access point, switch, or bridge to a wired network or ISP. A good idea is often to start with the connection point nearest the Internet and work back through the network, eliminating possible problem sources as you go.

Testing to Isolate the Problem

You are sure you understand the problem and you are relatively certain of one or more causes for the problem. The next step is to identify which of the potential causes is the real cause. Using the following four-step process can help you to isolate the cause of a problem:

- **Remove or uninstall any recent hardware or software additions or changes**   In a majority of cases, the problem is typically caused by a conflict or incompatibility between one or more components and a recently added or modified piece of hardware or software. By removing or undoing this change, you may be able to quickly resolve the issue.

- **Check out a working station or device**   Check the configuration, setup, or the working environment of a "known-good" system or device. **Known-good** is a working term that refers to a computer or device you know to be working properly. You may find something that has been inadvertently or purposefully changed on the problem station by comparing it to a good one.

- **Replace failing hardware with known-good units**   If all initial testing fails to identify the source of the problem and you believe the problem is being caused by hardware, the next step is to begin replacing hardware devices with units you *know* to be *good*. A *top-down approach* is the better way to proceed: start with the highest level device in the series of hardware related to the problem, such as the Internet gateway, and then work back toward the problem station.

- **Begin eliminating components to isolate the problem**   Although this step is used mostly to isolate the cause of a hardware-related problem, it can be used for software issues as well. If all else has failed to identify and isolate the cause of a problem, begin removing one component at a time (retesting after removing each component) until the problem ceases. You can then put your diagnostic focus on the last component removed and how it was causing the issue.

Where to Look for Help

A variety of sources can provide you with information to help you troubleshoot, diagnose, and resolve a PC or network issue. The following is a list of a few of the better sources:

- The documentation (user's guide) that came with the system or component (you did read and save this, didn't you?)

- The manufacturer's web site's support area

- SkyVision's "How To Troubleshoot Network Problems" at www.sky-vision.net/whitepapers/How_To_Troubleshoot_Network_Problems.pdf

- Windows Networking.com's white paper, "Troubleshooting Wireless Network Connections," at www.windowsnetworking.com/articles_tutorials/Troubleshooting-Wireless-Network-Connections.html

- The PC Guide—virtually everything there is to know about PCs at www.pcguide.com.

Fixing the Problem

The title of this section essentially describes the action of this step. Once the source of the problem is identified and verified, the next step is to apply the fix. However, before you install the hardware, software, or make any needed configuration changes, you should take the time to record the details of the troubleshooting and diagnostics steps you performed to arrive at your conclusions. The best procedure is to write this information in the appropriate maintenance logs as soon as possible after determining what you believe are the cause and the solution of a problem.

Install or apply the required changes following the manufacturer's instructions (from the documentation or from their web site) for preparation and procedure carefully and specifically.

Testing the Solution

After the problem has been identified, isolated, and resolved or repaired, you should thoroughly test to verify that the fix was performed properly and does, in fact, resolve the problem. The testing procedure must ensure that not only is the affected workstation now working properly, but also any station with which the workstation may interface and the network on the whole. Simply testing the repair is not enough: the idea is to ensure the problem is fixed, so you never have to revisit it—or, at least, this should be the goal.

Anytime you modify any portion of a network topology, configuration, or structure, the entire network should be retested to ensure all its parts still function as they should. New network problems can commonly stem from what were believed to be corrections, enhancements, or additions made to a network. To make sure you haven't started a chain reaction of network problems, test every aspect of the network that may have been even remotely impacted by any change.

Documenting the Process

There is no guarantee that you will be the next person to work on a particular device or computer. For this reason, when a network is installed, a maintenance log should be created. The **maintenance log** should contain detailed information about the initial hardware and software configuration of the network, as well as a benchmark of its throughput time. The maintenance log should be updated each time diagnostics, research, repairs, upgrades, or additions are applied to the network or one or more of its nodes. In fact, a separate maintenancc log should also be created for each node.

Creating the maintenance log at the time a network is first installed establishes a baseline and a record of the devices, connections, configurations, and performance of the network at its beginning. This baseline provides a measurement point against which future performance can be measured. Maintaining a record of all maintenance actions, including those times when diagnostic testing didn't identify a problem, provides a recorded history that can be a valuable resource to the next technician to work on the network. Table 13-1 illustrates a sample of a network maintenance log. The information recorded at the network level can be summarized more than that recorded in the maintenance log for the particular PC or device.

Date	Action	Results	Technician	Follow Up
1/13/05	Installation	See baseline test	RP	Ad-hoc testing
1/14/05	Ad-hoc testing	5×5	RG	Monitor
2/26/05	Implement 802.11i Security Pack	Initial test passed	CP	Monitor with analyzer

Table 13-1 Example of a Network Maintenance Log

❓ Line Check 13.1

1. What are the six steps included in a network troubleshooting procedure?
2. Why is gaining an understanding of the "real" problem so important?
3. Why is documentation so valuable in the future?

What Do You Think?

Which of the six steps in a wireless network troubleshooting procedure would you say may be the more important in the short run? Is your choice the same for the long run?

Troubleshooting Wireless Network Problems

The overall process used to troubleshoot a wireless local area network (WLAN) is essentially the same used to troubleshoot any network. However, you should consider some specific issues when **troubleshooting** a WLAN. In the following sections, the more common of the problems and issues that can cause a network or node fault are discussed for the following devices:

- Access points
- Network adapters
- Antennas

In addition to the specific problems that these devices can develop, it can also be necessary to troubleshoot a WLAN for overall network performance issues. This area is also covered in this section.

Access Point Issues

When attempting to identify a WLAN problem that is not obviously a workstation or user issue, a good place to start is with the access point(s). The method you should use to test an access point depends on whether or not the access point is connected to a wired network.

To test an access point connected to a wired network (including an Ethernet link, a cable or DSL bridge or modem, or a wireless receiver) to verify it is responding to the wireless network, perform the following:

1. On a Windows workstation connected to the wired side of the network, open a command prompt:

2. Click the Start button, click Run, and type **CMD** in the Open text box, as shown in Figure 13-3.

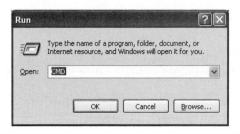

Figure 13-3   The Windows XP Run dialog box

3. At the command prompt displayed, type **ping** *IP address*, using the IP address of the access point, as shown in Figure 13-4. (See the section "Using **Ping** to Test a Connection.")

4. If the ping command times out or returns any other error condition, verify the IP address being used. If the IP address is correct, you must assume either a cabling issue exists between the wired node and the access point or, more likely, that the access point is not responding to the wired network.

```
C:\WINNT\system32\CMD.exe                                          - □

C:\>ping 192.168.0.101

Pinging 192.168.0.101 with 32 bytes of data:

Request timed out.
Request timed out.
Request timed out.
Request timed out.

Ping statistics for 192.168.0.101:
     Packets: Sent = 4, Received = 0, Lost = 4 (100% loss),

C:\>
```

Figure 13-4   The results of a ping command to a nonresponding device

To determine if the cause of the problem may be a general failure of the access point or simply a connection problem with a wired network, do the following:

1. Ping the access point from a wireless workstation to verify the access point is functioning.

2. If you are unable to successfully ping the access point, it has apparently failed and you can focus your diagnostic efforts on it, following the manufacturer's troubleshooting guide.

3. If you are able to ping an access point from a wireless node, the problem is likely in its connection to the wired network. If the wireless client is unable to ping the access point, the access point could be malfunctioning. Reset the access point by unplugging its power cord from the power source; wait about five minutes; and plug it in again. Ping the access point from the wireless and wired sides again.

4. If both of the pings fail, either the access point is physically or electronically faulty or it was configured or reconfigured incorrectly. Check the configuration first and, if it's okay, follow the manufacturer's troubleshooting guide to determine the problem on the access point itself.

5. If the access point is directly connected to the Internet gateway device of a service provider, contact the provider's technical support and have them ping the access point, modem, or bridge to determine on which side of the connection the issue exists.

If the problem is a configuration issue, which is far more common than a hardware problem, some major configuration settings should be verified, as follows (note, the following list is in alphabetical order and not in order of importance or severity):

●   **Channel assignment:** One issue related to connectivity problems between a wireless node and an access point is the signal strength on a particular channel. If the signal strength of the assigned channel suddenly becomes too weak to sustain a connection or the signal strength drops off intermittently, first try changing the assigned channel. If this fails to clear up the problem, check out the physical environment of the area within range of the access point or workstation. It could be that a cordless telephone, a microwave oven, or another 2.4 GHz device is creating interference.

Another channel assignment consideration, especially in densely populated areas, such as where houses are close together, or in apartments or condominiums, is that the signals from an access point in one home may be interfering with the signals in another nearby home if the two access points are using the same or overlapping channel assignments. The default channel assignment for most access points is Channel 6. In a case where two access points are interfering with one another, changing the channel assignment of one or both will likely eliminate the problem.

●   **DHCP settings:** Newer access points typically include a **DHCP** *server function*, which is used to assign private IP addresses and other IP configuration data to the wireless nodes that establish an association with the access point. In fact, some access points incorporate DCHP assignments into their security scheme and will not associate with devices to which they haven't provided an IP configuration. Another issue is the use of a nonprivate IP pool, which can cause IP address mismatch problems when communicating with the wired portion of a network or sharing the same router when two segments are using the same address pool range.

- **MAC filtering:** Many newer access points include a feature that can limit the wireless nodes allowed to associate with an access point to only those included in an approved or allowed MAC address list. This security-oriented feature, called **MAC filtering**, is intended to block the unauthorized access to a network's resources by unlisted devices. However, MAC filtering (also known as allowed client list) can also be the cause of connectivity issues on a WLAN. Out of the box, this feature is typically disabled, but if, somehow, during the configuration of the access point, it is enabled, with the allowed list empty, no nodes will be able to associate with the access point. Also, in a multiple access point environment, each access point through which a wireless node is to connect must be configured separately. If in use, MAC filtering can also cause connectivity problems when a new network adapter is installed in an existing node, a new node is added to the network, or when a wireless network-ready peripheral device is added to the network and the allowed client list is not updated.

- **SSID:** It is unlikely that the SSID on an access point would be changed inadvertently, but if a node is moved from the range of one access point into the range of another access point, the SSID of the relocated node must be reset to that of the new access point. If the SSID is configured differently on two wireless devices attempting to communicate, the nodes will be unable to create an association.

- **Signal strength:** If an access point can be pinged by a wired node, but not from a wireless node, some form of a **signal strength** issue is likely the cause. You should check the signal strength by using the Windows wireless connection status dialog box (as shown in Figure 13-5),

13

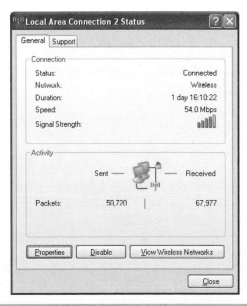

Figure 13-5   The Windows XP wireless connection status dialog box

Figure 13-6   Wireless network adapter's monitoring software

or monitoring software (as shown in Figure 13-6) provided by the manufacturer of the access point or wireless NIC. The interface of monitoring software differs for each manufacturer. However, the various monitors essentially provide about the same features to assist you with configuration, setup, and some low-level troubleshooting.

If signal strength is the issue, check the distance of the node from the access point and any obstacles or obstructions that may lie in the path between the two devices.

● **WEP settings:** Another reason two wireless devices may have connectivity problems could be the Wired Equivalent Privacy (WEP) settings for transmitting encrypted data. WEP is a standard IEEE 802.11b security protocol (see Chapter 11 for more information). If two devices have different WEP settings, it is likely they cannot connect. Different manufacturers implement WEP differently on their wireless products, which can mean the configuration data must be entered on each device using different formats. WEP functions only if all its configuration settings are an exact match. Refer to the manufacturer's documentation or web site for specific information on how WEP is implemented on a particular device.

Network Adapter Issues

The performance and connectivity issues common to all forms of wireless NICs and network adapters tend to revolve around their connections to a PC. The first step you should use when troubleshooting a wireless NIC or network adapter is to reseat the expansion card and ensure an external USB or serial interface connection has a snug fit. If this fails to solve the problem, here are a few more steps to use to diagnose the problem:

1. If the signal strength is reported as being low on either the Windows wireless connection status dialog box (see the previous Figure 13-5) or the manufacturer's proprietary device monitor (such as the one in the previous Figure 13-6), test the connection by moving the PC around inside the range of the access point.

2. Verify the distance of the PC from the access point to which it should be associated.

3. Verify the device driver installed on the PC is the latest and the version is appropriate for the PC's processor, OS, and chip set, according to the manufacturer's web site.

4. Check the connection or replace the USB cable on an external network adapter (if one is in use).

5. Verify the firmware of the access point and/or the network adapter is up-to-date, according to the manufacturer's web site.

6. Replace the wireless NIC with a **known-good** card.

Antenna Issues

The placement of any standalone wireless network antennas can also contribute to or be the cause of WLAN problems. Typically, a problem related to an antenna will fall into one or more of the following two areas:

- **Range** An antenna can be installed beyond the maximum distance for effective communications for the devices it is to support. Check the manufacturer's documentation or web site for information on the placement and use of a particular antenna.

NOTE

Cisco Systems has a handy Microsoft Excel spreadsheet you can use to calculate the maximum distance for placing an antenna in a WLAN at **www.cisco.com/warp/ public/102/us-calc.xls**.

- **Line of Sight** Generally, line of sight (LoS) is not an issue for WLAN antennas. However, the construction materials of a facility can sometimes block or weaken an RF signal, causing transmission problems. Table 13-2 lists some construction materials and the effect each has on a transmitted RF signal.

Material	Signal Penetration
Paper/Vinyl	Little or no effect
Solid Concrete/Precast Concrete	One to two walls
Concrete blocks	Three to four walls
Wood/Drywall	Five to six walls
Metal	Reflects signal
Chain link fabric or wire mesh	Blocks signal

Table 13-2 The Impact of Various Building Materials on RF Signals

WLAN Performance Issues

While all the specific device issues previously discussed can directly cause WLAN problems, sometimes the problem is more generic and manifests itself as generally poor performance of the entire WLAN. Users may complain about slow throughput, intermittent connection problems, or application issues. These problems can be caused by a failing or faulty access point, or another WLAN device, but they might also be caused by one of the following issues:

- **Retransmitted frames**   Nearly any problem that impacts the signal strength in a way to weaken or block it can immediately increase the number of retransmitted frames on a WLAN. Frames that aren't acknowledged by the receiving station are automatically retransmitted. As the number of retransmitted frames increases, the effective bandwidth available decreases, resulting in reduced performance on the overall network. Add to this the amount of broadcast and beacon frames also being transmitted and retransmitted and, soon, all user nodes are impacted. The underlying condition causing this problem can be related to a specific device or an overlooked or recently modified environmental element.

- **RF interference**   Radio frequency interference (**RFI**) can be the cause of an increase in the number of retransmitted frames on a WLAN. *RFI* can be caused by external signals, such a nearby radio transmitter, or a nearby WLAN operating on the same or an overlapping RF channel. A signal noise level of −85 dBm in the area of a WLAN can impact the performance of the network and cause a retry rate of about 10 percent, which is the point at which users begin to see a performance difference. You can use a network analyzer (see the section "Wireless Network Troubleshooting Tools") to pinpoint the source of the RFI and resolve it. The solution to most RFI issues is to increase the signal-to-noise ratio (SNR) for the WLAN. For example, if you determine that the interference problem only exists when the lunchroom microwave is running or one or more cordless phones are in use, you can reassign the RF channel for the network. If the RF interference cannot be avoided or corrected, you can increase the signal strength (gain) of the antennas or simply reduce the distance between the network's access points.

- **Saturation**   If the number of users on a WLAN has increased beyond the number it can effectively support or if the users are consistently downloading large files, the network could be approaching, if not passing, its capacity. Typically, one or more access points are saturated more than others, which can increase the retry rate and reduce the throughput performance of the network. To resolve this issue, the network's layout and configuration may need to be realigned, creating smaller clusters around access points.

- **Facility changes**   As companies grow or downsize, facility changes are quite common. A new wall is built, more partitions are installed, and more people are hired. These changes can impact the range and coverage of a WLAN, and, sometimes, even raise the noise level of the signal. To avoid any network performance issues resulting from physical changes in the environment, a site survey should be conducted periodically to verify the configuration and operating characteristics of the network.

? Line Check 13.2

1. What factors could contribute to a loss of connectivity between an access point and a wireless workstation?

2. In what way can enabling MAC filtering inadvertently during configuration cause a network problem?

3. How closely must the WEP configuration data match on a WLAN's devices of a wireless network?

13

Wireless Network Troubleshooting Tools

A variety of hardware and software tools are available to help you to troubleshoot, diagnose, and isolate WLAN RF signal issues. These tools can be used to measure and analyze a wide range of WLAN RF conditions, including noise, retry rates, data speed, frame types, rogue stations, hidden stations, and more. The primary types of tools you can use to troubleshoot a WLAN are:

● Network analyzers

● Operating system administrator tools

● Protocol-based utilities

Network Analyzers

A wireless network analyzer is, most commonly, either a piece of specialized software that is installed and run on a portable PC equipped with a wireless radio transceiver or a specialized handheld PC with built-in software. A **network analyzer** tests for a wide range of wireless network performance and security characteristics, producing a graphical user interface (GUI), as shown in Figure 13-7. A few of the better known software wireless network analyzers are AirMagnet (from AirMagnet, Inc. at www.airmagnet.com), AiroPeek (from Wildpackets, Inc. at www.wildpackets.com), and Sniffer Wireless (from Network General at **www.sniffer.com**). Nearly all network analyzer packages provide the following functions:

● **Monitoring:** Network analyzers passively monitor and capture all data traffic transmitted within range of the PC on which the analyzer is installed, and temporarily store it on the PC's hard disk. Because the operation of the analyzer is passive, it makes no impact on the performance of the network.

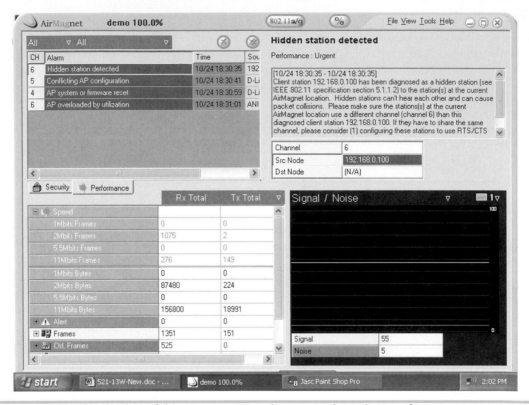

Figure 13-7 The display of the AirMagnet wireless network analyzer software system

- **Decoding:** Each frame captured by the analyzer, including 802.11 control, management, and data frames, is decoded and its data, protocol type, and frame configuration are examined.

- **Filtering:** The analyzer also examines each frame for certain data on which it performs statistical analysis relating to performance, security, and throughput.

Windows Administrator Tools

The Windows XP OS includes a variety of administrator tools, which can help you to troubleshoot a single workstation on a wireless network. In the following sections, we look at how these tools are applied in a few troubleshooting scenarios for a Windows XP workstation.

Troubleshooting the Wireless NIC

In general, if a Windows XP workstation is failing to connect to a wireless network, the issue is likely related to compatibility, the device driver, or configuration. Here are the steps used to check out these areas:

1. If an internal PCI network interface card (NIC) is installed, verify the card is listed on the windows XP Hardware Compatibility List (HCL), now also referred to as the Windows Marketplace Tested Products List, included on the Windows XP installation CD or on the Microsoft web site at **www.microsoft.com/whdc/hcl/**. If your NIC is not listed, replace it with a compatible card.

2. Verify the device driver installed for the wireless network adapter is compatible with Windows XP. This information should also be in the HCL or available on the manufacturer's web site. If a more recent or compatible driver is available, install it before you perform any other troubleshooting steps.

13

Wireless Zero Configuration Service

Windows XP includes a feature called Wireless Zero Configuration service (WZC) that allows a wireless-enabled device to automatically establish a connection when moving between different wireless modes without the need for reconfiguration. *WZC* automatically configures the wireless device with the IP configuration data needed to associate with a new access point, including any activated security settings. This allows a wireless device to move between different wireless environments, such as home, work, airports, and other hot spots, without requiring the user to intervene.

How can you tell if the WZC service is running on your Windows XP system? Follow these steps:

1. Open the Control Panel, either from the Start menu or by choosing Run, and enter **control.exe** in the Open box.

2. Open the Network Connections or Network and Internet Connections icon.

3. Right-click the icon for your wireless connection and choose Properties from the pop-up menu. If the dialog box that appears includes a Wireless Networks tab (see Figure 13-8), the WZC service is running.

If the Wireless Connections tab is not present, either an issue exists with the device driver for your network adapter or your driver doesn't support the service. This must be resolved before the service can start. Another possible reason the wireless Connections tag may not be displayed is because your system has not been upgraded to Windows XP service pack 2 (SP2).

Device Driver Issues

Note the following as you work on various device-driver issues:

1. If the wireless network adapter or NIC was installed using the manufacturer's installation disk and instructions, device driver problems should be rare, unless the driver is out-of-date or incompatible with Windows XP. However, if you believe the device driver may

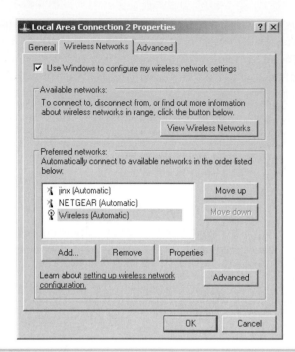

Figure 13-8 The Properties window for a Windows XP wireless connection

be the problem, use the following steps to troubleshoot the device driver. Depending on which style of Desktop view you have, right-click the My Computer icon on either the Start menu or on the Desktop. Select Manage from the pop-up menu to display the Computer Management Window (see Figure 13-9).

2. In the left pane, choose Device Manager to display the device tree in the right panel (see Figure 13-10).

3. If the list includes an Other Devices entry, expand that selection. If the wireless network adapter is included under Other Devices, likely the device drivers for the wireless network adapter or NIC have not been installed or are incompatible with Windows XP.

4. If there is no Other Devices entry, or if the wireless network adapter or NIC is not listed under that entry, expand the Network adapters entry.

5. If the wireless network adapter or NIC is included under Network adapters, double-click it to display the Properties window for the adapter (see Figure 13-11).

6. Select the General tab. If the network adapter device driver is installed and compatible, the Device Status window should include the statement "This device is working properly."

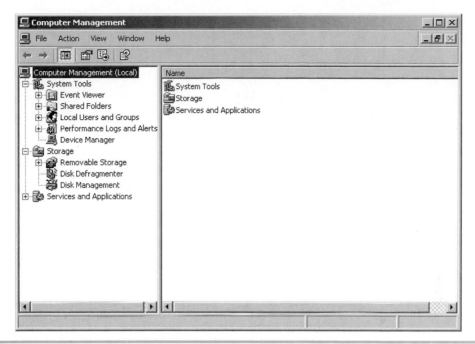

Figure 13-9   The Windows XP Computer Management window

If a device or device-driver problem exists and the device is not working properly, an error code should be displayed in the Device Status box. To determine the meaning of the error code, go to **http://support.microsoft.com/** and search for the error code.

Protocol-based Utilities

Windows XP provides a suite of TCP/IP protocols and utilities that can be used to troubleshoot connection problems, ranging from testing the connection at the network adapter or NIC to verifying the IP configuration of a workstation. These tools are discussed in the following sections.

Using Ping to Test a Connection

The TCP/IP **ping** utility is an excellent tool for testing the connection of a workstation on its LAN or WLAN. Ping includes a variety of options to help you troubleshoot a number of potential connection issues. Table 13-3 lists the steps in a sample ping testing series in which the local workstation is named rons_pc, the local IP address is 10.51.111.105, the default loopback address is 127.0.0.1 (localhost), and the access point (WLAN_AP1) is located at address 10.51.111.10.

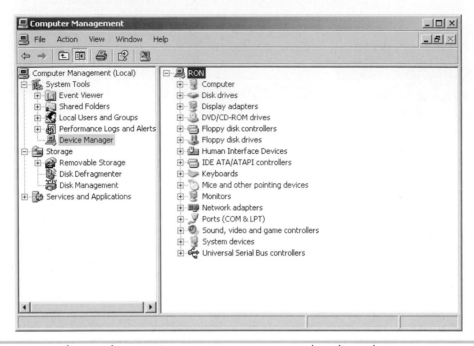

Figure 13-10   The Windows XP Computer Management window shows the Device Manager tree.

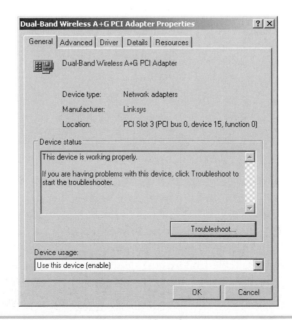

Figure 13-11   The Windows XP Properties window for a wireless NIC

Ping Command	Device Being Tested	Problem Identified by Ping Failure
ping 127.0.0.1	Loopback address (NIC or network adapter)	Corrupted network adapter or NIC, or TCP/IP configuration
ping localhost	Loopback name (NIC or network adapter)	Corrupted network adapter or NIC, or TCP/IP configuration
ping 10.51.111.105	Local IP address (NIC or network adapter)	Corrupted network adapter or NIC, or TCP/IP configuration
ping rons_pc	Local name (NIC or network adapter)	Corrupted network adapter or NIC, or TCP/IP configuration
ping 10.51.111.10	Access point's IP address	Faulty hardware or network adapter, or NIC device driver
ping WLAN_AP1	Access point's name	NetBIOS name resolution failure

Table 13-3   Ping Commands and What a Ping Failure Indicates on a WLAN or LAN

The ping utility can also be used to troubleshoot problems with connecting to a WAN or the Internet. Table 13-4 lists a series of ping commands that, if used in sequence, can help to identify the source of a connection issue.

NOTE

To obtain the IP addresses of the default gateway and DNS server, run the ipconfig /all command from a command line prompt. From the Start menu, choose Run, and then type **cmd** to open a command window. Then, type **ipconfig /all**.

Ping Command	Device Being Tested	Problem Identified by Ping Failure
ping 10.51.111.1	Default gateway	Default gateway down or faulty connection
ping 10.51.111.5	DNS server	DNS Server down for faulty connection
ping 198.45.24.104	Web server/site IP address	Local or ISP router issues, or the web server is down
ping www.mhhe.com	Web site name	Local or ISP DNS Server issues, or the web server is down

Table 13-4   Ping Commands and What a Ping Failure Indicates on a WAN

Using ipconfig to Display the IP Configuration

Ipconfig (ifconfig in Linux) can be used to display a PC's current IP configuration, showing its IP address, MAC address, network (subnet) mask, default gateway, and more. Ipconfig can also be used to release and renew the DHCP configuration of a PC. The ipconfig tool shows a computer's TCP/IP configuration. This TCP/IP utility can be useful when you need to verify a PC's setup and configuration. Figure 13-12 shows the output from the ipconfig /all command on a Windows XP system.

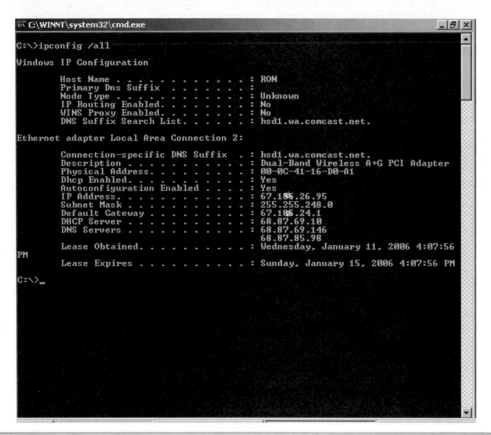

Figure 13-12 The results of the ipconfig command

Using tracert to Test Connectivity

The most common use of the **tracert** (traceroute in Linux) is to determine the path taken by messages sent from a workstation to a specified destination IP address or domain name.

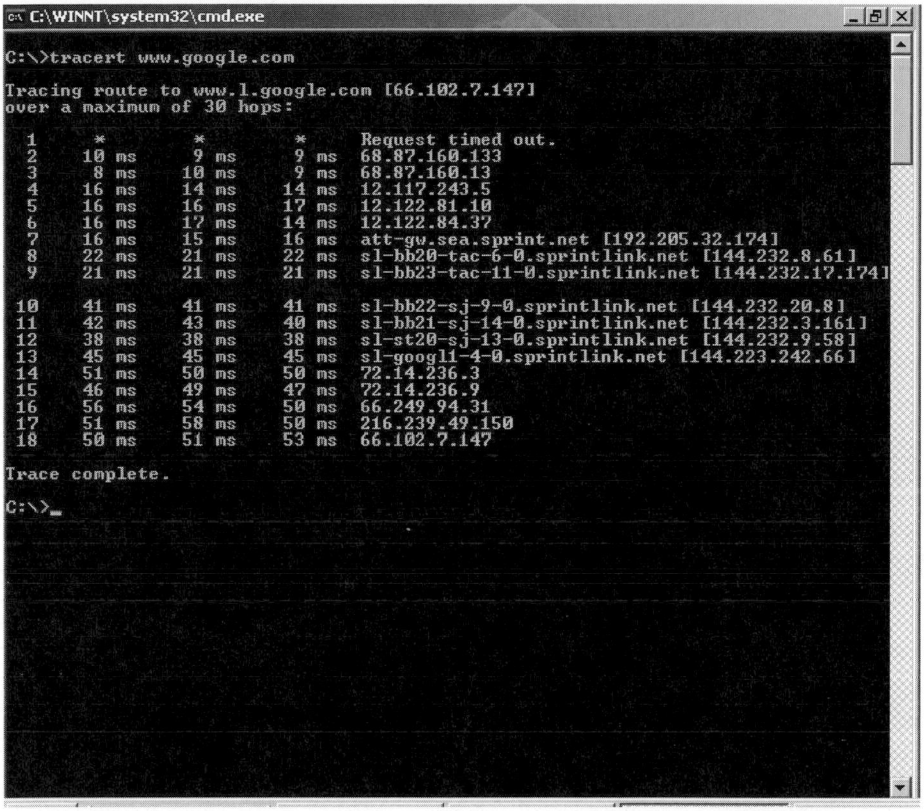

```
C:\WINNT\system32\cmd.exe                                          _|8|X|

C:\>tracert www.google.com

Tracing route to www.l.google.com [66.102.7.147]
over a maximum of 30 hops:

  1      *        *        *     Request timed out.
  2    10 ms     9 ms     9 ms  68.87.160.133
  3     8 ms    10 ms     9 ms  68.87.160.13
  4    16 ms    14 ms    14 ms  12.117.243.5
  5    16 ms    16 ms    17 ms  12.122.81.10
  6    16 ms    17 ms    14 ms  12.122.84.37
  7    16 ms    15 ms    16 ms  att-gw.sea.sprint.net [192.205.32.174]
  8    22 ms    21 ms    22 ms  sl-bb20-tac-6-0.sprintlink.net [144.232.8.61]
  9    21 ms    21 ms    21 ms  sl-bb23-tac-11-0.sprintlink.net [144.232.17.174]

 10    41 ms    41 ms    41 ms  sl-bb22-sj-9-0.sprintlink.net [144.232.20.8]
 11    42 ms    43 ms    40 ms  sl-bb21-sj-14-0.sprintlink.net [144.232.3.161]
 12    38 ms    38 ms    38 ms  sl-st20-sj-13-0.sprintlink.net [144.232.9.58]
 13    45 ms    45 ms    45 ms  sl-googl1-4-0.sprintlink.net [144.223.242.66]
 14    51 ms    50 ms    50 ms  72.14.236.3
 15    46 ms    49 ms    47 ms  72.14.236.9
 16    56 ms    54 ms    50 ms  66.249.94.31
 17    51 ms    58 ms    50 ms  216.239.49.150
 18    50 ms    51 ms    53 ms  66.102.7.147

Trace complete.

C:\>_
```

Figure 13-13   The display produced by a Windows XP tracert command

The display of the tracert command lists the IP address and name (if available) of each internetwork router through which a message passes en route to its destination (see Figure 13-13). When troubleshooting a connectivity problem on a workstation, tracert can help you diagnose whether the station is able to communicate with the default gateway and beyond. You can use either the destination's IP address or its domain name, if appropriate.

Using arp to Verify Address Pairings

The TCP/IP *arp* utility is used to verify the contents of a workstation's arp cache. The arp cache stores the IP and MAC address of other network nodes to which a PC transmits messages. In Figure 13-14, notice the display of the arp command lists the PC's IP address and the IP and MAC (physical) address of one or more stations to which a station has recently transmitted a message.

```
C:\WINNT\system32\cmd.exe                                    _ |8| X|

C:\>arp -a

Interface: 67.185.26.95  --- 0x10003
   Internet Address        Physical Address      Type
   67.185.24.1             00-01-5c-22-2f-82     dynamic

C:\>_
```

Figure 13-14   The results of an arp command

Line Check 13.3

1. What are the functions performed by a wireless network analyzer?

2. How extensive should the testing performed be when verifying a change or modification to a network?

3. If a workstation seems unable to connect to the network media or to an access point, what TCP/IP utility would you first use?

What Do You Think?

Of the various steps included in the troubleshooting procedure for a wireless network, which is the most important to ensure the network continues to meet the long-term needs of the organization?

Chapter 13 Review

Chapter Summary

Understand Network Troubleshooting Procedures

- To consistently identify the root cause of a networking problem, you should use a structured troubleshooting procedure.

- The six steps of a comprehensive wireless network troubleshooting procedure are: identify the problem, identify probable causes, test to isolate, repair or resolve the issue, test for success, and document any action taken.

- The best immediate source of information about a network problem is the user. When interviewing the user: listen, don't jump to conclusions, and make sure you completely understand exactly what the user believes is the problem.

Troubleshooting Wireless Network Problems

- A wireless network problem is typically caused by one of four general sources: user error, a network adapter, an access point, or the transmission medium.

- Communication problems on a wireless network are typically caused by a small set of common issues: channel assignment, DHCP settings, MAC filtering, SSID settings, signal strength, and WEP settings.

- The issues common to wireless NICs and network adapters revolve around their connections to a PC. To diagnose a NIC or network adapter problem, replace the wireless NIC with a known-good card, replace the USB cable on an external network adapter, verify the device driver is the latest and appropriate for the PC, verify the firmware is current according to the manufacturer's web site, and verify the distance of the PC from the access point.

- A wireless network analyzer is specialized software running on a portable PC with a wireless network interface card. A network analyzer tests for data speed, frame types, rogue stations, and hidden stations.

- A maintenance log should be created when the network is installed and updated each time a diagnostic, research, repair, upgrade, or addition is applied to the network.

- The maintenance log establishes and maintains a baseline and a record of the devices, connections, configurations, and performance of the network over its life.

Wireless Network Troubleshooting Tools

- A variety of hardware and software tools can be used to measure and analyze a wide range of WLAN RF conditions.

- The primary types of tools that can be used to troubleshoot a WLAN are: network analyzers, operating system administrator tools, and TCP/IP protocol-based utilities.

- A network analyzer tests for a wide range of wireless network performance and security characteristics. A network analyzer can be used to monitor, decode, and filter network traffic.

- Windows XP includes administrator tools to troubleshoot a single workstation on a wireless network.

- The Windows XP Wireless Zero Configuration service allows a wireless-enabled device to automatically establish a connection when moving between different wireless modes without the need for reconfiguration.

- Windows XP provides a suite of TCP/IP protocols and utilities that can be used to troubleshoot connection problems, including ping, ipconfig, tracert, and arp.

Key Terms

DHCP *(440)*
Known-good *(435, 443)*
MAC filtering *(441)*
Maintenance log *(437)*
Network analyzer *(445)*
Ping *(439, 449)*
RFI *(444)*
Signal strength *(441)*
Tracert *(452)*
Troubleshooting *(430, 438)*

Key Term Quiz

Use the terms from the Key Terms list to complete the following sentences. Don't use the same term more than once.

1. _____ is a security-oriented feature intended to block the unauthorized access to a network's resources by unlisted devices.

2. The process of determining the cause and source of a network problem is _____.

3. To verify the connectivity of a device on the network, use the _____ command.

4. On a Windows XP workstation, the command used to display the network path between a station and a destination address is _____.

5. The protocol that can be used to automatically assign an IP configuration to a network workstation is _____.

6. The record of the installation and maintenance actions performed on a network is a(n) _____.

7. A(n) _____ can be used to monitor the activities of a wireless network.

8. When diagnosing a wireless connectivity problem, verify the _____ between a workstation and the access point to which it is associated.

9. The way to determine if a hardware device is the source of a problem is to replace the suspected device with one that is _____.

10. A common interference source on a wireless network is _____.

Multiple Choice Quiz

1. Many access points include a feature that will allow the access point to associate with only certain nodes. What is this feature called?

   A. Selective authorization

   B. Approved node access list

   C. MAC filtering

   D. Selective access

   E. None of the above

2. What TCP/IP protocol is used to automatically assign IP configuration data to a wireless network node by an access point?

   A. ARP

   B. DHCP

   C. SNMP

   D. IPCONFIG

3. What type of electrical nose interference is transmitted through the air?

   A. EMI

   B. SNR

   C. RFI

   D. NEXT

4. What characteristic of a wireless network should be checked when a wireless station is exhibiting intermittent connection issues?

   A. Frequency

   B. IEEE 802.11 standard in use

   C. Modulation

   D. Signal strength

5. What manual record should be maintained in detail for every wireless or wired network?

   A. Event log

   B. Maintenance log

   C. Repair log

   D. Security log

6. Which of the following would not necessarily be included in the troubleshooting process when a node on the distant edge of an access point's range begins to suffer intermittent connectivity problems?

   A. Access point power

   B. Antenna type

   C. Brand of access point

   D. Signal strength

7. What TCP/IP utility can be used to test whether one node on a network can be reached from another node on the same network?

   A. ping

   B. arp

   C. ipconfig

   D. tracert

8. What software tool can be used on portable, as well as desktop, PCs to monitor and control the actions of a wireless network?

   A. Diagnostic packages

   B. Network analyzer

   C. System analyzer

   D. Event logs

9. When replacing a suspected hardware device, what characteristic should the replacement device have?

   A. Different brand or model

   B. Different IEEE 802.11*x* standard

   C. A device that is known-good

   D. A working device from another like system

10. What TCP/IP utility can be used to display the internetwork path used between a workstation and a remote IP address on a Windows XP system?

A. ping

B. arp

C. ipconfig

D. tracert

Lab Projects

1. After the instructor has purposely changed the configuration of your wireless network's access point, the wireless NIC or network adapter in a wireless node, or both, perform a structured troubleshooting procedure to determine the cause of the problem(s). Make a written record of each step in the procedure, identifying what actions you took, and what you were able to accomplish on each step.

2. Download a demonstration version of a network analyzer, such as AirMagnet (**www .airmagnet.com**), and install it on a portable PC. Move the portable PC around to each desktop PC on a wireless network and record the signal strength, data speed, throughput rating, and the frame success rate at each position. You may also want to compare any other statistics created by the network analyzer and determine if an unforeseen problem already exists or is brewing on the network.

Case Problems

1. Using the Internet, visit the web site for the manufacturer(s) of the wireless devices installed in your school's wireless network, or the wireless network in your home or office. Determine the device driver and the firmware version for each device is current and compatible with the OSs in use on the network. If any need to be updated, obtain the instructions for performing the required tasks and, with your instructor's permission (where appropriate), update the devices or software that should be updated.

2. In two adjacent rooms or on opposite ends of a single large room, install two 802.11 WLANs using the same standard for both. Place the access point for each WLAN near (but, not next to) the common wall between the rooms. Configure both WLANs uniquely, with the exception of setting both to use the same wireless channel. Using portable PCs equipped with the proper network adapters, determine if interference between the two networks is causing any level of communications problems. Change the channel settings of the two WLANs until you find two channels on which no interference is created.

Advanced Lab Project

Working in small teams of two or three students, do the following:

1. Have one team member introduce faults or problems into the setup and configuration of a wireless workstation. This can be done any number of ways, including removing the NIC, deleting protocols or services, changing the DHCP settings, and so forth.

2. The other team member(s) should follow the troubleshooting process described in this chapter, performing all the steps listed, including documentation. The problem-causing team member is to play the role of the user.

3. Change roles after each problem is diagnosed and resolved until all team members have had a turn in each role.

Chapter 14

Wireless WANs

LEARNING OBJECTIVES:

In this chapter, you learn how to:

Use the basics of WANs and their technologies.

Understand WWAN components and technologies.

Assess WAN communications technologies.

Connect over virtual private networks.

Review the IEEE 802.16 standard.

In the networking world, the definitions of the various types of area networks can be overlapping and downright confusing at times. Where a local area network (LAN) stops and a metropolitan, enterprise, or wide area network (WAN) begins is often vague, at least in terms of their exact definitions. On top of that, just how wide a WAN can be and exactly which type of technology is used can also be contradictory and confusing.

The focus of this chapter is to dispel some of the vagueness and confusion by explaining, in the context of wireless networks, just what WANs, metropolitan area networks (MANs), and a couple other area networks are, the technology used in each, and how they work.

Wide Area Network (WAN) Basics

The definition of a WAN has changed a bit over the past few years, although, generically, today's WAN still fits its original definition. At one time, a WAN was a network that had a larger geographical coverage, such as a company's network that links its West Coast office with its East Coast headquarters. On the other hand, the Internet itself was commonly presented as the prime example of a WAN. If you search the Internet for a definition of a WAN, you will find dozens of variations on essentially the same theme: A WAN is

- A network of computer devices
- Linked by telecommunications equipment
- A larger geographical area
- Bigger than a LAN
- A network that covers an area larger than a single building or campus
- An interconnection of at least two LANs

What is odd about the currently available definitions of a WAN is that not one defined it as a communications network, which is essentially what all networks are, regardless if they are physical networks (such as a wired Ethernet or Token Ring network) or logical networks (such as a wireless ad-hoc network).

A *WAN* is a physical or logical communications network with the capability to create links between independent devices to facilitate an interchange of data over a common transmission-interconnected topology implemented over a wide geographical area. Perhaps, the key semantic in this definition is the most important word in the whole definition: wide. As we discuss in this chapter, the term "wide" can mean different things to different people, companies, and even governments.

Regardless of how you interpret the definition of a WAN and the scope of the word "wide," basically a WAN is an interconnection of local networks that are linked using some form of communications technology. For example, in the WAN shown in Figure 14-1, two LANs connect through their respective routers into a communications cloud that provides the WAN services.

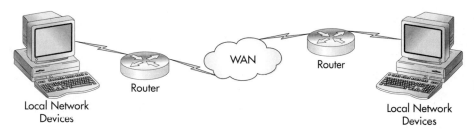

Figure 14-1 The components of a simple WAN

The cloud metaphor is commonly used to depict WAN communications services because no one specific type of communications technology is used end-to-end, and the ownership and control of these services are commonly provided by a combination of vendors. The cloud represents the services and links provided by the various communication services providers that provide the long-distance connectivity.

NOTE

In virtually all network diagrams that include a WAN component, the WAN communications link is shown as a cloud. Why a cloud, you ask? The cloud represents the portion of the network provided by a communications services provider. The cloud also represents a wide variety of different communications services that could be used to create the link represented by the cloud in the diagram. In some cases, it could be dial-up services, frame relay, high-speed backbone services, or a radio frequency (RF) wireless service. It is safe to surmise that the cloud shrouds the communications link in mystery, but only because it could easily change.

As is the case on a LAN, the communications technologies used in a WAN can be generically grouped into two basic classes: wireless and wired (which includes fiber-optic cabling, the most common type of "wire" used in high-bandwidth, long-haul connections). With few exceptions, however, nearly all wireless networks are eventually interconnected into wired communications links at some point.

Autonomous Systems

An autonomous system (AS) is a grouping of connected IP networks commonly managed, maintained, and controlled by one or more companies or other entities. An AS implements a common routing policy on the Internet, as defined in Request for Comments (RFC) (1930). Each AS is assigned a unique and registered AS number (ASN) that identifies its routing policy to the Border Gateway Protocol (BGP). *BGP* is the core routing protocol used on the Internet, using network and routing policies to determine its routing decisions.

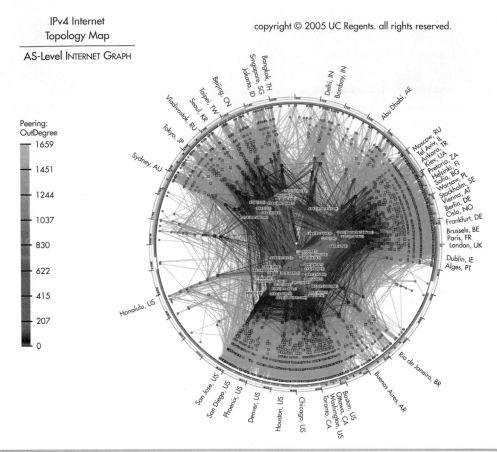

IPv4 Internet
Topology Map

AS-Level INTERNET GRAPH

Figure 14-2 A map showing global Internet connections (Image courtesy Cooperative Association for Internet Data Analysis [CAIDA] at the University of California, San Diego)

As the popularity of the Internet and mobile telephony have grown, so has the amount and complexity of the communications services that provide world-wide connectivity. Figure 14-2 illustrates only the major autonomous systems (AS) using IPv4 around the world (as of 2005). (See the sidebar on the previous page, "Autonomous Systems.")

The following sections discuss the wireless and, briefly, the wired technologies used in WAN communications.

Wireless WAN Technologies

As the various wireless communications technologies rapidly evolve, the nature of **wireless wide area networks (WWANs)** is being constantly redefined. If we define a WAN as a network on which data can be transmitted over extended geographical areas, given the capabilities of current technology, we run the risk of defining a WAN much too narrowly in the near future. However, if we can agree to define all transmitted content—data, voice, video, or graphic images—as "data," and we also agree that any wireless communications technology carrying our "data" from one LAN to another is a wireless WAN technology, we can put the two definitions together and come up with a fairly generalized definition of a WWAN:

A WWAN is a network that uses wireless communications technologies to interconnect geographically separated LANs for the purpose of exchanging transmitted data.

If only it were this simple! Our WWAN definition can also be used to define a newly emerging wireless network structure, the public wireless LAN (PWLAN). However, we can differentiate a WWAN from a PWLAN by their usage and application. A *WWAN* is intended to interconnect two private LANs, while a PWLAN is intended primarily to provide Internet access to anyone roaming into its range in a public setting.

PWLANs are most commonly associated with *hot spots*, which are public access areas in which a wireless service is available for forming ad-hoc network connections, commonly with either 802.11b or 802.11g. The major difference between a WWAN/WLAN and a PWLAN has to do with how the network is used and the nature of its traffic. WLAN and WWAN traffic tends to relate more to the business of a workgroup or an organization. On the other hand, *PWLAN* traffic rarely relates to any other user and is almost always a connection to the Internet.

Wireless WAN Connections

One of the characteristics that distinguish one type of wireless network from another is the form of wireless service in use. Like all forms of communications, wireless links essentially connect one point with another. However, variations on this theme allow connections to be defined in four basic configurations:

- Point-to-Point (P2P)

- Point-to-Multipoint (P2MP)

- Multipoint-to-Point (MP2P)

- Multipoint-to-Multipoint (MP2MP)

Each of these connection types is discussed in the following sections.

Point-to-Point (P2P)

A **point-to-point (P2P)** wireless connection is more commonly used to provide a two-way communications link between two wireless LANs. However, *P2P links* can also be used to provide access directly to an Internet backbone service. A P2P link is commonly referred to as **last mile** because it often provides the last link in the series of service connections that connect a building, home, or office to the primary service backbone. Figure 14-3 illustrates the concept of a last mile connection. The wireless link between two buildings provides the link for one

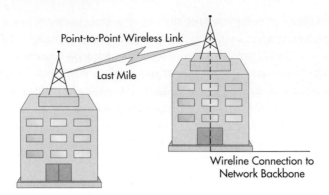

Figure 14-3   A wireless link can provide a last-mile connection to a network backbone.

building to the wired backbone. The last mile approach allows multiple buildings or locations to have access to a single fiber-optic head end, which eliminates the cost of pulling fiber-optic or other cabling to each building.

NOTE

Some last-mile service providers try to put a more positive spin on this service by calling it first mile.

A P2P link can be established between two buildings for connecting to an Internet source or to connect two buildings into a WLAN. In addition to an antenna, a wireless bridge is required to link the wireless system into the building's network, regardless of whether it is wired or wireless. Figure 14-4 shows examples of P2P equipment, including a P2P (line of sight) antenna and wireless Ethernet bridges.

Figure 14-4   P2P wireless antennas, including a point-to-point antenna and wireless Ethernet bridges (Photo courtesy of Proxim Corp.)

Point-to-Multipoint (P2MP)

A **point-to-multipoint (P2MP)** wireless link is used to provide broadcast services from a single transmitter to many locations or to create a last-mile link for multiple locations, as illustrated in Figure 14-5. The building that includes the direct link to the carrier's backbone is connected to multiple other buildings using wireless links. From the viewpoint of each of the remote buildings, the connection is essentially P2P, but the single antenna on the central building services multiple links. Of course, it is also possible to place multiple antennas on the central building and support P2P connections for each remote location, but when you consider that a WWAN, such as the one shown in Figure 14-5, operates essentially the same as a WLAN, a *P2MP* arrangement allows the system to take advantage of the economies of scale inherent in a multipoint system, such as the burstiness of the network's activity. Figure 14-6 shows examples of the antennas used in a P2MP system.

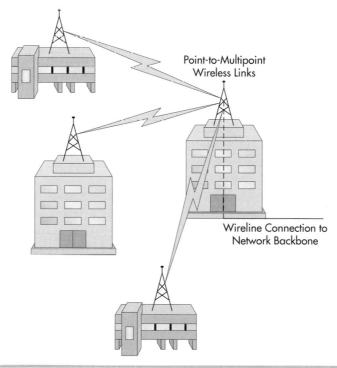

Point-to-Multipoint
Wireless Links

Wireline Connection to
Network Backbone

Figure 14-5 A P2MP WWAN

The wireless technologies used in both P2P and P2MP systems run the gamut from unlicensed services, such as ISM and UNII, to licensed services, such as MMDS and LMDS, with more to come in both groups.

Figure 14-6 Examples of P2MP antennas with the central (point) antenna on the right and the multipoint antenna on the left (Photo courtesy of Proxim Corp.)

Multipoint-to-Point (MP2P)

A multipoint-to-point (MP2P) system isn't that much different from a P2MP. A MP2P wireless system is application-based, rather than being based on any particular wireless technology. The other differentiation between P2MP and MP2P is which end of the connection is transmitting and which is receiving.

One example of a MP2P system is the Wireless Medical Telemetry System (WMTS). The *WMTS system* uses three frequency bands—608 to 614 MHz, 1.395 to 1.4 GHz, and 1.429 to 1.432 GHz—to receive or transmit information regarding the health or status of certain patients. Authorized physicians, hospitals, and other medical professionals can equip their patients with a radio transmitter that is connected to probes and sensors attached to a patient's body. Periodically, the patient's unit transmits its readings to the central system (on a closely coordinated frequency), which then analyzes the data and determines if any specific medical action is required. It isn't foreseen, at least not yet, that more than a few dozen patients would be connected to the WMTS system at any one time. Yet, even with only a few patients wearing transmitters, WMTS creates a MP2P system, such as that illustrated in Figure 14-7.

Multipoint-to-Multipoint (MP2MP)

A common application for multipoint-to-multipoint (MP2MP) wireless systems is video teleconferencing, although this application is essentially two or more MP2P systems combined back-to-back. Multipoint video conferencing allows geographically diverse locations to join in a real-time video teleconference, seeing and hearing all other participants, regardless of their location.

Another example of an MP2MP application is an 802.11 hot spot, in which roaming users are provided connections to P2P, MP2P, and MP2MP systems. Figure 14-17 on page 488 illustrates

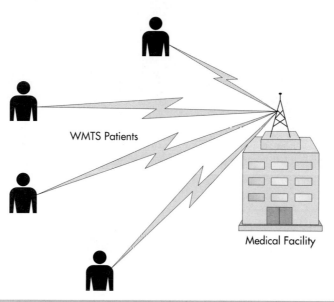

WMTS Patients

Medical Facility

Figure 14-7 The WMTS system is a MP2P system.

14

a city scene in which wireless networks are used to provide P2P and both forms of multipoint systems. Also depicted in this figure is a growing application of last-mile wireless links, an application referred to as multiple tenant units (MTU). In the lower-right corner of Figure 14-8 is a building with a P2P (last mile) wireless connection that provides Ethernet service to the building. Inside the building, a router or LAN switch is used to distribute bandwidth to each apartment, office, or floor of the building and the wired or wireless network at each location.

Line Check 14.1

1. Define a wireless wide area network.

2. What are example applications for P2P and P2MP WWANs?

3. Explain the concept of "last mile."

What Do You Think?

The WMTS is an example of a MP2P application. What other current or future multipoint applications can you describe or envision?

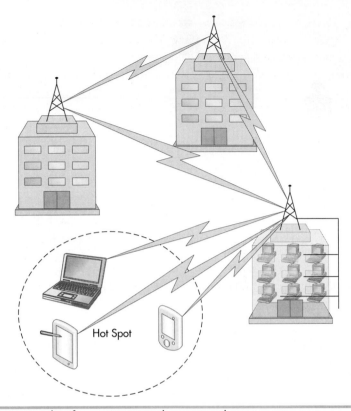

Figure 14-8 An example of a MP2MP wireless network supporting various wireless link applications

WWAN Devices

WAN devices are especially designed to handle the special needs of communicating on a WAN, which is much different than communicating on a LAN. For one thing, the bandwidth, throughput, and message-handling capabilities of WAN equipment must be much more reliable and fault-tolerant than is generally required on a LAN.

The most common devices included in a WAN infrastructure are

● Access server

● Router

● WAN switch

Access Servers

An *access server*, which is also commonly referred to as a remote access server (RAS) or a network access server (NAS), is a dedicated device that manages access to a network by users not physically connected to the network. Access servers provide authentication, authorization, and accounting (AAA) services controlling which remote users are authorized to access a network's resources based on the authentication process.

Access servers can be used to manage and control both inbound and outbound traffic. Inbound access through an access server is most commonly via a dial-up modem, ISDN, or virtual private network (VPN) connections (see the section "Virtual Private Networks"). Outbound, an access server can be used to concentrate several users onto a single communications link, such as a dial-up modem or an ISDN link.

Routers

We've discussed routers a few different times in this book, so a lengthy explanation should be unnecessary. However, the basic function of a *router* is to provide switching and forwarding services to both inbound and outbound WAN packets.

Depending on the type of communications link used to access the WAN, the router may require additional hardware—in the form of interface module cards or boards—or the use of one or more of the termination devices required for the communication service in use.

14

WAN Switches

A **WAN switch** is most generally found in the switching centers of a communications service provider, such as the telephone company or a backbone services provider. *WAN switches* are used to bridge various communications modes and formats to and from each other, such as frame relay to SMDS, as a part of a switched circuit. In Figure 14-9, WAN switches are used to bridge between frame-relay circuits and an ATM backbone through the WAN.

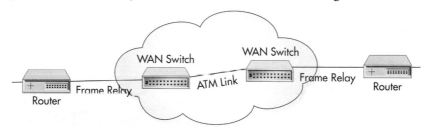

Figure 14-9   WAN switches are used to bridge between communications services in a WAN.

? Line Check 14.2

1. What are the purpose and function of an access server?

2. What is the device used to switch and forward network traffic across a WAN?

3. Where are WAN switches typically located?

WAN Communications Technologies

Eventually all networks, including WWANs, become a part of a wired network at some point. The telecommunications backbone of the United States, for example, consists of several routes of high-capacity, high-speed, fiber-optic, and copper cabling that connects the major communications hubs throughout the country. Figure 14-10 shows the fiber backbone for a single communications service provider in Minnesota.

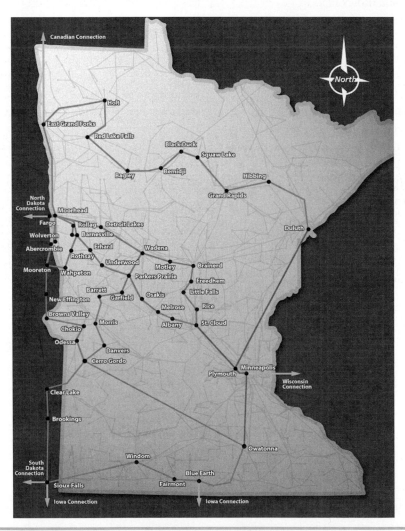

Figure 14-10   The fiber backbone of one Minnesota telecommunications services company (Image courtesy of Aurora Fiber Optic Networks)

When you want to download a web page from a site that is hosted in a different part of the country, your request is forwarded by your network router along a path which is, at the time, a better route to use than others. Your request travels across the Internet backbone of your service provider or their service provider, or even *their* service provider, until it eventually is forwarded to the network on which the remote web server is located. Figure 14-11 illustrates an example of what a large company's network structure may look like. On the left and right sides of the drawing are the LANs in each of this fictional company's offices located thousands of miles apart. The infrastructure, topologies, and media used in these networks don't matter in the context of a WAN—what does matter is the cloud in the middle of this drawing.

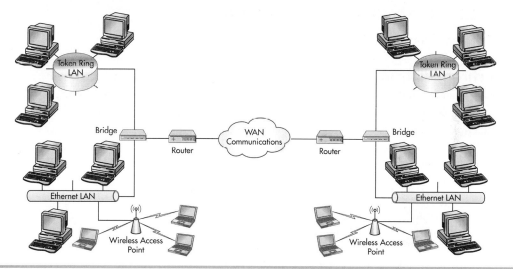

Figure 14-11   A larger company's network structure connects one set of LANs to another set of LANs using WAN communications.

The primary communications services used in the creation of a WAN are discussed in the following sections.

Wired WAN Communications Technologies

It is possible that a wireless WAN can be completely wireless; this just isn't practical for most homes and small businesses, primarily because of the cost of air time and the sophisticated equipment required. If you have satellite television service at your home, it comes fairly close to being a totally wireless network, except for the cable that ties the broadcast source to the satellite uplink and the cable connecting your television to your receiving disk. The U.S. National Aeronautics and Space Administration (NASA) most likely has a completely wireless network in use, but just think of the scope it must have.

At some point, all networks, including common wireless networks, connect to a cable-based, high-bandwidth communications service. A variety of transmission technologies and services are implemented on these lines, with the most common being

- Asynchronous Transfer Mode (ATM)

- Dedicated Digital Service (DDS)

- Frame Relay (FR)

- Integrated Services Digital Network (ISDN)

- Switched Multimegabit Data Services (SMDS)

- Synchronous Optical Network (SONET)

Asynchronous Transfer Mode (ATM)

ATM is an international telecommunications standard used in the telephone industry to transmit voice, video, and data. ATM is a cell-switching service that transmits data in small, fixed-length data units, called *cells*. ATM can be installed as the backbone service in a private network, but it is more commonly used for high-speed transfer within the telephone system. Figure 14-12 illustrates how ATM can be implemented to facilitate an entire network.

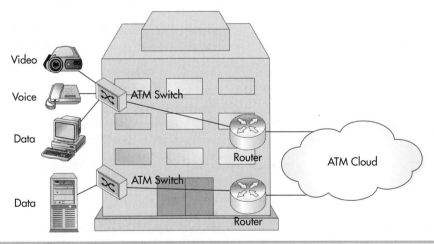

Figure 14-12 ATM can be implemented throughout a network.

ATM is an asynchronous cell-switching technology that combines circuit-switching and packet-switching, incorporating the best features of each system. ATM's bandwidth is scalable and can be implemented at only a few megabits (millions) per second (Mbps) or as much as several gigabits (billions) per second (Gbps). Today, ATM can be scaled from T-1 (1.54 Mbps) to OC-48 (2.45 Gbps). In some situations, ATM can also support 10 Gbps and should soon be available up to 40 Gbps.

Digital Data Service (DDS)

A digital data service (DDS) line is also commonly referred to as a leased line, a reference to the fact that this type of service line is leased from a telephone or communications service provider. A *DDS* can provide a variety of bandwidth in either a dedicated or switched configuration:

Dedicated DDS (DDDS)   A *dedicated line* provides a direct link between two communications points, typically within the same company or organization. Dedicated lines, which are always available, can be used to transfer data, voice, or video. However, a dedicated line is not a single run of cable strung between the two end points, although in rare situations, it could be. Typically a *dedicated DDS line* is a permanent virtual circuit (PVC) path created through the telephone system's Public Switched Telephone Network (PSTN). This means the transmitted signals could be carried on copper or fiber-optic cables, or both. To the end users, though, the link appears to be a single, continuous line. An example of a dedicated DDS link is a T-1 carrier leased by a company to connect two of its buildings that are about five miles apart.

14

Switched DDS (SDDS)   The primary difference between a switched DDS link and a dedicated DDS link is this: a switched link is created when it is needed, much like the circuit created when you make a telephone call. Arrangements with a service provider for a switched line involve the configuration of the line, when it is activated, such as a committed bit rate (CBR) or the minimum bandwidth and the type of communications service to be applied to the link. When the line is activated between two end points, a switched virtual circuit (SVC) is created through the PSTN for the duration of a singular communications session. ISDN is an example of a switched DDS service.

Frame Relay

Frame relay is a commonly used packet-switching WAN communications service that operates only on the data link and physical layers. *Packet-switched networks* transmit variable-length protocol data units (PDUs) dynamically between a source station and a destination station. The PDU moves across the PSTN by being switched from one circuit to another until it reaches its destination. If this sounds familiar, Ethernet and Token Ring are packet-switched networks and the Internet Protocol (IP) is a packet-switched protocol. Because frame relay operates primarily on Layer 2, it doesn't use IP addresses to route frames from one point to another. Frame relay is strictly a point-to-point service and is implemented on a switched DDS link.

Integrated Services Digital Network (ISDN)

Integrated Services Digital Network (ISDN) is an international communications standard that defines the use of telephone lines to provide for the transmission of digital voice, data, audio, and video transmission on PSTN lines operated by regional telephone service providers. *ISDN*, in any one of its three interface types, is based on 64 Kbps telephone line channels (DS0). What differentiates one ISDN interface from another is the number of 64 Kbps channels included.

Basic Rate Interface (BRI)   Basic Rate Interface (BRI) is the most commonly used form of ISDN in homes and small offices. *BRI* operates over an existing copper wire loop for digital voice and data support. BRI transmits data on a 128 Kbps Bearer channel (B-channel) made up of two 64 Kbps channels and a 16 Kbps Delta channel (D-channel) that carries control signals. BRI, also known as 2B+1D, requires a terminal adapter, which is also referred to as an inverse multiplexer (mux).

Primary Rate Interface (PRI)   An ISDN Primary Rate Interface (PRI) carrier is the equivalent of a standard T-1 carrier and is most commonly used by larger organizations that require both higher bandwidth and a higher number of distribution channels to carry voice, data, or both. PRI uses 23 B channels and one 64 Kbps D channel.

Broadband ISDN (B-ISDN)   Broadband ISDN (B-ISDN) defines ATM and cell-switching over virtual circuits on the PSTN. *B-ISDN* uses fiber-optic backbone services and is projected to integrate the transmission of voice, data, and graphics on a single high-speed line.

Switched Multimegabit Data Services (SMDS)

Switched Multimegabit Data Services (SMDS) was the first broadband service developed for general use in the U.S. *SMDS* is a packet-switched WAN network technology that communicates over the public switched data network (PSDN) of the telephone companies on either fiber-optic or copper wiring. SMDS operates on DS-level circuits at either 1.544 Mbps on a DS-1 carrier or 44.736 Mbps on a DS-3 carrier. SMDS is also protocol-friendly in that its frame size is large enough to encapsulate Ethernet (802.3) and Token Ring (802.5) data units.

Another similar service to SMDS is the Connectionless Broadband Data Service (CBDS). Originally, *CBDS* was the European equivalent of SMDS, but it is now offered in North America for certain applications. CBDS, like SMDS, is a high-speed switched transmission service, but offers lower-speed services in addition to its high-speed offerings.

Synchronous Optical Network (SONET)

Synchronous Optical Network (SONET) is a standard for interconnecting fiber-optic transmission systems, which operates on the physical level of the OSI model. SONET allows data streams, transmitted at different rates, to be multiplexed on to a common transmission link. The SONET standards define the optical carrier (OC) bandwidth levels, ranging from 51.8 Mbps (OC-1) to 9.95 Gbps (OC-192). See Table 14-2 for more information on OC transmission rates. SONET was originally developed as a U.S. fiber-optic transmission standard, but has been included in the international standard, Synchronous Digital Hierarchy (SDH).

Carrier Circuits

When bandwidth for a WAN is discussed, it is usually referenced by the type of carrier circuit used to connect one location to another, typically a building to a switching center or hub. Depending on

Circuit Designator	Bandwidth	DS0 Equivalent
DS0 (Digital signal 0)	64 Kbps	1
DS-1 (T-1)	1.54 Mbps	24
DS-1C	3.15 Mbps	48
DS-2 (T-2)	6.31 Mbps	96
DS-3 (T-3)	44.74 Mbps	672
E-1 (European)	2.05 Mbps	30
E-2	8.45 Mbps	128
E-3	34.37 Mbps	512

Table 14-1   Wire-based Carrier Circuits

14

the bandwidth required, different sizes and types of carrier circuits can be obtained from the Regional Bell Operating Company (RBOC) or its local exchange carrier (LEC), meaning the telephone company in your region; an ISP reselling the LEC's lines; or a regional, national, or international backbone services company.

Tables 14-1 and 14-2 list the most commonly subscribed carrier circuits, plus a few we can only dream of having. The base unit for a carrier circuit is a *DS0*, the equivalent of a single telephone circuit, such as the line to your house, which is an indicator of the number of separate signal streams that can be transmitted over the circuit.

Carrier Designator	Bandwidth
OC-1	51.84 Mbps
OC-3	155.52 Mbps
OC-12	622.08 Mbps
OC-24	1.24 Gbps
OC-48	2.48 Gbps
OC-192	9.95 Gbps
OC-256	13.27 Gbps
OC-768	51.85 Gbps

Table 14-2   Optical Carrier (Fiber-optic) Carrier Circuits

Line Check 14.3

1. What type of circuit is created in a DDDS?

2. Define BRI and PRI ISDN services in terms of the number of D and *B* channels each use.

3. What is the bandwidth difference between OC-1 and a T-1 circuits?

 ## What Do You Think?

Why would you consider any of the communications services included in this section when designing a wireless WAN?

Wireless Communications Technologies

WWANs are connected using a variety of wireless communications technologies. However, because the focus of this book is wireless local and wide area networks, let's look a bit deeper into RF communications.

RF Communications

Without repeating all the information contained in Chapters 1 and 4 of this book, we should briefly review the primary RF bands in the context of a WWAN. One or more of these wireless services can be used effectively to link two or more WLANs together. The primary limitation, as in all RF links, is the transmission range of a particular service being considered. Table 14-3 lists the primary RF bands commonly used in a WWAN.

Wireless RF Media Characteristics

The wireless media portion of a wireless system represents the physical layer of the communications system, and, similar to wired or cabled networking media, wireless media have certain characteristics that can determine the effectiveness of one frequency band or service in comparison to others.

The characteristics that can impact the performance, throughput, and effectiveness of wireless media are the following:

- Bandwidth issues
- Frequency

Frequency Range	Purpose	Licensing	Effective Range (LoS)	Application
900 MHz	Spread Spectrum	Unlicensed	30 meters	Private and public WLAN
2.4 GHz	Spread Spectrum	Unlicensed	1.2 kilometers	Private and public WLAN
2.5 GHz	Multichannel Multipoint Distribution Service (MMDS)	Licensed	3 kilometers	Fixed wireless & Internet access (last mile)
5.8 GHz	Spread Spectrum	Unlicensed	4 kilometers	Private and public WLAN
23 GHz	Microwave	Licensed	4 kilometers	Private WLAN
28 – 31 GHz	Local Multipoint Distribution Service (LMDS)	Licensed	5 kilometers	Fixed wireless & Internet access (last mile)
38 & 39 GHz	General communications	Licensed	5 kilometers	Fixed wireless & Internet access (last mile)
60 GHz	General communications/ broadband	Licensed	1.7 kilometers	Fixed wireless & Internet access (last mile)
80 & 95 GHz	General communications/ broadband	Licensed	7.1 kilometers	Fixed wireless & Internet access (last mile)

Table 14-3   WWAN RF Frequency Bands

- Interference reduction
- Non-line-of-sight and near-line-of-sight (NLOS)
- Modulation type

Bandwidth   One of the first problems the users of a wireless network notice is bandwidth and how it impacts their throughput. A definite and direct relationship can occur between bandwidth and throughput on any network, whether wired or wireless.

One of the most common misconceptions about bandwidth is a difference exists between the rated or raw data speed of a circuit and the actual data rate users realize. Users tend to see a network connection as being proprietary with all of the network's bandwidth expressly available to them alone. First, bandwidth is a shared entity on almost every network. If the network has 11 Mbps of raw data-rate bandwidth and 11 users who are constantly transmitting 12-byte (approximately 100 bits) messages, chances are each user is only realizing less than 1 Mbps of bandwidth. Remember, some bandwidth is also eaten up by network administrative tasks and overhead, such as CSMA/CD, protocol management, and the like.

The bandwidth of any medium represents its maximum capacity or its raw data-transfer speed. Throughput, on the other hand, is the time required to transfer a user's data from one point to the next. As more points (hops) are involved between a user and the destination address, the slower throughput becomes.

Part of the problem is this: in an effort to enhance the desirability of their equipment, wireless device manufacturers advertise the raw data speeds of their devices, such as 11 Mbps or 54 Mbps. However, if a wireless user realizes only around 5 Mbps of throughput when transferring a file or downloading a web page, they believe the problem to be a failing of the network.

In many cases, the issue is the duplex mode used by the wireless network or its devices. A half-duplex (two-way communications, but only one-way at a time—such as a citizens' band radio) effectively drops the available bandwidth by half, which means on an 11 Mbps 802.11b network, the maximum throughput cannot be greater than 5.5 Mbps.

To operate in full-duplex (two-way communications, two ways at a time—like a telephone) mode, a wireless device requires two transceivers. Unfortunately, at least at this time, full-duplex devices are available only for P2P applications but, eventually, network adapters should emerge with this capability for WLANs, as well.

Another issue for wireless networks is distance. A trade-off definitely occurs between data rate and distance on a wireless network. For example, an 802.11b system operating *in the clear* (meaning outdoors where no obstacles exist), can transmit at 11 Mbps for about 150 meters (approximately 500 feet), but at 396 meters, the data speed drops to 2 Mbps, and at about 450 meters (about 1,500 feet), the data rate drops to 1 Mbps.

Of course, these considerations are part of the planning for a fixed-position wireless network, but roaming users experience a decrease in throughput as they move further away from an access point.

Wireless WAN Frequencies
As previously discussed, there are a variety of wireless services, each operating on a different licensed or unlicensed frequency (see Table 14-3).

Interference Reduction
One of the criteria that should be used for determining the quality of a wireless device is the noise- and interference-reduction capabilities built into it. Generally, a wireless device's interference- and noise-reduction capabilities are stated as its signal-to-noise ratio (SNR).

Unfortunately, environment has a direct impact on the SNR performance of a WLAN device, but unlike bandwidth and throughput, SNR typically decreases as the distance increases. Regardless of your environment, many wireless devices have a nominal SNR rating, which is measured under perfect conditions in a laboratory, so don't expect to realize the same SNR in your network. In most situations, however, an SNR above 25 is adequate, if that level provides the user with adequate throughput.

Multipath is the condition that exists when a transmitted signal reflects off physical objects and multiple signal paths are created between the transmitter and receiver (see Figure 14-13). The types of multipath conditions that can be created are illustrated in Figure 14-13. The best condition is, of course, LoS. However, obstacles in the transmission path, such as houses, trees, buildings, rocks, mountains, and the like can cause the signal to diffract, reflect, scatter, and be completely blocked (a condition known as *shadowing*). Multipath can also be caused by two antennas transmitting with the same polarity in the same vicinity.

14

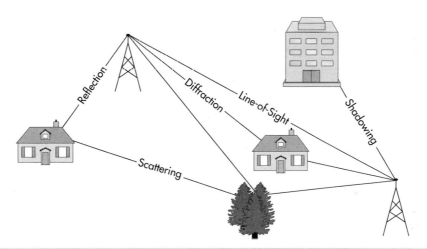

Figure 14-13 Multipath conditions can create signal errors.

The primary problems caused by multipath are:

- **Signal fade:** This is a reduction in signal strength.

- **Phase cancellation:** If two of the deflected signal paths are exactly 180 degrees out of phase, they will cancel each other.

- **Delay spread:** Parts of the signal arriving with a variable amount of delay can overwrite each other.

The most commonly used interference reduction method is multipath elimination, of which the following are the most common means of reducing or eliminating a multipath condition:

- **Antenna polarization:** A wireless device that features selectable antenna polarization allows two conflicting antennas to be configured to opposite polarities.

- **Smart antenna:** Some wireless devices include firmware or software that allows the antenna's transmission beam to be adjusted to avoid objects or create a better LoS alignment.

- **Smart radio:** This feature allows the radio transmitter in a wireless device to automatically select the frequency with the least interference and, if needed, also adjust the power level of the transmitted signal.

Line of Sight (LoS) Issues   LoS is generally not an issue for most WLAN products, unless infrared (IR) devices are in use. Where LoS can become an issue is in P2P and P2MP applications in which broadband wireless devices are implemented.

Many P2P devices are indicated as NLoS, which, unfortunately, can have two meanings. In most cases, *NLoS* refers to non-line-of-sight, which means LoS is not a general requirement for the device. For example, nearly all WLAN devices, such as network interface cards (NIC) or network adapters are NLoS or non-line-of-sight. However, NLoS can also refer to near-line-of-sight, which means two wireless devices must be aligned within a certain degree of LoS to communicate. Near-line-of-sight can also refer to the equipment's capability to transmit without interference through certain objects, such as trees, heavy rain, fog, snow, or any object that partially blocks the transmission path.

Wireless devices define a broadcast area, which is referred to as a Fresnel (pronounced "freh-nell") zone. A *Fresnel zone* defines the visual LoS area over which the signals transmitted by an antenna spread out. Any obstruction in the Fresnel zone can cause the transmitted signal's strength to weaken. Figure 14-14 illustrates the effect of an object intruding on the Fresnel zone of a transmitter. While most RF signals aren't necessarily blocked by the object, it can weaken the signal, which could result in a signal too weak to receive.

Just how much an object will block an RF signal has to do with its water content. Because walls are dry, RF signals pass through them easily. On the other hand, a tree has a high level of water content and, because some RF waves are easily absorbed into the water—especially 2.4 GHz signals—the signals fail to pass through the tree.

NOTE

Microwave ovens use a 2.4 GHz frequency to cook food. The water in the item being cooked absorbs the RF waves. The energy released by this action creates heat, which then cooks the food, often from the inside-out.

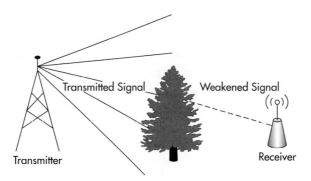

Figure 14-14   An object inside the Fresnel zone of a transmitter can weaken its signal.

Modulation   *Modulation* is the process used to transform the amplitude, frequency, or phase (or a combination of the three) of a signal for transmission over a particular medium. For example, a dial-up modem both modulates and demodulates analog and digital data for transmission over telephone lines and for use by a computer, respectively.

Wireless network technologies use one of three forms of spread-spectrum modulation:

- **Direct-sequence spread-spectrum (DSSS):** *DSSS* reduces the amplitude of a signal and spreads the signal, so it is wider than the bandwidth of the original signal. For example, a signal transmitted on an 11 MHz medium is modulated into a 22 MHz DSSS signal. A multicarrier DSSS or High Rate DSSS (HR/DSSS) is used in 802.11b systems.

- **Frequency-hopping spread-spectrum (FHSS):** *FHSS*, which is incompatible with DSSS, shifts the signal between different frequencies in the transmission. Wireless networking standards incorporate either narrowband frequency hopping or wideband frequency hopping. FSSS is the modulation technique used in Bluetooth and HomeRF.

- **Othogonal Frequency Division Multiplexing (OFDM):** *OFDM* is the modulation method used in 802.11a (in the 5 GHz band) and 802.11g (in the 2.4 GHz band). OFDM transmits as many as 52 carrier streams simultaneously, with each signal traveling on its own frequency.

Cellular Technologies

Cellular telephony and mobile telephone technology have advanced to the point that they now rival wireless data networking technology in many respects. With the advancement toward the third generation (3G) of mobile wireless communications technology, the prospect of integrated voice and data networks is a reality.

Cellular Networking Protocols   Officially and internationally, what is commonly called 3G is the International Mobile Telecommunications 2000 (IMT-2000) system, which is described in a standard of the same name by the International Telecommunications Union (ITU). However, in the U.S., most of North America, and in Asia, IMT-2000 is still referred to as 3G. In Europe, it is more commonly known as the Universal Mobile Telephone System (UMTS). In the late 1990s, the ITU began the process of developing a standard global mobile telecommunications system—IMT-2000—that combines the best of 3G and UMTS.

Table 14-4 shows the protocol development evolution that has led the mobile telephony industry to the present day and into the future.

The vision behind IMT-2000 is this: eventually, multiple levels of voice and data networks will be in place, with many of them already deployed and interconnected, to facilitate the transfer of data within a single building or globally to a wide range of enabled handheld and mobile devices. Figure 14-15 illustrates the various levels of ITU's vision for IMT-2000. The levels depicted are:

- **In-building:** This level is called a *picocell*, which is effectively a CDMA2000 EV-DV hot spot.

- **Urban:** This level is a *microcell* and encompasses multiple picocells. The urban level is, essentially, a city center, in much the same way that cellular telephone service functions today, only with new protocols.

- **Suburban:** This level is a *macrocell* and provides linkage for data and voice transfers to multiple microcells and picocells.

- **Global:** In the sense that you can already make cellular telephone calls to some parts of the globe, the global level is already under way. The global level encompasses all lower-level cells.

Wireless Application Protocol (WAP)   The Wireless Application Protocol (WAP) combines wireless telecommunications and the Internet into a single applications environment. *WAP* is a standard protocol set developed and published by the *WAP Forum*, a standards and trade organization made up of manufacturers and developers from both the wireless and the Internet market.

WAP defines an application framework and protocols to support the deployment of the framework on mobile telephones (see Figure 14-16), pagers, PDAs, and compact PCs. Virtually all the most popular OSs for these devices provide support for WAP, including PalmOS, Windows CE, OS/9, and the JavaOS.

WAP devices typically include a microbrowser, which is either proprietary or a much smaller version of some standard web browsers, such as Opera, Minimo (Mozilla), and Pocket

Generation (Duration	Time Frame	Services	Protocols
1G	1984–1996	Analog voice	Nokia Mobile Phones (NMP) Total Access Control system (TACS) Advanced Mobile Phone System (AMPS) Personal Handyphone System (PHS)
2G	1992–2001	Digital voice	Global System for Mobile (GSM) Time Division Multiple Access (TDMA) Motorola iDEN Technology (iDEN) Personal Digital Cellular (PDC) Code Division Multiple Access (CDMA)
2.5G	1984–1996	Packet radio data	General Packet Radio Service (GPRS) Global Spatial Data Model (GSDM)
2.75G	2003–2005	Light multimedia	Enhanced Data GSM Environment (EDGE)
3G	2003–Present	Full multimedia and data	Wideband CDMA (W-CDMA) Universal Mobile Telecom System (UMTS) Time Division Synchronous CDMA (TD-SCDMA) CDMA2000/Evolution Data Optimized (EV-DO) CDMA2000/Evolution Data Voice (EV-DV) IMT-2000
3.5G	2005–Present	Full multimedia and data	High-Speed Downlink Packet Access (HSDPA)
3.75G	2006–Present	Full multimedia and data	High-Speed Uplink Packet Access (HSUPA)
4G	2008 (est.)	Full multimedia and data	Software Defined Radio (SDR) Orthogonal Frequency Division Multiple Access (OFDMA)

Table 14-4   The Generations of Mobile Voice, Data, and Multimedia Development

Internet Explorer. WAP includes support for the Hypertext Markup Language (HTML) and Extensible Markup Language (XML), the primary platform for WAP applications is the Wireless Markup Language (WML). *WML* is specifically designed for small-screen displays and single-hand navigation, often without the use of a keyboard. WAP also supports WLMScript, which is similar to JavaScript, but requires less memory and processor power. Because of its growing

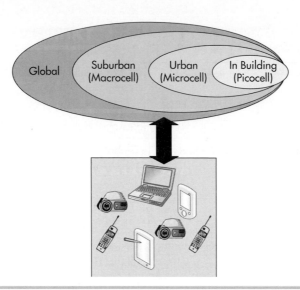

Figure 14-15 The vision of the ITU for IMT-2000

Figure 14-16 A mobile (cellular) telephone with an Internet microbrowser (Photo courtesy of Sendo)

popularity, most WAP developers are working to reduce the power and memory requirements, and to improve their display quality under Man-Machine Interface (MMI) initiatives.

 ## Line Check 14.4

1. What can cause multipath conditions in a wireless network?
2. What are the two possible meanings for NLoS and how are they different?
3. What is WAP and how is it used?

 ## What Do You Think?

Do you foresee a time when technology advances to the point that cellular-based communications and WWAN communications combine? How would the combined technology work?

Virtual Private Networks

A **virtual private network (VPN)** is an extension of a LAN that can be accessed by authorized users over a WAN under security techniques and facilities that maintain the privacy of the resources on the LAN. A *VPN* can be established for a variety of reasons, but the most common forms of VPNs are:

- **LAN access:** An *access VPN* provides a remote user with the capability to join a LAN to access the network's resources from wherever they are, whenever they need. Typically, a connection to an access VPN is made over the Internet using a national dial-up account, a mobile IP device, or a point-to-point wireless connection. This type of VPN is commonly used by employees in remote offices, telecommuters, or traveling employees.

- **Intranet VPN:** An *intranet* is a network with access limited to authorized employees for the purpose of accessing company resources. An *intranet VPN* is used to link dispersed facilities and employees of a company to the primary company data and device resources.

- **Extranet VPN:** An *extranet VPN* extends a company's intranet to include customers, suppliers, business partners, and other persons with the need to access limited resources on a company's network.

Figure 14-17 illustrates the combinations of access methods that can be used to access a VPN.

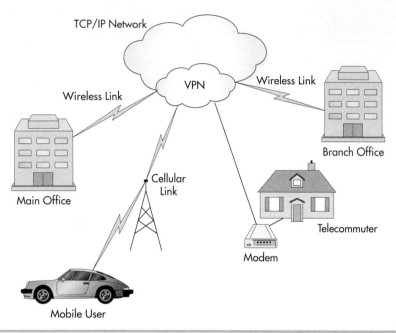

Figure 14-17   The various means used by different locations and users to access a VPN

VPN access is secured with a combination of protocol, hardware, and software. *VPN protocols* are tunneling protocols, such as PPTP and L2TP. *Hardware devices* can include VPN gateway appliances, firewalls, routers, and access servers. *VPN software* is most commonly in the form of VPN servers running at the main network location and VPN clients running on the distributed nodes.

IEEE 802.16/Wireless Metropolitan Area Networks (WMAN)

The **IEEE 802.16** *standard* defines the implementation of wireless networks for metropolitan area networks (MANs). In the past, many companies attempted to use 802.11 equipment to extend their wireless networks beyond a building or campus. However, because of the performance and security limitations of 802.11 and its limited capability to support large numbers of users, a broadband wireless access standard was needed.

The use of wireless broadband is seen as an excellent solution to support the growing demand for Internet access and integrated data, voice, and video data streams. Broadband wireless can be used to enhance a variety of communications applications, including the extension of fiber-optic networks—increasing the capacity of cable and digital subscriber line (DSL) networks—and to provide an extended connection area for ad-hoc networking to public areas. Broadband wireless networking is seen as both a first mile and a last mile solution.

In April 2002, the 802.16 Working Group for Broadband Wireless published its first standard, the Air Interface for Fixed Broadband Wireless Access Systems, defining a wireless network operating in the 10 GHz to 66 GHz frequencies. The intent of 802.16 is to provide wireless network access to homes, small businesses, and commercial buildings. The primary wireless networking industry group supporting the 802.16 standard is the Worldwide Interoperability for Microwave Access (Wi-Max) Forum, which is made up of many leading wireless networking manufacturers, such as Intel, Nokia, and Proxim. Figure 14-18 illustrates where the 802.16 standards fit into the overall structure of 802.x networking.

14

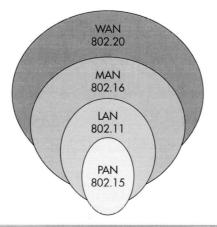

Figure 14-18 The relationships and hierarchy of the IEEE 802.x networking standards

802.16 Standards

In June 2004, the IEEE 802.16 working group approved a new standard (802.16—2004) that superseded and encompassed its earlier standards (802.16, 802.16a, and 802.16d), primarily to clear up the confusion caused in the industry by the overlap of the earlier standards. The 802.16–2004 standard, also called *Fixed Wi-Max*, consolidates the WMAN standards toward the goal of the complete **Wi-Max** standard.

The 802.16 standards, which started with 806.16a in January 2003, define non-line-of-sight (NLoS) wireless MAN operations in the 2 GHz to 11 GHz RF bands that provide a shared bandwidth of up to 75 Mbps. At the lower frequencies, 802.16 antennas and base stations can be located on houses and shorter buildings, instead of mountaintops and tall buildings.

A common 802.16 WMAN implementation includes a base station placed on a building or tower that provides P2MP communications to user stations located on office buildings or homes. An 802.16 transmitter has a range up to 30 miles but, typically, an 802.16 cell (transmitter) has a range radius of about 4 to 6 miles to ensure its NLoS and throughput performance.

Backhaul

Backhaul is a communications term that refers to the connection that carries traffic to a networking switching center or to a backbone service, such as the link that provides a connection to the Internet cloud for a WMAN, as illustrated in Figure 14-19. One of the primary applications foreseen for 802.16 networks is providing a connection to a backhaul link for backbone, and Internet services to homes and businesses with wired or wireless (802.11) networks internally and to commercial or municipal hot spots.

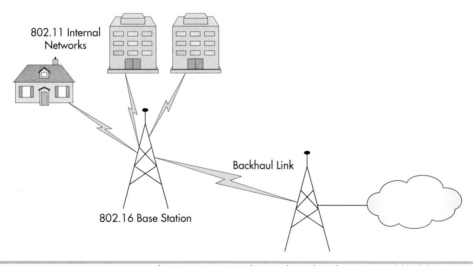

Figure 14-19 An 802.16a wireless MAN providing subscriber homes and buildings with an Internet backhaul

802.16 Working Groups

Other 802.16 standards are under development. Table 14-5 lists the 802.16 working groups currently active and the area on which each is focusing.

Working Group	Focus
802.16a	2–11 GHz
802.16b	Patent policy and procedures
802.16c	10–66 GHz interoperability
802.16d	Wi-Max
802.16e	Mobile WMAN
802.16f	Management information base (MIB)
802.16g	Management policies
802.16h	Wireless high-speed unlicensed MANs (WirelessHUMAN)

Table 14-5   The 802.16 Working Groups

14

802.16 Operations

The 802.16 standards defined the use of the **Demand Assignment Multiple Access (DAMA)-Time Division Multiple Access (TDMA)** method that adapts as required to changes in demand patterns from multiple subscriber stations. DAMA-TDMA operates in two modes: mode *A* supports continuous transmission stream traffic, such as multimedia, audio, or video streams. Mode *B* supports bursty traffic, such as Internet access.

In addition to defining its PHY wireless medium (radios, transmitters, and antennas), the 802.16 standard also defines the MAC layer on which data are transmitted in frames, as well as the methods used for controlling and monitoring access to the wireless medium.

The 802.16 standard defines a P2MP system in which the downstream transmissions (base station to subscriber stations) is relatively a simple RF transmission process. However, upstream transmissions (subscriber stations to base station) are a bit more complicated because the subscriber stations are competing for access to the medium. TDMA is used to divide data streams into time slots to allow maximization of the medium's bandwidth. *DAMA-TDMA* defines a logical channel that includes the stream of time-slotted frames from a single subscriber with an allocation of 2 Mbps to 155 Mbps per logical channel.

The 802.16 standard also defines a convergence layer that operates above its MAC layer. The *convergence layer* provides support for functions required by specific service types, including bearer services for digital multimedia, audio, video, multicasting, voice, Internet access, ATM, and frame relay.

Quality of Service (QoS)

An issue in all broadband services is **quality of service (QoS)**, which is mechanisms built into a protocol or communications service that attempt to maintain a certain level of consistent performance. Without QoS mechanisms, a transmitted data, video, or voice stream could lose data or break up because of interference or inadequate bandwidth. *QoS* provides a network with the capability to maintain a specific service level, which is typically above its specified minimum performance levels.

WMAN transmissions are susceptible to attenuation, interference, and disruption from stationary and moving objects, such as buildings, trees, rain, snow, and moving or parked cars and trucks. To overcome these problems, the 802.16 standards include QoS mechanisms to increase the robustness of P2MP transmissions for either obstructed LoS or near LoS environments. However, different types of transmissions require different forms of QoS.

The quality of a voice or video transmission isn't affected by a few lost frames, but quality can definitely be impacted by latency or multipath conditions. On the other hand, data transmissions aren't impacted greatly by latency, but transmission errors and lost frames are. The 802.16 standards apply the appropriate QoS mechanisms for each type of data transmission to ensure the quality of the transmission.

The most common of the QoS mechanisms employed by 802.16 standards are:

- **Adaptive modulation:** This QoS mechanism uses the content of a transmission and the quality of a link to determine the data rate.

- **Adaptive duplexing:** The 802.16 includes both frequency-division duplexing (FDD) and time-division duplexing (TDD) and can adapt its transmission mode to a link. If a link has a structured pair of channels available, FDD, which requires two channels (one to receive and one to transmit), can be used. *FDD* is a legacy method still in by some cellular systems. Where a structured pair of channels isn't available, *TDD*, which uses time slotting to use a single channel for both transmitting and receiving, can be used.

❓ Line Check 14.5

1. What is the general focus of the 802.16 standards?
2. What is the latest 802.16 standard?
3. What is the purpose of QoS mechanisms on a communications service?

What Do You Think?

If WMAN systems are widely installed, what existing systems might they displace?

Chapter 14 Review

Chapter Summary

Use Wide Area Network (WAN) Basics

- A WAN is a physical or logical communications network implemented over a wide geographical area.

- The cloud metaphor is commonly used to depict WAN communications.

Understand Wireless WAN Components and Technologies

- A WWAN is a network that uses wireless communications technologies to interconnect geographically separated LANs for the purpose of exchanging transmitted data.

- The basic types of WWANs are P2P, P2MP, MP2P, and MP2MP.

- A P2P wireless connection is used to provide a two-way communications link between two wireless LANs.

- A P2P link is commonly referred to as "last mile" because it often provides the last link in the series connections to a primary backbone service.

- A P2MP wireless link provides broadcast services from a single transmitter to many locations.

- A MP2P wireless system is application-based, rather than being based on any particular wireless technology.

- A MP2MP wireless system allows geographically diverse locations to join into a real-time video teleconference, seeing and hearing all other participants, regardless of their location.

- The most common devices included in a WAN infrastructure are access servers, routers, and WAN switches.

- An access server is a dedicated device that manages access to a network by users not physically connected to the network.

- The basic function of a router is to provide switching and forwarding services to both inbound and outbound WAN packets.

- WAN switches are used to bridge various communications modes and formats to and from each other.

Assess WAN Communications Technologies

- Eventually all networks become a part of a wired network at some point.

- The more common transmission technologies and services used in WAN communications are ATM, DDS, FR, ISDN, SMDS, and SONET.

- The media in a wireless system represents the physical layer of the communications system.

- The characteristics of wireless media that can impact the performance, throughput, and effectiveness of a wireless media are bandwidth, frequency, interference, NLoS, and modulation.

- Cellular telephony and mobile telephone technology have advanced rival wireless data networking technology, providing for integrated voice and data networks.

- WAP combines wireless telecommunications and the Internet into a single-application environment.

Connect over Virtual Private Networks

- A VPN is an extension of a LAN that provides access to external authorized users over a WAN under security techniques and facilities that maintain the privacy of the resources on the LAN.

IEEE 802.16/Wireless Metropolitan Area Networks (WMAN)

- The IEEE 802.16 standard defines the implementation of a wireless metropolitan area networks (WMAN).

- The 802.16 standards define the use of DAMA-TDMA that adapts as required to changes in demand patterns from multiple subscriber stations.

- An issue in all broadband services is QoS, which are mechanisms built into a protocol or communications service that attempt to maintain a certain level of consistent performance.

- The most common of the QoS mechanisms employed by 802.16 standards are adaptive modulation and adaptive duplexing.

Key Terms

Backhaul *(490)*
Demand Assignment Multiple Access/Time Division
  Multiple Access (DAMA/TDMA) *(491)*
IEEE 802.16 *(488)*
Last mile *(465)*
Multipath *(481)*
Quality of service (QoS) *(492)*
Point-to-multipoint (P2MP) *(467)*
Point-to-point (P2P) *(465)*
Virtual private network (VPN) *(487)*
WAN switch *(471)*
Wi-Max *(489)*
Wireless wide area network (WWAN) *(464)*

Key Term Quiz

Use the terms from the Key Terms list to complete the following sentences. Don't use the same term more than once. Not all terms will be used.

1. _____ is a condition that can occur when a transmitted wireless signal bounces or reflects from solid objects.

2. A _____ is a network that uses wireless communications technologies to interconnect geographically separated LANs for the purpose of exchanging transmitted data.

3. A _____ link is used to carry traffic to a backbone service or the Internet.

4. _____ features maintain consistent performance on a communications medium.

5. A _____ is used to bridge communications modes and formats as a part of a switched circuit.

6. A central base station that services multiple subscriber stations is set up in a _____ topology.

7. The standard for a WMAN is _____.

8. Two wireless stations that communicate directly in a NLoS arrangement are set up in a _____ topology.

9. Wireless P2P links are often referred to as _____ because they provide a connection between the primary communications carrier and a subscriber's network.

10. A _____ VPN is a LAN system that enables remote users to securely access the network's resources.

Multiple Choice Quiz

1. What device is used to bridge different communications carriers on a switched network?

    A. Hub

    B. LAN switch

    C. Router

    D. WAN switch

2. What is the term used to define the mechanisms included in network services that maintain consistent performance for a network's medium?

    A. Last mile

    B. QoS

    C. LoS

    D. NLoS

3. Which of the following best defines the topology of a WWAN in which a single base station provides wireless communications links to multiple subscriber stations?

    A. Point-to-point

    B. Multipoint-to-point

    C. Point-to-multipoint

    D. Multipoint-to-multipoint

4. Which of the following IEEE networking standards defines the PHY and MAC layers of a WWAN?

    A. IEEE 802.11

    B. IEEE 802.15

    C. IEEE 802.16

    D. IEEE 802.20

5. What is the condition that can result from a wireless transmission reflecting off solid objects in its LoS path?

    A. Attenuation

    B. Multipath

C. Interference

D. Crosstalk

6. What is the acronym for the type of network that uses wireless communications technologies to interconnect geographically separated LANs for the purpose of exchanging transmitted data?

A. LAN

B. WAN

C. WLAN

D. WWAN

7. What is the term commonly used to describe the communications link that connects a building to a primary carrier service medium?

A. Last mile

B. QoS

C. LoS

D. NLoS

8. Which of the following best defines the topology of a WWAN in which a single base station provides a wireless communications link to a single subscriber station?

A. Point-to-point

B. Multipoint-to-point

C. Point-to-multipoint

D. Multipoint-to-multipoint

9. What term is commonly used for the communications link used to carry subscriber traffic to the Internet?

A. Backhaul

B. Point-to-point

C. QoS

D. Backbone

14
REVIEW

10. Which of the following technologies enables remote users to securely access and share the resources on a company's intranet?

   A. WLAN

   B. WWAN

   C. VPN

   D. QoS

Lab Projects

1. Using a portable PC (notebook or Pocket PC) equipped with a wireless network adapter, stand outside a building in which a wireless network is installed.

   A. Are you able to detect the signal of the wireless network inside the building?

   B. Are you able to connect to the WLAN inside the building?

   C. What is the farthest distance at which you are still able to connect to the WLAN?

   D. Are there any security concerns associated with your findings in the previous points A, B, and C?

2. If possible, connect to the Internet from an available public hot spot and access your school network or your personal e-mail accounts. Is this an example of a WLAN or a WWAN connection? Why?

Case Problems

1. You are a WWAN consultant and have been asked to create a conceptual design for a WWAN for a school district in a medium-sized city. The school district wants to implement the WAN in a sequence of four zones, with from five to six schools in each zone. Create the conceptual design for a single zone considering the following information gathered during the preliminary requirements analysis:

   A. In each zone, the closest two campuses are approximately five miles apart.

   B. Each zone has one high school, one middle school or junior high school, and three to four elementary schools.

   C. Usage is highest at the high schools and drops by half to each lower education level. On a scale of 1 to 10, a high school's usage was rated at 8, a middle school's usage was rated at 4, and an elementary school's usage was rated at a 2. This relative usage pattern appears to be consistent in each zone.

D. The city government and the incumbent local exchange carrier (ILEC) have recently agreed to work together to install a fiber-optic local loop throughout the city. The loop is within five miles of at least one school campus in each zone.

E. Each school building has a wired Ethernet LAN, and the library and cafeteria in each high school have 802.11b wireless hot spots.

F. The primary purpose of the WWAN project is to provide backhaul to the city government's IT services, which provides backbone connection services to the school district.

2. Contact the IT services department at a local hospital to learn if that facility is using WMTS or any other WWAN system. What equipment is installed to support the WWAN and what has their experience been with this system? You may want to invite the head of the medical facility's IT department to speak to your class.

Advanced Lab Project

If you have 802.11a or 802.11g access points or WLAN bridges available, create a link that spans an outdoor space between two buildings, provided this space is not wider than the effective range of your wireless devices. After you establish the link, answer the following questions:

1. What is the strength (how many bars?) of the link?

2. Is the link affected by people, vehicles, or other objects obstructing the LoS between the devices?

3. What security issues are involved with this type of a link?

4. Are ad-hoc users able to connect to the link from within the range of either device?

5. Is one device more dominant than the other? Why?

Appendix A

Network Standards and Technologies

Perhaps the primary reason the Internet has grown as it has is that in its infancy, networking models, practices, protocols, and standards were developed on which it could grow. Without these elements, networking as we know it today would be so segregated along proprietary lines that it would essentially be nonfunctioning.

This appendix provides an overview of the building blocks on which local and wide area networking, and all networking in between, is built, including the OSI model, networking topologies, and media access methods.

Networking Models

With the Internet and local area networking (LAN) rapidly gaining popularity, it quickly became obvious that networking devices from different manufacturers had to be able to communicate with one another to ensure end-to-end data transmissions across a network. Without some form of networking standards, the promise of the Internet and the capability of local networks to interconnect to the Internet could be lost to infighting among manufacturers.

The Open Systems Interconnection (OSI) reference model provided a framework on which manufacturers and software developers could produce networking devices and services that could be intermixed on a network, regardless of their source. The following sections trace the formation of the two primary networking models in use and the technologies based on these models. The topics included are

- Development of a networking standard

- A seven-layer model

- Moving through the layers

- The TCP/IP model

In the late 1970s, the British Standards Institute expressed the need for a standard communications infrastructure for distributed computing to the International Organization for Standardization (ISO). In 1977, the ISO created the Open Systems Interconnection subcommittee and assigned the task of developing alternative proposals to the American National Standards Institute (ANSI).

Coincidentally with these developments, Honeywell Information Systems had been developing structured distributed communications architectures to support distributed database system designs, which resulted in a seven-layer framework it called the Distributed Systems Architecture (DSA).

Honeywell was a participant in the early ANSI meetings and presented its seven-layer DSA conceptual model, which was chosen as the only proposal to be submitted to the

OSI subcommittee. The OSI subcommittee agreed that the DSA model satisfied most of the OSI requirements and felt the model could easily be expanded in the future to include any new developments. So, in March 1978, the OSI reference model, which was in essence the Honeywell model, was published as the international standard for distributed communications and networking.

With the Internet and local area networking (LAN) rapidly gaining popularity, it quickly became obvious that networking devices from different manufacturers had to be able to communicate with one another to ensure end-to-end data transmissions across a network. Without some form of networking standards, the promise of the Internet and the capability of local networks to interconnect to the Internet could be lost to infighting among manufacturers.

Two primary network models provide the standard frameworks that guide the development of the hardware and software used to provide network functionality and interoperability: the OSI reference model and the TCP/IP model. These models provide a framework on which manufacturers and software developers can produce networking devices and services that could be intermixed on a network, regardless of their source.

The OSI reference model, or simply the *OSI model*, defines seven discrete layers (see Figure A-1) of functions and data formatting that should be used to ensure conformity, compatibility, and interoperability between the protocols and devices involved with the transmission and processing of data transmitted across a network.

A

Distributed Computing

Distributed computing can be defined in a variety of ways, but each of these definitions revolves around one central theme: the connection of users and resources to create a shared, transparent, and scalable computing environment. The objective of *distributed computing* is the creation of a shared resource network of computers, which is more reliable and powerful than a single computer or an interconnection between individual computers.

The World Wide Web is an example of a distributed computing environment on which you use the resources of a remote system to access and download information. When you are browsing the Web, the browser running on your computer is interacting with web servers running on other computers. To make the connection with the remote web server systems, your browser had to interact with domain name servers, which are, themselves, interconnected into a distributed system.

Another type of distributed computing system is one that manages and utilizes idle processing and storage space on up to thousands of networked computers to create a computing environment with sufficient CPU power and storage for large processing-intensive software.

(Continued)

This type of arrangement is illustrated in the following graphic that depicts the interconnection of three government and university computing resources to provide high-end processing power to users at a remote research facility.

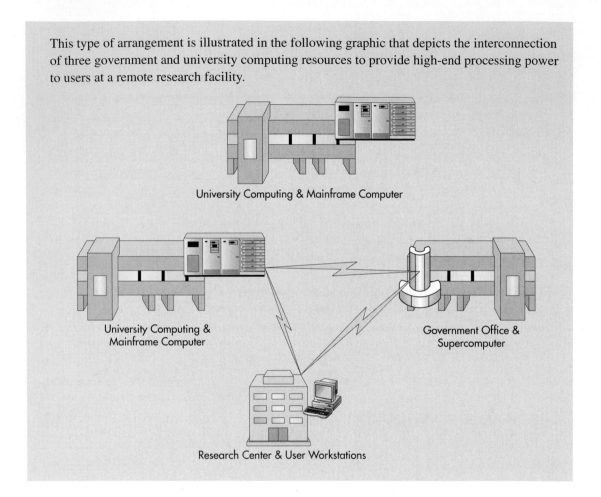

Figure A-1 The seven layers of the OSI reference model

Important to understand is that the OSI model is not software, but rather a standard guideline that should be followed by manufacturers and developers when designing hardware or software to carry out one or more functions involved in the transmission of data across a network.

Each of the seven layers of the OSI model specifically defines the purpose and objectives of the functions that operate at that layer, as well as the input and output formats of data messages received or passed out of the layer. An overview of each of the seven layers of the OSI model (as shown in Figure A-1), in order from the top layer (Layer 7) to the bottom layer (Layer 1), is provided in the following sections.

Layer 7: The Application layer

First, the name of this layer does not refer to application software, such as word processors, spreadsheets, games, and the like; it refers to application support and an interface for computer-based applications to network services. The purpose of the *application layer* is to provide transparency and accessibility to network services for user software.

Although this may seem to contradict the preceding point, networked computers do have application-layer software that provides access to a network for computer applications. For example, a web browser, an e-mail client, and a File Transfer Protocol (FTP) client contain application-layer elements that provide an interface between network protocols and services and the user, such as transmission, format, and display support for Hypertext Markup Language (HTML) and Post Office Protocol (POP) files or messages.

The application layer receives data either from the applications running on a user's computer or from the presentation layer. For outgoing messages, Layer 7 ensures that required data is present and formats the data for processing by functions defined on lower layers. For incoming messages, the application layer prepares the data for use by the appropriate protocol—HTTP (Hypertext Transfer Protocol), FTP, or others.

Layer 6: Presentation Layer

The presentation layer could just as easily be called the conversion layer because the functions defined on this layer are concerned with converting the data itself for use by the application layer or for processing by the functions defined on lower layers.

The primary purpose of the *presentation layer* is to ensure data compatibility between open systems and to perform the tasks associated with data representation between communicating

Protocols

A *protocol* is an established set of rules that prescribe the interactions and formats that are to be used to transform, transmit, or process data in a communications environment. Typically, a protocol is limited to performing a single task, although the task itself may be complex.

systems. Simplistically, this means Layer 6 functions ensure that potentially incompatible systems communicate using a mutually agreeable data representation.

Among the functions performed by Layer 6 protocols are

- **Code or format conversions** Personal computers generally use the American Standard Code for Information Interchange (ASCII, pronounced "ask-ee"), and many mainframes and other computers use the Extended Binary Coded Decimal Interchange Code (EBCDIC, pronounced "ebb-suh-dic"). When an ASCII computer communicates with an EBCDIC computer, functions defined on the presentation layer ensure each receives the data in its format—this is essentially the job of a translator between a Japanese ballplayer and American sportswriters.

- **Data compression** When data is required to be compressed for transmission, the presentation layer functions perform the compression and, at the receiving end, the decompression of the data.

- **Encryption** The encryption and decryption of data for transmission can be done on any of three of the OSI layers, and which layer is used for encryption depends on how much of the transmitted data needs to be encrypted.

  - **Layer 6 encryption** The encryption that occurs on the presentation layer affects only the data that needs to be protected. The data is encrypted prior to being placed into the message format for transmission; the remainder of the message remains unencrypted.

  - **Layer 4 encryption** The *transport layer* encrypts every character of a message prior to passing it on for transmission.

  - **Layer 1 encryption** When the physical layer encrypts a message unit, every bit is encrypted for transmission.

NOTE

The functions of the OSI's Layer 6 are typically performed by routines embedded in a computer's operating system (OS). Many people visualize the OSI model as a set of working protocols that exist completely outside any single computer. However, many of the activities defined on the OSI model's Layers 6 and 7 are integrated into a computer's OS software.

Layer 5: Session Layer

In communications terminology, a telecommunications session exists as long as two systems are communicating. The session begins when one station requests connection information from another station, mutually compatible session rules are agreed to, and the connection is established, or as the telecom folks say, "nailed up."

If you understand the concept of a session, it shouldn't be too hard to guess what the session layer of the OSI model defines. The *session layer* defines the mechanisms used for managing the communications between end-user processes, including the transmission mode, line checks, and session teardown and restart processes.

The functions defined on the session layer are typically involved in a transmission only at the beginning and end of a session. At the beginning of a session, Layer 5 functions verify the receiving station is present and available, and they notify it of the intent to communicate. At the end of a communication session, the Layer 5 functions determine if the transmission was successful and break down the session.

Included in the information provided to the remote station at the beginning of a communication is the type of transmission to be used:

1. **Simplex** In a simplex transmission, only one station transmits and all other devices only receive. The communications flow is one-way only. An example of simplex communications is a public address system.

2. **Duplex** Duplex transmissions allow two communicating stations to communicate, but depending on the type of duplex communications in use, the transmission can carry signals from only one or both of the communicating stations:

   - **Half-duplex** Half-duplex communications allow both stations to transmit data, but only one at a time. If the communications line is in use by one of the stations, the other must wait until the line is clear to transmit its data; otherwise, a collision will occur and all the data will be lost. A citizen's band (CB) radio is an example of a real-life half-duplex system.

   - **Full-duplex** A full-duplex communication allows both stations to transmit simultaneously without fear of collisions on the line. The telephone system is an example of full-duplex communications.

Figure A-2 illustrates the basic differences among these three communications modes.

In summary, the functions defined on the session layer perform three primary steps for each communications session:

1. Establish and negotiate the connection.

2. Maintain the connection and restart the session if it fails.

3. Release the connection when the session is completed.

Layer 4: Transport Layer

The functions defined on Layer 4 of the OSI model perform essentially what the name *transport layer* implies—the transmission of data between communicating stations. While that's the end

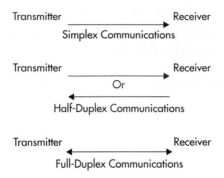

Figure A-2 The transmission differences among the three basic communications modes

result of Layer 4 activities, several other communications-related functions are also defined at this layer.

Layer 4 functions also provide for guaranteed, error-free transfers of data between communicating devices, although the services that provide guaranteed, error-free transmissions can be ignored, if desired.

Transport-layer protocols provide reliability in a number of ways:

- **Connection-oriented communications** This type of communications session requires interaction between the communicating stations to guarantee each transmitted message segment is received. Figure A-3 illustrates the elements of a connection-oriented session between two stations. Typically, a connection-oriented session requires the receiving station to acknowledge the receipt of each message unit before another unit is transmitted. If the acknowledgment is not received in a certain amount of time, the message is retransmitted. In certain instances, a connectionless session may be desired to eliminate the overhead a connection-oriented session imposes.

- **Error-free transmission** Although truly error-free data communications are virtually impossible, the transport layer uses a checksum or another checking device to verify the number of bits or the value of the data in the message received. A checksum is not foolproof, but if the receiving station calculates a different checksum from that in the message, chances are good an error occurred in the transmission. If an error is detected or suspected, the receiving station requests the erroneous message to be retransmitted.

- **Flow control** Because not every communications device has the same processing power or the same-sized receiving buffer, it is possible for the sending station to overpower the receiving station by transmitting too much or too fast. When this happens, the receiving station can interrupt the transmission flow long enough for it to process the data it has

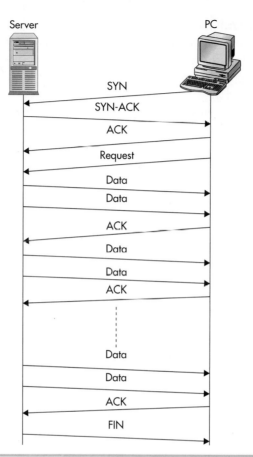

Figure A-3 A connection-oriented session requires the two stations to maintain a dialog using specific types of message frames.

received and catch up. If the situation is that the receiving station doesn't have enough space to hold the message block being transmitted, it can request a smaller block size. The receiving station could also request a larger block size, if it has enough memory to handle it.

● **Ports** Just as the first line of an address on a letter indicates which occupant of a residence the letter is for, a Layer 4 port number can be used to indicate which application or service a particular message is to be processed by. This allows more than one network-enabled application to be monitoring a network connection and processing only the messages specifically addressed to each.

Layer 3: Network Layer

The primary function of the OSI model's *network layer* is to route a message across an internetwork to its destination network. To do this, the network layer defines a group of related functions that can be applied to accomplish this action:

● **Routing**   The main activity of routing is *path determination*, which means a routing device must use the information it possesses about the network and its neighboring devices to determine which of the paths (routes) it could forward a message to is the better choice at any particular time. Included in the routing functions of Layer 3 devices are address handling, subnetting, supernetting, and other address-related activities.

● **Switching**   As illustrated in Figure A-4, a Layer 3 device can have one or more connections to a WAN or the Internet and multiple connections to one or more LANs. *Layer 3 switching* involves forwarding messages between the incoming and outgoing connections on a Layer 3 device. Switching is also performed by certain types of Layer 2 devices.

● **Route setup**   Some network architectures require Layer 3 devices to perform call setup, much like a Layer 4 or 5 device, prior to forwarding messages across a network.

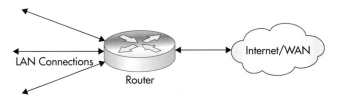

Figure A-4   A Layer 3 device (router) interconnected among a WAN and several LAN connections

Layer 2: Data-link Layer

The *data-link layer* of the OSI model has two major responsibilities:

1. Prepare formatted message units for transmission as a stream of bits over the physical medium.

2. Format raw transmitted data into message units that are free of transmission errors and pass them to the network layer.

The data-link layer also provides flow control and error control support to Layer 1 devices and provides physical addressing support to facilitate message delivery on local networks.

The data-link layer is commonly associated with two sublayers: the Logical Link Control (LLC) layer and the Media Access Control (MAC) layer. While technically not OSI layers—because they are defined in Ethernet standards—these two layers further define the functions performed on Layer 2 for LAN message traffic.

Logical Link Control   On an Ethernet network, the data-link layer is divided into upper and lower functions. The *LLC sublayer* defines the functions of the upper portion of Layer 2 activities, including

- **Service Access Points (SAPs)**   A *SAP* is a logical link or port to a Layer 3 protocol. On a LAN with multiple network protocols running, each of the Layer 3 protocols has its own unique SAP, which allows each protocol to communicate with any or all of the other protocols. For example, if a LAN is supporting both TCP/IP and Novell's SPX/IPX, each protocol has a SAP assigned, so incoming and outgoing messages can be directed to the appropriate Layer 3 protocol for processing. Figure A-5 illustrates how each layer defines SAPs to provide communications between itself and the layers above and below it.

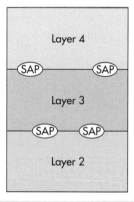

A

Figure A-5   Each layer in the network model defines SAPs for communications between layers.

- **Logical link addressing**   The message unit formatted on the LLC sublayer contains two link addresses: the Destination SAP (DSAP) and the Source SAP (SSAP), which are used to direct a message unit to the appropriate Layer 3 protocol to forward the message.

- **Data-link communications**   The LLC sublayer provides connection-oriented link support for data being forwarded on the MAC sublayer, which uses connectionless transmission. LLC also supports connectionless communications, but only in cases where the MAC sublayer protocols provide for message reliability.

● **Message sequencing** The original data in a message is likely to have been divided into more than one message unit to conform to the message formatting defined on each OSI layer. For LAN protocols to order the message into its original form, the message pieces are assigned a sequence number.

Media Access Control The functions performed on the MAC sublayer, which are defined by protocol-specific standards, include the following:

● **Media Access Control** The MAC sublayer defines the methods used to access the transmission medium and the recovery methods used when an error or collision occurs on the medium.

● **Bridging** The MAC sublayer provides for a communications link between Layer 1 activities and the LLC sublayer.

● **Physical Addressing** The unique physical addressing of each network device is defined on the MAC sublayer.

The functions of the MAC sublayer are defined as topology- and protocol-specific, but they are usually independent of the physical medium in use.

Layer 1: Physical Layer

The *physical layer* of the OSI model defines the electrical, mechanical, and communications means used to transmit data across a physical medium, including electrical and electromagnetic specifications, network hardware, and the physical or wireless connection medium. In simpler terms, the physical layer defines exactly what is required to transmit data as electromagnetic ones and zeros. This includes broadcast frequencies, the processes used to connect and terminate a connection to a communications medium, and the rules used to resolve broadcast contentions on the physical medium.

Moving Through the Layers

When a user sends a request to download a web page or an e-mail message, the processes used to format, manage, and transmit the message are essentially the same, regardless of the type of network medium in use. Some of the actions are slightly different to account for the different media, but whether the message is being transmitted from a wireless or wired network, a certain sequence of events must take place to ensure the message is processed properly at the receiving end.

Note, as a network message moves through the services and protocols of each layer of the OSI model, as illustrated in Figure A-6, the format of the original message is restructured—perhaps divided into smaller pieces—and picks up some additional information on each layer. Remember, as a message is processed for transmission, it is being passed between different communications protocols. For the logic of each successive step to know what it is working with, certain information must be passed along to each lower or higher function. In addition, when the message arrives at the receiving end, a corresponding process for each of the processes is on the sending side and they need input, so the message can be properly handled and forwarded.

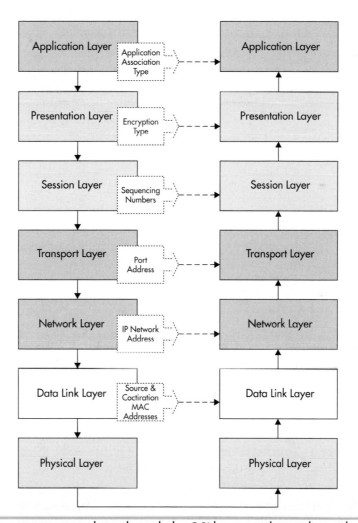

A

Figure A-6   A message moves down through the OSI layers on the sending side and up through the OSI layers on the receiving side.

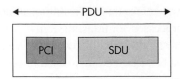

Figure A-7 A PDU consists of a protocol-specific PCI and the original message as the SDU or payload.

The process used to add this vital information to the message is called *encapsulation.* As a message moves down through the layers of the OSI model, the functions on each layer reformat and rename the message or its parts to facilitate all later processing of the message.

When a message begins its trek toward its destination, it is a generic application data unit. As each succeeding protocol layer processes the message, it adds specific information to the message in the form of a message header, or what is called its Protocol Control Information (PCI), as illustrated in Figures A-7 and A-8. The data received by the protocol is a service data unit (SDU), or what is called the *payload.* Together, the PCI and the SDU form the message unit passed to the next protocol layer as a protocol data unit (PDU).

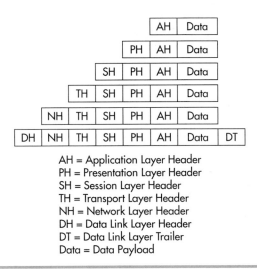

AH = Application Layer Header
PH = Presentation Layer Header
SH = Session Layer Header
TH = Transport Layer Header
NH = Network Layer Header
DH = Data Link Layer Header
DT = Data Link Layer Trailer
Data = Data Payload

Figure A-8 Information is added to a message unit as it passes down through the OSI model's layers used by the corresponding layer on the receiving end.

As illustrated in Figure A-8, a header is added to the message on each layer as it passes down through the OSI layers. In some cases, additional information is also appended to the message in the form of a tail or trailer. When the message is received at the other end of the transmission, the headers (and tails) are removed as the message unit is passed up through the layers. The information contained in the headers and tails contains parameters and flags that assist the receiving end layers to process the PDU.

As additional information is added to a PDU as it progresses down or up through the protocols or services defined on the OSI layers, the PDU's format and name also changes to indicate its current status. Table A-1 lists the name of the PDU produced on each layer of the OSI model.

Layer	PDU Name
Application	Application Data Unit
Presentation	Presentation PDU
Session	Session PDU
Transport	Segment
Network	Packet or Datagram
Data Link	Frame
Physical	Bits

Table A-1   OSI Encapsulation PDUs

A

NOTE

An analogy that may help you understand how the layers of the OSI are designed to work together is this: the Lower Layers (Layers 1 through 4) construct a highway that the Upper Layers (Layers 5 through 7) can use.

The TCP/IP Model

While the OSI is the generally accepted network model, other models have emerged that more closely relate to the functions of certain networks. Predominant among the other networking models is the TCP/IP model, which more specifically defines the functions involved to transmit messages across the Internet. The *TCP/IP model* defines a four-layer model intended to reflect how data flows from a transmitting host across the Internet to a receiving host. Unlike the OSI model, which is a generic specification of the functions to occur on each level, the TCP/IP model is built around a specific group of protocols.

As shown in Figure A-9, the TCP/IP model combines or restructures the layers defined in the OSI model. The TCP/IP model has four layers (as opposed to the seven layers of the OSI model). The layers of the TCP/IP model (top to bottom) are

- **Application layer**   The TCP/IP model's application layer combines the OSI model's application, presentation, and session layers. In the TCP/IP model, an *application* is any process that occurs above the transport layer. Such processes are commonly performed by communications or data-handling processes in a communicating application or by a

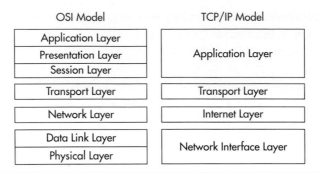

Figure A-9 The TCP/IP model in comparison with the OSI model

computer's OS. Examples of TCP/IP protocols that operate on the application layer are: e-mail protocols, such as the Simple Mail Transfer Protocol (SMTP) and the Post Office Protocol (POP); web page transfer protocols, such as the Hypertext Transfer Protocol (HTTP); and file transfer protocols, such as the File Transfer Protocol (FTP).

- **Transport layer** This layer essentially mirrors the transport layer of the OSI model. The TCP/IP model's transport layer performs the activities associated with transferring data across the network from one host to another. Two TCP/IP protocols operate on the transport layer: the Transmission Control Protocol (TCP) and the User Datagram Protocol (UDP).

- **Internet layer** In the context of internetworking, the TCP/IP Internet layer performs essentially the same activities as the OSI model's network layer. However, because of the emphasis on internetworking in TCP/IP protocols, all communications pass through the Internet layer. The primary TCP/IP protocols that operate on this layer are the Internet Protocol (IP) and the Internet Command Message Protocol (ICMP).

- **Network Interface layer** This layer, also called the *network access layer*, combines the functions and standards of the OSI model's data-link and physical layers. In fact, the TCP/IP's network interface layer doesn't define any new protocols, technologies, or standards. Instead, it relies on those defined by the OSI model and other networking standards. The TCP/IP network interface layer defines how IP interacts with common data-link protocols, such as Ethernet, Token Ring, FDDI, HSSI, and ATM, as well as existing physical media standards, such as the cable termination pin-outs, voltage levels, and cabling requirements defined by RS-232C, V.35, and IEEE 802.3.

IEEE 802 LAN Standards

The 802 specifications of the Institute of Electrical and Electronics Engineers (IEEE—pronounced "eye-triple-ee") don't specifically define a model in the same way as the OSI and TCP/IP models. Each of the 802 standards defines the specific characteristics, properties, and functions that should occur on the data-link and physical layers of a LAN. Table A-2 lists the various 802 standards.

IEEE Standard	Defines
802.1	Internetworking
802.1d	Spanning Tree Protocol
802.1s	Multiple Spanning Trees
802.1q	Virtual LAN (VLAN) Frame Tagging
802.2	Logical Link Control
802.3	Ethernet (CSMA/CD)
802.3u	Fast Ethernet
802.3z	Gigabit Ethernet
802.3ae	10-Gigabit Ethernet
802.4	Token Bus
802.5	Token Ring
802.6	Distributed Queue Dual Bus (MAN)
802.7	Broadband Technology
802.8	Fiber-Optic Technology
802.9	Voice/Data Integration (IsoEnet)
802.10	LAN Security
802.11	Wireless Networking
802.11a	54 Mbps Wireless Network
802.11b	2211 Mbps Wireless Network
802.11g	54 Mbps Wireless Network
802.11n	100 Mbps Wireless Network
802.12	Demand Priority Access LAN (100BaseVG-AnyLAN)
802.15	Wireless Personal Area Network (WPAN)
802.16	Wireless MAN (WMAN)

A

Table A-2   The IEEE 802 Subcommittees and Standards (*Continued*)

IEEE Standard	Defines
802.17	Resilient Packet Ring
802.18	LAN/MAN Standards Committee
802.20	Fixed Wireless Broadband

Table A-2   The IEEE 802 Subcommittees and Standards

The IEEE 802 standards are developed and maintained by a committee formed in February 1980, which is where the number 802 comes from. The 802 committee is divided into several subcommittees, which develop and manage each of the specific LAN standards listed in Table A-2.

Networking Topologies

In the context of a computer network, a *topology* is essentially the pattern used to organize the devices connecting to the network. A network's topology represents its general shape and organization, and how its nodes connect to the network media.

The four basic network topologies are

● Bus topology

● Star topology

● Ring topology

● Mesh topology

Bus Topology

The *bus topology* (see Figure A-10), which is also called the *linear bus topology*, is built around a single "backbone" cable that runs the length of the network, creating a network bus (or communications path) structure. Nodes attach to the network by connecting to the network backbone and, in a pure bus topology, computers attach directly to the backbone.

The bus topology was the structure used for early Ethernet networks installed on either a thin or thick coaxial backbone cable. Computers and other nodes connected to the bus using a pass-through connector on a network adapter or attaching to a network adapter that pierced the backbone cable.

Transmitting Signals on a Bus

While a bus topology may be the least expensive way to structure a LAN, some inherent problems are associated with communications over an end-to-end cable. First, if the backbone

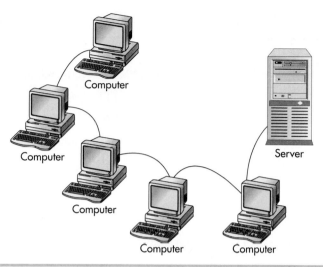

Figure A-10   The basic bus topology

cable passes through a computer's network adapter, a risk exists that a loose connection could interrupt the bus. The same issue occurs if the backbone cable is broken or damaged.

When a signal is transmitted on a communications bus, the signal spreads out to fill the bus. This means when a computer located in the center of the backbone cable transmits a signal, the signal travels to both ends of the cable. If the ends of the cable aren't terminated to absorb the signal, the signal reflects back from the cable ends, essentially destroying or severely garbling the original signal. This situation would be much like speaking in a small room that produces echoes. The echo would eventually be so distracting to a listener that what the speaker is currently saying would be lost. The problem with the reflected signal on a bus is it again travels to the other end of the cable and continues reflecting back and forth, virtually forever, rendering the bus unusable. This condition is called *ringing*.

To avoid ringing on a bus topology, the ends of the cable must be terminated with an electronic circuit or device, either connecting to the cable itself or at the last computer connection, to absorb errant signals. The terminators absorb the electrical energy and stop the reflections.

Advantages of a Bus Topology

In addition to being relatively inexpensive to implement, a bus topology also has these advantages:

- The bus topology is easy to use, easy to understand, and simple to implement.

- Additional nodes are easily added to a bus network by adding additional taps on the network backbone.

- The transmission length of the backbone cable can also be extended to longer distances using a signal repeater.

Disadvantages of a Bus Topology

A bus topology has these disadvantages:

- Because the backbone supplies all of a network's bandwidth, adding additional nodes can slow the network for all nodes.

- The nodes compete for transmitting rights on the network backbone.

- A break in or damage to the backbone cable can cause signal reflections that will busy out the network bus.

NOTE

Pure bus topology networks are less common today than a few years back. In some situations, though, variations of bus topology are still used, such as when distributing network access to the floors of a multistory building from a network head end on the roof or in the basement.

Star Topology

The *star topology*, illustrated in Figure A-11, is any network arrangement that involves a central clustering device directly connected to a number of network nodes. In the illustration in Figure A-11, a wireless network access point serves as a clustering device for a group of wireless workstations. The access point provides connectivity to the network for each of the computers. The star topology is commonly used in networking today.

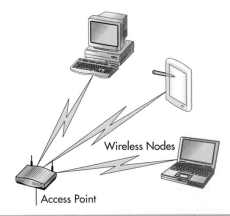

Wireless Nodes

Access Point

Figure A-11 Wireless network devices arranged in a star topology

The star topology is rarely used in its purest form for LANs in a business or education situation. However, the star topology is the recommended topology for installing what is called structured wiring in a home automation network.

Star clusters are used with both ring and bus topologies to create the star-bus and the star-ring hybrid topologies. As illustrated in Figure A-11, wireless networks are commonly structured in a star arrangement with a wireless access point. Figure A-12 illustrates a star-ring hybrid network structure.

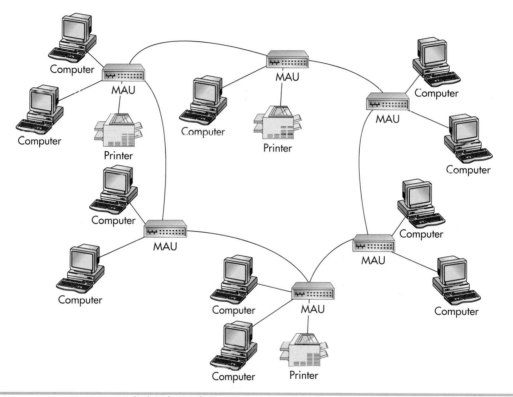

A

Figure A-12   A star-ring hybrid topology

Advantages of the Star Topology

The star topology, regardless of how it's implemented, has some advantages:

- If one computer or cable fails, only that one node (not the entire network) is affected.
- Transmissions are virtually collision-free.

- The use of centralized networking devices (hubs, servers, and so forth) reduces the overall network costs and enables network administration to also be centralized, which makes network management much easier.

- A variety of network media can be used to attach to the centralized devices, making it easier to merge legacy and new networks.

- Data transfer speeds of 4, 16, 100, and 1000 Mbps are now specified in IEEE 802.5.

Disadvantages of the Star Topology

The disadvantages of a star topology are

- If a central device, such as a hub or a server, should fail, the entire network is affected.

- In a wired network environment, cable costs can be higher than they would be in a bus or ring topology because of the length of the cabling used to connect nodes to a central device.

- Throughput speed is given up for collision-free transmissions.

Ring Topology

The ring topology became popular with the introduction of IBM's Token Ring Networking architecture. Although a *ring topology* (see Figure A-13) is commonly depicted as a loop or circle, a ring network may look much like a star topology, with devices configured into a logical ring. What makes a ring network structure work isn't so much its shape as how the network nodes access the network.

A ring topology is closely associated with the Token Ring networking, with hub-like devices called multistation access units (MAUs or MSAUs) providing the ring management. In a typical ring network structure, the nodes are clustered to an MAU, which connects to the physical ring or backbone medium. As discussed earlier, this arrangement creates a hybrid form of the ring topology commonly referred to as a star-ring or a star-wired ring topology. The ring topology is also the basis of the Fiber Distributed Data Interface (FDDI), in which a campus or metropolitan area is attached to a fiber-optic cable loop for network access.

Advantages of the Ring Topology

A ring topology provides some advantages in comparison to other topologies, including these:

- A single node cannot monopolize the network and its resources.

- A ring network has the capability to continue to function even after the network's capacities are reached, although it functions much more slowly than normal.

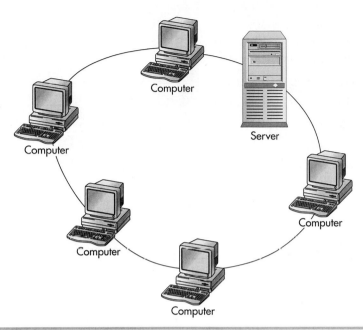

Figure A-13   The basic ring topology

A

Disadvantages of the Ring Topology

A ring topology has these disadvantages:

● The failure of a single node can impact the operation of the entire network.

● Troubleshooting and isolating a problem on a ring network can be difficult.

● Adding additional nodes disrupts the entire ring.

Mesh Topology

As illustrated in Figure A-14, a *mesh topology* directly connects each node of a network with all other nodes. The additional links of the network create a mesh structure that provides redundant paths across a network for each node. In the event that any one node fails, or if any of the network links is broken or damaged, the redundant links provide fault tolerance to support the continued operations of the network.

Typically, in a network implemented on a mesh topology, only the key connectivity devices, such as switches and routers, are connected into the mesh to prevent the failure of a single device from taking down all, or a portion of, the network. In some ways, a wireless network installed on a star-bus topology that has overlapping access points can provide a mesh-like fault tolerance.

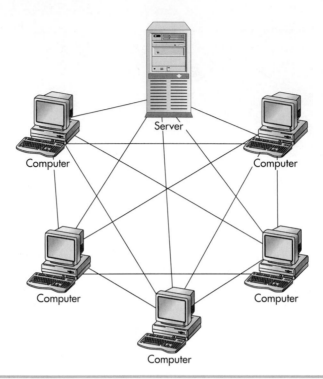

Figure A-14 A mesh topology

The advantages of a mesh topology are its path redundancy and fault tolerance; its disadvantages are cabling costs (in a wired network environment) and troubleshooting issues.

Media Access Methods

A LAN consists of a network medium shared by a number of connected computers, printers, workstations, and other network-enabled devices. A LAN allows a relatively large number of devices to share and use the resources connected to or stored on the network. A computer connected to a network has a veritable wealth of information, software, and hardware at its disposal, just like all the other computers connected to the network. The problem with this information-processing utopia is, in most cases, only one network device can access the network at a time, regardless of the network technology or topology in use.

If two or more network devices attempt to transmit on the network medium at a time, the transmitted signals overlap each other and neither is usable. To prevent this situation from occurring, each network technology includes an access method that defines how a connected device gains access (permission to transmit) to the network's shared medium. The access method creates a cooperative environment for all the devices connected to the network, so they don't interfere with each other's transmissions.

The two most commonly used access methods are integral parts of the most popular networking technologies: Ethernet and Token Ring.

Ethernet Access Methods

The IEEE 802.3 standards define the Ethernet access method—Carrier Sense Multiple Access with Collision Detection, or as it is more commonly known, CSMA/CD. The key to understanding how CSMA/CD controls access to the Ethernet media is basically described in its name.

Essentially, Ethernet is based on a shared bus topology, which means multiple computers and devices share a common network medium. This arrangement can and does cause problems if any or all of the connected devices don't follow Ethernet's rules for transmitting on the medium.

In Ethernet's simplest form, when a network node wants to transmit a message (service request, e-mail transmission, or interactive game actions, among others), it "listens" to the network cable to determine if the network is busy (a signal is present) or idle (no signal is present). This works something like when you want to see if a multiple-extension telephone in your home is available to make a call. If, when you pick up the receiver, you hear a dial tone, you know the line is clear and you can make your call. However, if you hear a voice, you know the line is in use and you must wait to place your call.

When an Ethernet network node transmits a message, called a *frame*, all the other nodes are "listening" or sensing the bus to determine one of two things: (1) is a message on the bus addressed to it? or (2) is the bus idle so the node can transmit on the bus? Because a transmitted signal can be sensed anywhere on the network medium, all nodes can easily determine if either of these two conditions exist.

If a node wants to transmit an Ethernet frame and the medium is clear, that node receives the exclusive transmission rights to the medium and all other nodes must wait until the medium is clear to transmit on the line. However, if a transmitted signal is present on the medium, the access rules require a node to wait until the medium is clear to transmit its frames.

For Ethernet network nodes, the method used to determine if the transmission medium is clear is CSMA. *CSMA* is used in place of a bus controller, such as that used in a computer to control transmissions across the internal bus structures of the computer. Instead, each node is bound by an honor code not to transmit over another node's transmissions.

A transmission on the network medium has a certain electrical property that can be measured (sensed) by each device, and the network medium also has a default electrical property when it is idle. So, to determine if the network medium is busy or idle, a node merely tests the medium with a sort of built-in voltage meter to see which condition the medium is in. The electrical value for a transmitted message is referred to as a *carrier signal*, or *carrier* for short. Allowing each node to check the medium for a carrier signal helps to prevent transmission collisions on the network, theoretically.

By and large, the carrier-sensing method used in Ethernet to prevent transmission collisions works, but inadvertent situations exist where collisions do occur quite innocently. If two or more nodes determine the network is idle at exactly the same instance, each node, thinking it now has

A

permission to transmit, may attempt to transmit frames on the network medium. This multiple access transmission creates line contention and, typically, leads to transmission collisions. *Line contention* occurs when multiple nodes are attempting to transmit on the medium at the same time, and a collision occurs when more than one transmission is trying to occupy the medium at the same time. On a large LAN, two nodes may be located at the extreme ends of the network and the transmission time between the nodes may be sufficiently long for one node to access the medium before it can detect a transmission by the other node.

Collision Detection

When two devices sense the medium is clear and attempt to transmit at the same time, a collision occurs. Using the collision detection method, both devices test the line after transmitting to see if a collision has occurred. If a collision is detected, both nodes stop transmitting immediately and wait a random length of time before attempting to retransmit their messages. Because the algorithm used by each node to calculate its wait time is based on randomized values, it is unlikely these two nodes will experience another collision in the near term, which doesn't rule out a collision at some point in the future.

On a fairly large network, the amount of contention for access to the medium can create a situation where collisions can become commonplace, which is why the performance of an Ethernet network can decline as more nodes are added to the network. The estimation is that as much as 40 percent of an Ethernet network's capacity should remain free to avoid line contention and frequent collisions.

The downside of collision detection is it is reactive. In other words, the collision is dealt with only after it occurs. However, the collision avoidance method attempts to be more proactive.

Collision Avoidance

The *collision avoidance method* attempts to avoid collisions before they occur by requiring each node to signal its intention to transmit before it does so. Before transmitting frames on the network, a node transmits a jam signal, and then waits a certain amount of time to allow every station to receive the jam signal before transmitting its payload. When a node is preparing to transmit on the medium, if it detects a jam signal from another node, it ceases its transmission activities and waits until the line is clear to transmit its jam signal. A fair analogy for collision avoidance would be the practice of raising your hand to indicate you want to speak in class.

Collision avoidance was first implemented in Apple Computer's AppleTalk networking system. However, collision avoidance is commonly used on network systems where the activity on the media cannot be easily determined, such as a wireless network.

Token Passing

The *token-passing media-access control method* is based on the principle that only the network node possessing the token is allowed to transmit on the medium. If you and a group of your friends arranged yourself in a circle and used some object, such as a baton or even a pencil, to indicate who "had the floor"—that is, who could speak—you would be, in effect, practicing token passing. In this arrangement, when one speaker finishes talking, the token is passed around the circle until it comes to the next person with something to say. Only the person with the "token" is allowed to speak, and all others must remain silent.

By limiting access to the transmission medium to only a single node, collisions are virtually impossible. Token passing is a collision avoidance technique because only the node possessing the one and only network token is enabled to transmit on the network.

Because token passing networks, such as Token Ring, token bus, FDDI, ARCnet, or Apple Computer's TokenTalk, transmit data in a circular, sequential form from one MAU or node to its next active upstream neighbor (NAUN), transmitted signals effectively travel around the ring, one node to the next. When a node wants to transmit to the network, it must wait for whichever node currently has the token, which is a special type of control frame, to finish its business and pass the token on. The first node to grab the token as it goes by can begin transmitting. If one node wants to communicate directly with another node and receive a return message, the token must be included in the message, so the receiving node will have the capability to respond.

In practice, obtaining the token isn't as haphazard as it may sound. Inside the token frame, is a priority field, called the *Start of Frame Sequence*, which is used to determine which node has priority for the use of the token. Each station compares the priority for all other nodes to its own priority and, if another node has a higher priority, the node is transmitted on to that node.

A

NOTE

Despite the line contention and transmission collisions that frequently occur on carrier sensing networks, carrier-sensing access methods, such as the CSMA/CD used in Ethernet, are generally faster than token-passing access methods, because they are typically installed on higher-bandwidth lines. Even though token passing networks are collision-free, they tend to have slower performance.

Appendix B

WLAN Protocols and TCP/IP Utilities

This appendix reviews the protocols of the TCP/IP suite commonly associated with a WLAN. In addition, it covers the common TCP/IP utilities you need to know.

Media Access Transmission and Protocols

Media access protocols provide and control access to a network's media. Without some method to control which node is transmitting on the network medium, the result would be RF signal chaos as signals from competing nodes collide.

A Media Access Control (MAC) protocol, such as the Carrier Sense Multiple Access/Collision Avoidance (CSMA/CA) used on 802.11 networks, provides the methods used to either prevent or recover from signal collisions on the physical media.

When lighting strikes a lake, the electrical charge from the lighting is transmitted throughout the water of the lake, which acts as an electrical conductor. Wireless communications work similarly in that, when an RF transmitter emits its signals, the signals spread out to fill a particular broadcast pattern, as shown in Figure B-1.

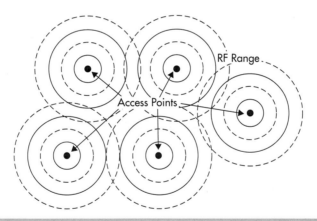

Figure B-1   Broadcast pattern

Transmitting an RF Signal

When a wireless network interface card (NIC) or network adapter transmits an RF signal, which is an electromagnetic charge representing a stream of data bits, the signal spreads and may enter the receiving range of one or more receiving devices, such as a wireless access point. Regardless of where the transmitting node is located within the range of the receiving station, its signals travel to the edge of its broadcast range.

Problems occur when two nodes attempt to transmit at the same time. The two signals can overlap, interfere, or cancel each other, perhaps resulting in a single unintelligible signal.

In wireless networking, MAC protocols are used primarily to avoid these problems and, when they do occur, to recover from them. Wireless MAC methods are grouped into these general categories: collision avoidance, collision detection, and Ready-to-Send/Clear-to-Send (RTS/CTS).

Collision Avoidance

MAC is focused on either collision avoidance or collision detection and recovery. On wireless networks, the focus is on collision avoidance. Unlike nodes on a wired network, a wireless node can't always detect when a neighboring node is transmitting to a base station (access point or other receiving station). So, an emphasis is made on preventing two or more wireless stations from transmitting on the medium at the same time.

The access method commonly used on wireless Ethernet networks is CSMA/CA. Fixed wireless access methods are defined in the MAC functions of each communication service and several mobile wireless networks implement Mobile Assisted Channel Allocation (MACA) or some variation of MACA.

Collision Detection

On wireline networks, the MAC methods are focused on detecting collisions and correcting them, rather than avoiding collisions altogether. The primary MAC protocol is CSMA/Collision Detection (CD) and its functions are much different from those of CSMA/CA.

If we use the same analogy used earlier to illustrate how wireless signals propagate, we can see how the electrical charge in a wireline transmission also spreads out to fill the medium. When water under pressure (in other words, a current) runs into a hose, the water fills up the hose. When an electrical charge is placed on a copper wire, which is, an excellent electrical conductor, the electrical charge spreads out to all parts of the wire, as illustrated in Figure B-2, just like the water in a hose.

B

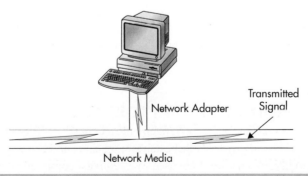

Figure B-2   Spreading of the electrical charge

Copper network cabling has two major component types: conductor and insulator. The *conductor* is the metal portion of the cable, usually at the cable's center, that allows the electrical charge to pass through it. The *insulator* is wrapped around the conductor and resists the electrical charge, which, in many ways, keeps the electrical charge limited to the conductor.

When a network adapter transmits an electrical charge, representing a stream of data bits, the charge is carried throughout the conductor, end to end. Even if a network node is attached to the center of a network cable, its signals travel to each end of its conductor. At the ends of the cable, without some device to absorb the signals, the signals bounce back on themselves, muddling the signal beyond recognition.

If two nodes attempt to transmit at the same time, the two electrical charges collide to become a single unintelligible electrical signal. MAC protocols are used either to avoid or recover from these situations.

RTS/CTS

Another technique employed to avoid collisions on a wireless network is RTS/CTS. Although available typically as an option on home or small office wireless local area network (LAN) products, *RTS/CTS*, when used, can be an effective way to improve the performance of a WLAN by controlling when a station has access to the medium.

With RTS/CTS implemented, a wireless station does not transmit network messages until it has been able to establish what is called a RTS/CTS "handshake" with another wireless device, typically a base station or a peer station. The concept of a handshake between communicating devices was originally defined in the serial communications process (EIA/TIA 232). In this process, the station wanting to transmit on the network transmits a Request To Send (RTS) frame to the receiving station, which, if available for communications, responds with a Clear To Send (CTS) frame. If the receiving station is unable to respond for any reason, it simply ignores the RTS frame, which means the station wanting to transmit must restart the handshake process. The CTS frame serves two purposes: it notifies the sending station that the medium is clear and provides for the other stations within the range of the receiving station to stay off the medium for a certain amount of time to allow the transmission to take place. After the receiving station receives the sending station's transmission, it issues an acknowledgement (ACK) frame, which lets the sending station know its data was received and releases the other stations, so they may request the use of the medium.

Connection Management Protocols

Within the Transmission Control Protocol/Internet Protocol (TCP/IP) protocol suite are a group of connection management protocols that establish, manage, and control transmissions across a network. Essentially, two methods are used to establish a communications connection or session: using a dial-up link or using a LAN or other network link. However, the actions performed at the protocol level in either of these connection types are similar and, in some cases, exactly the same.

The connection management networking protocols operate on Layers 4 and 5, Transport and Session, respectively. However, the protocols in which we are most interested are the Layer 4 protocols: TCP and the User Datagram Protocol (UDP). The primary differences between these two Layer 4 protocols are reliability management functions and the use of different connection types.

Reliability

TCP includes a variety of mechanisms to help provide for the reliability of transmitted data. The mechanisms employed by TCP are

- **Checksum**   Before TCP passes a message segment to the network layer protocols, it calculates a checksum and places it in the segment's header. The checksum is recalculated by the receiving station and compared to the checksum in the header. If the two checksums match, the assumption is the data arrived intact and complete. If they are not equal, a request is made to have the segment retransmitted.

- **Duplicate data discard**   When data is transmitted across the Internet or over long distances on any wide area network (WAN), it is possible for some of the data to be duplicated for one reason or another. To prevent duplicate data from being passed on to the application layer, TCP discards any already received data.

- **Retransmission of data**   Whenever a possible data error or missing data is suspected in a message segment, TCP transmits a request to have the segment retransmitted.

- **Sequence control**   Message segments can arrive at the receiving station out of sequence because some of the segments may have been forwarded over different routes. TCP tracks the sequence of message segments arriving, so the data passed on to the application layer is in its proper form.

- **Timer control**   When the sending station forwards a packet, TCP allows only a set amount of time for the message to arrive at its destination and be acknowledged. If any of the required transmission control functions fail to take place in the allotted time, TCP normally initiates (from the sending station) or requests (from the receiving station) a retransmission of the segment.

A fairly major part of the reliability function in TCP is the establishment of a reliable connection at the start of the communication session. For a session link to be considered reliable, a handshake process must be performed. The TCP handshake is a bit different from that used between a wireless node and a base station. The TCP handshake, which is a three-way handshake, uses a SYN (synchronizing), SYN/ACK, and ACK sequence.

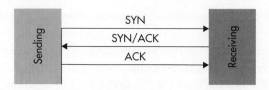

Figure B-3 SYN message information

As Figure B-3 and Table B-1 show, the station wanting to transmit sends a SYN message to the receiving station with a sequence of n. If the receiving station is available, it replies with a SYN/ACK with an ACK sequence of n+1 and a SYN sequence of x to accept the sender as a session partner.

Step	ACK Sequence	SYN Sequence	Event
1	–	n	Sender sends TCP SYN packet to receiver
2	n+1	x	Receiver replies with SYN ACK
3	n+2	x+1	Sender replies with ACK
4	–	–	Session begins

Table B-1 SYN Message Explanation

At the end of the session, another handshake process is used to tear down the session, but rather than SYN packets, finish (FIN) packets are used. The sequence of events is similar to that used to establish the session, with each request requiring an ACK in reply, as illustrated in Figure B-4 and Table B-2.

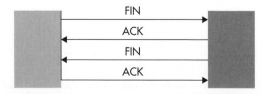

Figure B-4 FIN packets

Step	Event
1	At end of transmission, sending station transmits FIN packet
2	Receiving station sends ACK
4	Receiving station sends FIN packet
5	Sending station sends ACK and breaks connection

Table B-2   FIN Message Explanation

In a way, the second FIN packet sent by the receiving station asks the question, "Are you sure?" to which the sending station, if it meant to end the session, replies with an ACK and breaks the connection, ending the session.

Another component of the reliability of a TCP session is the reliable delivery of packets during the session. Using a connection-oriented communications mode (see the next section), the receiving station sends an ACK packet after it determines an arriving packet doesn't require retransmission for any reason.

Connection-Oriented Protocols   A protocol is connection-oriented if it performs one or both of two activities:

- Transmissions are made over a negotiated, established link
- Error-detection

Connection-oriented protocols establish an end-to-end connection by negotiating the parameters of the connection. The communicating stations must agree or compromise on the authorization of the data transfer, the synchronization method to be used, and that each station is ready to transfer or receive data.

Data transfers made by a connection-oriented protocol can be compared to sending a registered postal letter. When a registered letter is delivered to its destination, the receiver signs a receipt, which is sent back to the sender. The receiving station must acknowledge each block of data transmitted through a connection-oriented protocol before the next data block is transmitted.

Because of the time involved to ensure the reliable delivery and receipt of each message block, connection-oriented protocols are slower than connectionless protocols, which don't include any of the control and error-recovery processes used by a connection-oriented protocol (see the section "Connectionless Protocols").

B

TCP Reliability and Wireless Networks Wireless network standards are sensitive to any added demand on the medium. When stations communicating through TCP retransmit packets, the anticongestion mechanisms built into the 802.11 standards increase throughput by allowing less data to flow to ensure its reliability. So, in effect, TCP and 802.11 can fight each other, all in the cause of reliable data transfers.

Eliminating TCP can be one solution to this problem, such as implementing a gateway or router on the network. However, the Wireless Transport Protocol (WTP), which is a part of the Wireless Application Protocol (WAP) protocol suite, uses connection-oriented connections and depends on TCP/IP to provide a seamless connection to the Internet. So, eliminating TCP is not a real solution and the contention between it and 802.11 is likely to be a continuing condition faced by wireless networks.

Connectionless Protocols A connectionless protocol does establish a connection link but, beyond that, despite what its name may imply, this type of protocol doesn't use or require the connection management and control functions of a connection-oriented protocol. In effect, a *connectionless protocol* is more like a straight and open pipeline between two communicating stations.

Connectionless protocols, such as UDP, Ethernet, and Novell's IPX, assume whatever is transmitted on the link will be received by the receiving station. Connectionless protocols don't include error-recovery functions and they depend on other protocols for this safeguard. Because a connectionless protocol doesn't include any of the link establishment, management, and control functions performed by a connection-oriented protocol, it is much faster. And, where the connection-oriented protocol can be compared to a registered letter, a connectionless protocol is more like the faith you have when you drop a letter into a post box. You assume the postal service will carry and deliver the letter to its destination.

A connectionless protocol can be used in situations where other protocols, typically application layer protocols, are tending to the reliable delivery of the data or in cases where the transmission is less critical or small enough for transmission errors not to be an issue.

Point-to-Point Communications

The primary function of a data communications protocol is to transmit data from one point to another, typically using a dial-up or another form of virtual circuit (VC). A *VC* is a communications link created specifically for a single transmission or communications session and torn down (removed) after the session completes.

The primary data communications protocols are those protocols that carry data from a transmitting source to a receiving destination. As a group, point-to-point protocols essentially carry data in its transmitted format from Point *A* to Point *B*.

Point-to-Point Protocol Originally developed as an encapsulation protocol for transmitting IP packets over dial-up connections, the Point-to-Point Protocol (PPP) has become the de-facto standard for transmitting packets from native network protocols, such as IP, IPX, and Compaq's DECNet, over many forms of point-to-point links.

In operation, PPP can be compared to a delivery truck. In the same way that a package is placed inside the truck's cargo area for delivery to a destination, PPP encapsulates the original message unit into its payload area, and then carries the payload to the receiving station, where the payload is extracted for processing and handling by its native protocol.

PAP and CHAP

PPPs are often used to log a remote user into a network. In most PPP situations, the Password Authentication Protocol (PAP) and the Challenge Handshake Authentication Protocol (CHAP) are used to provide access control to remote users attempting to log into a network.

Under PAP, a control database of user names and their associated passwords is stored on a server. When a user attempts to log in to the network, the user name and password are verified against the database to determine if they are valid. If the user name and password aren't included in the database, the logon is denied.

CHAP, like PAP, is also used to verify a user name and password for logging on to a network. However, CHAP goes a couple of steps further by encrypting the user name and password. The login procedure on the user's computer obtains a random one-use-only value (called a *nonce*) and an ID code from the CHAP server. The user's computer uses the random value to create a hash total, which is sent as a part of the login request. If the CHAP server determines the values match it was expecting, the login is allowed to proceed. Otherwise, the login is denied.

PPTP and VPN

Some point-to-point clients access a network through a Virtual Private Network (VPN). A *VPN* is a private network that connects to remote users over the public internetwork (Internet), which saves the cost of private, dedicated lines to the remote user locations. A VPN also allows a remote user the freedom of connecting from random locations, rather than requiring the remote user to come to a fixed location to connect to a private network.

A VPN is commonly used to connect remote offices to a central office network or to allow traveling employees or telecommuters to log into the network and access the same services and resources available to employees at the home office.

The primary flaw in the concept of a VPN is this: the Internet is an open network, without much protection against interception and unauthorized access. Because the connection made over a VPN is a point-to-point connection, the technology of PPP along with some additional security capabilities are combined into the Point-to-Point Tunneling Protocol (PPTP).

PPTP allows a private network to create "tunnels" through the Internet to carry private transmission to and from the network. *Tunneling* refers to the process used to encrypt and place a message packet inside another carrier packet. Point-to-point protocols load data units into a payload area for transmitting the data across a point-to-point connection. The primary difference between PPP and PPTP, and other tunneling protocols, such as the Layer 2 Tunneling Protocol (L2TP), is that the data placed in the payload portion of a PPTP packet is encrypted.

B

In effect, tunneling establishes a virtual tunnel of privacy, in that only the communicating stations can decrypt the payload, between two stations. Nonsecure packets are placed inside secure packets. Where PPP was like a delivery truck, PPTP is an armored car.

Internetworking Protocols

An *internetwork* is a network of networks. The best example of an internetwork is the Internet, which is comprised of literally millions of networks from around the world. Each local network has the choice of whether to connect to an internetwork and more than you would probably guess choose not to. However, for those local networks that choose to connect to the Internet, they must follow one primary rule: they must be running the standard internetworking protocols. For the Internet, the standard protocol suite or protocol family is the TCP/IP suite of protocols.

The TCP/IP protocol, which is also referred to as the IP protocol suite, consists of a family of interoperable protocols and services that can be used on a LAN or WAN, but are essentially required to communicate over the Internet.

TCP/IP includes at least one protocol for each layer of the TCP/IP reference model to help ensure that, as data is processed and prepared for transmission across a network, the protocols in use function seamlessly—almost like one large protocol, rather than a series of related protocols.

As listed in Table B-3, the TCP/IP suite has protocols to perform the specifications defined for each layer of the TCP/IP reference model.

TCP/IP Layer	OSI Layer(s)	TCP/IP Protocols
Application	Application, Presentation, Session	FTP, DNS, Telnet, HTTP, NNTP, POP3, SMTP, IMAP
Transport	Transport	TCP, UDP
Internet	Network	IP, ICMP, IGMP
Network Interface	Data Link, Physical	ARP, RARP, DHCP, BOOTP, Ethernet, Token Ring, FDDI, Frame Relay, X.25

Table B-3 Protocols in the TCP/IP Suite

Application Layer Protocols

Application layer protocols interface with user applications to provide linkage to Internet and Network Layer services. The primary protocols found on the TCP/IP Application layer are

- **Domain Name System (DNS):** Maps network domain names to their IP address equivalents.
- **File Transport Protocol (FTP):** Facilitates the reliable and secure transfer of whole files across a network.

- **Hypertext Transfer Protocol (HTTP):** Facilitates the transfer of Hypertext Markup Language (HTML) files between an HTTP client (such as a browser) and an HTTP server (such as a web server).

- **Internet Mail Access Protocol (IMAP):** An e-mail protocol that enables a user to access and manage e-mail in the user's mailbox on an e-mail server.

- **Network News Transfer Protocol (NNTP):** Facilitates the transfer, posting, and retrieval of Usenet messages across a network.

- **Post Office Protocol, version 3 (POP3):** An e-mail protocol that interacts with an e-mail server to move e-mail from an e-mail user's mailbox to their computer's e-mail client and to remove all transferred mail from the user's mailbox on the e-mail server.

- **Simple Mail Transfer Protocol (SMTP):** Facilitates the transmission and receipt of e-mail messages across a network. Relies on POP3 and IMAP to queue messages in users' mailboxes.

- **Telecommunications Networking (Telnet):** Facilitates virtual terminal services and access to host computers by remote users.

- **Trivial FTP (TFTP):** Facilitates the nonsecure transfer of files across a network.

Transport Layer Protocols

The two primary transport layer protocols are the Transmission Control Protocol (TCP) and the User Datagram Protocol (UDP). *TCP* provides reliable and guaranteed transmission of data across a network, while *UDP* transmits data as a stream without any error-correction or flow-control mechanisms.

In addition to providing reliable transmission control, TCP features

- **Flow control:** Mechanisms that allow the receiving station to advise the transmitting station that the maximum transmission unit size may need to be reduced to avoid overflowing its input area.

- **Full-duplex communications:** TCP is able to transmit and receive data and control messages simultaneously.

- **Multiplexing:** TCP can process multiple service interactions with multiple higher-layer protocols simultaneously in a single session.

UDP is a connectionless transport layer protocol used primarily as an interface service between the Internet layer (such as IP) and higher-layer protocols. UDP provides little in the way of message reliability services, but it can be used to transport data when a higher layer protocol or application is able to provide these services. UDP is commonly invoked as the transport layer protocol by such services as the Network File System (NFS), the Simple Network Management Protocol (SNMP), DNS, and TFTP.

B

TCP Error-Detection   A key part of TCP's reliability is error recovery. *Error recovery* is a connection-oriented process that provides not only for error-detection, but also the means to retransmit any data suspected of error. For the most part, error recovery means simply retransmitting a message either thought to have an error or not received completely.

NOTE

Error recovery is not the same as error correction. If a segment is determined to contain a transmission error, the segment is retransmitted and no attempt is made to correct data errors.

The mechanism used to determine if error recovery should be invoked is error checking. Error checking has three methods:

- **Checksum:** This error-checking process calculates a ones-complement value for the data stored in a segment's payload and stores the result in the message header before transmitting the segment. At the receiving end, the same calculation is performed and compared to the value in the message header. If the values match, processing continues; otherwise, a request is sent back to the transmitting station to retransmit the segment.

- **Cyclical Redundancy Check (CRC):** Although not calculated by TCP, the *CRC,* which is added to a message segment on the network interface layer, is a calculated binary profile of the data in the message payload. Like the checksum, if the CRC value calculated by the receiving station differs from that in the segment header, the segment is flagged for retransmission and passed back to the transport layer protocol.

- **Parity:** *Parity checking*, which can be applied as either odd-parity or even-parity, uses the process where the transmitting station tallies the number of binary bits with a value of one. If the tally results in an even or odd number, depending on which parity method is in use, a parity bit is set to one to force the number of one bits to either an even or odd tally. For example, if the number of bits with a value of one is 1128 and odd-parity is in use, a parity bit is set on (to a value of one) to force the tally to 1129, an odd number. If, in this same example, even-parity was in use, no parity bit would be necessary because the tally is already an even number. When the parity checking is in use, the sending station tallies the number of bits in the segment and, if needed, adds a bit to ensure that the number of total bits is either an odd or even number, whichever method is in use. The receiving device also counts the bits (including the parity bit) and verifies that the correct number of bits arrived and that its tally is appropriately even or odd. If the bit tally doesn't match the parity type in use, a request is sent back to the transmitting device to retransmit the segment.

Another method used to determine if a segment should be retransmitted is the use of a time-out timer. After transmitting a segment, TCP waits a preset amount of time, such as

100 milliseconds, for an acknowledgment to be returned by the receiving station. If this time expires before an acknowledgment is received, the sending station assumes the segment has been lost and automatically retransmits it.

Ones Complement

In computing, negative numbers are represented using the ones complement method. To represent its negative value, all of the one bits in a binary value are replaced with zeroes and all of the zero bits are replaced with ones. The quirky result of this method is that there is both a positive and negative zero. The following table illustrates this process.

Binary Value	Decimal Value
00000100	+4
00000011	+3
00000010	+2
00000001	+1
00000000	+0
11111111	−0
11111110	−1
11111101	−2
11111100	−3
11111011	−4

And, no, −0 plus +1 does not equal +0.

B

TCP Flow Control   In addition to providing connection-oriented reliability features, TCP also provides flow control to ensure the receiving station receives all transmitted messages. *Flow control* is used to avoid a situation where the speed or size of the transmitted data overflows the receiving station's incoming data area and segments are lost as a result, a condition called *congestion*. The objective of flow control is to ensure the integrity of transmitted messages.

To avoid congestion, the receiving station transmits a control message to the transmitting station when it determines its incoming data area is nearly full. The receiving station requests that the transmitting station stop sending messages until it (the receiving station) can process the data in its incoming area and catch up. Once the receiving station is able to clear its incoming area, a control signal is sent to the transmitting station to resume transmissions.

Three forms of flow control are employed to prevent congestion: buffering, congestion avoidance, and windowing.

- **Buffering**   The *buffering* type of flow control allocates extra buffer space (incoming data space) to handle any bursts of excessive data flow until it can be processed. The disadvantage of the buffering method is if the extra buffer space overflows, no attempts are made to stop or stem the flow of data. If insufficient buffer space is allocated and congestion occurs, any additional data flow could result in lost data transmissions.

- **Congestion avoidance**   While the objective of all flow-control methods is to avoid congestion, the *congestion avoidance* method enhances the buffering method by monitoring the receiving buffers and, before the buffers overflow, notifies the transmitting station to stop transmitting until the data in the buffers can be processed, freeing up buffer space. When buffer space is again available, the transmitting station is notified that it can restart its transmissions. The size of the receiving buffer determines how often the transmission is interrupted.

- **Windowing**   The *windowing* flow-control method is used to control the size of the transmitted block as a means to prevent congestion. In the context of flow control, a *window* refers to the number of segments transmitted before an acknowledgment is required. Windowing is a dynamic flow-control method. If the session is progressing satisfactorily with a window size of 1, the receiving station can request the window to be increased to 2. The window size can be steadily increased until congestion occurs, at which time the window is reset to 1 and the windowing process restarts.

TCP and UDP Sockets   A facility supported by transport layer protocols is the creation of a linkage between application layer protocols that allows these protocols and the application software they support to communicate directly with each other. The mechanism used to establish this linkage is a *socket*. TCP and UDP sockets are called *stream sockets*, which consist of a number representing the transport layer protocol (TCP or UDP) in use, the destination IP address, and a port number identifying the application or protocol that should process the packet payload on the receiving end.

A *port* is a logical device used to identify a specific application on a server. Each port is identified through a port number, assigned by the Internet Assigned Numbers Authority (IANA). Port numbers are divided into three groups by the IANA:

- **Well-known ports:** *Well-known ports* includes the most commonly used ports, ranges in number between 0 and 1023. However, only operating systems (OSs), system processes, or privileged software can apply or access the ports in this group.

- **Registered ports:** *Registered ports* includes port numbers 1024 to 49,151, which are used by user and application programs to create logical ports and sockets between proprietary programs.

- **Dynamic ports:** *Dynamic ports*, also called private ports, include port numbers 49,152 through 65,535. These ports are unregistered and can be used dynamically by application software to create private logical connections on the fly.

Table B-4 lists a sampling of well-known port numbers. To see a complete list, visit the IANA web site (**www.iana.org**).

TCP/UDP Port Number	Application/Service/Protocol
1	TCP Port Service Multiplexer (TCPMUX)
5	Remote job entry (RJE)
20	FTP—Data
21	FTP—Control
22	SSH (Secure Shell) Remote Login Protocol
23	Telnet
25	SMTP
43	WHOIS
53	DNS
69	TFTP
80	HTTP
110	POP3
119	NNTP
143	IMAP
156	SQL Server
161	SNMP
179	Border Gateway Protocol (BGP)
194	Internet Relay Chat (IRC)
389	Lightweight Directory Access Protocol (LDAP)
546	Dynamic Host Configuration Protocol (DHCP) Client

Table B-4   Well-known Port Numbers

B

An example of how a socket is used between two communicating applications is as follows:

1. On her PC, Carly opens her FTP client software and chooses an FTP server to which she wants to connect.

2. The FTP client interacts with FTP and TCP to create a segment to be transmitted to the FTP server requesting permission to create a session. In this segment, TCP assigns the port number of 21 (see Table 4-2) along with the IP address of the FTP server and the IP address of Carly's PC (or the router on her network) to create a TCP socket that is transmitted in the TCP segment.

3. On the remote network, the incoming message is directed to the FTP server, which responds with a message using a socket consisting of the port number 20 and a login request message.

Internet Layer Protocols

While TCP and UDP deal with the transport of packets over a communication link, Internet and network layer protocols are primarily concerned with the delivery of the packets. The Internet layer protocols provide the addressing structures that allow packets transmitted across a network or Internet to be routed across the network and delivered to their destinations.

The primary TCP/IP Internet layer protocols are

- **Internet Protocol (IP)**   *IP* is a connectionless protocol that depends on the connection-oriented services of TCP to maintain the connection over which packets are transmitted. With the connection management taken care of, IP focuses on the logical addressing of packets and the delivery of packets to the appropriate destination network. IP converts TCP segments and UDP datagrams into packets and, in the process, often reduces the overall size of the message to be transmitted by fragmenting the message unit into a series of sequentially numbered packets.

NOTE

IP is currently released in two versions—IPv4 and IPv6—each of which defines a different addressing structure.

- **Internet Command Message Protocol (ICMP)**   In the course of transmitting data under a protocol's control, one communication device may need to pass information, control codes, or status information to another. The Internet Control Message Protocol (ICMP) is an Internet layer protocol used for this purpose. *ICMP* is also used as the underlying protocol in many TCP/IP utilities and services, including Ping and Trace (these utilities are discussed in the sections "Ping" and "Trace").

● **Internet Group Management Protocol (IGMP)** The Internet Group Management Protocol (IGMP) provides a means for a networked computer to inform its most adjacent router of its membership in a multicast group. *Multicasting* allows one computer or server on the Internet to transmit to multiple other computers that have subscribed to a multicast group. Multicasting has a variety of applications, including such actions as updating the address book on a portable computer, transmitting a company's newsletter to registered subscribers, distributing digital magazines, and net-broadcasting a streaming multimedia "show" to a preregistered audience.

Address Resolution Protocols

Note, two primary address resolution protocols are the Address Resolution Protocol (ARP) and the Reverse Address Resolution Protocol (RARP).

The *ARP* is used to map an IP address to a physical address, typically a MAC address. An *IP address* is used to route a packet from one network to another, but once the packet reaches its destination network, the physical address associated with the destination IP address is used to deliver the packet to a specific node. ARP is used to resolve (translate) the IP address to its MAC address equivalent.

ARP is also used between nodes on a local network running TCP/IP. Each node maintains a table, called *ARP cache*, which maps each of the IP addresses on the network to its MAC address. If a MAC address is unknown for an IP address, the node transmits an ARP request that, essentially, asks the node with a certain IP address or a certain MAC address to identify itself, and its logical and physical addresses.

Thin clients or diskless workstations connected to a network do not store their assigned IP configuration data and must request this information each time they start up or connect to the network. On many of those networks not running DHCP, *RARP* is used to obtain a workstation's

B

Network Broadcasts

Network broadcasts are a common occurrence on several network types. Broadcasts are used most often to discover unknown information, such as the physical or logical address of a networked computer, bridge, or switch on the same network.

If you wished to deliver a written message to a stranger in a crowded room, you could go around the room asking each person if he or she was the one to whom the message was intended, or you could find a way to make an announcement to the entire room, asking if the addressee would identify himself or herself. The latter method, while far less discreet, is the most efficient and effective way to accomplish your task.

Network devices use broadcast messages for essentially the same purpose as the announcement made to a crowded room. If the address of another computer is unknown, a broadcast message is placed on the network in hopes that the unknown computer will respond with its address information.

IP configuration. During startup, the node broadcasts its MAC address requesting its IP address from the network's RARP server.

Stations that do not store their IP configuration data, such as a diskless workstation, use RARP to discover their IP address when they power up. As you may have guessed, RARP uses a process that is the reverse of ARP. Instead of sending out its IP address to discover the matching MAC address (which is what ARP does), RARP broadcasts its MAC address hoping to get back its IP address. For this to work, there must be a RARP server, to supply the IP address, on the network.

Node Configuration

The primary protocols used to configure a network node on a TCP/IP network are the Bootstrap Protocol (BOOTP) and the Dynamic Host Configuration Protocol (DHCP). These protocols are used to assign IP address configuration data to a network device signing onto the network.

BOOTP   *BOOTP* is used for some of the same purposes as RARP, except that diskless workstations or thin clients may also use BOOTP to request not only their IP configuration, but the IP address of the BOOTP server, and even the file it needs to complete its boot process and startup procedures. The IP address assigned to a network computer by BOOTP must manually be preconfigured on the BOOTP server by the network administrators.

DHCP   On the other hand, *DHCP* is more commonly used on private networks and networks with a limited number of available IPv4 addresses. DHCP allows a network computer to request its IP configuration from a DHCP server when the node starts up and connects to the network. DHCP is an extension of BOOTP, which provides the node with its IP address. However, DHCP provides a more complete IP configuration data, including an IP address that is assigned to the node for a fixed period of time, rather than until the computer boots up again.

The IP address assigned to a network computer by DHCP is "leased" to a network computer for a fixed time, which is either determined by the DHCP server or set by the network administrators. In addition to assigning an IP address, DHCP also provides other IP configuration settings, including the IP address of the default gateway the node is to use to access an internetwork (if any), the IP address of the DNS server to be used, and, in some cases, the DNS domain of the client computer. This set of IP configuration data represents the full set of information that would have to be entered manually to configure a computer for a TCP/IP network, if DHCP were not in use.

A DHCP server assigns client IP addresses from a pool of available addresses. The pool of addresses may include fewer IP addresses than network computers, which is part of the purpose behind DHCP in the first place. Operating under the assumption that not all computers need to be active on a network at any one time—an assumption that was often true in the early days of networking—DHCP assigns active (logged on) computers IP configuration data to use while they are on the network. Because DHCP data is leased to nodes, when the lease expires, much like an apartment, the IP address can be assigned to a different computer.

The use of private IPv4 addressing has virtually eliminated the need to lease IP addresses to nodes, but the lease period is still included in DHCP assignments, typically with a default lease period of 72 hours. The assumption is that network computers will be restarted at least that often. However, in most cases, when a lease expires, it is automatically renewed.

Many Internet service providers (ISP) use DHCP for their dial-up service subscribers. In this situation, the ISP likely has more subscribers than it has connection points. If the difference in numbers is at all significant, some subscribers may be unable to obtain a connection until another subscriber's DHCP lease expires. The lease period for a dial-up DHCP assignment may be minutes rather than hours.

The advantages of DHCP to a network administrator are

1. Complete TCP/IP configuration data is assigned to network computers automatically.

2. IP configuration data typically remains assigned to a computer as long as the client remains logged on to a network.

3. A limited IP address pool can be shared by network computers that don't require permanent IP address assignments.

4. IP addresses automatically become available to other computers at the end of the lease period or when a computer logs off a network, whichever comes first.

Routing Protocols

B

Routing is the logical and physical action that transmits a message unit from one switching point to the next as the message unit, typically a packet, is forwarded toward its destination address. Although this may seem obvious, routing is performed by a router.

Routing Protocol Functions

For the most part, routers are used as the primary interface point between a LAN and a WAN but, on occasion, a router can also be used within a large LAN, regardless of whether the network is wireline or wireless. In a small wireless network, a router is used as the Internet gateway and provides a variety of switching, security, and privacy services. In larger wireless LANs and WANs, routers can be arranged so they create hierarchical layers with multiple local-level routers linked to higher-level routers.

Routing protocols are used to maintain the information used by a router to make its determination of the path that should be used to forward a packet toward its destination address.

A router maintains a table of statistics, called *metrics*, used to calculate the quality, reliability, and speed of a link connected to one of a router's interface ports. Because network environments are highly dynamic, this information needs to be updated frequently. Routers use routing protocols to inform its neighboring routers (immediately upstream) of any changes it detects or is informed about on the network.

Commonly used routing protocols, each using a different set of metrics and algorithms to make its path determinations, are

- **Routing Information Protocol (RIP)** While the standard RIP is one of the oldest routing protocols in use, dating back to the late 1950s, several proprietary routing protocols also go by this name. *RIP* is a distance vector protocol, which means it uses the distance (measured in the number of hops [routers] a packet much pass through to reach its destination) as its primary metric. The current open standard version of RIP is also known as *IP RIP*.

- **Open Shortest Path First (OSPF)** In addition to the distance metric, *OSPF* also factors in the condition of a link (its link-state) when making its path determination. The number of hops (distance), link speed, congestion, and other factors are used to determine the "cost" of a link, with the lowest cost link generally preferred.

- **Interior Gateway Routing Protocol (IGRP)/Enhanced IGRP (EIGRP)** These two distance-vector routing protocols are used within a large organization's private network, called an autonomous system (AS).

- **Border Gateway Protocol (BGP)** *BGP* is the routing protocol used on routers between the routers of private networks, such as those of ISPs. An AS is likely to use an interior gateway protocol (IGP), such as RIP or IGRP, and link to a higher-level router running BGP.

Wireless Network Routing Protocols

A wireless LAN typically doesn't need to include a routing protocol, at least on smaller wireless LANs. Most wireless LANs link to a wireline network at either a gateway/router or at an access point. In either case, a wireless LAN provides a connection to routing services. However, ad-hoc networks can be spread over fairly large areas and may require some routing, especially when communicating peer-to-peer.

- Wireless networks, especially larger ad-hoc networks, use a variety of specialized routing protocols that manage metrics particular to an ever-changing wireless environment. Wireless ad-hoc routing protocols fall into one of the following three groups:
    - Table-driven routing protocols
    - Hierarchical state routing protocols
    - On-demand routing protocols

Table-Driven Ad-Hoc Routing Protocols When using a *table-driven routing protocol*, each wireless node maintains routing information to the other network nodes of which it is aware. Routing information is updated whenever a node detects a topology change, meaning whenever a node enters or leaves the network. Each of the more common table-driven routing protocols uses slightly different algorithms, metrics, and methods in its routing calculations and topology change updates. On an ad-hoc network, the route to a particular node may be through at least one other node.

Some of the existing table-driven ad-hoc routing protocols are

- **Dynamic destination-sequenced distance vector routing protocol (DSDV)**   *DSDV* maintains a routing table that includes all known nodes on the network, along with the distance to each node. Because there can be more than one path to a node, each path to a particular node is ranked with a sequence number to help ensure the better path is used first and to avoid routing loops.

- **Global state routing (GSR)**   *GSR* is similar to DSDV, but it maintains a neighbor list, a topology table, a next hop table, and a distance table. The neighbor list contains a list of the nodes that respond to routing message updates—the assumption being that if the node responds, it must be a neighbor; the topology table contains the link-state information for each reachable node; the next hop table contains the first intermediate node to which packets must be forwarded to reach a particular node; and the distance table contains the link address that provides the shortest distance to each node.

- **Wireless routing protocol (WRP)**   *WRP* maintains four related routing information tables: a distance table, a routing table, a link-cost table, and a message retransmission list (MRL) table. The distance table contains the distance vector for each destination, counting each intermediate node as a hop; the routing table contains a relative distance metric for each of the intermediate nodes, as well as potential destination nodes; the link-cost table contains the metric cost to each node; and the MRL contains a list of the nodes that did not respond to update messages and need to be retransmitted.

Hierarchical State Routing   The hierarchical state routing (HSR) protocol performs a logical clustering of ad-hoc nodes to create a hierarchy of clusters and a node central to each cluster, called a *cluster head.* Each cluster can also create subclusters within itself. Routing information is maintained on the paths to the cluster head, which then, in turn, forwards a packet on to its final destination. Routing information is traded between cluster heads, which decreases the amount of routing information overhead on the medium and improves throughput for the entire network.

In an adaptation of the HSR method, the zone-based hierarchical link-state routing protocol (ZHLS) divides an ad-hoc network into a series of nonoverlapping zones, and then maintains both zone-level and node-level topology tables.

On-Demand Routing Protocols   On-demand routing protocols, such as the Ad-hoc On-demand Distance Vector (AODV) routing protocol, don't maintain routing information tables. Instead, they issue a route discovery frame whenever they need a path to a particular node.

Another common on-demand routing protocol is the Cluster-based Routing Protocol (CBRP), which operates something like a hierarchical routing protocol, only without the table maintenance, and the Dynamic Source Routing Protocol (DSRP), which maintains a routing cache (an informal form of routing table), but only updates the cache as it needs routing information to a particular node.

TCP/IP Utilities

The TCP/IP protocol suite also includes a variety of utility protocols that can be used to verify a computer's IP configuration, check a network connection, troubleshoot the route between two internetwork addresses, or log on to a remote host. The TCP/IP utilities are valuable tools for a network administrator, regardless of whether the network is wired or wireless.

The primary TCP/IP utilities are

- ipconfig
- nslookup
- ping
- telnet
- trace

IPCONFIG

Ipconfig is used to display the IP configuration of a computer's network adapter, as shown in Figure B-5.

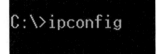

Figure B-5   Use of ipconfig

The ipconfig command, in its default mode, displays the IP address, subnet mask, and default gateway address assigned to a computer's network adapter. Figure B-6 shows the results of the ipconfig command with the "/all" parameter that displays all the configuration information for a computer's network adapter, including its physical addressing and DHCP information.

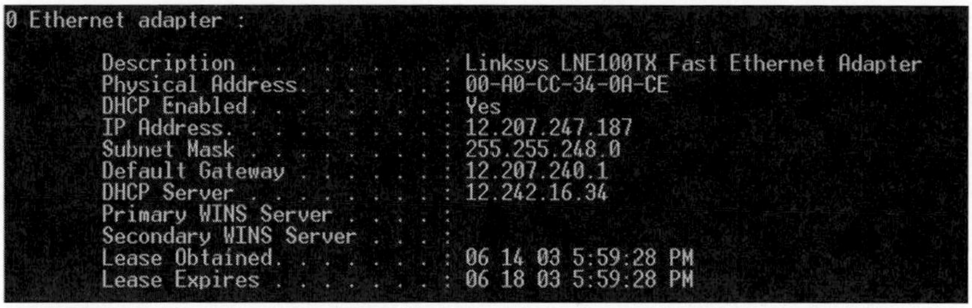

```
0 Ethernet adapter :
        Description . . . . . . . : Linksys LNE100TX Fast Ethernet Adapter
        Physical Address. . . . . : 00-A0-CC-34-0A-CE
        DHCP Enabled. . . . . . . : Yes
        IP Address. . . . . . . . : 12.207.247.187
        Subnet Mask . . . . . . . : 255.255.248.0
        Default Gateway . . . . . : 12.207.240.1
        DHCP Server . . . . . . . : 12.242.16.34
        Primary WINS Server . . . :
        Secondary WINS Server . . :
        Lease Obtained. . . . . . : 06 14 03 5:59:28 PM
        Lease Expires . . . . . . : 06 18 03 5:59:28 PM
```

Figure B-6   Ipconfig command with the "/all" parameter

Ipconfig can be used to manage and override the DHCP information on a computer through the use of several command parameters, as shown in Table B-5.

Ipconfig Parameter	Action
/all	Displays all IP configuration data
/renew_all	Renews the DHCP leases for all of a computer's network adapters
/release_all	Releases the DHCP leases for all of a computer's network adapters
/renew N	Renews only the lease for adapter N
/release N	Releases the DHCP lease for adapter N

Table B-5   Ipconfig Parameters

NOTE

Ipconfig is the official TCP/IP name for this command. However, the same command is implemented under different names on some systems. ipconfig is used by Windows OSs, but ifconfig is used on UNIX and Linux systems; and config is used on Novell NetWare systems.

nslookup

The nslookup (Name System Lookup) utility is used to display the DNS information for either an IP address or its associated host name. This command is commonly used to verify that an IP address or an Internet domain name is listed in the DNS databases.

Several nslookup sites are located on the Internet that provide you with a variety of DNS servers and options. Figure B-7 illustrates the output produced by one such site (**www.infobear.com/nslookup**).

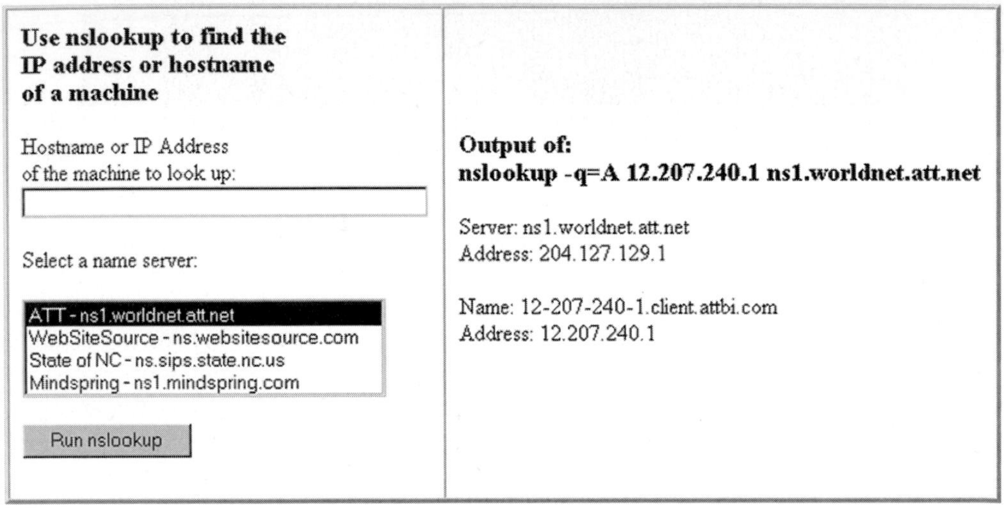

Use nslookup to find the IP address or hostname of a machine

Hostname or IP Address of the machine to look up:

[   ]

Select a name server:

ATT - ns1.worldnet.att.net
WebSiteSource - ns.websitesource.com
State of NC - ns.sips.state.nc.us
Mindspring - ns1.mindspring.com

[Run nslookup]

Output of:
nslookup -q=A 12.207.240.1 ns1.worldnet.att.net

Server: ns1.worldnet.att.net
Address: 204.127.129.1

Name: 12-207-240-1.client.attbi.com
Address: 12.207.240.1

Figure B-7 An nslookup web site

PING

Although some claim ping stands for Packet Internet Groper, most believe its name refers to its action, which is much like the ping signal used in submarine sonar systems. The *ping* utility transmits an ICMP echo request to a specific IP address. If the IP address is online and connected to the network, it should reply with an ICMP echo response. Then, ping displays the time interval between the request and the reply.

Ping is most commonly used to determine if the network adapter in one computer is able to "see" another computer on a network or the internetwork. However, some network firewalls will not pass a ping echo request, in which case no reply is received and the ping times out.

Ping also works with DNS to resolve a domain name to its IP address, which lets you enter a domain name in place of its IP address to test whether it can be reached across the network. Figure B-8 illustrates the display produced by the ping command, used to ping a domain name. Note, the ping command also displays the IP address of the domain, which it uses to transmit the echo request.

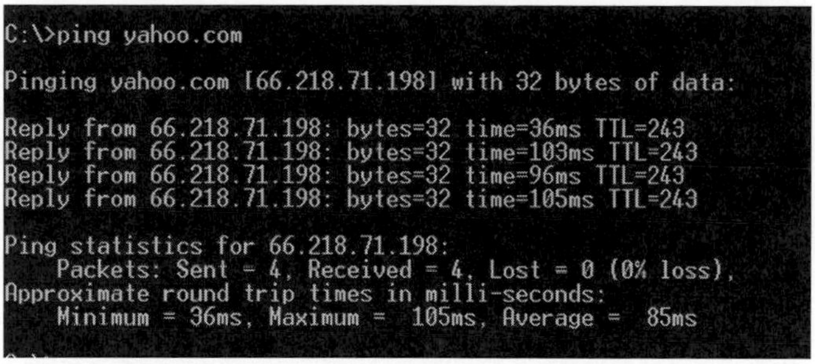

Figure B-8   Result of the ping command

Telnet

Telnet (Telecommunications Networking) is a command used to request logon services from a remote server or computer on a network or across the internetwork. The Telnet function cannot be used to create a login on a remote computer, but it can be used to log on to the remote computer on which a login exists. Figure B-9 illustrates the start of a Telnet session.

B

Figure B-9   Telnet session

TRACE

The *trace command*, which is implemented variously as trace, traceroute, and tracetracert, is used to verify or troubleshoot the routing used between a network computer and a remote computer or network gateway.

Trace identifies the routers through which an ICMP message is passed to reach the destination address or domain name entered, along with the amount of time, in milliseconds, that transpires between the hops from one router to another. Trace displays up to 30 hops along a path. Figure B-10 illustrates the output from a tracert performed on a domain name (on a Windows computer).

NOTE

Like ipconfig, different OSs use different commands to initiate a trace function. On Windows and Novell systems, the command tracert is used. On UNIX/Linux systems, the command traceroute is used.

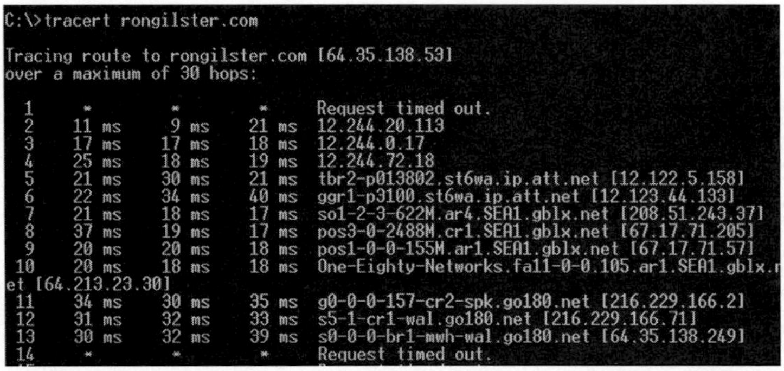

```
C:\>tracert rongilster.com

Tracing route to rongilster.com [64.35.138.53]
over a maximum of 30 hops:

  1     *        *        *     Request timed out.
  2    11 ms     9 ms    21 ms  12.244.20.113
  3    17 ms    17 ms    18 ms  12.244.0.17
  4    25 ms    18 ms    19 ms  12.244.72.18
  5    21 ms    30 ms    21 ms  tbr2-p013802.st6wa.ip.att.net [12.122.5.158]
  6    22 ms    34 ms    40 ms  ggr1-p3100.st6wa.ip.att.net [12.123.44.133]
  7    21 ms    18 ms    17 ms  so1-2-3-622M.ar4.SEA1.gblx.net [208.51.243.37]
  8    37 ms    19 ms    17 ms  pos3-0-2488M.cr1.SEA1.gblx.net [67.17.71.205]
  9    20 ms    20 ms    18 ms  pos1-0-0-155M.ar1.SEA1.gblx.net [67.17.71.57]
 10    20 ms    18 ms    18 ms  One-Eighty-Networks.fa11-0-0.105.ar1.SEA1.gblx.r
et [64.213.23.30]
 11    34 ms    30 ms    35 ms  g0-0-0-157-cr2-spk.go180.net [216.229.166.2]
 12    31 ms    32 ms    33 ms  s5-1-cr1-wal.go180.net [216.229.166.71]
 13    30 ms    32 ms    39 ms  s0-0-0-br1-mwh-wal.go180.net [64.35.138.249]
 14     *        *        *     Request timed out.
```

Figure B-10   Output of a tracert

Appendix C

Network Addressing Basics

Your home has an address, which is used by the postal service to forward and deliver mail to you and the other occupants at that address. The method used by networks to deliver messages to a destination isn't all that much different than the process used by the postal service to make sure you get your magazines, bills, letters, and junk mail.

To get your mail to you, every part of your address has either a name or a number, and in some cases, both. In the U.S., we use a ZIP code to identify numerically a region of the country, a particular state and county, and a city or part of a city. This five-digit number packs in quite a bit of information, when you think about it. And, by adding four more digits to the ZIP code, the postal service can identify not only your street, but your house or apartment as well. So, using a nine-digit numeric code, the postal service is able to identify every location to which they deliver mail. As the population of the U.S. continues to grow, it is conceivable that, at some point, one or more digits will need to be added to the ZIP code, or a new system will be devised to replace it.

A network can be likened to a city and the postal service to the cabling, network devices, and protocols that facilitate the delivery of messages to and inside the network. A network has addressable nodes, each of which is assigned a unique and specific address, just like a house or apartment. When a message is transmitted to a particular node from anywhere in the world, its address is used to locate its network (like its country), and then its particular part of the network (state and/or county), and, finally, its exact location (house). Without unique addresses for either the postal service or a network, mail or messages could not be reliably delivered to their destinations. For example, the third house from the southeast corner of Second and Main in Walla Walla, Washington, U.S.A., is a bit troublesome for efficient sorting and processing, although it does identify the location of a house—generally. Because network nodes can be moved to new locations, such as from being node 6 on port 4 on hub 4 to being node 7 on port 3 on hub 5, a node's current location might not be the most reliable address to use to deliver e-mail to a particular user.

For these reasons, both the postal service and networking engineers have devised addressing schemes that allow a destination site to be specifically identified to anyone or anything wanting to send information to a particular place, whether through the mail or across a network.

Network Addresses

On a network, the lowest level of addressing is a physical address, which is very much like the address of your house or apartment. A *physical address* uniquely identifies a network node, but unlike a house address, physical network addresses are unique among all other physical addresses in the entire global internetwork. Literally hundreds or thousands of 123 Main Street addresses can exist around the world, which have to be further identified by their city, state, and country, but a physical network address is able to stand alone as globally unique.

In networking, two levels of addresses are used to identify a particular node: physical and logical. A *physical address* is assigned to a networking device when it is manufactured. Network administrators, using a variety of assignment methods, assign logical addresses to network nodes. You take a look at physical addresses in the following section of this appendix. You learn about the two standards used for logical addresses, IPv4 and IPv6, in the later sections "Logical (IPv4) Addresses" and "The New Logical (IPv6) Addressing Scheme."

Physical Addresses

The Media Access Control (MAC) sublayer of the OSI model's data-link layer defines a structured physical addressing scheme, which conforms to specifications in the 802.3 networking standards published by the Institute of Electrical and Electronics Engineers (IEEE). Using this standard, every addressable networking device is assigned a globally unique address—a MAC address— by its manufacturer. MAC addresses are embedded in the electronics of networking devices when each device is manufactured. MAC addresses, or physical addresses, are globally unique and serve as a permanent identification for each networking device. In many ways, a MAC address is much like a student ID number, Social Security number, or other permanently assigned ID number, which is used to identify you specifically.

In the IEEE 802 specifications, a MAC address is defined to have two parts: a manufacturer's code and a serialized device ID code (see Figure C-1). As illustrated in Figure C-1, a 48-bit MAC address is represented as six two-character hexadecimal elements. The first three two-character elements are the manufacturer's ID number, which is assigned to the manufacturer by the IEEE. Table C-1 lists some of the more common manufacturer's ID codes. The remaining three two-character elements are the unique device ID number assigned to the device when it is manufactured.

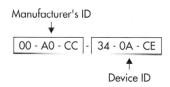

Figure C-1   A MAC, or physical address, is made up of two parts: the manufacturer's ID number and a unique device ID number.

NOTE

Table C-1 is far from an all-inclusive list. In fact, many manufacturers have several ID codes assigned. To see the entire list of manufacturer's ID codes, visit: http://standards .ieee.org/regauth/oui/index.shtml.

C

ID Code	Manufacturer
00 00 0C	Cisco Systems
00 00 1D	Cabletron
00 00 94	Asante
00 55 00	Intel
00 60 C5	3Com
00 80 A3	Lantronix
00 80 C7	Xircom
00 80 C8	D-Link
08 00 07	Apple
08 00 09	Hewlett Packard
10 00 5A	IBM

Table C-1 MAC Address Manufacturer ID Codes

Hexadecimal Numbers

The hexadecimal number system is based on powers of 16, and its counting digits range 0–F. Table C-2 lists the hexadecimal digits and their decimal value equivalents.

Hexadecimal Digit	Decimal Value	Hexadecimal Digit	Decimal Value
0	1	8	8
1	1	9	9
2	2	A	10
3	3	B	11
4	4	C	12
5	5	D	13
6	6	E	14
7	7	F	15

Table C-2 Hexadecimal Digits and Their Decimal Value Equivalents

The best way to convert a decimal number into a hexadecimal number or from hex to decimal is to use a calculator, such as the Windows Calculator in Scientific view (see Figure C-2).

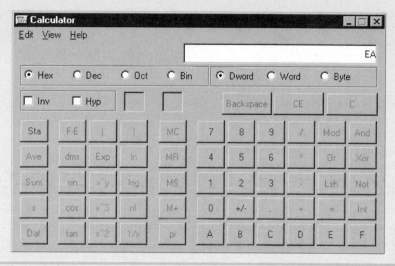

Figure C-2   The Windows Calculator in Scientific view can be used to convert between different number systems, including decimal to hexadecimal.

However, although the need to convert between decimal and hexadecimal rarely comes up, if you need to covert between decimal and hexadecimal, use the following process:

1. Divide the decimal number by 16 (the base value of hexadecimal) and write down the remainder.

2. Divide the answer from Step 1 by 16 and write down the remainder to the left of the previous remainder.

3. Repeat Step 2 until the remainder is less than 16.

For example, to convert the decimal number 234 to hexadecimal:

1. Divide 234 by 16 to obtain the result 14 with a remainder of 10.

   The remainder of 10 presents us with a bit of a challenge. How do we write 10 as a single digit? In hexadecimal notation, because the single-digit values are 0–15, the letters *A, B, C, D, E,* and *F* are used to represent the hexadecimal equivalents of the decimal values 10, 11, 12, 13, 14, and 15, respectively. So, a remainder of 10 is recorded as the digit *A*.

2. Now divide 14 by 16, which results in 0 and a remainder of 14, which is recorded as an *E* in hexadecimal.

   The result of converting the decimal value 234 to hexadecimal is the hexadecimal value EA.

C

Try This!

From the following list, find your operating system (OS), and then follow the subsequent steps to find and display the MAC address of your computer:

- **Windows 98, Windows 98 SE, or Windows Me**   Click the Start button and open the Run option. In the text box on the Run function display, enter the command **winipcfg** and click OK. The MAC address is included in the displayed information as the "Adapter Address."

NOTE
If the first two digits of the MAC address are 44, the adapter shown is a dial-up adapter. Use the drop-down box to choose your network adapter.

- **Windows NT 4.0, Windows 2000, or Windows XP**   Click Start. Choose the Run option, enter the command **cmd** in the Run function's text box, and click OK to open a command prompt window. At the command prompt, enter the command **ipconfig /all** to display the configuration data for all the network adapters for your computer. The MAC address for each adapter is displayed as the Physical Address. The screen to the right shows an example of the information displayed by the ipconfig command:

- **Unix or Linux**   At a command prompt, enter the command **ifconfig –a** to display the network configuration for each adapter for the computer. The MAC address is displayed on the first line for each adapter as the HWAddr.

- **Macintosh OS before version 10.2**   From the Apple menu, select System Preferences, and then select Network. Choose Show: Built-In Ethernet from the pull-down list. Choose the TCP/IP tab to display the configuration data. The MAC address is displayed as the Ethernet Address.

- **Macintosh OS version 10.2 and newer**   From the Apple menu, select About This Mac. Choose More Info and click the System Profile tab. Included in the information shown for Network Overview: Built-In is the MAC address, listed as the Ethernet Address.

Typically, MAC addresses are assigned to network adapters or network interface cards (NICs) that connect directly to a network's media in an Ethernet, Token Ring, or 802.11 wireless network.

In case you're worried about the networking world running out of MAC addresses, consider that most of the larger manufacturers have more than one ID number assigned and, within each manufacturer's ID number, 16,777,215 device IDs can be assigned to networking devices. Given that the first six characters are fixed (as the manufacturer's ID), at the present time, approximately 281 million device IDs or MAC addresses can be potentially assigned.

Logical (IPv4) Addresses

A *logical address* differs from a physical address in that a logical address is temporarily assigned (in comparison to the permanence of a MAC address) and usually has some relationship to the logical addresses assigned to other network nodes in its vicinity. The relationship among logical addresses is generally derived from the hierarchical structure of networks. The nodes of Network A are assigned from a block of addresses that have been set aside for the use by that network. So, network A's nodes are logically (which can mean arbitrarily, in many cases) assigned addresses that relate to Network A. Figure C-3 illustrates the logical and hierarchical relationship of network addresses.

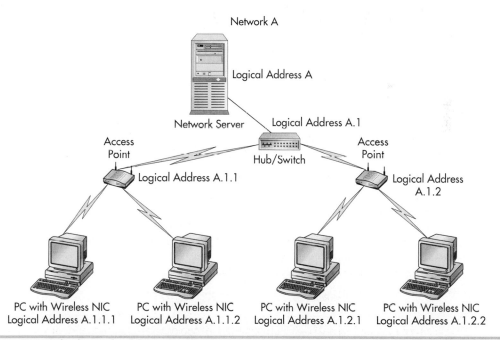

Figure C-3   The logical address assignments on a wireless base station set (BSS) network

The logical addresses assigned to the devices in Network *A* in Figure C-3 reflect how one device relates to another. Notice how the hub or switch connected to the network server is assigned the logical address A.1. If another hub or switch were installed on this network and connected to the server (*A*), it would likely be assigned the logical address A.2. The wireless access points connecting to the network through logical address A.1 are assigned logical addresses A.1.1 and A.1.2, and so on down through the PC connecting to the access points.

Where the true logical nature of this type of addressing scheme shows up is in a situation where the PC currently assigned logical address A.1.1.1 is moved, so it now connects to the network through the access point with the address A.1.2 and is assigned the address of A.1.2.3. The PC's MAC address (or rather the MAC address of the PC's NIC) remains constant, but the station is assigned a new logical address.

The most commonly used logical addressing scheme is the one defined by the Internet Protocol (IP), which is the primary Layer 3 protocol of the TCP/IP protocol suite. IP addresses have been in use on internetworks and the Internet from their beginnings. Before connecting a LAN to the Internet became common, LANs were able to function internally using only MAC addresses. However, as LANs began to connect to WANs and the Internet, many adopted the TCP/IP protocol suite for their native network protocols. This adoption allowed them to use IP addresses for LAN nodes and to provide a seamless addressing scheme across an entire internetwork.

IPv4 Address Structure

In the early days of the Internet, when it became apparent that some form of structure and an assignment procedure were needed to allocate IP addresses to the various organizations and companies wanting them, IP addresses were divided into address classes. Initially, the assignment process allocated IP addresses according to the quantity of IP addresses an organization might need, given its size and the extent of its networks.

The address allocation process and the number of addresses in each address class went through several iterations before the current and most commonly used (at press time) IP address standard, IP version 4 or IPv4, was adopted.

An *IPv4* address consists of 32 bits arranged into four 8-bit groupings. Each of the 8-bit groups is called an *octet*, which refers to its 8 bits. While network devices and computers work with the binary data that defines an IP address, humans can deal far more easily with the decimal value represented in each octet. Each octet is able to represent in binary the decimal values 0–255. The address on the top line of Figure C-4 illustrates the makeup of an IPv4 address, with its four octets separated by periods or dots. This form of expressing a network address is called a *dot-delimited format*.

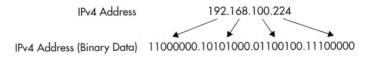

IPv4 Address   192.168.100.224

IPv4 Address (Binary Data)   11000000.10101000.01100100.11100000

Figure C-4   The dot-delimited and binary data formats of an IPv4 network address

Binary Numbers

The binary number system consists of only two digital values: 1 (one) and 0 (zero). Binary values represent various powers of 2. For example, 2^3 is 8, 2^{10} is 1,024, and each position of a binary number represents an increasing power of two, reading right to left, as follows:

Binary number values:	2^7	2^6	2^5	2^4	2^3	2^2	2^1	2^0
Decimal number equivalent:	128	64	32	16	8	4	2	1

So, in an 8-bit binary number, such as 01010101, the positions with ones indicate the value of that column is added into the result and a zero is used as a placeholder for those columns not contributing value to the result. In this number, the result is determined in this way:

0 times 2^7 (128) = 0
1 times 2^6 (64) = 64
0 times 2^5 (32) = 0
1 times 2^4 (16) = 16
0 times 2^3 (8) = 0
1 times 2^2 (4) = 4
0 times 2^1 (2) = 0
1 times 2^0 (1) = 1

Adding these values together, the decimal value being represented is 85.

NOTE

If this seems like a strange way to represent a small number (or any number), remember, a computer can only hold electrical charges to represent zeros and ones.

C

IPv4 addresses contain two parts: a network ID and a host ID, as shown in Figure C-5. Exactly how much of an IPv4 address is allocated to a network ID or a host ID depends on the address class of the address (IPv4 address classes are discussed in the sections following this discussion). The *network ID* is generally associated with the device that serves as the gateway to a larger network, such as the Internet. A *host device* is any addressable node connected within a network, such as a desktop PC. Hosts are addressed inside of networks, and networks are addressable across the internetwork. In the example shown in the previous Figure C-3, the server (address *A*) could be configured as the device associated with the network ID, and all the other devices "behind" it would be associated with host IDs.

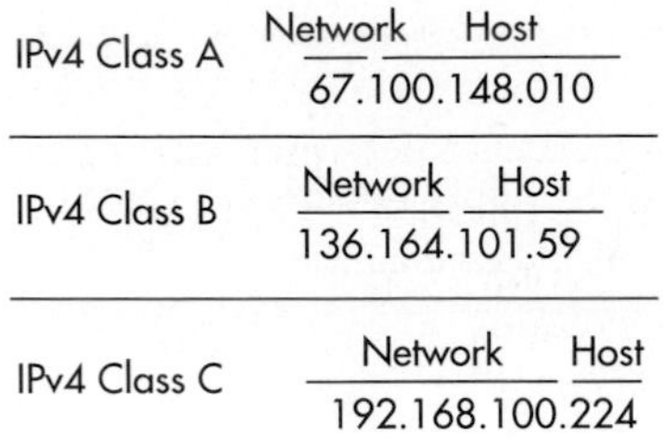

Figure C-5 IPv4 addresses contain a network ID and a host ID, regardless of the address class.

IP Address Classes

Back in the 1970s, when the early forms of Internet routing were being implemented and the Internet was growing popular, the need to control the allocation of Internet (IP) addresses became quickly apparent. The allocation scheme devised, and one still in use for IPv4 addresses today, divided the available IP addresses into three primary address classes, each intended to provide sufficient numbers of IP addresses to serve the needs of large corporations, medium corporations, and small companies, respectively. In addition, smaller blocks were set aside to accommodate the special needs of multicasting, and research and development. The three primary address classes were designated as Class *A*, Class *B*, and Class *C*. The additional two special purpose classes were designated as Class *D* and Class *E*.

Class *A* addresses were designated for large corporations that convinced the issuing authority that they should be allocated large blocks of IP addresses, such as AT&T, IBM, General Electric, and the like. Because there are fewer large corporations, relatively fewer Class *A* address blocks exist. Class *B* addresses were allotted to mid-sized organizations that believed they needed large blocks of IP addresses, but couldn't justify the need for as many as the larger corporations. Because more medium-sized companies exist than large corporations, more Class *B* blocks are available than Class *A* blocks. Class *C* addresses were initially treated as the minimum allocation for smaller organizations that needed only a relatively few addresses. And, because a large number of smaller companies exist, there are more Class *C* address blocks than either Class *A* or Class *B*.

Class A Addresses   A Class *A* IPv4 address is identified in two ways: one by routers and computers, and the other by humans, respectively:

- **The high-order bit is set to zero**   The first bit (the high-order bit) of the first (leftmost) octet is set to 0, and the bit pattern of a Class *A* address is 0*nnnnnnn.nnnnnnnn.nnnnnnnn .nnnnnnnn* (where 0 is the high-order bit and *n* represents the binary values of the other bits in the IP address).

- **The value in the first octet is 0–127**   The binary value range of the first octet in a Class A address is 00000000 to 01111111.

Like all IP addresses, Class *A* addresses include network ID and host ID components. The network ID uses the rightmost seven bits of the first octet (remember, the class ID bit occupies the first [leftmost] bit). The remaining three octets (24 bits) in a Class *A* address are used for the host ID. Because of this arrangement, only 127 Class *A* network IDs are available, but each network ID can address 16,777,214 host IDs.

Table C-3 summarizes the number of network IDs and host IDs available in the three primary address classes.

IP Address Class	Networks	Hosts
A	126	16,777,214
B	16,384	65,532
C	2,097,152	254

Table C-3   IPv4 Address Classes

NOTE

Class *D* and *E* addresses are not assigned, but are held for special purposes. Also, no unassigned Class *A* or Class *B* address blocks are available for allocation, which is the primary reason for the development of IP version 6 (IPv6) (see the section "The New Logical (IPv6) Addressing Scheme").

The structure of a Class A IPv4 address is shown in Figure C-6. In this figure, the 0 is the class ID bit; *n* represents the bits used, in addition to the class ID bit, for the network ID; and *h* represents the bits used for the host ID.

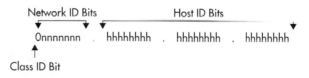

Figure C-6   IPv4 Class A address structure

Class B Addresses   In a Class *B* IPv4 address, the first two bits are used to identify the IP address class. They are used as the class ID bits and always contain the binary value 10. Class *B* addresses are represented by the values 128–191 in the first octet, or the lowest and highest binary values that can be represented in 8 bits, when the first two bits are always 10. The value 128 is expressed in binary as 10000000, and the value 191 is expressed in binary as 10111111.

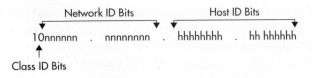

Figure C-7   IPv4 Class *B* address structure

As shown in Figure C-7, Class *B* addresses use 2 bits for the class ID, 14 bits for the network ID, and 16 bits for the host ID, which yields addressability for 16,384 network IDs and 65,532 host IDs per network (see the previous Table C-3).

Class C Addresses   A IPv4 Class *C* address, as you can probably guess, uses 3 bits for its class ID, which is always the binary value 110 and the values 192–223 in the first octet. Class C addresses use 24 bits to identify the network ID (including the class ID bits) and 8 bits to identify the host ID (see Figure C-8). The binary values of the first octet of a Class *C* address range 11000000–11011111.

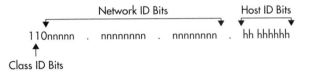

Figure C-8   IPv4 Class *C* address structure

As shown in the previous Table C-3, a IPv4 Class *C* address block is capable of addressing 2,097,152 network IDs and 254 host IDs on each network.

Class D Addresses   Class *D* IPv4 addresses are reserved for multicast uses. A multicast transmits data from one source to a list of subscribers' IP addresses, such as on a pay-per-view event over the Internet. Class *D* addresses use four class ID bits at the beginning of the first octet, which are always set to 1110. The first octet of a Class *D* address has a range of 224–247, which is represented in binary as 111000000 to 11101111.

Class *D* addresses are not divided into network and host IDs. Only the first 4 bits are used to identify the address as a Class *D* address, and the remaining 28 bits are used for a multicast address. Figure C-9 illustrates the structure of a Class *D* IPv4 address.

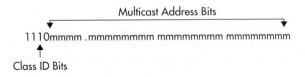

Figure C-9   IPv4 Class *D* address structure

Class E Addresses   Class *E* IPv4 addresses are reserved for research and experimental use. A Class *E* address also uses the first 4 bits of the first octet for its class ID, which always contains the binary value 1111. The first octet of a Class *E* address is a value in the range of 248–255, which is represented in binary as 11110000–11111111.

IP Address Summary   Table C-4 summarizes the structure and range of the IPv4 address classes.

IPv4 Class	Class ID Bits	First IP Address	Last IP Address
A	0xxx	0.0.0.0	127.255.255.255
B	10xx	128.0.0.0	191.255.255.255
C	110x	192.0.0.0	223.255.255.255
D	1110	224.0.0.0	239.255.255.255
E	1111	240.0.0.0	255.255.255.255

Table C-4   IPv4 Address Class ID Bits and Address Ranges

NOTE

As shown in Table C-4, IPv4 addresses are shown using a dot-delimited format, with a period (dot) used to separate each octet, which is expressed as a decimal value.

Reserved and Special-Purpose Addresses

In addition to IPv4 Class *D* and Class *E* addresses, some address ranges have been set aside from Classes *A*, *B*, and *C* for specific uses or purposes. These addresses, which were included in the ranges listed earlier in Tables C-3 and C-4, reduce the number available for assignment in each class. The following subsections discuss these specific uses or special purposes.

Zero Addresses   The IPv4 Class A address range that begins with 0.0.0.0 and ends with 0.255.255.255 is not technically available for use over the Internet. *Zero addresses*, which is what this range of addresses is commonly called, are used by LAN servers to broadcast messages to all the nodes on the LAN.

Broadcast messages aren't transmitted to a particular destination, but to every node on a network. If broadcast messages were allowed on the Internet, they would likely tie up the Internet with useless traffic. For this reason, Internet routers ignore all messages with a zero destination address.

C

IP Loopback Addresses Another IPv4 address range unavailable as network or host addresses is the range 127.0.0.0–127.255.255.255. Although IPv4 reserves only the single address 127.0.0.1 as the loopback address, the entire range is set aside for loopback usage. Back when it was believed that we would never run out of IP addresses, it was easier to set aside the entire 127.*x.x.x* block for loopback purposes, and the routers and NICs were configured accordingly. At this point, leaving this block reserved continues to be easier than trying to reconfigure every router and NIC in use.

The *loopback address* provides a testing mechanism for network adapters and NICs. A computer's network adapter won't forward a message addressed to 127.0.0.1 or any other loopback address to the network. Instead, these messages are returned to the sending application to complete a test on the network adapter.

NOTE

While IPv4 assumes any IP address with a network ID of 127 is a loopback address, the issue of the addresses lost for other uses is solved in IPv6, which assigns only the address 0:0:0:0:0:0:0:1 as the loopback address. For more information on IPv6, see the section "The New Logical (IPv6) Addressing Scheme."

Private Addresses Within the IPv4 specification, the need to address nodes on a LAN without routing messages across the Internet is addressed by the allocation of private addresses. For the most part, IPv4 addresses are public addresses, except, of course, for those reserved for other purposes. A *public IP address* is a routable address that can be transmitted across an internetwork, such as the Internet. A *private address* has been identified for use only within a LAN, and gateway routers don't forward private addresses to the Internet.

A range of IPv4 addresses has been set aside from each of the primary three address classes to provide private network addresses for TCP/IP LANs that are intranets, don't connect to the Internet, or implement network address translation (NAT) when transmitting to the Internet. Table C-5 lists the address ranges reserved for private networks.

IPv4 Address Class	Private Address Range
A	10.0.0.0–10.255.255.255
B	172.16.0.0–172.31.255.255
C	192.168.0.0–192.168.255.255

Table C-5 IPv4 Private Address Ranges

No hard and fast rules exist about which of the private address blocks an internal network should use. The decision typically boils down to two criteria: the number of addresses required and the preferences of the network administrators. Essentially, any of the available private address ranges may be used on any network.

Special Addresses Summary   Table C-6 reflects the net effect of the reserved or set-aside IPv4 addresses on the number truly available for use on a network within each address class.

IPv4 Class	Overall Range	Total Networks Defined	Reserved Range(s)	Net Networks Available
A	0.0.0.0–127.255.255.255	126	0.0.0.0–0.255.255.255 10.0.0.0–10.255.255.255 127.0.0.0–127.255.255.255	123
B	128.0.0.0–191.255.255.255	16,384	171.16.0.0–171.31.255.255	16,368
C	192.0.0.0–223.255.255.255	2,097,152	192.168.0.0–192.168.255.255	2,096,896

Table C-6   Summary of IPv4 Address Classes and Reserved Addresses

Routing and Subnet Masks

A *subnet mask* is the mechanism used to extract and identify the network ID portion of an IPv4 address. When a router or switch is determining to which of its interface ports a message should be forwarded, it compares the network ID portion of the destination address to the entries in its routing table to make this determination.

NOTE
Subnetting is covered in the section "Subnets and Supernets."

The Role of Boolean Algebra
The use of a subnet mask applies *Boolean algebra*, which uses three logical operators, OR, AND, and NOT, to determine a comparative result. Although Boolean algebra is more generally associated with true and false conditions, it can also be adapted to filter binary bits to extract a binary result in which true is represented with a 1 and false with a 0.

Subnet masks apply the AND operator of Boolean algebra in a process called *ANDing*, which is the process used to combine two binary number sets. Basic principles are in use when Boolean ANDing is used in conjunction with a subnet mask:

1 AND 1 = 1
1 AND 0 = 0
0 AND 1 = 0
0 AND 0 = 0

In Boolean algebra, only a true and a true can yield a true. Any other combination of true and false yields only a false, as shown in the preceding example. In terms of binary numbers, where one represents true and zero represents false, only a one and a one yields a one. Every other combination of ones and zeros or zeros and zeros always results in a zero.

Applying a Subnet Mask

A subnet mask has the same 32-bit, four-octet format as any IPv4 address, and each of the three primary IPv4 address classes has a default subnet mask (see Table C-7).

IPv4 Address Class	Default Subnet Mask
A	255.0.0.0
B	255.255.0.0
C	255.255.255.0

Table C-7 Default Subnet Masks for IPv4 Address Classes

Notice the number 255 is placed only in the octets of the mask that match the positions occupied by the network ID in the standard specification of IPv4 address classes.

Here's how the subnet mask works.

To determine the network ID in the Class *B* address of 191.70.55.130, the default subnet mask for Class *B* addresses (255.255.0.0) is combined with the IP address using the Boolean ANDing operator:

```
191        70        55        130        IP address (decimal)
10111111   10000110  00110111  10000010   IP address (binary)
255        255       0         0          Subnet mask (decimal)
11111111   11111111  00000000  00000000   Subnet mask (binary)
191        70        0         0          Result (decimal)
10111111   10000110  00000000  00000000   Result (binary)
```

IPv4 Address	Subnet Mask	Result
1	1	1
0	1	0
1	1	1
1	1	1
1	1	1
1	1	1
1	1	1
1	1	1

Table C-8   The ANDing Operation of the First Octet

Tables C-8 and C-9 detail the ANDing operation performed on the first and third octets, respectively.

IPv4 Address	Subnet Mask	Result
0	0	0
0	0	0
1	0	0
1	0	0
0	0	0
1	0	0
1	0	0
1	0	0

Table C-9   The ANDing Operation of the Third Octet

As shown in the upcoming Table C-10, the effect of applying the default subnet mask to this Class *B* address was to zero out the parts of the IP address that represent the host, leaving only the network ID portion of the address, which was 191.70.0.0. This result can now be used by a router or switch to determine to which of its interface ports this message should be forwarded by looking up the network ID in its routing or bridging table.

IPv4 Classless Interdomain Routing

In some networking situations, the classful (as defined by the IPv4 class ID bits) limitation on the number of bits used to identify the network address may not be adequate as networks expand and become segmented into many smaller networks. This segmentation has become necessary as we continue to run out of IPv4 address blocks.

To satisfy the need to identify more networks within the limited IPv4 address space, Classless Interdomain Routing (CIDR—pronounced either "cedar" or "cider," depending on whom you ask) was developed in the early 1990s. The original intent behind CIDR, which is also called *supernetting*, was to reduce the number of routing-table entries on Internet backbone routers, especially on Class *C* networks. Reducing the number of routing table entries is beneficial because doing so reduces the amount of bandwidth that must be dedicated to maintaining the routing table entries, as well as the time required to look up an address in the routing table. CIDR allows *route aggregation*, or the capability to represent a block of Class *C* IPv4 networks in a single routing table entry. Essentially, *CIDR* replaces the classful limitations of IPv4 addressing with a network prefix designation that indicates the number of bits used to identify the network ID portion of an IPv4 address. As currently defined and implemented, CIDR defines network prefixes from 13 to 27 bits, which allows blocks of IPv4 addresses to be assigned to networks as small as 32 hosts or as large as 524,288 hosts. For example, CIDR allows a Class *C* address to define a network ID using fewer or more than the classful 24 bits defined in the IPv4 standards. Using CIDR is place of the legacy classful addressing enables a network administrator to organize IP address assignments to meet an organization's specific requirements.

A CIDR address includes the standard 32-bit IPv4 address and adds a network prefix designator (added to the end of the address), which indicates how many bits are used for the network ID, or what is also called the *network prefix*. For example, in the CIDR address 190.254.57.1 /17, the /17 indicates the first 17 bits are used to identify the unique network, leaving the remaining bits to identify the specific host.

What the network prefix indicates specifically is how many one bits (from left to right) should be used in the subnet mask applied to the IP address to extract the network ID. In the previous example, where the network prefix was /17, the first 17 bits of the subnet mask are set to ones and the remaining 15 bits are set to zeros. The result, in binary, is

```
11111111.11111111.10000000.0000000
```

The decimal value for this subnet mask is 255.255.128.0. CIDR provides one ease-of-use benefit, in that the network administrator doesn't need to precalculate the subnet mask. All that's required is to indicate the number of bits used in the network ID.

The number of bits indicated in the network prefix depends on the number of hosts the network requires. Table C-10 lists the number of hosts that can be addressed for each of the available CIDR network prefix values and the subnet mask that is the equivalent of each network prefix.

CIDR Prefix	Host Addresses	Equivalent Subnet Mask
/27	32	255.255.255.224
/26	64	255.255.255.192
/25	128	255.255.255.128
/24	256	255.255.255.0
/23	512	255.255.254.0
/22	1,024	255.255.252.0
/21	2,048	255.255.248.0
/20	4,096	255.255.240.0
/19	8,192	255.255.224.0
/18	16,384	255.255.192.0
/17	32,768	255.255.128.0
/16	65,536	255.255.0.0
/15	131,072 hosts	255.254.0.0
/14	262,144 hosts	255.252.0.0
/13	524,288 hosts	255.248.0.0

Table C-10   CIDR Network Prefixes, Numbers of Host Addresses, and Subnet Masks

C

The New Logical (IPv6) Addressing Scheme

Even with the foresight of the founding fathers of the Internet, the world has begun to outgrow the number of available IPv4 addresses that can be assigned, to the point where even some small blocks of IPv4 addresses are becoming hard to get. To avoid an addressing crisis and to facilitate the continued growth of the Internet, the Internet Engineering Task Force (IETF) has designed a new version of the Internet Protocol (IP), IPv6, to replace the current version, the 20-year-old IPv4.

IPv6 defines IP addresses using a 128-bit number that is expressed using *couplets* (two-byte [16 bit] sets) separated with colon, for example:

```
21DB:01D3:0A02:2FCB:07AC:02FF:AE23:9D59
```

The IPv6 address structure potentially allows for as many as 340,282,366,920,938,463,463,374, 607,431,768,211,456 individual addresses, which should be sufficient to handle at least the near-term growth of the Internet. However, we also thought that about the IPv4 addresses at one time.

IPv4 Deficiencies

When IPv4 was first implemented in 1981, it was considered revolutionary, and it has provided the foundation for the growth of networking and especially the Internet. However, the developers of IPv4 were unable to anticipate a number of events that are rapidly making it obsolete, including

- **The rapid growth of the Internet**   The Internet and the need for IP addresses have grown exponentially over the past 10 years. With IP addresses becoming scarce, private addresses and the use of NAT have allowed networks to continue to expand internally. However, private addressing and NAT do not support standards-based network security or the proper mapping of some higher layers (meaning OSI layers 4–7) protocols, which can cause address translation problems when two LANs using private addressing try to connect.

- **The growth of routing tables**   Although you haven't read about routing and routing tables to this point, note that the way IPv4 addresses were allocated to flat networks in the past, and the way they are used to represent hierarchical networks today, has caused the routing tables of the Internet's backbone routers to commonly hold over 350,000 routing entries. Considering that routing tables are held in a router's memory and must be searched for each message segment being forwarded, the size, power, and configuration of global Internet routers has, at best, been a moving target.

- **Classful addressing**   For the most part, IPv4 implementations are configured either manually or using an automatic configuration scheme, such as the Dynamic Host Configuration Protocol (DHCP), and a class-based address assignment scheme for even private addresses, which can be a complex and arduous task for a network administrator.

- **Security concerns**   Improved security on the Internet is needed to protect more and more private communications and transactions being transmitted over the public network. Under IPv4, the Internet Protocol security (IPSec) services are optional and have been implemented with a variety of proprietary versions, which can vary in effectiveness.

What Happened to IPv5?

When it was originally conceived in 1994, what is now IPv6 was called IPng, which stood for Internet Protocol Next Generation. *IPng* added many new features to IPv4, including the capability to address more networks and hosts, but one of the features retained was the version field inside the IP packet format. This 8-bit field contains the number 4 for IPv4 packets. One would think, with the newer version of IP, the number 5 would indicate IPng packets.

Back in the 1970s, however, the Internet Stream Protocol (ST), which was used for experiments to transmit voice and video packets, and its later version (ST2) were assigned the protocol version code of 5. Thus, when it came time to implement IPng, the next number available was 6, and so IPng became IPv6. It's as simple as that.

IPv6 Solutions

IETF devised IPv6 to address the problems listed in the preceding bulleted list. The primary solutions offered by IPv6 include

- **The rapid growth of the Internet**   IPv6 defines a 128-bit address space, which offers the potential for 3.4×10^{38} individual addresses. In practice, however, some of these addresses will be consumed to address network segments within larger networks.

- **The growth of routing tables**   IPv6 defines a classless addressing structure, which achieves many of the same benefits, in terms of the number of routing entries required, realized in the CIDR classless structure. In addition, IPv6 defines only two individual addresses for special purposes: 0:0:0:0:0:0:0:0 (reserved for protocol usage) and 0:0:0:0:0:0:0:1 (loopback testing), which avoids setting aside large blocks of reserved addresses for singular purposes.

- **Security concerns**   IPv6 implements IPSec along with Encapsulating Security Payload (ESP) and Authentication Header (AH), which support security and privacy through the application of encryption and tunneling across the Internet.

IPv6 Address Types

A functionally oriented address type is one that can be structured specifically to support a particular type of transmission or communication. Although IPv6 does not define address classes, it does define three functionally oriented address types.

- **Multicast**   *Multicast addresses* perform the same function in IPv6 as they did in IPv4, which is to transmit a single message stream from one source to a preset list of destination addresses.

- **Unicast**   A *unicast address* is essentially a standard IP address. A *unicast transmission* is transmitted from a single source to a single destination address.

- **Anycast**   *Anycast* defines both an addressing scheme and a routing method. The anycast addressing scheme identifies a one-to-many association between each destination and multiple hosts. However, in any transmission only one of the related hosts is sent information. Anycast routing forwards messages to the nearest router.

Subnets and Supernets

One of the methods developed to work around the shortage of IPv4 addresses is the use of *subnetworks*, which are logical subdivisions of larger networks divided into addressable smaller networks. A subnetwork is often confused with a network segment, or the physical segmentation of a network created by the installation of a LAN switch, bridge, or router. While a network segment can be accessed in much the same way as a subnet, a *subnet* is strictly a logical addressing technique that, typically, doesn't require changes in the topology of a network.

NOTE

In networking parlance, a *host* is the same as a node, which is generally a computer connected to the network. However, a host could also be a hub, a printer, or another network-connected device.

Subnetting a network enables the network administrators to fit the structure of the network to that of the organization and to simplify the network's routing and switching. However, the primary benefits of subnetting a network are the creation of smaller broadcast domains and the creation of individually addressed subnetworks that can be managed separately.

NOTE

A *broadcast domain* is all or a subdivision of a network on which all nodes receive all broadcast messages, which are transmitted without a specific destination address.

Every network or subnet has two specified addresses: a network address and a broadcast address. The *network address* represents the addressable address for a network or subnet. The *broadcast address* is used to transmit messages to every host on a network or subnet.

Although technically it can be done, there is little reason to subnet a Class *A* address. Subnetting is much more common with Class *B* and Class *C* networks. Table C-11 and Table C-12 list the number of subnets and hosts in each subnet for the number of bits borrowed for the subnetwork ID for Class *B* and Class *C*, respectively.

A trade-off is definitely to be made between the number of subnetworks (subnets) possible and the number of hosts that can be addressed in each subnet after bits are shifted from one to the other.

NOTE

The numbers included in Tables C-11 and C-12 for subnets are reduced by the two required addresses that must be set aside for network and broadcast addresses. Also, at least 2 bits must be reserved for host addresses.

Reasons to Subnet a Network

Before subnetting was developed, the only means available to logically divide an IPv4 network was through classful addressing assignments. However, as discussed in the section on CIDR (see the previous section "IPv4 Classless Interdomain Routing"), the need to extend network addressing emerged as available IPv4 addresses became scarce.

Bits Used	Subnet Mask	Subnets	Hosts
2	255.255.192.0	2	16,382
3	255.255.224.0	6	8,190
4	255.255.240.0	14	4,094
5	255.255.248.0	30	2,046
6	255.255.252.0	62	1,022
7	255.255.254.0	126	510
8	255.255.255.0	254	254
9	255.255.255.128	510	126
10	255.255.255.192	1,022	62
11	255.255.255.224	2,046	30
12	255.255.255.240	4,094	14
13	255.255.255.248	8,190	6
14	255.255.255.252	16,382	2

Table C-11 Class B Subnets

Bits Used	Subnet Mask	Subnets	Hosts
2	255.255.255.192	2	62
3	255.255.255.224	6	30
4	255.255.255.240	14	14
5	255.255.255.248	30	6
6	255.255.255.252	62	2

Table C-12 Class C Subnets

C

Subnetting can be used in a number of situations (besides extending the usability of an IPv4 address block), including

- **Network administration** The creation of separate logical address ranges allows for better and easier monitoring and management of the network.

- **Mixed network technologies** Subnetting can be used to create a logical separation between hosts on an Ethernet network and hosts on a Token Ring network.

- **Performance** On shared media networks, such as Ethernet, all hosts in the same broadcast domain share the bandwidth of the medium and commonly suffer from frequent transmission collisions. Dividing the network into smaller subnets creates smaller collision domains, which yields better performance on the network as a whole.

- **Improved security** Subnetting increases the security level between subnets, a benefit that extends to the entire network.

Extended Network Addressing

The underlying concept of subnetting is the use of an extended network address. An *extended network address*, which includes a network ID and a subnet number, can be applied to individual computers and other network devices. The extended network address provides for the two-level addressing supported on virtually every implementation of IPv4. With the addition of the host ID, a three-level addressing scheme is created.

To illustrate how subnetting works in practice, consider the following example:

High Tech College (HTC) is planning the installation of a LAN in its main building. The LAN is to support nearly all the college's administrative offices, student services areas, library, and six lecture halls. The financial aid office and the human resources office, which both store personal financial and other confidential data, want their desktop computers to be restricted from all other parts of the network. HTC has been allocated a single Class *C* network address block, which, by default, provides for 254 peer hosts on the network that can communicate directly with each other.

A Class *C* address uses 24 bits to address the network and 8 bits to address each host. However, to create subnets for (at least) the financial aid and human resources offices, a subnet number must be added to the network address. A 1-bit subnet number allows the addressing of two subnets.

To direct traffic specifically to one of the two subnets, an additional 1 bit must be added to the default subnet mask. Where the default subnet mask for a Class *C* network is 255.255.255.0, with an additional bit added in the 25th position, two subnets can be identified, subnet 0 and subnet 1, with the subnet masks of 255.255.255.0 and 255.255.255.128, respectively.

However, if all the other areas of HTC's main building are also to be subnetted, additional bits must be added to the subnet mask to allow for the additional subnets. HTC's network administrator wants to allow for up to eight subnets, which requires the use of 3 bits in the subnet number (for subnets 0 through 7) and subnet masks ranging 255.255.255.0–255.255.255.224. By assigning 3 of the 8 host ID bits to the subnet number, 5 bits remain for the host ID within each subnet, allowing for potentially 31 hosts per subnet.

The Class *C* address to be used is 204.200.115.0. Table C-13 shows the resulting extended network addresses and the host addresses within each subnet.

Network address (24 bits)	Subnet Number (3 bits)	Extended Network Address	Hosts
204.200.115.0	0	204.200.115.0	204.200.115.1–204.200.115.31
	1	204.200.115.32	204.200.115.33–204.200.115.63
	2	204.200.115.64	204.200.115.65–204.200.115.95
	3	204.200.115.96	204.200.115.97–204.200.115.127
	4	204.200.115.128	204.200.115.129–204.200.115.159
	5	204.200.115.160	204.200.115.161–204.200.115.191
	6	204.200.115.192	204.200.115.193–204.200.115.223
	7	204.200.115.224	204.200.115.225–204.200.115.255

Table C-13   Extended Network Addresses for a 3-Bit Subnet Number

Calculating Subnet and Hosts

Before a network administrator modifies the subnet masks in use on a network, he should have some idea of the number of subnets or hosts a particular subnet mask will make available. Of course, the administrator could use trial-and-error, and try different numbers of bits for the subnet number and host ID, but a quicker and easier way exists to determine this important information.

The formula $2^n - 2$ can be used to determine either the number of subnets or the number of hosts within a network or subnet. In this formula, n represents the number of bits used for either the subnet number or the host ID, depending on which is being calculated. After the number of subnets and the number of hosts are calculated, multiplying one by the other yields the number of total hosts available for the address class and the subnet mask in use.

Network and Broadcast Addresses

You may also be wondering why 2 is subtracted in the formula $(2^n - 2)$. On any network or subnet, two addresses are reserved for the ID address of the network or subnet (the address yielded when the subnet mask is applied) and a broadcast address used to broadcast messages to all nodes on a network or subnet. Host IDs that are all zeros or all ones are not allowed, but are reserved for use as network or subnet addresses (zeros) or broadcast addresses (ones).

On a network without subnets, the network address typically has a zero host ID, such as 204.200.159.0. However, on a subnet, the address is generally either zero or a multiple of the number of hosts available on the subnet, as shown in Table C-14. Because the network or subnet requires these addresses, the network (or subnet) ID address and the broadcast address are unavailable to be assigned to hosts.

Subnet ID Bits	Subnets	Host ID Bits	Hosts Per Subnet	Total Hosts Available
1	1	7	126	126
2	2	2	62	124
3	6	5	30	180
4	14	4	14	196
5	30	3	6	180
6	60	2	2	120

Table C-14   Hosts Available for 1 to 6 Subnet Number Bits

For example, if 3 bits are used for the subnet number, then the calculation is $2^3 - 2$, or $8 - 2$, or 6, which means six subnets are available. If 3 bits are used for the subnet number, then 5 bits are available for the host ID and the calculation is $2^5 - 2$, or $32 - 2$, or 30, indicating that each subnet has 30 host ID addresses available for assignment. On six subnets with 30 hosts each, there is a total of 180 addressable hosts.

Lost Addresses

In the preceding example, only 180 hosts can be assigned in the six subnets. So, what happened to the other 74 hosts that should be available on a Class *C* address block, which, by definition, supports 254 addresses? When subnetting is applied to a classful address block, the total number of possible hosts is reduced.

Here's an example showing how this happens:

Dixie's Doilies, Inc., a small but growing manufacturer, has been allotted the Class *C* network address of 181.52.206.0 (meaning an entire Class *C* address block). The network administrator wants to subnet the network, so at least 12 subnets with at least 8 hosts are on each subnet. Using the information in Table C-14, she determines the best subnetting plan for the DDI network is to use 4 bits for the subnet number and 4 bits for the host ID, which will create 14 available subnets with 14 available hosts on each subnet. This arrangements makes 196 hosts available on the network, which exceeds DDI's current requirement for 96 hosts.

NOTE

Table C-14 doesn't list 7 or 8 bits used for the subnet number because at least 2 bits must be used for a host ID.

Although the network will be limited to 196 hosts (instead of the 254 hosts when subnetting is not used), the advantage of creating smaller broadcast domains and increased security is worth it, especially when all 254 hosts aren't required.

Using 4 bits for the subnet number converts the default Class C subnet mask (255.255.255.0) to a subnet mask of 255.255.255.240. According to the calculation for the number of subnets, this creates $(2^4 - 2)$, and there are 16 possible subnet IDs, two of which cannot be used. The available subnet addresses are listed in Table C-15.

Subnet Bits	Network ID	Node Addresses	Broadcast Address
0000	181.52.206.0	None	None
0001	181.52.206.16	181.52.206.17–181.52.206.30	181.52.206.31
0010	181.52.206.32	181.52.206.33–181.52.206.46	181.52.206.47
0011	181.52.206.48	181.52.206.49–181.52.206.62	181.52.206.63
0100	181.52.206.64	181.52.206.65–181.52.206.78	181.52.206.79
0101	181.52.206.80	181.52.206.81–181.52.206.94	181.52.206.95
0110	181.52.206.96	181.52.206.97–181.52.206.110	181.52.206.111
0111	181.52.206.112	181.52.206.113–181.52.206.126	181.52.206.127
1000	181.52.206.128	181.52.206.129–181.52.206.142	181.52.206.143
1001	181.52.206.144	181.52.206.145–181.52.206.158	181.52.206.159
1010	181.52.206.160	181.52.206.161–181.52.206.174	181.52.206.175
1011	181.52.206.176	181.52.206.177–181.52.206.190	181.52.206.191
1100	181.52.206.192	181.52.206.193–181.52.206.206	181.52.206.207
1101	181.52.206.208	181.52.206.209–181.52.206.222	181.52.206.223
1110	181.52.206.224	181.52.206.225–181.52.206.238	181.52.206.239
1111	181.52.206.240	None	None

Table C-15   Subnet Addresses from a 4-Bit Subnet Number

In this example, as shown by the information in Table C-15, the subnets at .0 and .240 are reserved for use as the overall network ID and the broadcast address, so the 32 host addresses associated with these subnets are lost for use.

Variable-length Subnet Masks

In our discussion on subnet masks to this point, all the subnets have had the same number of hosts because the same subnet mask is used in every case. In a majority of networks, this arrangement is acceptable and serves the needs of the organization, despite the loss of a certain number of host addresses. However, in other situations, a need occurs to have all host addresses available.

Variable-length subnet masks (VLSM) assign a different subnet mask to each subnet, one that typically varies from the standard or default subnet masks. *VLSM* assigns host addresses to subnets in a way that meets the needs of the subnet and not according to the general subnetting rules. VLSM, which is also known as *classless addressing*, combines the concepts of subnetting and CIDR (supernetting).

If the network described in the preceding section (14 subnets of 14 hosts each) were assigned to meet the needs of the network, subnet 1 is assigned 14 hosts, subnet 2 is assigned 28 hosts, subnet 3 is assigned 2 hosts, subnet 4 is assigned 14 hosts, and subnet 5 is assigned 28 hosts.

Because subnets are logical subdivisions of a network structure, VLSM is able to reorganize the subnets, so the largest subnet is defined first. VLSM would define subnet 2 (28 hosts) first followed by subnet 1 (14 hosts), and then subnet 3 (2 hosts). This arrangement makes better use of the available addresses and helps eliminate wasted addresses.

VLSM assigns a different network prefix to each subnet. For example, subnet 1 (14 hosts) needs a network prefix of /28; subnet 2 needs a network prefix of /27; subnet 3 needs a network prefix of /30, and so forth. Table C-16 shows the VLSM definition of the subnets.

Subnet	Subnet ID	Network Prefix	Host Addresses
Subnet 2	181.52.206.0	/27	181.52.206.1–181.52.206.30
Subnet 5	181.52.206.32	/27	181.52.206.33–181.52.206.62
Subnet 1	181.52.206.64	/28	181.52.206.65–181.52.206.78
Subnet 4	181.52.206.80	/28	181.52.206.81–181.52.206.94
Subnet 3	181.52.206.96	/30	181.52.206.97–181.52.206.98

Table C-16   VLSM Subnetting

Appendix D

Network Media

Network media are the physical communications links used to connect nodes on a network. Every network uses at least one form of network medium, whether it is copper wire, fiber-optic cable, infrared beams of light, or radio frequency (RF) signals.

It may seem odd that wire and cable are included in the media topics being discussed in a wireless networking book, but to understand wireless networking fully, you must have an understanding of wired networking. Remember, eventually, all network transmissions end up on a cable of some kind, even wireless networks.

Which physical cable are chosen for use in a given wired networking situation depends on the requirements of the network, and the properties and characteristics of the cable. However, before we get too deeply into the specific types of cabling used for networking, you should understand some basic concepts.

Cable Properties

Perhaps the first thing to discuss about network cabling is its basic construction. Essentially, all wire that carries electrical or light impulses consists of a conductor and at least one layer of insulation. A *conductor* is a material that transfers electrical (or light) impulses efficiently. An *insulator* is a material that does not transfer electrical impulses. Copper is an excellent conductor, which is why it is commonly used for electrical and communications cabling. Rubber, plastic, and silicone are good insulating materials, and they are the most commonly used insulators on electrical and communications wire.

NOTE

Just like any other professionals, networkers have a language all their own that is rampant with semantics. For example, take the terms "cable," "cabling," "wire," and "wiring." *Cable* typically is used to mean a single run of a communications cable. *Cabling* is used to describe more than a single run of communications cable. *Wire* is used interchangeably with "cable" but, technically, it means the conductors inside the cable. *Wiring* is something used to transmit electricity.

Of the three cable media used in wired networking environments, two use copper to carry electrical impulses and one uses glass or plastic to transmit light impulses. Currently, wired networks install more copper wiring than glass or plastic, primarily because of cost.

What you need to know about physical network media, aka cable, centers on their physical properties and construction features. Here are some of the basic concepts you need to understand about all cable types:

- **Attenuation** In nearly all cable and RF media, there's a distance limit at which the signal on a wire weakens and no longer can be recognized.

- **Cancellation**   The electromagnetic fields of two wires placed in close proximity can cancel each other. This is generally a good thing and helps control the signals being sent over the individual wires, but too much cancellation can destroy the integrity of the signal carried on either wire.

- **Crosstalk**   If the electromagnetic (or what's called inductive) or electrostatic (capacitive) properties of two conductor wires become coupled, interference is caused by the transmitted signals being carried on the separate wires becoming superimposed on one another. What commonly happens is this: on two wires that are placed too closely together, the electromagnetic field on one wire creates (induces) a current on the other wire. The effects of crosstalk are reduced if shielded cabling is used or if the distance between the two conductors is increased. Two common types of crosstalk that occur on twisted-pair cable are

  - **Near-end crosstalk (NEXT)**   *NEXT* crosstalk occurs when bare conductor wires become crossed or crushed within a short distance of a connector. The wires don't need to touch each other; they just need to be close enough to exchange electromagnetic and electrostatic fields. Crosstalk can also be caused by wires being placed too close to other voltage sources, such as electric wiring, or by wet cable or improper installation, as well as several other ways.

  - **Far-end crosstalk (FEXT)**   *FEXT* occurs for the same reasons as NEXT, but it is detected at the far end of the cable from where a signal originates.

NOTE

The number of wire twists per inch (the *twist rate*) used on each pair in Cat 5 and 5e cables is varied to reduce crosstalk. To further reduce the chance of crosstalk, the specifications for stripping and crimping connectors, the amount of pull force (measured in foot-pounds), and the bend radius for Cat 5 and 5e are stringent.

- **Electromagnetic interference (EMI)**   Virtually all electrical devices emit electromagnetic waves that can cause interference and impair the signals of other devices. However, the impact of EMI on transmission cables can be reduced in other ways. For example, in a building, cables should not be run near electrical lines or near notoriously noisy (meaning something that emits a lot of EMI) devices, such as fluorescent light fixtures, electrical motors or pumps, and, if installed in an elevator shaft, elevator motors.

- **Radio frequency interference (RFI)**   Radio waves broadcast from nearby transmitters can be picked up by electrical devices and cause RFI. *RFI* can be a problem for unshielded cabling because these cables are designed specifically to keep electrical charges inside the cable, which increases their tendency to absorb RFI and EMI. Wireless media can also suffer from RFI if the signals from a nearby transmitter overlap the transmissions of a wireless network.

Network Physical Media

All network cabling has a set of general characteristics that guide you in picking the most appropriate cable for a given situation.

- **Bandwidth** *Bandwidth* is the amount of data a cable can carry in a certain period of time. Bandwidth is often expressed as the number of bits (either kilobits or megabits) that can be transmitted in a second. For example, UTP cable is nominally rated at 10 Mbps, or 10 million bits per second.

- **Cost** Cost is always a major consideration when choosing a cable type. The Network+ exam deals with this characteristic on a comparative basis. The relative cost comparisons for the major cable media are

  - Twisted-pair (TP) cable is the least expensive, but it has limitations that require other hardware to be installed.

  - Coaxial cable is a little more expensive than TP, but it doesn't require additional equipment and it is inexpensive to maintain.

  - Fiber-optic cabling is the most expensive, requires skilled installation labor, and is expensive to install and maintain.

- **Maximum segment length** Every cable is subject to a condition called *attenuation*, which means the signal weakens and can no longer be recognized. Attenuation occurs at a distance specific to every type of cable. This distance (measured in meters) is the maximum segment length for a cable medium or the distance at which signals on the cable must be regenerated. Segment length is a function of propagation (transmission) speed, which determines the time (travel distance) required to detect a collision by the Ethernet media access method, Carrier Sense Multiple Access/Collision Detection (CSMA/CD).

- **Maximum number of nodes per segments** Each time a device is added to a network, the effect is like another hole being put in the cable. Like leaks from pinholes in a balloon, having too many devices attached to a network cable reduces the distance at which attenuation begins. Therefore, each type of cable must limit the number of nodes that can be attached to a cable segment.

- **Resistance to interference** The different cable media have varying vulnerability to electromagnetic interference (EMI) or radio frequency interference (RFI) caused by electric motors, fluorescent light fixtures, your magnet collection, the radio station on the next floor of your home or office, and so on. As the construction of the cable and its cladding (coverings) varies, so does its resistance to EMI and RFI signals.

NOTE

Just for clarification, a network segment is created each time you add a network device that regenerates or redirects message signals.

Table D-1 summarizes the characteristics of the various wire media types.

Cable Type	Bandwidth	Maximum Segment Length	Maximum Nodes per Segment	Resistance to Interference
Thin coaxial	10 Mbps	185 meters	30	Good
Thick coaxial	10 Mbps	500 meters	100	Better
UTP	10–1,000 Mbps	100 meters	1,024	Poor
STP	16–1,000 Mbps	100 meters	1,024	Fair to Good
Fiber-optic	100–10,000 Mbps	2,000 meters	No limit	Best

Table D-1   Wire Media Characteristics

In a wired network environment, the most commonly used cable types are (with the most commonly used listed first):

● Twisted pair cable

● Coaxial cable

● Fiber-optic cable

Twisted Pair Cable

The most commonly used physical media for networks is twisted pair cable (see Figure D-1). The twisted pair cable used in most computer networks consists of four pairs of wire that are twisted around each other, creating a twisted wire pair.

The twisted-pair cabling used for a data network (CAT 5 and above) is terminated with an RJ-45 connector jack or plug. A connector jack (see Figure D-2) is the receptacle half of a connection, and a plug (Figure D-3) is the insert half of the connection. When used in a telephony network or to support many security devices, twisted pair cabling is terminated with an RJ-11 connector (see Figure D-4).

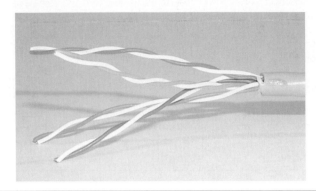

Figure D-1 A twisted pair cable with its outer jacket removed to show its four wire pairs

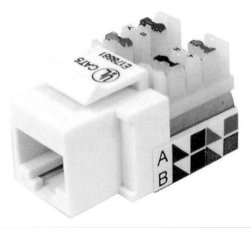

Figure D-2 An RJ-45 connection jack

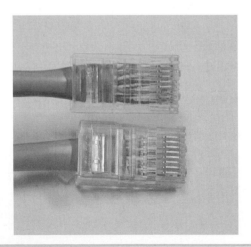

Figure D-3 RJ-45 connection plugs

Figure D-4   There are different styles for RJ-11 plugs. The standard RJ11 (shown in the inner two plugs) is the most commonly used.

Twisted pair cable is available as unshielded or shielded cable. Shielded twisted pair (STP) cable has additional layers of foil wrapped around the wire pairs to cut down on crosstalk and cancellation between the wires. Unshielded twisted pair (UTP) cable, shown in Figure D-2, provides no additional shielding for the wire pairs inside the outer jacket. Because of its low cost, UTP is the most common type of twisted pair cabling for data networks.

Category-rated Cable

UTP cable includes four wire pairs grouped into five rating categories (each referred to as a Cat, short for category):

- Cat 1 or 2 UTP is not used in data networking.

- Cat 3 UTP supports data speeds (bandwidth) up to 10 Mbps. Cat 3 is the minimum standard for Ethernet networks.

- Cat 4 UTP is most commonly used for 16 Mbps Token Ring networks. However, Cat 4 STP is also commonly used in this application.

D

- Cat 5 UTP supports bandwidth up to 100 Mbps. Cat 5 and Cat 5e (enhanced) are the recommended minimum cable types for data networks according to the Electronics Industry Association/Telecommunications Industry Association (EIA/TIA) 568 standards.

- Cat 6 and Cat 7 support up to 1,000 Mbps or 1 gigabit (one billion bits) per second (Gbps).

Straight-through vs. Crossover Cables

When connecting different devices together, different wire patterns are used, depending on the type of devices being connected. Because of the data transmit and receiving methods, the wires used for transmitting and receiving data signals must be crossed for some devices. For example, when a PC is connected directly to a network hub or switch (or something similar), a straight-through cable can be used. However, when a PC is directly connected by a cable to another PC, a crossover cable must be used. Tables D-2 and D-3 show the pin-outs for a straight-through cable and a crossover cable, respectively.

PC			Connectivity Device		
Pin	Function	Polarity	Pin	Function	Polarity
1	Transmit	+	1	Receive	+
2	Transmit	−	2	Receive	−
3	Receive	+	3	Transmit	+
6	Receive	−	6	Transmit	−

Table D-2   The Pin-Outs Used on a Straight-Through Cable

The EIA developed a color code and wire standard to interconnect devices that use RJ-45 interfaces with twisted pair cable. The reason this standard was developed was to provide the industry with a standard that would identify how a sending and receiving device should assign pin-outs. If the sending and receiving devices use the same pins to send and receive, the

PC			Connectivity Device		
Pin	Function	Polarity	Pin	Function	Polarity
1	Transmit	+	3	Receive	+
2	Transmit	−	6	Receive	−
3	Receive	+	1	Transmit	+
6	Receive	−	2	Transmit	−

Table D-3   The Pin-Outs Used on a Crossover Cable

send channel on one device would connect to the send channel on the other device. To send information, the sending station's transmit channel must connect to the receiving station's receive channel.

For example, some devices are wired with pins 1 and 2 as the transmit channel, and other devices assign pins 1 and 2 as the receive channel. In these cases, a straight-through cable can be used. However, when the sending device uses pins 1 and 2 as the transmit channel, and the receiving device also uses pins 1 and 2 as its transmit channel, the cable must be configured to cross this connection, which is accomplished through a crossover cable.

IEEE Ethernet Cable Standards

UTP cable is given different designations in the standards that define Ethernet networking developed by the Institute for Electrical and Electronics Engineering (IEEE). In the Ethernet world, cables are designated with a coding scheme that describes their characteristics, primarily their attenuation points.

The most common of the Ethernet cable specifications are listed in Table D-4:

Cable Specification	Ethernet Specification	Cable Type	Maximum Speed	Maximum Segment Length
10Base2	Ethernet	Thin coaxial cable (RG-58)	10 Mbps	185 meters (607 feet)
10Base5	Ethernet	Thick coaxial cable (RG-8)	10 Mbps	500 meters (1,640 feet)
10BaseT	Ethernet	Unshielded twisted-pair (UTP/Cat 3-7)	10 Mbps	100 meters (328 feet)
100BaseT	Fast Ethernet	UTP (Cat 5, Cat5e, Cat 6, and Cat 7)	100 Mbps	100 meters (328 feet)
100BaseFx	Fast Ethernet	Multimode fiber-optic cable	100 Mbps	2,000 meters (1.24 miles)
		Single-mode fiber-optic cable	100 Mbps	100 kilometers (62 miles)
1000BaseT	Gigabit Ethernet	UTP (Cat 5e, Cat 6, and Cat 7)	1 Gbps	100 meters (328 feet)
1000BaseFx	Gigabit Ethernet	Single-mode fiber-optic cable	1 Gbps	100 kilometers (62 miles)
1000BaseSx	Gigabit Ethernet	Multimode fiber-optic cable	1 Gbps	220 meters (721 feet)

Table D-4 Common Ethernet Cable Specifications

D

The Ethernet cable designations have three parts to them: the bandwidth, the transmission mode, and the material or the attenuation distance. For example, the 10, 100, and 1000 represent 10 Mbps, 100 Mbps, and 1,000 Mbps, respectively. "Base" indicates this standard uses baseband transmission to transfer data. The last one or two characters represent either the material, as in *T* for twisted pair and *F* for fiber-optic, or the attenuation distance of coaxial cable, in which the 2 represents "approximately 200 meters" (meaning an actual 185 meters) and the 5 represents 500 meters.

Baseband technology transmits data over a single carrier frequency, using the entire capacity of the cable and requiring all connected network nodes to participate in every message transmitted on the network. The other technology used for transmitting data over a cable is *broadband* which uses multiple frequencies to transmit several signal paths at once.

Plenum-rated Cable

Many local and national fire, building, and electrical standards specify plenum-rated cable to be used in certain applications. The difference between standard category-rated cable and plenum-rated cable is in the wire-pair coatings and the outer jacket of the cable, which makes *plenum cable* more resistant to heat and fire. Performancewise, the two cables have the same transmission specifications.

The outer jacket of a plenum cable meets the specific American National Standards Institute (ANSI) requirement for being flame retardant and for low smoke and fume emissions. If a building in which network cabling has been installed catches fire, plenum cable does not burn as easily or produce as much smoke as standard cable if it ignites. The downside to plenum cable is that plenum cable burns at a higher temperature and can cost as much as three times more than standard cable.

Coaxial Cable

Coaxial cable, like that used in your home cable television system, has a solid-core conductor wrapped with several layers of insulation and shielding materials. Figure D-5 shows the makeup of a coaxial cable. Around the center copper conductor wire is a layer of dielectric material that provides an electrostatic buffer between the conductor wire and the metal shielding of the cable. Around the dielectric layer is wrapped a layer of either foil or a metal mesh or braid, or both. In a coaxial cable, two currents flow: the signal current flowing on the center conductor wire and a grounding current flowing in the opposite direction. The outer jacket of the cable is plastic or a silicone material that protects the cable from cuts and nicks.

You probably have coaxial cable, which is used to connect your cable TV service or your cable Internet access, in your home. This type of coaxial cable is a 50-ohm cable, officially known as RG-59 or RG-6. The type of coaxial cable used for networking is 75-ohm, RG-58 (thin coaxial cable) or RG-8 (thick coaxial cable). The connectors used to terminate the cable must be compatible with 75-ohm cabling.

Figure D-5   A coaxial cable that has been stripped and one that is terminated with a BNC connector

As shown in Figure D-6, a coaxial cable used in a data networking system is terminated with what is called a bayonet-Neill-Concellman (BNC) connector. *BNC* connectors provide a secure connection because the jack and the plug mate lock with a twist-lock mechanism. In many networking situations, such as peer-to-peer networking, a BNC T-connector is used to "daisy-chain" the nodes to each other.

Figure D-6   A BNC T-connector is used to create a continuous connection from one network node to the next.

D

Fiber-optic Cable

Fiber-optic cable (Figure D-7) uses a glass or plastic fiber strand to transmit data as light impulses. Fiber-optic cable is available in two types: single-mode and multimode. *Single-mode fiber-optic cable* is designed to carry a single beam of light over long distances. *Multimode fiber-optic cable*, which is the type most commonly used in LANs, CANs, and MANs, carries multiple light beams concurrently.

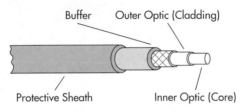

Figure D-7 The composition of a multimode fiber-optic cable

Multimode fiber was the first type developed and, although not originally designed to carry multiple signals, a discovery showed it could. Further development led to the single-mode cable. Because it carries multiple beams, multimode cable has a shorter distance limit when used in networks, which is why it is typically used only in horizontal building runs and single-mode fiber is used for longer distances.

Multimode fiber-optic cable is capable of carrying virtually all standard network bandwidths and certainly those in the Ethernet standards (10 to 1,000 Mbps), with an attenuation point of 2,000 meters, or the equivalent of about 1.25 miles.

Fiber-optic cable is more expensive than UTP and is more difficult to work with. However, its advantages are its capability of carrying data over much greater distances and its resistance to interference.

Fiber-optic cable has a variety of connectors that can be used, but in most data networking situations, either an ST or SC connector is used. These connectors align and fix in place the center strand of the cables or devices being joined.

Glossary

0-9

802.11 High Rate—see 802.11b

802.11 Legacy—the original IEEE wireless network standard that included both RF and IR media.

802.11a—an IEEE wireless standard that defines up to 54 Mbps of data transfer in the 5 GHz RF band using OFDM.

802.11b—an IEEE wireless standard that defines 1 Mbps, 2 Mbps, 5.5 Mbps, and 11 Mbps of data transfer in the 2.4 GHz RF band using DSSS signaling.

802.11i—the 2004 IEEE wireless network security standard that included WPA, an update to WEP.

802.11g—an IEEE wireless standard that defines up to 54 Mbps of data transfer in the 2.4 GHz RF band, which makes it compatible with 802.11b systems.

802.11n—an emerging IEEE standard that has a target throughput rate of 100 Mbps.

802.15—an IEEE standard that defines the standards for a variety of technologies and applications for personal area networks (PANs).

802.16—the IEEE standards for wireless MANs.

802.1x—The network security standard for all IEEE networks.

A

Access point (AP)—A WLAN device that provides communications support to wireless workstations and, in some cases, an interface to a wired network.

Ad-hoc mode—Ad-hoc WLAN structures provide connections between devices without involving an access point.

AM—see Amplitude modulation.

Amplitude modulation (AM)—a radio wave modulation method that alters the height (amplitude) of a transmitted radio wave.

AP—see Access point.

Authentication—the process used to provide verify a user's login and to allow or deny access to a network.

B

Backhaul—a communications link is used to carry traffic to a backbone service or the Internet.

Baseband—a telecommunications system that carries digital data on a single channel on the transmission medium.

Basic service set (BSS)—A wireless network configuration that includes an access point that provides a bridging function to a wired network.

Bluetooth—a telecommunications industry standard that specifies mobile devices can be interconnected over a short-range wireless connection.

Bluetooth SIG—see Special interest group.

Bridge—a device used to link two network segments or networks in separate buildings.

BSS—see Basic service set.

C

CA—see Certificate authority.

Certificate authority (CA)—a private company that issues and verifies digital signatures and public and private keys.

Circuit-switching—a switching technique that uses mechanical and electronic switching to establish a circuit path between the source and destination for a single session.

Coaxial—a standard cable type that has either a solid copper wire or a stranded copper wire core that is covered by a dielectric plastic sheath, which is then covered by a braided copper or aluminum wire sheath.

D

DAMA/TDMA—see Demand Assignment Multiple Access/Time Division Multiple Access

dB—see Decibel.

dBm—see Decibels relative to one milliWatt.

Decibel (dB)—a logarithmic ratio between two signals, voltage, or current levels.

Decibels relative to one milliWatt (dBm)—a measure of the signal strength in RF frequencies, where one milliWatt (mW) equals 1/1000 of a watt.

Demand Assignment Multiple Access/Time Division Multiple Access (DAMA/ TDMA)—an 802.16 standard that adapts as required to changes in demand patterns from multiple subscriber stations.

Denial of service (DoS) attack—a network attack intended to monopolize a network's processing capabilities and deny service to the network's users.

DHCP—see Dynamic host configuration protocol.

Diffused IR—an IR technology that spreads its signal up to 180-degrees, allowing it to reflect off surfaces in an enclosed space.

Direct-sequencing spread-spectrum (DSSS)—a spread spectrum modulation method that uses amplitude modulation to combine the waveforms of the data and carrier signals.

Directed IR—an IR transmission method that requires direct and unobstructed line-of-sight.

Directional antenna—a type of RF antenna that produces a radiation pattern that can be aimed to provide coverage to a single area.

DoS—see Denial of service.

DSSS—see Direct-sequencing spread-spectrum.

Dynamic host configuration protocol (DHCP)—a TCP/IP protocol that assigns an IP address and other IP configuration data to a network node.

E

EAP—see Extensible authentication protocol

EIRP—see Equivalent isotropically radiated power.

Equivalent isotropically radiated power (EIRP)—a measure of an antenna's power output calculated by adding the power received to the gain produced and subtracting any loss from cabling or connectors.

Electromagnetic interference (EMI)—a disruption of RF signal quality caused by an electromagnetic emissions from an electrical device.

EMI—see Electromagnetic interference

Enterprise network—A network that connects the resources for an entire company or corporation.

ESS—see Extended service set.

Extended service set (ESS)—a WLAN configuration in which the access points communicate with each other to extend the network.

Extensible authentication protocol (EAP)—a wireless network protocol that expands on authentication methods provided by the Point-to-Point Protocol (PPP).

F

FCC—see Federal Communications Commission.

FDM—see Frequency division multiplexing.

Federal Communications Commission (FCC)—the U.S. agency that regulates wireless communications.

FHSS—see Frequency-hopping spread spectrum.

FM—see Frequency modulation.

Frequency—The number of wavelengths occurring in an oscillating radio wave in specific time.

Frequency division multiplexing (FDM)—applies a different frequency to each of the signal streams being combined onto a single transmission medium.

Frequency-hopping spread spectrum (FHSS)—a spread spectrum modulation method that transmits signals by constantly switching the carrier signal between frequency channels using a switching sequence known by both the transmitter and the receiver.

Frequency modulation (FM)—a modulation technique that alters the vibration rate of the signal, represented by the number of wavelengths transmitted in the signal in one second.

G

Gain—the extent to which an amplifier boosts the strength of a signal.

Gateway—a networking device most commonly used to connect two dissimilar networks, such as a LAN to a WAN.

H

HAN—see Home area network.

HCI—see Host controller interface.

Home area network (HAN)—A network that provides a communications connection between devices inside a home

Host controller interface (HCI)—A Bluetooth protocol that provides a command interface to the link controller (LC), the link manager protocol (LMP), and access to hardware status and control data.

Hertz—A hertz represents one electromagnetic wave cycle per second. MHz stands for megahertz (or million cycles per second).

Hot spot—any general area where a user can connect to a wireless network to access the Internet.

I

IBSS—see Independent basic service set.

IEEE—see Institute of Electrical and Electronics Engineers.

Independent basic service set (IBSS)—a PC with wireless access point capability that is used to support an ad-hoc network.

Industrial, scientific, and medical (ISM)—an unlicensed 2.4 GHz RF band originally created to support industrial, scientific, and medical uses, but now used for a wide variety of wireless communications, including WLANs.

Infrared (IR)—the band of light just below visible light.

Institute of Electrical and Electronics Engineers (IEEE)—a leading professional association for the advancement of technology.

Interoperable—Devices and software elements that have the capability to communicate and interact with each other effectively.

Infrastructure mode—An WLAN configuration in which the wireless stations communicate through an access point.

Infrared Data Association (IrDA)—an independent trade organization that creates and publishes standards aimed at establishing an interoperable, low-cost data connection using IR technology.

IR—see Infrared.

IrDA—see Infrared Data Association.

IrPHY—the physical layer interfaces and functions of the IrDA standards.

ISM—see Industrial, scientific, and medical.

Isotropic—a conceptual antenna type that exists at some point in space and radiates a global signal pattern.

K

Known-good—typically a hardware device that is known to be in good working order used to replace a suspected bad device for testing and troubleshooting purposes.

L

L2CAP—see Logical link control and adaptation protocol

Last mile—a term used by service providers to describe the link between a customer's premises and a backbone link.

LED—see Light-emitting diode.

Link management protocol (LMP)—a Bluetooth protocol that provides for the creation and management of links to other Bluetooth devices.

Light-emitting diode (LED)—an electronic component that uses electricity to cause a reaction between its materials to release photons.

Lightning arrestor—a device used to help protect cabling and electrical devices connected to an antenna from damage by an electrical surge or a lighting strike.

Line-of-sight (LoS)—a term used to describe a direct path between two communicating devices.

LMP—see Link management protocol.

Logical link control and adaptation protocol (L2CAP)—a Bluetooth protocol that provides for networking functions, such as high-level multiplexing, packet segmentation and reassembly, and the management of quality of service (QoS) data.

LoS—see Line-of-sight.

M

MAC—see Media access control.

MAC filtering—a security-oriented feature intended to block the unauthorized access to a network's resources by devices whose MAC addresses are not listed in the allowed list.

MAN—see Metropolitan area network.

MANET—see Mobile area network.

Media access control (MAC)—defines the methods and addressing schemes used to access a network medium.

Metropolitan area network (MAN)—a network structure that provides service to an area inside a city.

Mobile area network (MANET)—a wireless network for mobile devices using discovery and linking protocols.

Multipath propagation—a condition that can occur when portions of a transmitted signal are deflected, reflected, or blocked by objects in the transmission path that causes parts of a signal to arrive later than other parts of the signal.

Multiplexing—A transmission method that intersperses message segments from multiple sessions onto the single medium.

N

NAT—see Network address translation.

Network adapter—A device that interconnects a PC to a network's medium.

Network address translation (NAT)—a network service that uses a single public address to shield the assigned IP address of a network node from the Internet.

Network interface card (NIC)—A network adapter installed inside a computer's system unit in an expansion slot.

Network analyzer—a hardware device or software program that is used to monitor and analyze the activities of a network.

NIC—see Network interface card.

O

OFDM—see Orthogonal frequency division multiplexing.

Omnidirectional—a type of RF antenna that produces a radiation pattern that is essentially a circular pattern around the antenna.

Orthogonal frequency division multiplexing (OFDM)—a transmission method that splits an RF signal into multiple substreams for simultaneous transmission on separate frequencies.

P

P2P—see Point-to-point.

P2MP—see Point-to-multipoint.

Packet-switching—a logical switching method that uses the address embedded in the data packet to switch (forward) a message to its destination.

Packet Internet groper (Ping)—a TCP/IP utility that ise used to test whether one node on a network can be reached from another node on the same network

PAN—see Personal area network.

PC Card—A device that mounts in a PCMCIA 68-pin connection, commonly on the exterior of a portable PC's system unit. (see Personal Computer Memory Card International Association)

PCI—see Peripheral components interconnect.

PCMCIA—see Personal Computer Memory Card International Association.

Peripheral components interconnect (PCI)—a motherboard bus structure commonly used for network adapters.

Personal Computer Memory Card International Association (PCMCIA)—a trade organization that defines standards for hot-swappable PC Card devices. (see PC Card)

Peer-to-peer WLAN—A wireless ad-hoc network that does not include an access point.

Personal area network (PAN)—a network that interconnects personal productivity devices for a single user.

Personal operating space (POS)—the result of using wireless technology to create a PAN around a single user.

PHY—see Physical layer.

Physical layer (PHY)—The physical (medium) layer of a networking standard.

Piconet—an ad-hoc logical structure used by Bluetooth to form networks from as many as eight devices.

Ping—see Packet Internet groper.

PKI—see Public key infrastructure.

Polarization—the orientation of the current of a transmitted signal.

Point-to-point (P2P)—a communications link that connects one station directly to another.

Point-to-multipoint (P2MP)—a communications mode that connects a master station with two or more slaves.

POS—see Personal operating space.

Private key—an encryption key known only to the parties in an Internet transaction.

Public key—an encryption key known to everyone.

Public key infrastructure (PKI)—an encryption system that uses digital signatures and public and private keys to verify and authenticate the sender and receiver in an Internet transaction.

Q

QoS—see Quality-of-service.

Quality-of-service (QoS)—a capability of a network to provide better service to selected network traffic using a selection of technologies

R

Radio frequency identification device (RFID)—low-power wireless transmitters that can be embedded in several applications to identify items.

Radio frequency interference (RFI)—random and extraneous radio waves transmitted by broadcast or electrical sources.

Radio wave—an electromagnetic wave with distinct frequency and amplitude properties that is propagated through the air.

RC4—see Ron's code 4.

Receive signal strength indicator (RSSI)—a measurement indicating which of two or more access points is providing the strongest signal on each channel.

Repeater—a networking device used to overcome attenuation on the medium.

RFI—see Radio frequency interference.

RFID—see Radio frequency identification device.

Ron's Code 4 (RC4)—a stream cipher that uses a variable key-size stream cipher with byte-oriented operations; the encryption cipher used in WEP.

Router—a networking device that uses Layer 3 addressing to forward messages on an internetwork.

RSSI—see Receive signal strength indicator.

S

Scalability—a network's capability to change as needed to meet the expanding needs of an organization or home.

Scatternet—an ad-hoc logical structure formed by Bluetooth protocols from multiple piconets.

SDP—see Service discovery protocol.

Service discovery protocol (SDP)—a Bluetooth protocol that provides the means for one Bluetooth device to discover the services provided by another.

Service set identifier (SSID)—a keyword used by wireless network adapters to associate with wireless access points on a single WLAN.

Signal-to-noise ratio (SNR)—a measurement indicating a ratio between signal strength and interference at a particular location.

Site survey—The process used to verify the capability for a facility or space to support a WLAN.

SMA—see SubMiniature version A.

Small office/Home office (SOHO)—a small network built around a device that provides an Internet connection to a remote server or intranet (see VPN).

SNR—see Signal-to-noise ratio.

SOHO—see Small office/Home office.

Spanning tree protocol (STP)—a protocol applied by WLAN switches to prevent undeliverable messages from clogging up the network.

Special interest group (SIG)—in the context of the Bluetooth technology, the Bluetooth SIG is responsible for the development, promotion, testing, and conformance issues surrounding the Bluetooth technology.

Spread-spectrum—a modulation technique characterized by its use of a wide frequency spectrum.

SSID—see Service set identifier.

STP—see Spanning tree protocol.

SubMiniature version A (SMA)—along with TNC, a common connector type used with the cabling for antenna systems.

Switch—an intelligent device that is able to forward messages across a network using a variety of factors, including the Layer 2 address of the destination node.

T

TDM—see Time division multiplexing.

Temporal key integrity protocol (TKIP)—an encryption protocol defined by the IEEE 802.11i security standard for WLANs.

Threaded Neill-Concelman (TNC)—a threaded version of the BNC connector commonly used with antenna systems.

Time division multiplexing (TDM)—a transmission technique that divides the medium into a series of time slices.

TFO—see Total final output.

TIM—see Traffic indication map.

TKIP—see Temporal key integrity protocol.

TNC—see Threaded Neill-Concelman.

Total final output (TFO)—The amount of power in the signal transmitted by a transmitter to an antenna.

Trace—see Trace route.

Trace route (tracert/trace)—a TCP/IP utility used to display the internetwork path used between a workstation and a remote IP address.

Tracert—see Trace route.

Traffic indication map (TIM)—The field used by an access point to notify a wireless node that a queue of messages has been created while the node was in sleep mode.

Troubleshooting—The process of determining the cause and source of a problem.

U

Ultra wide band (UWB)—a transmission technology in the 3.1 to 10.6 GHz RF band.

Unlicensed National Information Infrastructure (UNII)—an unlicensed RF band used for wireless networking and broadband multimedia that is allocated to the 4.9 GHz to 5.825 GHz band. Commonly referred to as 5 GHz.

UNII—see Unlicensed National Information Infrastructure.

UWB—see Ultra wide band.

V

Virtual local area network (VLAN)—a logical structure that can supersede physical placements of network nodes.

Virtual private network (VPN)—a networking system that allows remote users to connect to an internal network over public communications links to securely access the network's resources.

VLAN—see Virtual local area network.

VPN—see Virtual private network.

W

WEP—see Wired equivalent privacy.

Wi-Fi—see 802.11b.

Wi-Fi protected access (WPA)—the pre-standard version of the 802.11i standard that defined TKIP.

Wi-Max—the industry name given to the 802.16 standards.

Wired equivalent privacy (WEP)—the 802.11b legacy security standard that has two parts: a 24-bit initialization vector (IV) and a WEP key that is either 40-bits or 104-bits in length, yielding a total length for the key of 64-bits or 128-bits.

Wireless fidelity (Wi-Fi)—see 802.11b.

Wireless local area network (WLAN)—A network connecting over a wireless medium to interconnect wireless devices within a specified geographical space.

Wireless wide area network (WWAN)—a network that uses wireless communications technologies to interconnect geographically separated LANs for the purpose of exchanging transmitted data.

WLAN—see Wireless local area network.

WPA—see Wi-Fi protected access.

WWAN—see Wireless wide area network.

Z

ZigBee—a low-power, low-cost, simpler RF communications standard, often compared to Bluetooth.

Index

Authentication frames, 284
Authentication framework, 372
Authentication Header (AH), 575
Autonomous systems (AS), 463, 464
Autorité de Régulation des Télécommunications (ART) (France), 132
Available Networks window, 71
Avoidance
    collision, 526, 531–532
    congestion, 542
    CSMA/CA, 145

B

B-channel (bearer channel), 476
B-ISDN (Broadband ISDN), 476
Baby monitors, 120
Backfire, 339
Backhaul, 490
Bandwidth
    cables affecting, 586
    of enterprise WLANs, 417
    and RF communications, 479–480
    shared, 248
Bandwidth modeling, 266
Barker code, 59
Baseband communications, 142–146
    for Bluetooth, 236
    in Bluetooth, 217
    infrared baseband, 142
    and MAC, 145–146
    radio frequency baseband, 143–145
Baseband layer (Bluetooth), 218
Basic Rate Interface (BRI), 476
Basic Service Set (BSS), 43–44, 81
    and IEEE 802.11b WLAN standard, 175
    as WLAN configuration, 277
Battery packs, 261
Bayonet Neill Concelman (BNC) connectors, 347, 593
Beacon frame, 281, 284
Beacon interval (access points), 292
Bearer channel (B-channel), 476
Bel, 331
Bell, Alexander Graham, 331
Bell Laboratories, 347

BGP (*see* Border Gateway Protocol)
Binary numbers, 563
Binary Phase Shift Keying (BPSK), 143, 178
Biomechanical devices, 20, 21
Blackberry (device), 18, 19
Blatand, Harald, 215
Blocking state, 87, 315
Bluejacking, 229
Bluetooth (device), 214–235
    and bluejacking, 229
    and connecting to other Bluetooth devices, 228–230
    incompatibility with standards, 65
    infrared networks vs., 234–235
    name origin of, 215
    for networking, 223–227
    operational layers of, 217–220
    pairing of, 229
    profiles for, 230–234
    protocols for, 217–220
    and Telefonaktiebolaget LM Ericsson, 216
    and toothing, 229
    transmitters for, 221–223
Bluetooth (historical figure), 215
Bluetooth Profiles, 216, 230–234
Bluetooth SIG (*see* SIG)
Bluetooth Special Interest Group (*see* SIG)
Bluetooth Specification, 216
BNC (*see* Bayonet Neill Concelman connectors)
BNC T-connector, 593
Body area network (*see* Personal Area Networks)
Boolean algebra
    applied to subnet masks, 569–570
    XOR operations, 92
Bootstrap Protocol (BOOTP), 546
Border Gateway Protocol (BGP), 94, 463, 548
BPL (Broadband over Power Line), 205
BPSK (*see* Binary Phase Shift Keying)
Braun, Karl, 326
"Break before make," 46
BRI (Basic Rate Interface), 476
Bridges, 16, 84–86
    configuration of, for WLAN, 313–314
    for enterprise WLANs, 412–413
    Ethernet, 16, 313–314, 466
    learning, 84, 313
    multiport, 86

Propagation
multipath, 115–116
of radio waves, 111
Proprietary standards, 7
Proprietary wireless network monitors, 73
Protected Extensible Authentication Protocol
(PEAP), 375, 394
Protocol analyzers (sniffer), 261, 391–392
Protocol-based utilities, 449, 452–454
Protocol Control Information (PCI), 514–515
Protocol data units (PDUs), 475
Protocol support (router), 312
Protocols, 91, 506 (*See also specific types, e.g.:*
Connection management protocols)
PSE (Power Sourcing Equipment), 90
Pseudonoise (PN), 134
Pseudorandom (PR), 134
PSK (*see* Phase Shift Keying)
PSP (power savings polling), 66
PSTN (Public Switched Telephone Network), 128, 204
PTS (Post-och telestyrelson) (Sweden), 132
Public internetwork (Internet), 537
Public IP address, 568
Public Switched Telephone Network (PSTN),
128, 204
Public wireless LAN (PWLAN), 465
PWLAN (public wireless LAN), 465

Q

QAM, 174
QoS (quality of service), 491
Quadrature Phase Shift Keying (QPSK), 143, 173
Qualcomm, Inc., 296
Quality of service (QoS), 491

R

Radiated power (RP), 336
Radiation, electromagnetic, 118–120
Radiation pattern, 329–330
Radio-controlled (RC) aircraft, 120
Radio frequency (RF) communications, 2, 3,
50–51, 109–147
and analog/digital waves, 117
band licensing, 25

and bandwidth, 479–480
bandwidth allocation, 24–25
in Bluetooth, 217
characteristics of, 478–484
control of, 119
and electromagnetic radiation, 118–120
evolution of, 131–136
interference, 26
multipath propagation of, 115–116
and multiplexing signals, 124–127
and radio waves, 111–115
and signal switching, 127–131
signal transmission for, 120–124
standards for, 124–131
and wavelength and frequency relationship,
116–117
and WLAN design, 246–248
in WWANs, 478
(*See also under* RF)
Radio Frequency Identification (RFID), 19–20
Radio frequency interference (RFI), 26, 444, 585, 586
Radio grade (RG) cables, 346
Radio layer (Bluetooth), 218, 237
Radio modulator/demodulator (modem), 4, 58
Radio receivers, 119
Radio waves, 111–115, 118, 119
propagation of, 111
properties of, 111–115
transmitting data with, 121
RADIUS (*see* Remote Authentication Dial-in
User Service)
Random number generators, 367
Random number seeds, 367
Range (antennas), 443
Range modeling, 265–266
RARP (Reverse Address Resolution Protocol), 545
RBOC (Regional Bell Operating Company), 477
RC (radio-controlled) aircraft, 120
RC cars, 120
RC4, 394
RCA, 394
Read/write unit, 19
Ready-To-Send/Clear-To-Send (*see* RTS; RTS/CTS)
Real-time communications, 129
Reassociation request frame, 284
Reassociation response frame, 284
Receive signal strength indicator (RSSI), 267

W